MEDIEVAL DUBLIN IV

This volume is dedicated by
the Friends of Medieval Dublin
to the memory of Dr Philomena Connolly, 1948–2002

Medieval Dublin IV

Proceedings of the
Friends of Medieval Dublin Symposium 2002

Seán Duffy

EDITOR

FOUR COURTS PRESS

Typeset in 10.5 pt on 12.5 pt Ehrhardt by
Carrigboy Typesetting Services, County Cork for
FOUR COURTS PRESS LTD
7 Malpas Street, Dublin 8, Ireland
e-mail: info@four-courts-press.ie
and in North America for
FOUR COURTS PRESS
c/o ISBS, 920 NE, 58th Avenue, Suite 300, Portland, OR 97213.

A catalogue record for this title is available
from the British Library.

ISBN 1–85182–743–9 hbk
ISBN 1–85182–744–7 pbk

This book is published with the active support of
Dublin City Council/Comhairle Chathair Átha Cliath

Dublin City
Baile Átha Cliath

Printed in Ireland by Betaprint, Dublin.

Contents

LIST OF CONTRIBUTORS   6

EDITOR'S PREFACE   7

'AFTER HEARING OF PHIL CONNOLLY'S DEATH' *by Gréagóir Ó Dúill*   8

APPRECIATION OF PHILOMENA CONNOLLY *by Katharine Simms*   9

Excavations at the medieval cemetery of St Peter's church, Dublin
TIM COUGHLAN   11

The contribution of insect remains to an understanding of the environment
  of Viking-age and medieval Dublin
EILEEN REILLY   40

The defence of Dublin in the middle ages
JAMES LYDON   63

The role of St Thomas's abbey in the early development of Dublin's
  western suburb
CATHAL DUDDY   79

Health status in medieval Dublin: analysis of the skeletal remains
  from the abbey of St Thomas the Martyr
LAUREEN BUCKLEY   98

The growth and decline of a medieval suburb? Evidence from
  excavations at Thomas Street, Dublin
EDMOND O'DONOVAN   127

Women in medieval Dublin: their legal rights and economic power
LYNDA CONLON   172

Land use in medieval Oxmantown
EMER PURCELL   193

A much disputed land: Carrickmines and the Dublin marches
EMMETT O'BYRNE   229

English patron, English building? The importance of St Sepulchre's
  archiepiscopal palace, Dublin
DANIELLE O'DONOVAN   253

Dublin's southern frontier under siege: Kindlestown Castle, Delgany,
  County Wicklow
LINZI SIMPSON   279

List of contributors

LAUREEN BUCKLEY is a freelance osteoarchaeologist.

LYNDA CONLON is a student in Trinity College, Dublin.

TIM COUGHLAN is an archaeologist with Irish Archaeological Consultancy Ltd.

CATHAL DUDDY holds an M.A. from University College, Dublin and is a member of the Franciscan community.

SEÁN DUFFY is a Fellow of Trinity College, Dublin and Chairman of the Friends of Medieval Dublin.

JAMES LYDON is a Fellow Emeritus of Trinity College, Dublin where he held the Lecky Chair of History.

EMMETT O'BYRNE holds a Ph.D. from the Department of Medieval History at Trinity College, Dublin.

DANIELLE O'DONOVAN is a Ph.D. student in the Department of the History of Art and Architecture at Trinity College, Dublin.

EDMOND O'DONOVAN is a senior archaeologist with Margaret Gowen and Co. Ltd.

EMER PURCELL is a postgraduate student in the Department of History at University College, Cork.

EILEEN REILLY is an environmental archaeologist with Margaret Gowen and Co. Ltd.

LINZI SIMPSON is a senior archaeologist with Margaret Gowen and Co. Ltd.

Editor's preface

The fourth annual Friends of Medieval Dublin Symposium took place in Trinity College, Dublin, on Saturday 25 May 2002. The large attendance on the day – comprising people of all ages and backgrounds – indicates that interest in Dublin's medieval past has not waned and the lively discussions to which individual papers gave rise is proof that debate on the subject is alive and well. It was until recently a hobby horse of enthusiasts on the subject of medieval Dublin to speculate as to the location of the site of the original Viking *longphort*, and massive excavations such as those conducted at Temple Bar fed into that debate and are reflected in the published proceedings of earlier Symposia in this series. But, now that the era of large-scale excavation within the walls of the medieval town is a thing of the past, development and excavation has shifted elsewhere, and new foci of debate are emerging.

One of the most discernible features of the debate at the 2002 Symposium was instead, therefore, the question of the location of the early Christian ecclesiastical settlement of *Duiblinn*, and the vestigial remains of various ditches and possible enclosures that have been – and, as I write, continue to be – unearthed to the south of the medieval town, where development is proceeding apace, suggest that we may soon have answers to this weighty question. These subjects – where was the precise location of the Viking ship-camp that developed into the town of Dublin? And where exactly was the monastic site from which this country's capital city takes its name? – are not matters of dry academic argument but rather the very foundation-stones of Dublin's history, and it is a privilege to be involved in seeking answers to them.

I would like, therefore, to thank all who contributed to making the fourth Symposium the success it was, particularly the Department of Medieval History at Trinity College, which covered the costs, and Margaret Gowen & Co. which funded the reception afterwards. Almost all the speakers at the Symposium surrendered to my bullying and produced manuscripts which it has been an honour to prepare for publication, while several others unable to speak on the day allowed me to include their work. My colleague, Dr Katharine Simms, kindly agreed to write an appreciation of the late Dr Philomena Connolly, who contributed to *Medieval Dublin II* (2001) and to whom this volume is dedicated, while Gréagóir Uasal Ó Dúill willingly assented to the inclusion of his very moving poem, composed on the occasion of Phil's untimely death. The volume is nearly twice the size of its predecessors, and I am most grateful to Mr John Fitzgerald, Dublin City Manager, for the continuing financial support that makes the series affordable, and to Michael Adams and his team at Four Courts Press for not allowing size to matter (*too* much).

Seán Duffy
Chairman
Friends of Medieval Dublin

After hearing of Phil Connolly's death

The sky flat grey, pewter cold and closed,
The wind unvarying in its varying presence
Is a bass ground, a tactile wash.
You walk the edge – an ancient *geas* –
As close to the edge as you dare.

Your eyes are bent on the water's treacherous advance
On the breaking of water, blacklettered on the parchment sand,
In suddenly swallowed drying out disappearances
And the spew of ragworm burrows.
You try to interpret the fugitive evidence of the ebb.

A black excrescence out beyond the surfline
Dives, where salmon pause before the uphill race,
Rears shoulder high, juggling its prey, settles, watches you.
The horizon has jumped in closer in a squall of rain.

At extreme edge of vision your eye becomes
Barely conscious of glints and flashes out on the sky,
        above the metal sea,
Your mind engages to see the gannet dive,
Each body shines, incandescent, with a light
Gathered from some source unknown to you:
Perhaps the flashing fear of the rushing mass of mackerel fry,
Or the phosphorescence of a dying ocean wave.

A bird flies through the hall and out again
Into the stormy night.

GRÉAGÓIR Ó DÚILL
June 2002

Gréagóir Ó Dúill, a colleague of Phil's as archivist in the Public Record Office of Ireland 1971–6, is now assistant director of the Poets' House, Falcarragh, Co. Donegal.

Philomena Connolly, an appreciation

14 December 1948 to 12 June 2002

Historians and archivists throughout Ireland and beyond were shocked to hear of Phil Connolly's tragically sudden death in the prime of a very active and productive career.

The eldest of three children of Cornelius and Gabrielle Connolly, she was born in Dublin and educated in the progressive Sandymount High School before successfully obtaining licence from Archbishop John Charles McQuaid to ignore the Catholic Church's ban then in force and study for her B.A. in History and Political Science at Trinity College, 1965–69. Specialising in medieval history was more unusual then than now. Only four took the Junior Sophister course 'The changing society of the later middle ages', and only Phil and myself proceeded to the Senior Sophister option 'Anglo-Irish relations in the later middle ages' under Professor Lydon, who nicknamed us, as a result of frequent spirited though amiable arguments over historical issues 'the irresistible force and the immoveable object'.

As postgraduates we formed part of a larger group of Trinity medieval historians, senior and junior to ourselves, and Phil became a major influence in creating a sense of community among us, organising the joint production of a spoof medieval chronicle in Latin and medieval French, or infecting us with her own enthusiasm for the latest recorded medieval music.

Directly after graduating Phil took a Diploma in the Study of Records and the Administration of Archives at Liverpool (awarded 1970), and next year she was appointed an archivist in the Public Record Office of Ireland, then in the Four Courts, though later relocated to Bishop Street, and known from 1988 onwards as the National Archives. She combined her work there at the outset with research for a Ph.D. thesis under Professor Otway-Ruthven on the Irish expeditions of Prince Lionel of Clarence (awarded 1978). With her professional training she was enormously helpful to fellow-postgraduates, pouring over puzzling manuscript readings with us, and drawing our attention to documents relevant to our own topics that she came across, not only through her job at the National Archives but also because she generously shared the fruits of her research trips to the London Public Record Office. She brought a great gusto and sense of fun to the study of medieval people, making the less disciplined among us wonder at her predilection for the study of Anglo-Norman administrative records, but to her every Chancellor, Treasurer and Exchequer clerk was an individual, with human needs and human failings, an approach shown, for example, in her article on 'The proceedings against John de Burnham, Treasurer of Ireland 1343–49'.

Having started work so young, in recent times Phil was the longest-serving archivist in the National Archives, and had thus been colleague, friend and mentor to a whole generation of archivists in Ireland and to some now holding positions around Britain. She possessed an unequalled knowledge of the holdings of the National Archives and its predecessor institutions, enabling her to bring to light and publish many neglected caches of medieval records which had survived the disastrous fire at the Four Courts in 1922.

Though specialising in medieval material, she also had a vast knowledge of the nineteenth-century administrative records, and had recently been cataloguing documents relating to the 1798 Rebellion. Given the demands of her day-to-day work as an archivist, the speed and efficiency with which she made source after medieval source accessible in published form was breath-taking, and required a constant dedication of her all-too-short periods of leave to this work. For years she devoted an afternoon a week in term-time to giving lessons in Palaeography and Diplomatics to postgraduate students in the Medieval History Department in Trinity. Her *Medieval Record Sources* was based on this long teaching experience and has proved an invaluable guide to novice researchers.

Before she died so suddenly she was planning both an edition of the remaining unpublished calendars of the justiciary rolls, and a future calendar of the reconstructed records of the medieval Irish Chancery. There must be few who could be so truly described as an irreparable loss, both to friends and colleagues and to the discipline she served so selflessly.

KATHARINE SIMMS

Excavations at the medieval cemetery of
St Peter's church, Dublin

TIM COUGHLAN

INTRODUCTION

The site of the excavation is located at the corner of Stephen Street Upper and Longford Street Great, Dublin (fig. 1). It is proposed to develop this site by constructing a five-storey office development with basement-level car-parking. Prior to excavation the site consisted of a car-park with no standing buildings extant on the site. Preliminary site investigations by Martin Reid in 1999 in the northeast corner of this site identified the remains of twenty articulated inhumations. This burial horizon was delimited to the west by the stone foundations of a medieval boundary wall *c*.1.2m wide. Further testing was carried out in the southeast corner of the site by Dermot Nelis, and subsequently by the author, which indicated that burials extended into this area also. Martin Reid had established that cellars had removed all archaeological material in the west of the site.

The excavation of the site was carried out in two phases (fig. 2). The first phase was concentrated in a 10m by 11m area in the southeast corner of the site. However, the subsequent granting of planning permission for a full basement in the development required that all archaeological deposits across the site be excavated. This work was carried out during Phase 2 in the areas to the north and west of Phase 1. Phase one excavations were carried out between March and June 2001, with Phase 2 being carried out from January to April 2002. Post-excavation work is ongoing at the time of going to press, so that full appraisal of the excavation results has not been completed. The following represents an outline of the more significant results identified to date.

HISTORICAL BACKGROUND

The site is located in the parish of St Peter in Royal Exchange Ward, Dublin. It lies southeast of the walls of the medieval town, at the southern end of the important medieval routes known respectively as Sheep Street (modern Ship Street Great) and St George's Lane (modern South Great George's Street). Close to the location of the present excavation are the sites of the medieval

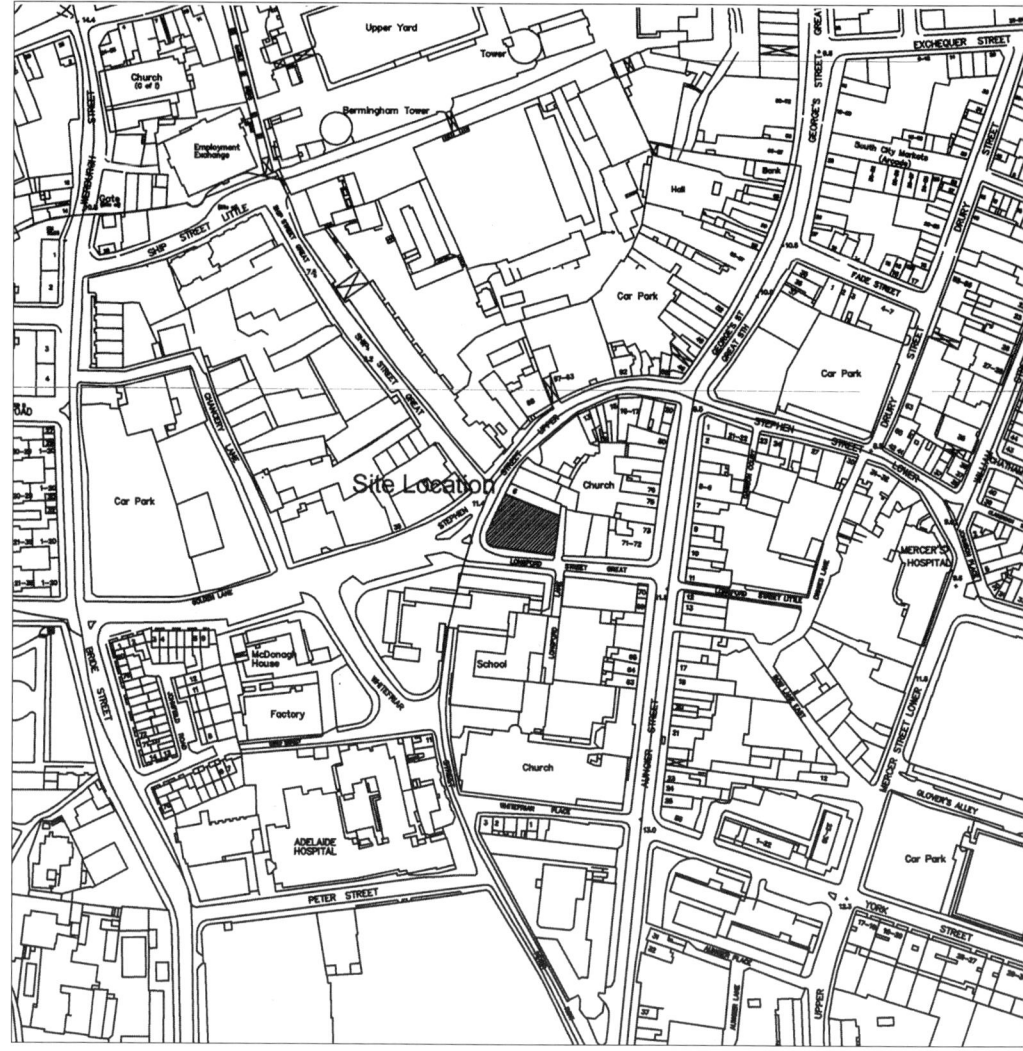

1 General site location

churches of St Stephen and St Peter. St Stephen's church and leper hospital was located at the site of the modern Mercer's Hospital and gave its name to the street.

Early medieval
The name Dublin (Dubhlinn), meaning black pool, is generally accepted as referring to the pool or pond that was located directly southeast of the site of the present Dublin Castle. The name, it is suggested, was applied to an early

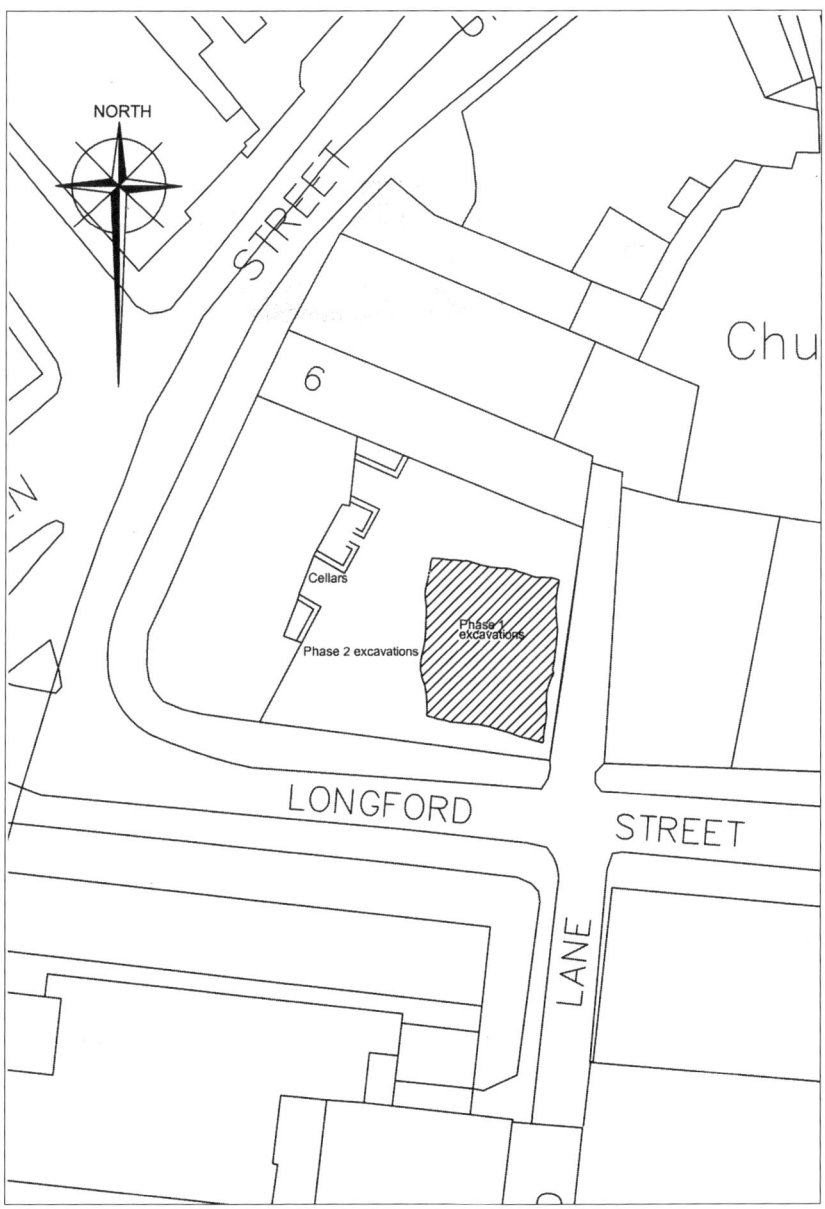

2 Site location showing excavation areas

Christian monastic settlement south of the black pool (1990, 58). In the early medieval period and pre-dating the establishment of the Norse settlement, there are references to abbots and bishops of Dubhlinn (Simms 1990, 44). The site of this ecclesiastical foundation is a matter of conjecture. Myles V.

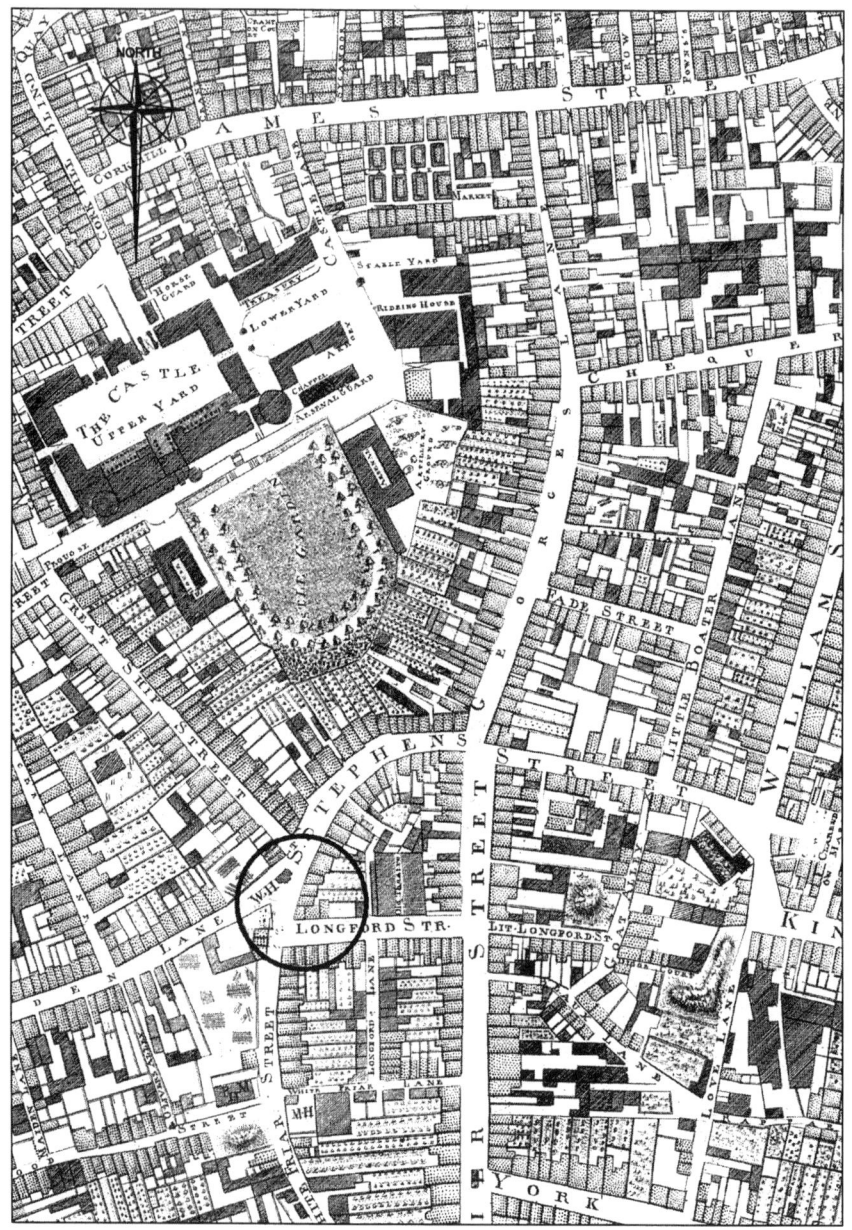

4 Rocque 1756, showing site location

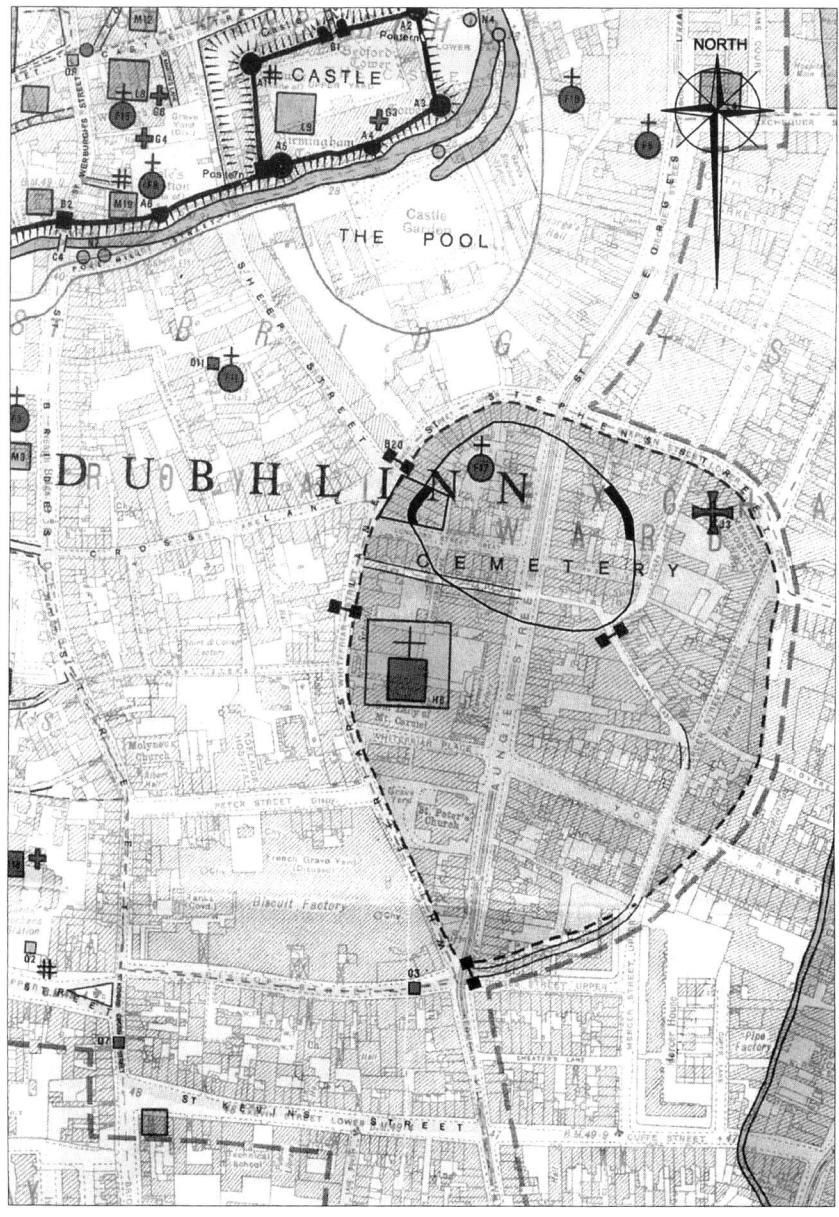

5 After Clarke 1978 – with excavated ditch overlaid

Ronan was the first modern scholar to detect that there is a distinctive curvature to the street pattern formed by Stephen's Street, Whitefriar Street and Peter's Row, which is visible on both Speed's map, and the 1756 map of Dublin by Rocque (fig. 4), and is still preserved in the modern street pattern (fig. 5). Ronan referred to this as a 'rath-like site surrounded by a ring of old streets which still retains its remarkable outline', and Howard Clarke subsequently suggested that it might be the ecclesiastical enclosure of Dubhlinn (1990, 62). The curvature is indeed characteristic of early medieval ecclesiastical enclosures, for example, Duleek, Kells or Armagh.

This outline corresponds to the medieval parish of St Peter's, and may originally have demarcated the line of an enclosure that contained a church dedicated to that saint, a popular figure in the early medieval period. It should, however, be pointed out that there are no less than five churches south of the walled town of Dublin lying to the east of the river Poddle, some of which may have been founded before 700 (Clarke 1990, 63). Only two, St Peter's and St Stephen's, are within the bounds of the proposed enclosure. The site of another of them, the church and graveyard of St Michael le Pole, located west of St Peter's and outside the suggested enclosure, was excavated in 1981 by the Dublin Archaeological Research Team (Gowen 2001, 13–51). The earliest phase of occupation of the site was represented by gullies, postholes and cut-features that may date to the eighth or ninth centuries. Several burials, for which an eighth- or ninth-century date has been suggested, were uncovered over these layers (ibid., 34–36). This may imply an early site, with Christian activities and burials continuing into the Viking period.

Anglo-Norman and later medieval
The exact site of the original church of St Peter is not known. On the earliest surviving map of Dublin (John Speed 1610, fig. 3), it is placed in the block defined by the curving line of Stephen Street to the north, with St Stephens's church to the east, and by the Carmelite monastery of Whitefriars to the south. St Peter's if not actually side-by-side with St Stephen's was certainly situated very close to it. Certainly the church at St Peter's was in existence prior to the arrival of the Anglo-Normans, as it is referred to in an important early twelfth-century poem preserved in the *Book of Uí Mhaine* (Clarke 2002, 17). The earliest Anglo-Norman reference is contained in a papal bull of Alexander III dating to 1179 (ibid.) where it is cited as the property of the priory of Holy Trinity at Christ Church. It functioned as one of the original parochial churches of Anglo-Norman Dublin, frequently referred to as St Peter's de la Hulle (St Peter's of the hill). It was, however, too poor to be taxed in the 1290s (ibid.), and by 1370 it was in such a state of disrepair that it was described as 'ruined to its foundations' and a papal indulgence was granted of 1 year and 40 days to repair it (Donnelly 1905, ii, 135).

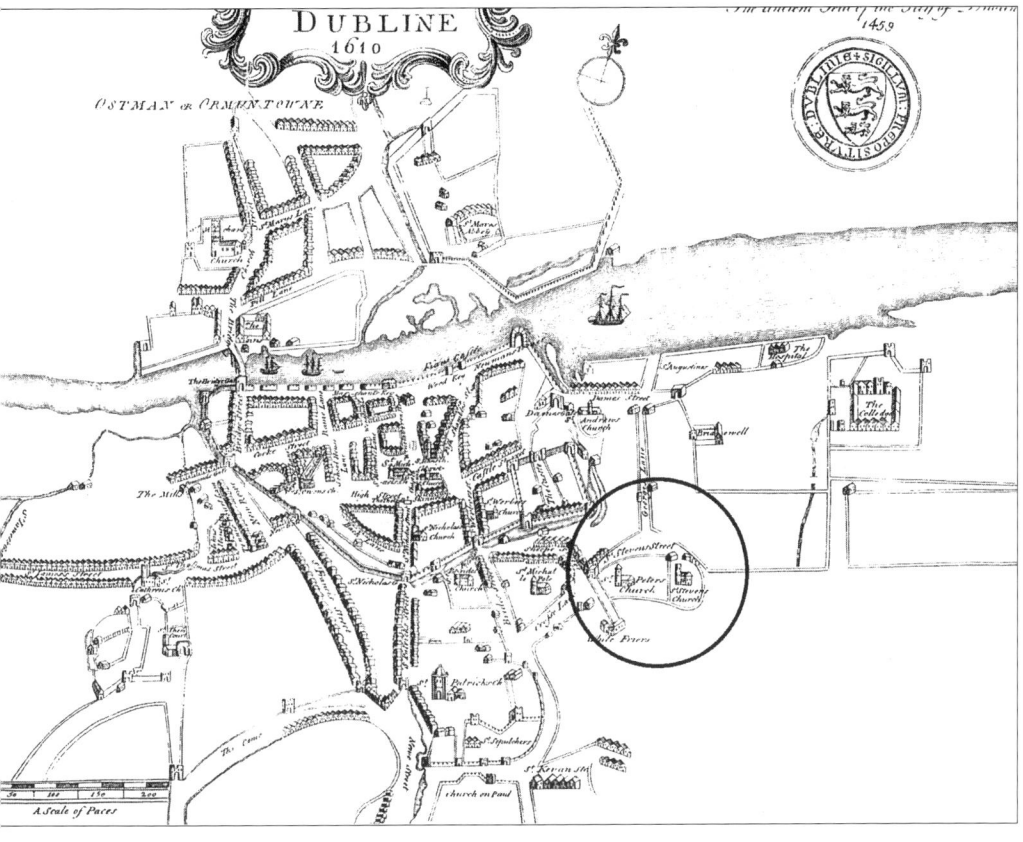

3 John Speed, 1610, with site location circled

Post-medieval

By the time of the Restoration in the 1660s both the churches of St Peter and of St Stephen were in very bad repair if not in ruins. Land and finance for the building of a new parish church were provided by the first earl of Longford. In the early seventeenth century Sir Francis Aungier, Master of the Rolls to James I, acquired much of the property of the dissolved Carmelite friary, and converted the monastic buildings into his residence. His descendant, also Francis, was created earl of Longford in 1677 and began to turn his Dublin property into a building estate. Between 1660 and 1685 the first extensive planned suburban development of Dublin city took place on the estate owned and administered by Francis Aungier (Burke 1972, 368). The boundaries of Aungier's estate, as described in 1724, included a portion of the site of the church of St Peter's on the Hill (or Mount) (Burke, 368).

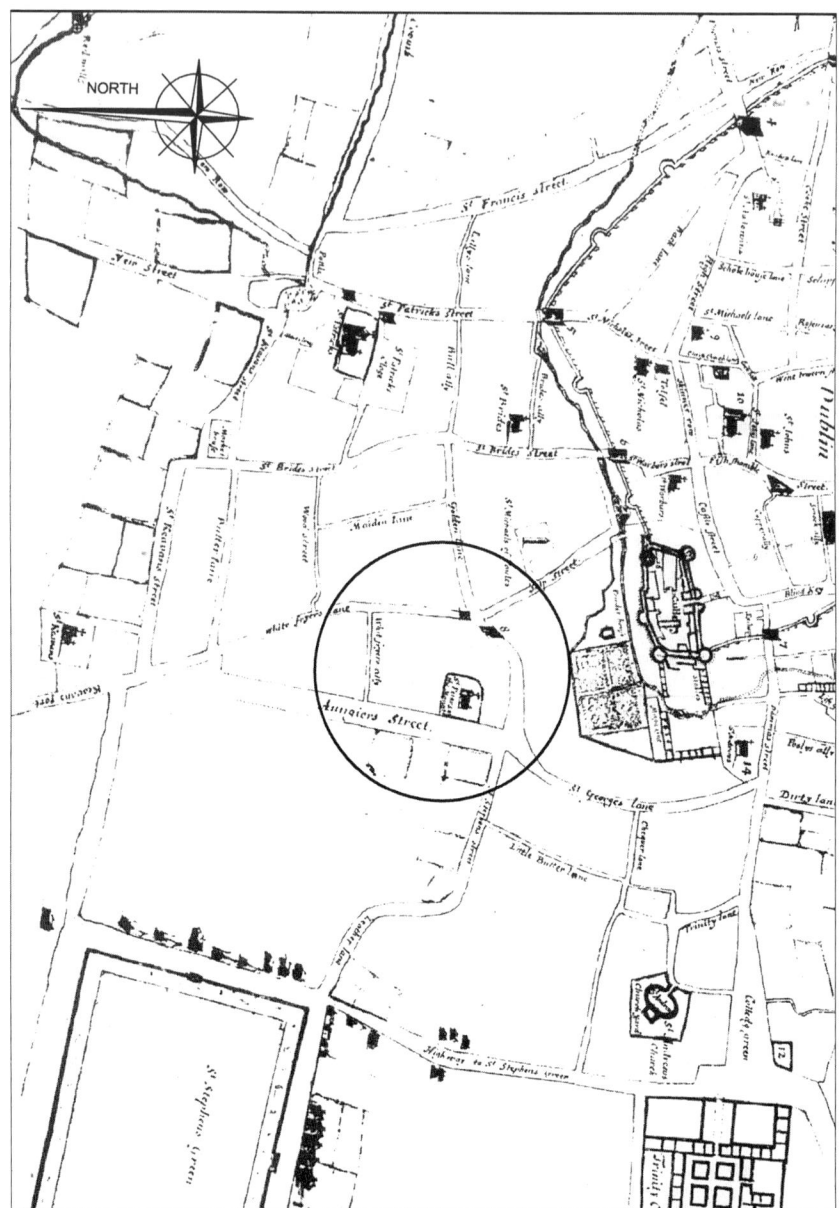

6 De Gomme, 1673, with site ringed

Part of this site was never in the possession of Aungier and his title to an adjacent piece of property is doubtful. According to Speed's map of 1610 and de Gomme's survey of 1673 (fig. 6), the south-eastern section of the street block that is now bounded by St Stephen's Street, Aungier Street and Longford Street was the location of the church and churchyard of St Peter's on the Mount. According to Burke (ibid.) Speed's plan suggests that in 1610 the churchyard of St Peter extended eastwards from Stephen Street to the western boundary of St Stephen's churchyard and occupied all the area between Stephen Street and Goat Alley, with Beaux Lane forming the southern boundary of properties fronting the south side of Great Longford Street. Francis Aungier laid out Aungier Street, Longford Street and Cuffe Street, and if Speed's depiction is taken as accurate, Aungier Street was opened through the churchyard of St Peter to the lands of Whitefriars, and Aungier either took possession of or was granted the part of St Peter's churchyard that was east of the new street (ibid.). He then provided the site for the new church of St Peter's on Aungier Street. The medieval church of St Peter on the Mount and a portion of its graveyard evidently became an enclave within the Aungier estate.

The present excavation site would therefore appear to be located at the western edge of the putative early medieval ecclesiastical enclosure. Speed's map and also the late seventeenth-century developments of the earl of Longford would suggest that the area had remained undeveloped, part of the monastic precinct originally of St Peter's and later of the Carmelite priory.

THE EXCAVATION RESULTS

The total excavated area on the site measured a maximum of 23m east-west by 21m north-south. The archaeological horizon was sealed by 1.2m–1.4m of rubble overburden, which was removed by mechanical digger. During the course of the excavation a total of 150 individual burials were identified. It is difficult to apply broad phases of activity on a site where each burial represents a single phase/event; however three main levels of activity were identified, with many phases of activity within each level. These are: Level 1, the ditch (earthen enclosure); Level 2, the walled enclosure; and Level 3, post-medieval activity. This paper will only deal in detail with levels 1 and 2. Activity in level 3 will only be referred to where it has impacted on earlier levels.

THE DITCH/EARTHEN ENCLOSURE (fig. 7)

The earliest features on the site were identified at or just above subsoil level. The subsoil itself consisted of a mixed yellow-grey clay with gravel and it was sealed by a thin band of yellow loam that probably represented an original sod

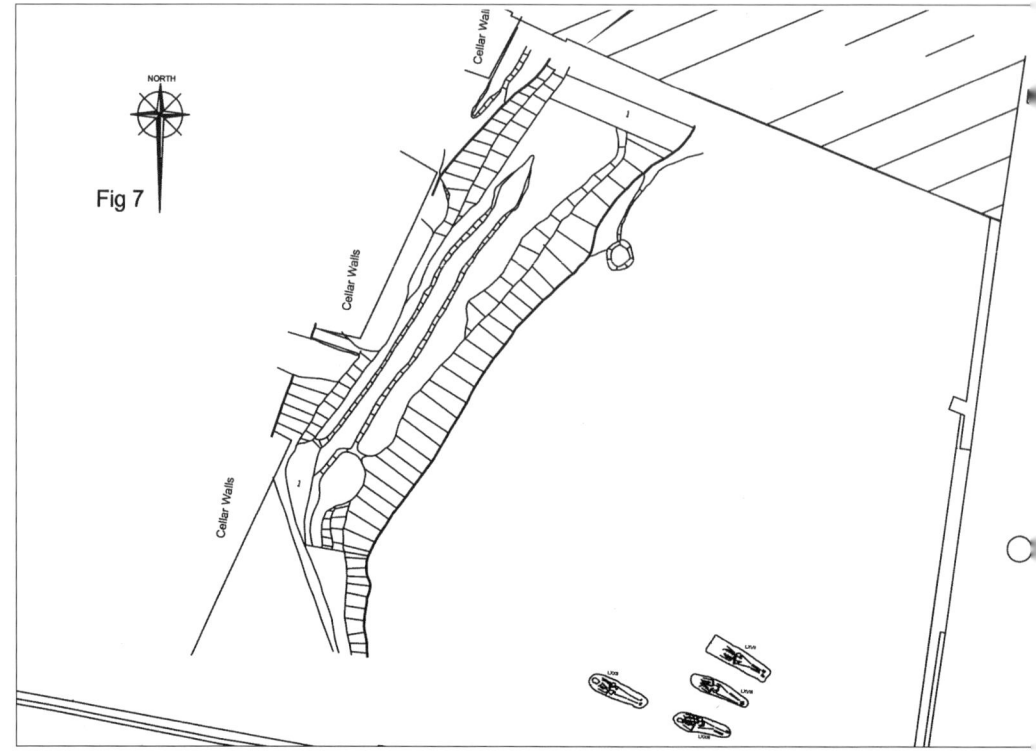

7 Plan of excavated earthen enclosure

layer. A number of small pits were recorded at this level but their associations
are unclear. The main feature was a large ditch that was identified in the
western half of the excavated area (plate 1). The ditch was orientated roughly
northeast–southwest but turned to a north–south orientation at the southern
end of the site. It had been cut at the original sod level. It had a maximum
width of 5m at the top and 2.4m at the base and was a maximum of 2.2m
deep. There was no evidence within the excavated area of the excavated
material from the ditch being re-deposited to form a bank, so it can only be
assumed that if there was a bank associated with this ditch it must have been
located outside/to the west of the ditch. At the base of the ditch a narrow
channel was dug along the inner (eastern) edge. It is likely that this feature
functioned to drain water, so it would appear that the ditch was clearly not
intended to act as a moat.

The ditch was multi-phased and there was evidence for at least three re-
cuts (fig. 8), and attempts to keep a deeper channel as a drain at the base of
the ditch can be seen at all stages. However, the channel moved to the outer
(western) edge. It is not known if there was a significant reason for this. The

Plate 1 Excavated ditch from south

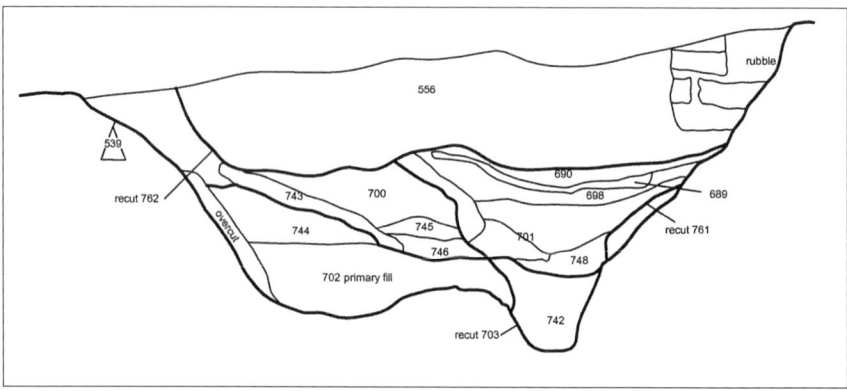

8 Excavated ditch section

answer may be quite simply that it was preferable to throw the excavated spoil from the re-cuts outside the enclosure rather than inside, and as such it is easier to dig on that side. The main deposits filling the ditch consisted of heavy clays, often quite stony. It is possible that this represented material from a clay bank that fell back into the open ditch. The fills of the re-cut channels were, however, comprised of silt and organic mixes, the silt confirming the presence of water. The organic material on the other hand may represent the remains of occupation debris that either was dumped into the ditch directly with the intention of draining away, or built up as a result of the drain being clogged. It would seem apparent that the drainage channels were diverted out of the ditch along its northern edge at some point where they would flow away with the natural terrain. It is possible that the ditch diverted a natural water source but there appears to be none recorded in this specific area.

The ditch clearly forms part of a large enclosure. But is this enclosure Clarke's early monastic settlement of Dubhlinn? During the course of the excavation it was felt that this may indeed be the case given the scale of the ditch and its orientation running parallel to the present street frontage. If there had been an outer bank it is likely that the route around the enclosure would have been close to the present street. Towards the end of the dig, however, in the southern area of the site, the ditch turned quite sharply to the southeast. This indicated that the ditch would enclose a smaller area than that required for the early Christian enclosure suggested by Clarke.

Fieldwork carried out by John Ó Néill of MGL Ltd on two sites to the east of the site under discussion found traces of a ditch (pers. comm.). His work consisted of a series of test trenches to the rear (i.e., west) of a building fronting onto Digges Lane, and a small excavation to the rear of a property fronting onto Longford Street Little. He found a ditch of similar proportions to that on our site although he has not been able to excavate a full section through it to date. His ditch runs in a northwest-southeast direction. It is Ó Néill's opinion that his ditch represents the eastern boundary of St Peter's, and as such is a continuation of the excavated ditch at Stephen Street. When his results are looked at in conjunction with the author's and overlaid on Clarke's map of medieval Dublin (fig. 5) it becomes quite evident where the probable original boundary of St Peter's was. The sharp turn at the southern end of Digges Lane corresponds with the turn at the southern end of the excavated ditch on Stephen Street. It is clear that St Peter's was within its own enclosure.

It is still possible that Clarke is correct in his claim of a large early Christian settlement being demarcated by a larger enclosure which is mirrored in the surviving street pattern. Could St Peter's be an enclosure within an earlier larger enclosure? It is possible that an earlier (early Christian) large enclosure was subdivided into a number of smaller medieval enclosures – these being St Peter's, St Stephen's and possibly St Mary's Carmelite friary (Whitefriars) to the south. Or perhaps the street pattern indicates only the boundaries around the later institutions. The location of the ditch in the excavation at Stephen Street suggests that there is room for an additional outer ditch to be located inside the modern street frontage provided there was no associated outer bank. As this street alignment is assumed to follow the course of a ditch/enclosure, it remains possible that it follows another ditch outside that under discussion. It can only be hoped that further archaeological fieldwork will confirm the presence and the precise location of the early Christian enclosure.

Burials within the earthen enclosure
There were only four identified burials associated with this earthen enclosure (fig. 7). All four were orientated west-east and are thus most likely to be Christian burials. They were in simple graves beside one another at the southern end of the excavation area. Two of the burials were missing their skulls–LXVII (plate 2) and LXVIII. There was no obvious evidence of a re-cut/robber cut in either grave or its fill. But it remains unclear whether these skulls were removed as trophies, since there was no obvious disturbance to the thoracic vertebrae as one would expect if either had been decapitated, and the bodies would need to be decomposed in order to remove the skulls without disturbing other parts of the skeleton.

All four skeletons have been initially identified as adult males between the ages of 25 and 45. Jenny Coughlan has looked at their pathologies in an attempt to determine whether they are significant in terms of the population. She has identified that Burial LXVII showed evidence for a non-specific infection of the leg bones showing healing new bone formation, suggesting that it was active at time of death but was perhaps of long standing. There was also fusion at the sacroiliac joint (between the hip and the sacrum) and at the right elbow. There was very little degenerative joint disease with only the lower lumbar vertebrae affected. Burial LXVIII had two healed rib fractures

Plate 2 Skeleton lxvii

Plate 3 Western boundary wall

(obviously trauma but not associated with death) and mild/moderate degenerative joint disease through the thoracic vertebrae. Burial LXXII contained *os acromiale* at the left scapula. This is non-fusion of the acromion process to the spine of the scapula and is suggested to be associated with stresses through the rotator cuff muscles during development: a lot of individuals, probably archers, from Henry VIII's warship, the *Mary Rose*, had this condition (pers. comm., J. Coughlan). There were also healed rib fractures, osteoarthritis at the right big toe and mild degenerative joint disease through the vertebrae. Burial LXXIII had compression fractures through the lower spine (probably caused by a fall or some other trauma) and mild degenerative joint disease through the vertebrae. Ms Coughlan concluded that these individuals were involved in some from of activity which resulted in the visible bone trauma, but that this activity was not associated with any of their deaths. It is difficult to suggest at this stage whether these individuals were unusual in terms of pathology until all the data is collated. It is not unusual, however, to find such fractures in a population.

Dating of the earthen enclosure

There were no finds or datable artefacts from the lower fills of the ditch. A small amount of disarticulated human bone was found at the base and, in conjunction with the four burials, it is hoped that C14 dates will be forthcoming, although this work had not been completed at the time of writing. There were pottery sherds recovered from the upper fills of the ditch and this pottery has been tentatively dated to the early twelfth century. This suggests that we are possibly looking at a rough date of 1100 for the construction of St Peter's church and earthen enclosure, which gives us a similar date to that of the early material excavated at St Michael le Pole (Gowen 2001, 36). The earthen enclosure at St Peter's possibly continued to function until the late twelfth/early thirteenth century.

THE WALLED ENCLOSURE

The second major phase of activity on the site was characterised by the final infilling of the ditch and the construction of a mortared stone boundary wall. This had the effect of reducing the area of the enclosure (fig. 9). The western boundary wall survived at foundation level only (plate 3). This wall extended for 8.50m and had a maximum width of 1.2m. This wall was orientated north-south and had been exposed previously by Martin Reid. The wall was built tight against its construction cut. The wall stood a maximum of three courses high (0.5m). It was not properly faced and was constructed of large, medium and small-sized uncut limestone and had a rubble core. Part of the lower course of the wall had sunk into the soft upper fills of the underlying ditch. The wall clearly represents the foundation level and none of the original above-ground portion of the wall survives. Neither did any of the structure of the southern boundary wall survive, but a robber trench was identified during the excavation that marked its line (plate 4). The stone in the wall was robbed in the late medieval period and re-used elsewhere. This wall was slightly narrower than the western boundary measuring only 0.9–1.0m in width. As there was no direct stratagraphic link between the western and southern boundaries because of later disturbance it can only be assumed that both walls are contemporary. The fact that all of the associated burials are within the area enclosed by these walls would suggest that they are.

It had been hoped that the south-western corner of the enclosure would be identified during the course of the excavation. However a post-medieval drain truncated the site at the point where both walls were anticipated to meet. It became apparent during the excavation that the two walls never met and that

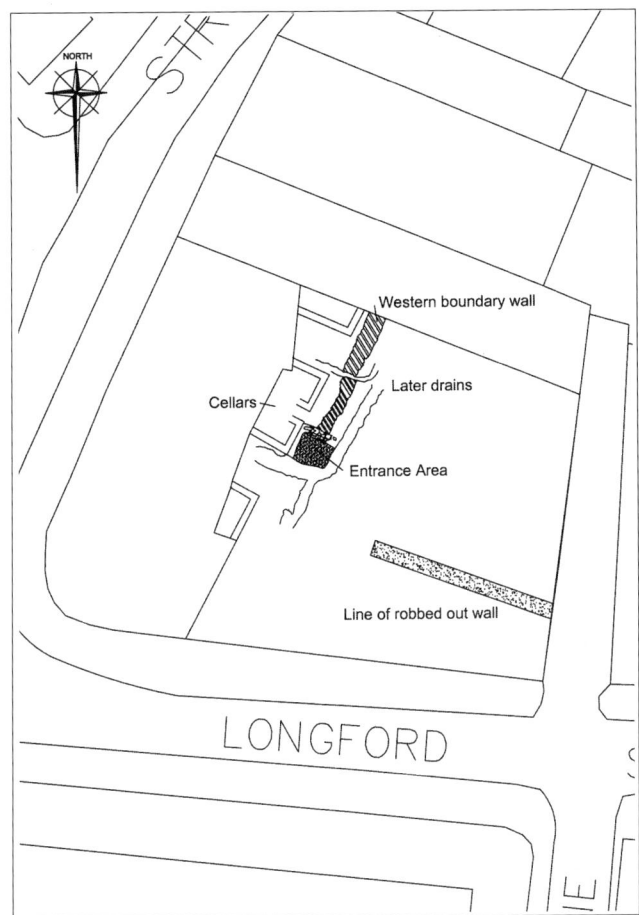

9 Plan of excavated walled enclosure

there was an entrance to the enclosure in this south-western corner. Only a small portion of this feature survived due to the post-medieval disturbance. The entrance consisted of a roughly built, un-mortared, east-west orientated stone wall (plate 5). It only survived for a maximum length of 2.8m due to disturbance from post-medieval cellars to the west and the graveyard to the east. It was only one course high and 0.68m wide. It appeared that this wall was abutted by the main western boundary wall. At first it was felt that this small portion of wall may have been part of an early structure – possibly directly associated with the church building. However, immediately to the south of the wall was a series of deposits of compacted coarse gravel and stones. These formed a solid, and probably quite dry, pathway into the cemetery itself. The line of the pathway can then be traced through the main burial areas. The burial distribution clearly shows areas with no burials and in the west and south of the graveyard it is quite likely that these areas represented

Plate 4 Southern
boundary robber
trench

pathways or access routes. During the course of the excavation these areas
also showed evidence for stone and mettled surfaces.

The entrance wall probably never stood particularly high and was possibly
more an elaborate form of kerbing than a large structure. This can be seen in
its construction – loosely clay-bonded – and also in the fact that subsequent
burials running along the line of the western boundary wall cut through
portions of the wall, suggesting that it had been covered over with soil and
was no longer clearly evident. This is supported by the fact that subsequent
deposits of small stone and roughly mettled surfaces were also cut by the later
burials and sealed the wall remains.

The burials within the walled enclosure

A total of 146 burials were recorded within the excavated area of the walled
enclosure (fig.10). No detailed phasing of the burial activity can be accurately

Plate 5 E–W entrance wall

established given their large number. The burials were interred in a green-brown clay soil and there appeared to be two main deposits of this soil, although this was difficult to discern, again due to the large amount of distur-bance from the burials themselves. It is possible that the soil was imported, as suggested at the excavation of the church of St Michael le Pole (Gowen 2001, 41). All of the deposits and burial fills contained mixed medieval pottery, and it is likely that following the completion of analysis quite a broad range of dates will be evident across the site. The burials were not formally laid out with the exception of those along the line of the western boundary wall (plate 6). In the main group of burials in the eastern half of the site it was found that later burials cut through earlier interments without care (plate 7): it would seem to have been more important to ensure the opening of new graves than to preserve earlier remains. This implies that there were no grave mark-ings and that the significant factor in death was to be in the graveyard rather than in a specific plot. There were instances of attempts to re-inter disturbed remains with some degree of reverence by placing legs with legs, skulls with skulls, etc., and it is hoped that further analysis of the burial record may facilitate the re-uniting of some of the disarticulated remains with their articulated parts.

The twenty-one burials along the western boundary wall were, however, more evenly spaced, and an attempt appears to have been made to preserve remains *in situ* while facilitating further burial. The significant feature which

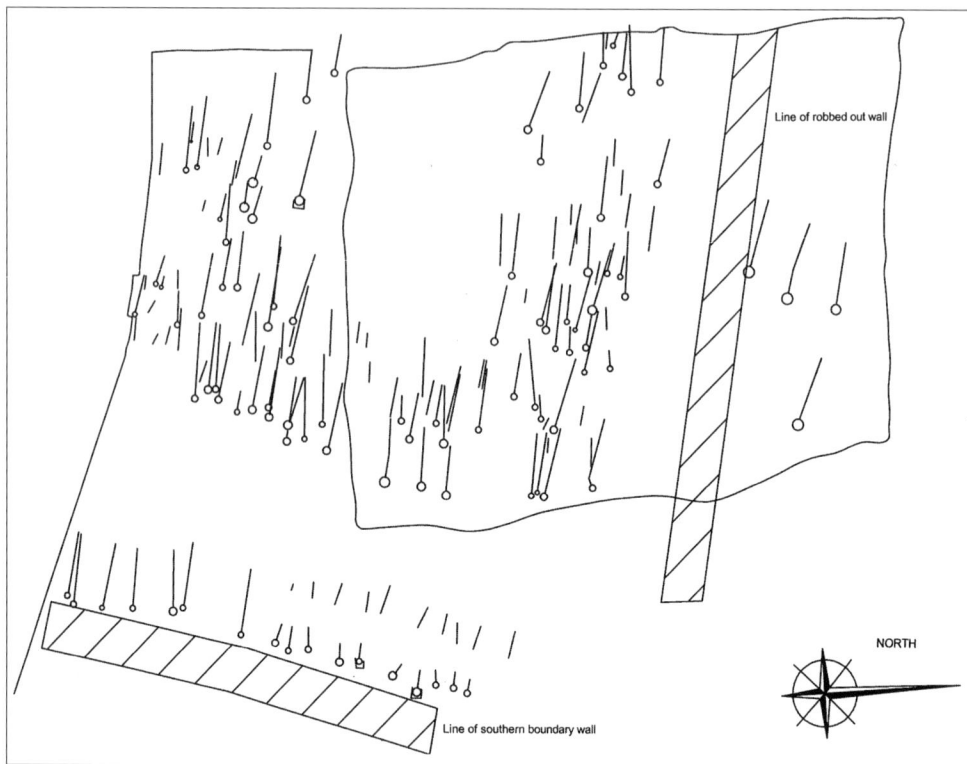

Line of robbed out wall

NORTH

Line of southern boundary wall

10 Burial location plan

caused disturbance in this region was a post-medieval drain that bisected 14 of the 21 burials (plate 6). It is probable that marks were made on the western wall, above the heads of those interred, showing their position. Perhaps these were the graves of more esteemed members of the community who continued to command respect after death. This theory is in some way supported by the fact that five of the burials lay to the south of/across the entrance and their graves cut sections of the entrance wall and the gravel pathway, but the bodies continued to be interred side by side without disturbing each other. Initial examination of the 21 remains shows that 11 were adult males, 6 adult females, and 4 were sub-adult.

Two of the graves in the excavation were stone lined, one along the western boundary wall – Burial LXXXIV – and the other in the northeast corner – Burial CVII. The stone-lined coffin of Burial CVII was roughly trapezoidal in plan (plate 8) and had an internal length of 1.73m. The stones are mortared and they have been roughly dressed on their internal face. A small bed of mortar was evident beneath the skull, which acted as a pillow. The stones of the grave also narrowed around the skull to support it laterally. A narrow

Plate 6 Three truncated burials

ridge of mortar evident around the top of the stones clearly shows that originally there was a lintel, which has subsequently been robbed out. A large number of disarticulated remains were re-interred in this grave. It is not clear whether these represent remains disturbed during the construction of the stone coffin or whether they were placed there following the removal of the lintel. The second stone-lined burial, LXXXIV, was badly disturbed by a post-medieval drain (plate 9). Only the upper body and the lower legs survived. The stones were set vertically against the sides of the grave-cut and the body was then interred. It was a simpler construction than that of burial CVII and there was no surviving evidence of a lintel.

Dating of the walled enclosure
It is probable that the walled enclosure replaced the earthen enclosure during the early thirteenth century. It is difficult to date this accurately until all the excavation results have been analysed. There was little indication of coffins with only some nails being identified within some graves, and these may not have been directly associated with coffins. There were a number of examples of shroud pins and buckles but in general the burials were simple and no artefacts of significant value were found with any of them. It is not likely that

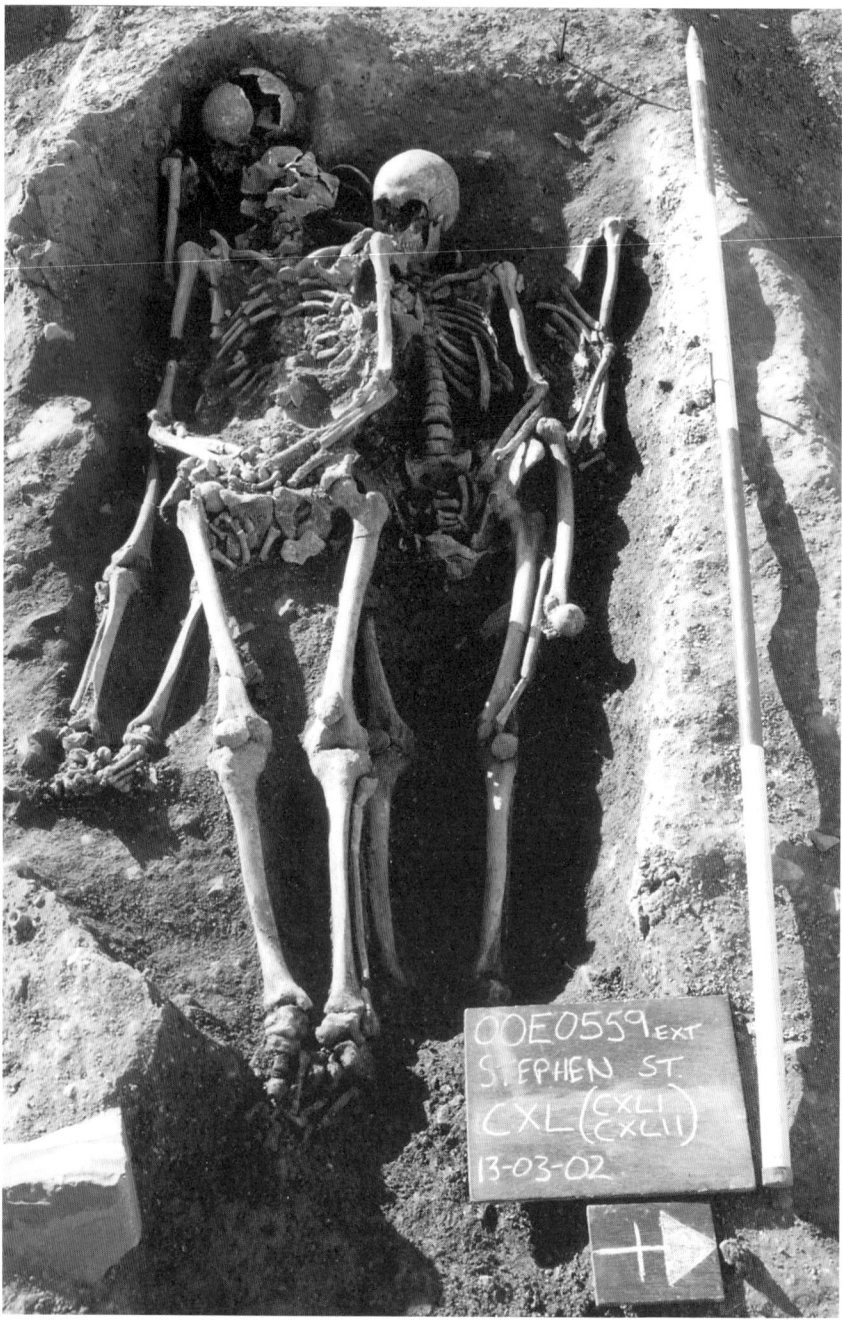

Plate 7 Overcrowding of burials

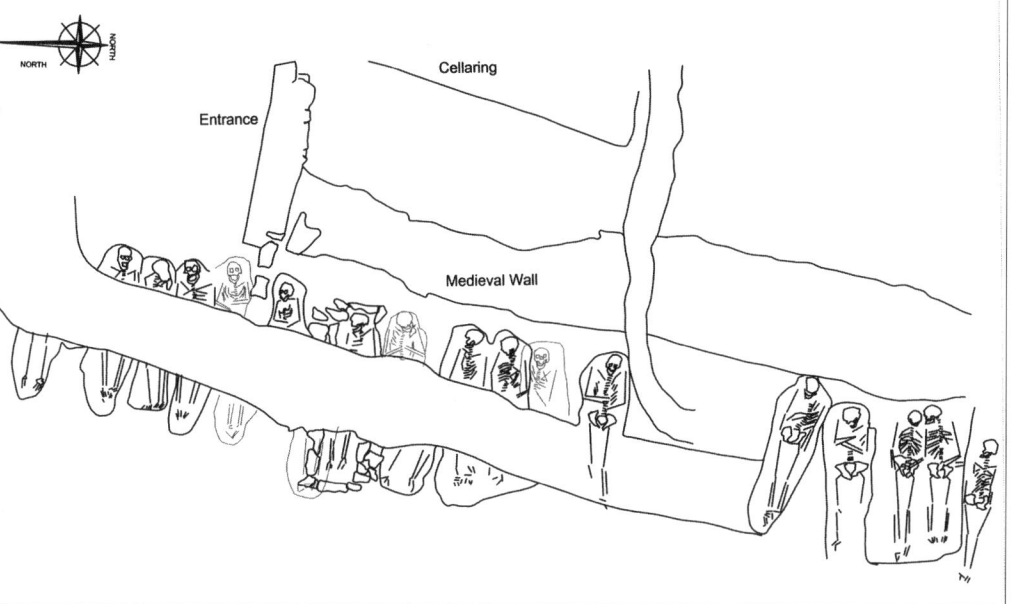

11 Plan of burials along western boundary wall

the burials represented people of particularly high social status, and as such it is possible that the cemetery continued in use even if the church had fallen into ruin. It is probable that the graveyard was not in use after the early seventeenth century. There were certainly no burials identified during the excavation later than the post-medieval activity on site, the Aungier estate having begun to be laid out as a suburban development from 1660.

PRELIMINARY ANALYSIS OF THE INHUMATIONS

Excavations undertaken in advance of construction at Stephen Street, Dublin identified a total of 149 discrete inhumations. The remains of a single additional child inhumation were identified during osteological analysis bringing the total number of individuals analysed to 150. Analysis was undertaken both to establish basic demographic information (sex, age and stature) and to identify skeletal changes that could be linked to occupational, pathological or nutritional stresses. Only preliminary results are offered at this stage. Of the 150 burials analysed, 42 (28%) were identified as sub-adult, the remaining 108 (72%) adult. These broad age groups can be further subdivided based on stages of skeletal and dental development (sub-adults) and degeneration (adults).

Plate 8 Stone lined grave CVII

Plate 9 Stone lined grave LXXXIV

Sub-adults The category of sub–adult includes all individuals up to sixteen years of age at time of death. A breakdown of these burials reveals that there were three infants (one year or less) deposited within the cemetery. A further eleven individuals could be aged as young children (2–6 years) and six as older children (7–11 years). In addition, eleven individuals could only be placed in the broad 'child' category. Of these, six were found to fall between the young and old child age groups (5–8 years) while the remaining five were too poorly preserved to age accurately. Nine of the sub–adult individuals were identified as adolescent (12–16 years). The remaining two burials were identified as sub-adult based on skeletal development (non–fusion of the epiphyses) but could not be aged with any greater accuracy due to poor preservation.

Adults In general, the degenerative changes used in the ageing of adult individuals are less predictable and secure than the developmental sequences available for sub–adult ageing. This means that adult age categories tend to be broader and ageing of older adult individuals is difficult. Of the 108 adults, 23 were aged as young adult (17–25 years) and nine were aged as middle adult (26–35 years). A further 35 could be assigned a young middle adult age (26–35 years) and 13 were placed in the old middle adult age category (36–45 years). Only two individuals were determined to be older adult (46+) while the remaining 26 individuals were aged as adult only due to poor preservation.

Sexing Skeletal traits that identify sex only develop with the onset of puberty; however, sub–adult remains, even those that have reached puberty, often show little sexual differentiation. In this population sex was only assigned to adult individuals. In all, 54 males and 11 probable males, 17 females and three possible females were identified. A further 23 adult remains could not be sexed due to either ambiguous sexual traits or poor preservation.

Dental health Teeth do not remodel through time, and, as such, any changes that occur through life remain as a permanent record of health, diet and hygiene. At Stephen Street the most commonly encountered condition affecting the teeth was calculus (mineralised plaque). Caries, abscesses and periodontal disease were also well represented in this population.

Pathology Only a small number of diseases visibly affect bone and these are most commonly restricted to long-standing periods of disease and/or nutri-tional deficiency. Most acute episodes of nutritional or pathological stress either resolve themselves or result in death before the bone elements become involved. The most commonly encountered conditions in the study of archaeological material include joint disease, infection, metabolic disorders, neoplastic disease and trauma. The Stephen Street skeletons displayed evidence for all these conditions. As is often found in the study of past populations, joint disease was the most commonly encountered pathological condition in this group, followed by non-specific infection and metabolic disorders (*cribra orbitalia*). The category of trauma was represented by healed fractures (long-bones and ribs), unhealed fractures (ribs) and blunt/sharp-force trauma. An old middle adult of undetermined sex displayed a well-healed depression on the left parietal and a healed fracture to the mastoid portion of the right temporal. The level of healing indicates that this insult occurred a significant time prior to death. Sharp-force trauma to the cranium and vertebrae of a young middle adult male, on the other hand, showed no evidence of healing and would have occurred in or around the time of death.

Conclusion While it appears that this population suffered from a normal range of stresses and deficiencies, without detailed analysis of prevalence rates it is difficult to draw any meaningful conclusions about the health of the Stephen Street skeletons.

SUMMARY

It is evident from the initial results of the excavations at Stephen Street that the site has provided a significant insight into the history of St Peter's Church. It is now clear that the church was first surrounded by an earthen enclosure. The excavated section of ditch does not appear to represent the remains of the suggested early Christian enclosure of Dubhlinn that is widely believed to be responsible for the curving street pattern on Stephen Street. Is the St Peter's enclosure located within a larger early boundary? Or is St Peter's directly responsible for the street patterns, as is suggested by John Ó Néill's findings near Digges Lane, the eastern side of the enclosure? The subsequent walling of the enclosure follows a typical Anglo-Norman building trait of stone construction. The walling of the enclosure created a narrowing of the boundaries, possibly indicating a decline in the importance of the church within medieval Dublin.

Unfortunately the excavation failed to identify the exact location of the church itself. It is likely to be in the area immediately to the northeast of the excavation, as suggested by a number of historical maps. It is also unfortunate that, as yet, there are no indications as to the identity of any of the 150 remains interred in the cemetery. Further dissemination of the results will hopefully give us a clearer picture of the dates of the various phases of the church and the nature of the interred population within its cemetery.

ACKNOWLEDGEMENTS

I would like to thank Jenny Coughlan BSc for contributing the preliminary analysis of the human remains. I would also like to thank the staff of IAC Ltd. for their help with the preparation of this article and in particular

Andrew Taylor for his work on the figures and Caitríona Gleeson for her time
spent on the historical background.

BIBLIOGRAPHY

Aalen, F.H.A. & Whelan, K. (eds). 1992. *Dublin city and county: from prehistory to present.*
    Dublin.
Bardon, C. & J. 1988. *If ever you go to Dublin town.* Belfast.
Bennett, D. 1991. *Encyclopaedia of Dublin.* Dublin.
Bennett, I. 1990–2000. *Excavations: summary accounts of archaeological excavations in
    Ireland.* Bray.
Burke, N.T. 1972 An Early modern Dublin suburb, the estate of Francis Aungier, earl of
    Longford. *Irish Geography*, 6.
Clarke, H.B. 1978 *Dublin 840–c.1540: the medieval town in the modern city.* Ordnance
    Survey, Dublin. 2nd edn Royal Irish Academy 2002. Dublin.
——— 1985 The mapping of medieval Dublin: a case study in thematic cartography. In
    Clarke, H.B. & Simms, A. 1985, ii, 617–43.
——— & Simms, A. (eds.). 1985. *The comparative history of urban origins in non-Roman
    Europe: Ireland, Wales, Denmark, Germany, Poland and Russia from the ninth to the
    thirteenth century.* B.A.R. Int. Ser. 255. Oxford.
——— (ed.). 1990. *Medieval Dublin: the making of a metropolis.* Dublin.
——— 1990. 'The topographical development of early medieval Dublin', in Clarke, H.B.
    (ed.) *Medieval Dublin: the making of a metropolis*, 51–69. Dublin.
——— 1998. '*Urbs et suburbium*: beyond the walls of medieval Dublin'. In Manning, C. (ed.)
    Dublin and beyond the Pale. Studies in honour of Patrick Healy, 45–58. Dublin.
——— 2002 *Dublin Part I, to 1610.* Irish Historic Towns Atlas, no. 11. Royal Irish Academy.
    Dublin.
Clarke, M. 1983. *The book of maps of the City Surveyors of Dublin 1695–1827.*
Craig, M. 1952. *Dublin, 1660–1860.* Dublin.
Department of Arts, Heritage, Gaeltacht and the Islands. 1999. *Frameworks and Principles
    for the Protection of the Archaeological Heritage.* Dublin.
Donnelly, Rev. Dr. 1911. *Short Histories of Dublin Parishes. Part IX.* Dublin.
Dublin City Development Plan. 1999.
Duffy, S. 2000. *Medieval Dublin I.* Dublin.
——— 2001. *Medieval Dublin II.* Dublin.
Fitzpatrick, S.A.O. 1907. *Dublin, a historical and topographical account of the city.* London.
Gilbert, J.T. 1854–9. *A History of the city of Dublin* 3 volumes Dublin.
Gowen, M. 2001. 'Excavations at the site of the church and tower of St Michael le Pole,
    Dublin' in Duffy, S. (ed.) *Medieval Dublin II*, 13–52. Dublin.
Griffith, M.C. 1991. *Calendar of inquisitions formerly in the office of the chief remembrancer of
    the exchequer prepared from the MSS of the Irish Record Commission.* Dublin.
Halliday, C. 1884 *The Scandinavian kingdom of Dublin.* Dublin (repr. Shannon, 1969).
Little, G.A. 1957. *Dublin before the Vikings. An adventure in discovery.* Dublin.
M'Cready, C.T. 1892. *Dublin street names, dated and explained.* Dublin.
Museum of London Archaeology Service. 1994. *Archaeological site manual.* London.
National Monuments Acts 1930–1994.
Reid, M. 2000. *Report on archaeological testing at Stephen Street Upper/Longford Street
    Great.* Unpublished report lodged with Dúchas, the Heritage Service.

Shaw, H. 1850. *The Dublin pictorial guide & directory of 1850*. Dublin.

Simms, A. 1990. Medieval Dublin in a European context: from proto-town to chartered town'. In Clarke (ed.) *Medieval Dublin the making of a metropolis*, 37–50. Dublin.

Simpson, L. 1999. *Director's findings: Temple Bar West* Temple Bar Archaeological Report 5. Dublin.

—— 2000. 'Forty years a-digging: a preliminary synthesis of archaeological investigation in medieval Dublin. In Duffy, S. (ed.) *Medieval Dublin I*. Dublin, 11–68.

Walsh, C. 2001. 'Dublin's southern town defences, tenth to fourteenth centuries: the evidence from Ross Road'. In Duffy, S. (ed.) *Medieval Dublin II*, 88–127. Dublin.

Cartographic Sources:

John Speed, Map of the City of Dublin, 1610.

Bernard de Gomme, 1673.

Charles Brooking, Map of Dublin, 1728.

John Rocque, Map of the City of Dublin, 1756.

The contribution of insect remains to an understanding of the environment of Viking-age and medieval Dublin

EILEEN REILLY

INTRODUCTION

This paper examines the important contribution that sub-fossil insect remains can make to an understanding of the environment of Viking-age and medieval Dublin. The study of insect remains is one aspect of the increasingly important area of environmental archaeology and can contribute to a more holistic understanding of archaeological contexts. Environmental archaeology seeks to use other scientific disciplines to answer classic archaeological questions of the 'why, how and what' of prehistoric and historic human activity. Environmental archaeology has a particularly significant role to play in the interpretations of urban sites because the matrix of these sites is made up primarily of organic remains – plants, wood, insects, animal bone, shell.

So what of insects in particular? What can they tell us about the prevailing micro- and macro-level environmental conditions in Dublin during the Viking and medieval periods? About the use of structures at a macro-level? About the use of domestic space within structures? About the use of hinterland resources? About the seasonality of that use? And about the hinterland itself and the nature of the landscape around the town? The study of insects can contribute to the answer to all of these questions, particularly as part of an integrated environmental/archaeological strategy, and a number of case studies will be presented in this paper to illustrate this. However, it is important to start with a brief introduction to the subject as a whole and its development and subsequent contribution to urban archaeological research.

HISTORY OF THE SUBJECT

The study of sub-fossil insect remains (often called paleo-entomology or archaeo-entomology) began in Britain in the late 1950s. Its earliest exponents were Russell Coope, a geologist, and Peter Osborne, an entomologist at the Quaternary Research Laboratory in Birmingham University (Ashworth et al.

1997). Here, work on late glacial material had produced fossil insect remains, many of which, through painstaking comparative work, proved to be species that were by then extinct in Britain. The original idea behind looking at fossil insects was to provide an addition biostratigraphical dating technique for the Quaternary, based on the prevailing wisdom among entomologists at the time that insects were rapidly evolving and therefore fossil insects that did not compare to modern specimens must be extinct species. However, Coope's work proved that many of these species while extinct in Britain were in fact still found in other parts of the world (Coope et al. 1961).

Mutual Climatic Range (MCR)

Coope argued for the constancy of species in recent geological time and that faced with climatic stress species changed their distribution patterns rather than evolving into new species (Coope 1978). Thus, the importance of insect remains as a tool for understanding past climatic change was established. Coope developed a model using the thermal preferences of these species and produced a graph of climatic change over the last 14,000 years (Coope et al. 1971). This remarkable graph compared well to those produced from Greenland ice cores and other climatic proxies and became known as the Mutual Climatic Range method (Atkinson et al. 1987). In 1968, Coope and Osborne together devised the Paraffin Flotation method of recovering insect remains and inspired a significant number of researchers to look beyond the use of fossil insects for purely palaeoenvironmental studies into their application to the archaeological record and to landscape change brought about by human influence.

Importance of sub-fossil insect studies to archaeology

The importance of insect remains, particularly beetles, in archaeological contexts lies in the ability to extrapolate important habitat data from the presence and associations of particular species, which sheds light on micro- and macro-level environmental change. All orders of insects can be looked at including bugs, flies, parasites, mites, and even ants. But it is beetles that have proved most useful in archaeological contexts. Flies are particularly important in forensic archaeology and are used in forensic pathology at crime scenes to establish time of death and in some instances original locations in cases where bodies have been moved. On methodology, fossil insect remains are usually, though not always, disarticulated. Whole-insect entomologists will use a set of well-established keys (e.g. the Royal Entomological Society keys or *Die Käfer Mitteleuropas*) plus a comparative collection to identify a particular beetle to species. However, with archaeological material a key is often rendered useless as the diagnostic body parts is missing. The main diagnostic body parts are the head, thorax and elytra (plate 1); however, legs, antennae and male

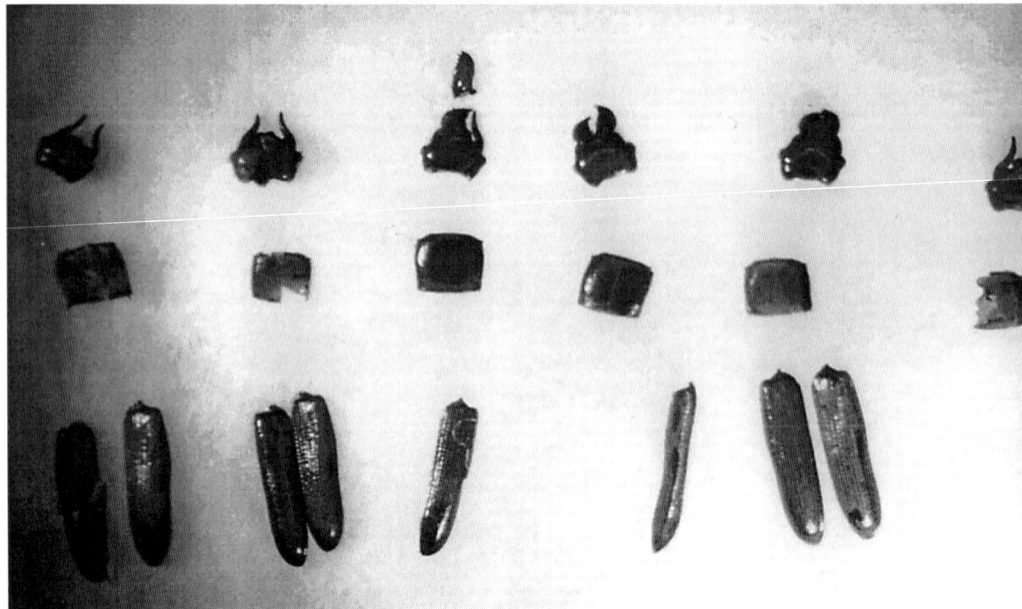

Plate 1 *Prostomis mandibularis* found in Bronze Age contexts from Derryville Bog, Co. Tipperary – heads, thoraces and elytra recovered

genitalia may be needed for an exact identification and these softer or more delicate body parts often do not survive. Identification to genus level is often the highest level of identification possible. However, it is very important to stress the value of good reference collections and many beetles can be taken beyond genus level through painstaking comparisons with modern and archaeological reference material.

URBAN ARCHAEOLOGY AND INSECTS

With the large-scale urban excavations of the early 1970s, such as those that took place at York, the need was quickly identified for an integrated strategy to interpret properly the huge volumes of organic archaeological remains being uncovered. Indeed, as Harry Kenward, the leading archaeo-entomologist in Britain, noted, environmental archaeology was seen as one solution to the problems of watching briefs and restricted rapid excavations such as the original excavations at 5–7 Coppergate and 6–8 Pavement (Kenward and Hall 1995). Such sites were difficult to interpret in the field and it was hoped that biological analysis would permit identification of deposits. A number of individuals, many of whom were former students of Russell Coope or

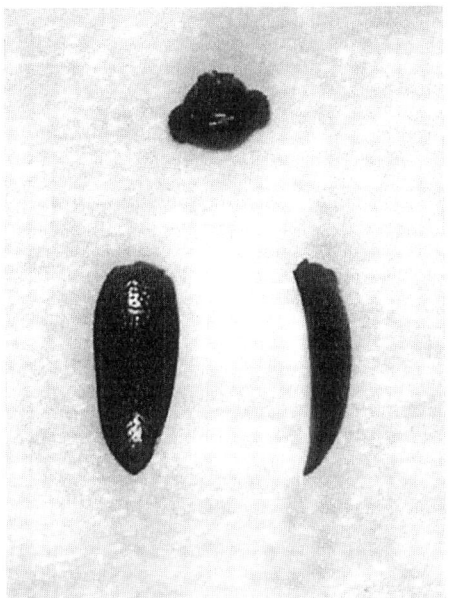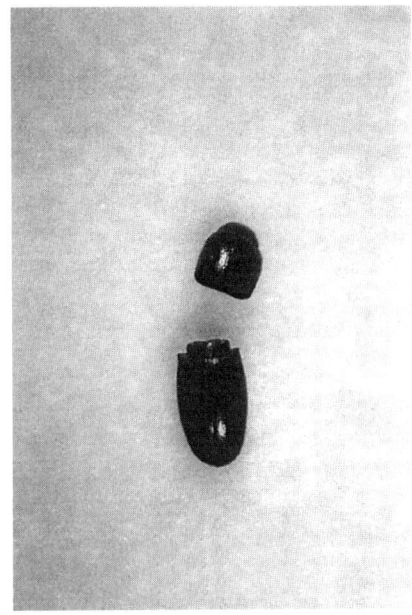

Plates 2a & 2b Decomposer species part of the 'house' fauna – *Mycetea hirta* and *Aglenus brunneus* (from Back Lane, Dublin)

influenced by him, as well as botanists, soil scientists and archaeologists, came together to combine their skills and apply them to this issue of properly integrating the archaeological and environmental information. Ultimately, in the case of York, the Archaeological Environmental Unit was born and has continued to set the standard for others to follow.

Archaeo-entomologists acknowledge the enormous contribute made by Harry Kenward, in particular, to this area of research. He has examined literally thousands of contexts and identified key marker groups of species that occur again and again together in those contexts. He has identified so-called 'house' fauna, made up mostly of decomposer species of beetles, pre-ferring generally drier conditions (plates 2a and 2b); he has also identified groups that generally occupy fouler conditions, be that manure/animal waste or human waste (see Kenward and Hall 1995; Hall and Kenward 1998). He was the first to coin the phase 'urban insect fauna', a general term for these consistent patterns of associations, but more recently he has concluded that 'intensive human occupation fauna' would be a more appropriate term (for more detailed discussion on these terms see Hall and Kenward 1990; Kenward and Hall 1995; Kenward 2001). This is because the so-called urban fauna are being increasingly detected on sites that would otherwise be considered 'rural', Deer

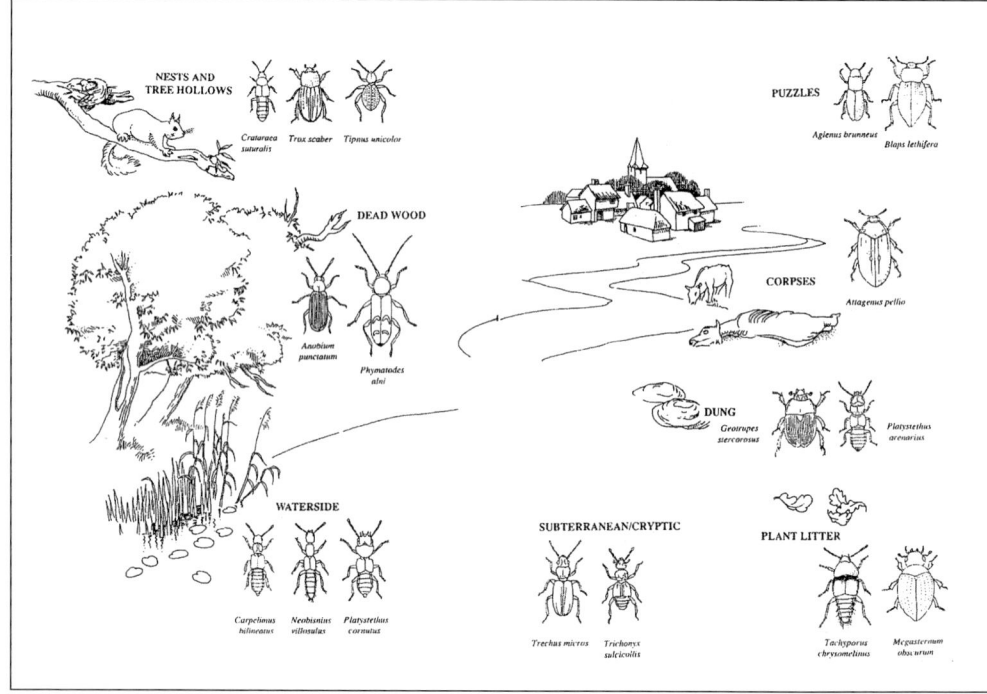

NESTS AND TREE HOLLOWS

Crataraea suturalis *Trox scaber* *Tipnus unicolor*

PUZZLES

Aglenus brunneus *Blaps lethifera*

DEAD WOOD

Anobium punctatum *Phymatodes alni*

CORPSES

Attagenus pellio

DUNG

Geotrupes stercorosus *Platystethus arenarius*

WATERSIDE

Carpelimus bilineatus *Neobisnius villosulus* *Platystethus cornutus*

SUBTERRANEAN/CRYPTIC

Trechus micros *Trichonyx sulcicollis*

PLANT LITTER

Tachyporus chrysomelinus *Megasternum obscurum*

1 Origins of the urban insect fauna (after Kenward and Allison 1994)

Park Farms, Co. Antrim, a rath dating from the eighth century AD being one very clear example of this (Kenward and Allison 1994a). The intensity and longevity of occupation play important parts in the diversity and richness of urban insect assemblages, not necessarily location.

Urban-rural connections
One of his many research interests was trying to detect the 'rural' origins of the insect communities observed in urban archaeological contexts (Kenward and Allison 1994b, 60–1, fig. 26, and fig. 1 above). This was achieved through a combination of looking at the current habitat preferences of certain key species, the types of archaeological contexts being excavated, and the matrix of those contexts using other biological analyses. Many of these species ended up in towns occupying artificially created niches that in effect mimicked their natural habitats. Some, as I will describe later, have become synanthropic over time, that is, dependent to some degree on humans for their survival. This has important implications for their present-day distribution and indeed their survival into the future.

In Ireland, palaeo- or archaeo-entomology is not as well established as most other environmental proxies. There are a number of reasons for this, the most obvious being the lack of an Irish-based researcher in the past. Occasionally, British-based researchers have examined Irish sites (e.g., Coope 1981; Kenward and Allison 1994a) and Roy Anderson, an entomologist based in Queen's University Belfast, examined insect remains from the ditch at Haughey's Fort, Co. Armagh (Anderson 1989). However, up until the mid-1990s the number of sites where sub-fossil insects had been examined could be counted on one hand. This situation has greatly corrected itself over the years with both Irish-based researchers and increasing numbers of British-based researchers working on Irish material.

Background to sub-fossil insect studies in Dublin

Wood Quay A great number of urban sites have been excavated in Dublin over the years and some have produced huge amounts of well-preserved organics, most notably within the Viking town precincts but also extending into the early Anglo-Norman areas of the town (fig. 2). Despite the lack of an Irish-based palaeo-entomologist, some samples from the Wood Quay/Fishamble Street excavations directed by Dr Patrick Wallace were examined by Dr Jim O'Connor of the Natural History Museum (O'Connor 1987). These samples produced the then earliest known examples of a species called *Blaps leithifera*, a scavenger in vegetable waste and products such as flour and grain stored in granaries, barns and old cellars, a species otherwise unknown from Ireland (O'Connor 1979). It is classified in Britain among archaeo-ento-mologists as a relict-urban species and is considered by Harry Kenward a key species of the house fauna group (Kenward and Hall 1995). Its earliest finding in Britain is from the Roman period and it is considered strongly synanthropic (Horion 1956; Koch 1989). Other insect species noted from these samples were generally not taken beyond family level and the samples were not provenanced, making comparisons difficult.

Christchurch Place Samples were examined by Russell Coope from an eleventh-century house and pit in Christchurch Place, excavated by Breandán Ó Ríordáin in the late 1970s (Coope 1981). These samples were highly productive and most beetles were identified to either species or genus level. While the two samples were taken in order to obtain a contrast between the relatively sheltered 'indoor' environment of the house and the outdoor con-text of the pit, the pit assemblage appeared to be simply a sub-set of the house assemblage, indicating that the pit was used for the disposal of household waste rather than cess (human waste). The indoor assemblage indicated that while the floor was comprised of a deep litter of mouldering vegetation it was

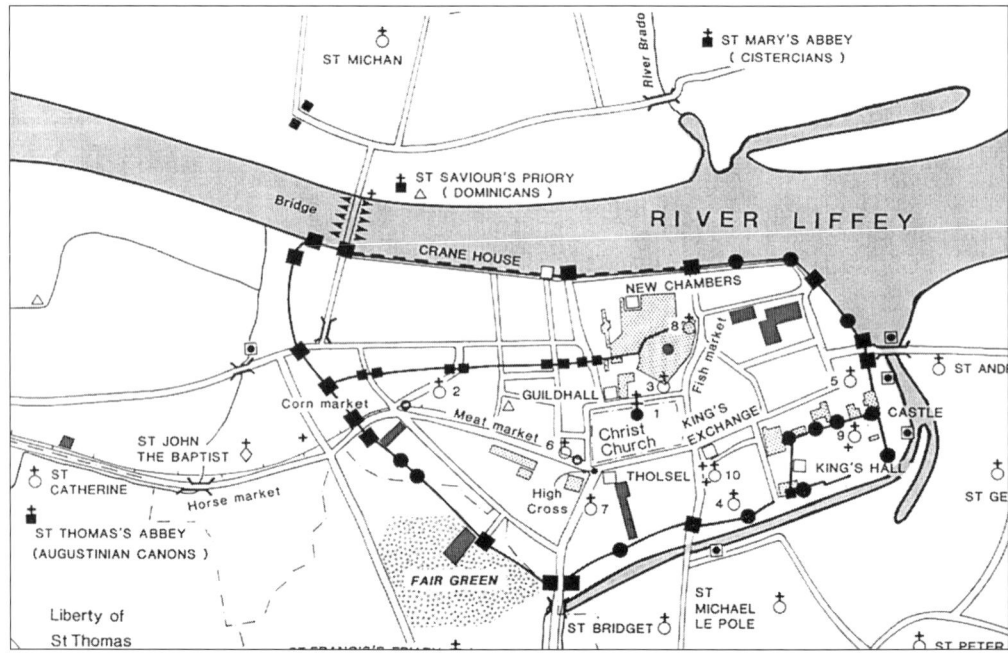

2 Medieval Dublin showing sites discussed in this paper (after Clarke 1978)

far from what one could call foul and indeed the build-up of vegetation may have been deliberate in order to increase warmth within the building. The presence of the beetle *Aglenus brunneus* in huge numbers from the indoor sample certainly indicated that vegetation was, as Coope says, a 'damp layer with texture akin to the mouldy hay left behind after the removal of haystacks, not a sodden mass'. There were certainly very few foul indicators and only one dung-feeding taxon present. The samples also produced a couple of examples of the long-horn beetle, *Gracilia minuta*, a species on the Red Data book in Britain and considered vulnerable. Its main habitats are thin branches/twigs of species such as hazel, blackthorn, elm and lime (Harde 1966; Hyman 1992). It was a pest of wicker work and hence its occurrence in Dublin and York in early-medieval contexts. Its present status in Ireland is less well known and its semi-synanthropic nature has perhaps contributed to its present vulnerability, as the use of wickerwork disappeared from human habitation building styles.

This work gave us a first insight into the complexity of the material that made up the floor layers, pit-fills and middens excavated in Dublin. In particular, it proved that the floor level was not simply made up of decaying plant material, but was perhaps the result of deliberate choice made by the occupant to improve internal warmth in the building.

Recent sub-fossil insect studies in Dublin

The site at Essex Street West, excavated by Linzi Simpson from 1996 to 1998 (see Simpson 1999; 2002), provides a good opportunity to examine some of the question raised at the start of this paper. Here it was possible to examine a larger number of samples in a more systematic way. The detailed stratigraphy established by the excavation team meant that sample choice could be more focused on addressing specific questions. Data from a number of other recent excavations will be examined here also including Back Lane, excavated by Tim Coughlan; Thomas Street, excavated by Edmond O'Donovan and Iveagh Markets, excavated by Franc Myles.

USE OF BUILDINGS

One of the first questions addressed – what some building were being used for – was well illustrated by four structures that occurred in the late ninth century levels at Essex Street West (fig. 3). The archaeological evidence was very much pointing in the direction of animal pens, given the morphology of these structures, with only CM/CC indicating a more complex two-phase history that involved animals and humans. CL, in particular, a small enclosure with no evidence for an entrance way or a roof, produced an assemblage indicating that the structure was indeed not roofed as the 'house fauna' element was poorly represented. Also, the diversity of decomposers indicates an area relatively open but with a constant build-up of decomposing plant matter. This factor and the presence of a variety of dung beetles and other foul-loving and moisture-preferring decomposer-species beetles would tentatively point to the use of this structure as an animal enclosure.

Regarding CM, the archaeological evidence identified two distinct phases, the first suggesting its use as an animal pen, the second indicating human occupation. The sample taken came from organic build-up associated with the first phase. Plant decomposers dominated the sample, with significant numbers of those with a tendency towards the moister and therefore fouler end of the decomposer spectrum, with strong indications of the presence of animal dung. However, the 'house fauna' group is reasonably well repre-sented. In particular, *Tipnus unicolor*, usually found in mouldy hay in barns, in roofing material, or decaying timber, but invariably indoors in medieval contexts, was recovered. Its presence may suggest that the structure was roofed at some stage; although this is tenuous. There is also a strong 'hinterland' element in the form of various plant feeders, in particular, a number of weevils that feed at the roots of grasses in coastal locations, species

3 Layout of late 9th-century levels, Essex Street West, Dublin

found on meadow plants, and yet others found on various weed species. The palaeo-botanical evidence indicated a similar range of biotopes. This combination of plant feeding insects and animal dung is generally taken as an indicator of manure (Hall and Kenward 1998). Two examples of *Tenebrio molitor/obscurus* were also recovered. It is cited as a pest of stored products, being found in flour mills and barns today (Brendell 1975). Overall, the assemblage pointed towards animal use of the structure at the time this layer was deposited with some indication that it was roofed. However, this may also be the product of taphonomy caused by post-depositional mixing of the two phases of occupation.

CC was perhaps the most intriguing structure at this level. Two distinct levels of occupation were again tentatively identified by the archaeology and suggested by the finds. The first phase of the main circular part may have been roofed and had a small curious annex attached onto the west wall, which was open to the south. The samples examined for insect remains came from this annex and produced a very clear signature group of beetles indicating the

Plate 3 Structure CC, late 9th century, Essex Street West

presence of animal dung and a deep litter of plant material. The combination of these two features certainly indicated an animal pen; however, included in the assemblage were twenty examples of *Pulex irritans*, the human flea (plate 3). On its own, or within house structures, it is strongly associated with the 'house' fauna of medieval buildings (Kenward and Hall 1995). In this struc-ture however, it was somewhat problematic because the annex was thought most unlikely to be a human occupation structure. One possibility lies though in the origin of *Pulex irritans* as a pest of humans. One theory is that the original main host of the 'human' flea was the wild pig. Today, it is virtually eliminated as a parasite of humans but it continues to be a pest of domestic pigs (Allison and Kenward 1990). The close association between humans and pigs throughout prehistoric and historic times may have meant that this species transferred easily between the two. This would indicate that the annex may have been used as a pig pen, or fallowing pen.

BI, a mid-tenth to early eleventh-century structure, clearly built as a house originally, was later converted into an open-air pen and a house to the south, AY, presumably became the human occupation site. The insects gave a very clear picture of decomposing plant material, dung and general foul con-

4 Plan of Structure BN,
early 10th to mid-11th
century levels, Essex
Street West, Dublin

ditions. The plant remains produced a large number of goosefoot seeds, which
grow in nitrogen rich soils and are often indicative of manure heaps (Johnston
2000). The mixture of animal and human occupation continued into the later
tenth/early eleventh century and indeed into the twelfth century. From the
insect evidence alone, one could almost form the impression that more animals than humans were living in this area during the whole Viking period!
However, a certain bias is present if the insect evidence is examined alone due
to the fact that many of the houses in these levels were burned and therefore
no insect remains were recovered. There is ample evidence for intensive
human occupation from the plant macro-fossils and animal bone remains
from these levels (Johnston 2000).

USE OF DOMESTIC SPACE

A number of the houses that were unburned and could be examined for insect
remains as well as other biological evidence provided useful information on
the micro-environment within structures and the use of domestic space. One
such structure was BN, a Type 1 house (*sensu* Wallace 1992) dating from the

early tenth century, with three aisles and central hearth, internal roof supports, and entrance in the north and south wall (fig. 4). Here three deposits
were sampled from three different locations within the house: the main floor
deposit, which extended over much of the central aisle area and was sampled
from the northern end of the building; some possible roofing material, which
occupied the centre of the aisle close to the hearth; and material from the
western aisle.

The three deposits produced different and informative assemblages. The
northern material was described archaeologically as trampled organic matter.
Certainly it was decaying plant refuse; however, it would appear from the
insect evidence to be have been quite wet. The assemblage may have reflected
a general problem with drainage in this house (Simpson 2002). There were
very few true dung beetles present, so this layer still represented a house floor
deposit, but the number of true 'house fauna' species was quite small. As
most of these species prefer the dry end of the decomposing spectrum, this is
not too surprising. There were a small but consistent number of 'outdoor' or
hinterland species too. Most of these were beetles that are found on weeds and
plants of disturbed ground and grassland and for the most part probably had
a very local origin. Three examples of *Pulex irritans* were also recovered from
this sample. Nothing in this samples indicated the storage of animal or plant
produce in this part of the house and this may have been due to the
underlying damp ground.

The layer from near the hearth was described archaeologically as 'collapsed
roofing material'. This sample produced a disappointingly small assemblage
and this may be due to one of two factors: firstly, since the material sampled
was near the hearth area it would be drier and less organic that the rest of the
floor and would inhibit decomposition; secondly, roofing material would tend
to be drier than floor material that is being trodden underfoot and would be
subject to constant drying from the hearth below. Significantly, however, one
of the most characteristic species of any reasonably long-lived roof of this
period, *Mycetaea hirta*, is completely absent from this sample. The present
writer found it in large numbers in a pit in Thomas Street (O'Donovan 2002a,
this volume Reilly 1997a), which appeared to contain the remains of decaying
thatch material. By the use of modern comparative locations David Smith
established that it is a signature beetle of this ecological niche (Smith 1996).
The sample from Structure BN near the hearth also contained a wide variety
of plant feeders found on coastal grassland and urban flora, but none that
were particular to the kinds of plant material used in roof construction. In
effect, it appeared that the assemblage was reflecting either the sod element of
the roof, or floor material, rather than the thatch itself. One example of *Pulex
irritans* was also found in this sample, which seemed to be a common
inhabitant of this house, an unfortunate situation for its human occupants.
Obviously, the flea would not be living in roof material but its presence could

be explained by occupational debris from the house becoming mixed with the roofing material after it collapsed. Overall, there is actually very little in this sample to confirm that it is roofing material, a conclusion also reached by the palaeo-botanical results (Johnston 2000).

The third sample, interpreted archaeologically as possible bedding material, or the floor of a bedding area, taken from the western aisle, contains a typical profile for a 'house' sample. Significantly though, the impression that the underlying ground conditions were perhaps wetter than those seen at Christchurch Place is still attested to by the presence of some species more favourable of damper decomposing plant material. The plant feeders were generally indicative of urban flora and were not significant in pointing to the plant materials used for the bedding. However, the palaeo-botanical results indicated a wide variety of sources. This sample is most significant for the number of human fleas present, sixteen in total. In this case, however, unlike structure CC above, it can be safely assumed that these fleas were from a human host. Given the close association between humans and animals on this site it is not surprising that *Pulex irritans* could become strongly established. It is worth noting that no other species of flea was recovered from any of the contexts examined at Essex Street West. Two lice were recovered from this aisle material but could not be identified to species.

HINTERLAND RESOURCE AND SEASONALITY

On the issue of hinterland resource use, seasonality and the storage of foodstuffs, particularly in the early Anglo-Norman town, a number of pits from Essex Street West, Iveagh Markets and some structures from Back Lane produced very interesting findings that address these two issues. Two pits from Essex Street West, in particular, were sampled thoroughly – pit 3136, dated to the late twleth century and four of its seven identified fills were examined for insect remains; Pit 3065, dated to the very early thirteenth century, and two of its four fills were examined. It should be stated from the outset that the insect fauna produced from pits is, in many cases, simply a reflection of the houses and other structures around them. They can be expected to have a proportion of household waste, and therefore members of the house fauna will be well represented, but if their use is primarily as a cess pit there will also tend to be more foul-loving species. Both of these pits showed these two signature groups, with a tendency for the lower fills to be more reflective of what might be considered their primary use, i.e. a cess pit, while the upper fills tended to be more mixed, possibly reflecting secondary use. Indeed, in the case of the first pit, 3136, the upper three fills examined were more reflective of house floor origin than most of the samples taken from

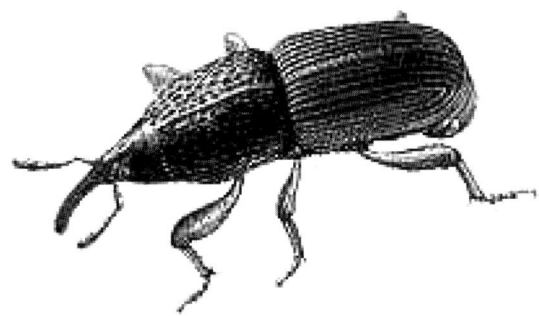

Plate 4 Stored products pests
– *Bruchus rufimanus* and
Sitophilus granarius

actual houses, the assemblage of the upper two layers comprising 50% house fauna. Species like *Blaps leithifera* and *Mycetea hirta* probably reflected the dumping of hay residue, floor sweeping and old thatch from buildings. This may have been done to dampen down smell emanating from cess-pits when opened during warmer months.

In the lower fills of this pit a number of examples of *Bruchus rufimanus*, a pest of beans, particularly broad beans, were found and it is most likely that they ended up in the pit as part of a cess deposit, having been ingested by humans (plate 4a). It was also found consistently in pits examined by the author in late Viking/early medieval contexts in Waterford (Reilly 1994). Another very important stored product pest that occurred in Pit 3065 is the grain weevil, *Sitophilus granarius* (plate 4b). Again, when found in cesspits, it is usually considered to form part of the cess indicator group (Osbourne 1983). It appears to be able to withstand the human digestive process and its occurrence in cess-pits appears to be as a result of ingestion by humans rather than dumping of spoilt grain. The writer has also recorded this species in samples taken from the medieval city ditch excavated at Iveagh Markets by Franc Myles and from one of the pits there, dated to the late thirteenth/early fourteenth century (Reilly 2001). It has also been recovered from a sixteenth-century context on George's Quay, Limerick (O'Donovan 2002b).

The presence of this species in various contexts has important implications for trade and the manner in which grain was stored in late Viking/medieval Dublin. *S. granarius* is rarely found away from synanthropic (human-associated) situations today and has never been recorded from archaeological layers other than in synanthropic contexts. It is flightless and appears to owe its current worldwide distribution to accidental transport by humans (Buckland 1990). It has been recorded from wheat, rye, barley, maize, oats, buckwheat, millet, chick peas and, less frequently, chestnuts and acorns (Hoffman 1954). It is unclear what its primary host was, the small grains of wild cereals being probably too small for successful breeding. It may, therefore, have originated in acorns and moved to cereals, possibly after first cultivation by humans. Its expansion westward may have been associated with the movement of agriculturalists and early storage of grain; however, its progress appeared to be dependent upon the presence of suitable permanent stores. It is significant that its earliest findings in Northwest Europe are all within the Roman Empire (Buckland 1990). Its first records in Britain date to the Roman period (Coope and Osborne 1968; Buckland 1981). Its recovery from the ditch and pit-fill in Iveagh Markets could either be from wind-blown or household refuse sources or with cess material dumped into the ditch and may be related to the presence of the Cornmarket, located nearby at the north-western end of Francis Street – the main location for trading of grain in the medieval city. Its finding in Limerick was clearly associated with the presence of a nearby mill, Nicholas Arthur's Mill, shown on Hardiman's map of Limerick *c.*1590 (Hill 1997). But it is simply unclear when it first arrived in Ireland. Its earliest recorded finding is from late Viking/early Anglo-Norman pit-fills in Waterford (Reilly 1994) and raises many interesting questions. Did it arrive with the first Viking settlers, who may have brought grain with them on their original raids? How was grain stored within the precincts of the Viking and medieval town? Was *S. granarius* already here in pre-Viking times, perhaps introduced during occasional Roman incursions into Ireland? Or did the proto-towns of the monastic period store and trade grain with settlements in England and Wales and was this its route eventually into the Viking towns during early trading and raiding of agricultural produce? It is clear that this is a species that could benefit from more thorough research, and could contribute to an understanding of the dynamics of agricultural trade in the early historic and medieval period.

An important hinterland resource indicator is *Cercyon depressus*, a strictly seaside or estuarine beetle, which is highly stenotopic to decaying seaweed (i.e. known only from that biotope). It is an increasingly rare species in Britain and is not recorded from Ireland in recent times (Hyman 1994; Anderson et al. 1997). It was found in both the lower contexts of the early thirteenth-century pit F.3065 in Essex Street West; House B and Structure E at Back Lane also produced small but significant numbers of *Cercyon depressus* (Reilly 1997b).

This species continued to be present throughout the early to mid-thirteenth century Anglo-Norman stave-built houses at Back Lane and was present in one of the rubbish pits of this period. In the pits of Essex Street West it occurred together with plant indicators and other species preferring estuarine habitats that clearly indicated the presence of seaweed on site. At Iveagh Markets, a number of other species of decaying seaweed and a ground beetle, *Dicheirotrichus gustavi*, an exclusively coastal species also, preferring saline locations, dunes and salt marshes (Koch 1989), were recovered in the ditch and pit-fills there. These species may confirm the presence of seaweed within the decaying plant matter. Fergus Kelly, in his study of early Irish agricultural documentary sources, details a number that refer specifically to the gathering and use of seaweed for a variety of purposes (Kelly 1998). These included its use as human food, soil fertilizer and animal fodder – one of the specific examples given was that cattle fed with seaweed would become thirsty, drink more and hence increase their milk yields. It is perfectly possible that practices relating to the gathering and use of seaweed from the pre-Viking period were carried on throughout the Viking and Anglo-Norman period and that the insects are simply a reflection of this.

SEASONALITY OF RESOURCE USE?

The two fills from pit 3065 produced two extremely interesting and diverse insect assemblages and perhaps reflect aspects of seasonal use of food resources. The lower fill had stored product pests, *Bruchus rufimanus* and *Sitophilus granarius*, and the palaeo-botanical results showed fewer fruit seeds in this layer (Johnston 2000). This may hint at deposition during a time when fruit was scarce, i.e. winter, spring or very early summer. In contrast the upper layer of this pit had the largest number of *Mycetaea hirta*, usually associated with thatch or other roofing material but also mouldy hay and straw. Coupled with the fact that this deposit had abundant fruit seeds and pips of apple, bilberry, blackberry/raspberry and various Prunus species, it may indicate that this layer was deposited in summer and autumn when these fruits were readily available. Hay or straw may have been thrown into the pit to dampen down smells, particularly in summer time. The pit was possibly sealed shortly afterwards giving us this very clear picture of the final use cycle of this pit.

THE ENVIRONMENT AROUND THE MEDIEVAL TOWN

The insect evidence above indicates the use of coastal resources, the possible grazing of animals on coastal grassland, and the gathering of meadow plants for use in house floors. This gives us some insights into the landscape sur-

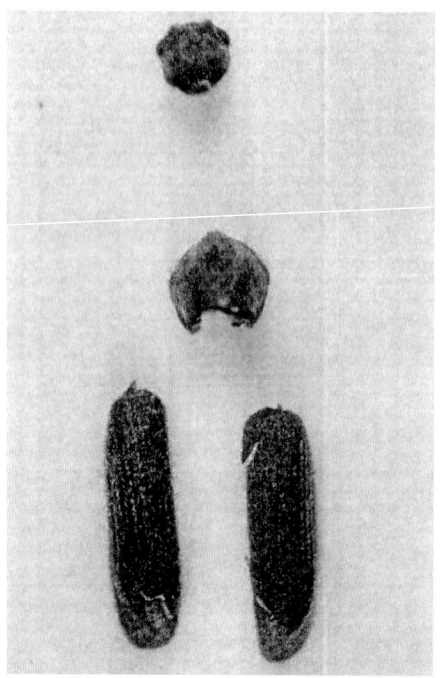

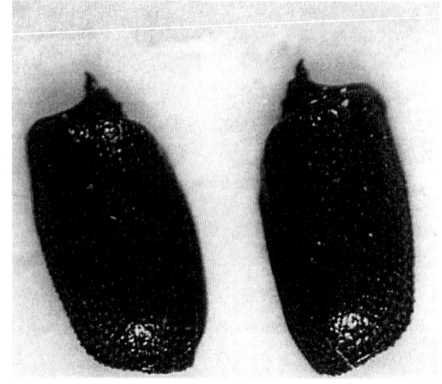

Plates 5a & 5b Wood-dependent species ('structural and/or worked wood') – *Anobium punctatum* and *Scolytus mali*

rounding the medieval town. A very important component of that landscape was woodland and here the insect evidence is extremely important in indicating not just woodland presence, but the nature of that woodland.

Insects recovered from house floors and structural timbers in Back Lane produced a very large numbers of wood-dependent taxa. These ranged from the structural wood pests like *Anobium punctatum* (woodworm beetle) (plate 5a) and *Lyctus linearis* (the powder-post beetle) and a surprising number of what are considered rare, threatened or, in an Irish context, possibly extinct woodland species. Structure E, for example, produced three different species of Scolytidae ('bark' beetles) – *Lepersinus orni*, *Scolytus mali* (plate 5b) and *Acrantus vittatus* – none of which are recorded on the current Irish list of Coleoptera (Anderson et al. 1997) and one of which, *A. vittatus*, is considered part of the 'relict woodland fauna' by researchers in this field (Girling 1985). All attack thin branches of tree species such as ash, willow, and fruit tree species, species invariably used in construction of wattle walls, mats and household implements in medieval times. Another rare beetle, *Saperda scalaris*, was recovered from this context (plate 7a). This is a long-horn beetle, the same family as *Gracilia minuta* found at Christchurch Place (Coope 1981), and is found generally in broad-leaved woodland. It is not recorded currently in Ireland (Anderson et al. 1997). From between the wall of Structure G and a property boundary built up against it a remarkable range of wood-dependent species were recovered (plate 6), including sixty-three examples of *Anobium punctatum, Lyctus linearis, Lepersinus orni, Acrantus vittatus, Mesites tardii* (plate 7b: found in broad-leaved woodland with a pronounced coastal preference (Alexander 1994)), and *Rhyncolus chloropus* (plate 7c), usually found in dead and decaying oak or pine (Bullock 1993). Of all of the above taxa, only *M. tardii, A. punctatum* and *L. linearis* are still recorded in Ireland. These findings clearly give us important insights into the nature and extent of woodland surrounding Dublin at this time.

A discussion by O'Sullivan on the nature of woodmanship in Anglo-Norman Dublin (1998) highlighted the differentiation between types of woodland gleaned from medieval documentation: *Silva* was timber woodland used for construction; *boscus* was underwood used for fuel and wattle and *bruaria* was poor, scrubby brushwood. The small but significant assemblage of wood-dependent beetles discussed above gives us a glimpse into these different types of woodland in the hinterland of Dublin. While *A. punctatum* and *L. linearis* established themselves worldwide as pests of structural timber because of the age and condition of the wood they infest, most of the other species are either inhabitants of recently felled, thin-bore twigs or branches (the scolytid beetles primarily), or dead wood and tree stumps (*R. chloropus, S. scalaris*). These species

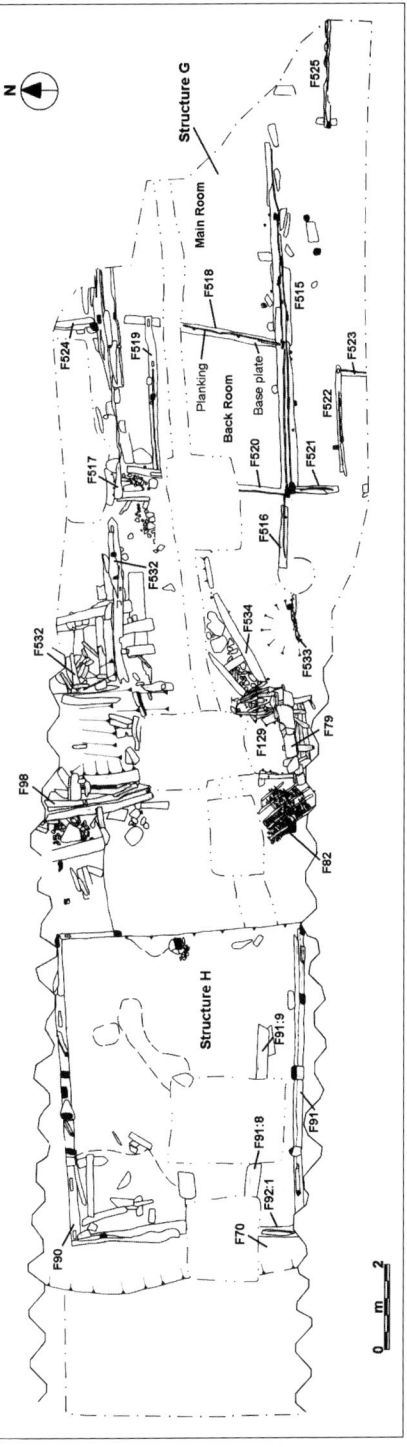

5 Structure G and H, early 13th century, Back Lane

Plates 6a, 6b & 6c
Wood-dependent
species ('wild wood'?) –
*Saperda scalaris, Mesites
tardii* and *Rhycolus
chloropus*

are more likely to have been brought into the town occasionally in timber, fire-wood or branches cut for wattle-making then to have become established as structural timber pests themselves. With the clearance of woodland over time and generally tidier forest management practices that included clearance of dead wood from forest floors, many of these species have simply disappeared from the record. This is important information not just for the archaeologist in terms of understanding the nature and use of surrounding woodland, but is of enormous value to the entomologist and ecologist in providing a glimpse into our once richer entomo-fauna. It is a very tangible way of seeing the dramatic effects of forest clearance from medieval times onward. The true extent of the loss of wood-dependent beetle taxa is not as well studied in Ireland as it is in Britain (e.g., Whitehouse 1997), however, research is ongoing and findings from some prehistoric sites have added yet more wood-dependent species that are no longer recorded in Ireland (e.g., Caseldine et al. 2001). It is certainly an area of research worthy of greater attention.

CONCLUSIONS

This paper has attempted to illustrate some of the interesting and important environmental evidence suggested by sub-fossil insect remains. They can contribute to the overall archaeological interpretation of the use of buildings, the use of space within buildings, and the living conditions of people at this time. They give us insights into the use of hinterland resources, the nature of surrounding woodland, links with the European mainland through the presence of imported species like *Sitophilus granarius* and, occasionally, the seasonality of resource use. While rich organic preservation does not always occur in the suburban areas of medieval Dublin except in pits – for example, the sites examined in Thomas Street and Iveagh Markets – many of the same species that occur in the organic-rich deposits within the walled Anglo-Norman precincts are found in the pit-fills of these suburban areas. This at least points to similar micro-environments within structures in these areas; structures that unfortunately have not survived in the archaeological record. In particular, the 'background' fauna noted within samples from Iveagh Markets showed a strong esturine and coastal bias, and this was well reflected in findings from within the Viking and the Anglo-Norman walled town. Our understanding of the suburban areas of Dublin could benefit greatly from increased integration of environmental analysis in tandem with archaeological excavation.

Finally, it is extremely important for archaeologists to note their contribution to our present understanding of the current Irish insect fauna. All of the findings of rare, threatened and extinct Coleoptera described in this paper have come from archaeological sites. These findings have the potential to contribute positively to future conservation strategies for certain threatened ecological niches.

ACKNOWLEDGEMENTS

This paper is based on findings from a number of urban sites in Dublin, Waterford and Limerick carried out primarily as a result of private-sector contract work (the samples from Peter Street, Waterford were analysed for my M.Sc. thesis). The author wishes to acknowledge the following archaeologists for access to their sites, for their interest and encouragement, and also for permission to reproduce plans and photographs from some of them: Tim Coughlan, Franc Myles, Edmond O'Donovan, Orla Scully and Linzi Simpson, with particular thanks owing to Margaret Gowen. To the following environmental archaeologists and specialists who have offered encouragement, discussion and constructive criticism where needed over the years: Professor Paul Buckland, Brenda Collins, Penny Johnston, Harry Kenward, Mick

Monk, Dr Robert Nash, Dr Martin Speight, Dr Ingelise Stuijts, John Tierney, Dr Nicki Whitehouse. A special thanks to Dr David Smith of Birmingham University for the use of the Gorham and Girling Coleoptera Collections, help in identifying difficult species and ongoing support and encouragement. Thank you also to his wife, Wendy, for her kind hospitality on my many visits to Birmingham. I wish to thank all the present and former staff of Margaret Gowen & Co. who, over the years, have provided the most stimulating and enjoyable of working environments that anyone could wish for, and Dr Seán Duffy, for his invitation to submit this paper and his patience and encouragement during the editorial process. Above all though, this paper is dedicated to Rónán.

BIBLIOGRAPHY

Alexander, K.N.A. 1994 *An annotated checklist of British lignicolous and saproxylic invertebrates*. National Trust Estates Advisors' Office, Cirencester (Draft).
Allison, E. & Kenward, H. 1990 Learning from archaeology: fleas from archaeological deposits. In *Interim* 15 (1), 27–33.
Anderson, R. 1989 Haughey's Fort: analysis of an insect death assemblage. *Emania* 6, 37–42.
Anderson, R., Nash, R. & O'Connor, J. 1997 *A revised and annotated list of Irish coleoptera*. Irish Biogeographical Society. Dublin.
Ashworth, A.C., Buckland, P.C. & Sadler, J.P. 1997 G Russell Coope: an appreciation. In A.C. Ashworth, P.C. Buckland and J.P. Sadler (eds.) *Studies in Quaternary entomology – an inordinate fondness for insects*, Quaternary Proceedings No.5, John Wiley & Sons, Chichester, 1–5.
Atkinson, T.C., Briffa, K.R. & Coope, G.R. 1987 Seasonal temperatures in Britain during the past 22,000 years, reconstructed using beetle remains. *Nature* 325, 587–92.
Brendell, M.J.D. 1975 Coleoptera: Tenebrionidae. *Handbooks for the identification of British insects*, V, 10. Royal Entomological Society of London. London.
Buckland P.C. 1990 Granaries, stores and insects: The archaeology of insect synanthropy. In D. Fournier & F. Sigaut (eds.) *La préparation alimentaire des céréales*. Rapports présentés à la table ronde, Ravello au Centre Universitaire pour les Biens Cultures, Avril 1988. PACT, Rixensart, Belgium.
—— 1981 The early dispersal of insect pests of stored products as indicated by archaeological records. *Journal of Stored Product Research* 17, 1–12.
Bullock, J.A. 1993 Host plants of British beetles: a list of recorded associations. *Amateur Entomologist* 11a, 1–24.
Coope, G.R. 1978 Constancy of insect species versus inconstancy of Quaternary environments. In L.A. Mound & N. Waloff (eds.) *Diversity of Insect Faunas*, 176–87. Symposium of the Royal Entomological Society, 9. Oxford.
—— 1981 Report on the Coleoptera from an eleventh-century house at Christ Church Place, Dublin. In H. Bekker-Nielson, P. Foote & O. Olsen (eds.) *Proceedings of the Eighth Viking Congress 1977*, 51–6. Odense.
Coope, G.R. & Osborne, P.J. 1968 Report on the Coleopterous fauna of the Roman well at Barnsley Park, Gloucestershire. *Transactions of the Bristol and Gloucestershire Archaeological Society* 86, 84–7.

Coope, G.R. Morgan, A. & Osborne, P.J. 1971 Fossil Coleoptera as indicators of climatic fluctuations during the last glaciation in Britain. *Palaeogeography, Palaeoclimatology, Palaeoecology* 10, 87–101.

Coope, G.R., Shotton, F.W. & Strachan, I. 1961 A Late Pleistocene fauna and flora from Upton Warren, Worcestershire. *Philosophical Transactions of the Royal Society of London* B244, 379–421.

Girling, M.A. 1985 An 'Old-Forest' beetle fauna from a Neolithic and Bronze Age peat deposit at Stileway. *Somerset Levels Papers* 11, 80–3.

Hall, A.R. & Kenward, H.K. 1998 Disentangling dung: pathways to stable manure. *Environmental Archaeology* 1, 123–6.

—— 1990 Environmental evidence from the Colonia. *The Archaeology of York*, 14/6. Council for British Archaeology, London.

Harde, K.W. 1966 Cerambycidae. In H. Freude, K.E. Harde & G.A.Lohse (eds.) *Die Käfer Mitteleuropas*, 9, 7–94. Goecke & Evers, Krefeld.

Hill, J. 1997 *The Building of Limerick*. Dublin.

Hoffmann, A. 1954 Coleoptérès Curculionides 2. *Faune de France* 59, 487–1208. Lechevalier, Paris.

Horion, A. 1956 *Faunistik der Mitteleuropäischen Käfer 5, Heteromera*. Munich.

Hyman, P.S. 1992 *A review of the scarce and threatened Coleoptera of Great Britain, Part 1* (Revised & updated by M.S. Parsons). UK Joint Nature Conservation Committee, Peterborough.

Hyman, P.S. 1994 *A review of the scarce and threatened Coleoptera of Great Britain, Part 2* (Revised & updated by M.S. Parsons). UK Joint Nature Conservation Committee, Peterborough.

Johnston, P. 2000 *Macroscopic plant remains from excavations at Temple Bar West*. Unpublished Technical Report for Margaret Gowen & Co. Ltd.

Kelly, F. 1998 *Early Irish farming*. Early Irish Law Series Vol. IV. School of Celtic Studies, Dublin Institute of Advanced Studies. Dublin.

Kenward, H. 2001 Species associations among insect remains from urban archaeological deposits and their significance in reconstructing the past human environment. *Journal of Archaeological Science* 28, 887–905.

Kenward, H.K. & Allison, E. 1994a A preliminary view of the insect assemblages from the early Christian rath site at Deer Park Farms, Northern Ireland. In J. Rackham (ed.) *Environment and Economy in Anglo-Saxon England*, 89–107. Council for British Archaeology Res. Report, London.

—— 1994b Rural origins of the urban insect fauna. In A.R. Hall & H.K. Kenward (eds.) *Urban rural connections: perspectives from environmental archaeology*. Symposium of the Association for Environmental Archaeology No.12, 55–79. Oxford.

Kenward, H.K. & Hall, A.R. 1995 Biological evidence from Anglo-Scandinavian deposits at 16–22 Coppergate, *The archaeology of York*, 14/7, Council for British Archaeology, London.

Koch, K. 1989 *Die Käfer Mitteleuropas. Ökologie 2*. Goecke & Evers, Krefeld.

—— *Die Käfer Mitteleuropas. Ökologie 1*. Goecke & Evers, Krefeld.

Caseldine, C., Gearey, B., Hatton, J., Reilly, E., Stuijts, I. & Casparie, W. 2001 From the wet to the dry: palaeoecological studies at Derryville, Co. Tipperary, Ireland. In B. Raftery & J. Hickey (eds.) *Recent developments in wetland research*, Seandálaíocht: Monograph 2, Department of Archaeology, UCD/WARP Occasional Paper 14, Dublin, 99–115.

O'Connor, J.P. 1987 Appendix V: Insecta. In G.F. Mitchell (ed.) *Archaeology and environment in early Dublin*, Medieval Dublin Excavations 1962–81, Series C.

—— 1979 *Blaps lethifera* Marsham (Coleoptera Tenebrionidae), a beetle new to Ireland from Viking Dublin. *Entomologist's Gazette* 30, 295–297.

O'Donovan, E. 2002a The growth and decline of a medieval suburb? Evidence from excavations at Thomas Street. In S. Duffy (ed.) *Medieval Dublin IV*, Dublin.

—— 2002b Abbey River/George's Quay, Limerick. In I. Bennett (ed.) *Excavations 2000: summary accounts of archaeological excavations in Ireland*, 193–4, Bray.

Osborne, P. J. 1983 An insect fauna from a modern cesspit and its comparison with probable cesspit assemblages from archaeological sites. *Journal of Archaeological Science*, 10, 453–463.

O'Sullivan, A. 1998 Woodmanship and the supply of underwood and timber to Anglo-Norman Dublin. In C. Manning (ed.) *Dublin and beyond the Pale. Studies in honour of Paddy Healy*, 61–69, Bray.

Reilly, E. 2001 *Analysis of insect remains from excavations at Iveagh Markets, Dublin* (Licence No.99E0261). Unpublished technical report for Margaret Gowen & Co.

—— 1997a *The insect remains (Coleoptera) from 3 pits, Thomas Street Excavations.* Unpublished technical report for Margaret Gowen & Co.

—— 1997b *The insect remains from Back Lane, Dublin, 1996/7 Excavation* (Licence No.99E0300). Unpublished technical report for Margaret Gowen and Company Ltd.

—— 1994 *A study of the insect remains from the Viking-medieval excavations at Peter St., Waterford.* Unpublished MSc thesis for the University of Sheffield.

Simpson, L. 2002 *Stratigraphic report on excavations at Temple Bar West, Dublin*, Licence Ref. 96E245. Unpublished report lodged with Dúchas, the Heritage Service.

—— 1999 *Director's findings. Temple Bar West*, Temple Bar Archaeological Report No. 5, Bray.

Smith, D. 1996 Thatch, turves and floor deposits: a survey of coleoptera in materials from abandoned Hebridean Blackhouses and the implications for their visibility in the archaeological record. *Journal of Archaeological Science* 23, 161–174.

Wallace, P.F. 1992 *The Viking age buildings of Dublin*, 2 vols. Royal Irish Academy, Dublin.

Whitehouse, N.J. 1997 Silent witnesses: an 'Urwald' fossil insect assemblage from Thorne Moors. *Thorne & Hatfield Moors Papers*, 4 19–54.

The defence of Dublin in the middle ages

JAMES LYDON

In his classic (and unique) analysis of the sources for the history of the borough institutions of medieval Anglo-Ireland, Gearóid Mac Niocaill emphasised that defence was a primary necessity, especially in ports where the quays were one of the weakest links in the defensive system.[1] This was certainly the case with Dublin, from its very beginning as a *longphort* founded by the Scandinavians in and after 841. Sited on a ridge above the Liffey, the new settlement was exposed to attack from the river, and archaeology has revealed that its earliest fortifications were earthen banks constructed along the riverfront.[2] While these may have made it difficult for attackers to find a ready foothold on the banks, they could not protect the city as it grew, and it is certain that before the end of the tenth century Dublin had a more advanced system of defence which enemies could not easily penetrate. In 989 Dublin (called a *dún*, a 'fortress') was besieged by Máel Sechnaill and it is recorded that the siege lasted for twenty days during which the Ostman inhabitants 'drank no water save brine'.[3] A stone wall was certainly in existence before 1100, though the date of its construction has so far not been established.[4]

When the English came to Dublin later in the twelfth century, the city was well protected with a large stone wall. Gerald of Wales describes how in 1171 the Norse of the Isles 'made an attack on the walls at the eastern gate' and how Richard Cogan 'made an unobserved sortie with a few men through the southern postern (*posticam australem*)'. Later he describes how Strongbow and his men, under siege by Ruaidrí Ua Conchobair (Rory O Connor), were 'hemmed inside the walls for about two months'.[5] The near-contemporary poem on the invasion, known as *The Song of Dermot and the Earl*, not only mentions 'the eastern gate', but also 'St Mary's gate' and the 'western gate',

---

1 Gearóid Mac Niocaill, *Na Buirgéisí XII–XIV aois* (Dublin, 1964), ii, 391. 2 See summary in Linzi Simpson, 'Forty years a-digging: a preliminary synthesis of archaeological excavations in medieval Dublin', in Seán Duffy (ed.), *Medieval Dublin I* (Dublin, 2000), pp 25–6. For a more recent analysis of some archaeological evidence see Claire Walsh, 'Dublin's southern town defences, tenth to fourteenth centuries: the evidence from Ross Road' in Seán Duffy (ed.), *Medieval Dublin II* (Dublin, 2001), pp 88–127. 3 Whitley Stokes (ed. and trans.), *The annals of Tigernach* (repr. in 2 vols, Llanarch, 1993), ii, 346. 4 Simpson, 'Forty years a-digging', pp 38–41. 5 A.B. Scott and F.X. Martin (eds), *Expugnatio Hibernica: the conquest of Ireland by Giraldus Cambrensis* (Dublin, 1978), pp

as well as remarking on the 'battlements' on the walls.[6] In 1171–2, while wintering in Dublin, King Henry II issued a charter granting land 'outside the eastern gate', and in 1185 the citizens of Dublin granted to Henry Mausenure and his heirs 'the western gate of Dublin to be lived in'. A few years later a new charter was issued; but now the gate is called 'the new gate', which implies rebuilding or reconstruction, possibly by Henry himself in order to improve living conditions.[7] As will be seen later, this kind of 'domestic improvement' to the defences of the city was not unusual in the thirteenth century. It is a clear indication that the city gates were regarded as valuable sites. In an expanding city, building sites were scarce and city gates, and even the city walls, could be used to provide accommodation. The function of gates was no longer primarily defensive.

It is evident, then, that Ostman Dublin was well defended by a stone wall that contained at least three substantial gates and probably gatehouses, and was well able to withstand a siege. Yet within those walls there was also a fortress that was a last line of defence, almost like the keep in later castles. In the *Song of Dermot* this is called 'the castle and the keep (*le chastel e le dongun*)', which Henry II delivered into the charge of Strongbow.[8] In Latin this same building is called a *castellum* in the sources, as in the early charter in which Strongbow granted two burgage plots 'before the gate of the castle (*contra portam castelli*)'.[9] What exactly those two terms, *chastel* and *castellum*, represented in physical fact has still to be determined. But there seems no doubt that a town defended by walls also had an inner defended place. In other words the *castellum* was to the *civitas* what the keep would be to a castle in Anglo-Ireland. In later times Dublin Castle certainly performed this function. But it seems that Ostman Dublin, too, with its walls and gates, was like a large fortress in which the castle occupied the place and function of a keep in a typical medieval castle.

In the early years of English occupation, there was a keen awareness of the need of armed men to defend the walls and city from attack. Grants of land in the vicinity of the city regularly included, among the services demanded, 'guarding the king's city of Dublin'. For example, a grant of three carucates of

76–7, 79.   **6** G.H. Orpen (ed. and trans.), *The song of Dermot and the earl* (Oxford, 1892), ll. 2332–3, 2341, 2350. See note, p.292. The *Annals of Ulster* describe how after Tigernán Ua Ruairc (Tiernan O Rourke) was killed in 1172, his head was brought to Dublin and was 'raised over the door of the fortress'. For an analysis of the earliest civic seal, showing evidence of possible city defences, see Seán Duffy, 'Ireland's Hastings: the Anglo-Norman conquest of Dublin', *Anglo-Norman Studies*, xx (1998), pp 69–74.   **7** J.T. Gilbert (ed.), *Chartularies of St Mary's abbey, Dublin*, 2 vols (London, 1884–6), i, 140–1; idem (ed.) *Historic and municipal documents of Ireland, AD 1172–1320* (London, 1870), p. 56.   **8** *Song of Dermot*, l. 2715. For a general overview of the medieval castle see James Lydon, 'Dublin Castle in the middle ages' in Seán Duffy (ed.), *Medieval Dublin III* (Dublin, 2002), pp 115–27.   **9** J.T. Gilbert (ed.), *Register of the abbey of St Thomas, Dublin* (London, 1889), pp

land in the honour of Lusk in 1207 specified that it was a knight's fee; but the military service required was to be rendered 'by guarding the king's city of Dublin'.[10] Another charter granted land to Jordan Locard on 8 November 1207 'by the service of one archer to be rendered in guarding the king's city of Dublin'.[11] As the capital of the lordship, the defence of Dublin was necessarily a matter of concern to the lord of Ireland, the king of England. When King John in 1204 ordered the construction of a new Dublin Castle, he told the justiciar that, among other purposes, it was 'if need be for the city's defence, with good dikes and strong wall'. But responsibility for the defence of the city, for maintaining the walls and if necessary extending them, was in law the responsibility of the citizens themselves. King John made this clear when ordering the building of Dublin Castle – he had already, he said, 'commanded that the citizens of Dublin fortify their city' and that the justiciar should 'compel them if they do not do so'.[12] In another letter of 1 September 1204 to the citizens of Dublin, thanking them for their 'good service', King John ordered them to 'attend to the fortifying of their city, every one for his part'.[13] But he continued to help the citizens in their task. In 1207, for example, he wrote to his 'barons and knights of Meath', urging them that 'for love of him they give an aid ... towards fortifying the king's city of Dublin'. He also wrote in similar terms to the 'barons and knights of Leinster'.[14] Clearly the government was involved in helping to provide money for the citizens in managing the defence of Dublin. In February 1215, for example, the justiciar was ordered to compel the citizens to account for 500 marks that they had received some years previously from the justiciar, John de Grey, 'to fortify their city'.[15]

From the beginning of the English occupation there is evidence that the citizens were working on the city defences. When Roger de Limminster in 1190 was granted by the city 'the place over the new west gate', he was also given what the charter called 'the two places which are on either side of the gate' – building sites, as it were, where he was allowed 'to build as much as he could without interference from the city'. For this Roger gave 'one ounce of gold to help repair the wall of the city'.[16] But apart from some repairs, there is no firm evidence of any extensions to the existing city walls. Rather, it was the great fosse which was constructed, in the early part of the century. On 8 August 1225, for example, the king ordered that the abbot of St Thomas's be paid compensation 'in regard to the lands occupied by the fosse thrown up around the city of Dublin'.[17] Similar compensation was also paid to landowners during the construction of Dublin Castle.

369–70. **10** H.S. Sweetman (ed.) *Calendar of documents relating to Ireland, 1171–1307*, 5 vols (London, 1875–86), i, no. 345. **11** Ibid., no. 346. **12** Ibid., no. 226. **13** Ibid., no. 228. **14** Ibid., no. 315. **15** Ibid., no. 529. **16** Gilbert (ed.), *Hist. & mun. doc. Ire.*, p. 56. **17** *Cal. Doc. Ire., 1171–1307*, i, no. 1314.

The absence of murage grants also suggests that no defensive building works were taking place on the walls in the early thirteenth century. The normal way of raising money to finance the building of borough walls was through a murage, a licence from the king to levy tolls on specified goods brought into the borough for sale.[18] But it was not until July 1221 that 'the men of Dublin' were first granted a murage 'to enable them to enclose their city for the security and defence of the city and of the adjacent parts'.[19] Even then the grant was severely restrictive, being levied only on wool, hides and wine, so that the amount of money raised would have been insufficient for any major building operations. The next murage grant, of 28 October 1233, was far more extensive and suggests that serious works were being considered. By the mid-century a 'new city wall' was certainly in existence.[20] Regular grants thereafter, no fewer than seven between 1250 and 1302, covered every imaginable import into Dublin, including luxury goods from abroad.[21] It seems, then, that extensive building operations were planned, including the construction of new walls. Archaeological evidence does support the building of some new wall and the addition of some towers, such as Buttevant and Isolde's.[22] But there is no evidence of money collected from murage being spent on the walls.[23] It seems to have been used for other purposes. For example, a letter of Edward I to the mayor and bailiffs of Dublin in 1290 confirmed that on the order of the treasurer, Nicholas de Clere, they had spent 'a great part of the money' arising from the customs lately granted 'in aid of enclosing their vill' on works at the exchequer; he therefore granted them a new murage for three years.[24]

A famous case involving a former mayor, the merchant Geoffrey Morton, illustrates very well how murage could be abused.[25] He had rented part of the wall and a defensive tower at the head of the bridge across the Liffey. He was responsible for maintaining the fabric at his own cost. But in 1308 he petitioned the king, claiming that the last great fire of Dublin had severely damaged the structure. He was therefore granted a murage by the king, a unique example of such a 'private' grant. Within a year there were complaints that he

---

18 See the references cited in J.S. Hamilton, 'Edward II and the murage of Dublin: English administrative practice versus Irish custom', in J.S. Hamilton and Patricia J. Bradley (eds), *Documenting the past: essays in medieval history presented to George Peddy Cuttino* (Woodbridge, 1988), pp 85–6.   19 Gilbert (ed.), *Hist. & mun. doc. Ire.*, p. 76.   20 J.T. Gilbert (ed.), *Calendar of ancient records of Dublin*, 19 vols (Dublin, 1889–1944), i, 95.   21 Hamilton, 'Murage of Dublin', p. 86; Mac Niocaill, *Na Búirgéisí*, ii, 448–50.   22 Simpson, 'Forty years a-digging', pp 53–56.   23 See Philomena Connolly, *Irish exchequer payments, 1270–1446* (Dublin, 1998), pp 1–197, which records issues from the Dublin exchequer and specifies where the money went.   24 Gilbert (ed.), *Hist. & mun. doc. Ire*, pp 190–91; *Cal. doc. Ire., 1171–1307*, i, no. 754.   25 For a thorough examination of the problem of this abuse of murage by Morton, in the wider context of his long career in Dublin, see Philomena Connolly, 'The rise and fall of Geoffrey Morton, mayor of Dublin, 1303–4', in Duffy (ed.), *Medieval Dublin II*, pp 233–51.

was not collecting murage on the goods of his friends, clear evidence that customs were collected by him on most goods coming into the city. But, the king was informed, he made no attempt to use that money in repairing either the tower or the walls 'in contempt of the king and to the manifest danger of the city'. By March the king was writing to the chief governor, complaining that the citizens had been defrauded, that now the quay as well as the tower were in ruins, and revoking the grant. It later emerged that as a result of Morton's rebuilding, fortifications had been destroyed: he had not only narrowed the width of the walls, replaced battlements with windows and put a new *solarium* on the tower, he had made it impossible for Dubliners to move along the wall to defend it from attackers.[26]

It seems, in fact, that what money was collected from murage in the thirteenth century was rarely if ever spent on city defences. If, as we saw, the government was concerned with the defence of Dublin in the early days of the English settlement, that concern vanished in the thirteenth century, when the extensive English settlement of Ireland seemed to extend what was called the 'land of peace (*terra pacis*)' well beyond the environs of the city. The citizens themselves had a casual attitude towards the walls, towers and even the great fosse. Despite complaints of damage caused by animals, grazing rights in the fosse were regularly hired out. As space within the city walls became scarcer, and therefore more valuable, the municipality began to raise revenues for the city's coffers by renting out defence towers, gatehouses, the cellars underneath, and any part of the many buildings in the city walls which might be used as a private dwelling or, more important, a shop.[27]

This casual attitude, as we might call it, to the city defences continued even into the fourteenth century. For example, on 27 August 1305 the city sealed a charter in the Guildhall granting to Nigel le Brun and his heirs, in perpetuity, the tower called *La Botavaunt* (Buttevant Tower), with an adjoining plot of land, saving to the city what the charter called 'free entrance and exit through the said tower and land for the protection of the said city as often as it shall be necessary'. Nigel and his heirs were to pay an annual rent of 4*s*. They were also to maintain the fabric of the tower, 'both above ground and below, in all necessary places, at their own cost, unless it is destroyed by common war, which God forbid'. Finally, Nigel, at his own expense, was to remove 'the common latrine which is there at present … to the west' and rebuild it there 'in as good a state as it was before, or better'.[28] While the city fathers showed some awareness that the tower was there to defend the city and made provision for free access if the need should arise, it is evident that this was a

---

26 Hamilton, 'Murage of Dublin', pp 92–3.　27 See, in general, examples in *Cal. anc. rec. Dublin*, i, 82ff.　28 N.A.I., D 19707. I am grateful to the late Dr Philomena Connolly for a copy of this charter.

routine requirement which they expected would never be realised – as unlikely as the 'general war' which might cause the tower to be destroyed. They seem more concerned with the inconvenience caused to the city inhabitants by interference with the public latrine.

There are many examples of such grants, including portions of the walls themselves hired out as building sites. As a result the walls quickly ceased to be entirely effective as defences and came to be primarily regarded as valuable stone properties which, like the grass on the fosse, could be turned to profit. Not only might houses built on the walls obstruct the free passage that was supposed to be maintained along the length of the wall, so that defenders could quickly move from tower to tower if the city were attacked, but the weight of the building might cause the wall to collapse and expose a gap which might be exploited by the enemy. This is exactly what happened in Waterford in 1170 when it was under siege by the army of Strongbow. Gerald of Wales describes that the siege was not making much progress, when someone noticed that a beam supported a house overhanging the wall. When this support was cut away, the house collapsed and, Gerald tells us, brought down a 'considerable part of the wall'.[29] The same thing happened in Dublin. When Geoffrey Morton claimed that a fire had accidentally burned the tower he had rented from the municipality and sought the famous murage grant, he failed to mention that he had built a great hall (*aula*). For this he used the city wall to form one side of the new building, putting a cellar under the wall itself and inserting joists in the wall in such a manner that they blocked the way by which men should have access to mount the wall for the defence of the city. It was the burning of those same joists in the Dublin fire that caused part of the wall to collapse.

It was the fact that Dublin was surrounded by the *terra pacis* (land of peace), seemingly safe and secure from attack, that made people so complacent about defence. Dublin Castle also reflects this same complacency. When King John ordered its construction in 1204, he made it plain that the new castle, 'if need be', was to be linked directly to the defence of the city. The justiciar was therefore ordered, as we have seen, to make it as strong as he could 'with good dikes and strong walls'.[30] The best site, high on the ridge, was chosen and a great clearance was made of all structures that impeded building operations. Even churches, St Paul's and St Martin's, had to be removed to allow the castle walls to be constructed.[31] In the early years of Henry III there is evidence that the fortifications of the castle were being maintained – in 1227, for example, the sheriff of Dublin was allowed £24 paid to Walter the carpenter

29 Gerald of Wales, *Expugnatio*, p. 67. 30 *Cal. doc. Ire., 1171–1307*, i, no. 226. 31 Margaret Murphy, 'Balancing the concerns of church and state: the archbishops of Dublin, 1181–1228', in Terry Barry, Robin Frame and Katharine Simms (eds), *Colony and frontier in medieval Ireland* (London, 1995), p. 54.

for 'making the towers' and nearly £9 for '6 loads of lead and the carriage thereof and converting it into gutters for the towers'.[32] But, as with the city, the absence of danger soon meant that the military function of the castle ceased to be uppermost. It was what might be called the 'domestic' function of the castle which became dominant – the residence of the justiciar when he was in Dublin; the place where the Irish council met regularly; the seat of the exchequer. This is best epitomised in the famous order of Henry III in 1243, when he was expected to pay a royal visit to Dublin, that a great hall should be constructed in the castle, 120 feet in length and 80 feet in breadth, a copy (the king said) of the hall at Canterbury. In the gable behind the dais a great rose window was to be made, 30 feet in diameter. Beneath that splendid window a picture of the king and queen with 'their baronage' was to be painted.[33]

Expenditure on what are called 'works' at the castle was accounted for frequently, but these are usually for the domestic side. Payments for 'a bucket for the well', 'repair of the bakehouse', 'glass for the windows of the exchequer' – these are typical. The sums involved are small, so that repairs to the defensive fabric of the castle were minimal.[34] As late as 1300–2 the sums expended in two years of works amounted to only £21. 5s. 8½d. and covered repairs to the old stable, the mint, the oriel between the chamber of the justiciar and the chapel, the roof of the great hall, mending gutters, plastering the walls of the chamber opposite the exchequer, repairs to the roof of the chapel and the old stable, to the chamber of the constable, to the kitchen and the houses of the exchequer, and glass for some windows – nothing remotely connected with defence.[35]

Occasionally there was a flurry when a political crisis threatened the security of the government. In 1264, for example, the justiciar and some other members of the government were taken prisoner by members of the Geraldine faction who had risen in revolt. A provisional government had to take over in Dublin and the first thing it did was to take measures to make the castle secure. More than £340 (a huge sum in those days, when the average wage of a soldier was still only 1*d.* per day, and the annual income of the government was less than £4,000) was spent on supplies and what the account simply calls 'the fortifications'.[36] On another occasion when the government was forced to take action against a dangerous enemy, the state of Dublin Castle was exposed as something of a disaster. When Hugh de Lacy invaded Ireland in 1223, Dublin was faced with a dangerous rebellion. It immediately ordered an inventory of stores in a number of royal castles, in case they

---

32 'Accounts on the great rolls of the pipe of the Irish exchequer', *Report of the Deputy Keeper of the public records of Ireland* [hereafter *PRI rep. DK*] no. 35, p. 30.   33 *Close rolls 1242–47*, p. 23; Roger Stalley, 'Irish Gothic and English fashion', in James Lydon (ed.), *The English in medieval Ireland* (Dublin, 1984), pp 74–5.   34 See for example *PRI rep. DK*, 35, pp 29, 30, 31, 34, 45.   35 *PRI rep. DK*, 39, p. 25.   36 *PRI rep. DK*, 35, p. 47.

needed to be defended against rebel attack. That for Dublin is revealing. The
only items listed that might be useful in defence were: '2 mangonels, 1 crossbow with a wheel, 1 crossbow for the foot, 4,500 quarrels'. There was also one
tent, which in some way might have been useful in a siege. Otherwise all the
items listed were from the kitchen, pantry, workshop, or miscellaneous items
like 'a great chain to guard the prisoners'.[37] There was not a trace of any other
arms or armour.

Both Dublin Castle, then, and the state of the city defences show that
generally throughout the thirteenth century Dublin was free from any real
worry about security and the need of defence. The city prospered and grew,
expanding into new suburbs and attracting an ever-increasing number of
merchants and traders, many of whom settled in the city.[38] The continuous
expansion of the Guild Merchant, the organisation that had a monopoly of
trade, is a sure indication of the growing numbers involved in commerce. In
1222–3, 73 were admitted; 78 in 1223–4; 125 in 1224–5; 224 in 1225–26.
There was no let-up in the years following: 159 were admitted in 1263–4.[39]
There were many other signs of the city's growing prosperity: the massive
land reclamation projects revealed by the archaeologists; the new stone
buildings, houses as well as churches, which quickly occupied all available
space within, and even on, the city walls; the proliferation of religious houses,
including some hospitals, that were visible signs of the patronage of wealthy
benefactors; even the simple fact that Dublin was served by not one, but
uniquely by two cathedrals. All of this prosperity was a measure of the
peaceful and secure conditions that Dublin enjoyed.

Before the end of the thirteenth century, however, this happy state of
affairs was to change dramatically. A petition from the tenants of the royal
manor of Saggart in *c*.1280 is particularly revealing. It painted a grim picture
of the destruction caused by raiding parties from the Irish enclaves in the
mountains just south of Dublin. 'Many of our fathers and brothers and
relatives have been killed', they told the king, and, 'for seven years past we
have been refugees from our houses, seeking alien refuges as beggars, so that
the great part of 13 carucates of your land and our tenements lie sterile and
uncultivated'. They claimed to have lost 30,000 sheep, 200 cattle, 100 afers,
200 pigs, and goods and possessions worth £100 and more. They end with the
plaintive wail that because 'we are the nearest to the mountains, we always
suffer the first evils'.[40] Not far away, just across the border in Kildare, the

---

37 *Cal. doc. Ire., 1171–1307*, i, no. 1227.   **38** For some figures from the late thirteenth
century 'great custom' which illustrate the extent to which the wool trade had grown see
the table in Mac Niocaill, *Búirgéisí*, ii, 523.   **39** Philomena Connolly and Geoffrey Martin
(eds), *The Dublin Guild Merchant Roll, c.1190–1265* (Dublin, 1992), p. 121.   **40** G.O.
Sayles (ed.), *Documents on the affairs of Ireland before the king's council* (Dublin, 1979), no
41. For the deteriorating situation in the Dublin and Wicklow mountains, the growing

escheator in his account for 1300 'answers nothing' for a manor in the king's hand, 'because situated in the march near the Irish, the manor is burned by them, and nobody has the courage to live there'.[41] On 30 April 1306 an important official in the Dublin administration, William de Moenes, actually surrendered his land of Bothercall which he farmed on the same royal manor of Saggart because, he said, he was so often preyed upon by Irish felons that he could no longer plough, sow, or make any use of the land.[42] Saggart was literally only just down the king's highway from Dublin.

The *terra guerre* (land of war) was now encroaching on lands in the immediate vicinity of Dublin. During the war in Leinster in 1294–5, the government had to employ men to guard the area around the city ('the parts of Dublin', as the exchequer account calls it).[43] Early in the fourteenth century the situation worsened and the city was immediately threatened. For many years the records of the exchequer recorded payment for the carriage of rolls and the king's treasure from the castle outside to the houses of the exchequer, from the beginning of each term and back again at the end of term.[44] But in Trinity term 1307 they were brought back to the castle 'at various times to avoid danger because of the war in Leinster'.[45] In 1308 they were brought back and forth from the castle 'every day in Trinity term because of the imminent war in Leinster'.[46] In December 1310 a large ward, under John fitz Thomas, was placed at Rathmore, to defend the land between Saggart and Ballymore 'because of the rebellion of the Irish felons of Leinster.[47] Six months later another ward was placed at Rathfarnham 'to guard the march of those parts against the Irish felons of the king'.[48] The danger could hardly have got much closer to Dublin.

Yet the government seemed to think that the danger had passed. By 1309 things were back to normal in the exchequer. Once more records and the royal treasure were carried from the castle to the exchequer each term, and not daily. This continued until Hilary term 1314, when the daily carriage was resumed 'because of the common war in Ireland'. There was by then, too,

---

threat to Dublin, and the history of subsequent wars versus the Irish of the mountains see James Lydon, 'A land of war' in Art Cosgrove (ed.), *A new history of medieval Ireland* (Oxford, 1987), ii, 256ff; idem, 'Medieval Wicklow – 'a land of war', in Ken Hannigan and William Nolan (eds), *Wicklow history and society* (Dublin, 1995), pp 158–81.   **41** *PRI rep. DK*, 38, p. 82.   **42** National Archives of Ireland (NAI), EX 2/1, p.162. In 1313 a tenant at Saggart was allowed to pay his arrears of rent in instalments because he was 'altogether impoverished and oppressed by reason of the robbery and burnings which the Irish of the mountains of Leinster, felons of the king, have lately made in the aforesaid town', Lydon, 'Medieval Wicklow', p. 171.   **43** Connolly, *Irish exchequer payments*, p. 125. A good indication of the dangers posed by the new rebellion is the fact that Dublin Castle was well stocked with 'wine, victuals, crossbows and other necessities' because of the war; ibid., 124.   **44** See for examples between 1302 and 1307 in ibid., pp 169, 172, 174, 179, 188, 194.   **45** Ibid., p. 195.   **46** Ibid., p. 204.   **47** J.F. Lydon, 'The enrolled account of Alexander Bicknor, treasurer of Ireland' in *Analecta Hibernica*, xxx (1982), p. 30.   **48** Ibid., p. 32.

what the record calls a 'garrison (*garnestura*)' of the houses of the exchequer, to whom a 'horn for blowing (*cornu flatili*)' was delivered, presumably to sound an alarm and summon help if attacked.[49] Later a watch was established in Dublin Castle 'to avoid and suppress the malice of Irish felons and enemies of the king in the parts of Leinster who were threatening to burn the houses of the exchequer', and a special watch of five crossbowmen was established at the exchequer between 30 April 1316 and 31 March 1317. Robert de Cotegrave, keeper of the works of Dublin Castle and of the houses of the exchequer, was also paid the large sum of £100 'for preparing and carrying out works there to avoid and suppress the malice of the Scots and their Irish allies, who were attacking the king's faithful people of the land of Ireland and were threatening to attack and besiege the castle'.[50]

The danger was now obviously very real. The main reason, of course, was that by then the Bruce invasion had established a very threatening Scottish position in Ireland.[51] The government had been quick to react, not least in preparing for the defence of Dublin. There the justiciar and the council decided that immediate action was called for. Brother Walter de Aqua, a Hospitaller, was assigned 'to direct the defence of the city of Dublin in aid of the mayor and commonalty there, in order to suppress the malice of the Scottish and Irish felons'.[52] The Irish of the mountains had responded positively to the success of the Scottish invaders and once again posed a serious threat to Dublin. Hugh Lawless complained to the exchequer that he could gain no profit from lands in Bray. Because of the arrival of the Scots, he said, the Irish of the mountains had gone to war against the king and had invaded, burned and altogether destroyed not only his lands, but 'all other lands and tenements of divers faithful of the king in those parts'.[53] On 8 December 1315 a large ward (6 men at arms and 80 foot) was placed at Tallaght 'to keep watch against the Irish there every night'.[54] This presented a security problem without precedent. The Dublin chronicle records that on 6 September 1316 'David O Toole came with 80 men and secretly hid himself in the wood at Cullenswood and in the morning came to Dublin, and lord William Comyn with his co-citizens of Dublin went out and manfully put them to flight for 6 leagues and killed about 17 and mortally wounded many besides'.[55] There could no longer be any doubt that the defence of Dublin should long since have been a top priority for the Irish government.

When King Robert of Scotland joined his brother Edward Bruce in Ireland in the winter of 1316 with huge reinforcements, the danger greatly increased. He and his great army moved south from Ulster in the direction of Dublin

49 Connolly, *Irish exchequer payments*, pp 209, 213, 217, 220, 223, 229, 233.   50 Ibid., p. 240.   51 For the Bruce invasion see Seán Duffy (ed.), *Robert the Bruce's Irish wars* (Stroud, 2002).   52 Connolly, *Irish exchequer payments*, p. 234.   53 Gilbert (ed.), *Hist. & mun. doc. Ire.*, p. 457.   54 Ibid., p. 372.   55 *Chartul. St Mary's, Dublin*, ii, 297.

and there was an immediate panic in the city. What are called the 'articles of grievance of the common folk of the community of Dublin', presented to the mayor, give a glimpse of that panic. They demanded that 'under penalty of grievous amercement', at least one man from each house, and more if necessary, should come to muster at the tolling of the public bell by day or night, 'while the land is troubled by Scots enemies, and by the common war of the Irish who daily threaten to burn the suburbs and do all possible damage to the city'. They also demanded that guards should be posted to each gate 'to save the city' and that no sally should in future be made through the gates unless by direct order of the mayor and under the command of the captains appointed to lead the city militia.[56]

This certainly gives the impression that Dublin was almost under siege, even before the Scots arrived in the vicinity. Other evidence supports this. On 26 May 1316 the Irish council ordered that militia should be raised in Saggart (30 men), Newcastle (30 men) and in all the other vills and hamlets 'from the river Liffey to the Leinster mountains' for the custody of those parts against the Irish of the mountains.[57] Dublin itself was ordered to provide food and supplies for the 300 men they had raised in the city for the same purpose.[58] The Scots, too, were rumoured to be threatening. One man collecting rents for the king in the manor of Swords was told that the Scots and the men of Ulster were approaching the area. He turned to go to Dublin for safety. But when he had almost reached the city he was told for certain that the Scots were 'hostilely invading that country', so he turned back in fear.[59]

Long before that, however, the English government had reacted positively to the news of the Scottish invasion of Ireland and in September 1315 a top official, John de Hothum, was despatched to Dublin as a special envoy of the king.[60] It was he who first ordered practical defence measures after the Scots advanced south and won an important victory at Kells. He feared that they would advance on Dublin. Given the state of the city defences, he knew that the castle would have to be the last refuge. So in December he ordered that the bell-tower of the church of St Mary del Dam be demolished, and the stones were used for repair work on Dublin Castle.[61] The gates were closed and even though the Scots moved on, away from Dublin, the gate 'del Dam' remained permanently closed for a year.[62] Hothum also ordered the mayor and bailiffs of Dublin to supply 10,000 bolts for crossbows to the castle garrison, as well as a large amount of lead for repairs. Most interesting, they were also ordered to provide 100 stones and eight hides of large white cows – these

56 Gilbert (ed.), *Hist. & mun. doc. Ire.*, pp 359–61.   57 Ibid., pp 375–7.   58 Ibid., p. 354.
59 Ibid., pp 450–1.   60 For Hothum and his mission see J.R.S. Phillips, 'The mission of John de Hothum to Ireland' in James Lydon (ed.), *England and Ireland in the later middle ages* (Dublin, 1981), pp 62–85.   61 Gilbert (ed.), *Hist. & mun. doc. Ire.*, pp 405–6: the Irish treasurer was ordered on 8 June 1319 to repair the belfry.   62 Ibid., p. 445.

almost certainly were to be used as missiles to be fired from catapults against besiegers of the castle.[63]

But the Scots moved on and it was not until King Robert approached Dublin again in February 1317 that another panic gripped the city. One sign of this was the arrest of the earl of Ulster who had arrived there shortly before. The father-in-law of King Robert, the earl was now suspected of being in collusion with him and probably planning the betrayal of the city to the Scots. So the citizens took the law into their own hands and threw him into prison.[64] By the time the Scots had reached Castleknock, overlooking the city, the mayor and citizens had taken extreme measures to defend the city against the expected attack. They burned all the suburbs, to make sure that the Scots would have no protection in approaching the city walls. A later inquiry revealed that this was done because 'the common council of the lord king in Ireland, after the aggression of the aforesaid Scots in the same land, for the salvation of the aforesaid city [Dublin] ordained and agreed that if the same Scots approached the city, the aforesaid mayor and community should destroy and burn the suburb of the aforesaid city, lest the aforesaid Scots find any refuge in the same suburb'.[65] In the short time available they also tried to repair the walls as best they could. They got part of the masonry they needed by raiding the Dominican friary of St Saviour's on the far side of the Liffey. The friars subsequently complained to the king and council in England that the mayor and citizens, 'for the defence and protection of their city', burned the houses of the friars, seized what timber they could, broke the walls and took the stone to the city, cut down all the trees in their garden, stole the timber and used it in their works, together with stone from the hearths, the shutters from the windows, the bolts from the doors, the table, lathes, all iron tools, and also malt, grain, and other victuals and goods.[66] The attempt by the citizens to repair the walls clearly had some measure of success, for in September 1318 they were pardoned the huge sum of £600 of ancient debts because of the expenses they had incurred in repair of the walls and towers for the defence of the city.

There is confirmation of the citizens' actions in the Dublin chronicle, where it is seen as part of a frenzied response when it was discovered that Bruce had reached the castle of Hugh Tirell at Castleknock, overlooking the city. The

---

63 Phillips, 'Mission of John de Hothum', p. 68; Gilbert (ed.), *Hist. & mun. doc. Ire.*, pp 327, 337, 343. Expenditure on 'works' and 'stores' for Dublin Castle greatly increased: Connolly, *Irish exchequer payments*, pp 234, 237, 240. 64 J.F. Lydon, in Duffy (ed.), *Bruce's Irish wars*, pp 79–80. 65 Gilbert (ed.), *Hist. & mun. doc. Ire.*, p. 411. The same inquiry revealed that as a result the loss annually to the city was over £100, damage of 500 marks, and loss of property amounting to the enormous sum of £10,000 'and more'. For years afterwards compensation was sought by the city, by individuals and religious communities who had lost valuable properties – for some examples see Sayles, *Affairs of Ireland*, nos. 112, 113, 114. 66 Sayles, *Affairs of Ireland*, no. 113.

writer tells how the mayor 'destroyed the church of St Saviour and carried off the stones of that place to make city walls, which were then extended to the north over the quay'. He describes how Bruce captured the castle of Hugh Tirell, taking him and his wife prisoners: 'And on that same night, by the consent of the citizens, Thomas Street was set on fire, but by misfortune the church of St John, with the chapel of Blessed Mary Magdalene were burned by the same fire and all the suburbs of Dublin were burned together, and the church of St Patrick together with St Mary's abbey were plundered by the same inhabitants'.[67] The chronicler describes that when Bruce on the day following 'learned that the city had been fortified', he abandoned Castleknock and moved to Leixlip. The ploy was effective and Bruce moved away from the city, never to return. Dublin had escaped. But the danger persisted, with the Irish a constant threat and the Scots still a presence in Ireland. The environs of Dublin had to be protected. The government had already initiated this policy in response to the threat posed by the Leinster Irish, in particular those in the Leinster mountains. As we saw, a large ward had been set up at Rathmore in 1310; and in December 1315, shortly after he arrived in Dublin, John de Hothum placed another large ward at Tallaght in the immediate vicinity of the city. This policy of warding was subsequently maintained and eventually led to the creation of the Pale in the mid-fifteenth century. In 1455, for example, the Dublin parliament ordered that barriers were to be made at the bridges at Lucan and Kilmainham against Irish enemies and English rebels, and other defences at all fords between the bridge of Lucan and the bridge of Dublin, and a heavy financial penalty was imposed on all who defaulted when summoned to help in the work.[68]

The citizens of Dublin had also to play a part in the expeditions mounted by the government directly against the Irish of the mountains. In 1354, for example, because there was what the record called a 'deficiency of the number of archers which the justiciar needed in furtherance of the war recently begun against the Obrynnes', John Serjaunt of Dublin was ordered to choose many 'strong and powerful archers in the city of Dublin and the neighbouring parts' to make up the deficiency. John, 'well arrayed for war with those archers and also certain hobelars [light horsemen]', joined the justiciar's army and 'in various conflicts and encounters with the said enemies bravely placed himself and the said archers and hobelars in the front of the army and fought valiantly'. But men, horses and arms were lost as a result.[69] In 1356 the city was allowed 100 marks of the annual farm for aiding the justiciar again in 'making war again

---

67 *Chartul. St Mary's, Dublin*, ii, 299, 352–3. **68** H.F. Berry (ed.), *Statute rolls of the parliament of Ireland, reign of Henry VI* (Dublin, 1910), p. 315. Two towers with two gates were also to be built at the two bridges and another tower 'by the wall of St Mary's abbey', all to be paid by means of a subsidy to be levied on the county: ibid., p. 403. **69** Connolly, *Irish exchequer payments*, p. 461.

upon O'Byrne and his sept, and divers other powerful Irish of Leinster'.[70] In a petition of 9 May 1356 the commonalty of Dublin pointed out that 'with a great number of armed men, hobelars, archers and footmen' they had gone out on a number of occasions to resist the O Byrnes and O Tooles 'and their accomplices invading the marches of Leinster in county Dublin'.[71] The city regularly sent men to join the justiciar on similar campaigns and they continued to supply men for warding.[72] The religious houses within the city were also compelled to supply men whenever military service was demanded.[73] They also took precautions themselves against potential threats to their lands by the Irish of the mountains. In his harvest account for 1344 for Clonkeen in county Dublin, the bailiff recorded payment to 'two men watching upon the tops of the mountains through fear of the Irish'.[74] They lit fires as a warning and this gave rise to what became known as 'smokesilver', a local subsidy to pay for the services of watchmen with bonfires keeping watch over the Irish.

The city had no real problem in finding men to fight. Long before this the English system known as 'watch and ward' had been introduced, whereby citizens had to provide armed men to guard and keep watch over the city at night, especially the towers and gates. In 1305, for example, the council divided the city into three quarters under three watchmen, each with three others under his direction. All citizens were obliged to contribute towards the cost.[75] Two years later parliament imposed English legislation concerning watch and ward 'in the great towns which are enclosed', with elaborate regulations governing the maintenance of the rule of law at all times.[76] In 1344 the seneschal of Christ Church accounted for 6*d*. paid 'to the serjeants in the watch' in Dublin.[77] By 1457 eight men were keeping watch each night.[78] There were other military obligations that helped. Each freeman had to possess arms. In 1454 the city enacted that no apprentice was to be accepted as a freeman unless he had a small bow, arrows and a sword, all of which he was to display to

70 Gilbert (ed.), *Cal. anc. rec. Dublin*, i, 8–19.   71 NAI RC8/27, pp 203–4. In an earlier petition in 1334, the mayor and commonalty petitioned to be freed from customs levied, because of 'great expenses' in defence of the city and 'surrounding marches', and also because they joined the justiciar against the Irish enemies for 21 days with 500 men on one occasion, and again later for 15 days. This cost them over £400 and, they claimed, most of their men, horses and arms: P.R.O., C81/218/8216.   72 See for example Connolly, *Irish exchequer payments*, pp 501, 546; for examples from the fifteenth century see Gilbert (ed.), *Cal. anc. rec. Dublin*, i, 327, 328, 357, 381, 393. The city also provided banners for the royal army: *PRI rep. DK*, 43, p. 66.   73 See for example the case of Christ Church: James Lydon, 'Christ Church in the later medieval world, 1300–1500', in Kenneth Milne (ed.), *Christ Church Cathedral Dublin: a history* (Dublin, 2000), p. 88; or *Chartul. St Mary's, Dublin*, ii, xxvi.   74 James Mills (ed.), *Account roll of the priory of the Holy Trinity, Dublin, 1337–46* (repr. Dublin, 1996), p. 64.   75 Gilbert (ed.), *Cal. anc. rec. Dublin*, i, 223. 76 H.F. Berry (ed.), *Statutes and ordinances and acts of the parliament of Ireland, King John to Henry V* (Dublin, 1907), p. 255.   77 *Account roll of Holy Trinity*, p. 92.   78 Mac Niocaill, *Búirgéisí*, ii, 390. In 1465 the number was reduced to two, who were to receive 4*d*. from each house and 3*d*. from each shop, as well as a gown from the mayor and bailiffs.

the authorities twice a year. In 1466 it was enacted that 'every householder and their men were to have weapons according to their degree'; constables were appointed to supervise training 'on holidays when the weather is according' and to punish 'any who quitted'.[79] Within the city, then, there was a steady supply of men trained in arms. In Waterford there is evidence that guns, too, were in use and we must presume that the same was true of Dublin.[80]

In the fourteenth and fifteenth centuries, then, the government was able to keep the immediate environs of Dublin safe from sudden attack, even though the Irish threat never went away. Even that danger seemed to be neutralised when the Leinster Irish submitted to Richard II during his expedition to Ireland at the end of the fourteenth century. In a famous ceremony in Dublin Castle, carefully recorded for posterity by a public notary and witnessed by a great assembly of notables (including the mayor of Dublin), Donnchad O Byrne swore on the gospels to keep the peace and did fealty to the king. The other important Leinster leaders had already done, or shortly afterwards did, homage to King Richard.[81] But the peace achieved by the king did not last. As early as 1402 the citizens of Dublin, led by the mayor, marched out of the city against the O Byrnes and in battle near Bray defeated the Irish and reputedly killed 493 of them.[82] As we have already seen, the government was later forced to defend bridges and fords that provided easy access to Dublin. The potential danger remained, right to the end of the middle ages. In 1515 a special report on the state of Ireland was realistic when it emphasised that only half of county Dublin was in any real sense subject to the king's laws.[83]

There was one spectacular development in the late fifteenth century that greatly increased the security of Dublin. The creation of the Guild of St George (or Fraternity of Arms) in 1474, in association with the city, provided up to 500 men, the first real standing army in medieval Ireland.[84] The primary purpose was to protect the Pale, the fortified and defended area of land within parts of counties Dublin, Kildare, Meath and Louth, that provided some measure of security within the Dublin area. The city could therefore act on the basis that permanent arrangements had been made for the defence of the city. Within the walls of the city Dublin Castle, too, was for a long time considered safe. The old complacency returned. While the castle remained the principal place where important political and military prisoners were confined, it could not always be relied on to fulfil adequately even that limited function. As early as 1313 four dangerous prisoners nearly succeeded in escaping over the walls 'by certain cords … which they made from sheets and coverlets'.[85] In

79 Ibid., p. 392; Gilbert (ed.), *Cal. anc. rec. Dublin*, i, 283, 326. St Edmund was appointed patron. 80 Mac Niocaill, *Búirgéisí*, ii, 396. 81 Lydon, 'Medieval Wicklow', p. 178. 82 Ibid., p. 179. 83 *State papers Henry VIII*, Part III, 1515–38, p. 8. 84 Edmund Curtis, *A history of medieval Ireland* (2nd edn, London, 1938), pp 334–335. 85 *Calendar of the justiciary rolls of Ireland, 1308–14*, p. 285. They were caught, drawn and hanged. It was the wife of one of them who 'came by night to Dublin and brought with her the said sheets and coverlets'.

1330 the newly crowned MacMurrough king of Leinster escaped over the walls with the help of a rope.[86] Ten years later the government got a rude shock when William de Bermingham and his son Walter, both leading supporters of the recent rebellion by the earl of Desmond, one of the greatest challenges to the authority of the crown in medieval Ireland, nearly succeeded in making their escape from confinement in the castle. Worse, they brought troops (40 mounted and 200 foot) into Dublin and up to the castle walls on the night of 2 July 1232 and when the troops receded they set alight a house in the suburbs with the intention of burning as many houses as possible.[87]

Despite the dangers revealed by such incidents, nothing was done to make the castle safer. Watchmen were maintained, though they do not seem to have been very effective.[88] Some payments for 'works' are also recorded, though few in number and mostly for repairs to houses and the great hall.[89] By 1380 the castle was described as 'ruinous', for which the negligence of the royal officials was blamed.[90] In 1430, John Cornyngham, clerk of the works of the castle, was paid £4. 6s. 8d. in part payment of the small sum of £13. 6s. 8d., 'because the king's castle of Dublin and the great hall and other buildings and towers within the castle, in which the books and records of the chancery, both benches, and the exchequer are kept, are ruinous and greatly in need of repair'; the record adds that 'for lack of repair of the hall, towers and buildings the books and records are greatly damaged by rain and storms'.[91] In 1407 the government was worried that 'by the deceit of untrue men, strangers, and others dwelling in the marches of Ireland who flock thither and enter the castle' it might be taken.[92] But nothing was done and by May 1520, when the earl of Surrey arrived to head the Irish government, the state of the castle was so ruinous that it was evacuated so that reconstruction could commence.[93] A new era was initiated, necessary because the arrival of heavy ordnance on the scene transformed the nature of siege warfare. No longer were men armed with crossbows and bows and arrows, or even primitive hand guns, sufficient to guard the city walls of Dublin or the castle within. The problems of defence which Dublin had encountered throughout the middle ages were now augmented by the new technology available to those who posed a threat to the city.

86 *Chartul. St Mary's, Dublin*, ii, 372.   87 P.R.O., C.250/46/23. I am grateful to the late Dr Philomena Connolly for a copy of this important record.   88 See for example Connolly, *Irish exchequer payments*, pp 428, 502, 525.   89 Ibid., pp 531, 545, 546, 552, 564.   90 P.R.O., E 101/245/3: Dr Connolly supplied me with a copy. The state of the castle was such that Mortimer, the king's lieutenant, could not live in his house there, nor could parliament or council meetings be held there, and the records continued to deteriorate.   91 Connolly, *Irish exchequer payments*, pp 568–9. The decision to spend the small sum was actually taken by the justiciar and council, which shows how low down on their list of priorities the castle came. 92 Art Cosgrove, 'The emergence of the Pale, 1399–1447', in *A new history of Ireland*, ii, 555. 93 D.B. Quinn, 'The reemergence of English policy as a major factor in Irish affairs, 1520–34', ibid., 654–5.

The role of St Thomas's abbey in the early development of Dublin's western suburb

INTRODUCTION

The prominence and influence of St Thomas's abbey in the life and character of medieval Dublin is reflected in the many studies devoted to it by historians and archaeologists up to the present day, including Berry (1892), Gwynn (1954), Davis (1986–7), Elliott (1990), and Walsh (2000). Gwynn examines some of the ancient documents of St Thomas's, dates some of them, and from the information gleaned, sheds light on its early history. He explains that St Thomas's was a royal abbey, whereby the community had to obtain royal assent for the election of a new abbot, who in turn was obliged to submit to the king (and swear fealty) before seeking 'restitution of temporalities' (Gwynn 1954, 4; 20). He says that the king himself endowed the abbey with favours. He traces all the abbots of St Thomas's abbey throughout the thirteenth century, and says that by 1227, at the time of the election of its second abbot, St Thomas's had accrued considerable wealth (Gwynn 1954, 19–26). He refers to the 'close and continuous' link between St Thomas's in Dublin and St Augustine's in Bristol, both of which were Victorine monasteries of Augustinian canons regular (Gwynn 1954, 15–19; 33).

Davis draws attention to the disputes arising between St Thomas's and the municipality of Dublin, brought about by the proximity between the abbey's liberty and the municipality itself (Davis 1986–7, 58, 63). Usually, disputes arose when the municipality defied the rights of the Liberty of St Thomas's abbey, rights derived from its being a separate 'secular' jurisdiction with its own court (Davis 1986–7, 58). Since it was a royal abbey, transgressions by the municipality were also an infringement on royal interests because the king had the right to the issues of profits of the temporalities of the abbey whenever the abbacy was vacant (Davis 1986–7, 60). Confirmation of the abbey's rights was made time and again during the course of its history, particularly whenever these rights were being challenged. However, she points out that while the municipality questioned and at times ignored the abbey's rights of jurisdiction, individual citizens were generous benefactors (Davis 1986–7, 63), and this observation is borne out by the evidence discussed below.

Walsh has uncovered physical remains of St Thomas's, possibly the abbey church itself, and uses the depiction of the abbey on early maps of Dublin to help her interpret these remains (Walsh 2000). She says the importance of her work on Earl Street, the first of three excavations in the area, lies in the fact that it situates part of the abbey within the modern streetscape of Dublin for the first time.

The western suburb of the city, until recently much neglected, is drawing increasing attention (Clarke 1998; Hayden 2000; Simms 2001; Duddy 2001; Clarke 2002). Clarke outlines the main features of the western suburb throughout its medieval history (Clarke 1998, 50–51). He points out that the western suburb was unlike others in that it rose higher than the *urbs*, and that it was essentially linear in character comprising 'the great street leading to Kilmainham' (later the Thomas Street/James Street alignment) and a parallel back lane, Crockers' Street (Croker Lane, now Marshal Lane) towards the north (Clarke 1998, 50–51). This 'great street' passed through the suburb connecting the interior and west of Ireland to Dublin city. He refers to it as 'the great artery for food and other necessities entering the city'. He finds that in 1204, King John established an eight-day annual fair there, and by 1215, the fair had been lengthened to fifteen days. This main route forked off, with one road passing into the city while the other (Bridge Street) crossed the River Liffey at Dublin Bridge close to the city. He mentions the presence of two parishes and two religious houses, including St Thomas's. He says that St Thomas's was the most dominant religious institution in the western suburb, although, looking from Newgate, the abbey complex itself was probably not so conspicuous as it lay down-slope from the ridge along which Thomas Street curves (Clarke 1998, 51; Simms 1979, 36). He attributes part of the business activity of the western suburb to the economic life and needs of St Thomas's (Clarke 2002, 7).

Hayden excavated Bertram's Court (at the Cornmarket) outside the western wall at Newgate (Hayden 2000,101–14). He found that the earliest pottery uncovered in the area belonged to the late twelfth or early thirteenth century and also that light industrial activity was carried on there in the early- to mid-thirteenth century (Hayden 2000, 103–105). There is evidence too that animals were housed in this area (Hayden 2000, 109). Using Speed's map, Simms shows that the medieval suburbs, including the western suburb, grew around 'the nucleus of ecclesiastical sites', and in this way she highlights the influence of monasteries on urban expansion (Simms 2001, 50–4). She talks about the great monasteries as 'urban developers', considering how the Anglo-Normans used them to develop and stabilise their newly conquered towns.

Using *The register of the abbey of St Thomas, Dublin*, the writer elsewhere sketched the development of the western suburb during its first century of growth (Duddy 2001, 157–75). The paper details the emerging contemporary street pattern, the growing presence of religious houses and parishes, the developing streetscape characterised by rows of burgage plots (tenements), and the appearance of urban dwellers. It is pointed out that the beginning of large-scale urban development in the western suburb coincided with the founding of St Thomas's there, and that St Thomas's continued to influence the developing suburb through its acceptance and supervision of grants of urban land in the form of burgages and urban rent. From the very beginning, St Thomas's had royal approval, and perhaps even a royal mandate, to take an active interest in urban expansion in the western suburb, as this paper illustrates, through receipt of a tenement among the original grants received at its foundation. Throughout its first century, St Thomas's seems to have exercised this role to the fullest extent, involving itself in the transaction of grants of an urban nature in every way. This paper describes the nature and operation of St Thomas's abbey, and attempts to show how the receipt of the initial grant led to the exploitation of similar grants, which in turn led to the urban development of the western suburb.

THE STUDY PERIOD

The documents contained in the primary source, *The register of the abbey of St Thomas, Dublin* (Gilbert 1889) date from the founding of St Thomas's in *c*.1177, to the beginning of the final quarter of the thirteenth century (Gilbert 1889, xii). Approximately thirty-one of the documents refer to the western suburb, and inform this study. Unfortunately, just two of these documents were dated by Gilbert, one to 1268 (corrected by Gwynn to 1266–7; Gwynn 1954, 4) and the other to 1272 (Gilbert 1889, 3, 353–4), and the writer has attempted elsewhere to date the remainder of the documents (Duddy, 1990). The method of dating used involves comparisons of information from the *Register* with that of other contemporary sources (Curtis 1932; Brooks 1936; McNeill 1950; Brooks 1953), noting the reigning monarch or current bishop and comparing witness lists and topographical references. Only approximate dates were forthcoming, but the results – marked by an asterisk (e.g. 1183*) – may help to convey a sense of chronology in the development recorded over the period. Since all but the two documents noted above seem to date to no later than the 1240s, there was a temptation to close the study period at the mid-thirteenth century. However, the documents of 1266–7 and 1272 offer an important insight into the western suburb that is only implicit in the earlier documents, namely its considerably rural character, that endured behind the developing urban streets. Therefore, the study covers the period from the foundation of St Thomas's in 1177 to 1272.

THE ORIGIN AND NATURE OF ST THOMAS'S ABBEY

The priory (soon to become 'abbey') of St Thomas the Martyr was founded in 1177 by order of King Henry II who had vowed – as part of his penance for the murder of the archbishop of Canterbury, Thomas Becket, in 1170, canonised in 1173 – to found and dedicate churches in honour of the saint. Being 'the king's special abbey', St Thomas's enjoyed particular attention from the king himself and those who wished to display their loyalty to him (Gwynn 1954, 20; Davis 1986–7, 57; Duddy 2001, 160). The status of the founder of any religious house was a decisive factor in determining the subsequent extent of its influence, and the king was inevitably the most important founder, with the greatest range of possessions, both of a spiritual and temporal nature. Indeed, under feudal jurisdiction, he was the supreme owner of all land, so that his accompanying sphere of influence was co-extensive with the kingdom. The king granted lands from his own estate, and indeed, during the early years of St Thomas's, most of the chief Anglo-Norman settlers granted property to St Thomas's from their territories in Leinster, Munster and Ulster (Gwynn 1954, 13–14). Most of the abbey's lands, apart from the church of St Thomas in Dublin and lands in Cork, were located in Meath because lands in County Dublin had already been distributed among the earlier religious foundations like St Mary's abbey (Gwynn 1954, 15). Nevertheless, according to Davis, for more than a decade, St Thomas's became the foremost grantee of land, tithes, churches and other property at the cost of such long-standing institutions as St Mary's or Christ Church (Davis 1986–7, 64).

St Thomas's was governed on an Erastian basis – not a conscious concept in medieval times – in which the ecclesiastical institution was integrated into the overall institutional structure of society (Elliot 1990, 63; Rodes 1977, xiii–xiv). The functions of the institution, whether it was holding responsibility for parishes (Gilbert 1889, 284, 317), alleviating the poor (Gilbert 1889, 281, 284, 294), or interceding for the dead (Gilbert 1889, 281, 374, 377, 383, 392, 395, 397, 407, 418), all of which were pertinent to St Thomas's, were as necessary as those of secular institutions. St Thomas's actually played the role of a secular institution in providing welfare services for the poor and may have replaced diocesan priests in parish churches. Through Erastianism, the ecclesiastical institution was subjected to state control because the collateral tie between Church and State was seen to form the one pattern of organisation. If the 'area management' was delegated to a body that answered to central government, then overall functional efficiency might be achieved. This did not mean that religious ends were subordinated to wordly ends, but rather both ends were commonly pursued. Therefore, St Thomas's was founded with ends in mind, that were advantageous to civil society, for example, the

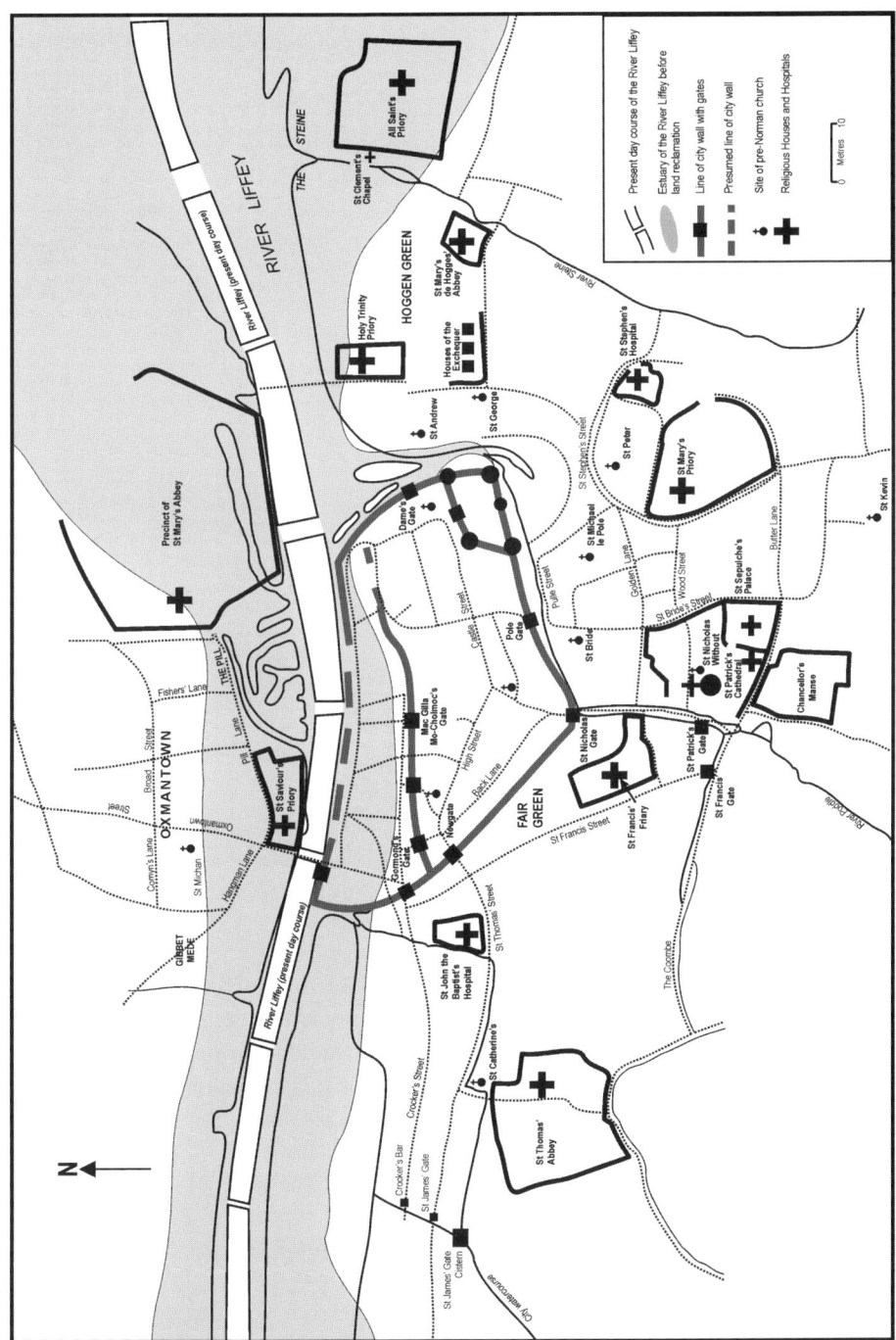

1 Sketch-map of the medieval city and suburbs showing St Thomas's Abbey in the western suburb (based on Clarke, 1998 and Simms, 1979)

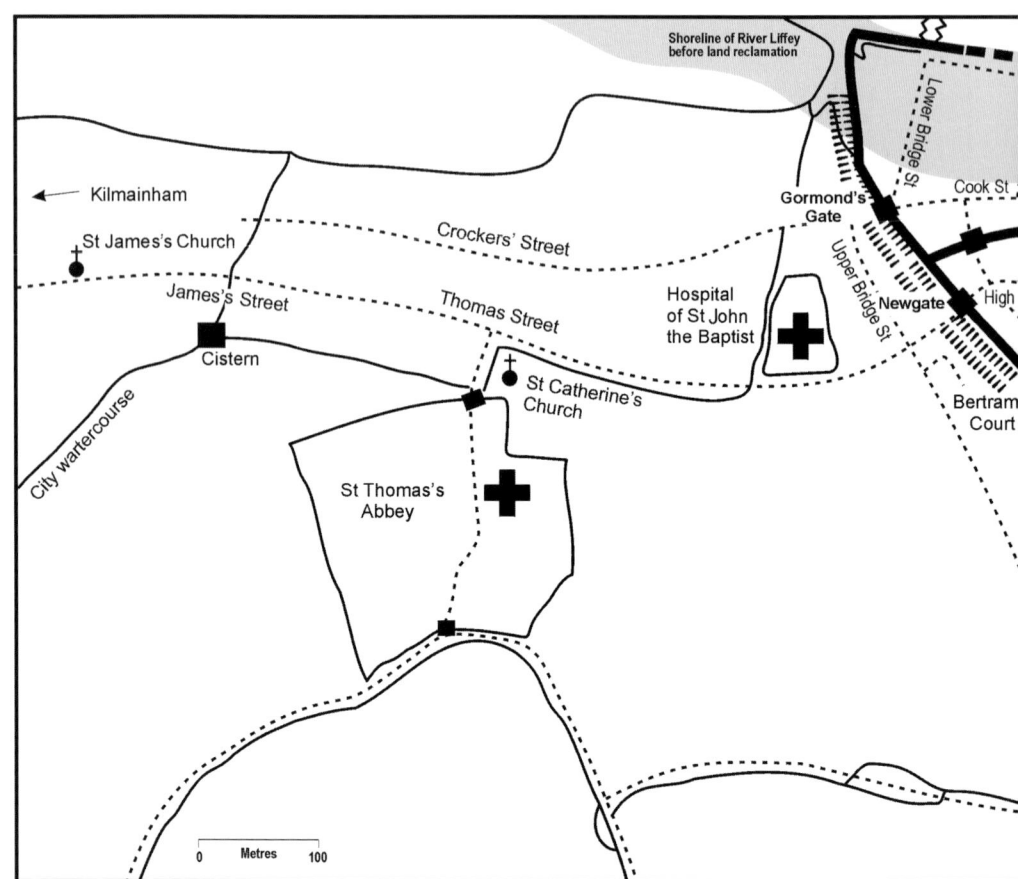

2 Sketch-map showing the location of St Thomas's Abbey in the western surburb *c*.13th century (based on Clarke, 1998 and Simms, 1979)

development of the suburb, but these ends were to be reached through the Christian ethic. The royal status of the endowment and the practical purpose behind the endowment ensured a most apt location for the efficient operation of the institution.

In addition, Murphy describes the archbishops of Dublin in the thirteenth century – all Englishmen – as 'the articulators of royal policy' and says that they strove to Anglicise the diocese in terms of personnel and structure (Murphy 2000, 73). She states that John Cumin (1181–1212), Henry of London (1212–28), and Luke (1229–55) were appointed by the crown as a reward for their loyalty while Fulk de Sandford was a papal appointee accepted by the crown (Murphy 2000, 75–6). She illustrates how John Cumin and Henry of London, who had both been civil administrators prior to their appointments, continued to act on behalf of the crown during their incumbencies (Murphy 1995, 42). Interestingly, John Cumin supported Henry II during the dilemma surrounding Thomas Becket to whom St Thomas's itself was dedicated, and it was most probably due to his loyalty that he received the archbishopric of Dublin. During the first seven years of his episcopacy, he continued to attend the king's court, and his awareness of St Thomas's special royal favour may have motivated him to look after its welfare (Gwynn 1954, 15–16). Thus, both Church and State acted as one, in order to set up Anglo-Norman ecclesiastical organisation in Dublin.

It seems that the Augustinian canons regular took charge of St Thomas's from the outset. Originally, a canon was a priest on the official list of diocesan clergy, as distinct from one serving in a monastery. The regular canon was a development of this; he was a celibate clergyman living a communal life, under a common superior, and also lived under obedience to a fixed Rule of life (Dickinson 1961, 76–77). Regular canons adopted the Rule of St Augustine, a brief Rule requiring the support of further customs and observances to ensure the regulated life. Regular canons were distinct from monks, and contemporaries recognised this (Gilbert 1889, 411). By the latter half of the twelfth century, regular canons were taking responsibility for parish churches in numerous cases (Dickinson 1961, 78), and Dublin's western suburb was one such case (Gilbert 1889, 284, 413). These regular canons were clergy in theory, and therefore were usually under the supervision of the local diocesan bishop, but St Thomas's was only nominally under the archbishop because it was under the king's direct influence as a royal foundation. In any case, John Cumin, archbishop of Dublin, acted with King Henry II's interests at heart (Murphy 1995, 44).

SOURCES OF ST THOMAS'S REVENUE IN THE WESTERN SUBURB

While this paper focuses on St Thomas's influence on urban expansion through its dealings in grants of urban property, it would be a grave mistake to think that the life of this religious community revolved around this single interest. Rather, the abbey's involvement in urban development was just one, albeit a significant, component among a range of activities. A minimum of security and well-being was required for the normal upkeep and running of the abbey, and so the canons had to possess and exploit various sources of revenue. Income from temporal and spiritual grants was the mainstay of St Thomas's.

Temporal income

The temporal income gained from the western suburb came through arable land (Gilbert 1889, 3, 284), woodlands (Gilbert 1889, 3), fisheries (Gilbert 1889, 281), mills, rents, and urban possessions such as houses. St Thomas's derived income from arable land throughout its first century since one record appears for 1192x5* (Gilbert 1889, 284–5) and another for 1266–7 (Gilbert 1889, 3). In St James's parish, the western suburb north of Thomas Street and James's Street, the arable land was exempted from all ecclesiastical tithes, an incentive to give that land to cultivation because St Thomas's would receive all of the revenue (Gilbert 1889, 284). Further to this, St Thomas's was free to rent any of this arable land to the parishioners there. Whether it did or not, no record has been kept, but seven acres of arable land were recorded in the later record of 1266–7 (Gilbert 1889, 3) by which time the lands of the abbey had been arranged in a network of open fields. The uses to which the other documented fields were put were not stated, as it was enough to record their relative locations only. They were hardly put to pasture since one of these fields was described as being next to a meadow (*in campo juxta Honimed*e). These fields may have been cultivated also. Mills were possessed by St Thomas's throughout the period of study and this was normal as Clarke indicates that mills were often a source of profit for laity and religious alike during the late twelfth and thirteenth centuries (Clarke 2002, 9). A reference was made in *c.*1196* (Gilbert 1889, 284; Clarke 2002, 18) when confirmation was given that the abbey's mills and arable land were to be exempt from tithes. In 1272, the abbey is recorded as renting mills to John de Hac, a layman. Another record of a mill appears as a locational reference for one of the fields in 1266–7: *in campo juxta molendinum* (Gilbert 1889, 3). Thus, St Thomas's was gaining revenue from its mills.

St Thomas's probably exploited the woodland recorded in 1266–7 with four different references made to it indicating the relative locations of the fields: *januam silve, sub silva, super silvam, in silva* (Gilbert 1889, 3). Assarting was the permanent clearance of trees for alternative, usually more productive use, for example, arable cultivation. No direct indication is given as to the uses to which the woodland was put, but an assart may have operated where seven acres of arable land were found in the woodland: *in silva vii acras terre arabilis* (Gilbert, 1889, 3; Robinson 1980, 285). In this way, St Thomas's was making efforts to increase its landed revenue. Provision was included in a tenurial agreement to ensure the property against the threat of fire by stressing that houses on the granted plot be rebuilt if they were burnt down (Gilbert 1889, 408). The clause may be taken as an indication of the building fabric used, namely timber. Thus, the seven acres of arable land were probably cleared woodland, the timber being sold for use as a building material, as well as domestic fuel and fuel for smiths' furnaces, bakers' ovens, and potters' kilns. In this way, timber may have accounted for a further source of income for St Thomas's.

Stone-built structures were rare in the early stages of the development of Anglo-Norman Dublin. Timber-built dwelling structures were more common in late twelfth-century Dublin, with just a few stone buildings. As time progressed, stone structures were becoming more prevalent although perhaps only for town walls, gatehouses, ecclesiastical buildings, religious houses and the dwellings of wealthy officials and merchants. A quarry (*lapicinium*) located beside one of the fields of the abbey was recorded in 1266–7 (Gilbert 1889, 3), and this was probably one of the sources of the city's supply of building stone. If the quarry was part of St Thomas's property, there is little doubt but that the canons operated it on commercial terms.

Fisheries were an additional source of St Thomas's revenue from temporalities. Some income from fisheries was derived from spiritual property, but one instance where the resource was granted in the form of temporal property is worthy of note. St Thomas's was granted a fishing boat for use on the river Liffey (Gilbert 1889, 281). The income was to be channelled back into the then priory of St Thomas for the upkeep of the canons and the works of charity they undertook. Nevertheless, any surplus could have been sold to generate extra revenue. St Thomas's also received a much sought-after custom on beverages sold throughout Dublin city and suburbs. Granted by the crown (Gilbert 1889, 281), it must have endowed St Thomas's with a constant and unfailing income, and it was from this issue as well as the rights over water that most legal disputes throughout the history of St Thomas's arose (Davis 1986–7, 63).

St Thomas's receipt of rents from laymen and women, many of them rents from urban possessions, was considerable (Duddy 2001, 162). One case is recorded in which the canons made their own efforts to secure income in rent from an urban possession (Gilbert 1889, 387–8). One of the donations which the citizens of Dublin granted to St Thomas's was in the form of rents (*redditus*) (Gilbert 1889, 281–2). A grant of burgage at foundation meant that one of St Thomas's sources of revenue was gained through urban property. The canons may have granted the holding to someone else so as to earn some income from the rent. The land Philip of Worcester granted to St Thomas's between *c.*1177 and 1189* seems to have been burgage tenure also (Gilbert 1889, 407–8). An example of direct exploitation of an urban possession by St Thomas's was its grant to Walo, brother of Gillebert Niger in *c.*1210* (Gilbert 1889, 387–88) which had formerly been received from Helia, son of John Gille. Between *c.*1190 and the 1240s*, St Thomas's received urban property in the western suburb from Thomas of Kenfig (Gilbert 1889, 409), Alice, wife of Gilbert de Livet (Gilbert 1889, 374), and Robert of Bedford (Gilbert 1889, 377–8).

The temporal property of St Thomas's amounted to a large estate by 1266–7 (Gilbert 1889, 3) as well as all the possessions of an agricultural and urban nature mentioned above. There was ample reason behind St Thomas's wish to have temporal property, primarily because this religious community required to be fed and clothed (*ad sustentacione*) as well as to maintain its public services (Gilbert 1889, 281). Basic temporal property thus was a necessity for the mere subsistence of the community, and it seems that St Thomas's was highly dependent on agriculture to sustain itself (Gilbert 1889, 3). However, extra wealth was encouraged in order to receive and accommodate guests (*ad susceptionem … hospitum*), including royal guests, benefactors and their retinue should they visit the city (Gilbert 1889, 281), and at one stage, St Thomas's included a set of buildings with a tower called the King's Lodging, presumably for such an occasion (Gwynn and Hadcock 1970, 172; Clarke 1998, 51). The education of young men was another duty of St Thomas's according to Gwynn, and may have been undertaken since the foundation (Gwynn 1954, 33).

Income from spiritual property

The spiritual component of St Thomas's revenue originated from the churches it possessed and tithes of various other benefices with which it had been endowed. The profit from receiving a spiritual grant is demonstrated in its receipt of St James's church and parish (Duddy 2001, 161–2). In *c.*1190 (Clarke 2002, 18), along with the site for the church of St James, Henry Tirel granted the tithes and alms of that holding to St Thomas's (Gilbert 1889, 383). In the same charter, he gave a tithe of fishing and a tithe of his knight's fee. Then, *c.*1196*, he granted the tithe of a mill situated in the parish of St James and along with that, a tithe of fishing from the pond next to the mill (Gilbert 1889, 392). As mentioned already, St Thomas's arable land and mills within the parish were given exemption from all ecclesiastical tithes, meaning that the abbey would receive all the revenue. St Thomas's jurisdiction over spiritual property in the form of parishes secured external profits in the form of tithes (on temporal property) and lay contact encouraged further donations and grants of temporal property. The new settlers were familiar with the arrangement whereby benefactors donated tithes from their harvests and from their other possessions found within the parish. Indeed, tithes may have formed the great part of parish revenues. In 1186, John Cumin, archbishop of Dublin, pointed out that it was the parishioners' duty to pay tithes (Murphy 1995, 47). The canons of St Thomas's were not necessarily parish priests, and the grant of St James's church and parish by John Cumin to the canons was related to the extra temporal revenue that would be received by them from this grant (Gwynn 1954, 18). The canons received the tithes on the parish land and, for example, tithes from mills and fisheries (Gilbert 1889, 383, 392).

In the foundation grant, St Thomas's received a tithe of the city of Dublin (Gilbert 1889, 281), surely a substantial sum. Moreover, in the long-term, this income would increase as the city expanded, and this would have been an added incentive for St Thomas's to encourage and become involved in the development of the western suburb.

THE INITIAL GRANT AS GUIDING INFLUENCE

The foundation grant was decisive because it set down a precedent for subsequent grants. Included in the original foundation grant of St Thomas's was a burgage, a custom on ale and mead sold throughout the walled city and suburbs, a tithe rent of the city, a boat for fishing on the Liffey, certain lands and holdings, rents and other donations including a stone house (Gilbert 1889, 281–2). It is the grant of burgage that interests us here and its signifi-cance is suggested in the fact that most of the subsequent gifts recorded in the documents concerning the western suburb are grants of urban property (Gilbert 1889). The initial grant often set the pattern advanced by subsequent benefactors, but a royal grant provided a special stimulus. The nature of this initial grant and the subsequent laying out of burgages in the same area, hitherto a rural landscape, suggest that the crown used its influence to stimulate borough development in the western suburb through this grant of burgage.

A decisive spirituality
Perhaps accompanying the initial temporal grant of burgage from the royal founder was an initial spiritual grant from the archbishop of Dublin. Responsibility for the parish of St Thomas the Martyr was received either simultaneously with the founding of St Thomas's itself or else very shortly afterwards – at least from 1179 (Sheehy 1962, 26–9) – and possibly encom-passed the whole western suburb as far as Kilmainham. The parish may be considered to be a decisive spirituality since the pastoral role of St Thomas's, facilitating and fostering close interaction between the canons and the laity in the western suburb, was made possible mainly through its responsibility for parish churches beginning with that of St Thomas. Care for a parish offered an additional source of revenue, and the likelihood of this revenue increasing the more the parish was colonised by burgages made the management of this parish a viable and even attractive proposition for St Thomas's. However, according to Reynolds, the main use of the parish was that it provided the framework for a level of co-ordinated development on the part of the religious (Reynolds 1977, 84), and given the overlapping objectives of Church and State at that time, this development by churchmen was to be in keeping with secular initiatives. Thus, the creation of the parish of St Thomas the Martyr

strengthened the chances of success of the urban development desired and initiated by the founder and first benefactors.

A certain level of early success must have been achieved because in *c.*1190 St Thomas's was endowed with a site for a church of St James from Henry Tirel followed in *c.*1196 with the actual church of St James (Clarke 2002, 18). It was also appropriated the parish of St James from John Cumin (Gilbert 1889, 284), and so the parish church of St James became the second parish centre within the western suburb (Gilbert 1889, 383, 284–5; Gwynn 1954, 16). Though the new parish encompassed the western suburb to the north of Thomas Street and James's Street, and from Newgate and Bridge Street to Kilmainham, the location of its church farther to the west indicates either successful population growth as far as the western margin of the suburb or substantial hopes for such growth, since a parish church relied on a supportive population. Such a linear suburb of 1km in length may have had a sizeable population and therefore would have required two parishes (Clarke 1998, 50). St Thomas's parish, reduced in size, and seemingly comprising the western suburb to the south of Thomas Street, is last recorded in 1205, and it seems likely that the parish church of St Thomas was rededicated to St Catherine early in the thirteenth century (Clarke 2002, 18).

SUBSEQUENT GRANTS OF AN URBAN NATURE

As evident from the sources of St Thomas's revenue detailed above, the canons received grants of urban property and, at first glance, seem to have maintained a passive rather than an active role in the receipt of grants, and were a medium through which the laity rendered service to God (*dedi et concessi … Deo … pro salute anime …*) (Gilbert 1889, 407). However, on further examination, St Thomas's is found to have been involved in grants on a number of planes, and in each case the conditions on which the grants were made are likely to have been favourable to the canons even when they themselves were neither grantors nor grantees, but overseers.

Nature of grants
The foundation grant of burgage as suggested above led to the phenomenon where most of the subsequent recorded grants relating to the western suburb are of an urban nature. The grants concern transactions where the canons were grantees, overseers, and grantors in that numerical order, but given the lack of certainty around the dates of the individual charters, it would be futile to allocate the percentage proportion of each type. Where the first two cate-gories are concerned, the evidence suggests that an equal share of those types was prevalent. On the other hand, most of the transactions made between laity and canons concerned a grant made by the laity to the canons. In two

instances, representing a very small proportion of the evidence (Gilbert 1889, 353–4, 387–8), the transactions dealt with grants made by the canons to the laity. And there are three instances where the canons receive spiritualities from other ecclesiastics (Gilbert 1889, 284–5, 294–5, 317–18).

The terms upon which solely lay transactions were made were very similar to those in which St Thomas's was grantor, but were different from those in which St Thomas's was grantee. The fact that transactions solely among the laity are recorded in the *Register* suggests that the canons acted as overseers of those grants. W., the clerk of Hamwoda, granted a plot in free burgage to three other laymen in the western suburb, and an annual rent of eight pence was to suffice for all service (Gilbert 1889, 384). Allewin of Winchester granted a plot in free burgage to Nicholaus Pistor of Hereford probably on Thomas Street, and an annual rent of ten shillings was due (Gilbert 1889, 398). W. Long granted a plot to John Albus on Thomas Street also, and an annual rent of eight shillings satisfied all service and the tenant had full power of sale (Gilbert 1889, 413–14). Adam son of Seilda granted land to Richard Faber on Thomas Street (Gilbert 1889, 408) and an annual money rent was due in payment for all service and freedom for the tenant to deal in his land. Thomas of Kenfig granted a plot to Roger Passe next to the Hospital of St John the Baptist at the Newgate (Gilbert 1889, 415), with an annual money rent for all service and liberty for the tenant to sell his land. Audoen Brun granted land to William Long on Thomas Street (Gilbert 1889, 386), and an annual rent in kind was agreed and the tenant had the normal burgage right to sell his land. William Albus granted half a burgage to Osbert Lecanum on Thomas Street (Gilbert 1889, 399), and once again, the normal burgage tenure was upheld with an annual money rent. Rembold son of John Tannere granted land to Alexander la Ware (Gilbert 1889, 417) with an annual money rent for all service and the freedom to sell his land. This seems to have been on Thomas Street also. Bartholomew granted land to Robert Thop in free burgage (Gilbert 1889, 385), the annual rent of four shillings being due for all service and the tenant being free to sell the land if he wished. Bartholomew granted half a burgage to William Liun of Chester (Gilbert 1889, 385–6), and again the annual rent was four shillings and the tenant had the usual freedoms. Other lay transactions concerning burgages in the western suburb are also recorded (Gilbert 1889, 377, 397–8, 412, 414). As overseers, it is reasonable to expect that the canons ensured that these transactions, relating to plots held in the vicinity of St Thomas's enhanced as much as possible the value of the abbey's property.

In two instances, St Thomas's acted as grantor in order to generate income. One of these was the grant of land it made to Walo, brother of Gillebert Niger mentioned above (Gilbert 1889, 387–8). The terms are consistent with those held by burgage tenure, and an annual rent was due for all service. The other concerns some of St Thomas's mills, which it rented to John de Hac in 1272 (Gilbert 1889, 353–4). In *c.*1215, St Thomas's granted lands in Bertram's Court to the hospital of St John the Baptist (Hayden 1999, 102). Indeed, St Thomas's may also have created burgages to be granted in the suburb as the evidence below suggests. Usually, the terms of transaction were very different when St Thomas's was grantee. The laity donated alms to St Thomas's to bring in spiritual revenue for themselves and their families such as the salvation of souls. Philip of Worcester granted to the abbey a plot in front of the gate of St Thomas (Gilbert 1889, 407–8). The usual annual rent was required, but St Thomas's was in receipt of it. Not only that but the canons owed nothing in secular service for holding the plot because it was received in alms (*in perpetuam et puram elemosinam*). Rather, the service due was spiritual (Pollock and Maitland 1968, 240–3).

The majority of grants involving the laity concerned an individual donor rather than a group of donors. Only occasionally was a group involved. In two instances, the group were citizens of Dublin (Gilbert 1889, 397–8, 404). In another, the donor granted land to a group of three laymen (Gilbert 1889, 384–5), while two further cases concerned a layman with the consent of his wife as donor (Gilbert 1889, 409, 415).

Receipt of grants from the laity
Most grants made directly to St Thomas's took the form of gifts and were made on the impetus of the donor. Although these were important because they increased the overall income of St Thomas's, they were not always decisive in that they were made within parameters that were already set down by the initial grants. The initial receipt of burgage seems to have encouraged borough expansion on a large scale in the western suburb.

Many grants were received from the laity within the context of the devotional structure of the time (Dickinson 1961, 66; Rodes 1977, 49–51), and incurred no expense to St Thomas's (Duddy 2001, 161). St Thomas's receipt of the plot from Philip of Worcester (mentioned above) was one such instance. St Thomas's received a plot in alms also from Alwin of Winchester (Gilbert 1889, 397). St Thomas's received a plot with house and yard in alms from Alice, wife of Gilbert de Livet, and was to receive the annual money rent in perpetuity (Gilbert 1889, 374). St Thomas's received a number of plots in alms (*in puram, integram, liberam et perpetuam elemosinam*) from Robert of Bedford (Gilbert 1889, 377[2.]–378). One of the plots may have been located in the fee (land) of St Thomas because it was held of Master Hugo of whom Rembold son of John Tannere also held a plot which was part of the fee of St Thomas (Gilbert 1889, 417). Indeed, all plots held between 'the great street and the cemetery of St Thomas' may have belonged to the fee received by St Thomas's at foundation. Both plots, Robert of Bedford's and Rembold's, if this suggestion is correct, provide evidence that St Thomas's was actively involved in both the creation and transferral of burgages in its original landed property within the suburb. Either way, it was profiting from the burgage development that was happening right next to the abbey lands.

A further four quarters (*quatuor quarterios*) of a burgage were included in Bedford's grant. Two of these fronted Thomas Street and extended to Crockers' Street, while another lay in Bertram's Court. Another plot was located on or very close to Crockers' Street and yet another was to be found in Bertram's Court. Other plots were received also but their whereabouts is uncertain. St Thomas's received a burgage at Dublin Bridge from Thomas la Martre (Gilbert 1889, 418), and once again, this was donated in alms (*liberam elemosinam*) and was exempt from secular service. The receipt of a burgage, given in alms, was financially good for St Thomas's as the terms of tenure cost it little (Gilbert 1889, 281) and yet facilitated the exploitation of an extra source of revenue. These terms favoured the canons immensely because the financial state of the abbey in turn affected the size and intensity of its sphere of influence. Nevertheless, not all burgages received by St Thomas's were given in alms. St Thomas's received a burgage from Thomas of Kenfig (Gilbert 1889, 409) under similar terms to those of the usual lay transactions (evidenced above and Duddy 2001, 163). It was not donated in alms, and so was not exempt from secular service. Rather, an annual rent of ten shillings was to be paid by St Thomas's, and this, as was normal with the usual burgage tenure, would satisfy for all service. In addition, St Thomas's was to pay an entry fine like many of its lay counterparts (Gilbert 1889, 382–3, 398).

THE RESULTING URBAN CHARACTER

Burgages, the basis for borough development and associated on some level with St Thomas's, were granted extensively throughout the western suburb and especially along Thomas Street during the period of this study. The effect of the laying out of burgages in the western suburb led to the emergence of Thomas Street, James's Street, and Bridge Street, a gradual transformation from a rural to an urban landscape. Three documents actually refer to *suburbium* when speaking of the western suburb (Gilbert 1889, 284, 385, 413), while another refers to the suburb of Dublin in the direction of the bridge (Bridge Street) (Gilbert 1889, 414) suggesting that suburban development was evident from an early stage. At Bertram's Court immediately outside the western curtain wall at Newgate, the burgage plots were already undergoing subdivision while those on Thomas Street were being laid out for the first time (Duddy 2001, 164–7). At this early stage, the demand for space at Bertram's Court must have demonstrated the great potential farther to the west of the city. The small but ever more densely populated suburb at Bertram's Court, as the first expression of city expansion beyond the restrictive curtain wall and into the western suburb, must have prompted city 'planners' to consider developing the western suburb on a grander scale. Plots were arranged in rows of long, rectangular strips along Thomas Street, James's Street, and Bridge Street. It also seems likely that plots located on the northern side of Thomas Street extended northwards to Crockers' Street (Croker Lane).

Many of the plots laid out on the new streets of the western suburb adjoined other similar plots (Duddy 2001, 167–9), like, for example, the plot which Allewin of Winchester granted to Nicholaus Pistor of Hereford that was located between the land of Levis, mother of William, and the land of Robert Sutor on the northern side of Thomas Street (Gilbert 1889, 398). In this way, intermittent rows of plots straddled the above-named streets. The evidence indicates that there were ten instances of three contiguous (adjacent) plots, two instances of two contiguous plots, and two instances of single plots on Thomas Street. Considering the four plots recorded for the southern edge of Thomas Street, there was one row of three contiguous plots and a single plot. On James's Street, there were at least eight plots including the plot for the church of St James. Of these, there were two instances of three contiguous plots and a single plot for the church. The location of the plot for the church and cemetery of St James at the western extreme of the developing western suburb surely reflects the westward drive of suburban expansion. On Bridge Street, six plots have been recorded and, of these, there were two instances of three contiguous plots. At Bertram's Court, each of the three grants of burgage have been recorded as contiguous, so that, in total, nine plots were accounted for in Bertram's Court. The findings above suggest that intermittent rows of burgage plots were to be found along the new streets of the developing western suburb at an early stage, and that these rows may have been continuous in a ladder pattern along the streets by the second half of the thirteenth century.

The sources of revenue of St Thomas's detailed above, as well as indirect references in the documents, give an idea of the land-use and activities carried on in the western suburb (Duddy 2001, 169–73). Many of the surnames of the recorded plot holders indicate the occupancy of urban dwellers, for example, Walter *Pistor*, Nicholas *Pistor* of Hereford, Robert *Sutor*, Richard *Figulus*, John *Textor*, John *Telarius*, Hugo *le Feutrer*, Richard *Faber*, Hosbert *Tanner*, and Richard *Carpentarius* (Gilbert 1889, 378, 398, 395, 413, 386, 387, 408, 412, 414) suggesting millers or bakers, a tailor, a potter, a weaver, another weaver, a felter, a smith, a tanner, and a carpenter respectively. The millers and/or bakers and the potter were all to be found on the northern side of Thomas Street. The potter's plot may have stretched as far as Crockers'

Street along which is thought to have been the potters' quarter (Clarke 1998, 50). The two weavers and the tailor were on one side or another of Thomas Street, while the tanner was on James's Street.

CONCLUSION

The early development of the western suburb owes much to St Thomas's. As a very special royal foundation, St Thomas's was always a popular beneficiary of the crown and its loyal supporters. As was usual with religious institutions of the time, and particularly so due to its association with the 'establishment', St Thomas's was integrated into the overall structure of society so that it served secular and religious needs alike. One of the secular needs included expansion of the city into the western suburb in a way that correlated with the Anglo-Norman mindset. The Victorine Augustinian canons regular, who occupied St Thomas's, profitably organised and managed themselves within such a system. Situated within the suburb itself, St Thomas's influenced the local pattern of land-use so as to maximise its own interests economically, doing so by harnessing temporal income such as grain production, mills and urban possessions, and spiritual income such as churches and parishes. The initial grant of a burgage plot to St Thomas's set a precedent, so that many of the subsequent local grants were also burgage plots. Furthermore, this initial grant from the crown was soon followed by the granting of a local parish to St Thomas's from the ecclesiastical authority. Consequently, St Thomas's was motivated, and encouraged, to involve itself in urban expansion in the western suburb. The grants of burgage made to St Thomas's, unlike grants made to lay people, usually incurred no expense for the abbey because they were given in alms. Yet, the receipt of these burgages facilitated the annual receipt of multiple revenues in the form of rents whenever the abbey, in turn, exploited their rent value by granting these burgages to other people. As well as receiving grants of burgage, St Thomas's acted as overseer to lay transactions and even created and granted burgages itself. This ongoing interest and involvement in urban property by St Thomas's abbey was a significant factor in the urban-making of the western suburb of medieval Dublin.

ACKNOWLEDGEMENT

I wish to thank Stephen Hannon for drawing the maps.

REFERENCES

Ballard, A. (ed.) 1913 *British borough charters, 1042–1216*. Cambridge.
Berry, H.F. 1892 On the use of signs in the ancient monasteries, with a special reference to a code used by the Victorine canons at St Thomas' Abbey, Dublin, *Journal of Royal Society of Antiquaries of Ireland*, 22, 107–125.
Brooks, E. St J. (ed.) 1936 *Register of the Hospital of S. John the Baptist without the New Gate, Dublin*. Dublin: Irish Manuscripts Commission.
Brooks, E. St J. (ed.) 1953 *The Irish Cartularies of Llanthony Prima & Secunda*. Dublin: Irish Manuscripts Commission.
Clarke, H.B. 1998 Urbs et suburbium: beyond the walls of medieval Dublin. In Manning, C. (ed.) *Dublin and beyond the Pale*. Studies in honour of Patrick Healy. Bray, 45–58.
Clarke, H.B. 2002 *Dublin, part I, to 1610*. Irish Historic Towns Atlas No.11, Dublin.
Curtis, E. (ed.) 1932 *Calendar of Ormond Deeds 1172–1350 A.D.* Vol. 1, Dublin: Irish Manuscripts Commission.
Davis, V., 1986–7 Relations between the abbey of St Thomas the Martyr and the municipality of Dublin, *c*.1176–1527, *Dublin Historical Record*, 40, 56–65.
Dickinson, J.C. 1961 *Monastic life in medieval England*. London.
Duddy, C. 1990 The role of St Thomas's abbey in the development of the extra-mural settlement of Medieval Dublin 1177–1272. Unpublished MA thesis. Department of Geography, UCD, Dublin.
Duddy, C. 2001 The western suburb of medieval Dublin: its first century, *Irish Geography*, Vol. 34(2), 157–75.
Elliott, A.L. 1990 The abbey of St Thomas the Martyr, near Dublin, In Clarke, H.B. (ed.) *Medieval Dublin: the living city*. Dublin, 62–76.
Gilbert, J.T. (ed.) 1889 *Register of the abbey of St Thomas, Dublin*. Rolls Series, London.
Gwynn, A. 1954 The early history of St Thomas's abbey, Dublin, *R.S.A.I. Jn.*, 84, 1–35.
Gwynn, A. and Hadcock, R.N. 1970 *Medieval religious houses: Ireland*. Repr. Dublin, 1988.
Hayden, A. 2000 West Side story: archaeological excavations at Cornmarket and Bridge Street Upper, Dublin – a summary account, In S. Duffy (ed.) *Medieval Dublin I*. Dublin, 84–116.
Hennessy, M. 1988 The priory and hospital of New Gate: The evolution and decline of a medieval monastic estate. In W.J. Smyth and K. Whelan (eds) *Common ground: essays on the historical geography of Ireland*, Cork, 41–54.
Murphy, M. 1995 Balancing the affairs of church and state: the archbishops of Dublin, 1181–1228. In T.B. Barry, R. Frame, and K. Simms (eds) *Colony and frontier in medieval Ireland*. London, 41–56.
Murphy, M. 2000 Archbishops and anglicisation: Dublin, 1181–1271. In J. Kelly and D. Keogh (eds), *History of the Catholic diocese of Dublin*. Dublin, 72–91.
McNeill, C. (ed.) 1950 *Calendar of Archbishop Alen's Register c.1172–1534*. Dublin: Royal Society of Antiquaries of Ireland.
Pollock, F. and Maitland, F.W. 1968 *The history of English law before the time of Edward I*, 2nd edn, ed. S.F.C. Milsom, vol.2, Cambridge.
Reynolds, S. 1977 *An introduction to the history of English medieval towns*. Oxford.
Robinson, D.M. 1980 *The geography of Augustinian settlement in medieval England and Wales*. B.A.R., British Series 80(I), Oxford.
Rodes Jr., R.E. 1977 *Ecclesiastical administration in medieval England*. London.
Sheehy, M.P. (ed.) 1962 *Pontificia Hibernica: medieval papal chancery documents concerning Ireland 640–1261*. vol. I. Dublin.
Simms, A. 1979 Medieval Dublin: a topographical analysis, *Irish Geography*, 12, 25–41.

Simms, A. 2002 Origins and early growth. In J. Brady and A. Simms (eds) *Dublin through space and time (c.900–1900)*, Dublin, 15–65.

Speed, John, 1611–12 'Dubline'. In *The theatre of the empire of Great Britaine*. London.

Walsh, C. 2000 Archaelogical excavations at the abbey of St Thomas the Martyr, Dublin. In S. Duffy (ed.) *Medieval Dublin I*. Dublin, 185–202.

Watt, J. 1998 *The Church in Medieval Ireland*, Dublin.

Health status in medieval Dublin: analysis of the skeletal remains from the abbey of St Thomas the Martyr

LAUREEN BUCKLEY

INTRODUCTION

These skeletons were excavated by Claire Walsh of Archaeological Projects Ltd in advance of a development. They were all recovered from medieval contexts, with most of the burials dating from the late thirteenth to the early fourteenth century. The burials are associated with the abbey of St Thomas the Martyr, the largest abbey in medieval Dublin. It is known that a number of high-status individuals were interred there. The results of the archaeological excavations have been previously published in *Medieval Dublin I* (Walsh 2000). This report of the skeletal analysis yields findings that support the presence of well-nourished individuals from wealthy backgrounds.

POPULATION CHARACTERISTICS

A total of 18 burials were recovered from this site. Four (22%) were juveniles, and fourteen were adults. The adults consisted of eight males and six females. These statistics are summarised in the chart below:

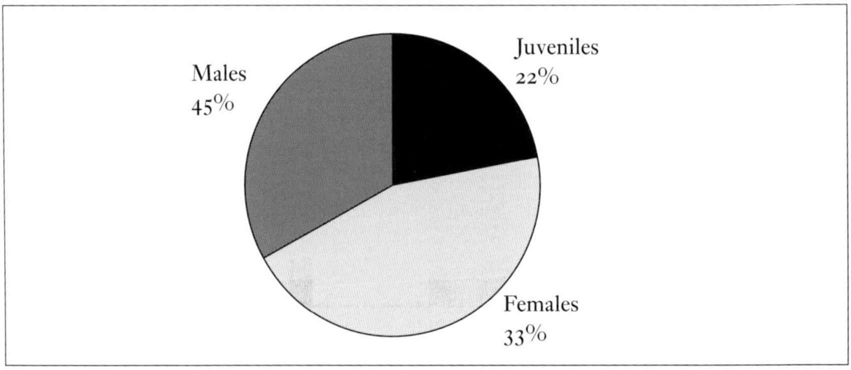

Chart 1: Population statisctics

The percentage of juveniles is small relative to what would have been a normal cemetery population of this period. However, as this was not a parish church or graveyard it would not be expected to reflect the configuration of the general population. The ratio of males to females is 1.33:1. Thus there is a higher proportion of males than expected from a normal population. This is not surprising considering that the cemetery is attached to an important religious house, although the formal graveyard of the canons to the west of the site was unexcavated. Even if the burials did not include canons the cemetery would be expected to contain burials of high-ranking individuals. Indeed prominent Anglo-Normans including Hugh de Lacy and his wife are reported to be buried in this graveyard as well as Basilia de Clare, the sister of Strongbow (Walsh 2000). As it is more likely that there would have been more males than females deemed to be high status, then it is unsurprising that the proportion of male skeletons is higher.

Age There were four juveniles found, one was aged 3–5 years, one was aged around 6 years, one was aged 4–8 years and one was aged 10–12 years. There was a notable lack of infant burials, and no infant bones were found in the disarticulated remains, which suggests that infants were probably buried elsewhere. However, the fact that this graveyard was the preserve of the rich and not the surrounding population might account for the lack of infants. Infants are susceptible to malnutrition and disease in the first five years of life and a normal cemetery of this period might have up to 50% infant skeletons. The distribution of adult ages is given in the chart below:

	Young Adult (17–25)	Middle Adult (25–45)	Older Adult 45+	Unaged
Male	0	5	2	1
Female	1	4	1	0
Total	1	9	3	1

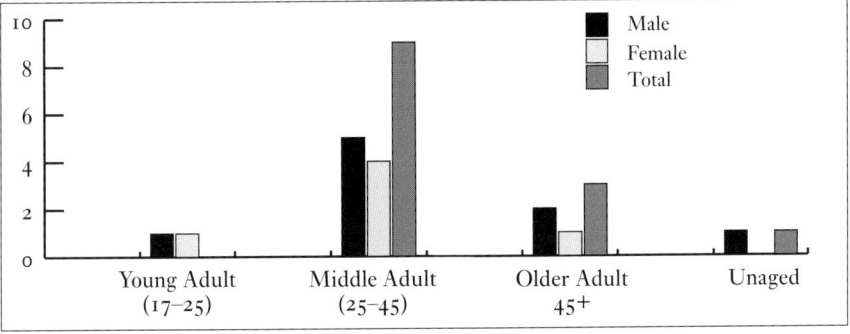

Table 1: Adult age groups

The number of individuals is too small to draw realistic conclusions about age
of death among males and females. All that can be said is that although there
was one young adult female and three older adults, the majority of individuals
died between the ages of 25–45. In the Dominican friary at Drogheda (Halpin
and Buckley 1995), which dates to a similar period to St Thomas's abbey,
most of the deaths occurred in the younger and middle adult age groups.
However in another Dublin monastic site, St Francis's friary (Buckley 1996A),
over half the burials were over 45 years of age.

Stature The average stature of the six females was 156cm and the average
stature of the eight males was 171cm. It can be seen from the table below that
this is very close to statures obtained from the Dominican friary at Drogheda
and other Early Christian and medieval sites throughout Ireland and is only a
few centimetres below the average height of the modern population.

Site	Period	Male stature (cm)	Female stature (cm)
Solar[1]	Early Christian	171	157
Kilshane	do.	173	160
Castleknock[2]	do.	170	158
Dominican friary/ Drogheda	13/14th century	171	155
St Thomas, Dublin	*13/14th century*	171	156
St Francis, Dublin	13/15th century	170.5	157.5
Tintern[3]	15th/17th century	170	159
Modern Population		174	161

1 Buckley (1996);   2 McLoughlin (1950);   3 Ó Donnabháin (1985)

Table 2: Average statures for males and females from various Irish populations

Congenital developmental abnormalities Congenital developmental abnormalities are abnormal developments of body tissues, which arise at birth or
shortly afterwards. In the skeleton they usually take the form of missing or
extra bones or a failure of the ossification process. Burial 13 had sacralised
lumbar vertebrae. In this condition the fifth lumbar vertebra is completely or
partially incorporated in to the sacrum. It should have no significant effect on
the individual. The only other abnormalities present in this group were congenitally absent teeth, which occurred in three individuals. It is not unusual
for the third molars not to develop but one individual also had a second molar
that had not developed.

Dentition Eleven adults had dentition present. There were two partial mandibles and two partial maxilla recovered from the disarticulated remains but they are not included in the dental analysis as they were too incomplete with very few teeth present. Not all the adults had complete dentitions but there were 253 observable sockets and 159 teeth present. Allowing for teeth lost antemortem and teeth not developed this represents 59% of the potential dentition from this number of individuals. However the sample size is too small to be able to make reliable statistical comparisons with other population groups. It is possible to make some general observations with the proviso that if a larger sample size becomes available a more accurate analysis can be obtained.

Attrition Molar attrition did not appear to be severe in this population. Only three individuals had heavy wear on the anterior teeth and one of these was an older individual. There appeared to be a moderate amount of wear on the first molars only of the middle adult group. There was only one individual, an older female, who had exposure of the pulp cavity caused by excessive attrition. It was difficult to assess the level of wear on the anterior teeth compared to the molars as there were few older individuals and there was a high rate of antemortem loss. The pattern of heavier wear on anterior teeth compared to the molars has been found at other medieval sites such as the Dominican priories at Drogheda and Carlingford (Buckley, 1994). It is thought to indicate a higher meat content to the diet (Henderson 1984). Medieval and later populations tend to have less severe attrition than prehistoric populations, which is indicative of a less abrasive diet, possibly because cereal was more refined.

Antemortem loss Teeth that have been lost antemortem are easily recognized as the sockets gradually heal over and the gap in the dentition is obvious. Occasionally the socket will not be completely closed indicating that the tooth loss occurred shortly before death. Six individuals from this site had lost 45 teeth during life. One older male, B12 had lost 26 teeth. Overall the rate of antemortem tooth loss per observable sockets was 18%. This is much higher than at other medieval sites. However, in this case the sample size is so low that a few older individuals may be biasing the results and they would not be considered to be reliable. Apart from two individuals that had lost several teeth, the most common tooth lost was the first molar followed by the second premolars. There are many factors involved in antemortem tooth loss and there is no distinct variation in the rate of tooth loss over various time periods.

Calculus Calculus is a deposit of mineralised plaque that builds up when conditions are non-acidic (Hillson 1990, 300). It is a frequent finding on teeth from archaeological sites and its prevalence in a population should be noted. Eight individuals with dentition had evidence of calculus deposits, which in most cases varied from light to moderate. Only two individuals had heavy deposits and even then it was only on a few individual teeth. The presence of calculus generally indicates poor oral hygiene but it was not excessively heavy in this population.

Periodontal disease Periodontitis is a disease caused by plaque micro-organisms, which leads to inflammation of the supporting structures of the teeth. Eventually resorption of the underlying bone occurs and this may result in tooth loss. The exact cause of periodontal disease is unknown but a number of factors including poor oral hygiene and a diet rich in soft carbohydrate food may predispose to it. Periodontal disease may increase irregularly during an individual's lifetime but in general is more severe with increasing age. Its presence in a population is determined by assessing the amount of alveolar recession around the tooth roots. However, teeth can continue to erupt from the jaw due to excessive attrition, so scoring of periodontal disease was carried out in those individuals who had definite recession of the alveolar crests between the teeth, not individuals where the cemental enamel junction appeared to be higher above the alveolar bone. Seven individuals had some degree of alveolar recession but it was only severe in four, most of which were older individuals. Even if the sample size had been bigger it would not be possible to make a direct comparison of periodontal disease between medieval sites as there are many factors to be considered including the age profile of the population and the status of the population group.

Caries Dental caries or tooth decay develops when acidic conditions prevail in the mouth as this causes demineralisation of enamel, cement and dentine. The bacteria in plaque thrive in acidic conditions especially when sucrose, or starches which can be converted into sugars, are present. The sugars are fermented by the plaque bacteria to produce energy and acid is produced as a by-product. Thus both plaque and sugars are necessary to produce the acid conditions that result in tooth caries. Five individuals from this group had eleven carious teeth. The percentage of affected teeth was 7%. Although this is not a fully reliable figure it is similar to the 6.5% found at the Dominican friary, Drogheda and the 6.3% found at the Franciscan friary, Dublin.

Dental abscesses A dental abscess arises when the pulp chamber is exposed by caries or attrition allowing an infection to set in at the root of the tooth. The build up of pus usually finds an escape through an opening in the bone and this is usually obvious in the dry bone specimen. This pyogenic material may spread through the bloodstream to cause infections in other organs of the body. There were three individuals with abscesses from this site. Two had only one abscess each and the other individual had two abscesses.

SKELETAL PATHOLOGY

Nutritional deficiencies There are a number of bone conditions that give indirect and direct evidence of nutritional deficiencies in the population, including cribra orbitalia, tibial periostitis and enamel hypoplasia.

Cribra Orbitalia This is a bone condition characterised by pitting of the anterior portion of the orbital surface of the frontal bone and is usually attributed to iron-deficiency anaemia. When the blood is anaemic, the bone marrow will proliferate in an attempt to make up by quantity what the blood lacks in quality. The bone marrow expands at the expense of the compact bone, which becomes thinner and more porous. Seven skulls from the articulated remains had observable orbits and only one had evidence of cribra orbitalia. There were a further five skulls from the disarticulated remains but no lesions were found. Only one of the three juvenile skulls had cribra orbitalia. Overall the incidence of cribra orbitalia is 13%. This is very low compared with the 25% found at Francis Street and 18% found at the Dominican priory, Drogheda, which was also thought to have high status individuals. The iron-deficiency anaemia may not be caused by lack of iron in the diet; it may also be caused by parasitic infection of the gut, excessive haemorrhage or lack of vitamin C, which is essential for efficient uptake of iron. Its apparent low rate in this site may indicate that these were not a significant factor in the lives of the population buried here.

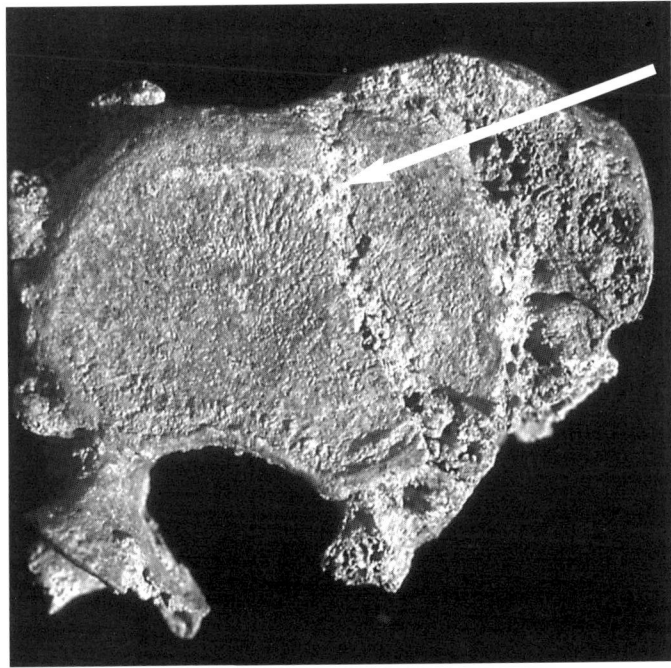

Burial 13: Healed fracture of the vertebral body T12 with semi-circualr buttress of bone on right side

Tibial Periostitis Periostitis is an inflammation of the outer layer of bone, the periosteum. It can arise as a result of infection of overlying tissues, such as a leg ulcer, or trauma or from spread of bacteria from an infection elsewhere. There is some association of tibial and fibular periostitis with vitamin C deficiency. Since it is associated with malnutrition its presence in a population is used as an indicator of biological stress. Fifteen individuals had tibiae present and only one was affected by periostitis. Burial 46, a middle adult male, had small areas of healed periostitis on the medial surface of the tibial shafts. There was also evidence for another healed lesion on the posterior surface of the right bone. It may be significant that this was also the individual that had cribra orbitalia.

Enamel Hypoplasia Hypoplastic defects take the form of lines, grooves or pits in the enamel of teeth crowns. They are thought to occur during development of the tooth when the enamel production is temporarily halted due to an acute infection or a period of dietary stress. The age at which the stress occurred can usually be determined, as the ages at which a particular tooth develops are known. Hypoplastic defects were present in eight adults and one juvenile and were extensive in only three individuals. In some cases only one or two teeth were affected. There were only two individuals where the hypoplasia had occurred below the age of two years. In the majority of individuals the episodes occurred between 3 and 5 years of age.

Degenerative Joint Disease Degenerative joint disease or DJD takes various forms but it is basically the degeneration of the normal smooth joint surface over time. Osteoarthritis is caused mainly by the accumulative affect of everyday stresses and strains on synovial joint surfaces. However there are many other factors involved such as age and genetic predisposition of the individual (Rogers and Waldron 1995). Sometimes it arises as a result of trauma to the joint. The changes that occur in the joint are an attempt by the bone to relieve mechanical stress. Initial changes are osteophytes or lipping at the joint margins, which are an attempt to increase surface area and so reduce stress. New bone can develop on the joint surface, which is also an attempt to strengthen the joint, and these are described as surface osteophytes. The surface of the joint can also appear pitted and porotic. Eburnation of the joint surface caused by bone rubbing on bone when the cartilage is destroyed is considered the final stage of the disease. This is generally referred to as severe osteoarthritic change although in practice there is little correlation between the bone changes in osteoarthritis and the severity of the pain felt by the individual (Rogers et al., 1990).

Vertebral DJD Osteoarthritis of the posterior joints of the vertebral column was present in ten individuals, five male and five female. However, in most cases the lesions were mild and affected only a few vertebrae. In fact in three cases only one vertebra was affected. In only three cases were severe lesions noted. In one, B58, a middle adult male, only the cervical vertebrae were affected. The other two individuals were older adults and had several vertebrae throughout the vertebral column affected.

Vertebral Osteophytosis The joints between the centra or bodies of the vertebrae are not synovial joints, so the term osteoarthritis cannot be applied to these joints. Degeneration of these joints usually involves the formation of osteophytes, new bone growth, at the joint margins and so the term osteophytosis is used. It is referred to as mild to severe depending on the size of the marginal osteophytes. Excluding the individual with DISH (see below), osteophytosis of the vertebral column was present in ten individuals and in most cases it was mild with only a few vertebrae affected. However, in the older individuals with severe osteoarthritis there was severe osteophytosis of some vertebrae also. Degeneration of the joint surface is sometimes also associated with osteophytosis. The surface of the vertebral bodies appears very pitted and reactive and

T6–T12 Burial 13: Fused on anterior and right side of vertebral bodies

these changes are thought to reflect degeneration of the intervertebral disc (Rogers and Waldron 1995). Usually the lower cervical and lumbar vertebrae are affected. In this site the two older individuals with severe osteophytosis or osteoarthritis of the vertebrae had degeneration of the vertebral body surfaces with the cervical and lumbar vertebrae being affected.

Schmorl's nodes Schmorl's nodes, which are small depressions in the surfaces of the vertebral bodies, are caused by heavy manual labour or lifting heavy weights particularly when the labour is carried out during adolescence. They are usually present in the lower thoracic and lumbar vertebrae and rarely appear above the fifth thoracic vertebra. Eight individuals, five male and three female, from this site had Schmorl's nodes. Two of the females had only two vertebrae affected with mild depressions, the other female and all the males had several vertebrae, affected and in two individuals the depressions were very deep. Three males with extensive Schmorl's nodes also had one or two vertebrae, usually lumbar vertebrae, that were compressed on one side or the other. The compression was slight, not enough to consider a diagnosis of a crush fracture but it does give evidence for excessive strain on the spine. All three individuals also had severe vertebral osteophytosis.

Non-vertebral osteoarthritis Eight individuals had osteoarthritis of non-vertebral joints although in two cases only one costo-vertebral joint was affected. All the individuals had osteoarthritis of one or more costo-vertebral joints. The next most common joints with degenerative lesions were the shoulder joints. Five individuals were affected and it was bi-lateral in four cases. There were two individuals with osteoarthritis of both hips, two with both wrists affected and three with one or both elbows affected. One individual had degeneration of the proximal joint surface of a metacarpal but this was due to trauma to the bone. In almost all cases the degenerative changes were mild or moderate. There were no very severely affected joints and this probably reflects the relatively young age of the population. However, even the two older individuals were only moderately affected although they did have several joints with changes. In particular burial 12, the older male, had degenerative joint disease of both shoulders, the left elbow, both wrists and both hips.

Trauma There was no evidence for weapon wounds on these burials but there were some healed fractures noted. Burial 54, a middle adult female, had a healed fracture of the left femur. The fracture had occurred in the middle of the bone and was well healed by a callous of smooth bone. However, the broken ends of the bone had overlapped due to the pull of the strong muscles in the thigh and this had resulted in the left femur being 3cm shorter than the right. In modern medicine, traction is applied to pull the broken ends of the bone back into position, but obviously no such treatment was applied in this case; however, as no complications such as osteomyelitis had occurred the patient was able to survive. A fracture known as spondylolysis had occurred at the fifth lumbar vertebra of B46, a middle adult male. In this type of fracture the neural arch becomes detached from the body of the vertebrae due to stress acting on a congenital weakness at this point. The broken ends of the fracture never heal but the spine is usually stabilized by muscles and ligaments. Problems only occur if the detached vertebral body slips forward slightly, as this can cause a lot of pain. Another type of fracture of the spine is known as a crush fracture of the vertebral body. In this type of fracture, severe stress such as lifting a heavy weight can cause a weak vertebral body to collapse downwards partially or completely. Usually the weight is centred on the anterior part of the vertebrae and a wedge-shaped vertebral body is the result. In burial 13, however, there is a crush fracture of the twelfth thoracic vertebra but the stress is centred on the right side. This has had the result of compressing the right half of the body, pushing it down until it partially broke away from the left half. However, since the vertebrae were not displaced the fracture has repaired itself and the two parts of the vertebrae are firmly joined. In the same way as broken long bones form new bone around the two broken ends, new bone has formed on the right side of the vertebrae. The new osteophytes are so large they are like buttresses of bone that are shoring up the broken bone. This fracture is well healed and the new bone so smooth that the incident occurred some considerable time before death and presumably the patient was well cared for until he recovered. Burial 13 was a large big-boned male with the highest stature of the group, 182cm. Presumably the muscles needed to cover this frame made him appear very strong and he may have been called upon to exert this strength frequently for the benefit of others. Unfortunately even strong men have their breaking point and he may have overexerted himself in trying to lift a very heavy weight. The only other fracture noted was to the proximal joint surface of a fifth metacarpal in B45.

Diffuse Idiopathic Skeletal Hyperostosis (DISH) The thoracic vertebrae of burial 13, T6–T12 were completely fused together and some of the ribs were also fused to the vertebrae. The sixth to the tenth thoracic vertebrae were fused by one long osteophyte on the anterior and right side of the vertebral bodies only. This osteophyte was smooth and had the appearance of 'dripping candle wax'. The posterior vertebral joints were unfused and the vertebral disc space was maintained. The eleventh and twelfth thoracic vertebrae were fused all around the vertebral body by large buttresses of bone that have been described above. Fusion of at least four continuous vertebrae as described above, along with fusion of the ribs is typical of a condition known as diffuse idiopathic skeletal hyperostosis (DISH). Fusion occurs on the right side only of the middle thoracic vertebrae as the descending aorta prevents ossification on the left side. Another feature of DISH is the development of enthesophytes (ligament ossifications) on extraspinal bones. Unfortunately very few bones survived from this individual and the points where enthesophytes usually occur were missing. However, there was one enthesophyte present on the humerus, which was probably the insertion for the biceps muscle. The cause of DISH is uncertain but males are usually more affected than females and the usual age of onset is over 50 years. It has been found in high proportions in monastic cemetery sites (Stroud and Kemp, 1993; Waldron 1985), and there is thought to be some association with obesity and maturity onset diabetes. However, it has also been suggested that some individuals are 'bone formers' and ossification may result from an exaggerated response to stimuli in some people when similar stimuli would produce a modest response in other people (Resnick and Niawayama 1988). It seems likely that this individual, B13, was a bone former and that the body's response to the fractured twelfth vertebra triggered the overproduction of new bone which led to the development of DISH.

Osteochondritis Osteochondritis is a defect in subchondral bone characterised by usually circular or oval depressions in the articular surface of a bone with pitting in the surface of the depression. The usual age of onset is 15–20 years and is more common in males than females (Rogers and Waldron 1995). It was present in one male, B46, and it occurred on the proximal joint surface of the right ulna. The cause of osteochondritis is unknown but it is thought to be due to trauma.

Enthesophytes The majority of individuals from St Thomas's abbey appeared to have a robust, well-developed bone structure with strong, well-developed muscular markings. In some individuals over-development of muscles had led to ossification of tendinous and ligament insertions, known as enthesophytes. The most common sites for enthesophytes tend to be the iliac crest, the olecranon of the ulna, the linea aspera and the insertion for the Achilles tendon on the calcaneum. The two older individuals, B12 and B57 had enthesophytes on the iliac crests and on the olecranon of the ulnae. Burial 58 had a large exostosis on the posterior surface of the left tibia, near the proximal end. This may have been an enthesophyte for the popliteus muscle of the calf. The twelfth rib on the left side of this individual was also fused to the vertebra by smooth ossification of the radiate ligament.

Summary and conclusions These burials were recovered during excavation, in advance of development, of a site that was associated with the abbey of St Thomas in medieval Dublin. The abbey, also known as Thomas Court, was reported to be the burial place of high status individuals such as the wife of Hugh de Lacy. A total of eighteen burials and some disarticulated remains were recovered. The burials consisted of four juveniles and fourteen adults. Eight of the adults were male and six were female. It is not unusual for a higher proportion of males to be recovered from monastery sites. None of the juveniles were under three years of age and therefore the cemetery population does not reflect the population of the surrounding city. Although the group is small and therefore a reliable statistical analysis of the results cannot be obtained, some general trends, which may be re-enforced or contradicted if a larger sample is recovered, were noted.

Dental attrition did not appear to be severe, suggesting that the bread and cereals consumed were more refined than in Early Christian times. Calculus deposits were not heavy which suggests that there may have been some attempt at dental hygiene. Caries rates were relatively low, consistent with findings from other medieval priories. There was little indication of biological stress, with only one individual having iron-deficiency anaemia and possibly vitamin C deficiency. There was evidence of acute infections or nutritional distress during early childhood in several individuals. However as no episodes of stress occurred under the age of two years it is unlikely that nutritional deficiencies occurred around the time of weaning. The episodes of hypoplasia may reflect common childhood infections. Degenerative joint disease was present in many individuals but in most cases they were only mildly affected. A few older individuals had more severe and extensive joint degeneration. Schmorl's nodes, indicative of early adolescent manual labour, were present mainly in the male skeletons. There was no evidence of weapon wounds and any fractures that occurred had healed completely with no complications such as bone infection. One very tall and strong male had suffered a fractured vertebra, which had healed but unfortunately had led to the development of DISH, which had fused several vertebrae and ribs in his back.

In fact although this group is small, there is every indication that they did not suffer the biological stress and deficiencies that normal populations would have endured. They appeared to have had adequate nourishment; in fact the presence of DISH may indicate a very rich diet. They took care of their teeth and did not suffer too badly from degenerative diseases, which tend to be exacerbated by a physical lifestyle.

REFERENCES

Brothwell, D.R. 1981 *Digging up bones*. Oxford.
Buckley, L.A. 1991 A study of the human skeletal remains from a cemetery at Kilshane, Co. Dublin. Unpublished M.Sc. thesis. Queen's University Belfast.
Buckley, L.A. 1994 Carlingford abbey, Carlingford, Skeletal Report. Unpublished.
Buckley, L.A. 1996 Solar, Co. Antrim, Skeletal Report for DOENI. Unpublished.
Buckley, L.A. 1996 Francis Street, Dublin. Skeletal Report. Unpublished.
Buikstra, J.E. and Ubelaker, D.H. 1994 *Standards for data collection from human skeletal remains*. Arkansas Archaeological Survey Research Series. no.44.
Halpin, A., and Buckley, L.A. 1995 'The Dominican priory, Drogheda, County Louth'. *R.I.A. Proc.* 95C, no. 5.
Henderson, J. 1984 The human remains. In *Excavations on the site of the Dominican friary at Guildford in 1974 and 1978*. ed. R. Poulton and H. Woods, Surrey Archaeological Society, Guildford, vol. 9, 58–71.
Hillson, S. 1990 *Teeth*. Cambridge.

Lovejoy, C., Meindl, R., Pryzbeck, T. and Mensforth R. 1985 Chronological metamorphosis of the auricular surface of the ilium: a new method for the determination of adult skeletal age at death. *American Journal of Physical Anthropology* 68:15–28.

McLoughlin, E.P. 1950 *Report on the anatomical investigation of the skeletal remains unearthed at Castleknock in the excavation of an Early Christian cemetery during the summer of 1938*. Stationery Office. Dublin.

Ó Donnabháin, B. 1985 A study of the human remains from Tintern abbey, Co. Wexford. Unpublished thesis, National University of Ireland.

Resnick, D. and Niwayama, G. 1988 *Diagnosis of bone and joint disorders*, 2nd edn. Philadelphia.

Rogers, J., Watt, I. and Dieppe, P. 1990 Comparison of visual and radiographic detection of bony changes at the knee joint. *British Medical Journal* 300, 367–8.

Rogers, J. and Waldron, T. 1995 *A field guide to joint disease in archaeology*. Chichester.

Stroud, G. and Kemp, R. 1993 Cemeteries of St Andrew, Fishergate. The archaeology of York. The medieval cemeteries 12/2. York. Council for British Archaeology for York Archaeological Trust.

Trotter, M. and Gleser, G.C. 1952 Estimation of stature from long bones of American Whites and Negroes. *American Journal of Physical Anthropology* 10, 463–514.

Trotter, M. and Gleser, G.C. 1958 A re-evaluation of estimation of stature based on measurements of stature taken during life and long bones after death. *American Journal of Physical Anthropology* 16, 79–123.

Waldron, T. 1985 DISH at Merton priory: evidence for a new occupational disease. *British Medical Journal* 291:1762–3

Walsh, C. 2000 Archaeological excavations at the abbey of St Thomas the Martyr, Dublin. In *Medieval Dublin I*. ed. S. Duffy. Dublin.

APPENDIX: INVENTORY OF BURIALS

A full description of burials recovered is given in this inventory. For each skeleton, the age, sex and estimated living stature is given in the top line, followed by a full description of any pathology noted and a suggested diagnosis where possible. The dentition is recorded in the following manner, where P=tooth present; PM=tooth lost after death; CA=tooth congenitally absent; AM=tooth lost during life; C=caries; A=abscess:

			A									A					
CA	P	P	P	P	P	PM	PM		P	P	P	P	P	P	P	CA	
18	17	16	15	14	13	12	11		21	22	23	24	25	26	27	28	
48	47	46	45	44	43	42	41		31	32	33	34	35	36	37	38	
P	P	AM	P	P	PM	PM	PM		PM	PM	P	P	P	AM	AM	P	
		C										C	C				

The juvenile dentition is given in the following manner, where U=unerupted; E=erupting:

U	E	P	P	P		P	P	P	E	U
55	54	53	52	51		61	62	63	64	65
85	84	83	82	81		71	72	73	74	75
U	E	P	P	PM		PM	P	P	E	U

Burial 12, Older male: 170cm

This skeleton was mostly complete, although many bones were fragmented. It was mainly the back of the skull that survived with the occipital bone and posterior halves of both parietal bones present. However both temporal and zygomatic bones and fragments of the frontal bone were also present. The maxilla and mandible were virtually complete. The vertebral column was complete but in poor condition and there were eleven ribs from the left and ten from the right side. Both clavicles were almost complete although their lateral ends were damaged and both scapulae were present. The left humerus was virtually complete but fragmented at the proximal end and the proximal end was missing from the right humerus. Both ulnae and the left radius were complete but only the shaft remained from the right radius. The left and right capitate and hamate, left trapezium and right lunate remained from the wrist bones. All the metacarpals were present and there were nine proximal, three middle and three distal hand phalanges. The pelvis was virtually complete although it was slightly damaged. The left femur was fragmented at the distal end but the right femur was virtually complete. Only fragments from the shafts of the left tibia and fibula were present but the right tibia was virtually complete. Only the left first metatarsal and one proximal phalange survived from the foot bones.

Skeletal pathology In general this was a large-boned individual with well developed muscle insertions on the iliac crests of the pelvis and on the olecranon of the left ulna. Most of the pathology noted was degenerative changes brought on by general wear and tear, the affects of which tend to increase in severity with the age of an individual. There was severe osteoarthritis affecting all the cervical vertebrae apart from C1. Most of the vertebrae had eburnation of the joint surfaces. Osteoarthritis was also present to a mild degree in the upper thoracic vertebrae but was severe in the lower thoracic and upper lumbar vertebrae. It was also present to a mild degree in the lower lumbar vertebrae. Osteophytosis was also present throughout the vertebral column and was severe in the lower cervical and mid-lumbar regions. The body of the third lumbar vertebrae was compressed on the right side. There was further evidence of degenerative disease between the vertebral bodies with many of the superior and inferior surfaces of the centra being very porotic and reactive. Some of the vertebrae had deep erosive lesions, which may have been Schmorl's nodes. Other joints apart from the vertebrae showed evidence of degenerative disease although the changes were mild to moderate and not as severe as in the vertebral column. The joints affected included both hips, both shoulders, the left elbow, both wrists and both sterno-clavicular joints. The ribs were also arthritic with both the joints at the head and transverse process affected on each side. The first costal cartilage was ossified and fused to the end of the first rib. Ossification of cartilage tends to occur as an individual ages and this is taken to indicate old age.

Dental pathology

AM	AM	AM	AM	AM	AM	AM	AM		AM	AM	AM	AM	AM	AM	AM	AM
18	17	16	15	14	13	12	11		21	22	23	24	25	26	27	28
48	47	46	45	44	43	42	41		31	32	33	34	35	36	37	38
AM	AM	AM	AM	AM	AM	AM	AM		AM	PM	PM	PM	AM	AM	AM	AM

All the teeth in the maxilla and most of the teeth in the mandible had been lost during life and the sockets were well healed over. The sockets for the three mandibular teeth, which had been present at the time of death, were very shallow and were probably on the point of being lost from the jaw.

Burial 13, Probably older adult, male: 184cm

This burial was very disturbed and incomplete. Only the base of the skull, the occipital bone and both temporal bones were present. A fragment of the left side of the maxilla remained. The seventh cervical, first thoracic and parts of four lumbar vertebrae were recovered with this burial. However seven lower thoracic vertebrae were recovered with F22 and labelled disarticulated. Examination of these vertebrae revealed that they had pathological lesions that matched lesions on the ribs recovered with burial 13 and therefore it is highly likely that these are some of the missing vertebrae from this burial. Only three ribs from the left and two from the right were present. Fragments of both scapulae were present. The left humerus was complete but the right humerus was missing its proximal third. Both ulnae were virtually complete and the proximal third of the left radius was present. Only the left third metacarpal and one proximal phalange remained from the hand bones. The sacrum was present but incomplete and only the shaft of a right femur and a left patella remained from the leg bones.

Skeletal pathology The lower thoracic vertebrae T6–T12 were all fused together. T6, T7 and T8 were solidly fused by a large vertical osteophyte down the entire length of the vertebral bodies. This osteophyte had the appearance of 'dripping candle wax', and was mainly on the centre and right side of the vertebral bodies. These are features typically seen in cases of diffuse idiopathic skeletal hyperostosis (DISH). The neural arches were unfused. Other features also seen in DISH include enthesophytes, which are ossifications of ligament insertions on the bone. In this skeleton there was an exostosis on the right humerus, which may have been ossification of the insertion of the biceps muscle. On the ninth thoracic vertebrae the osteophyte was broken off but originally would have continued down the vertebrae, fusing T9 to T8 and T10. There was also a small amount of fusion on the left side between T9 and T10 with the disc space being maintained. The tenth thoracic was fused to the eleventh thoracic all around the surface of the vertebral bodies. T11 was fused to T12 on the right side by a very large C-shaped osteophyte and on the left side by a similar large osteophyte. Severe osteophytosis was also present on the second and fifth lumbar vertebrae. It could be seen that the body of the twelfth thoracic vertebrae had been broken during life and the fracture had healed. The fracture line was in the middle of the centrum running from the anterior to the posterior surface. The right side of the centrum is compressed and has dropped to a slightly lower level than the left side. However the fracture is well healed. It seems that the large osteophytes on T11 and T12 are the bodies attempt to stabilize the fracture. Fractures on a long bone are healed by new bone being produced, which seals the two broken ends and binds them together. There is often considerable overlap of bone and a large callus can be produced. In these two vertebrae the new bone is acting like buttresses, to shore up the broken vertebra and thus stabilise it. It is very likely that the broken vertebra was the trigger for the development of DISH in this individual. Little is known about the cause of DISH but it does tend to occur in higher status individuals particularly in monastery sites. It may be associated with affluence and a better diet. However it often occurs in individuals that are large, heavy boned, i.e., they tend to produce bone easily. This individual was very large and the need to produce large amounts of bone to heal a broken vertebra may have led to the overproduction of bone resulting in a large number of vertebrae being completely fused. Some of the ribs in B13 were also fused to the vertebrae. There is evidence for smooth ossification of the costo-vertebral muscles both on the vertebrae and on two of the ribs. The fifth lumbar vertebra was sacralised, i.e., incorporated into the sacrum. There were also early indications of degenerative joint disease at both elbows.

Dental pathology

PM	P		AM	AM	PM
23	24		25	26	27

There was considerable alveolar resorption. An unidentified molar was also present but most of the crown had been destroyed by caries.

Stray mandible A stray mandible was present in the bag of disarticulated bone labelled F22. It is recorded here but it cannot be certain that it belongs to burial 13.

48	47	46	45	44	43	42	41		31	32	33
PPM	PM	P	P	P	P	PM	PM		P	P	

There was heavy wear on the anterior teeth and heavy calculus deposits on the buccal and lingual surfaces. There was considerable alveolar recession around the roots of the second premolar and first molar.

Burial 22, Late middle adult, male: 177cm

This skeleton was virtually complete apart from the skull, which was very fragmented. The occipital, both temporal and most of both parietal bones were present but there were only a few fragments of frontal bone and some fragments of maxilla and mandible from the facial area. The vertebral column was complete and in good condition apart from the fifth cervical vertebra which was missing. There were eleven ribs from each side and the manubrium and body of the sternum were present. Both clavicles and scapulae were present. Part of the proximal end of the left humerus was missing but the right humerus and both radii and ulnae were complete. The left and right capitate, lunate and scaphoid were present from the wrist bones as well as the left hamate, the right trapezium and right triquetral. All the metacarpals apart from the fourth and fifth left were present and there were eight proximal and four middle hand phalanges. The pelvis, including the sacrum was complete. Both femurs and tibiae were complete and the shafts of both fibulae were present. The right patella was present. All the tarsals and metatarsals were present although some of the joint ends of the metatarsals were missing. There were two proximal foot phalanges.

Skeletal pathology There was mild osteoarthritis on the superior articular surfaces of the fourth lumbar vertebra. Mild osteophytosis was present on the eight thoracic and fourth and fifth lumbar vertebrae. The condition was moderate to severe on the ninth and tenth thoracic vertebrae. Schmorl's nodes which are indicative of a heavy workload during adolescence were present on the lower seven thoracic vertebrae. There was osteoarthritis on one left rib on the transverse articular process.

Dental pathology

					P	P			P	P	P	P	P	P	P
					13	12	–		21	22	23	24	25	26	27
48	47	46	45	44	43	–	–		–	32	33	34	35	36	37	38
P	P	P	P	P	P					PM	P	P	P	P	P	P
C																

Attrition: there was a moderate degree of wear on the first molars and light wear on the second and third molars. The upper left central incisor and canine had small chips out of the enamel at the occlusal surface. This indicates that the teeth were probably used as tools. *Calculus:* deposits were light on the buccal and lingual surfaces of the left mandibular canine, premolars and first and second molars and the maxillary first and second molars. However they were moderate on the canine, first premolar and first molar on the right side of the mandible. *Caries:* there was a large cavity on the mesial side of the lower right third molar, at the cervical margin. *Hypoplasia:* linear enamel hypoplasia was noted on the lower premolars and the episodes occurred between 4–5 years of age.

Burial 27, Male: 164cm
This consisted mainly of the lower half of a skeleton. The manubrium of the sternum, the complete left ulna, most of the right ulna, the distal half of both radii, the left hamate and pisiform, all the metacarpals and six proximal, two middle and one distal hand phalanges were all that remained from the upper half of the skeleton. There were only a few fragments of upper thoracic vertebrae but the three lower thoracic and all the lumbar vertebrae were complete. There were four ribs from each side. The pelvis was virtually complete although the pubic bones were missing. Both femurs, tibiae and the left patella were complete. The proximal ends were missing from both fibulae. The left and right talii, calcanea, the left cuboid and first cuneiform and the left first, second, third and fourth metatarsals survived from the foot bones as well as one proximal phalange.

Pathology There was a small osteophyte on the superior edge of the third lumbar vertebra, on the left side.

Burial 45, Female, middle adult: 158cm
This skeleton was almost complete apart from the lower legs. The skull was complete except for the left side of the maxilla, which was missing. The vertebral column was complete and there were eleven ribs from the left side and twelve from the right side. Both clavicles were complete and both scapulae were present. All the arm bones were complete, all the metacarpals were present and there were nine proximal and two middle hand phalanges. The left ilium and ischium were virtually complete and the right ilium and ischium were incomplete. Most of the sacrum was present. Both femurs and the right patella were complete but there were only fragments of the tibiae and fibulae.

The left and right calcanea, cuboids, right navicular and all the metatarsals as well as seven proximal foot phalanges were present from the feet but were partially decayed.

Skeletal pathology There was slight to moderate osteoarthritis on the posterior joints of the middle thoracic vertebrae. Mild osteophytosis was present on the third lumbar vertebra. Schmorl's nodes were present on the inferior surfaces of the centra of the eleventh and twelfth thoracic vertebrae. There was slight damage to the proximal end of the left fifth metacarpal, possibly a small fracture of the joint surface. The surface was very reactive and pitted. The lateral ends of both clavicles had a slight degree of porosity indicative of early degenerative changes. There were also osteoarthritic changes on one rib on the left side.

Dental pathology

CA	PM	P	P	P	P	P	PM								
18	17	16	15	14	13	12	11								
48	47	46	45	44	43	42	41		31	32	33	34	35	36	37	–
CA	CA	P	AM	P	P	P	P		P	PM	P	P	AM	P	P

Anomalies: most of the teeth were stained black, probably due to lying in waterlogged conditions, which made it difficult to examine them. Three teeth were congenitally absent. Both third molars on the right side had not developed. It is not unusual for third molars to be undeveloped but the second molar on the right was also missing and this is not a common occurrence. The mandible of this individual was unusually small. *Antemortem loss:* the two lower second premolars were missing but they appeared to have been lost during life, rather than being undeveloped. *Attrition:* there was moderate wear on the anterior teeth. The lower first molars were heavily worn but there was light to moderate wear on the upper first molar and lower left second molar. *Calculus:* deposits were light on the buccal and lingual surfaces of the lower teeth and moderate on the upper canine and first molar. *Periodontal disease:* there was a slight degree of alveolar recession around the roots of the lower canines and molars and the upper canine and premolars. *Hypoplasia:* linear enamel hypoplasia was noted on the canines and there were pits of hypoplasia on the lower left canine.

Burial 46, Late middle adult, male: 165cm

This skeleton was complete and in good condition. The front of the skull was fragmented but the occipital, left parietal and left temporal bones were complete. Most of the right parietal and right temporal bones were present but there were only a few fragments of frontal bone. The left side of the maxilla and the mandible were present. All the vertebrae except the first thoracic vertebrae were complete. There were twelve pairs of ribs and the sternum was complete. Both clavicles and scapulae were virtually complete. All the arm bones were complete and the left and right hamate, left lunate and trapezoid, right capitate and scaphoid remained from the wrist bones. All the metacarpals were present and there were ten proximal, five middle and four distal hand phalanges. The pelvis and all the leg bones were complete, apart from the left patella, which was missing. All the tarsals and metatarsals apart from the right fourth metatarsal were present and there were four proximal and one distal foot phalanges.

116   *Laureen Buckley*

Skeletal pathology   Spondylolysis had occurred at the fifth lumbar vertebra. There was mild osteoarthritis on the fourth, fifth, sixth and twelfth thoracic vertebrae. Osteophytosis was mild on the middle thoracic vertebrae and moderate on the lower thoracic vertebrae. There was severe osteophytosis on the superior surface of the third lumbar vertebra. Schmorl's nodes were present on all the thoracic vertebrae from T_5 down and on the first three lumbar vertebrae. Osteoarthritis was present on the joints of the first right rib. There were early degenerative changes at the shoulder joints with slight porosity of the proximal surfaces of both humerii and of the lateral ends of both clavicles. There was also slight marginal lipping of the glenoid area of the right scapula. Both elbow joints had mild osteoarthritis with marginal lipping around the distal articular surface of the humerii and the proximal surfaces of the ulnae and radii. The right elbow was slightly more affected than the left. There was also marginal lipping around the distal surfaces of both ulnae and radii. The right ulna had osteochondritis on the superior part of the proximal joint surface. Cribra orbitalia was present in the right orbit. Both tibiae had evidence for healed periostitis on the medial surface of their shafts. The right tibia also had a small slightly raised area on the lateral surface in the proximal half of the bone. This might represent a small healed wound.

Dental pathology

PM	P	P	P	P	PM		PM	P	P	P	P	PM	P	CA
16	15	14	13	12	11		21	22	23	24	25	26	27	28
47	46	45	44	–	–	–	31	32	33	34	35	36	37	38
P	P	P	P				PM	PM	P	P	P	P	P	P
														C

Anomalies: the upper left second deciduous molar was retained. This usually only happens if the premolar does not develop but in this case both premolars had developed normally. *Attrition:* there was heavy wear on the upper anterior teeth and moderate wear on the lower teeth. The first molars had a moderate degree of wear and there was very little wear on the second and third molars. *Calculus:* there were moderate deposits on the buccal surfaces of the upper teeth and the lower left canine and first premolar. *Caries:* there was a moderate sized cavity on the buccal surface of the lower left third molar, at the cervical margin. *Periodontal disease:* there was a moderate degree of alveolar recession around the roots of the upper premolars and considerable recession around the lower premolars and molars and the upper left molars. *Hypoplasia:* linear enamel hypoplasia was present on the incisors, canines and upper premolars.

Burial 47, Late middle adult, female: 149cm

This skeleton was virtually complete although the skull and vertebrae were in poor condition. The back of the skull, consisting of the occipital, both temporal bones and most of both parietal bones was present but very little remained from the frontal bone and only the right side of the maxilla remained from the facial bones. The mandible was also present. The vertebral column consisted of the upper three cervical vertebrae, fragments of the lower cervical and upper thoracic vertebrae and the lumbar vertebrae. There were ten ribs from the left side and seven from the right side present. Both clavicles were present and there were fragments only of both scapulae. The left humerus was present but the proximal half was fragmented. The shafts of the left radius and ulna were present and the right radius and ulna were complete. The left and right scaphoid and hamate, left lunate and capitate and right trapezium remained from the hand bones along with all the metacarpals and ten proximal and four middle hand phalanges. The left and right ilium and ischium were present but incomplete and most of the sacrum was present. The proximal third was missing from the left femur and the right femur was complete. Both tibiae and the right fibula were complete and the shaft of the left fibula was present. All the tarsals apart from the left first cuneiform were present, all the metatarsals were present although partially decayed and there were three proximal foot phalanges.

Skeletal pathology There was mild osteoarthritis on the inferior articular surfaces of the twelfth thoracic vertebra and mild osteophytosis on the inferior surface of the body of the eleventh thoracic vertebra.

Dentition

CA	P	P	P	P	P	P	PM									P	P
18	17	16	15	14	13	12	11									27	28
48	47	46	45	44	43	–	–		–	32	33	34	35	36	37	38
P	P	P	P	PM	PM				P	P	P	P	P	P	P

Attrition: there was moderate wear on the lower first molar and light wear on all other molars. *Calculus:* deposits were light on the buccal surface of most teeth but were moderate on the buccal surfaces of the lower left second premolar and first molar and the upper canine and first premolar as well as the lingual surfaces of most of the lower teeth. Deposits were heavy on the buccal and lingual surfaces of the lower incisor and canine. *Periodontal Disease:* there was a small degree of alveolar recession around the roots of most teeth and moderate recession around the lower left premolars and molars. *Hypoplasia:* linear enamel hypoplasia was present on the upper incisor and canine.

Burial 48, Young adult, female: 152cm

This skeleton was almost complete except for the skull, which was very fragmentary. Part of the occipital bone, both temporal bones, and the right parietal bone were present. Only a few fragments remained from the frontal bone. There was no maxilla but the mandible was complete. The upper cervical vertebrae and one lower thoracic vertebra were missing but the rest of the vertebral column was complete. There were eleven ribs from each side. Both clavicles and scapulae were present. The distal end was missing from the left humerus but the right humerus was complete. Only part of the shaft of the left ulna remained and the right ulna was almost complete apart from the distal third. The right radius was complete. All the metacarpals apart from the left first and right fifth were present and there were two proximal phalanges. The left ilium and ischium were present from the pelvis and the right ilium and ischium were complete. Both femurs, tibiae and the left patella were complete but the proximal thirds were missing from the fibulae. All the tarsals apart from the right navicular and second and third cuneiform were present and all the metatarsals except the first metatarsals were present.

Dental pathology

4^8	47	4^6	45	44	43	4^2	4^1		3^1	3^2	33	34	35	3^6	37	3^8
P	P	P	P	P	P	PM	PM		PM	P	P	P	P	P	P	P

Attrition: there was very little wear on any teeth. *Calculus:* deposits were light on the buccal surfaces and moderate on the lingual surfaces of the molars. *Hypoplasia*: linear enamel hypoplasia was noted on the left first premolar.

Burial 49, Juvenile 4–8 years

The skull was very fragmented and incomplete but the squamous occipital bone, both parietal bone, both temporal bones and fragments of frontal bone were present. The right side of the mandible was also present. The axis, atlas and one other cervical vertebra were all that remained from the vertebral column. There were eight ribs from the left side and two from the right side present. Both clavicles and scapulae were present and the shafts of both humerii were virtually complete. The left radius and right radius and ulna were also present but were not complete. Parts of both ilia remained from the pelvis. Both femurs, tibiae and the left fibula were complete.

Pathology The metopic suture was unfused. Cribra orbitalia was present in the left orbit.

Dentition

47	46	85	84	83	82	41
U	E	PM	PM	PM	PM	U

The crown of the second permanent molar was only half formed.

Burial 50, Early middle adult, male: 165cm

This burial was virtually complete apart from the feet, which were missing. The skull was complete apart form the orbital area of the frontal bone, the right zygomatic bone and part of the right side of the maxilla. The vertebral column was complete apart from the third and fourth cervical vertebrae, which were missing. There were seven ribs from the left side and six from the right side. Both clavicles and scapulae were present. The humerii, left ulna and right radius were complete but the distal ends were missing from the left radius and right ulna. All the metacarpals except for the first right were present but were not all complete. There were eight proximal hand phalanges. Both ilia and ischia were present from the pelvis and the sacrum was virtually complete. The left femur and patella were complete and the right femur was damaged at the distal joint surface. The left tibia was virtually complete and the shaft of the right tibia was present. Fragments of the left fibula shaft remained.

Skeletal pathology There was slight compression of the right side of the centrum of the twelfth thoracic and first lumbar vertebrae. Schmorl's nodes were present on the lower six thoracic vertebrae and in the first and third lumbar vertebrae. Arachnoid pits were present in the internal surface of the skull.

Dental pathology

P	PM	PM	P	P	P	P	P	P	P	P	P	P	AM	P	PM
18	17	16	15	14	13	12	11	21	22	23	24	25	26	27	28
48	47	46	45	44	43	42	41	31	32	33	34	35	36	37	38
P	P	PM	P	P	P	P	P	P	P	P	P	P	P	P	MP
	C	A											C		

Attrition: there was moderate wear on the upper second molar and light wear on the other molars. *Calculus:* deposits were light on the buccal surfaces of most of the maxillary teeth but they were heavy on the right incisors and canine. Deposits were moderate on the buccal surfaces of the lower incisors and light on the lingual surfaces. *Caries:* The crown of the lower first left molar, 36, was completely destroyed by caries and only two stumps of roots remained. The lower right second molar, 47, had a large cavity on the mesial side of the crown. *Abscess:* there was an external abscess at the lower right first molar. Part of the root of this tooth was missing. *Hypoplasia:* linear enamel hypoplasia was present on most of the incisors, the canines and the upper premolars.

Burial 51, Early middle adult, male: 173cm

This skeleton was virtually complete but the joint ends of many bones were missing or damaged. The skull was fragmented but virtually complete with the occipital, both parietal bones, both temporal bones and the frontal bone present. Also present was the right zygomatic bone and the maxilla and mandible. The vertebral column was complete and there were eight ribs from the left side and eleven from the right side present. Both clavicles and scapulae were present and there were fragments of sternum. The left humerus was almost complete but the distal end was missing. The proximal end of the right humerus was fragmented. The left ulna was virtually complete apart from the distal third and the proximal half of the right ulna was present. The proximal end was missing from the left radius and only the proximal half of the right radius was present. Only the first and fifth right metacarpals and two proximal and two middle hand phalanges remained from the hand bones. The pelvis was virtually complete although the pubic bones were missing. Both femurs were complete and both tibiae were present but fragmented around the joint ends. Only the shaft of the right fibula survived. The left talus and calcaneum was all that remained from the foot bones.

Skeletal Pathology There were mild osteoarthritic changes in the posterior joints of the middle thoracic vertebrae. Mild osteophytosis was noted in the lower cervical and mid lumbar region and there was severe osteophytosis on the fifth lumbar vertebra. The fourth lumbar vertebra was slightly compressed on the left side. Schmorl's nodes were present in the lower five thoracic vertebrae.

Dentition

C															C	C
P	AM	P	P	P	P			PM	P	P	P	P	P		P	P
18	17	16	15	14	13	–	–	21	22	23	24	25	26		27	28
48	47	46	45	44	43	42	41	31	32	33	34	35	36		37	38
P	P	P	P	P	P	P	P	P	P	P	P	P	P		AM	P
		A														C

Attrition: there was moderate wear on the premolars and the first molars and light or no attrition on the remaining molars. *Calculus:* deposits were light on the buccal surfaces of the maxillary teeth and moderate on the lingual surfaces of the mandibular teeth. *Caries:* there was a small cavity on the buccal side of the crown of the lower left third molar. The upper left second and third molars and upper right third molar all had moderate sized caries in their occlusal fissures. *Abscess:* there was considerable porosity on the alveolar bone surrounding the buccal root of the lower right first molar, suggesting that an abscess was forming at the root and may have been about to open on the external side of the mandible. *Periodontal disease:* there was a slight degree of alveolar recession around the roots of most teeth but it was moderate around the lower right molars, lower left first molar and upper right first molar. There was severe recession around the lower left second molar and upper right second molar. *Hypoplasia:* linear enamel hypoplasia was present on all the canines and premolars as well as the lower right second molar.

Burial 52, Juvenile 6 years
This consisted of the middle of a skeleton only. The skull, vertebrae and ribs were missing and there were no upper arm bones. Part of the shafts of both radii and ulnae were present. The left and right ilia were almost complete. Both femurs were present, the right femur was complete but part of the proximal end was missing from the left femur. From the length of the femur it is estimated that the juvenile was around 6 years of age at the time of death.

Burial 53, Early middle adult, female: 165cm
There was no skull or cervical vertebrae remaining on this skeleton. However, apart from two mid thoracic vertebrae, most of the remaining vertebral column was complete and in good condition. There were nine ribs from the left and eleven from the right side and the sternum was complete. Both clavicles and scapulae were present and all the arm bones were complete. The right first metacarpal and left second, third, fourth and fifth metacarpals were present from the hand bone along with two proximal and one middle phalanges. The pelvis was virtually complete but the left pubic bone and part of the left ischium were missing. Both femurs and tibiae were complete and the fibulae were missing their proximal ends. The foot bones consisted of the left and right calcanea, talii and naviculars, the left second and third cuneiform bones, the left first, second and fourth metatarsals and all the right metatarsals.

Skeletal pathology There were mild osteoarthritic changes on the upper two thoracic vertebrae and moderate changes on the upper right articular surface of the fourth thoracic vertebra. There was moderate osteophytosis on the inferior surface of the fifth lumbar vertebra and pitting and erosion of the inferior surface of L5 and the superior surface of the sacrum on the left side. Schmorl's nodes were present on the third, fifth and sixth thoracic vertebra and on the second, third and fourth lumbar vertebrae. The indentations were very deep.

Burial 54, Middle adult, female: 153cm
The skull and neck were missing but otherwise this skeleton was complete and in good condition. The vertebral column was complete from the second thoracic vertebrae down.

There were twelve pairs of ribs and the manubrium of the sternum was complete. Both clavicles and scapulae were present. The left humerus was complete and the distal half of the right humerus was present. The radii and ulnae were virtually complete but the distal ends were missing from the left radius and ulna and the proximal end was missing from the right radius. The hand bones consisted of the left and right hamate, the right capitate and trapezium, all the metacarpals and ten proximal, three middle and two distal hand phalanges. The pelvis was complete and all the leg bones apart from the right patella were present and complete. All the tarsals apart from the right navicular and second and third cuneiforms were present and all the metatarsals were present although some were decayed. There were three proximal foot phalanges.

Skeletal pathology Schmorl's nodes were present in the ninth and tenth thoracic vertebrae. The left femur had a healed fracture in the mid-shaft region. There was considerable overlap of the broken ends of the bone with the bone being shortened by over 3cm compared to the right femur. The healing was complete with the new bone smoothly covering the entire area with no sign of infection. There was a small exostosis on the posterior surface of the bone that probably indicates some injury to the leg muscle at the time of the fracture.

Burial 55, Juvenile 3–5 years

This skeleton was in poor condition. The occipital bone was almost complete and both parietal, both temporal and the frontal bones were present but incomplete. The mandible was almost complete. There was no vertebral column and five ribs only remained from each side. The left clavicle and scapula were present. Most of the shaft of both humerii, radii and ulnae were present. There were no pelvic bones remaining. The leg bones were in poor condition but most of the shaft of the left femur was present but the right femur was very fragmented. The left tibia and fibula shafts were virtually complete but only the distal end of the right tibia remained.

Dentition

87	86	85	84	83	82		71	72	73	74	75	76	77
U	U	P	P	P	P		PM	PM	PM	P	P	U	U

Burial 56, Juvenile 10–12 years

This consisted mainly of the skull and legs only. The skull was virtually complete with the occipital, left and right parietal, sphenoid and left and right temporal bones complete. The maxilla and mandible were also present. The first five cervical vertebrae were present from the vertebral column. Both femurs were present and almost complete but the proximal end was missing from the left femur and the distal end was missing from the right femur. The left tibia was very fragmented but the right tibia was complete. Only fragments of both fibula remained. Both calcanea, the left talus and a left metatarsal remained from the foot bones.

Dentition

U	P	P	U	PM	E	P	PM		P	P	E	E	P	P	P	PM
18	17	16	15	14	13	12	11		21	22	23	24	25	26	27	28
48	47	46	45	44	43	42	41		31	32	33	34	35	36	37	38
U	P	P	E	E	P	P	P		PM	P	P	PM	P	P	P	U

The canines are not fully erupted and the crowns of the third molars are not fully formed. *Calculus:* there were moderate deposits on the buccal surfaces of the lower right incisors and canines and heavy deposits on the buccal surfaces of the lower left lateral incisor and upper right incisors. *Hypoplasia:* linear enamel hypoplasia was noted on the upper left incisors, the canines, lower right first premolar, and the lower molars. There were grooves of hypoplasia on the lower first molars.

Burial 57, Older female: 161cm

The skull was virtually complete although the facial bones were missing. Only part of the right side of the maxilla remained and the mandible was virtually complete. The vertebral column was in poor condition with only the cervical and first thoracic vertebrae complete and only the bodies of the remaining thoracic vertebrae present. There were nine ribs from the left and eleven from the right present. Part of the manubrium remained. Both clavicles and scapulae were present but incomplete. The left humerus was complete but only the proximal half of the right humerus was present. The left radius and ulna were present but the distal thirds were missing. The right radius and ulna were complete. All the metacarpals except for the left and right third and right first metacarpals were present and there were five proximal and two middle hand phalanges. The left ilium was almost complete and most of the right ilium was present. Both ischia were incomplete and only fragments of the sacrum remained. Both femurs and tibiae were complete and there were fragments of both fibulae shafts. There were no foot bones remaining.

Skeletal Pathology There was severe osteoarthritis with eburnation of the joint surfaces, affecting all the cervical vertebrae apart from the first. The first thoracic vertebra was also affected but the neural arches of the remaining thoracic vertebrae were not present. The arch of the second lumbar vertebrae was present and it had moderate osteoarthritis. Osteophytosis was present to a mild degree on the sixth cervical and on T5, T9 and T10. However it was severe on T8 and on all the lumbar vertebrae. The eleventh thoracic vertebra had destruction near the anterior edge of the centrum on the superior surface. The lumbar vertebrae also had a crescent shaped area of erosion on the superior and inferior surface, near the anterior edge. There was mild marginal lipping around both acetabula. Mild osteoarthritic changes were also present at the right shoulder joint and the left elbow. Some ribs from both sides had evidence of osteoarthritis and the heads of the first ribs were very arthritic. There were ossified ligament insertions on the olecranon of the ulnae and on the iliac crests. The first costal cartilage on the right side was fused to the manubrium.

Dental Pathology

			A	A											
?	PM	PM	AM	P	PM	P	PM								
18	17	16	15	14	13	12	11								
48	47	46	45	44	43	42	41	31	32	33	34	35	36	37	38
AM	AM	AM	PM	PM	PM	PM	AM	AM	AM	AM	PM	AM	AM	AM	AM

Attrition: there was very heavy wear on the remaining teeth. *Antemortem loss:* at least 12 teeth had been lost during life. The roots for the remaining teeth in the mandible were very shallow and the teeth were probably on the point of being lost. *Caries:* the pulp cavity of the remaining maxillary tooth, the first premolar was exposed but this was probably due to excessive wear rather than caries. *Abscess:* there were two abscesses with external openings at the roots of the upper incisors. *Periodontal disease:* there was considerable recession around all sockets in the maxilla and mandible.

Burial 58, Middle adult, male: 174cm

This skeleton was virtually complete and in good condition. The skull was complete apart from the facial bones and the vertebral column was complete. There were eleven ribs from the left side and nine from the right side present. Part of the sternum was also present. Both clavicles were complete and both scapulae were present. All the arm bones were complete. The left and right capitate, all the metacarpals and seven proximal and one middle hand phalanges were present from the hand bones. The left ilium was almost complete and the right ilium was very fragmented. Only the first sacral vertebrae remained. Both femurs and both tibiae were complete but the fibulae were not present. Both calcanea, the left cuboid, the right talus, navicular and third cuneiform as well as all the metatarsals and one proximal phalange survived from the foot bones.

Skeletal pathology Severe osteoarthritis was present in the posterior joints of the mid cervical and lower cervical/first thoracic vertebrae. Osteophytosis was present in the lumbar vertebrae only and was severe in the lower three lumbar, which had large cup-shaped osteophytes on the superior and inferior surfaces of the vertebral bodies. The fourth lumbar vertebrae had very large osteophytes indeed. There was an exostosis on the posterior surface of the left tibia, near the proximal end of the bone. This may represent an injury to a muscle. The right tibia had a similar osteophyte to a much lesser degree. There was porosity of the lateral ends of both clavicles, especially the right clavicle and there was also porosity of the proximal end of the right humerus. The twelfth rib on the left side was completely fused to the vertebrae by a very smooth new bone growth.

Dental pathology

														C		C
PM P	P	P	P	P	PM	P			PM	PM	PM	P	P	P	P	P
18	17	16	15	14	13	12	11		21	22	23	24	25	26	27	28
48	47	46	45	44	43	42	41		31	32	33	34	35	36	37	38
P	P	P	P	P	P	PM	PM		PM	P	P	P	P	P	P	PM
C																

Attrition: there was a moderate degree of attrition on the first molars and light wear on the remaining molars. *Calculus:* deposits were moderate on the buccal surfaces of most teeth but heavy on the buccal surface of the upper left molars and upper right canine. There were moderate deposits on the lingual surfaces of most teeth but deposits were heavy on the lingual surfaces of the upper left molars and lower left molars. *Caries:* there was a small cavity on the mesial surface of 26 at the occlusal edge. The upper third molar, 28, had small cavity on the buccal surface, at the cervical margin and the lower third molar, 48, had a small cavity also on the buccal surface at the cervical margin. *Periodontal disease:* there was a slight degree of alveolar recession in the mandible and in the right side of the maxilla and a moderate degree of recession in the left side of the maxilla. *Hypoplasia:* linear enamel hypoplasia was noted in the upper right premolars and first molars and the upper right central incisor.

DISARTICULATED BONE

A minimum of seven individuals, based on the number of skulls, were found among the disarticulated remains. However, three of the articulated skeletons were missing their skulls and some of these could have been disturbed in medieval or post-medieval periods and reburied in pit 21. Therefore the minimum number of extra individuals from the disarticulated remains must be considered to be four. Although the bones are described here they are not included in the analysis of the remains as so little of the skeletons remained.

F1 This consisted of one right tibia shaft possibly from an adolescent and an animal bone.
F2 This consisted of one fragment of frontal bone.
F3 This was an animal vertebra.
F8 This consisted of a fragment of an ulna shaft and an animal bone.
F11 This contained the acromion and lateral border of a left scapula, the right ischium from a pelvis and a fragment of mandible. The proximal half of a left ulna from a juvenile was also present. **Dentition:**

42	41		31	32	33	34	35
PM	PM		PM	PM	PM	PM	P

There were also a number of animal bones from this context.
F14 This consisted of an almost complete right femur. There was also some animal bone.
F17 This consisted of animal bone.
F19 The long bones consisted of the distal third of a left femur, the distal two-thirds of a right humerus, the shaft of a left humerus, a complete left radius and the proximal two-thirds of a left ulna. Also present were an almost complete left ilium and a right ilium from a male. There were also some skull bones including a complete left parietal and the posterior half of a right parietal bone from the same skull.
F20 This consisted of a right parietal bone from a juvenile, a fragment of occipital bone and one left and three right ribs.
F21 This context contained a number of skulls and some long bones.
Skull A: This consisted mainly of the occipital bone with a few fragments of parietal bone. An animal jawbone was also present. **Skull B:** This consisted of a calvarium (the occipital), both parietal, both temporal and the frontal bones. It appeared to be from a male skull. **Skull C:** This consisted of an almost complete occipital bone with a right parietal bone fused at the lamboid suture. Also present was the right side of a frontal bone from the same skull. The skull was probably from a female individual. **Skull D:** This consisted of a complete frontal, sphenoid, right parietal, part of left

parietal, right temporal bone and a fragment of the left temporal bone from a female skull. **Skull E:** This consisted of a complete female cranium with only the left zygomatic bone missing.

Dentition:

PM	PM	P	P		PM	PM	PM	P		PM	PM	PM	PM	PM	PM	PM	PM
18	17	16	15		14	13	12	11		21	22	23	24	25	26	27	28

There was very little wear on the remaining teeth. **Skull F:** This skull was fragmented and included the right side of the frontal bone with the right orbit complete and part of the left side with the orbit incomplete. The right temporal bone and part of the right temporal bone was also present. This appeared to be a male skull. Also present was a small fragment of a child's frontal bone. **Skull G:** This skull consisted of a complete occipital bone, a right temporal bone, the right wing of sphenoid, a complete right parietal bone and a fragment of the left parietal as well as a fragment of the right side of the frontal bone with no orbits present. It appeared to be the skull of a male. **Skull H:** This consisted of a complete occipital, both parietal, the right temporal and the frontal bone, all in one piece. The sutures were well fused. Also present were the left temporal bone and most of the sphenoid.

Long bones The bones present included a complete right femur, a complete right tibia and the proximal end of a left femur. There was also a left patella and a fragment of acetabulum present.

F24 This consisted of the proximal end of a right humerus, probably from a male, the medial border of a left scapula and a fragment of ulna. There were also a number of animal bones from this context.

F29 The long bones included the proximal half of a right femur, the mid-shaft area of a right tibia, a distal third of a left tibia and a left ulna. There were also two fragments of parietal bone and the left side of a mandible. **Dentition:**

42	41		31	32	33	34	35	36	37	38
P	P		P	P	P	P	P	P	P	CA

There was very little wear on the teeth and calculus deposits were slight to moderate. Linear enamel hypoplasia was noted on the lateral incisor, canine and premolars.

Juvenile bones: Also present in this context were the proximal third of a right femur and the proximal half of a left humerus from juveniles.

F42 This consisted of the anterior part of a male skull, with the frontal, both parietal and right temporal bones, part of the shaft of a left humerus, the proximal end of a left radius and a left ulna and the second cervical vertebra. **Skeletal Pathology:** The metopic suture was retained on the skull. There was severe osteoarthritis affecting the left inferior articular surface of the cervical vertebra. **Dentition:**

C										
P	P	P	PM	P		PM	P	P	P	P	PM
15	14	13	12	11		21	22	23	24	25	26	–	–

42	41		31	32	33	34	35	36	37	38
P	P		P	P	P	P	P	P	P	P

Attrition: There was heavy wear on the upper teeth. The second left incisor had an unusual wear pattern. It was worn obliquely on the distal half of the tooth and had the appearance of a rodent tooth. *Calculus:* there were moderate calculus deposits on the buccal surfaces of the lower premolars and molars and the lingual surfaces of the incisors and canine. Deposits were light on the buccal surfaces of the lower incisors. *Periodontal* disease: there was a slight degree of alveolar recession in the mandible. *Hypoplasia:* linear enamel hypoplasia was noted on the lower left lateral incisor. Some animal bone was also found in this context.

F44 This consisted of animal bone.

The growth and decline of a medieval suburb? Evidence from excavations at Thomas Street, Dublin

EDMOND O'DONOVAN

INTRODUCTION

Dublin was the largest and most important town in Ireland during the medieval period. It was also the chief administrative seat of the Anglo-Normans, although the size of the walled town is smaller than many of its regional counterparts, such as Kilkenny. Dublin differed from other Irish towns in the fact that a significant proportion of the inhabitants lived outside the walls in the medieval suburbs. This paper looks at the nature of the archaeology recorded on an excavation at 119–121 Thomas Street (O'Donovan 1997, 31) and how the evidence compares with the emerging picture of the medieval suburb that developed outside the Newgate on Thomas Street (Clarke 1998; and Duddy above). Thomas Street is the principal street in the western suburb. It is aligned upon the Slige Mór, the great pre-Norman routeway to the west of Ireland that divided the island in two (Clarke 2002, 1). The street has been laid out along the axis of a natural ridge extending from within the city and was an important medieval thoroughfare that rapidly developed after the Anglo-Norman invasion. The archaeological excavation at 119–121 Thomas Street, directed by the writer, lies on the north side of the street 400m beyond the Newgate, straddling the edge of the ridge, which falls to the north down towards the River Liffey (fig. 1).

HISTORICAL AND ARCHAEOLOGICAL BACKGROUND

The abbey of St Thomas the Martyr, Dublin The abbey was established by William fitz Audelin at the command of Henry II in 1177. It received royal favour as it was founded in atonement for the murder of the archbishop of Canterbury, Thomas à Becket (Gwynn and Hadcock 1988, 172). The abbey was wealthy and powerful and in 1305 King Edward I confirmed the power to hold court, hence the name Thomas Court (Elliott 1990). At its dissolution the abbey held in excess of 2000 acres in manors beyond the city and had an

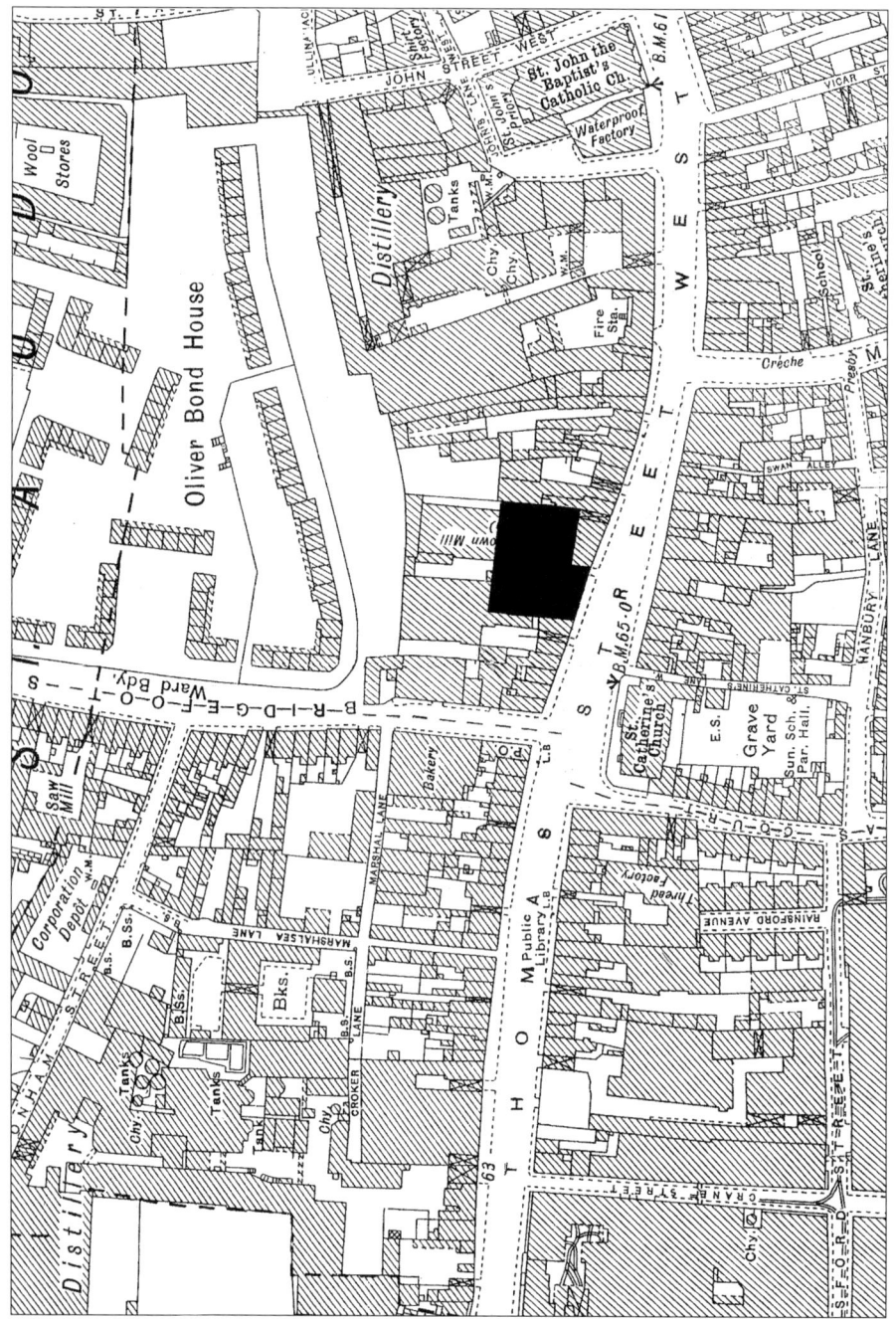

1 Site location

interest in some 46 rectories. There are no standing medieval remains of the Augustinian house, although archaeology has recently shed light on elements of its layout around Hanbury Lane and South Earl Street (Walsh 2000). The local street names, Thomas Court and Thomas Street, are of course another indication of the abbey's former existence. The lands surrounding the abbey became known as the Liberty of St Thomas (a judicial district comprising the lands of the abbey, independent from the jurisdiction of the city). The canons of St Thomas were granted lands at Donore and the liberty subsequently became known as the Liberty of St Thomas and Donore.

The hospital of St John the Baptist The priory and hospital of St John the Baptist lay at the eastern end of Thomas Street, on the site of the modern church of St John. It was positioned just outside the Newgate, the fortified gate that commanded the western entrance into the town. The hospital was founded between 1185 and 1188 by Ailred the Palmer and his wife and became known as 'Palmer's hospital' (Gwynn and Hadcock 1988, 212). It was run by brothers and sisters, the latter administering alms and food directly to the poor of Dublin. It was well loved in medieval Dublin, as demonstrated by the many bequests of land and property received from prominent citizens throughout the centuries.

Medieval settlement in the western suburb (fig. 2) The Anglo-Normans rapidly developed Thomas Street. The combined inertia of the Slige Mór and the foundation of the religious houses suggest that the primary suburban development occurred shortly after the invasion but was under way in the late twelfth century. There are references being made to 'Vicus Sancti Thome' by 1200 AD (Brooks 1936, no. 127). Documentary sources in the thirteenth century clearly indicate that the street was laid out in regular-sized property plots, some of which were inhabited. In 1264–5, a reference relating to Matilda de Yvielt mentions a burgage with edifices and appurtenances (ibid. no. 26), suggesting that the property plots on Thomas Street were occupied by dwellings. Further historical references in a grant to Roger Elys in 1273–4 (ibid. no. 39) refer to 'land with edifices and appurtenances in St Thomas's Street … between the land of Robert Ewelyn on the west and the land of the said Richard [Brabassun] on the east, being 19 feet on the front and extending in length from the great way (Thomas Street) to the land of the said Robert Ewelyn at the rear'. Such references to long burgage plots are mirrored in the emerging results from archaeological excavations (Carroll 1997). Medieval occupation deposits were uncovered and include evidence for iron-working on a plot extending south off Thomas Street opposite the hospital of John the Baptist (ibid. 55).

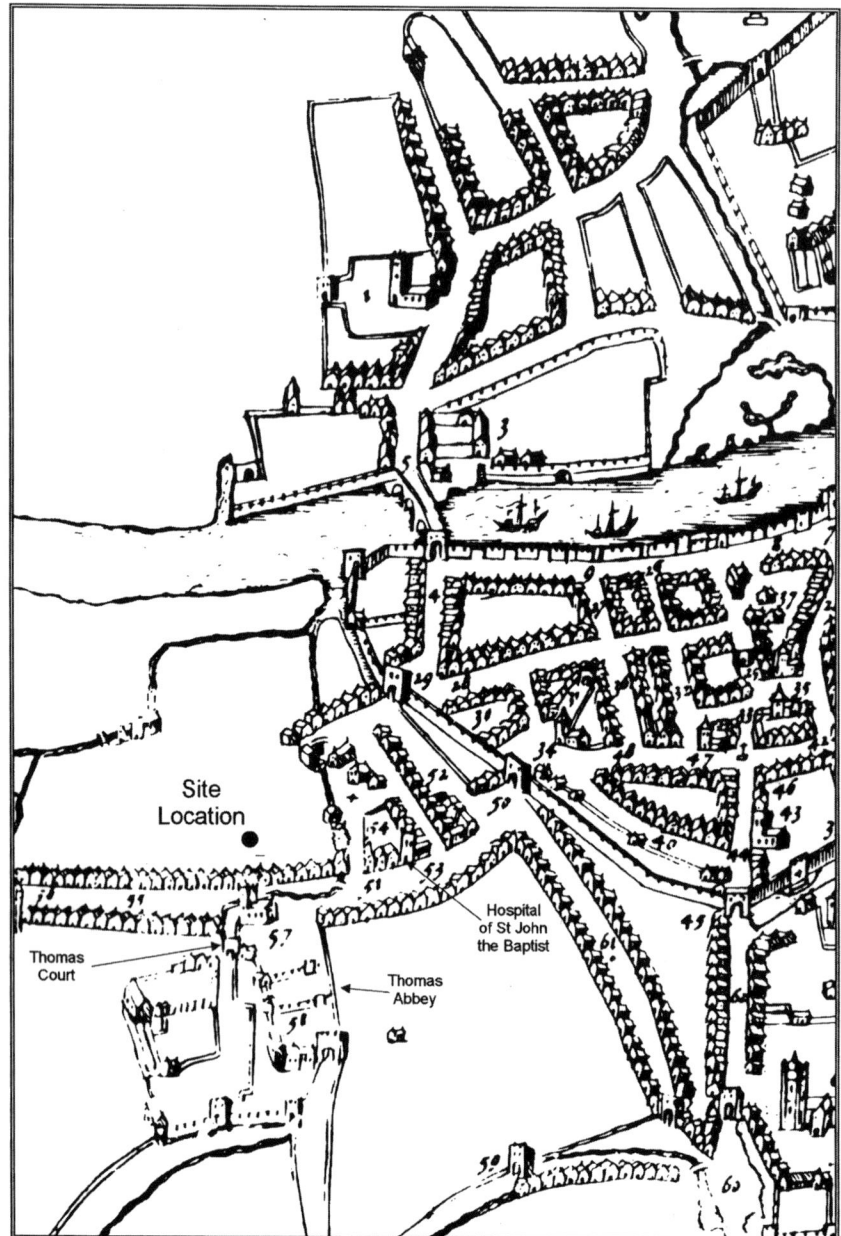

2 Speed's map of Dublin, 1610

Millers and potters in the western suburb Milling was an important component of medieval life both in terms of the production of food and in revenues tied to long-standing rights associated with mills and mill-races. The city had many mills located in the surrounding suburbs. The topography of the western suburb of Dublin was especially suited to milling owing to the presence of several natural watercourses that could be diverted over the natural ridge on which Thomas Street is laid out. Gilbert records the presence of a mill at Mullinahack north of the hospital of St John the Baptist, at the close of the twelfth century (1854–9, i, 351), demonstrating a long milling tradition on the watercourse. Joyce translated Mullinahack as *Muileann-a'-chaca*; muilleann is the Irish word for mill and the remainder of the phrase was politely interpreted by Joyce as indicating a state of disuse at the mill (1995, 166–7), whereas, of course, the name translates as 'the mill of the excrement'. It is not, however, known why the twelfth-century Irish inhabitants of Dublin would attribute such a name to this particular mill.

The watercourses were culverted over time and disappeared from the streets as the channels were conduited and re-channelled. The Camac river approached from the south-west and originally supplied the Viking town with fresh water (Sweeney 1991, 34). A second watercourse, identified as 'Crockers Barres', ran along Crockers' Street (Potters Street, the present day Oliver Bond Street and Marshal Lane). Crockers' Street was an important street in medieval Dublin located to the north of Thomas Street, orientated east/west. It was here that the potters had their kilns, well outside the city walls and beyond where they might have posed a fire hazard. A reference dated to 1435 refers to the 'fossam de les Croker Barres' (the ditch of the Crocker Barres) that was close to the 'pratum Cradocii' (this was a field which belonged originally to the Cradoc brothers, who may have been Welsh). This field was later granted to the hospital of St John the Baptist and it is recorded as having been located to the north of Crockers' Street (Brooks 1936, nos 2, 3, 146).

Speed's map of Dublin (1610) and early post-medieval Thomas Street
The oldest existing map of Dublin, by John Speed, is dated 1610. It illustrates the layout of the streetscape in some detail including the suburbs. The map records the character of the late medieval city. It depicts buildings lining Thomas Street from the town wall at the Newgate to Thomas Court, with the exception of land surrounding St Catherine's church on the south side of the street. To the north of Thomas Street lies open ground where the Camac flows into the Liffey. The Poddle/Glib watercourse flows through the abbey on the west side of St Catherine's church along the northern side of the street before turning north by the hospital of St John the Baptist. It is difficult to identify Crockers' Street on the map. Medieval mills are illustrated at St Thomas's abbey and to the west of the hospital of St John at Mullinahack.

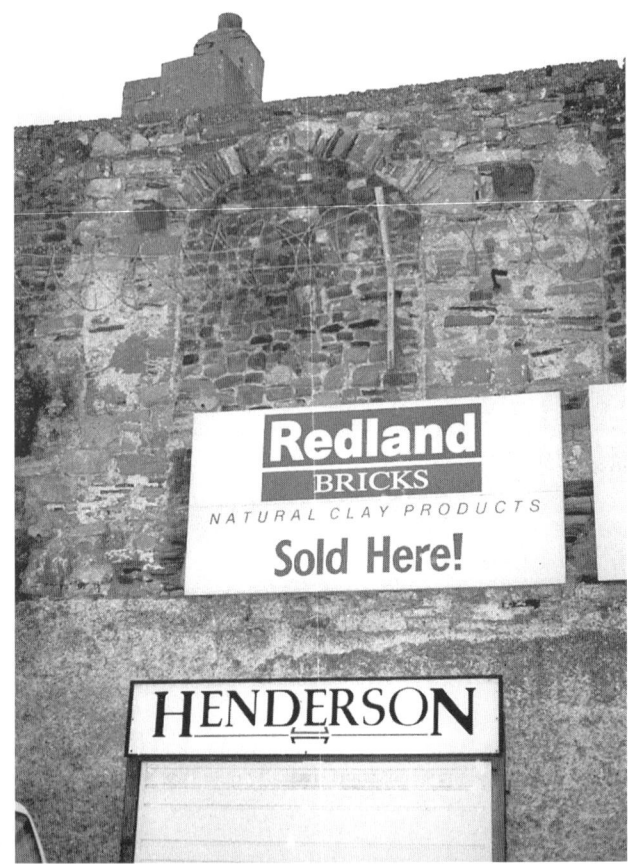

Plate 1 Blocked
opening, *c.*16th/
E 17th century, 68
Thomas Street

Crockers' Street is thought to have begun near Mullinahack Mills and extended westward along Oliver Bond Street. The documentary sources in 1558 refer to gardens on Thomas Street (Griffith 1991, 159), and later in 1609 a reference states that there are 'empty plots in Thomas Street' (ibid., 159). These empty plots contrast with Speed's illustration, which suggests a stylistic approach as opposed to purely depictional mapping. A fragment of a sixteenth/early seventeenth building survives on the southern side of Thomas Street in the yard of Chadwick's Builders Suppliers (No. 68, Thomas Street). Corbelling and segmental relieving arches are present in the side wall of the yard. These features are indicative of Irish houses of the period (plate 1).

Rocque's map of Dublin (1756) and later post-medieval Thomas Street
The Liberties was an industrial centre in Dublin in the seventeenth century (Whelan 1992, 407). This was based upon the tradition of milling established in the medieval period and the inertia this created, but also to an influx of

3 Rocque's map of Dublin, 1756

French Huguenots, and Dutch and Flemish Protestant settlers in the mid-seventeenth century and into the eighteenth century (Craig 1980, 86). This created the impetus for the re-building of much of the area, involving the demolition of many of the earlier Tudor and medieval buildings and their replacement by the 'Dutch Billy', brick gable-fronted buildings owing their architectural origin to northern Europe. John Rocque's map of Dublin, dated 1756, shows the extent of these changes and the evolution of the modern city. The abbey of St Thomas had been completely built over by the mid-eighteenth century (fig. 3).

SUMMARY OF EXCAVATION RESULTS

Introduction

The medieval archaeology at 119–121 Thomas Street The predominant medieval archaeological feature identified at the site was simple pits cut into the underlying natural boulder clay and gravel. Less numerous medieval pit forms, lined with either stone or timber, accompanied these. Thirty-two pits were recorded at the site and ranged from 1 to 2.5m in depth (plate 2). Medieval garden soils and areas of burning lay above the old ground surface. Pottery was the principal dating tool and 1,760 sherds were recovered from the site. Metal and other ceramic artefacts and animal bones were also recovered and a small number of the principal features on the site are described below to illustrate the archaeological character of the excavated features. The archaeological deposits are the physical remains of the daily lives of the inhabitants of the medieval suburb. The archaeology dates from as early as the thirteenth century and is domestic in character, although evidence for small-scale craft industry was also identified. Modern basements and buildings fronting onto Thomas Street disturbed much of the western half of the site along the immediate street front.

Post-medieval archaeology at 119–121 Thomas Street Post-medieval features that were recorded, overlying and cut into the medieval features on the site, included wells, pits and deposits of clay (garden soil). The archaeological activity is derived from domestic occupation to the rear of dwellings fronting onto Thomas Street. These archaeological deposits were subdivided into two distinct phases of activity dating from the seventeenth (early post-medieval) and eighteenth century (later post-medieval). Layers of post-medieval clay remained undisturbed *in situ* on the south-eastern side of the site over earlier medieval garden soils.

Modern archaeology at 119–121 Thomas Street The site was substantially altered in the middle of the nineteenth century with the construction of the Blanchardstown Mills and constant re-building of houses and shops fronting onto Thomas Street. The depth of the basement of this industrial building involved a reduction in ground level and the removal of earlier archaeological deposits to varying degrees across the site. The medieval and early post-medieval deposits only survived in the south-eastern corner. The construction of the Mills involved the relocation of substantial amounts of soil from the south to the north end of the site (Gowen 1996, 22–3).

The excavation

The medieval timber-lined pit (plate 3) An oak-lined pit measuring 0.65m north/south and *c*.2m east/west, survived to a height of 0.48m in the

Plate 2 Cutting 1, interlocking pits, 119–121 Thomas Street

Plate 3 Medieval timber lined pit

waterlogged deposits. The original function of the feature is not clear, although it was not a cess pit. The box structure was built with overlapping planks held in position by vertical corner posts. The posts were converted into squared timbers with a single rectangular projecting side tenon, giving both timbers a T-shaped cross section. The ends of both timbers were cut into a four-faceted pencil point and driven 0.40m into the subsoil. The walling of the box structure rested on the base of the pit. The west side-wall of the box was built from five horizontal planks roughly nailed together. The north and south walls were built from vertically set planks. The east wall did not survive. Two of the oak planks (F148:13 and F148:15) were dendrochronologically dated. The best estimated felling date established for the timbers was AD 1207 ± 9 years (F148:13) and AD 1206 ± 9 years (F148:15) (Brown 1997). The co-relation value between the tree ring series is very significant. It is highly likely that both planks were from the same tree. All of the planks in the pit show very irregular close-set growth rings, which does not favour their interpretation as reused ship timbers, as one would expect good quality and regular growth-ring patterns in timbers used for these purposes. The growth pattern suggests the timber was harvested from slow irregular locally grown oak trees (David Brown pers. comm.).

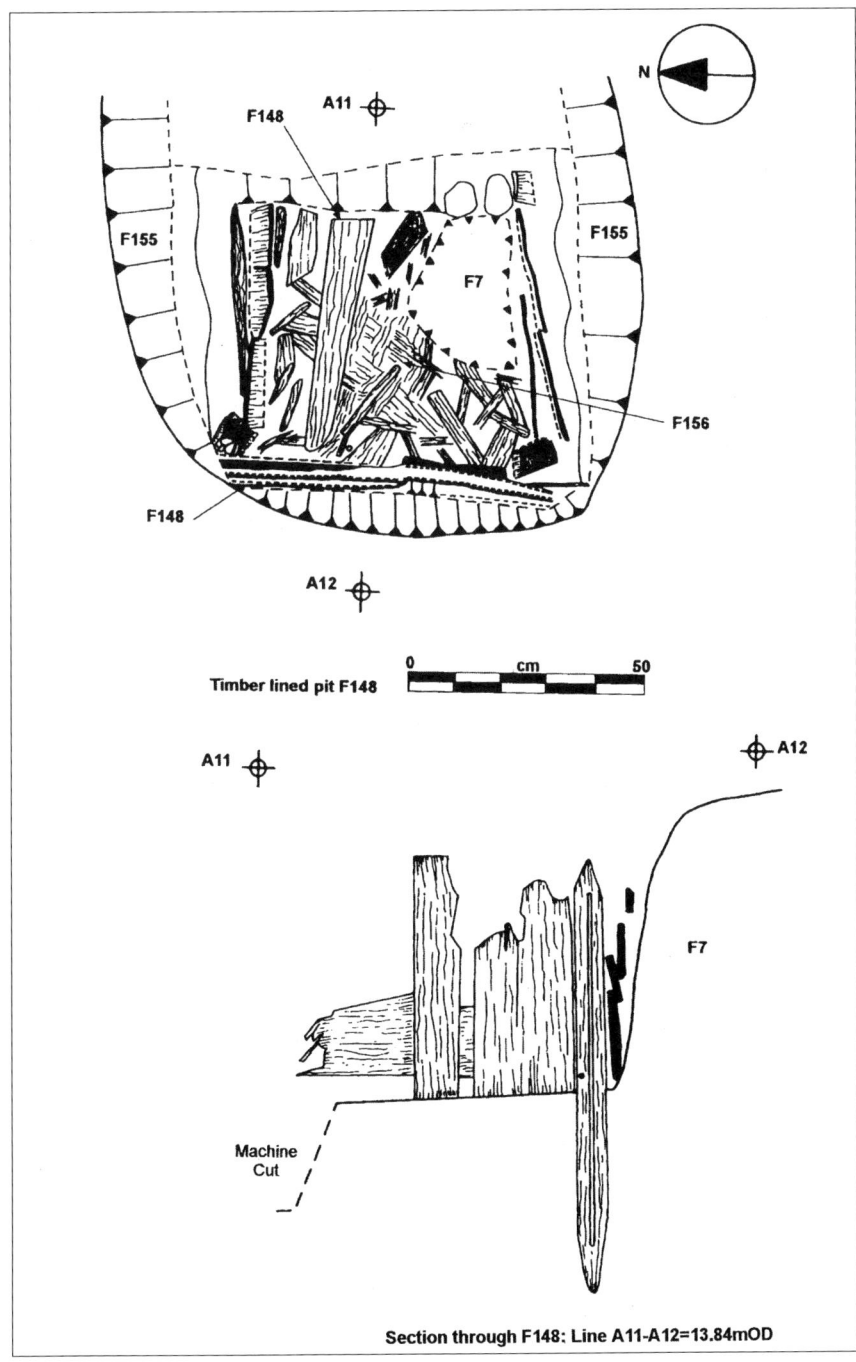

Timber lined pit F148

Section through F148: Line A11-A12=13.84mOD

4 Timber lined pit

Plate 4 Medieval layer of wood in a cess pit

Of the fifteen structural timbers used in the construction of the timber box, only the two T-sectioned upright posts were definitely reused. The tenons and nails present on these posts had no function in the structure. The rough construction of the remainder of the pit suggested that it may also have been built from reused timbers, although this is by no means certain, as the nails present on these structural timbers were used to hold the planking together and no clear vestigial wood-working details could be identified. If the dated timbers are secondary to the feature, which is unlikely as the softer sapwood was still present on the timbers, they still confirm an early thirteenth-century phase of activity in the vicinity of the site.

The base of the pit was lined with a thin (0.05m) deposit of organic and small poorly preserved wood chips, ranging from to 0.04 to 0.06m in diameter (fig. 4). A sample of the wood chips was submitted for analysis (Ingelise Stuijts, pers. comm.) and yielded 31 degraded oak (quercus) chips, seven ash (fraxinus) chips and one fragment of wild cherry (prunus avium, 5 years old). Macro plant analysis (Collins 1997) and beetle studies (Reilly 1997) were carried out on samples taken from the deposit and the results from the analysis of the beetles from the fill indicated that the organic material contained decayed thatch. Wood

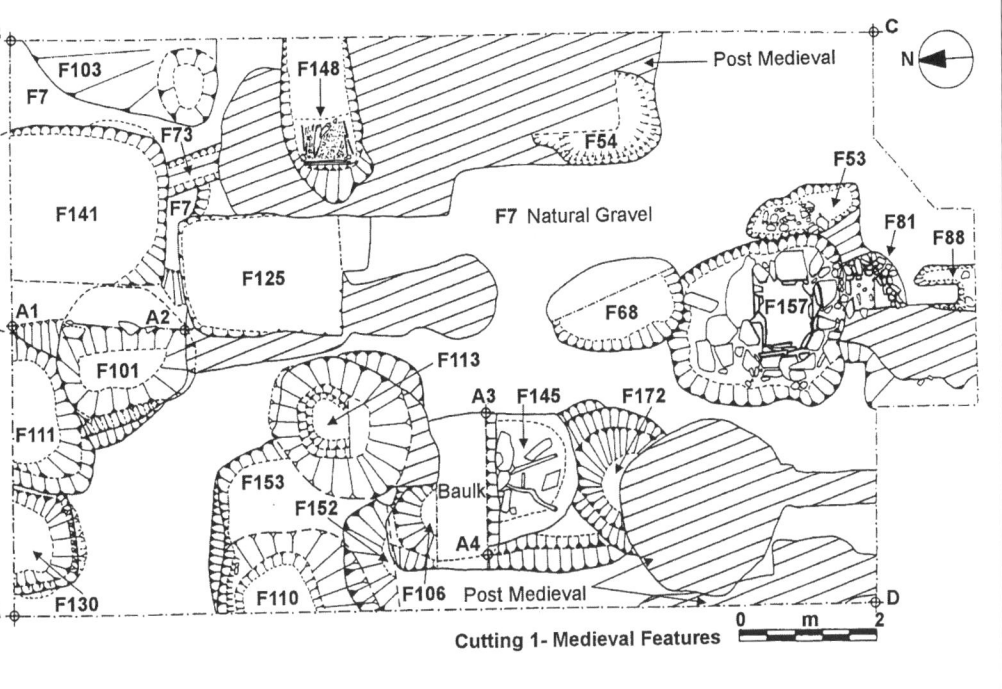

5 Cutting 1, interlocking pits

chipping was a common flooring material in the Middle Ages and hence the fill in the pit appears to have been derived from rotted house debris. Some pieces had very large insect channels. It was suggested that these were made by pale-worms, which are common in waterlogged wooden structures. An oak (quercus) artefact (96E286:148:17) from the pit is likely to have functioned as a wooden bucket handle.

Interlocking unlined medieval pits A dense concentration of six inter-locking pits was located in the middle of the western side of the site. The pits were all roughly circular in plan and ranged from 2.10m to 3m in diameter and from 1.40m to 2.10m deep (plate 4). The earliest pits were of a similar size (1.75m in diameter and 2.10m deep) and were filled with an organic cess deposit containing many sherds of pottery, animal bone and wood. A later pit measured 3m north/south, 1.9m east/west and 1.8m deep. The base of the pit was filled with soft organic cess. A layer of wood was located on top of the cess deposit, indicating that the pit had gone out of use. The wood consisted of six irregular fragmentary oak planks and oak bark with average dimensions of 0.37m in length and 0.09m in width. The rings from the planks suggest slow growth indicating poor growing conditions (Ingelise Stuijts, pers. comm.).

A single 12-year-old roundwood of regularly grown crab apple branch (Pyrus/Malus) was cut during the summer, as the growth ring was almost complete. The wood was not arranged to form any structure. The remainder of the pit was filled with green gravelly re-deposited boulder clay. A further three steep-sided circular pits, measuring 1.30m in diameter and 1.35m deep were identified to the north of this. These pits were also filled with thin layers of organic sealed by upper fills of stony grey gritty clay (fig. 5).

The stone-lined 'trough' and other unlined pits The medieval activity at the southeast end of the site centred on a large sub-rectangular stone-lined pit that functioned as a well or water trough. It measured 2.50m north/south, 2.30m east/west, 2m deep and had a stepped base lined with irregularly shaped flag-stones. The deposits contained animal bone and medieval pottery, including an almost complete pottery jug (96E280:168:76) and a decorated leather scabbard (96E280:160:1). The silty nature of the fills and their waterlogged state suggests that the stone 'trough' held standing water prior to being infilled. The trough was sealed by a buff gravelly re-deposited natural clay.

A medieval cesspit A sub-circular pit was cut into the upper fill of the stone-lined water 'trough'. The pit was steep-sided with a flat bottom and measured 1.75m in diameter and 0.90m deep. The base of the pit was filled with a thin deposit of brown organic cess (0.07m thick). Overlying the organic and on the sides of the pit was a dense deposit of ash and charcoal, dumped household rubbish. The upper deposit in the pit was a green/grey clay mixed with stones (*c.*0.05m in diameter) filling the remainder of the feature. Analysis of the soil (Collins 1997) indicates that the basal deposit consisted of poorly humified cess. A coprolite was identified in the fill. The thin charcoal deposit overlying the cess appears to have been derived from dumped raked-out hearth material from a local source. The main uppermost deposit indicates backfilling with re-deposited natural, possibly to create a firm ground surface after the feature went out of use as a toilet and rubbish pit.

Medieval barrel pit (plate 5) A roughly rectangular pit was cut into the natural boulder clay. The feature measured 1.50m north/south and 1.18m east/west. Timber barrel-staves were placed in the pit and held in position by groups of tightly wound hazel binding rods. The void behind the barrel-staves was back-filled to create a circular, timber-lined pit. The barrel pit was 0.87m in diameter at the top and tapered to 0.74m in diameter at its base. It was truncated and survived to a depth of 0.60m. Fifteen of the barrel-staves survived *in situ*. There were no wooden timbers lining the base of the structure. Five or six of the barrel staves were removed by later activity. The staves originated from at least two different barrels. The staves varied in width

Plate 5 Medieval barrel pit

from 0.015 to 0.06m. The groove to hold the base of the barrel, which was vestigial in this structure, was 0.05m above the bottom of each stave. None of the barrel staves were decorated and two are described in the small finds report. The staves in the barrel pit were reused. They were held in position by eighteen thin hazel-bound hoops tightly woven around the timber-lined pit, bound by willow strips. The hoops were made from half split hazel rods (Corylus), 4–7 years old and measured 0.03m in diameter. The binding strips were made from willow branches (Salix), 1–2 years old, measuring 0.005–0.007m in diameter. The use of hazel and willow was the most common method of fastening barrels in the medieval period. The fifteen barrel-staves recovered from the feature were all made from regularly growing oak (Quercus), showing stable growing conditions. The wood was very hard and its quality suggests that it was not locally grown and was imported specifically for coopering (Ingelise Stuijts, pers. comm.). The widest single barrel stave (96E280: 169:7) was submitted for dendrochronological dating, but yielded only 73 annual growth rings when measured, too low a value for dating (Brown 1997).

THE SMALL FINDS

Pottery
by Clare McCutcheon and Catherine Johnson

Introduction A total of 1,760 sherds of pottery were recovered from the site, of which 1,365 (78%) dated to the medieval period (mid-12th–14th centuries AD). The material was entirely domestic refuse and no fragments of kiln waste were recovered, although Crockers' Street, parallel to Thomas Street, was so named from at least the 1190s (Brooks 1936). All of the wares recovered are widely known from archaeological sites in Dublin and elsewhere in Ireland and detailed descriptions of fabrics and forms are already published or readily available (e.g., Papazian 1997; McCutcheon 2000). Several semi-complete or representative pieces were selected for illustration and are discussed below.

Irish Medieval Wares

Leinster cooking ware 'Leinster Cooking Ware is the single most widespread medieval pottery type in Leinster' (Ó Floinn 1988, 340). The majority of vessels in this assemblage are standard cooking pots with everted rims (fig. 6:1). Of interest, however, are the fragmentary remains of at least one jug (figs 6:4 and 6:6). The jug had a strap handle, probably with a row of central stabbing. The rim had continuous thumbing and the jug possibly had a pulled spout. A similar piece was recently recovered from excavations at Francis Street/Swift's Alley, Dublin. This had a large pulled spout, thumbed rim and stabbed handle (McCutcheon forthcoming). The base of a possible jug was also recovered at Thomas Street (fig. 6:6). Not enough of the base was present to show the characteristic sand marking of the Leinster cooking ware, nor was it fire-blackened. A row of thumbing was present above the line of the base. Jugs are uncommon, particularly in north Leinster (Ó Floinn 1988, 328), which makes this assemblage all the more interesting.

Dublin-type cooking ware (fig. 6) This is a generic term, used to cover unglazed, micaceous cooking ware, which is clearly not Leinster cooking ware (McCutcheon in prep.). Some of the vessels are hand-built and some are wheel-thrown and, in addition, there is a wide variety in the fabric, from very coarse to fine. This reflects the Dublin-type wares, but no attempt has been made to define specific cooking wares contemporary with the glazed wares. This category of Dublin-type cooking ware, therefore, dates from the late twelfth through the thirteenth century. Figures 6:1, 6:3, 6:7, and 6:8 illustrate a number of variations on the standard everted rim cooking pot. In one (plate 6 and fig. 6:2) there is a suggestion of a rim seating, which may have held a lid, while in another (fig. 6:7) faint lines of horizontal scoring are probably decorative. In contrast, a large cauldron (plate 7 and fig. 6:9) shows a definite

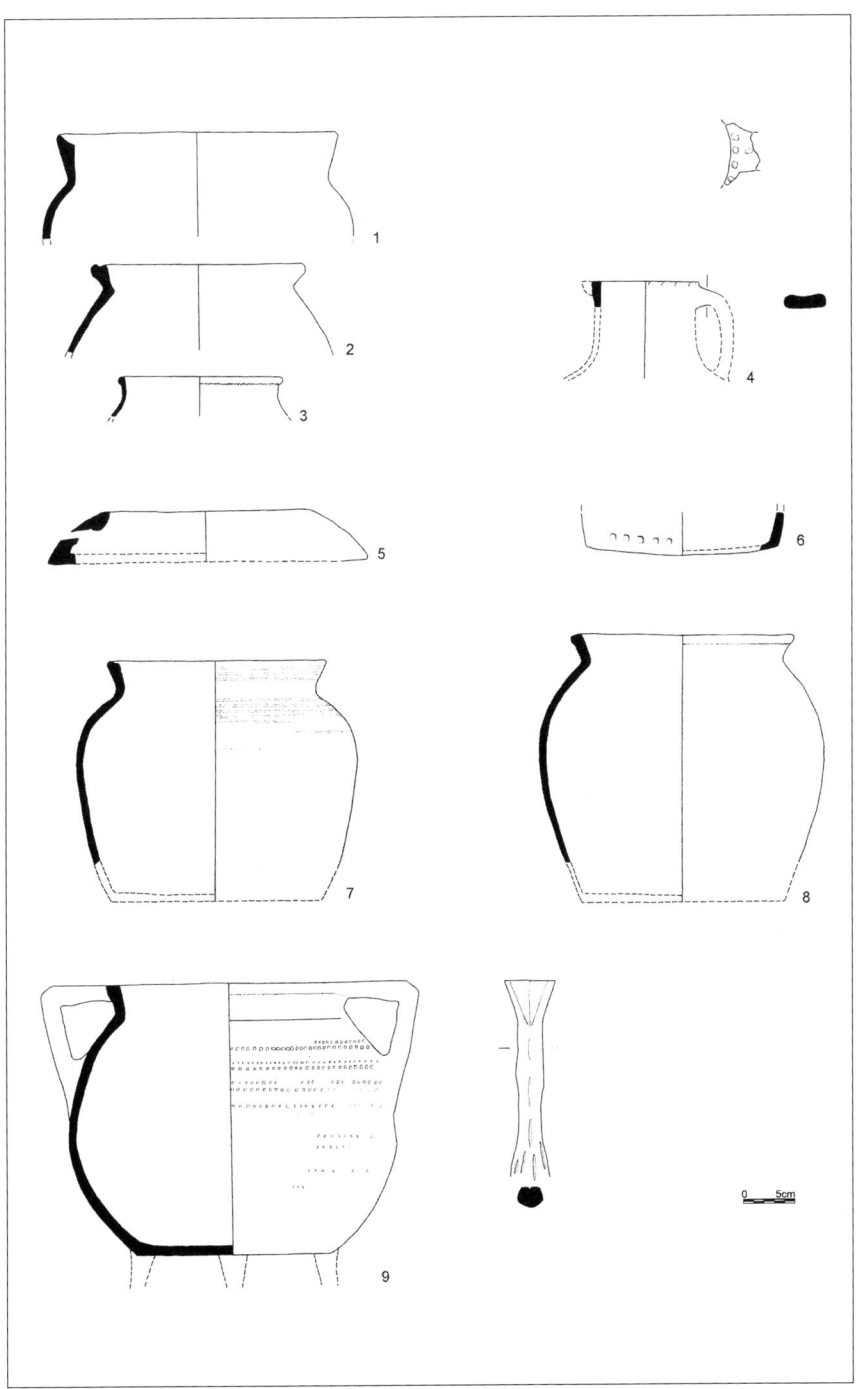

6 Dublin and Leinster wares

Plate 6 Dublin–type cooking ware pot, with evidence for lid

variation on the standard everted rim pot. Horizontal lines of square rouletting cover most of the body of the pot. Two angular handles extend straight out from the rim, paralleling contemporary metal cauldrons. The rod handle has decorative slashing on it. An almost identical piece with slashed handle and squared rouletting was recovered at the Wood Quay excavations (McCutcheon in prep.). It is assumed that three pods or feet were added to complete the vessel (Pearce et al. 1985, fig. 69). An unusual vessel is an incurved dish (fig. 6:5), similar to West Country vessels (McCarthy and Brooks 1988, 125, figs 1558 and 1559). This is a shallow, flat-based vessel with slightly inward-sloping walls and a single hole perforated through the side near the base (ibid.). Their exact function is unknown but is variously described as being connected with cheese-making and bee-keeping (ibid.). While the fabric appears similar to 'Vale Fabric Type 2', i.e., chocolate coloured (ibid., 369), the presence of mica flakes in the Dublin vessels probably indicates a clay source near Dublin. Similar vessels have been found at Wood Quay and Francis Street/Swift's Alley (McCutcheon in prep.; *eadem* forthcoming).

Dublin-type coarse ware A large quantity of this hand built, coarse fabric ware was found, but no semi-complete piece could be reassembled. There are many similarities in style between this ware and the Ham Green B ware, including bridge spouts, stabbed handles, rim finish and thumbed bases.

Plate 7 Dublin–type cooking ware cauldron with handles and everted rim

Dublin-type ware This wheel-thrown glazed ware is the main category of thirteenth-century pottery in Dublin. As noted above, a large quantity of Dublin-type ware was reassembled, and therefore the vessel count, rather than the sherd count, reflects more accurately the quantity of material. Two semi-complete vessels are illustrated (plates 8, 9 and figs 7:4, 7:5), along with an unusual strap handle (fig. 6:1). The larger of the jugs (plate 8 and fig. 7:4) has a small pulled spout, strap handle and a flat, plain base. There is an applied, thumbed, horizontal decoration around the rim, and this is often found in Dublin-type wares. The top of the rim shows a number of fractures prior to firing, but these obviously did not affect the function of the vessel. The handle has continuous vertical slashes, again a design regularly found both in Dublin and in other locally made medieval wares in Ireland, although the design appears to be more popular in Cork (McCutcheon 1995 (b)). The second jug (plate 9) has a much more pronounced, pulled spout, evidence for a strap handle, and a thumbed base. Decoration consists of incised straight and wavy lines. The detached handle (fig. 7:3), in contrast to the commonly found incised decoration, has two vertical rows of applied thumb strips.

Dublin-type fine ware The assemblage of this temper free glazed ware was very fragmentary, as evidenced by the large quantity of sherds representing a small number of vessels. The development of late forms is shown by the presence of a bowl and a probable chafing dish.

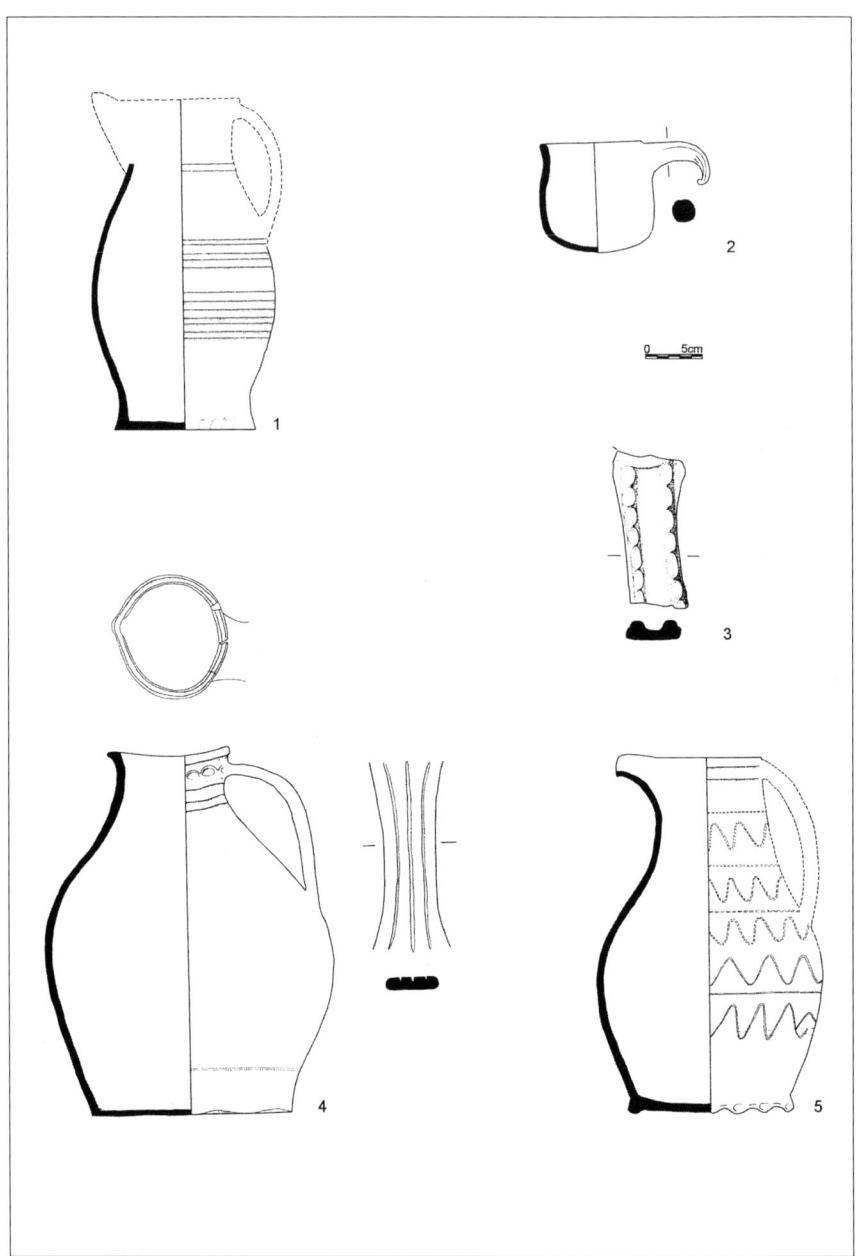

7 Dublin and imported wares

Plate 8 Dublin–type ware jug

English Medieval Wares
The fabric of the Bristol ware has been described in detail and petrologically analysed by Vince (1988, 258–64).

Ham Green A small quantity of this hand-built glazed ware was recovered. The forms have been discussed at length (Barton 1963; Ponsford 1991). The small quantity of this ware reflects the essentially thirteenth-century date of the Thomas Street assemblage.

Redcliffe Redcliffe ware, also from Bristol, is the wheel thrown successor of the Ham Green wares. By the mid-thirteenth century 'it is thought that Ham Green was put out of business by these new products' (ibid., 95). Very little is found in Dublin assemblages, a reflection of the successful local pottery industry. In contrast, similarly dated assemblages in Cork, for example, may contain up to 10% of Redcliffe ware (McCutcheon 1997, fig. 27a). A semi-

Plate 9 Dublin–type ware jug

complete jug was recovered from Thomas Street (plate 10 and fig. 7:1), but unfortunately the handle/rim/spout section is missing. The fabric of this jug has the characteristic 'sandwich' appearance with cream/buff external surfaces and a grey core. The jug is decorated with a series of horizontal incised lines around the body and the slightly splayed base has a pattern of groups of four thumb marks. Generally, these vessels had strap handles.

Continental Medieval Wares
Saintonge mottled green and unglazed wares Saintonge wares were imported from the Bordeaux area throughout the thirteenth and fourteenth centuries as a by-product of the wine trade (Clarke 1983, 19; Deroeux and

Plate 10 Redcliffe ware jug

Dufournier 1991, 163). The fabric is a fine, white earthenware and the mottled glaze was achieved by the addition of copper filings to the clear lead glaze. The vessel represented is a jug, probably a tall wine jug, with flat base, bridge spout, strap handle and a simple decoration of vertical, applied thumbed strips. The unglazed sherd probably represents a three-handled pitcher, known as a *pégau*. These large, squat vessels were also probably used for wine.

Paffrath This ware was first described by Dunning (1959, 76) and appear to have been used as ladles or mugs. The pottery type is also known as blue/grey wares and was made near Cologne in Germany from the late tenth to the fourteenth centuries (plate 11 and fig. 7:2). In Ireland they are consistently found in early thirteenth-century contexts, e.g. Waterford (Gahan and McCutcheon 1997, 320) and Patrick Street, Dublin (Papazian 1997, 125).

Unidentified The number of sherds recovered represents a minimum of four vessels, three jugs and a cooking pot. They could not be positively identified as to fabric, and are simply grouped here as medieval, possibly thirteenth-century, given the association.

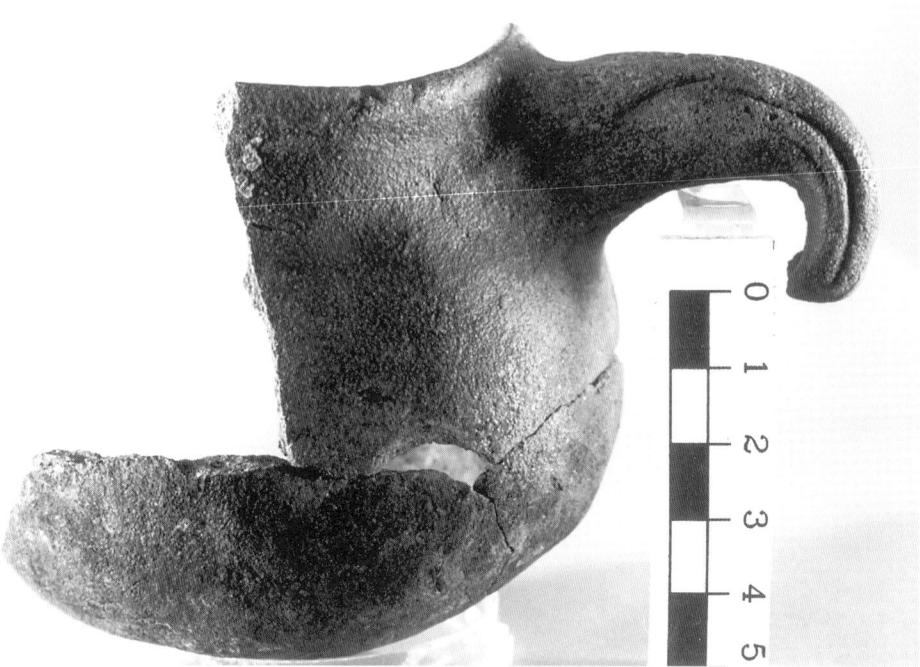

Plate 11 Paffrath ware ladle/mug

Conclusions: Medieval (table 1)

As stated above, the assemblage reflects a domestic context rather than kiln waste in spite of proximity to the known pottery-production area of Crockers' Street, which lay north of and parallel to Thomas Street. The Dublin-type jug (**fig. 2:4**) with fractures on the rim, shows that what might now be classified as a 'second' or reject was still used, as these faults did not affect the function of the vessel. The presence of the Paffrath ladle and a small quantity of Ham Green ware indicates some residual material from the early thirteenth century. The presence of the Redcliffe jug and the Dublin-type fine ware shows that the assemblage continued beyond the mid-thirteenth century, but the complete absence of any of the Saintonge decorated wares may indicate a terminal date of the late thirteenth century for the assemblage.

Post-Medieval Wares (table 2)

The late medieval and post-medieval pottery identified and presented in table 2 are all types well represented in assemblages from Dublin and elsewhere (Meenan 1994; McCutcheon 1995 (a)). A quantity of nineteenth- and twentieth-century chinaware and stoneware was also recovered. These

Table 1 – Medieval Wares

Type	Sherds	MNV	Form	Date
Leinster Cooking Ware	152	11	10 cooking pots, jug	12th–14th
Dublin-type cooking ware	336	22	19 cooking pots, cauldron, baking dish, incurved dish	12th–13th
Dublin-type coarse ware	378	15	12 jugs, 3 pipkins	L12th–E13th
Dublin-type ware	107	17	11 jugs, 4 storage vessels, pipkin, bowl	13th
Dublin-type fine ware	323	6	>4 jugs, bowl, ?chafing dish	L13th–14th
Ham Green B	12	1	Jug	L12th–M13th
Redcliffe	5	1	Jug	M13th–14th
Saintonge mottled green glazed	14	1	Jug	13th–14th
Saintonge unglazed	1	1	?Pégau	L13th–14th
Paffrath	4	1	Ladle	L12th–E13th
Unidentified	33	4	3 jugs, cooking pot	medieval
Total	**1,365**	**80**		

wares are not generally included as part of a post-medieval pottery assemblage, the cut off date being *c*.1800. A small quantity of white earthenware was found and this is assumed to be from Beauvais, although recent research by D. Gaimster suggests that this ware may also have been made in Frechen (J.G. Hurst pers. comm.). Of interest are the Westerwald vessels, which represent a range of material from the seventeenth and eighteenth centuries. Two of the jugs were largely reassembled. Both have the characteristic mottled grey salt glaze and stamped medallion decoration, one with a heart in a lozenge-shaped medallion (**fig. 8**), the other with foliage motifs in a heart-shaped medallion. In addition to the distinctive cobalt blue colouring, both have manganese purple, which was added to the blue style of decoration in 1665 (Noël Hume 1970). The chamber pot is of the eighteenth-century type, with incised design and flat rim.

Table 2 – Post-medieval wares

Type	Sherds	MNV	Form	Date
Beauvais	3	2	jugs	16th
Saintonge	2	2	chafing dish, unidentified	16th
Mature Valencian lustreware	1	1	bowl ?	16th
Seville coarseware	7	1	olive jar	17th
Merida type	2	1	jar ?	17th
Cologne	3	1	jug	16th
Frechen	1	1	jug	16th
Westerwald	38	>5	4 jugs, chamber pot	17th–18th
Tin glazed earthenware	30	8	3 wall tiles, chamber pot, ointment jar, 3 bowls	17th–18th
North Devon gravel free	7	1	jug	17th
North Devon gravel tempered	24	3	pancheon, chamber pot, cooking pot	17th
North Devon sgraffito	5	3	plate 5	1630–1700
North Devon slipware	1	1	plate	18th
Anglo Netherlands slipware	9	2	2 plates	17th
Blackglazed ware	59	5	2 bowls, two storage vessels, jug	18th–19th
White salt glazed stoneware	11	3	saucer, bowl, cup	18th
Bristol/Staffordshire slipware	12	7	3 plates, 3 ointment jars, bowl	18th
Mottled ware	131	13	11 tankards, cup, plate	18th
Glazed red earthenware	47	8	jug, 4 plates, handled bowl, wide bowl, storage jar	18th–19th
Porcelain	2	2	saucers	18th–19th
Total	**395**	**70**		

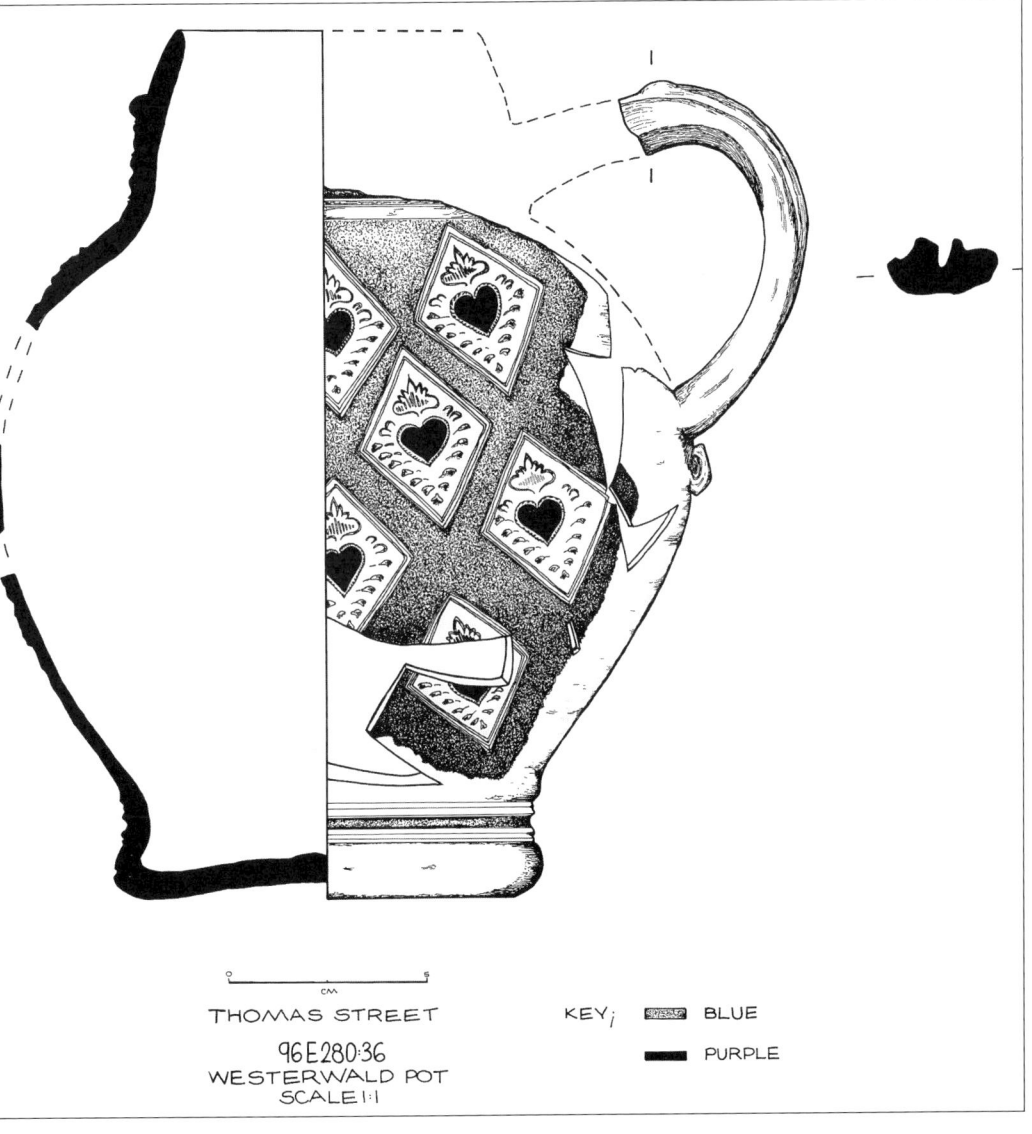

THOMAS STREET

96E280:36
WESTERWALD POT
SCALE 1:1

KEY: BLUE

PURPLE

8 Westerwald jug

Conclusions: Post-Medieval

The post-medieval wares date from the late sixteenth to the nineteenth century, but predominantly from the seventeenth and eighteenth centuries. North Devon wares are found on practically every Irish site of seventeenth-century date and the success of their production was, to a certain extent, a consequence of the exploration and exploitation of the American colonies. In

Dublin, the main eighteenth-century wares are varieties of black glazed pottery. Their predominance in Dublin can be attributed to the proximity of the production centres of Liverpool and the Buckley area of North Wales but black glazed wares were also made locally in Dublin. The later eighteenth century saw the success of the Staffordshire potteries, with a variety of manufacturing techniques. Two sherds of porcelain were also found. Porcelain was exported in vast quantity from China from the seventeenth century onwards (Hurst et al. 1986, 9).

The Small Finds
by Catherine Johnson

Introduction (fig. 9) This site was issued with the excavation number 96E280. For convenience, the excavation number has been omitted, so that the finds are referred to by the feature number, followed by a colon, followed by the find number within the feature. Only a selection of the datable medieval finds are listed in this paper. The advice of Michael Kenny, Paul Mullarkey and Raghnall Ó Flóinn of the National Museum of Ireland is acknowledged.

Metal non-ferrous
Buckle 17:160 (plate 12 and fig. 9:4) is a well-made copper alloy buckle, with an oval lipped and bevelled frame. The bar is offset and constricted for the pin. The external dimensions of the frame are 29x28mm and the internal measurements are 22x18mm. The pin, which is now bent, is 20mm long and tapers from 3.5mm to a point. Integral with the frame is a forked spacer, which would originally have had two separate pieces of sheeting soldered onto it to form a hollow plate. The spacer is 45mm long, 21mm wide and 2mm thick. The top of the spacer is cut into a stepped pattern and the two prongs taper from 3mm wide to a point. This item belongs to a group of distinctive, high quality buckles with integral forked spacers, onto which composite plates are soldered. They appear to be a specifically English form and are very rarely found on the continent (Egan and Pritchard 1991, 80). In Britain they are widespread from the mid-fourteenth to at least the early fifteenth century (ibid. 55). A similar buckle was recovered from excavations at Patrick Street, Dublin, from fourteenth- to sixteenth-century contexts (Hayden and Walsh 1997, 135). There may well have been a type of quality control in operation with regard to these buckles, and the spacer may be the 'double point' referred to in the regulations of the London Girdlers' Guild, recorded in 1344 (ibid. 80). This type of buckle represents the best quality, as well as the most labour-intensive, of the mass-produced buckles of the time (ibid. 82).

Buckle/brooch 17:161 (**plate 13 and fig. 9:3**) is a plain circular frame with pin, which could have served either as a brooch or a buckle on clothing or a

Plate 12 Copper alloy buckle　　　**Plate 13** Copper alloy buckle/brooch

harness. The frame and pin are of copper alloy and both are corroded. The frame is incomplete and approximately one quarter of it has disintegrated into tiny fragments. There is a small external projection, which may be corrosion or a small knob or lip. The frame has an external diameter of 28mm, an internal diameter of 24.5mm and a circular section. The pin has a rectangular section, tapering from 3mm wide x 1.2mm thick, and is looped around the frame. It is 32mm long. This is a common medieval form, which continued in use into the post-medieval period (Egan and Pritchard 1991, 64).

Metal ferrous: iron
Awl? 17:158 is a grit-encrusted iron object, tapering at both ends, from 10x8mm at the centre to 4.5x3mm and 4x5mm at the ends. The object appears to have a rectangular section. Length 78mm. The object was recovered from a medieval context.

Metal ferrous: lead
Hinged lid 68:24 (plate 14 and fig. 9:2) is a single piece lead hinged lid, with an incomplete central circular bowl, 26mm in diameter, 4mm deep and 1mm thick. The convex face of the bowl is decorated with raised dots in raised

Edmond O'Donovan

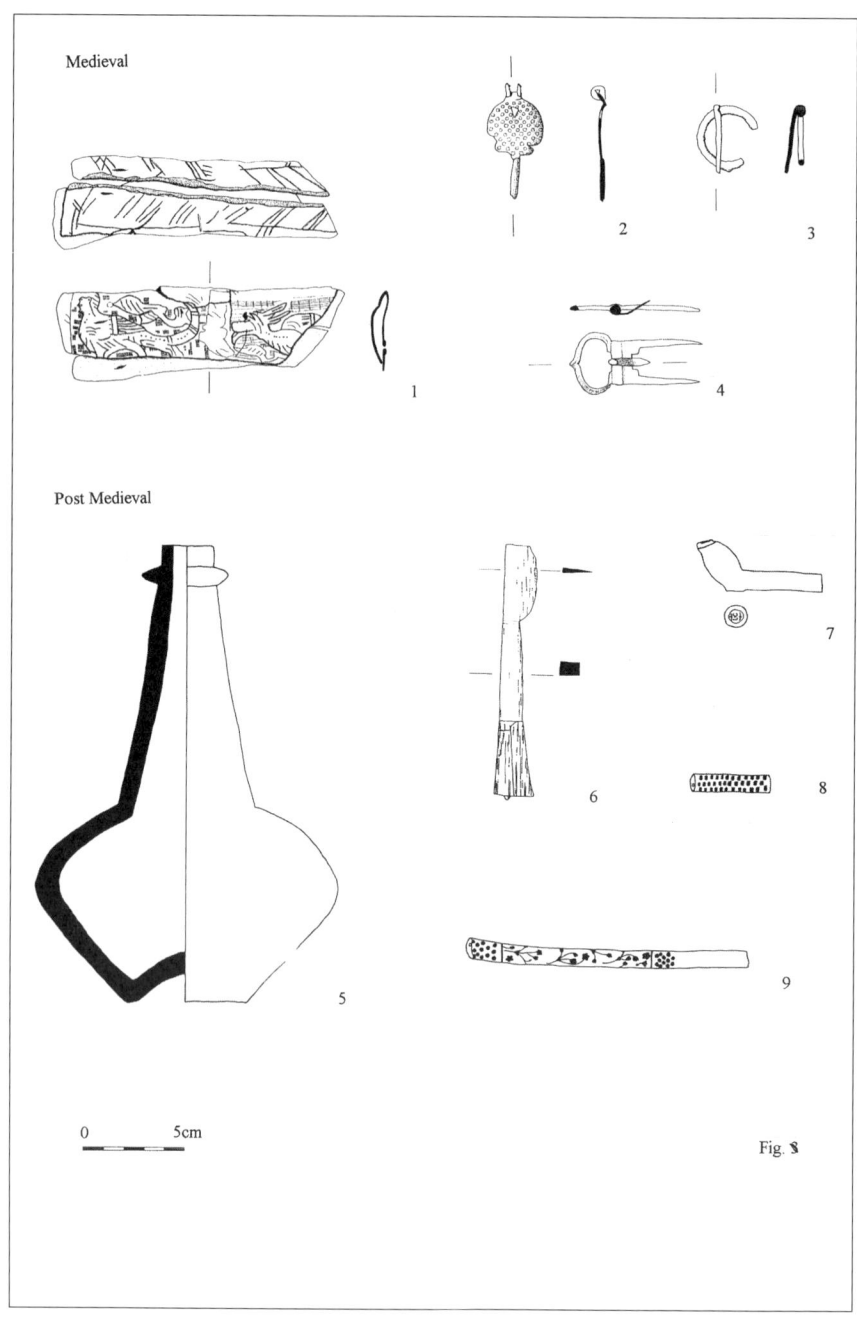

9 Small finds

Plate 14 Lead hinged lid

Plate 15 Decorated leather scabbard

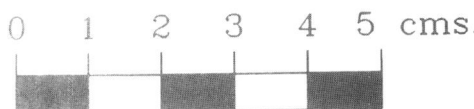

linked circles. The bowl also has a 4mm-long triangular-shaped hole. On the edge adjoining the hole is a pair of 7mm diameter pierced lugs, which act as a hinge. Facing the hinge, on the other side of the bowl, is a 20x2.5x2mm. prong, with a lozenge shaped section. The prong is broken at the end. I am grateful to Raghnall Ó Flóinn for drawing my attention to the fact that the prong is probably sprue residue, formed when the molten lead was poured into the mould through a sprue. The fact that this residual piece of metal was not removed from the object, and that the rough edges were left on the hinge, indicates that the object was a reject. The lid was probably intended for either a lead weight box or a mirror case, such as the lead, tin or copper alloy mirror cases recorded from excavations in London (Egan and Pritchard 1991, 358–362). The lead tin examples from London have a pre mid-fourteenth century date (ibid. 365).

Leather
Scabbard 160:11 (plate 15 and fig. 9:1) is an incomplete, decorated sheath
measuring 135mm long by 31mm wide, with a centre back seam and edge/
grain stitches. The sheath is now in two fragments. One half of the back
appears to have been cut away along the fold and the second half is torn along
the fold. The sheath was also cut diagonally across the width. There is an
8mm-long slit on either side of the upper back, to allow suspension from a
belt or thong. Both front and back of the object are decorated. The decoration
is divided into panels corresponding to the division between knife and blade,
which is a convention of such objects (Cowgill et al. 1987, 40). The back of
the sheath has engraved linear decoration and the front has embossed
zoomorphic decoration, on a background of punched dots arranged in blocks.
The decoration on the handle section depicts a long-bodied bird with curly
tail feathers/plant tendrils. The blade section is decorated with a winged
beast, unfortunately truncated when the leather was cut. A leather sheath
comparable to the one from Thomas Street was recovered from thirteenth-
century levels during excavations at High Street, Dublin (Maxwell 1980, 35
and National Museum of Ireland 1973, plate 13). The sheaths are very similar
both in the layout of the decoration and the appearance of the embossed
animal and bird motifs. De Neergaard has noted that from the mid-thirteenth
into the fourteenth centuries many decorated scabbards feature zoomorphic
decoration, which is occasionally embossed and frequently has a background
of stamped dots (Cowgill et al. 1987, 41). Parallels for the long-bodied bird
can be found among the sheaths recovered from London excavations. One of
these sheaths dates to the early/mid-thirteenth century (ibid., no. 378).
Another is unstratified (ibid., no. 475). An unstratified scabbard from the
same excavations has an embossed winged beast (ibid., no. 489).

Glass
Bottles: 15:8 One complete bottle was recovered from the excavations. It was
a dark green wine bottle of mid-seventeenth century type. The bottle was
fashioned with a globular-shaped body 140mm in diameter, and a long neck
measuring 115mm. The overall height of the bottle is 220mm and it has a very
small kick-up, 45mm in diameter. There is a triangular sectioned string ring
for holding down the cork. This type of bottle was in use during the mid-
seventeenth century. In his reference work on artifacts of colonial America,
Noël Hume includes an English wine bottle, very similar to this, with a seal
dated 1661 (Noël Hume 1991, 63, fig. 8).

Ceramic building materials
Medieval crested ridge tiles The assemblage included five sherds of crested
ridge tile, a type that was first introduced into Ireland by the Anglo-Normans
in the thirteenth century (Wren 1997, 149). Two of the tiles (nos 49:12 and

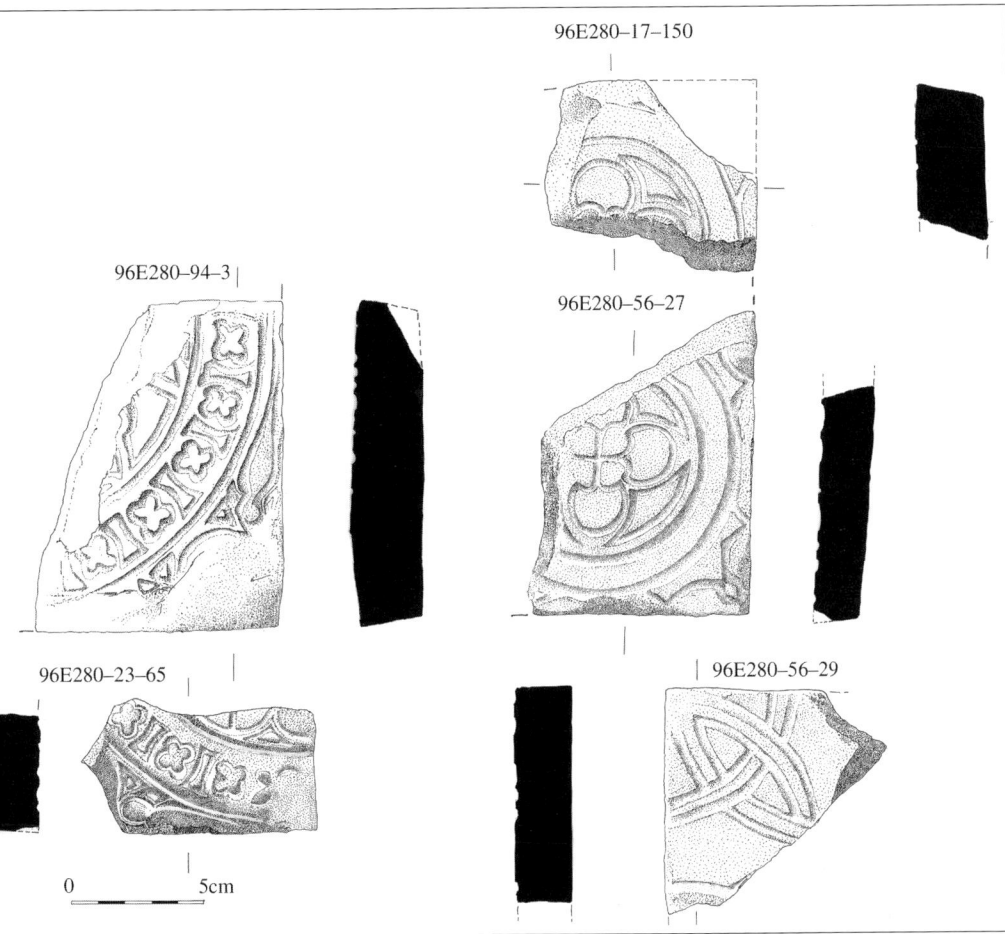

96E280–17–150

96E280–94–3

96E280–56–27

96E280–23–65

96E280–56–29

0   5cm

10 Floor tiles

79:6) have flat-topped crests. Production of tiles with flat-topped crests began in central and northern Leinster in the thirteenth century and continued until the fourteenth century (ibid. 1997, 149). The crests are missing on two of the fragments (nos 1:79 and 97:12). The external surface of no. 1:79 was decorated with incised vertical lines and has a mottled green glaze.

Pantiles Thirty-eight fragments of red roof tiles were recovered but none were complete. All are unglazed, with smooth upper and sandy underside. The tiles were highly fired to a red/orange colour. Pantile production began in the seventeenth century (Wren 1997, 152). Tiles were made locally, as well as imported, and tile wasters were recovered from excavations at Dublin Castle (ibid. 152).

Medieval floor tiles (fig. 10) Forty-four fragments of medieval floor tiles were recovered. The decorated tiles are described below, following Eames and Fanning's typology (Eames and Fanning 1988). Ten floor tile fragments (nos 20:43, 61:42, 97:168, 173, 175, 177 and 179; 100:77, 103:1 and 111:3) could not be categorised due to their small size or because the top surface was missing. Five tiles (nos 52:261, 71:110, 88:20, 92:88 and 93) were either unglazed or the glaze had worn away. The prefix letter indicates the type of decoration (T=two-colour, L=line-impressed, R=relief, M=mosaic) and the serial number following refers to the decorative motif on the tile. **Mosaic tile** 23:66 is a plain, triangular shaped tile (type M5), broken along one side. It has a complete, black/brown glaze, which has dribbled onto the two remaining edges, dimensions: 118x115x28mm. In their reference work, Eames and Fanning list type M5 tiles from one site only, namely St Canice's cathedral, Kilkenny (Eames and Fanning 1988, 79). **Two-colour tiles:** Four fragments were recovered. Three fragments (nos 71:111, 71:115 and 100:78) were not identifiable to type. The remaining fragment is either of type T59 or T60. **Line impressed mosaic tiles:** 93:1 is a triangular-shaped mosaic tile with line impressed decoration, depicting the hindquarters of the lion rampant sinister in 4-foil. An upper corner of the tile, which would have shown the animal's head, is missing. Only one of the three edges is complete. The tile has a speckled green glaze, which has dribbled slightly onto the edges. There are no triangular-shaped line-impressed mosaic tiles in Eames and Fanning's typology. This shape occurs only amongst two colour decorated mosaic tiles, as well as plain ones, such as no. 23:66 (see above). The decoration is a truncated version of that found on tile no L4 (Eames and Fanning 1988, 119). The Thomas Street tile was cut across the centre before firing, as indicated by the presence of glaze on the edge of the tile. Line-impressed tiles: The assemblage included twenty-two fragments of line-impressed tile. Of these, eleven could not be identified because the fragments were either too small or the tile surface was too badly damaged to do so. The remaining eleven fragments represent nine different motifs, all of them previously recorded. L4 (no. 82:81 and possibly 97:170); L18 (no. 52:254); L35 (no. 1:80); L43 or 44 (no. 17:150); L44 (no. 58:27); L46 (no. 79:7); L52 (no. 56:29); L64, 65, 66 or 67 (no. 111:2); L76 (no. 23:65); L77 (no. 98:77).

Clay pipes
Bowls: Twenty-four pipe bowls were recovered, and include both spurred and flat-heeled varieties. Only one (no. 1:52) is stamped. Four of the bowls have decoration in the form of milling around the rim. All date to the seventeenth/early eighteenth century. **Decorated clay pipe stems:** Three stems were highly decorated. No. 1:42 (fig. 9:8) has very ornate relief floral and linear decoration. The surface of no. 1:57 (fig. 9:9) is completely covered with a relief 'butterfly' motif. No. 58:15 is stamped with fleur-de-lis in

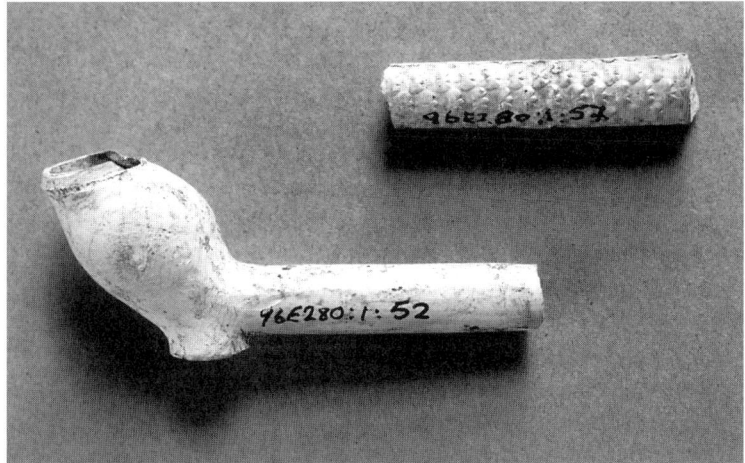

Plate 16 Clay pipe bowl and decorated stem

lozenge-shaped panels, with horizontal bands of milling. The fashion for decorating stems with diamond-shaped fleur-delis stamps was most popular in the mid-seventeenth century (Noël Hume 1991, 305). Nos 1:53 and 1:76 have simple bands of milling.

Wood

Wooden plate/bowl: 109:1; 2 (fig. 11:1) are two fragments of a turned wooden utensil. The plate/bowl is fashioned from ash and appears to be sub-rectangular in shape, measuring 117mm in diameter. The base is 11mm thick and flat. The sides of the vessel are missing, although they extend from the base at a 45-degree angle. **Wooden Object** 148:1 (fig. 11:3) is a piece of worked oak of unidentified function, possibly a bucket handle. It is 283mm long, 6mm thick, and tapers from 53–5mm at the ends to 35mm in the centre. The object has a rectangular section and all surfaces are smooth and flat. Both ends are cut into a wide V-shape and each has an 11mm-wide circular perforation. A pair of small V-shaped notches, cut into the long axis of the wood, do not mark mid-point but are 123mm from one end and 160mm from the other end. There is a patch of rust-coloured stain on one face, close to the notched area, which indicates contact with a metal object. This object came from a context with dated to 1206/7 ± 9 AD.

Barrel staves (fig. 12): No. 169:1 is an incomplete barrel stave. The upper end of the stave did not survive and it is concave in horizontal section. The stave has a V-shaped groove at its base when the base of the barrel would have attached. The grove is 3mm wide and 5mm deep located 50mm from the base of the stave, which was chamfered at a 45-degree angle. Adze marks on the

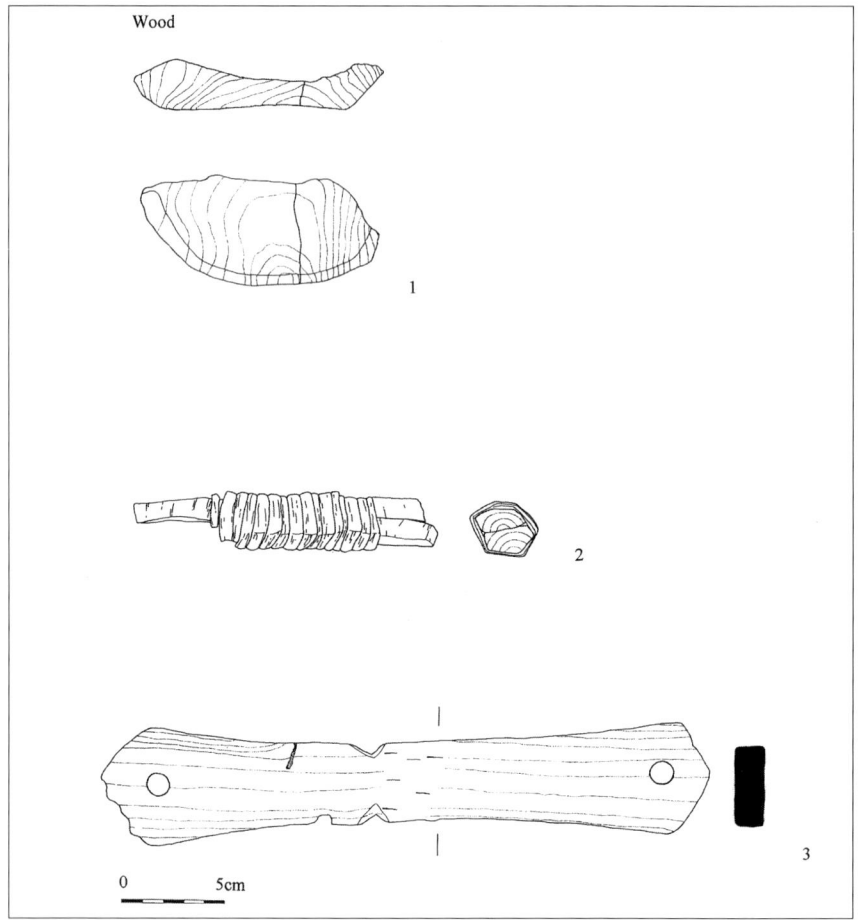

11 Wooden objects

interior of the stave are present above the groove. Length: 620mm. Width at base: 100mm. Width at top: 110mm. Thickness: 15mm. Oak, radial conversion. No. 169:9 is an incomplete barrel stave. The upper end of stave did not survive and it is concave in horizontal section. The stave has a V-shaped groove at its base when the base of the barrel would have attached. The grove is 4mm wide and 4mm deep located 50mm from the base of the stave, which was chamfered at a 45-degree angle. Adze marks on the interior of the stave are present above the groove. This barrel stave differed from the others. Two wooden dowels inserted through the bottom of the stave held the base of the barrel in place. Portions of two dowels were still in situ in the dowel holes. The dowels were 10mm in diameter and were made from hazel (Corylus; Ingelise Struijts, pers. comm.). Length: 510mm. Width at base: 70mm. Width at top: 75mm. Thickness: 15mm. Oak, radial conversion.

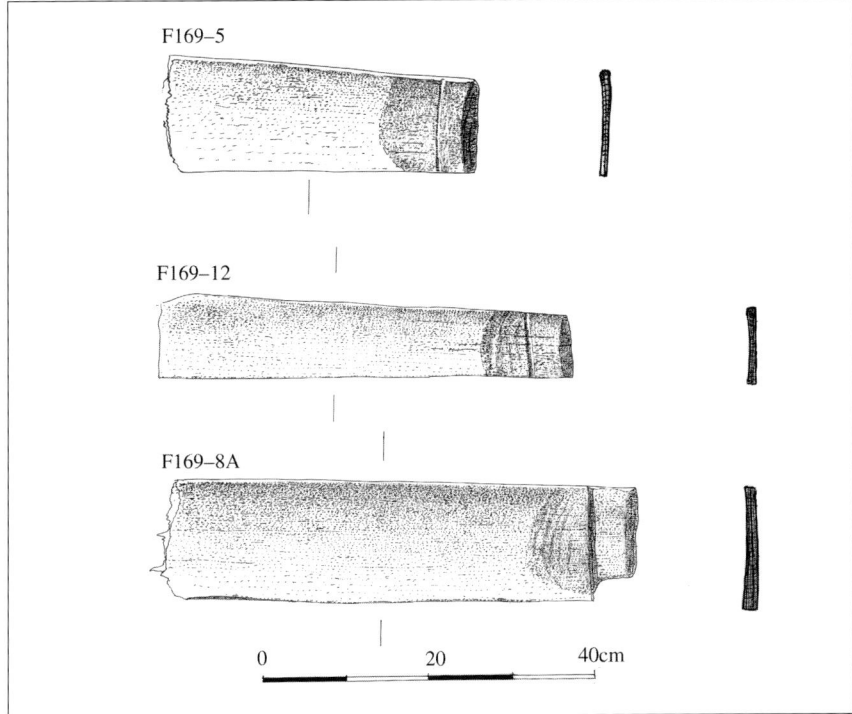

F169–5

F169–12

F169–8A

0   20   40cm

12 Barrel staves

Miscellaneous objects
Coprolite 103:28–29 Two pieces of oval-shaped coprolite or human medieval excrement were recovered from a cesspit. They measure 35x25x20mm and 40x20x18mm.

DISCUSSION

The location of the excavation The site was located outside the city walls on Thomas Street, at the western end of the 'great new street' (Gilbert 1889, 404). Its proximity to the powerful new abbey of St Thomas the Martyr, the ancient Slige Mór and the presence of numerous watercourses, was pivotal to the area's growth and expansion. No archaeological deposits were identified at the Oliver Bond Street end of the properties and the excavation clearly identified that the focus of archaeological activity fronted onto the northern side of Thomas Street.

The nature of the archaeological activity The excavation revealed two distinct phases of archaeological activity (medieval and post-medieval). These phases of activity did not represent single events, but a series of episodes of activity within the two chronological periods. This is demonstrable on site through the relative stratigraphy and interlocking features implying a sequential chronology for the site.

The medieval period (1200–1400?) Three archaeological feature-types were uncovered during the excavation: rubbish/cess pits, stone and timber-lined pits and occupation deposits or garden soils. The excavation located fifteen rubbish/cess pits. These features varied in size from 1.75 to 3m in diameter and from 0.9 to 2.25m deep. Some pits were completely filled with black organic cess and their function was obvious. Other cess pits had been cleaned out or emptied, back-filled with natural soil and only retained a thin layer of the original organic deposits at the base. The deliberate back-filling of pits was evident in four examples. The analysis of the beetles from these pits confirmed the presence of decomposer and foul-indicating species. In other cases where the pits had been cleaned out, the re-deposited material accumulated over a period of time along with domestic rubbish. This is indicated by the presence of animal bone, pottery and house fauna insect-remains (Reilly 1997). Three medieval features were typologically distinguishable from the rubbish/cess pits. These consisted of the plank-lined pit, the wooden barrel pit and the stone-lined pit. Both the barrel pit and stone-lined pit had silty fills and appeared to have functioned as water troughs or wells. A near complete jug (96E280: 168:76), missing its handle, was found in the basal fill of the stone-lined pit. It is tempting to speculate that the jug was deposited into the pit while collecting water as the handle broke away. The nature of the function of the timber-lined pit is not clear. The analysis of the beetle remains indicated that the fill in the feature consisted of decayed thatch and other house refuse, suggesting the presence of buildings in close proximity. The clay building material (floor tiles and roof tiles) also indicates the proximity of buildings that are likely to have once fronted onto Thomas Street. This, however, does not shed light on the primary use of the feature.

Objects, dates and economy The domestic material culture of the thirteenth century has been well illustrated by the National Museum's excavations in Dublin (Wallace 1981) and more recently during other excavations throughout the city, such as at Essex Street West (Simpson 1995) and Patrick Street, Nicholas Street and Winetavern Street (Walsh 1997). The artefacts excavated on the Thomas Street site compare closely to the artefacts from these excavations and date to the period from 1200 to 1400 AD. The earliest activity on the site has been dated to the late twelfth or early thirteenth century. This is based upon the results of the dendrochronological determinations from the timber-lined pit. The early date for the site is supported by the evidence from the pottery. Dublin-type cooking ware (L12–13th), Dublin-type course ware

(L12–E13th) and the Paffrath ladle (L12–E13th) were all found on the site. The sherds of Paffrath ware from this site form part of a drinking cup imported from Germany. The terminal medieval event on the site was the accumulation of a series of layers of 'garden soil' which produced artefacts such as the bronze ring brooch (96E280: 17:1) and the belt buckle (96E280: 17:2), indicating a later medieval date for these deposits. The line-impressed floor tiles were the only find type that dated from the early fourteenth to early sixteenth century, suggesting fifteenth- and sixteenth-century occupation on the site. The pottery assemblage recovered in the excavation totalled 1,374 sherds. The medieval pottery ranged from the late twelfth to the fourteenth century. The site lies to the south of the supposed location of Crockers' Street (Oliver Bond Street) that is thought to be one of the manufacturing locations of the medieval potters of Dublin. The wide range of types and provenance of the wares represented, including locally manufactured cooking vessels, glazed jugs and imported pottery from England, France and northern Europe demonstrate that the pottery represents local household use. No kiln waste was present and rather than being indicative of manufacturing, the pottery has a domestic character. The small finds include a range of artefacts also dating from a similar time span. These included a belt buckle (96E280: 17:160), ring brooch (96E280: 17:161), leather scabbard (96E280: 160:11) and a lead mirror case (96E280: 68:24). The lead mirror case had its casting tang still attached to it. A finished object would have had the tang removed and as such it can be suggested that it is unfinished and likely to have been manufactured locally. A small quantity of slag was recovered from several features that dated from the medieval period. This supports a picture of craft activity being carried out.

All bones recovered from medieval features during the excavation were collected for analysis (Cremin 1997). The number of bones recovered from each individual feature was low and they were amalgamated into one sample, giving rise to the problem that the sample is clearly not contemporary. The medieval activity took place over at least a period of two hundred years. The analysis of the animal on a grouped basis introduces the problem that the functional evolution at the site may remain unrecognised in the faunal record. The pattern established from the study of the bones suggests that the assemblage relates primarily to meat consumption (domestic habitation) and not slaughtering. The bone assemblage did not indicate the presence of large numbers of horn cores or metatarsals, normally associated with tanning. The range of animals present reflects the domestic meat diet consumed in the Anglo-Norman period and compares closely to the pattern established at Essex Street West (Bermingham 1995) and Waterford (McCormick 1998), although the overall bone count is low. The relative lack of faunal remains may indicate that the place of consumption was located a short distance from where the bones were found.

The function and culture of medieval Thomas Street The archaeological evidence, both from the excavated remains, finds and faunal evidence, is indicative of medieval domestic settlement coupled with small-scale local manufacturing (evidence from the lead mirror case and slag). The artefacts of these first inhabitants of Thomas Street compare closely with the material cultural remains excavated from Anglo-Norman levels in the city (Wallace 1991). This comparison suggests that the suburban dwellers were akin materially to their counterparts within the walls. After the Bruce invasion of 1315–18, many of the citizens of Dublin sought and received compensation from the king for the damage rendered to the suburbs in preparation for a siege (Clarke 1998, 47). The level of compensation demonstrates not only that the citizens need not have lived within the confines of the town wall, but also that many of the inhabitants of the town resided and traded in the suburbs of the city in the early fourteenth century. The early dendrochronological dates from Thomas Street indicate that this focus or shift of settlement beyond the city walls was well under way by 1200 and was not confined to a small number of plots extending from the Newgate, but as far west as St Thomas's abbey. Historical references and dendrochonological dates from a large number of sites and excavations demonstrate that the early thirteenth century was a period of dynamic growth. This is demonstrable with the construction of many large Castles, such as at Dublin (*c*.1210–28 AD; Lydon 2002), Kilkenny (*c*.1200–25 AD; McNeill 1997, 242), Carrickfergus, period II (1215–23 AD, ibid. 1997, 239) and Limerick (built by 1212, Barry 1987, 65) and bridges such as Baals Bridge in Limerick (*c*.1210–20 AD, O'Donovan, 2000) and water-fronts at Drogheda (*c*.1204–5+9 AD, Sweetman 1984) and Dublin (*c*.1200 AD, Halpin 2000). This considerable expansion must also have been accompanied by a parallel growth of population as is evident on Thomas Street. No evidence for Irish or late Vikings Age objects was identified in the excavations at Thomas Street, although it is not clear how these groups, if they were inhabiting the locality, would distinguish themselves in the archaeological record by 1200 AD, if at all.

The late medieval hiatus (1400–1600) There is little evidence for later medieval, fifteenth- or early sixteenth-century, archaeological activity on the site. The pottery types, such as the Saintonge, Redcliffe and Leinster cooking ware date from as late as the fourteenth century, although they may by the same token be as early as the thirteenth century. Post-medieval clays were deposited directly over the medieval clays. The absence of any identifiable phase of late-medieval activity suggests in the first instance that the site was abandoned by at least the fifteenth century. This break in the occupation of the site could reflect a wider decline experienced by the city and within Anglo-Norman settlements throughout the country. Duffy describes the Anglo-Norman presence in Ireland in the early fourteenth century as 'a colony in retreat' (1997, 134). Various factors were responsible for this, including the revolt of the Irish, the Bruce invasion, and plague. In hasty preparation for the Bruce siege to the city in 1317, Robert de Nottingham, mayor of Dublin, burnt and demolished the suburbs (Clarke 1998). The Black Death reduced the population of Europe dramatically in the fourteenth century and Dublin was stricken with plague like other Irish towns. It is very likely that this catastrophe led to a dramatic shrinkage of population with a greater proportional de-population of the suburbs as the city contracted back to its core.

The growth or decline of the medieval suburb? The principal dating evidence for the archaeological site and its decline in the later medieval period is primarily based upon the pottery. The apparent lack of late medieval pottery on the site compares with the picture established from urban excavations where there is a paucity or complete absence of late medieval pottery, within the walls of Dublin (McCutcheon 1995, 63–5), Waterford (Gahan and McCutcheon 1997) and Cork (McCutcheon 1997, 77, Table 3.). McNeill notes this gap in the archaeological record 'from the early fourteenth to the sixteenth century' and is sceptical about the implied abandonment of urban habitations following the Black Death (2002, 553). In spite of the devastation of the plague, all settlement cannot have ceased and surely as dramatic an interpretation as urban abandonment is untenable.

So how do we explain the gap in the pottery assemblage? Derricke's famous image of Irish feasting in the sixteenth century points to the possible Gaelicisation of material culture and a corresponding increase in the utilisation of skins for cooking as opposed to local cooking wares and the use of wooden vessels in place of the pipkins and ceramic jugs (1985). Perhaps a reassessment of the lack of evidence for pottery in the period is warranted. In his article 'concerning chronology' Joseph Raftery (1981) analysed apparent gaps in elements of the Irish archaeological record. His principal contention was that the establishment of critical dates in artefact sequences 'pigeonholes' artefact types and establishes immovable benchmarks around which typologies are constructed. The well-dated historical and dendrochonologically dated structures listed in the previous paragraph have given a secure context for Anglo-Norman material culture in the early thirteenth century. However, given that the medieval period saw little technological development in firing pottery, it may be that late medieval pottery is functionally and typologically similar to the pottery stratigraphically associated with well-dated structures, such as the Anglo-Norman timber waterfronts in Dublin (Wallace 1981). If late medieval pottery is typologically similar to the earlier wares then sherds found in unassociated or isolated pits automatically are dated to within the established dating framework. This presents us with an alternative interpretation of the Thomas Street site where the suburb survives the tumultuous events of the medieval period and remained occupied down to the post-medieval period.

Clearly, further excavation and research is required to clarify the chronology and the wider implications for settlement in the late medieval period.

Post-medieval (1600–1800) settlement Many features (pits and gullies) were identified dating to this period. These features were dated exclusively by their association with artefacts. These included diagnostic pottery types such as North Devon Gravel tempered ware, North Devon sgraffito, German stonewares, clay pipes and glass bottles. The features dated from the later sixteenth, seventeenth and eighteenth century, representing clear evidence for settlement on the street.

ACKNOWLEDGEMENTS

The paper draws on unpublished specialist work carried out as part of the post-excavation analysis of the site. These reports by Clare McCutcheon (pottery), Cathy Johnson (pottery and small finds), Eileen Reilly (beetles), Brenda Collins (seeds), Andrea Cremin (animal bones) and Dr David Brown (dendrochronology) have been summarised in this paper. Dr Ingelise Struijts provided the wood identifications. The author acknowledges the collaborative approach that is required in the analysis of archaeological excavation and the effort by the archaeologists on site, Stephen Gilmore, Cormac McSparran, John Conway, Paul McCooey, Claire Callaghan, Maybelline Gormley, Brian Shanahan, Donal Fallon and David Bailey. The excavation was conducted by Margaret Gowen & Co. Ltd. with the helpful administration of Dolores Cotter and Nessa Walsh. Illustrations in the paper were prepared by Shirley Markley, Avril Purcell, Simon Dick and Nina Koberol. All credit for the conclusions in the paper is theirs, any omissions or errors are my own.

BIBLIOGRAPHY

Barry, T.B. 1987 *The archaeology of medieval Ireland*. London.
Barton, K.J. 1963 The medieval pottery kiln at Ham Green, Bristol. *Transactions of the Bristol and Gloucestershire Archaeological Society* 82, 95–126.
Bermingham, N. 1995 Animal bones. In L. Simpson (ed.) *Excavations at Essex Street West, Dublin*, Temple Bar Archaeological Report, no. 2, 104–16, Dublin.
Brooks, E. St J. 1936 *Register of the hospital of St John the Baptist without the New Gate, Dublin*. Dublin.
Brown, D. 1997 Appendix VI Dendrochronological dating. In E. O'Donovan, Archaeological excavations at 119/121 Thomas Street. Unpublished report submitted to Dúchas, the Heritage Service and the National Museum of Ireland. 17/10/1997, Margaret Gowen & Co. Ltd.
Carroll, J. 1997 Vicar Street/58–59 Thomas Street, Dublin. In I. Bennett (ed.) *Excavations 1997: summary accounts of archaeological excavations in Ireland*. Bray.

Clarke, H.B. 1983 The historical background to North Sea trade, 1200–1500, in P. Davey and R. Hodges (eds), *Ceramics and trade*, 17–25. Sheffield.

—— 1998 Urbs et suburbium: beyond the walls of medieval Dublin. In C. Manning (ed.) *Dublin and beyond the pale: Studies in honour of Patrick Healy*, 45–58, Bray.

—— 2002 *Irish historic towns atlas No. 11, Dublin Part I, to 1610*, Royal Irish Academy, Dublin.

Collins, B. 1997 Appendix IV Plant remains. In E. O'Donovan, Archaeological excavations at 119/121 Thomas Street. Unpublished report submitted to Dúchas, the Heritage Service and the National Museum of Ireland. 17/10/1997, Margaret Gowen & Co. Ltd.

Cowgill, J., de Neergaard, M. and Griffith, N. 1987 Knives and scabbards. In *Medieval finds from excavations in London*. HMSO, London.

Craig, M. 1980 (reprint) *Dublin 1660–1860*. Dublin.

Cremin, A. 1997 Appendix III Animal bone. In E. O'Donovan, Archaeological excavations at 119/121 Thomas Street. Unpublished report submitted to Dúchas, the Heritage Service and the National Museum of Ireland. 17/10/1997, Margaret Gowen & Co. Ltd.

Deroeux, D. and Dufournier, D. 1991 Réflexions sur la diffusion de la céramique très décorée d'origine française en Europe du Nord-Ouest XIII–XIV siècles. *Archéologie Médiévale* 21, 163–77.

Derricke, J. 1985 (reprint), In Quinn D.B. (ed.) *The image of Ireland*. Belfast.

Duffy, S. 1997 *Ireland in the middle ages*. Dublin.

Dunning, G.C. 1959 Pottery of the late Anglo-Saxon period in England, in G.C. Dunning, J.G. Hurst, J.N.L. Myers and F. Tischer, Anglo-Saxon pottery: a symposium. *Medieval Archaeology* 3, 31–78.

Eames, E.S. and Fanning, T. 1988 *Irish medieval tiles*. Royal Irish Academy. Dublin.

Egan, G. and Pritchard, F. 1991 Dress accessories. In *Medieval finds from excavations in London*. HMSO, London.

Elliott, A.L. 1990 The abbey of St Thomas the Martyr in medieval Dublin. In H.B. Clarke (ed.) *The living city*, 62–76. Dublin.

Gahan, A. and McCutcheon, C. 1997 The medieval pottery. In M.F. Hurley and O.M.B. Scully (eds) *Late Viking age and medieval Waterford. Excavations 1986–1992*, 285–336, Waterford.

Gilbert, J.T. 1854–9 *A history of the city of Dublin*. 3 vols. Dublin.

—— 1889 *Register of the abbey of St Thomas, Dublin*. London.

Gowen, M. 1996 119–121 Thomas Street, Dublin. In I. Bennett (ed.) *Excavations 1995: summary accounts of archaeological excavations in Ireland*. Bray.

Griffith, M.C. 1991 *Calendar of inquisitions formerly in the office of the Chief Remembrancer of the exchequer prepared from the manuscripts of the Irish Record Commission*. Dublin.

Gwynn, A. and Hadcock, R.N. 1988 (reprint) *Medieval religious houses: Ireland*. Dublin.

Halpin, A. 2000 *The port of medieval Dublin, archaeological excavations at the Civic Offices, Winetavern Street, Dublin, 1993*. Dublin.

Hayden, A. and Walsh, C. 1997 The small finds. In C. Walsh (ed.) *Archaeological excavations at Patrick, Nicholas and Winetavern Streets, Dublin*, 132–44, Dingle.

Hurst, J.G., Neal, D.S. and van Beuningen, H.J.E. 1986 *Pottery produced and traded in north-west Europe 1350–1650*. Rotterdam.

Joyce, P.W. 1995 (reprint) *Irish names of places*. Dublin.

Lydon, J. 2002 Dublin Castle in the middle ages. In S. Duffy (ed.) *Medieval Dublin III. Proceedings of the Friends of Medieval Dublin symposium 2001*, 115–27, Dublin.

Maxwell, N. 1980 *Digging up Dublin*. Dublin.

McCarthy, M.R. and Brooks, C.M. 1988 *Medieval pottery in Britain A.D. 900–1600.* Leicester.

McCormick, F. 1998 The animal bones. In M. Hurley *et al.* (eds) *Late Viking Age and medieval Waterford: Excavations 1986–1992,* 819–53, Waterford.

McCutcheon, C. 1995 (a) The pottery. In L. Simpson (ed.), *Excavations at Essex Street West, Dublin,* 40–54, 59–67, Dublin.

McCutcheon, C. 1995(b) Cork type pottery: a medieval urban enterprise. Unpublished MA thesis, National University of Ireland.

McCutcheon, C. 1997 Pottery and roof tiles. In M.F. Hurley (ed.), *Excavations at the North Gate, Cork, 1994,* 75–101, Cork.

McCutcheon, C. 2000 Medieval pottery in Dublin: new names and some dates. In S. Duffy (ed.) *Medieval Dublin I, Proceedings of the Friends of Medieval Dublin Symposium 1999,* 117–25, Dublin.

McCutcheon, C. forthcoming, The pottery. In C. Walsh, *Excavations at Francis Street / Swift's Alley, Dublin.*

McCutcheon, C. in prep. The medieval pottery from the waterfront excavations at Wood Quay, Dublin.

McNeill, T.E. 1997 *Castles in Ireland. feudal power in a Gaelic world.* London.

McNeill, T.E. 2002 Lost Infancy: medieval archaeology in Ireland, *Antiquity,* 76, no. 292, June 2002, 552–6.

Meenan, R. 1994 The post-medieval pottery, in L. Simpson (ed.), *Excavations at Isolde's Tower, Dublin,* 54–77. Dublin.

National Museum of Ireland 1973 *Viking and medieval Dublin.* Exhibition Catalogue, Dublin.

Noël Hume, I. 1991 *A guide to artifacts of colonial America.* New York.

O'Donovan, E. 1997 119–121 Thomas Street, Dublin. In I. Bennett (ed.), *Excavations 1996: summary accounts of archaeological excavations in Ireland.* Bray.

O'Donovan, E. 2000 Broad Street / George's Quay / Abbey River, Limerick. In I. Bennett (ed.), *Excavations 1999: summary accounts of archaeological excavations in Ireland.* Bray.

Ó Floinn, R. 1988 Handmade medieval pottery in S.E. Ireland–Leinster Cooking Ware. In G. MacNiocaill and P.F. Wallace (eds.), *Keimelia,* 325–49. Galway.

Papazian, C. 1997 Medieval and later pottery from site G, in C. Walsh (ed.), *Archaeological excavations at Patrick, Nicholas and Winetavern Streets, Dublin,* 124–8, Dingle.

Pearce, J.E., Vince, A.G. and Jenner, M.A. 1985 *London-type ware.* London.

Ponsford, M. 1991 Dendrochronological dates from Dundas Wharf, Bristol and the dating of Ham Green and other medieval pottery, in E. Lewis (ed.), *Custom and Ceramics,* 81–103. Wickham.

Raftery, J. 1981 Concerning chronology. In D. Ó Corráin (ed.) *Irish antiquity: essays and studies presented to Professor M.J. O'Kelly,* 82–92, Dublin.

Reilly, E. 1997 Appendix V Insect remains. In E. O'Donovan, Archaeological excavations at 119/121 Thomas Street. Unpublished report submitted to Dúchas, the Heritage Service and the National Museum of Ireland, 17/10/1997, Margaret Gowen & Co. Ltd.

Simpson, L. 1995 *Excavations at Essex Street West, Dublin,* Temple Bar Archaeological Report, No. 2, Dublin.

Sweeney, C. 1991 *The rivers of Dublin.* Dublin.

Sweetman, P.D. 1984 Archaeological excavations at Shop Street, Drogheda, Co. Louth. *R.I.A. Proc.,* 84(C), 171–224.

Vince, A.G. 1988 Early medieval English pottery in Viking Dublin. In G. MacNiocaill and P.F. Wallace (eds) *Keimelia,* 254–70. Galway.

Wallace, P. 1981 Anglo-Norman Dublin: continuity and change. In D. O Corráin (ed.) *Irish antiquity: essays and studies presented to Professor M.J. O'Kelly*, 247–68. Dublin.

Walsh, C. 1997 *Archaeological excavations at Patrick, Nicholas and Winetavern Streets, Dublin*. Dingle.

—— 2000 Archaeological Excavations at the abbey of St Thomas the Martyr. In S. Duffy (ed.) *Medieval Dublin I. Proceedings of the Friends of Medieval Dublin symposium 1999*, 185–202, Dublin

Whelan, K. 1992 Beyond a paper landscape–John Andrews and Irish historical geography. In F.H.A. Aalen and K. Whelan (eds) *Dublin city and county: from prehistory to present*, 379–424, Dublin.

Wren, J. 1997 Roof tiles. In C. Walsh *Archaeological excavations at Patrick, Nicholas and Winetavern Streets, Dublin*, 149–52, Dingle.

Women in medieval Dublin: their legal rights and economic power

LYNDA CONLON

Women certainly feature quite extensively in the surviving records of Dublin, and their neglect in studies thus far has served to displace a far from negligible portion of medieval Dublin society from our view.[1] On a very basic level, the seemingly routine references to women as 'the wife of', the necessity to define them by their relationship with men, suggests that their own identity was subsumed, to some extent, within that of her husband or father. This practice would suggest that women were commonly regarded as occupying a distinctly marginal position in society. However, even a brief perusal of the records would indicate that, in reality, their activity and attendant power, was inconsistent with the docility desired of their sex.

This study aims to examine the manifestation of this power: women's right to control and alienate land, their right to bequeath property, and their ability to participate in the workforce. An analysis of the actual power of women can be approximated through an analysis of each of these aspects. The efforts to contain these rights in order to assure female docility will also be a concern of this study.

WOMEN AND PROPERTY RIGHTS

Although women are frequently portrayed in the secondary literature as almost entirely without political and legal rights, and under the constant surveillance of father, guardian or husband, the restricted legal rights allowed to them did include the power to control and alienate land to a certain extent. While their opportunities to acquire property may have been fewer than those of males, they were entitled to hold land either by right of inheritance or through purchase. The inventory of Joan, daughter of William Douce, is one of the most impressive examples of a woman taking considerable advantage of these opportunities. Joan's inventory, recorded in May 1381, included a lengthy catalogue of properties within the city: a messuage and four shops in

---

1 A useful beginning was, however, made in Jessica McMorrow, 'Women in medieval Dublin: an introduction', in *Medieval Dublin II*, ed. Seán Duffy (Dublin, 2001), pp 205–15.

St Audoen's parish, a messuage with two cellars in the parish of St John, a shop with a garden in the Scarlet Lane, four shops with a garden in St Francis Street, five shops (two roofed with tiles) in St Thomas Street, a stone house and messuage in Kisher's Lane, and a stone house with a garden on the west side of the same lane.[2] In the absence of any references to a husband, progeny, or widowhood, it is quite likely that Joan was a single woman. Though it could be considered unusual for a woman to hold so much property before her widowhood, it was certainly not unknown for women to acquire and hold land independently before their marriage.[3] Women such as Joan seem to have enjoyed full legal autonomy over their lands and were free to dispose of them as they wished, which indeed Joan did, granting two shops in Thomas Street to Richard Glasewryght forever, and a stone house with garden and solar to William Dercer forever.[4] While the means by which Joan acquired her land are not stated, the wills and charters of Dublin do feature evidence of single women either receiving property in the form of a gift from their father, or inheriting the land. For example, the *Calendar of Christ Church Deeds* features at least two instances of apparently unmarried daughters receiving grants of land from still living fathers.[5] Examples of unmarried heiresses are also scattered through the records.[6]

Though women were permitted to acquire property through purchase, given the more restricted occupational opportunities available to them (which will be addressed later in this study), the principle means of acquiring property was through inheritance. Dublin men, in their wills, left land and other valuables to their female kin – their mothers,[7] sisters,[8] daughters and more remote female relatives,[9] as well as their wives. However the women who inherited land often received only a life interest with reversion to male kin or the church if they died childless. Patrilineal inheritance, which favoured sons at the expense of daughters, was common in Dublin. However, in the absence of male heirs, women could inherit, as stated in the 'Ordinance of the Common Council of Dublin' for the year 1305: '… Inheritance by daughters of citizens without sons and by sons to the exclusion of daughters'.[10] This ordinance

2 H.F Berry, 'History of the religious guild of S. Anne, St Audoen's, Dublin', *R.I.A. Proc.*, xxv (1904–5), pp 47–8, no. 20.   3 Mavis E. Mate, *Women in medieval English society* (Cambridge, 1999). Mate notes that leaving property to daughters who wished to remain single became more common in the early sixteenth century but it is not known how widespread it was or when it began (at p. 93).   4 Berry, 'Guild of S. Anne', pp 47–8, no. 20. 5 M.J. McEnery and Raymond Refaussé, *Calendar of Christ Church deeds* (Dublin, 2001), nos. 581, 619.   6 For example, *Calendar of ancient deeds and muniments preserved in the Pembroke Estate Office* (Dublin, 1891), p. 22, no. 63.   7 *Christ Church deeds*, no. 290; H.L. Lawlor, 'A calendar of the Liber Niger and Liber Albus of Christ Church, Dublin', *R.I.A. Proc.*, xxvii (1907–8), pp 31–2; Berry, 'Guild of S. Anne', p. 73.   8 Lawlor, 'Calendar of the Liber Niger and Liber Albus', pp 31–2, no. 58; Berry, 'Guild of S. Anne', p. 73, no. 95.   9 *Christ Church deeds*: examples of bequests made to a niece (no. 291), and a female cousin (no. 309).   10 J.T. Gilbert (ed.), *Calendar of ancient records of Dublin*, 19 vols (Dublin, 1889–1944), i, p. 229.

highlights the fact that in Dublin, as elsewhere in medieval society, the inheritance rights of sons almost always took precedence over those of daughters.

Often if a woman was inheriting land in the absence of a direct male heir, she was seen primarily as a conduit, a means of transmitting the land rather than granting her the right to enjoy the land for herself.[11] There are numerous examples throughout the records, however, where women are clearly referred to as 'daughter and heiress'. Perhaps most noteworthy is the existence of what seems to be a matrilineal inheritance among the deeds of St Anne's guild: 'Katherine Hodd, daughter and heiress of Alson Colman, daughter and heiress of Joan Colyer …'.[12] As the sole heir, daughters could stand to inherit considerable amounts of property, as was the case with Margaret Flemyng in 1483. On her death, Margaret's mother, Margaret Whitacre of Dublin, widow, bequeathed to her daughter (and her husband John Kerny) 'all and every kind of my messuages, tenements, arable lands, barns, dove-cotes, gardens, parks, fields, pastures, rights of pasture, moors, rents and services with all and singular their appurtenances, being in the vill of Drogheda'.[13] On occasion, daughters were expressly provided for in the wills of parents. For example, on his death in 1482, Robert West left to his daughter Alice and her heirs 'a house upon the Quay … which is called the house next "le Crane"', while bequeathing to his son Richard all other 'messuages, lands and tenements, rents, services and possessions with their appurtenances which I have in the city of Dublin or elsewhere'.[14]

Also worthy of consideration are the dowry arrangements that the fathers of medieval Dublin made for their daughters. The dowry or marriage portion that came with the bride was of great importance and could be considered to be her portion of the family wealth, received on the occasion of her marriage instead of when her parents died. Testators were often aware of their obligation to the daughters; for example, in the will of Richard Boys, he left the house in which his mother dwelled to his daughter in aid of her marriage.[15] Such obligations were also fulfilled by the provision of a cash 'marriage portion', as in the case of Thomas fitz William who bequeathed £40 to each of his seven daughters 'to marriage', though not all of them subsequently received that amount.[16] In 1320, Alice, a widow, released a frontage with a messuage to Andrew fitz Richard, on his marriage to her daughter Eva.[17]

---

11 For example, in the case of John Gogh the preference for a male heir was explicitly stated. Were his son Nicholas to die 'without heirs male of body lawfully begotten', he willed that his property remain to his daughter Elizabeth 'and the heirs male of her body begotten'. If Elizabeth died without a male heir, John willed his property to 'John Swetman and his heirs for ever': H.F. Berry (ed.), *Register of wills and inventories of the diocese of Dublin in the time of Archbishops Tregury and Walton, 1457–1483* (Dublin, 1898), p. 40. 12 For example, in *Christ Church deeds*, nos. 318, 338, 416 and 489; Berry, 'Guild of S. Anne', pp 73–4, no. 98. 13 Colm Lennon and James Murray (eds), *The Dublin city franchise roll, 1468–1512* (Dublin, 1998), pp 57–8, deed no. 17. 14 *Dublin city franchise roll*, p. 54, no. 15. 15 Berry, *Register of wills and inventories*, pp 10, 76–8. 16 Lawlor, 'Calendar of the Liber Niger and Liber Albus', pp 67–9, no. 216. 17 *Christ Church deeds*,

Under the sixth constitution of the 1172 Synod that sat at Cashel, a man's moveable goods were to be divided, upon his death, into three parts, leaving one part to the children, another to his lawful wife, and the third for the funeral (if there were no progeny, the wife was entitled to one half of her husband's moveable goods).[18] The right of the widow to one third of the husband's holding, as her dower, was widely acknowledged throughout the Dublin testaments: 'Alienora Doudall ... held the third part of the premises in dower';[19] 'the third part of all messuages and lands Anna Cruys late wife of James Fitz William ... as of dower of the same James';[20] 'Johanna ... shall have lands to the value of £10 yearly, in recompense of her dower'.[21] A particularly interesting case in 1464 concerned what appears to be a marriage agreement in which the prospective groom, Stephen Fitz William covenants to wed Ann Cruys and to secure her seven marks a year after his death (or ten marks should he die without issue) 'besides the dower at Common Law'.[22]

However, the land granted to the bereaved wife was usually done with a reversion on the widow's death to a named (normally male) heir, or to the church, thereby restricting their power to control or alienate it. In 1348, William Foyll left his wife Helena houses and land in Castle Street, with a garden in 'Teyngmouth-street' for life, 'with reversion thereof to his right heirs'.[23] Similarly in 1484, Thomas fitzSymon left to his wife Elizabeth his 'newly built house upon the Woodquay during the life of the aforesaid Elizabeth and after her death to my heirs'.[24] John Birte also left property to his wife, on this occasion the house in which he was living and two other houses in Castle Street, stipulating that she have only a life interest and that they should revert to the fabric of St Olave's church upon her death.[25] The majority of testaments in which property was bequeathed to the wife specified that the interest be 'during her life' only, though not all contained reversionary clauses.[26] On at least one occasion, provisions in the form of property were made for the widow only until the heirs came of age; she would thenceforth receive an annuity of three marks of silver during her life. Thomas Dowdall willed that 'all and singular my messuages, lands and tenements in Dublin with their appurtenances, which I have by the donation and bequest of Jonete ... Dowdall, my mother, should remain wholly after my death to Christine Pyppart, to have and to hold to the aforesaid Christine and her assigns unless my children have reached legitimate age'.[27] On the whole, however, it was something of a triumph that Dublin women, like many of

deed no. 557. 18 Berry, *Register of wills and inventories*, introduction, p. x. 19 For example, in *Christ Church deeds*, nos. 318, 338, 416 and 489; Berry, 'Guild of S. Anne', pp 73–4, no. 98. 20 Lawlor, 'Calendar of the Liber Niger and Liber Albus', pp 50–1, no. 174. 21 Ibid., p. 57, no. 194. 22 *Ancient deeds in the Pembroke Estate Office*, pp 55–6, no. 190. 23 *Christ Church deeds*, no. 239. 24 *Dublin city franchise roll*, pp 58–9, no. 20. 25 Ibid., pp 48–9, no. 3. 26 For example, *Dublin city franchise roll*, pp 66–7, no. 36 and p. 74, no. 49. 27 Ibid., no. 46.

their European counterparts, were entrusted with much of their deceased husband's holdings despite the patriarchal nature of their society.

However, the acquisition of land alone did not necessarily bring women either independence or power. The stark difference between the position of the single woman, the wife and the widow is of particular relevance with regard to property rights. Daughters were legally under the control and authority of their fathers, wives were subject to the power and authority of their husbands, and it was generally only widows who had any measure of legal autonomy. With regard to property, a husband, by right of guardianship, took over all the wife's property, and she was adjured to obey him in this as in all other matters. Under English common law, all property matters were the domain of the husband, for example, the notion of 'community of goods' between a husband and wife was not recognised.[28] Instead, the husband largely controlled, for the duration of the marriage, all of the properties owned by either his wife or himself. He could freely alienate, without his wife's consent, the properties he brought to the marriage. He could similarly alienate his wife's properties, although only with her consent. Essentially her land and its legal responsibilities were taken over and managed by him and she in turn had no power to sell, transfer or exchange her own property without her husband's consent. However the power exerted by common law in this respect would seem to have been wanting in Dublin. The express consent of the husband is an unusual feature among the records of Dublin. Only William Mareschal 'grants leave to his wife Joanna to alienate' lands, later 'ratifying' whatever shall have been done by her.[29] More frequently expressed however is the concurrence of the wife in deeds involving her property. An apt example is that involving William de Donheved and his wife Isabella. William 'with the consent of Isabella his wife' granted to Adam de Helmiswell and Mabilla, his wife, '1 mark rent … being Isabella's proportion of 3 marks'.[30] Certainly, the husband exercised some power over his wife's property. A significant enhancement to whatever control he held under common law was granted under the 'Common Law and Usages of the City of Dublin' which conceded the right of redemption by the husband of land sold by his wife before marriage.[31]

Land transfers undertaken by conjugal pairs also seem to have been quite common in Dublin. In a very large number of documents of sale, transfer, and bestowal of property the names of husband and wife appear jointly.[32] Unlike those examined by R.M. Smith in Redgrave, Park and Codicote, the Dublin

---

28 R.M. Smith, 'Women's property rights under customary law: some developments in the thirteenth and fourteenth centuries', in *Trans Royal Historical Society*, 36 (1986), p. 180. 29 *Christ Church deeds*, no. 12; Lawlor, 'Calendar of the Liber Niger and Liber Albus', p. 18, no. 30. 30 *Christ Church deeds*, pp 55–6, no. 114. 31 Gilbert, *Ancient records*, i, p. 225. 32 Incidences of conjoint transfers of land in medieval Dublin are too extensive to enumerate here, but certainly seem to have occurred with curious regularity when

records do not yield up any immediate suggestion that conjoint transactions were more likely to be surrendering land rather than acquiring it.[33] The partial participation of the married woman in the transfer of land would seem to challenge the conventional assumption that under the common law the wife's legal identity was completely subsumed within that of her husband.

Only in widowhood did a married woman regain full control over her own estates. At this stage she acquired full legal autonomy never previously enjoyed as a single or married woman. Widows seem to have been more active conveying property than those privileged single women who had inherited, purchased or been given land. The number of transactions by those 'in their viduity' would seem to suggest that husbands would often forego the opportunity to impose conditions on their widows. The volume of transfers to what would appear to have been non-kin would also suggest that property was occasionally bequeathed to the bereaved wife in perpetuity, to do with what she wished. With these rights came responsibility however, as widows with property were required to contribute to the watch and ward proportionately with their neighbours.[34] Widows in Dublin also appear to have been entitled to take their land with them to a second or third marriage, thus making them an attractive marriage prospect (there are no records of Dublin women relinquishing their land upon remarriage). One might cite the example of Matilda de Bree (future wife of the infamous Geoffrey Morton) who, as the widow of Robert de Bree, a former mayor of Dublin, inherited property in the city and subsequently acquired further land in the time of her widowhood. Described by Philomena Connolly as a 'good match' for the ambitious Geoffrey Morton, what is most significant is the fact that all the real property Geoffrey had on his death either came from Robert de Bree through Matilda or was actually bought by Matilda herself before her second marriage.[35] However, those widows who were bequeathed property 'for life' found their legal autonomy somewhat circumscribed. Their transient hold on the property effectively meant that the inheritance was non-alienable, severely restricting the widow's control over her bequest. The evidence of the testamentary bequests in the Dublin records would seem to suggest that the legal autonomy of the widow was very often inhibited in this respect. Seemingly contradictory evidence in the same records suggests that there was quite an active market in land transfers by women describing themselves as either 'widow', 'formerly wife of' or 'in her viduity'. As a result, the general freedom and independence of widows with regard to property rights cannot easily be deduced.

compared with contemporary records in England. **33** Smith, 'Women's property rights under customary law', p. 185. Indeed, at Redgrave between 1260 and 1319, wives were twice as likely to be found surrendering land with their husbands than acquiring it. **34** Gilbert, *Ancient records*, i, p. 223. **35** Philomena Connolly, 'The rise and fall of Geoffrey Morton, mayor of Dublin, 1303–4' in *Medieval Dublin II*, ed. Duffy, p. 236.

WOMEN AND TESTAMENTARY PRACTICE

Having relied extensively on testimentary evidence in an attempt to deduce some idea of the property rights of women, the potential of this documentary material has not yet been exhausted. A closer examination of the extant wills yields sundry contradictions and vagaries which serve to challenge some of the conventional assumptions regarding the status of women in the city. Even the very fact that married women constitute a clear majority of those women who died testate complicates the common perception of their right to dispose of property. Given the relative paucity of source material which so hinders the study of women in Dublin, a chance detail or expression in these documents can provide a valuable insight, which may otherwise prove elusive. The only surviving register of wills, the *Register of wills and inventories of the diocese of Dublin in the time of Archbishops Tregury and Walton*, covering a relatively limited chronological span in the fifteenth century, is supplemented to some extent by a further twenty-four wills preserved in a variety of ecclesiastical and municipal sources ranging in date from 1270 to 1500. Apart from the strictly testamentary evidence, the abundant references to 'heiresses', legatees by virtue of a filial relationship (the most common), a sibling relationship, or even on one occasion as a cousin, throughout the various records gives some idea of the involvement of women in testamentary practices.[36] Comparatively less common, though equally relevant, are the references to certain individuals as 'son and heir', suggesting that the testamentary power of women was utilized more often than the extant wills would suggest.

Freedom of testation was reserved to widows and unmarried women. The testamentary capacity of married women was severely constrained by comparison. While 'single' women were at liberty to dispose of their chattels by will, their married counterparts enjoyed no such autonomy, as they required the consent of their husband to make a will. By relinquishing the uxorilocal property to her spouse upon marriage a wife's need to make a will was considered obsolete. In 1306, this surrender was explicitly acknowledged in the case of William Telyng, charged with stealing a number of items from Agnes le Cartere. By way of defence, William asserted that 'as Agnes is his wife, of whose [goods he might take] as he pleased without making theft' no crime had been committed.[37] Just a year later, in the course of a testamentary dispute, this definite judgement on the issue was delivered: 'there is no need that a woman bequeath her goods to her husband, as the husband is lord as well of the wife as of her chattels'.[38] The repressiveness of common law in this respect was countered by the law of the church, which held that married

---

36 *Christ Church deeds*, no. 309.   37 James Mills et al. (eds), *Calendar of the justiciary rolls, or proceedings in the court of the justiciar of Ireland*, 3 vols (Dublin, 1905–56), ii, pp 499–500. 38 Mills, *Cal. justic. rolls Ire.*, p. 389.

women were fully capable of making a testament of their separate properties. The position of canon law was perhaps best exemplified by a complaint made to the king by the citizens of Dublin in 1347 stating that 'contrary to the usage of the city, married women there make bequests of their husbands' goods without their licence; and that excommunications have been issued by prelates and ecclesiastics against citizens who prevented their wives from making such gifts'.[39] Given the limited sample of wills available for examination, the fact that the majority of those left by female decedents were actually by married women does not necessarily represent the triumph of canon law over common law.[40]

Of the seventy-two testaments contained in the *Register*, fourteen certainly belonged to women married at the time of their death, three came from widows, and another seven belonged to women of unknown status (possibly unmarried).[41] Four more wills, one certainly attributable to a married woman, two to widows and another whose status is not declared, may be added to the above.[42] As a result, married women accounted for over half of the women writing wills.[43] The stipulation regarding the mandatory acquisition of a husband's consent is expressly complied with in only one case however.[44] Thirteen wills were therefore recognised and subsequently proven with no categorical mention of spousal consent.[45] Helmholz suggests that in cases where the husband served as executor of his wife's testament, such assent may readily have been presumed.[46] If spousal licence could be inferred in this manner, the extent of compliance with the rules of the common law certainly improves, and fourteen testaments may be regarded as having been assented to. In the case of Agnes Duff, however, the existence of a husband is confirmed only by the fact that the will is prefaced by a joint inventory. There is no specific statement of consent, nor is he named as an executor.[47]

Only a small proportion of the wills of married women adhered to the axiom which limited their right of bequest to items of personal adornment.[48]

---

39 Gilbert, *Ancient records*, i, p. 145.   **40** The *Register* contains seventy-four testaments. In addition to this, another twelve wills were located in the various ecclesiastical, municipal and parish records used in this study, giving a relatively small sample of eighty-six testaments in total, the earliest dated 1275, and the latest 1533. Berry, *Register of wills and inventories*.   **41** Women's wills comprised 30.77 per cent of the total wills in the register. **42** *Christ Church deeds*, p. 54; *Dublin city franchise roll*, pp 57–8; *Ancient deeds in the Pembroke Estate Office*, pp 59–60.   **43** This preponderance of married testatrixes seems to have been peculiar to Dublin. By the middle of the fifteenth century Helmholz concluded that wills of married women had actually become something of a rarity in England. R.H. Helmholz, 'Married women's wills in later medieval England', in Sue Sheridan Walker (ed.), *Wife and widow in medieval England* (Michigan, 1993), p. 170.   **44** The will of Jacoba Payn commences: 'In the name of God. Amen. I, Jacoba Payn aforesaid, by leave of my said husband, do make my testament in this manner' (Berry, *Register of wills and inventories*, pp 156–8).   **45** A number of wills omit details of executors. In the case of married women's wills, an executor or executors are nominated in fifteen of the sixteen cases. **46** Helmholz, 'Married women's wills in later medieval England', p. 167.   **47** Berry, *Register of wills and inventories*, pp 5–7.   **48** Berry asserts that a wife was sometimes

In 1457, Ellen Stiward left one set of beads, a wedding ring and a box to her daughter Katherine Whytt, while a second daughter received 'Agnes Broun's beads'.[49] Joan Dansay beqeathed a 'huke', a women's garment, to her daughter, and two coats and a pair of blankets to her maid servant.[50] Other women instead left animals, sums of money or utensils to family members.[51] Perhaps the most notable bequest of this nature was made by Katherine, wife of John le Gront, in one of the earliest extant testaments. She left to her husband 'the utensils with the moveables and immoveables in the house and out of it belonging to her'.[52] The relative liberality of this will was countered by the implicit restraints placed on Jacoba Payn less than two centuries later. Having bequeathed to her husband 'all the goods which were his, and his deceased former wife's', Jacoba was free to will only the garments and other ornaments he had given her. Her testament was the practical embodiment of the afore-mentioned axiom: she left only articles of jewellery, girdles, and 'other ornaments which are worn on my person' to her daughter Matilda.[53]

Though no such restraints were placed on the freedom of single women to bequeath their property, the majority of unmarried testatrixes simply chose to make provisions for funerary expenses and *pro anima* bequests.[54] Their relatively meagre wills give little point for further consideration. Joan White's bequest of 'one three-legged pan and one trough with two trundles for the use of my neighbours ... for the health of my soul' is an isolated peculiarity in this respect.[55] Only the will of Joan Douce distinguishes itself, by virtue of its sheer extent. Her benefactions extended to 'the cripple who lies opposite Nicholas Seriaunt's inn', the scholars of St Audoen's church, the prisoners of the city, and the building of bridges.[56] However, characteristic of all these wills was the singular failure of any unmarried woman to devise real property. This is particularly remarkable in the case of Joan Douce, whose extensive inventory of lands and houses was enumerated earlier. Any temptation to infer a general impairment of property rights on this basis must be resisted, however, as the sample is too small to support any such conclusion. In contrast, the

permitted 'to make a will of the reasonable part she is likely to have, should she survive her husband, and chiefly of the things granted her for adornment, as with regard to robes and jewels'. Berry, *Register of wills and inventories*, introduction, p. xiii.   **49** These four articles represent a relatively small fraction of the items enumerated in the inventory of Ellen Stiward. Her possessions included numerous animals, quantities of grain, pots, pans and basins, and pieces of jewellery: Berry, *Register of wills and inventories*, pp 1–2.   **50** Berry, *Register of wills and inventories*, pp 142–4.   **51** Ibid., pp 5–7, 65–6, 75–6, 133–6.   **52** There is no way of computing the exact value of such a bequest. However, the fact that a wife left 'utensils' to her husband is in itself significant. Epstein considered utensils to be an important legacy, their bequest to a wife by a husband being 'an additional way to tie the wife to the household': S. Epstein, *Wills and wealth in medieval Genoa, 1150–1250* (Cambridge and London, 1984), p. 107; *Christ Church deeds*, no. 106.   **53** Berry, *Register of wills and inventories*, pp 156–8.   **54** Ibid., pp 11–13, 27, 63–4, 104–5, 125–7, 164.   **55** Ibid., pp 47–9.   **56** H.F. Berry, 'Gild of S. Anne', pp 47–8.

relative autonomy of widows was clearly reflected in their testaments. In 1475, Joan Drywer left all her 'goods, terms, deeds, indentures, and muniments in any way belonging to me' to her two daughters, Isabella and Alice.[57] Joan Stevyn, relict of John Mastoke, bequeathed to her son and heir 'all and singular my messuages, lands, tenements, rents and services, with all their appurtenances which I have or of right ought to have'.[58] Of the four extant wills, only Dame Margaret Nugent omitted to bequeath any property.[59] Her primary concern seems to have been to discharge a rather substantial accumulation of debts, as she instructed all the articles in her inventory to be sold in an effort to settle these debts.[60] As before, such slight testamentary evidence severely compromises the validity of any general observations regarding a widow's right to hold or transmit property.

Voluntary bequests to female relatives (that is, after the legal obligation to provide for wife and children had been satisfied) were quite common. The motives behind such bequests seem a little unclear however. While Berry contends that they were a posthumous effort to enhance the prospects of marriage, Epstein believes that they were actually an attempt to redress the inequities suffered by women.[61] Both opinions are pertinent, though Epstein's view may require a little modification. Certainly, bequests to mothers and sisters may have represented an effort to compensate those who were rarely in a position to enjoy the security afforded by inheritance. Animals, quantities of grain, sums of money and various utensils were willed to mothers and sisters.[62] One testator even remembered his mother-in-law, leaving her 'a scarlet kirtell cloth'.[63] Daughters were more frequently provided for however, quite plausibly with a view to their preferment in marriage. The most common bequest seems to have been monetary, whether in the form of a rent, as a sum paid immediately, or at the marriage of the daughter.[64] Some fathers left substantial legacies. Jenet, daughter of John Chever, inherited 'a gold square, with 4 pearls and a gold clasp with white enamel, and a gold bar'.[65] Though quite possibly very precious, it did not compare for practical value with the inheritance of Joan Barret. Nicholas Barret gave his daughter two bells, a brass pot of two gallons, a large brass pan, six silver spoons, a red cow, a basin, a mattress, a pair of blankets, a pair of sheets, a new napkin and a pair of towels. He also left her the sum of £10. His anxiety to see his daughter married is almost palpable, and indeed it is virtually acknowledged at the end

---

57 Berry, *Register of wills and inventories*, pp 149–51. **58** Ibid., pp 159–62. **59** The fourth will, that of Margaret Whitacre, includes a lengthy bequest to her daughter, Margaret Flemyng. **60** Berry, *Register of wills and inventories*, pp 78–81. **61** Ibid., introduction p. xxxi; Epstein, *Wills and wealth in medieval Genoa*, p. 121. **62** Berry, *Register of wills and inventories*, pp 13–15, 31–4, 112–13, 154–5. **63** Berry, 'Gild of S. Anne', pp 50–1. **64** Berry, *Register of wills and inventories*, p. 3; *Christ Church deeds*, no. 633; Gilbert, *Ancient records*, pp 127–8; *Ancient deeds in the Pembroke Estate Office*, pp 67–9. **65** Berry, *Register of wills and inventories*, pp 146–8.

of the testament: 'And if it happen (which may it not) that my daughter Joan die before she be married, I will that the aforesaid sum of £10 be expended in the best possible way for the health of my soul'.[66]

The frequency with which women were appointed either sole or joint executrix implies a habitual faith in their ability to act in the best spiritual interests of the deceased. In a society inclined to value the activities of males above those of females, this confidence in the ability of the wife, daughter or mother is all the more significant. In the *Register of wills and inventories*, the bereaved wife was appointed executrix in all but one case. Only one widower, however, chose to appoint his daughter as executrix.[67] This sample may be supplemented by a further fifteen testaments, the earliest dated 1282 and the latest 1533. Again, the widow was almost invariably appointed executrix, either in a sole or joint capacity.[68] Clearly, the wife's prospect of being nominated as an executor was generally realised. In 95.45 per cent of cases in which the husband predeceased his wife, his spouse was subsequently appointed as an executor. However, only 29.54 per cent of testators were satisfied to allow women to act independently as their executors.[69] The appointment of a male friend or relative did not necessarily signify misgivings on the testator's part as to his wife's competence. One testator, for example, actually explicated that nothing was to be done by his executors, he having appointed his wife and two male associates as such, without the express consent of the former.[70] Margaret White in her appointment as 'overseer' of Richard White's testament exercised a similar prerogative.[71]

Given the paucity of testamentary material and the absence of supplementary evidence, any attempt to generalize is clearly hazardous. Though the extant wills cover a wide variety of social classes, the fact remains that they represent only a diminutive proportion of the medieval population.[72] It would be imprudent to apply what is true of this small minority to the population at large. However, the detail and variety of the contents of these wills certainly reveal fascinating insights about personal relationships, situations and attitudes to women.

WOMEN IN THE WORKFORCE

Any attempt to ascertain the occupational opportunities available to women in medieval Dublin is also impeded by the fragmentary character of the sur-

66 Ibid., pp 68–72. 67 Ibid., pp 49–51. 68 Only Richard Donogh failed to appoint his wife as executrix, favouring instead Sir Peter Rath, chaplain, and David Rowe: Gilbert, *Ancient records*, i, p. 131. 69 This calculation includes women as sole executrix, or as co-executrix with a female relative. 70 Lawlor, 'Calendar of the Liber Niger and Liber Albus', pp 31–2. 71 Berry, *Register of wills and inventories*, pp 31–4. 72 Fifty-six are wills of farmers (some of whom were also boat owners and fishermen); twelve of merchant

viving evidence. In the absence of the illustrative tax rolls of Paris,[73] the detailed town studies of late-medieval Italy,[74] the poll tax returns or manorial court rolls of medieval England, a study of the occupational structure of Dublin must rely instead on evidence assembled from a variety of disparate sources. Examined in aggregate however, the various sources prove a rather inadequate documentary basis for such a study. The opportunity to determine a continuity of experience of female participation in the workforce, for instance, is denied due to the sporadic nature of the material available. Any generalisations posited on the available evidence would be of a distinctly speculative nature. The relevant information culled from the extant sources does provide some insight into the position of women in the medieval Dublin economy. Though they frequently provide no explicit occupational details, the extant wills of Dublin inhabitants are valuable as an indicator of the occupational activities of the testator and their legatees. The frequent statutes issued by the municipal authority in an effort to control the city's economic and commercial concerns also give some indication of the prevailing attitudes to the participation of women in the labour market. On the basis of this information, it will be possible to assess to what extent the experience of Dublin women corresponds with that of their European counterparts, with particular regard to the familiar pattern of employment of women in the least lucrative, least skilled and most vulnerable types of work.[75]

The occupational designations of women within the medieval manorial economy can be ascertained to some extent by an examination of the earliest extant source, the fourteenth-century *Account roll of the priory of the Holy Trinity, Dublin.* Incorporating the three accounts of the seneschal of Holy Trinity and one of the bailiff of the manor of Clonkeen for the years 1337 to 1346, the *Account roll* proves illuminating in an otherwise overlooked area, that of women and paid work. Very little detail survives regarding levels of remuneration in the medieval economy, but the *Account roll* provides an exceptional insight into the wages of the manorial employee. Though the variety of labour in which women were engaged on the granges was quite extensive, their involvement in the drying and preparation of malt seems to have predominated. The drying of malt certainly appears to have been an exclusively female pursuit. In the account of John Comyn, Leticia Marcold received '4 crannocs 10 pecks' for drying malt and 'to make malt of it',[76] while

citizens of Dublin, and four belong to persons described by Berry as 'gentlefolk'. Berry, *Register of wills and inventories*, introduction, p. xxviii. **73** Seven tax rolls (*tailles*) survive from the years 1292 to 1313, and another partial set of rolls survives from 1421 to 1438. D. Herlihy, *Women, family and society in medieval Europe* (Oxford, 1995), p. 70. **74** Herlihy, *Women, family and society*, p. 87. **75** Ibid., p. 83; Judith M. Bennett, *Ale, beer and brewsters in medieval England: women's work in a changing world* (New York and Oxford, 1996), p. 33. **76** James Mills (ed.), *Account roll of the priory of the Holy Trinity, Dublin, 1337–1346*

a 'certain woman' was in receipt of 2s. 6d. for drying malt.[77] In the account of John Chamburleyn, 'Mariota' was remunerated 'in food' for 'drying and making malt', 'Sarra' received '7 crannocs, 6 pecks' for drying malt at Grangegorman, and an unnamed woman received 3s. 'for her salary' which seems to have entailed drying malt in addition to 'other necessary work within the manor' (of Clonkeen).[78] The fact that women were also involved in the subsequent brewing process is apparent in the record of a payment of 2s. to Mariota Dawenoy for 'a debt of ale' in 1339.[79] The subordination of women to their male counterparts in the workforce is perhaps most aptly demonstrated by the labouring wage paid to each. Women assisting on the construction site, drawing straw for the thatchers, carrying water, or engaged in other labour-intensive work such as binding sheaves at harvest time were paid a uniform $\frac{1}{2}d.$ per day.[80] Considering that the normal wage for their male equivalent was 1d. per day (though workers with special skills were paid more), these female labourers compared unfavourably with their contemporaries in Bristol or Yorkshire for example, where the differential between male and female rates of pay was an average of 75 per cent and 71 per cent respectively.[81]

An ordinance of 1538 resolving that 'no maner [of] person shall wash no foull clothes in the watir in Seynt Thomas strett, from the which unto the place reserved for the same purpose, which is by Seynt John ys pore house' fails to clarify whether the washing of clothes was pursued as a commercial activity in medieval Dublin, and if so, whether any particular gender division existed.[82] In the Parisian *taille* of 1292 for example, in addition to the thirty-eight laundresses (making it the fourth largest female occupation in the city), eight male *lavandiers* also appear.[83] Laundresses also seem to have been numerous in the town records for Brussels and London at the end of the fifteenth century.[84] In Dublin, however, only one individual is recorded as having been paid for laundering services, namely 'Ymna the Washerwoman' who received 6d. for washing the linen cloths of the prior's chamber.[85] The *Account roll* also contains the sole reference to women selling bread in medieval Dublin (Alice Raggley was paid 20s. 'for bread bought from her'), and to women working with textiles: Juliana Schipman was paid 12d. for making two rochets, and Johanna Textrix (the weaver) is listed among the rentals of the grange of Clonkeen. The only other assertion of women's involvement in the textile industry is the admission to the franchise of Anne Prendergast 'seamstress' by virtue of her apprenticeship to Thomas Fouler, a cook, and his

(Dublin, 1890–91, repr. 1996), p. 54.   77 Ibid., pp 35, 45.   78 Ibid., pp 62, 82, 84. 79 Ibid., p. 20.   80 Ibid., pp 37, 39, 38, 68.   81 B.S. Anderson and J.P. Zinsser, *A history of their own: women in Europe from prehistory to the present* (London, 1989–90), p. 360; Mate, *Women in medieval English society*, p. 30, Epstein, *Wage labor and guilds*, p. 118.   82 Gilbert, *Ancient records*, i, p. 404.   83 Herlihy, *Women, family and society*, p. 72.   84 Anderson and Zinsser, *A history of their own*, p. 361.   85 Mills, *Account roll*, p. 99.

wife Rose.[86] Given the dearth of evidence to the contrary, it would seem plausible to suggest that women in Dublin did not predominant in those occupations associated with textile production and decoration as they did in other European cities.[87]

What fragmentary evidence is available would seem to indicate that domestic service absorbed the largest part of the female workforce in Dublin, as was generally the case throughout Europe.[88] Indeed the payroll of Holy Trinity priory features an allowance of three pecks to a 'housemaid' on the grange of Gorman. A perusal of the surviving wills would certainly suggest that domestic service as in institution was comparatively widespread in the medieval city. Indeed, a statute was enacted in 1349 declaring that 'every man and woman of our realm of England, of whatsoever condition, free or servile, being able in body and under the age of sixty years, not living by trading, or practising a certain craft, or having a livelihood of his own private property, or land of his own, in the husbandary of which he can occupy himself, and not serving another ... be bound to serve him who shall think fit to require him, and receive only the wages, liveries, rewards or salaries which were customary to be offered'.[89] Unfortunately more specific information regarding wage or the sexual division of domestic labour is not forthcoming. There certainly seems to be no grounds for suggesting that household servants in Dublin were overwhelmingly female; however, to attempt any kind of estimate of a likely gender division would amount to no more than mere conjecture. The extent and means of remuneration, whether they received a money wage in addition to board and lodging, is not readily apparent.[90] Perhaps the acknowledgement of debts to servants and, indeed, the specific bequests made to these domestic aides in the wills of their masters and mistresses may reveal something of the extent to which these women were valued in the urban home.[91]

The matter of outstanding debts was frequently addressed in the final testaments of individuals. In addition to allowing for the payment of dues to the serving staff in general, specific mention was often made of, perhaps,

86 *Dublin city franchise roll*, p. 11.   **87** Women's dominance was concentrated particularly in the silk-related industries: Anderson and Zinsser, *A history of their own*, p. 372. **88** Ibid., p. 358.   **89** H.F. Berry (ed.), *Statutes and ordinances and acts of parliament of Ireland. King John to Henry V* (Dublin, 1907), p. 367.   **90** There certainly seems to have been some competition in the recruitment of domestic servants. A wage limit was established under a 1299 statute of Edward I which also prohibited the inveigling the servants of neighbours, which was also forbidden by the 'Laws and Usages of the City of Dublin': Berry, *Statutes and ordinances*, p. 217; Gilbert, *Ancient records*, i, p. 227.   **91** The wills of the twelfth and thirteenth century Genoese prove particularly informative on this topic. Of the 146 servants who were mentioned in the testaments, a remarkable 140 were women (72 were servants, 53 wet nurses, and 13 were classified as having 'stayed with' the testator). Epstein points out that the voluntary nature of such bequests to servants precludes the use of wills to establish a complete record of all the servants even within one particular house: Epstein, *Wills and wealth in medieval Genoa*, pp 127–8.

personal or more favoured servants. The amounts acknowledged ranged from
18*d*. to the far from inconsequential sum of 18*s*.[92] Bequests to servants are
possibly even more revealing, particularly when personal items are bestowed,
as in the case of Thomas Finglas who left Joan, 'his maid servant', 2*s*. 6*d*. and
a woman's shirt and robe, and to 'his female house servant' 4*s*. 4*d*., two pairs
of stockings and two robes.[93] Similarly, Joan Dansey left to Margaret, her
maid servant two coats and a pair of blankets.[94] Testators also occasionally left
monetary bequests to their servants, or more unusually, to the servants of
others. For example, John Walshe made a rather benevolent gesture to Jonet
and Katherine, the maid servants of an acquaintance, Robert Weste, willing to
them the sum of 40*s*. to be shared equally.[95]

Superficially, women also seem to have retained quite a high visibility in the
brewing industry in Dublin, both in production and sale alike, throughout the
medieval period. Certainly the records of the corporation suggest that in the
fifteenth century the majority of brewers were female, a trend that would
seem to have had parallels in England.[96] Judith M. Bennett contends that the
actual use of the term 'brewesteres' in these civic regulations was indicative of
the explicit involvement of women in the industry.[97] Though it would appear
to have been quite a common female economic activity, it seems utterly
improbable that women in Dublin were brewing to the exclusion of men.[98]
The evidence substantiating the active role of women in the industry is
predominantly in the form of regulatory materials, though specific references
to actual individuals engaged in the production or vending of ale can be found
scattered throughout the various sources. Indeed some of the earliest references
point to male rather than female involvement in the industry. An inquisition
taken at the archbishop's palace of St Sepulchre in the mid-thirteenth
century, for example, records an award of land made to John the Brewer
(*braciator*).[99] Similarly, a messuage of land in 'Teyngmoth' was sold to 'John
de Aston, brewer' at the start of the following century.[100] A rather nonpartisan
indication of the ambiguous gender division in the brewing process refers
to 'people' brewing ale 'for sale' (and breaching the assise of ale) in the
St Thomas abbey area of the city.[101] The possession of a specifically designated 'brewing pan' is noted in the inventories of John Palmer who died in
April 1476, and Nicholas Delaber who died two months later.[102] Domestic
brewing does not seem to have necessarily required a great degree of capital
investment; most people could actually brew ale easily in the opinion of

92 Berry, *Register of wills and inventories*, pp 38–41, 58–60, 60–61, 133–6.   **93** Ibid., pp
151–3.   **94** Ibid., pp 142–4.   **95** Ibid., pp 15–18.   **96** P. Clark, *The English alehouse: a social
history, 1200–1830* (London and New York, 1983), p. 21.   **97** Bennett, *Ale, beer, and brewsters*,
p. 3.   **98** Ibid., p. 15.   **99** Charles McNeill (ed.), *Calendar of Archbishop Alen's register,
c.1172–1534* (Dublin, 1950), pp 101–2.   **100** *Christ Church deeds*, no. 541.   **101** Mills, *Cal.
justic. rolls, Ire.*, pp 5–6.   **102** Berry, *Register of wills and inventories*, pp 34–6, 123–5.

Bennett, by 'purchasing malt, grinding it with a hand mill, boiling water in a pot, tossing in some malt, drawing off the wort into a second vessel, and adding yeast'.[103] It is thereby possible to account for the negligible references to 'brewing equipment' in the inventories of the city's inhabitants, as regular domestic pots and pans would have sufficed. John Kyng and Jacoba Payn, his wife, actually appear to have engaged in brewing on a commercial scale. Their inventory includes a brew pan, wooden brewing vats, a mortar and pestle, an oven and an array of pots, bowls, pans and basins. However, in her appended testament (examined earlier) Jacoba, having agreed to bequeath to her husband 'all the goods which were his, and his deceased wife's', refers to none of the aforesaid equipment, suggesting that the brewing business was, in fact, John Kyng's (or possibly his deceased wife's).

An examination of the efforts made by the corporation to control the production and sale of ale in the city in the fifteenth century certainly serves to promote the impression of female dominance in the industry. In 1455, the regulation of ale measures was addressed exclusively to 'al maner of women that syllyn ale withyn the francheys of Dyvelyng'.[104] The quality of ale was also subject to similar jurisdiction, 'women-brewers' were prohibited to adulterate the product by brewing with straw, and any 'woman brewer' found guilty of selling inferior ale was to be fined initially, and ultimately suspended from 'her occupation' for repeat offences.[105] Under the 'Laws and Usages of the City of Dublin', women brewers were ordered to pay two shillings yearly, perhaps akin to the obligatory custom due by fishmongers, butchers and bakers 'to be fre in ther crafte'.[106] What is particularly significant about the ordinances of the latter half of the century however is the introduction of a new category of persons to be regulated, 'the tapesteres'. In 1470, the price of ale at which 'the brewesteres of the said citte shall syll to ther custumeres' was established, and the amount which 'the tapesteres' may charge 'as wal within house as withowte howse' was also determined.[107] Eleven years later, it was prescribed that no brewers or brewsteres were to sell their ale to a tappester or tappesters. An attempt was also made at this time to control to some extent those to whom the tappesters may sell their produce 'within house'.[108] Evidence of taverns in the city is rather elusive however, and the role which

---

103 Bennett, *Ale, beer, and brewsters*, p. 18. It is quite likely that the majority of families would have brewed on a strictly domestic level, which only required pots and pans, relatively common features it would appear.   104 An act of parliament in Ireland in 1450 prohibited the sale of wine, ale or other liquors within any city or town there, unless with 'the King's measure' – the gallon, the pottle, the quart and the pint: Gilbert, *Ancient records*, i, p. 288.   105 Gilbert, *Ancient records*, i, pp 220, 222.   106 Ibid., pp 224, 311. 107 Ibid., pp 342–3.   108 Tappesters were to sell ale (within their house) only to those of good conversation and English birth. This particular ordinance also provides an apt example of the delineation between 'the brewer' and his female counterpart, 'the brewster': Gilbert, *Ancient records*, i, p. 360.

women played in the operation of these taverns is even more difficult to
determine. In 1542, three 'taverns' were enumerated in the rentals of Holy
Trinity, one in High Street, another, appropriately, in Winetavern Street and
'a new tavern' in Bridge street.[109] In each case, the tenancy was held by a
single male. It is plausible however, that married couples may have undertaken
the management of a tavern or cellar as a joint enterprise. In 1325, for
example, Thomas Bagod and Eglentine, his wife, leased two cellars in
Winetavern Street, one called 'la crowd'.[110] Though the method of
identifying professions or occupations by surname evidence is far from
infallible, it is nevertheless important to note the debt of 9*d.* due to a 'Marion
Tapister' in the will of Dame Margaret Nugent.[111] In any case, the sale of ale
by women in taverns was expressly prohibited by an enactment of 1549.[112]

The notion that guilds fostered a marked gender division of labour must be
examined in a strictly Dublin context. In some cities, the existence of guilds
certainly contributed to a narrowing of occupational opportunity for women,
severely restricting their entry in many instances.[113] Conversely however, the
dominance of women in a particular trade was occasionally consolidated by
the formation of guilds exclusively feminine in membership.[114] While the
Dublin guilds do not appear to have insisted on the systematic exclusion of
women, the extent of their participation in guild business was certainly circumscribed. The earliest charter of the Dublin merchant guild, for example,
expressly sanctioned the admission of 'those persons and others whomsoever,
gratefully adhering to them, into the Fraternity or Guild … of the Art of
Merchants of the City of Dublin, as brethren and sisters of the Fraternity or
Guild aforesaid'.[115] Here, though women were expressly permitted as mem-

---

109 *Christ Church deeds*, no. 1191.   **110** *Ancient deeds in the Pembroke Estate Office*, p. 8.
111 Berry, *Register of wills and inventories*, pp 78–81.   **112** Gilbert, *Ancient records*, i, p. 422.
113 In Italy, women were virtually excluded from the urban guilds, leading to minimal
participation of women in the labour force; in Cologne, the guild of clothiers, which
included tailors, cutters, linen makers and cloth sellers, had no female members: Epstein,
Wage labor and guilds, pp 82, 87. Epstein also notes that some Parisian trades blatantly
excluded women; the tapestry weavers, for instance, justified such an exclusion by claiming
that 'the métier is too laborious', while the lapidaries felt that 'their métier is very subtle':
Quotations from Réne de Lespinasse and F. Bonnardot, *Les métiers et corporations de la ville
de Paris: Le Livre des Métiers d'Etienne Boileau* (Paris, 1879); Epstein, *Wage labor and guilds*,
p. 275.   **114** In the city of Cologne, there were four exclusively female guilds–the yarn
makers, the gold spinners, the silk spinners, and the silk weavers: Herlihy, *Women, family,
and society*, p.76. In Paris, the statutes of five silk guilds (gathered by Etienne Boileau)
suggest that the membership may have been chiefly female: E. Amt, *Women's lives in
medieval Europe: a sourcebook* (New York and London, 1993), pp 194–5. In fact, the
Parisian *taille* of 1300 records that 12 of the 200 crafts listed were exclusively female:
Anderson and Zinsser, *A history of their own*, p. 371. However, by 1450 Herlihy suggests
that the five women's guilds at Paris were reorganized and absorbed into predominantly
male corporations: Herlihy, *Women, family, society*, p. 82.   **115** Stephen Fox Dickson, *A
translation of the charters of the Corporation of Merchants, or, Guild of the Holy Trinity*,

bers in their own right, subsequent provisions seem to imply a somewhat subordinate position for them within the organisation. For instance, the 'brethren' were given full power to elect, every year, two masters and two wardens from amongst themselves.[116] Webb, however, asserts that the entitlement of sisters to vote at elections was 'not clear'. The use of the term *fratres* in the charter (which may include both the brethren and the sisters) suggested to Webb that perhaps female members were afforded such power.[117] However the charter appears to be a very carefully crafted document, conceding certain rights and duties to the 'brethren and sisters', and other distinct privileges to the 'brethren' alone. This would suggest that the guild was specifically constructed in such a way as to deny women equal status with male members.[118]

The extant 'founding' charters of several of the craft guilds were drawn up in very similar terms to that of the Guild of Merchants.[119] Each guild was to be composed of 'as well men as women', and the outright exclusion of women was certainly not a feature of any.[120] Similarly, the right to elect the guild officials was almost universally confined to the 'brethren'.[121] Analysis of those actually joining the various guilds is rendered virtually impossible however by

Dublin (Dublin, 1832). The charter was granted on 30 June 1451. The guild merchant is generally considered to be the first guild established in the city, and was in operation as early as 1191.   **116** Fox Dickson, *Charters of the Corporation of Merchants*, p. 5. The translation provided by Fox Dickson is to the effect that 'the Brethren of the Fraternity or Guild ... may have full power (to elect) in every year, two Masters and two Wardens from amongst themselves'.   **117** J.J. Webb, *The guilds of Dublin* (Dublin, 1918; repr. New York and Dublin, 1977), p. 17.   **118** Fox Dickson, *Charters of the Corporation of Merchants*. For example, the fact that the 'brethren' were to meet together when necessary to council and advise those responsible for the government of the guild, or that the monopoly of trade was granted to the 'Masters and Wardens and Brethren'; while the 'brethren and sisters' were involved in the making of ordinances and had the power to remove and depose the chaplain suggests that the certain rights were implicitly denied to women.   **119** The surviving charters (or abstracts thereof) include that of the guild of shoemakers (1426): H.F. Berry (ed.), *Statute rolls of the parliament of Ireland. First to the twelfth year of the reign of King Edward the Fourth* (Dublin, 1914), pp 351–5; two charters of the smiths' guild: T.P. le Fanu, 'A note on two charters of the smiths' guild of Dublin', *R.S.A.I. Jn.*, lx (1930), pp 150–164; and fragments of guild records and charters scattered through the journals, namely H.F. Berry 'The Goldsmith's Company of Dublin (Gild of All Saints)', *R.S.A.I. Jn.*, xxxi (1901); idem, 'The ancient corporation of Barber-Surgeons, or Gild of St Mary Magdalene, Dublin', *R.S.A.I. Jn.*, xxxiii (1903), pp 217–238; idem, 'The Dublin gild of carpenters, millers, masons, and heilers, in the sixteenth century', *R.S.A.I. Jn.*, xxxv (1905), pp 321–41, idem, 'The merchant tailors' gild–that of St John the Baptist, Dublin, 1418–1841', *R.S.A.I. Jn.*, xlviii, part 1 (1918); William Cotter Stubbs, 'Weavers' guild', *R.S.A.I. Jn.*, xlix (1919), pp 62–88.   **120** The phrase 'as well men as women' was a common expression in the founding charters when describing those eligible for membership. **121** The sole exception to this rule may have been in the Guild of Carpenters, Millers, Masons, and Heilers, as Berry, having examined the records of that guild, stated that 'the fraternity was to meet for the election of a master and wardens for the ensuing year': H.F. Berry, 'The Dublin gild of carpenters, millers, masons, and heilers, in the sixteenth century', *R.S.A.I. Jn.*, xxxv (1905), p. 325.

the general paucity of matriculation lists, though Berry does note that the name of only one sister, Margaret Herforde, appeared in the lists of the Guild of Carpenters, Millers, Masons, and Heilers (and in 1536 she paid 12*d*. to the master).[122] Perhaps the most conventional means of admission to a guild was on completion of an apprenticeship to a guild member, a procedure that was heavily regulated under the terms of the initial charter. While eligible candidates for service were to be 'of free condition, of the English nation, and good conversation', there was no explicit bias against women (though much of the relevant text is couched in purely patriarchal terms).[123] In a number of cities, guilds permitted widows to participate in the business of their late husbands. The guild regulations of the fullers of Paris, for instance, expressly stated that 'if a master dies, his wife may practise the craft and keep apprentices, freely'.[124] Though certainly not prevalent in Dublin, the records are not entirely devoid of suggestions of such a practice. In 1438, Richard Codde, baker, left to Joan his wife 'his terms of apprentice'.[125] It is possible that such an act merely exemplified a desire for the widow to conclude any business left unfinished at the time of her husband's death. In this case, however, the fact that Richard Codde also left his term and estate in his bake house to his wife and his son Walter suggests that perhaps a more permanent situation was envisioned.

Having been admitted to guild membership, it would appear that women were subsequently allowed to achieve full status, that is, the privileges of mastership. In the first instance, civic regulations concerned with the proper behaviour of apprentices make both 'maysteres' and 'maistricces' liable to a fine in the case of their misconduct.[126] A valuable source of corroboration also exists in the form of *The Dublin City Franchise Roll*, which denominates six women in whose service individuals were recorded as being engaged. No trades or crafts are attributed to Agnes Wodbone, Joan White, Rose Downe, Genet FitzWyllam, Genet Voder or Anne Barbi, though five of the six are recorded as free women.[127] The apprenticeship of Anne Prendergast (a seamstress) to Thomas Fouler, a cook, and his wife Rose is the only intimation of a wife taking an active part in her husband's craft. *The Dublin City Franchise Roll* is equally enlightening with regard to the extent of female indenturing. The temporal limitations of the source however, which spans a relatively short period, must be borne in mind.[128] Similarly, the fact that questions have been raised as to exactly what proportion of the membership of the guilds the *Franchise Roll* represented, suggests that as a source it may prove potentially misleading. Over the 44-year-period, women constituted 18 per cent of those

---

122 Berry, 'The Dublin gild of carpenters, millers, masons, and heliers, in the sixteenth century', p. 327.   123 Berry, *Statute rolls, Edward IV*, p. 341.   124 E. Amt, *Women's Lives in Medieval Europe*, p. 196.   125 Berry, 'Gild of S. Anne', pp 48–50.   126 Gilbert, *Ancient records*, i, pp 328–9, 370.   127 *Dublin city franchise roll*, pp 12, 14, 19, 35, 36, 39.   128 A forty-four year period 1468–1502.

admitted to the franchise, 27 per cent of whom became free on completion of apprenticeship.[129] The number of occupations with which these 46 women were associated was 12. The Oxford poll tax return of approximately a century earlier listed 93 trades, 12 of which included women.[130] By comparison, in the thirteenth century Parisian taille women were represented in an extraordinary 172 occupations.[131] In the majority of cases (39), the women were apprenticed to individuals who could be positively identified as 'merchants'.[132] The remaining women were in the service of men engaged in a variety of trades including vintner, corviser, butcher, glover, yeoman, smith, armourer and cook.

A rather bleak impression emerges of the working women of medieval Dublin. Largely relegated to the least skilled and certainly least remunerative class of labour, Dublin women failed to predominate in any trade. The records suggest that brewing, essentially the province of women in England, was carried on equally by both men and women in Dublin. The art of silk-weaving, the other female bastion, was only introduced to Ireland at the end of the seventeenth century, thereby depriving the medieval Dublin woman of the prominence enjoyed by her European counterparts.[133] Corporation records also suggest that Dublin women may have occupied a subsidiary roll in the family business, often selling their husbands' goods.[134] A very small number of women transcended these traditional limitations however, among them two nurses and perhaps more exceptionally, Elizabeth Talbot, auditrix of the churchwardens' accounts in St Werburgh's parish.[135] Her appointment in 1493–4 indicates that at least some women in the city were literate and had a basic knowledge of accounting. It is unclear whether this was a paid position or if Elizabeth offered her services gratis. Regardless, it remains an unusual show of faith in the capabilities of a woman.

CONCLUSION

Inevitably, the study of women in Dublin must suffer as a result of the unfortunate gaps in the medieval records, and the general paucity of material available unfortunately precludes the identification of general trends and

129 *Dublin city franchise roll*, introduction, pp xvii, xxiii.   **130** Anderson and Zinsser, *A history of their own*, p. 406.   **131** Herlihy, *Women, family and society*, p. 71.   **132** In twenty-seven of these thirty-nine cases, the individual's stated occupation was 'merchant'. In the remaining twelve cases, the individual was recorded as 'merchant' elsewhere.   **133** M.H. Daly, 'A few notes on the gild system' in *Dublin Hist. Rec.*, xi, no. 3, (Dublin, 1950), p. 77.   **134** In 1451, for instance, the wives of butchers and fishermen were expressly prohibited to sell meat and fish. This prohibition was reiterated in 1456–7. By 1464–5, however, the corporation seems to have relented and there was no active opposition to the fishmongers' wives selling fish: Gilbert, *Ancient records*, i, pp 274, 293, 318–19.   **135** Berry, *Register of wills and inventories*, pp 34–6; *Christ Church deeds*, no. 315; J.L. Robinson, 'Churchwardens' accounts, 1484–1600, St Werburgh's church, Dublin', *R.S.A.I. Jn.*, xliv (Dublin, 1914), p. 132.

preferences. However, one thing that seems clear is that while women in Dublin lived under the system of English common law, it did not dilute their legal power in any way. In fact, many women seem to have been rather successful at circumventing it, if not simply disregarding it. The matter of married women's wills is particularly pertinent. Despite the fact that no explicit consent was stated, fifteen married women made wills, a direct violation of the common law. Similarly, though common law ruled that all property matters were the domain of the husband, and a wife had no right to sell or transfer her own land without his consent, the explicit statement of consent was a very unusual feature. It must be remembered, however, that the women who appear in these records represent only a very small fraction of the total female population, who may, as a whole, have been entirely compliant with English common law.

In this as in all other areas, it seems that every right or privilege conceded to the women of medieval Dublin was qualified in some respect. Those permitted to hold land, for instance, found their freedom to alienate it compromised by reversionary clauses and 'life interests'. Widows might enjoy testamentary freedom, yet often found that they had very little to bequeath, having being granted usufruct of lands rather than actual ownership. Similarly, a daughter might inherit land ultimately destined for male kin. She merely served as a conduit, a means of 'keeping it in the family', in the absence of a direct male heir. Women were permitted to participate in the labour force, yet they generally remained on the periphery of the professions, performing low-skilled, low-paid tasks. Even when they worked alongside men, evidence suggests that women were paid only half of what their male co-worker received. A significant proportion of women were certainly entitled to own land, to bequeath property and to participate in the economy; however, the numerous restrictions and conditions placed on these rights served to undermine their power, and ultimately led to a less active role for women in medieval Dublin society.

Land use in medieval Oxmantown[1]

EMER PURCELL

Oxmantown, as a place name, has survived on the north side of the city of Dublin for over eight hundred years. The name is a translation of *villa Ostmannorum*, meaning 'Ostmen's town', which was later corrupted to Oxmantown. Ostmen is derived from Old Norse *Austmenn*, 'men from the east'.[2] The term originated in Iceland where it was used to describe men who came to the island from the Scandinavian homeland of Norway or from the Norse colonies, such as the Hebrides. Tradition maintains that when the Anglo-Normans took control of Dublin, in 1170, they expelled the Hiberno-Norse or Ostman population from the town. The name Oxmantown itself highlights two significant aspects of the settlement; 'Ostman' indicates the perceived ethnic dimension to the settlement, and 'town' reflects the development of the suburb and its relationship with the main town on the south bank of the Liffey.[3]

This article is concerned with patterns of land use in the suburb from 1170 to 1610, the date assigned to Speed's pictorial representation of Dublin (fig. 1). There are inherent dangers in examining such a long period: centuries tend to become condensed, and generalisations all too common. A study with a shorter time frame avoids these dangers. The source material itself also imposes some restrictions. Although regular record-keeping began in the late twelfth century, there is no single comprehensive survey of Dublin for the medieval period. References to Oxmantown are scattered throughout a variety of sources. The uneven spread of material, on the suburb and the areas within it, prompts the question as to whether this is a reflection of activity or an accident of preservation. The disparate nature of the source material may explain the current lack of a detailed survey of land use in medieval Dublin. While the evidence is in no way comparable with that for many English towns, such as Winchester or Canterbury, there is still a considerable amount of information extant. When this material is gathered and sifted, it is possible to reconstruct, as in the case of Oxmantown, an impression of settlement patterns

---

1 In memory of Patricia O'Sullivan, 1968–99, Friend of Medieval Dublin. 2 *Austmenn* is plural of *austmaðr*, 'easterner'. 3 Emer Purcell, 'Oxmantown, Dublin: a medieval transpontine suburb', MPhil thesis, National University of Ireland (unpublished, 1999).

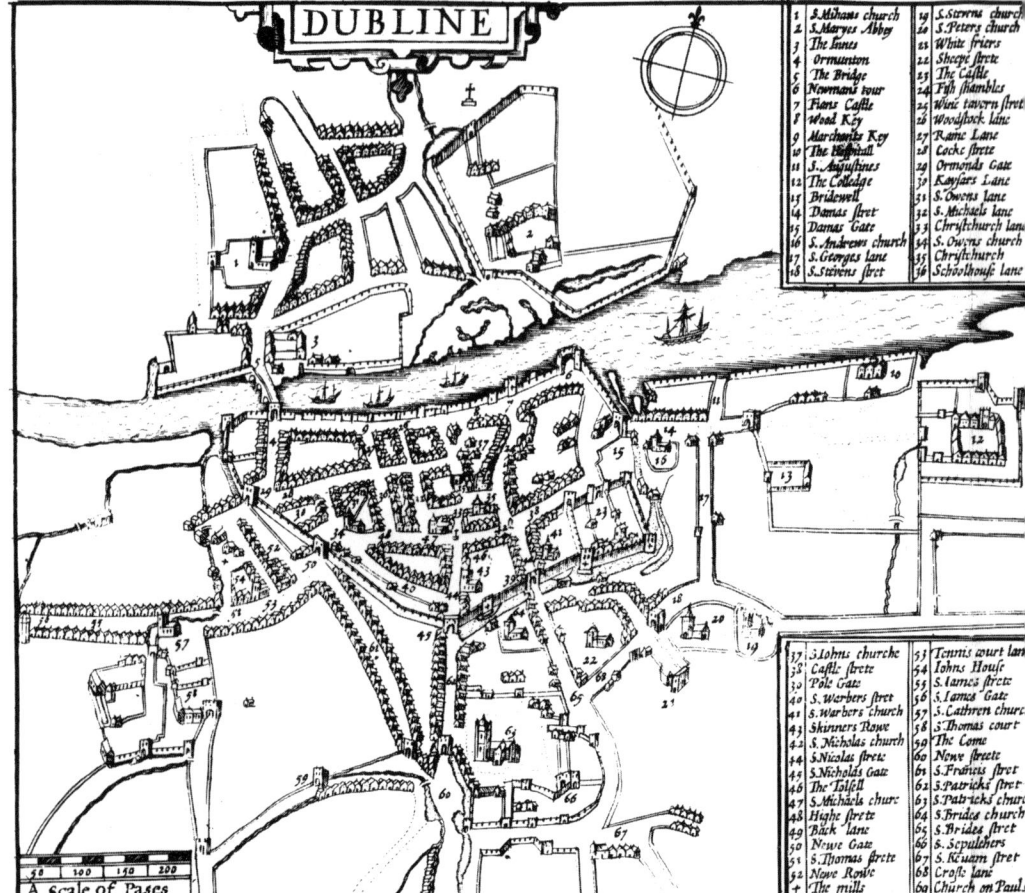

DUBLINE

1	S.Mihans church	19	S.Stevens church
2	S.Maryes Abby	20	S.Peters church
3	The Innes	21	White friers
4	Ormunton	22	Sheepe stret
5	The Bridge	23	The Castle
6	Newmans tour	24	Fish shambles
7	Fians Castle	25	Wine tavern stret
8	Wood Key	26	Woodstock lane
9	Marchants Key	27	Rame Lane
10	The Hospitall	28	Cocks stret
11	S.Augustines	29	Ormonds Gate
12	The Colledge	30	Kayfars Lane
13	Bridewell	31	S.Owens lane
14	Damas stret	32	S.Michaels lane
15	Damas Gate	33	Christchurch lane
16	S.Andrews church	34	S.Owens church
17	S.Georges lane	35	Christchurch
18	S.Stevens stret	36	Schoolhouse lane

37	S.Iohns churche	53	Tennis court lan
38	Castle strete	54	Iohns House
39	Pole Gate	55	S.Iames stret
40	S.Warbers stret	56	S.Iames Gate
41	S.Warbers church	57	S.Cathren churc
42	Skinners Rowe	58	S.Thomas court
43	S.Nicolas church	59	The Come
44	S.Nicolas stret	60	Newe streete
45	S.Nicholas Gate	61	S.Frances stret
46	The Tolsell	62	S.Patricks stret
47	S.Michaels churc	63	S.Patricks churc
48	Highe strete	64	S.Brides church
49	Back lane	65	S.Brides stret
50	Newe Gate	66	S.Sepulchers
51	S.Thomas strete	67	S.Keuam stret
52	Nowe Rowe	68	Crosse lane
+	The mills	69	Church on Paul

A Scale of Pases

1 John Speed, 1610, with Oxmantown lying north of the Liffey

and land use. The absence of a substantial study of the town core means that this discussion lacks the comparative basis that is found in examinations of the suburban development of many English towns. Individual land grants, or records of land transactions, are the main source of information. The purpose of this article is to demonstrate the potential value of these simple records as historical sources. References were transcribed and collated manually but, had time and resources permitted the use of a computer database – that is the entry of all details into a tailored programme – then perhaps a more comprehensive representation of land use may have emerged. Nevertheless, analysis of this material, even at a manual level, reveals patterns of land ownership and land use within the Oxmantown suburb.

In attempting to reconstruct medieval urban settlement one is faced with two possible methodologies: that pioneered by Salter and Urry, and used by

Keene based on historical records;[4] and that based on town-plan analysis as devised by Conzen and developed by Slater.[5] Keene's monumental work on medieval Winchester is based on the title deeds, but he also had a number of substantial surveys from which to work, for example, the tarrage survey of 1417.[6] The nature of the Dublin material makes reconstruction a difficult but not impossible task. Although the end result may not be as comprehensive as that for Winchester, nevertheless certain trends and patterns do emerge.

Conzen, using town-plan analysis, developed a method of reconstructing the medieval streetscape in the absence of reliable and comprehensive documentary source material. Such an analysis is based on 1:2500 scale Ordnance Survey maps and the identification of plan units composed of three elements: streets in the street system, plots in the street blocks, and buildings in the block forms.[7] This method has been refined and used to good effect by Slater in his study of English towns, and he has taken it a stage further. The cartographic evidence is examined in conjunction with fieldwork studies, where metrological analysis is made of the modern street plots and comparisons are made with the known medieval burgage or plot width.[8] In many cases these have proved to be identical.[9] Resources and time did not permit a detailed town-plan analysis of Oxmantown. Instead emphasis is placed on the historical record, fragmented though it may be, and it is occasionally supplemented by reference to the cartographic evidence.

LAND TENURE

Medieval Dublin had a complex system of land tenure. In Oxmantown the principal landholders were St Mary's abbey, Holy Trinity priory, and the city. Other religious foundations, located on the south bank, held land in the suburb: the abbey of St Mary de Hogges, the priory of All Saints (or All Hallows), St Thomas's abbey, and St John the Baptist's Hospital. Two significant events took place in the medieval period that affected donations to, and

4 H.E. Salter, *Survey of Oxford*, Oxford Historical Society 14, 20 (2 vols, Oxford 1960–9); W. Urry, *Canterbury under the Angevin Kings* (London, 1967); D. Keene, *Winchester studies 2: survey of medieval Winchester*, parts i & ii (Oxford, 1985).   5 M.R.G. Conzen, 'Alnwick, Northumberland, a study in town-plan analysis', in Institute of British Geographers, Publication No. 27 (London, 1960); idem, 'The use of town-plan analysis in the study of urban history' in H.J. Dyos (ed.), *The study of urban history; proceedings of the urban history group* (London, 1968), pp 113–30; T. Slater, 'The analysis of burgage patterns in medieval towns', in *Area* 13 (1981), pp 211–16; idem, 'English medieval town planning', in D. Denecke and G. Shaw (eds), *Urban historical geography* (1988), pp 93–105.   6 Keene, *Medieval Winchester*, pp 3–39.   7 Conzen, 'Alnwick, Northumberland', p. 5.   8 Slater, 'English medieval town planning', p. 96.   9 Ibid., for example, Stratford-upon-Avon burgage dimension specified in foundation charter 3.5 most modern plots conformed approximately to this size.

land held by, religious foundations. In 1279, the acquisition of lands and rents by religious houses was limited by the introduction of the statute of Mortmain. As is expressly stated in the contemporary *Laws and usages of Dublin*, 'prohibition of bequests by citizens to ecclesiastics as [they are] prejudicial to heirs and conducive to diminution of resources of the city'.[10] In 1299, Walter de la Haye, escheator of Ireland, deprived St Mary's of land because the monks had acquired it without the king's licence, that is, after the promulgation of the statute of Mortmain.[11] The record of the riding of the franchises in 1326 suggests that it may have been prompted by a desire to clarify the boundaries and rights of the city after this legislation.[12] At the end of the medieval period, the dissolution of monastic foundations and the subsequent documentation of the division of their lands provides an invaluable record, both in terms of the wealth of the institutions themselves and in the extent of lands held by them.[13]

In the medieval period, principal tenants often leased, or held, land from one another. In the 1230s, John of Coventry granted land that he held from the canons of All Saints, which lay beside land held by the friars of the hospital of St John the Baptist.[14] In 1261, the city leased to St Mary's abbey land formerly held by Geoffrey de Trivers. The monks then delivered the land to Henry Faber, son of William Palmer.[15] Quite often, religious houses were granted the annual rental value or income from a tenement, rather than the plot itself. An interesting charter records that in 1234, Margaret, daughter of Richard Gillemichelle, granted to St Mary de Hogges yearly rent of assise from a number of her tenements, including 3 marks and 26s. from her land in Oxmantown.[16]

It is clear that St Mary's abbey was one of the major landholders in Oxmantown. The tenurial rights of St Mary's over land on the north and south banks of the Liffey, and fishing rights on the river, were confirmed for the sum of 30 marks in 1200.[17] St Mary's held some of these lands prior to the arrival of the Anglo-Normans. In a similar fashion, lands held by Holy Trinity priory were confirmed in 1202. These include St Michan's and lands on either side of the church.[18] The gift, by Isake the priest, of St Michan's to

10 'Laws and usages of the city of Dublin', J.T. Gilbert (ed.), *Calendar of ancient records of Dublin*, 19 vols (Dublin, 1889–1944), i, p. 224.   11 J. Mills (ed.), *Calendar of justiciary rolls or proceedings in the court of the justiciar of Ireland 1295–1303*, i (Dublin, 1905), p. 226. 12 *Ancient records*, i, p. 134: 'that members of religious orders and others have acquired in fee, lands, tenements and rents within the city boundaries since the promulgation of the Statute of Mortmain [enacted 1279] and have without royal licence encroached on the citizens'.   13 N.B. White (ed.), *Extents of Irish monastic possessions 1540–41, from manuscripts in the Public Record Office, London* (Dublin, 1943).   14 J.T. Gilbert (ed.), *Chartularies of St Mary's abbey, Dublin*, 2 vols (London, 1884–5), i, *c*.1237–8, p. 495. 15 *Ancient records*, i, p. 93.   16 H.S. Sweetman (ed.), *Calendar of documents relating to Ireland, 1171–1307*, 5 vols (London, 1875–84), i, pp 327–8.   17 Ibid., p. 20.   18 C. McNeill (ed.), *Calendar of Archbishop Alen's register c.1172–1534* (Dublin, 1950), 1202, pp 29–30.

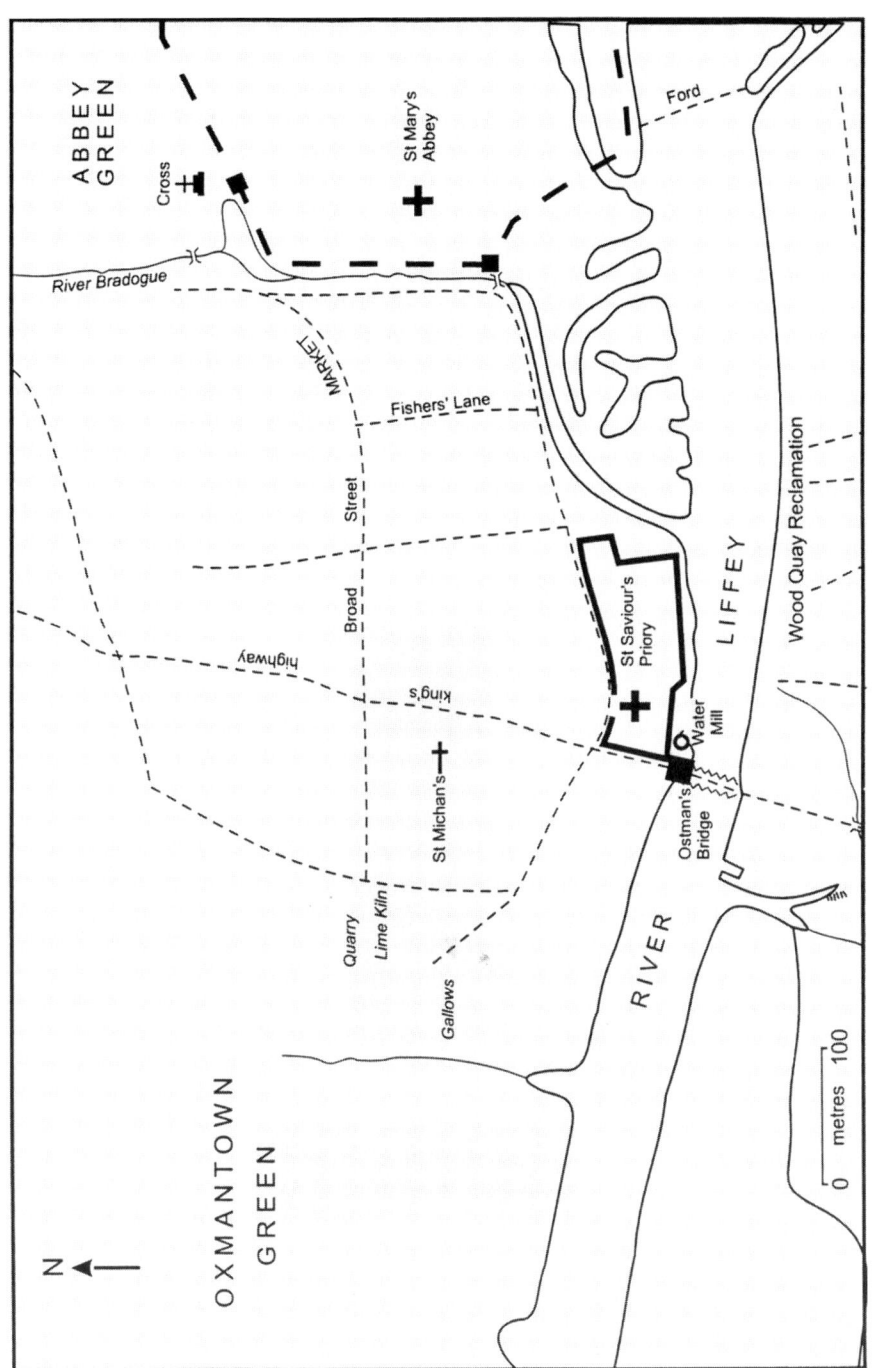

2 Sketch map of Oxmantown, c.1250 (Map based on Clarke and Simms, additions by Stephen Hannon, Geography Dept. UCD)

Holy Trinity is very interesting as it is included with a number of other grants made by prominent members of Hiberno-Norse families in Dublin: for example; the Mac Torcaills, the Mac Gillamaires, and the sons of Pole.[19] Management of communal resources, such as the River Liffey, as well as these substantial land grants, implies the existence of some form of controlling authority within the town in the Hiberno-Norse period.

Through an agreement with the city in 1213, St Mary's acquired the majority of its landholdings in Oxmantown. In exchange for lands held on the south bank, the monks received all the land between the Liffey and the Tolka.[20] The abbey made an initial down payment of 100 marks, and then an annual rent of 100s. St Mary's was the primary tenant, but the land remained under the jurisdiction of the municipality. In the late thirteenth century the abbey also entered into an agreement with the hospital of St John the Baptist: St Mary's exchanged land within the town walls for four tenements that St John's held in Oxmantown, including those belonging to the craftsmen, Matthew the carpenter and John the quarryman.[21] The emergence of St Mary's as a major landholder in the area probably resulted in a more stable Oxmantown. In the thirteenth century the abbey continued to hold land on the south bank. One of the monks' more substantial holdings comprised mills outside Dame's Gate in the Thingmouth area. In 1248, they received land to the value of 10s. as compensation for losses incurred by the king's mills at Dublin Castle.[22] The abbey mills continued in use until at least the fourteenth century.[23] The land occupied by the mills on the south bank was located almost directly opposite the abbey precinct and beside the ford that connected both banks. It is possible that the abbey had some rights over this crossing point on the Liffey, and this may explain why the monks retained land on both sides of the ford.

During the medieval period certain patterns of land ownership or land tenure emerge within Oxmantown. St Mary's abbey held land mainly, though not exclusively, in the eastern Broad Street/Fishers' Lane area of the suburb, while Holy Trinity held St Michan's church and a number of other plots in Oxmantown Street. Individual plots acquired by the other religious houses were dispersed throughout the suburb.

LAND GRANTS

Analysis of the distribution of land ownership is based on those land grants where location is positively stated, or where it is possible to determine by

19 Ibid. 20 *Chart. St Mary's*, i, pp 346–53. 21 E. St J. Brooks (ed.), *Register of the hospital of St John the Baptist without New Gate* (Dublin, 1936), 1283–4, pp 24–5. 22 *Cal. doc. Ire.*, v, no. 2941. 23 *Chart. St Mary's*, i, 1343, p. 15.

other means the location of the given plot. The potential value of land grants as historical sources depends upon a number of factors, the most important being their date. The earlier grants generally contain less specific detail. This is particularly true of Oxmantown, and it is complicated by the fact that most grants date from the fifteenth to the sixteenth century. An imbalance operates on two levels, both in terms of the number of grants and the amount of information they contain. As a result there is very little record of the development of the suburb in the late twelfth century. The extant thirteenth-century documents tend to contain less detail and seem to focus on the area to the east of Oxmantown Street.

Land grants have the potential to provide information on the following: plot size and dimensions, rental values and conditions of tenure, and information regarding land conveyance practice. They may also lend an insight into plot pattern, and issues of internal layout and access. Frequently, they specify the occupation of the grantor and grantee, as well as that of the former owner, so that it is possible to reconstruct the history of ownership and perhaps even of land use. Many land grants have abutment clauses that shed light on neighbouring plots. In the early thirteenth-century, plots are predominantly referred to as 'land' (*terra*) in Oxmantown rather than as a tenement or burgage: *c*.1235–7, William, son of Gilbert of Chester granted to St Mary's '2*s*. of rent annually received from the land which William, the tanner, holds of me in the town of the Ostmen, and lies between the land of Callach, the smith, and the land of Robert Ardene'.[24] Various terms are used in the land grants, such as 'messuage', 'tenement', and 'curtilage'. While 'messuage' does tend to occur more often in the early period, no real chronological pattern of usage emerges from an analysis of the present source material. The commonest description usually records the granting of a tenement or messuage with buildings and appurtenances. In the thirteenth century, Walter le Mercer granted 'all my rights and claims which I had, or was able to have, of land, tenements, rents, tenures, or dwellings, which Thomas of Lexington formerly held in the parish of St Michan's'.[25] This record is formulaic and suggests that in most cases standard terms or phrases were probably used. While the earlier grants are more concerned with the plot, that is the land itself, later grants often contain more detail about the contents of the tenement. In the fifteenth century William Tyrell, hooper, granted John Fanyn and Matilda Talbot, his wife 'the southern half of his dwelling-house, a right of way through the main door thereof, and a chamber which lies in the western part of the house, together with one-half of the garden, kiln, and well, adjacent thereto'.[26]

The laws and usages of Dublin specify the rent and dimension of burgage plots: 'the extent of each burgage within the city should not exceed sixty-four

---

24 Ibid., *c*.1235–7, p. 237; ibid., p. 234.   **25** Ibid., *c*.1246–7, p. 473.   **26** M.J. McEnery and R. Refaussé (eds), *Christ Church deeds* (Dublin, 2001), 1455, no. 958.

feet; yearly landgable, fifteen pence'.[27] Plot dimensions are more commonly
cited in the thirteenth-century land grants, the very grants that generally
contain the least detail regarding location. Tenements may have been less established in the suburbs and this may explain why it was important to specify
exact measurements. The issue is confounded by the fact that no consistent plot
size emerges from the numerous references to the dimensions in Oxmantown.
A greater availability of space in the suburb may have allowed flexibility in size,
though the lack of a comparative detailed analysis of burgage plots within the
walls must be acknowledged. A range of dimensions is specified: for example, 32
ft in breadth and 92 ft in length, is a common though not consistent size.[28] The
plots may have worked on a roughly 3:1 or 3.5:1 ratio, that is, length three
times the breadth.[29] It is important to stress that not all available plot sizes
conform to this measurement. Some very large plots were granted in the
thirteenth century, with dimensions of 70 ft in breadth and 92 ft in length.[30]
These larger plots may have been subdivided at a later date. Unfortunately
most of these grants fail to specify the street or location of the land.

The rental value of the plots also varied considerably. In the early 1270s,
Werburgh, daughter of Turkil, granted land to Thomas of Lexington for a
rent of 15s. 8d. The grant specifies that Werburgh had formerly let this land
to Matilda Blunde for a sum of 3s. 4d., representing an increase of over 12s.[31]
Many factors may have caused this significant rise in rent. The cost of a
tenement was related to its size, location and contents. It was governed by the
conditions of the lease itself, for example, the number of years. Stipulations
for building, maintenance and access also had a considerable impact. An interesting example occurred in the fifteenth century when Robert Blancheville
was granted Comyn's Lane provided that he make a gate at the end of the
lane.[32] One particular thirteenth-century grant lends a rare insight into
medieval land conveyance practice, in that it demonstrates that a number of
land grants were probably ratified at the same time. Walter de Suwell, vicar of
Howth, granted a rent of 10s. from his holding in Oxmantown to Thomas of
Howth. The witness list contains the following: 'John le Warre, mayor of
Dublin; Adam of Gloucester and Elias the Red, provosts; William the clerk,
Elias Burel, Richard Olof, Reginald of Gloucester, Richard Floc and Humphrey
the tailor, who were making an agreement between Roger Oweyn and Elias,
the butler, in the church of St Audeon, in whose presence seisin was delivered'.[33]
Witness lists themselves are a useful source of information. The names of the
mayors and provosts who witness the land grants in the cartularies of St Mary's

27 *Ancient records*, i, p. 224 (*c*.1305).   **28** *Chart. St Mary's*, i, *c*.1276–7, p. 499.   **29** Ibid.,
p. 227, 20ft by 76 ft.; ibid., p. 509, 28 ft by 96 ft. No dates are assigned to these grants, and
they are not witnessed by a mayor and provosts, which may suggest they date to the pre-1229
period.   **30** Ibid., *c*.1249–50, pp 489–90; ibid., *c*.1271–2, pp 511–12.   **31** Ibid., *c*.1270–1, p.
477.   **32** *Ancient records*, i, 1470, p. 341.   **33** *Christ Church deeds*, 1255, no. 495.

help to assign a date to these otherwise indeterminable records. Likewise, if the mayor or provosts are not listed, this suggests that the grant took place at some time before 1229, or at least before the 1230s, when it became common practice for their names to be attached. Names of other citizens, previously recorded, can also provide a rough indication of date. Medieval land grants tend to be witnessed by men from the street or neighbourhood of the given plot.

Many of the grants reveal information about plot patterns and complement the cartographical evidence. In the fifteenth century, Holy Trinity granted to John Tyrell 'a garden near the Fishers' Lane, in the parish of St Michan, stretching in length from said lane to the lane near the stone wall of St Mary's monastery'.[34] This description suggests that the plot had the advantage of frontage on both lanes. It also reveals something about the level of activity in these lanes themselves. Had the demand for land been greater, it is unlikely that the plot would have remained intact. Subdivision of plots occurred quite commonly and the more substantial holding was often located back from the street frontage. A transcript of a twelfth-century grant, dating to *c*.1172–6, addresses the issue of access caused by the division of plots: 'one messuage within the walls of Dublin, with the houses that are upon the messuage, that was Sunanha the Ostman's ... that messuage is the door to the door of Alberic, his brother, on the other side of the plot'.[35]

Land grants often contain references to the occupations of the parties involved in the transaction, as well as those of neighbouring tenants. Abutment clauses are invaluable in terms of the information they can provide on the location of the plot itself, the occupations of the owners, and former owners and land use. Abutment clauses formed a central part of Keene's study of medieval Winchester. He claimed that clauses occurred more frequently in the suburb of St Giles's than within the walls in the thirteenth century, because the physical boundaries were less well defined in the suburbs.[36] In the late twelfth century, *c*.1195, the following grant was recorded:

> Vincent de la Strande, with the assent of his wife, Helen, grants to Richard, the tanner, land in the northern suburb of Dublin, held from Thomas son of the Norman, situate between the bake house of the said Thomas and the land of Jordan de Luvethe, and between Gillechrist Mac an Suter, and the Liffey; rent 2 marks and a pound of cumin on change of heirs. Should grantee surrender the land, he shall pay 10 marks to grantor, unless the portion built upon between the street and the wall be then as at delivery thereof.

34 *Ibid.*, 1443, no. 938. *Chart. St Mary's*, i, p. 508, an earlier reference from *c*.1230–40 contains a similar description of another plot in Oxmantown that 'extends itself in length from one lane right up to the other lane'.   35 *Chart. St Mary's*, i, p. 480.   36 Keene, *Medieval Winchester*, pp 8–9.

The *in dorso* of this grant states: 'beyond the king's gate in the corner from beside Thomas Smothe's tenement'.[37] The exact location of this plot is difficult to determine, but if the Liffey was to the south then it lay on an east–west axis. This implies that the land of Gillechrist fronted on to Broad Street, while the land granted to Richard faced the riverfront. The wall referred to may be a quay wall. Alternatively it may be the wall of the bake-house. Presumably it was made of stone rather than wood because of the risk of fire. There were other stones houses in the suburb in the thirteenth century.[38] Two of the men mentioned in the above transaction, the grantee and one of his new neighbours, were tanners. Keene maintains that it is generally safe to interpret a surname as a craft occupation up until *c.*1350 and this guideline has been adopted.[39] Many of the early thirteenth-century land grants record craftsmen who have Hiberno–Norse names; for example, Margaret, daughter of Gilbert of Cork, granted the hospital of St John 12*d.* from land in Oxmantown which lay in between the land of Bridim fabri and Morine textris of the tenement of Richard Gillemichael.[40] These land grants clearly demonstrate that from the late twelfth century Oxmantown was composed of a mixed population; Ostmen, Irishmen and Anglo–Norman.

On one level land grants provide evidence as to individual plot histories and when several of these plot histories are put together an image of the street emerges. Certain streets display common characteristics that suggest that areas of specialised activity had developed. In the case of Oxmantown three concentrations emerge: fishing is associated with the eastern side of the suburb near St Mary's abbey; craftwork and shops are evident along Oxmantown Street; and cattle-related activity is associated with Oxmantown Green. Thus, an overall image or impression of the suburb may be reconstructed, and from this basis it is possible to assess Oxmantown's relationship with the medieval town core.[41]

One of the main characteristics of suburbs is the space that they provided for religious houses and their precincts. The religious institutions of Oxmantown – St Michan's church, St Mary's abbey, and St Saviour's priory – played an intrinsic part in the life of in the suburb. Therefore, it is important to treat them as such and not merely as separate institutions. For this reason they are discussed alongside the area of the suburb in which they were located. Keene holds a different view. In his study of Winchester, he maintains that their high walls separated religious houses physically and symbolically, and suggests that monastic communities were by their nature closed.[42] The very case he cites,

---

37 *Christ Church deeds*, *c.*1195, no. 475.   38 *Chart. St Mary's*, *c.*1241–2, no. 242. In this case the house was located on the riverfront near to St Saviour's.   39 Keene, *Medieval Winchester*, p. 250.   40 *Reg. St John the Baptist*, *c.*1241–2, pp 85–6; *Cal. Doc. Ire.*, i, *c.*1234, p. 327–8.   41 For a discussion of Oxmantown's relationship with the town of Dublin, see Purcell, 'Oxmantown', chapter 7.   42 Keene, *Medieval Winchester*, pp 139–40, explains

however, that of ribbon development in the city of Leicester (which is very similar to the pattern of St Thomas's suburb in Dublin) is evidence of their potential to encourage settlement.[43] Just as the Cistercian abbey of St Mary's encouraged the settlement of Broad Street, the foundation of St Saviour's priory stabilised the riverfront. This survey works from east to west, from St Mary's abbey to Oxmantown Green, and to a certain extent it also follows a chronological pattern, progressing from the thirteenth-century emphasis on St Mary's through to the development of Oxmantown Green in the early seventeenth century. For convenience the suburb is divided into four main areas: eastern Oxmantown including St Mary's and the area associated with fishing; the river front including St Saviour's priory; Oxmantown Street including St Michan's as a parish church and the concentration of craftworking and shops on both sides of this main street; and finally western Oxmantown including cattle-related activities and occupations associated with Oxmantown Green.

EASTERN OXMANTOWN

The dominant feature of the eastern side of Oxmantown was the abbey of St Mary's. Founded originally as a Savingnac house in 1139, it changed to the Cistercian rule in 1147. It is difficult to determine the exact precinct of the abbey in the cartographic evidence. The most informative description of the internal layout of the monastery dates from the sixteenth-century account of the division of the abbey after its dissolution.[44] Additional information is recorded in subsequent letters in the state papers and patent rolls detailing inquisitions held concerning the abbey's lands.[45] From these records it was possible to determine the contents and, perhaps with further analysis, the location of internal buildings within the precinct.[46] Two of St Mary's more

why he did not explore the religious foundations of Winchester more fully: 'they were also the centres for the administration of great estates and obtained many of their supplies independently of the Winchester markets'. **43** D. Keene, 'Suburban growth', in R. Holt and G. Rosser (eds), *The English medieval town: a reader in urban history, 1200–1500* (London, 1990), pp 97–119, at p. 117: 'There is little evidence that such foundations stimulated suburban growth, although the existence of a religious house a little way from the town as at Leicester might encourage a straggle of ribbon development, and the presence of a religious house outside a contracting town might halt the decay of the particular suburb where it lay ... By their occupation of valuable street frontage and the restriction on movement imposed by their precincts they may even have hindered commercial activity'. St Mary's abbey did impose a limit on the eastern expansion of Oxmantown. He expresses a similar view in *Medieval Winchester*, p. 144: 'In the early middle ages the great religious houses of Winchester seem not to have been a significant stimulus to suburban growth, but when the city was in decline they appear to have had a marked influence in determining the pattern of settlement outside the walls'. **44** *Extents Ir. mon. possessions*, pp 1–2. **45** *Chart. St Mary's*, ii, pp xli–iii. **46** P.J. Donnelly (ed.), *Remains of St Mary's abbey, Dublin* (Dublin, 1886), did include a superimposed plan of a

substantial buildings were leased after the dissolution; John Travers, held the church for the purpose of keeping artillery and munitions, and the abbot's lodge was granted to Lord Leonard Gray. The abbot's lodge was a substantial property within the precinct; it had other buildings and appurtenances attached, among them the abbot's chamber, the abbot's garden, and a stable. There was also a convent garden, a watermill, a horse mill, and a granary located near the outer gate. In addition there were two parks, Ash Park and Ankerest Park, the latter comprising an area of 3 acres, along with a haggard and a barn. The abbey had its own orchard called Comyn Orchard, and located within the walls there was also a tan house and a brew house.[47] The fact that St Mary's was also a liberty meant that it had its own court, prison and gallows. This evidence suggests that St Mary's had the potential to function as a separate settlement.

Many prominent residents of Oxmantown, as part of their donation to the house, requested that they be buried within the precinct in the abbey cemetery.[48] In the nineteenth century unscientific excavations of the area beneath the floor of the chapter house in Meeting House Lane uncovered some burials.[49] To the south of the chapter house a slype was also discovered.[50] The chapter house was built *c*.1190, probably at the instigation of Abbot Leonard. During the medieval period the chapter house served as a meeting place for the city council and in 1534 Silken Thomas famously stormed one such meeting.[51] St Mary's was a very wealthy abbey with a substantial church and precinct, and yet, other than the chapter house, it has left little physical trace. In the late nineteenth century, Donnelly related that a fragment of a gothic window was visible in a wall in East Arran Street, and two doorways at the rear of 25 and 26 Boot Lane (Upper Arran Street).[52] Donnelly also found a number of decorated floor tiles beneath the chapter house floor, and he dated them to the mid-fourteenth century.[53] These tiles were subsequently examined by Eames and Fanning.[54] In 1975, a portion of a cloister arcade and a number of other pieces of worked stone were discovered in Cook Street. Ó hÉailidhe suggested that this arcade was originally part of the monastery of St Mary's.[55] A wooden statue of the Virgin Mary dating to the sixteenth century, and now housed in the Carmelite friary in Whitefriar Street, is also thought to have come from St Mary's abbey.[56]

Cistercian monastery on Meeting House Lane. This was based on the location of the chapter house.   **47** Based on a compilation of evidence from the extents and letters in the statute and patent rolls.   **48** *Chart. St Mary's*, i, *c*.1260–1, pp 480–6, Thomas of Lexington; ibid., John Taylor, 1370, p. 16; ibid., Thomas Sueterby, 1463, p. 27.   **49** Donnelly, *Remains of St Mary's*, p. 4.   **50** Ibid., p. 4.   **51** Ibid., pp 14–17.   **52** Ibid., pp 4, 7.   **53** Ibid., p. 5.   **54** E. Eames and T. Fanning, *Irish medieval tiles, decorated medieval paving tiles in Ireland* (Dublin, 1988).   **55** P. Ó hÉailidhe, 'The cloister arcade from Cook Street, Dublin' in J. Bradley (ed.), *Settlement and society in medieval Ireland: studies presented to F.X. Martin* (Kilkenny, 1988), pp 379–95.   **56** Donnelly, *Remains of St Mary's*, pp 9–11.

Both Gwynn and Byrne have suggested the possibility of an English merchant settlement around St Mary's abbey.[57] In the pre-Norman period, the
foreign merchants who settled in Dublin came primarily from Chester and
Bristol. The evidence for these suggestions has been argued credibly elsewhere, in terms both of the archaeological and of the documentary evidence.[58]
Of particular interest are the links with Chester, which are probably older
than those with Bristol. Round drew attention to a charter dated *c*.1175, that
granted, or rather confirmed, trading rights to the men of Chester in Dublin.[59]
This document implies that strong trading links with Chester existed as far
back as the time of Henry I. Other evidence includes the cult of St Werburgh.
This cult originated in Chester but was also quite strong in Bristol. St
Martin's church in Dublin may have been re-dedicated to St Werburgh before
the coming of the Anglo-Normans. St Mary's links with Chester may be
stronger as the town lies in the middle of a group of Cistercian houses:
Basingwerk, Combermere and Buildwas. In 1154 St Mary's is listed as a
daughter-house of Combermere, but in 1156–7, by a decree of the abbot of
Savigny, St Mary's was made subject to the abbot of Buildwas. Given these
connections it is quite possible that a merchant community from Chester
settled around St Mary's. That both towns, Bristol and Chester, were granted
charters *c*.1171–2 and *c*.1175 respectively, argues that they had very strong
connections with Dublin.[60] The Dublin guild merchant roll show a strong
concentration of members from both Bristol and Chester.[61]

Did St Marys' abbey actively foster, or naturally attract, settlement? Recent
research in England suggests that the Benedictine order may have been
actively involved in urban settlement.[62] St Mary's Benedictine origins are
often cited to explain the unusual location of a Cistercian house in an urban
context. St Mary's daughter-house was located in Dunbrody, Co. Wexford.[63]

---

57 A. Gwynn, 'The origins of St Mary's abbey, Dublin', in *R.S.A.I. Jn.*, lxxix (1949), pp
111–27; idem., 'Medieval Bristol and Dublin' in *Ir. Hist. Stud.*, v (1947), pp 278–86; F.J.
Byrne, 'The trembling sod', in *A new history of Ireland: ii Medieval Ireland*, ed. Art
Cosgrove (Oxford, 1993), pp 1–42, at p. 26.   **58** P. Wallace, 'The English presence in
Viking Dublin', in M.A.S. Blackburn (ed.), *Anglo–Saxon monetary history: essays in memory
of Michael Dolley* (Leicester, 1986), pp 201–21.   **59** J.H. Round, 'Early Irish trade with
Chester and Rouen', in *Feudal England: historical studies on the eleventh and twelfth centuries*
(London, 1964), pp 353–4: 'Henry II. Licence to the burgesses of Chester to buy and sell
at Durham (recte Dublin) as they were wont to do in the time of Henry I'.   **60** *Ancient
records*, i, p. 1.   **61** P. Connolly and G. Martin (eds), *The Dublin merchant roll, c.1190–1265,
First supplement to the Calendar of ancient records of Dublin* (Dublin, 1992), Introduction,
p. xiv.   **62** K. Lilley, 'Coventry's topographical development: the impact of the priory', in
G. Demidowicz (ed.), *Coventry's first cathedral, 1043–1993* (Coventry, 1994), pp 72–96; T.
Slater, 'Ideal and reality in English episcopal medieval town planning', in *Transactions of
the Institute of British Geography*, xii (1987), pp 191–203; T. Slater and G. Rosser (eds), *The
church and the medieval town* (Aldershot, 1998).   **63** I. Doyle, 'The foundation of the
Cistercian abbey of Dunbrody, Co. Wexford and its historical context', in *Jn. Wexford Hist.*

Closer analysis suggests that many Cistercian houses, while they were not situated in urban areas, held properties in Irish towns, such as Cashel, Drogheda, and Waterford. Donkin and Graves have demonstrated Cistercian involvement in trade in England, while Carville has argued that trade was the main reason for Cistercian urban property in Ireland.[64] Many Irish Cistercian houses were granted the right to hold fairs or markets. Carville cites the example of Mellifont; the monks were granted the right to hold a Tuesday Fair at their village of Collon.[65] It is not inconceivable, given that St Mary's was one of the wealthiest monasteries in medieval Ireland, that its monks may also have held some form of market or fair.

Fr Ó Conbhuí has estimated that at its greatest extent St Mary's held approximately 30,000 statute acres. This figure includes the lands in the city and county of Dublin, as well as granges and vills further afield in counties Cork, Galway, Louth, Meath, and Roscommon.[66] The abbey demonstrated its wealth as early as 1213 when it gave the city 100 marks down-payment, and a yearly rent of 100s. for lands between the Liffey and the Tolka.[67] A measure of its wealth may also be ascertained by its contribution to the war with Hugh de Lacy: while the city gave £366, St Mary's gave £200.[68] St Mary's involvement in overseas trade must have made a significant contribution to the wealth of the monks. In addition to its own harbour, the abbey possessed ships, which travelled as far afield as Dieppe and Gascony.[69] In 1265 the abbot of St Mary's complained that one of his ships, having gone to Dieppe 'with merchandise to trade', was detained by the bailiffs at Yarmouth on its return journey to the grave loss of the abbot.[70] In 1293 a ship called the Roodship was granted to Peter Paris, a merchant of Youghal. This ship formerly belonged to the abbot of St Mary's and was forfeited on account of the robberies and transgressions of John le Jevene, a monk of the house.[71] In 1306 William de Baa and other monks of St Mary's, dwelling at Portmarnock, were charged with attempting to rob a ship when it was lost near Malahide. They 'took and carried away of the goods of the merchants, wax, tin and other goods'.[72]

Soc., xiv (1992–3). **64** R.A. Donkin, *The Cistercians: studies in the geography of medieval England and Wales* (Toronto, 1978); C.V. Graves, 'The economic activities of the Cistercians in medieval England 1128–1307', in *Analecta Cisterciensia* xii (1957), pp 3–60; G. Carville, 'The urban property of the Cistercians in medieval Ireland', in *Studia Monastica*, xiv (1972), pp 37–47. **65** Carville, 'Urban property', pp 42–43. Carville gives other examples but does not cite the primary source material for these references. **66** C. Ó Conbhuí, 'The lands of St Mary's abbey, Dublin' in *R.I.A. Proc.*, lxii, C (1961–3), pp 21–84, at p. 22. **67** *Chart St Mary's*, i, no. 287, pp 346–53. **68** *Cal. doc. Ire.*, i, 1225, p. 192. The abbey had difficulty in securing the repayment of this money; ibid., 1226, p. 213, and 1232–3, p. 301. **69** Ibid., iv, p. 353: 'Protection for the ship of the monks of the church of St Mary, Dublin, bearing on behalf of the Archbishop provisions to the king in Gascony'. **70** Ibid., ii, 1265, p. 126. **71** Ibid., iv, 1293–4, p. 63. **72** *Cal. justiciary rolls Ire.*, ii, 1306, p. 309.

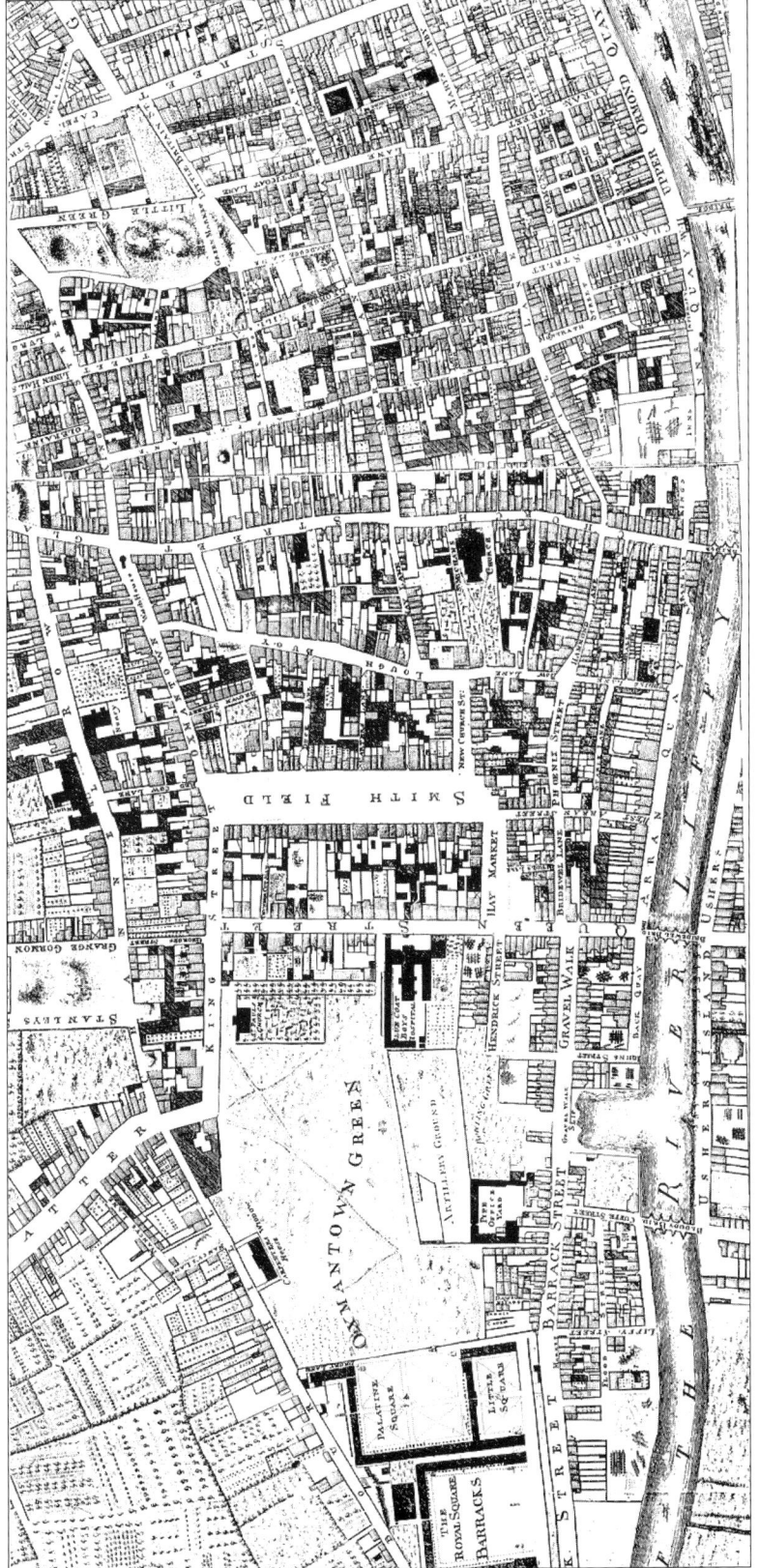

3 John Roque, 1756

The monks maintained the green area outside their gate as common pasture, and the inhabitants of Oxmantown presumably used this as well. A gate led from Abbey Green across the Bradogue and into Broad Street, and likewise at the southern end of the precinct wall a gate led across the Bradogue into Pill Lane (fig. 1). The Bradogue led to the harbour area of St Mary's and as was suggested earlier the monks may have had some control over the fording point in this section of the Liffey. These points of access and entrance to Oxmantown, and to the main town on the south bank, indicate that the abbey did indeed interact with its neighbours.

There is a strong possibility that there was a market place on Broad Street. It is important to note that there are no documentary references to a market in this area of the suburb. The suggestion is based mainly on the topographical evidence and the occurrence of similar Broad Streets in other towns, for example, Waterford and Oxford. Broad Street derived its name from a physical description of the street that broadened at its eastern end. In Oxmantown present-day St Mary's Lane actually narrows towards its eastern end into Little Mary Street. This is probably the result of an infill of the Abbey Green area. Halston Street has a strange curve that may be reflective of the mounds shown on Rocque's map, while further to the east Bolton Street curves into Capel Street and a triangle is formed with Ryders Row; again this is typical of market infill (see fig. 3). Surburban markets usually develop at the junction of two or more routeways leading into a town, as in the case of Northampton. Therefore, a more likely location for a market place in Oxmantown would have been the junction of Broad Street and Oxmantown Street. This may suggest that St Mary's abbey exerted an influence on the location of Oxmantown's initial market place. Further evidence of a market may be inferred by the reference to the cross on the green of St Mary's abbey in the 1192 perambulation of the town boundaries. Perhaps this cross was a market cross; it is still visible on Speed's map in 1610 (fig. 1). The cross may also have served as a boundary marker, signifying the division of territory between the liberty of St Mary's and the municipal liberty of Dublin. The likelihood that the monks had a surplus of goods from the tithes received from their grange lands, from their fishing rights, and from their involvement in overseas trade contributes to the argument for a market place. The agreement in 1213 between the abbey and the city demonstrates that the monks had a keen interest in developing their urban landholdings, or at least in maximising control over the lands in the vicinity of their abbey.

There appears to be a concentration of activity in the Broad Street area of the suburb in the thirteenth century. This may date to the pre-Norman period, although this concentration may merely be a reflection of the extant source material. Two land grants from c.1282–3 are very interesting, firstly because of their plot descriptions, and secondly because they demonstrate, on a small scale, the potential value of land grants and abutment clauses. Simon of Whitney and Philip of Bristol granted the following lands to St Mary's abbey:

> a certain part of my land in the town of the Ostmen ... that namely, which was formerly Vincent Maniwrench's (Ironworker), which lies between the land which was formerly Philip de Bristol's, on the eastern side and the lane next to the land formerly William Walrond's, on the western side, 66 ft., containing in width, and extending itself in length from the king's way towards the water of the Liffey.[73]

> a certain plot of land in the town of the Ostmen ... that, namely, which was formerly Gillemalass's, which lies between the land which was formerly Toryn Piscatoris's (Fisherman) on the eastern side, and the land of Vincent Maniwrench, on the western side, 33ft., containing width, and extends itself from the king's way towards the water of the Liffey.[74]

These are typical thirteenth-century land grants. Though they do not state the specific location of the plots, the description and co-ordinates may suggest that the land was located in Broad Street, i.e., 'extends itself in length from the king's way towards the water of the Liffey'. The east-west axis of the abutment clauses supports a Broad Street location. The width of these plots is worth noting for 33ft is exactly half of 66 ft and this may indicate that the original plots were subdivided. The reference to the river implies that the plots in Broad Street ran the length of the block to the riverbank. From these two land grants it is possible to reconstruct the history of four plots. William Walrond held the plot next to the plot donated by Simon of Whitney to Mary's, this plot was formerly held by Vincent the ironworker. On the other side of Simon's plot lay that granted to the abbey by Philip of Bristol, which formerly belonged to Gillemalass. The last plot in the sequence formerly belonged to Toryn the fisherman. His first name implies that he was Hiberno-Norse, and interestingly he lived in the area of the suburb associated with fishing.

The first mention of Broad Street occurs in 1262, when the mayor and commonalty granted a quarter of land with appurtenances to Adam Lawless.[75] In 1994/5, two areas within Fyffes' Yard, on the north side of Mary's Lane, were excavated.[76] The first revealed a high proportion of sherds of medieval pottery, in particular, Leinster cooking ware, dating mainly to the thirteenth century. Flanagan suggests that this may represent the sale of cooked meats in the area.[77] In the second area excavated, a number of pits containing a large

73 *Chart. St Mary's, c.*1282–3, p. 498.   74 Ibid., p. 502.   75 *Ancient records,* i, 1262, p. 94.
76 N. O'Flanagan, 'Fyffes' Yard, Beresford Lane' in *Excavations 1994,* ed. I. Bennett (Bray, 1995), p. 21; idem, 'Fyffes' Yard, Mary's Lane' in *Excavations 1996,* ed. I Bennett (Bray, 1997), pp 28–9.   77 Ibid., *Excavations 1994,* p. 21.

amount of butchered animal bones were found. One pit, with Saintonge and Leinster cooking ware, also had a number of butchered deer bones. This led the excavator to suggest that the area was associated with butchery and preparation of food.[78] In 1213, Ranulf, the butcher, held two parcels of land in Oxmantown.[79] The documentary material would suggest that Broad Street was built up, at the very least, from the early thirteenth century. The archaeological material from the Fyffes' Yard site provides evidence of thirteenth- and fourteenth-century activity, supplementing the lack of documentary material for the fourteenth century. Of more interest is the apparent absence of archaeological evidence of sixteenth- and/or seventeenth-century activity.[80] This would support the suggestion that, by this period, settlement may have contracted within the suburb to Oxmantown Street.

The second gate at the southern end of the abbey wall led to Pill Lane and the fishing area of Oxmantown. The importance of fishing in the eastern section of the suburb is clearly demonstrated by the name Fishers' Lane which is found *in dorso* on a land grant dated to 1320.[81] This is the second earliest recorded street in the suburb. The original grant in 1220 specifies 'land with buildings', which suggests that the site was already settled. In the early thirteenth century, John of Coventry granted a plot of land to Gilbert of Wales, 'lying between the land of William le Palmer, on one side, and Robert the fisherman, on the other, and holds from the king's way right up to the way next to the abbey'.[82] Robert the fisherman and Commedin the fisherman witnessed this grant. In the same period, land granted to Thomas of Lexington lay between that formerly owned by Thurstan the smith and Richard the fisherman.[83] The frequent occurrence of fisherman as an occupational name suggests that fishing was an important industry in this area of Oxmantown at least from the early thirteenth century. The development of St Mary's harbour was a major asset to the fishing industry. St Mary's held fishing rights on the Liffey, perhaps dating to the pre-Norman period, although Went maintains that these rights were granted in 1185.[84] They consisted of the right to have boats on the Liffey, as well as demarcated fishing territory on the north side of the river.

The right to have a boat to fish on the Liffey was a heavily guarded resource; most of the extant references have come about as a result of disputes or the attempts to appropriate these rights. Hamo de Valoignes tried to despoil

---

[78] Ibid., *Excavations 1996*, p. 29.   [79] *Chart. St Mary's*, i, 1213 p. 346.   [80] O'Flanagan, in *Excavations 1994*, p. 21; a renewed phase of pits that date to the late seventeenth century were also found.   [81] *Christ Church deeds*, no. 553. The actual deed dates to 1220 but the *in dorso* dates to 1320. The grant is concerned with land in Fishers' Lane itself.   [82] *Chart. St Mary's*, c.1230–60, pp 494–5.   [83] Ibid., c.1264–5, p. 474.   [84] A.E.J. Went, 'Fisheries of the River Liffey', in H.B. Clarke (ed.), *Medieval Dublin: the living city* (Dublin, 1990), pp 182–91, at p. 183.

the canons of Holy Trinity of their boat, with the result that in 1215 the king enquired of the Englishmen and the Ostmen as to whether or not they held the 'ancient rights'.[85] St Thomas's abbey was granted fishing rights in 1197, as was the city in 1200.[86] John, son of Dermot, granted salmon fisheries to All Saints, *c.*1240,[87] and he might have inherited this privilege from his father. In the thirteenth century, there is some evidence to suggest that St Mary's hired fishing boats from other religious houses.[88] In addition to this, the monks also rented out their boats to the inhabitants of Oxmantown. In 1425, John Dyer, a fisherman of a boat belonging to St Mary's, was accused of withholding the salmon tithes due to Holy Trinity.[89] This hiring and leasing of boats would have required a significant degree of organisation, control and monitoring, all of which suggests that fishing the Liffey was of considerable importance to the abbey.

The parish churches, including St Michan's, were entitled to tithes from all fish caught on the river.[90] At one stage in the fifteenth century, St Mary's attempted to claim the tithes of fish of St Michan's church.[91] According to a sixteenth-century case, the custom was to give half the tithes to the parish church where the fish were caught and the other half to the parish where the fishermen lived.[92] In 1500, it was ordained that Holy Trinity was entitled to fish on both sides of the river, 'except half of the tithes landed on the north side of the Fyr Pole which belongs to the abbot and convent of the Blessed Virgin Mary, and that marks should be erected to define the Fyr Pole'.[93] In 1503, the archbishop of Dublin, the prior of Kilmainham, and the abbots of St Mary's and St Thomas's, jointly rented the water of the Liffey for seven years at a yearly rate of 8 marks from the city.[94] A more detailed description of St Mary's fishing rights survives from 1517, including the right to place nets and stakes on the land and strand of the abbey on the north bank of the Liffey.[95]

Throughout the medieval period, there are references to men described as fishermen living in Oxmantown and in Fishers' Lane; these references extend from mention of fishermen of the thirteenth century – Robert, Richard, Commedin and Toryn – to men such as Richard Rounsell in 1581.[96] St Mary's harbour must have been a focal point for these fishermen. It is possible that

---

85 *Cal. doc. Ire.*, i, 1215, p. 99.   **86** J.T. Gilbert (ed.), *Register of the abbey of St Thomas, Dublin* (London, 1889), p. 281; *Ancient records*, i, p. 6.   **87** R. Butler (ed.), *Registrum Prioratus Omnium Sanctorum juxta Dubin* (Dublin, 1845), *c.*1240, p. 23.   **88** *Cal. doc. Ire.*, i, 1243, p. 391: 'The Abbot and monks of St Mary's, Dublin, represent that certain abbots of their order were wont to have boats on the Liffey; and other abbots had granted to them the use of boats to fish therein; but the men of Dublin will not allow them to enjoy this grant, nay are rude and affrontive to them'.   **89** H.J. Lawlor (ed.), 'Calendar of the Liber Niger and Liber Albus', in *R.I.A. Proc.*, xxvii, C (Dublin, 1908–09), pp 1–93, at p. 13.   **90** *Christ Church deeds*, 1324, no. 218.   **91** Ibid., 1435, no. 286.   **92** Ibid., 1577, no. 452.   **93** Ibid., 1500, no. 373.   **94** *Ancient records*, i, 1503, p. 390.   **95** Ibid., p. 175; *Chart. St Mary's*, ii, pp 31–4.   **96** *Chart. St Mary's*, p. 502; *Christ Church deeds*, 1581, no. 1356.

the monks employed some of the residents of nearby streets to load and unload goods and catches from these ships.

In 1218, Audeon le Brun and Richard of Bedeford granted a plot of land, 114 ft by 120ft, to the cathedral of Holy Trinity for the construction of the church of St Saviour.[97] In 1224, this church and site was granted to the Dominican friars, and the priory was dedicated to St Saviour in 1228.[98] The extents of the priory at the time of the dissolution relate that the church was to be demolished, and that 'its fabric was composed of timber, glass, iron, and stones'. There were other buildings within the precinct, including a cemetery and other accommodations containing 3 acres.[99] The size of the lands occupied by the priory had obviously increased from the initial grant made by le Brun and Bedeford. Many residents of Oxmantown, such as William Foyll, were buried in the priory cemetery.[100] Thirty human burials were found in an excavation in the 1960s when a ballroom was constructed on the site.[101] Excavations of a section of the Four Courts by McMahon, in 1984, discovered layers of humus material and human skeletons.[102]

In 1285, Edward I granted the friars thirty oak trees for the fabric of their church.[103] This wood was probably used for the construction of the church roof. McMahon's excavation uncovered a stone fragment of a quatre-foil indicating the presence of an aisled church. This fragment was dated to the thirteenth century and it fits nicely with the period of construction of the priory.[104] Decorated floor tiles were also found, many sharing similar patterns to those found at St Mary's.[105] Excavations also revealed a stone-built chancel and a sluice gate dating to the mid-thirteenth century.[106] Clarke suggested that the latter might be the remains of a millrace, which is interesting given that there are references to mills near the bridge on the north bank.[107] McMahon suggests that they may be part of a water conduit.[108] In the thirteenth century, *c*.1228–55, the Dominicans were awarded a special privilege by the city: 'permission to receive part of the city water supply, to be taken within the walls of the city at Newgate'.[109] This grant proceeds to specify that

97 M.P. Sheehy, 'The *Registrum Novum*, a manuscript of Holy Trinity cathedral: the medieval charters', *Reportorium Novum* 1, pt iii (1961–4), pp 249–81, *c*.1218, at p. 270. 98 M. McMahon, 'Archaeological excavations at the site of the Four Courts extension, Inns Quay Dublin', in *R.I.A. Proc.*, C, lxxxviii (1988), pp 271–319.   99 *Extents Ir. mon. possessions*, pp 53–4.   100 *Christ Church deeds*, 1348, no. 239.   101 McMahon, 'Archaeological excavations', p. 276.   102 Ibid., p. 291.   103 *Cal. doc. Ire.*, iii, p. 38.   104 McMahon, 'Archaeological excavations', p. 285 and p. 307.   105 Eames and Fanning, *Medieval Irish tiles*, catalogue numbers, L38, L49, L72, L73, L76, L78.   106 McMahon, 'Archaeological excavations', p. 285.   107 Ibid., p. 311.   108 Ibid.   109 *Ancient records*, i, p. 101.

the width of the pipes within the priory were not to exceed the size of a monk's little finger. The specification regarding the width of the pipes indicates the degree of municipal control exercised over the valuable supply of fresh running water. The friars were a mendicant order and their main means of support were the goods they received in return for sermons. It was customary that the mayor, on the day of his inauguration, crossed the bridge to St Saviour's to hear a sermon preached there by the prior. Each Sunday the friars preached three sermons in their own church, one in the Carmelite priory on the south bank, and two in nearby St Mary's abbey. For these services, the friars received 80 measures of wheat and 80 habits annually. This figure led O'Sullivan to conclude that there were probably 40 friars resident within the priory.[110]

During the medieval period, a ferry operated across the Liffey and the Dominicans were responsible for the collection of tolls. On Speed's map, there is a slipway visible in front of the priory, and to the east of this landing spot there are features that resemble steps (fig. 1). Most of the documentary references to the slipway date primarily to the period after the dissolution of the priory, and confirm that the Dominicans originally held the slipway and surrounding lands.[111] The physical presence of the Dominican priory on the north bank of the river may have stabilised the bank and encouraged further secular settlement in the area. It also aided the development of Pill Lane, though on Speed's map houses are located only on the northern side of this street (fig. 1). In the thirteenth century there is a concentration of land grants that specify their location next to the river.

There is little doubt that land reclamation first took place on the south bank. Reclamation on the north side of the river probably began on the eastern side of the bridge; with St Saviour's priory and particularly with St Mary's abbey, it was considerably more developed than the riverbank to the west. On Speed's map, land on the eastern side of the bridge extends further into the riverbed as compared with that on the western side (fig. 1). The construction of their own harbour, their involvement in overseas trade, and their ownership of seaworthy ships would suggest that it was in the interest of the monks of St Mary's to raise the level of the water at their quay-side to enable their ships to dock, although larger ships probably used the abbey's harbours in County Dublin, such as Portmarnock and Bullock, as they were more accessible than the Liffey. There was definitely a quay on the eastern side of the bridge by the late fifteenth century; the friars of St Saviour's were licensed to build a house over the slip in front of the chapel of Mary and 'beside the quay of the said city'.[112] Archaeological excavation of Arran Quay

110 B. O'Sullivan, 'The Dominicans in medieval Dublin', in Clarke (ed.), *The living city*, pp 83–99, p. 85. 111 *Ancient records*, i, 1557, p. 465. 112 *Ancient records*, i, p. 359.

revealed evidence for man-made reclamation on the north bank of the river, to the west side of the bridge. Two excavations were carried out; one directed by Alan Hayden along Arran Quay in 1990, and a second, directed by Simpson, near the corner formed by Hammond Lane and Church Street in 1993.[113] Hayden's excavation of Arran Quay uncovered a series of revetments built in to the river, and back-filled. These dated to the fourteenth century, although they shared common techniques with those of thirteenth-century date found at Wood Quay.[114] The first revetment on the south bank dates to *c.*1210, and two more revetments were set further out into the river before the construction of the stone quay wall *c.*1300.[115] The stone wall discovered by Hayden at Arran Quay dates to the late fourteenth or early fifteenth century, but he questions whether or not, even at high tide, this would have functioned as a quay.[116] Simpson's excavation revealed a timber structure that may represent the base of a millrace. More importantly, a number of timber-braced revetments were found, and these were dated by associated finds to the thirteenth century.[117]

Land reclamation took place on both sides of the river in the thirteenth and fourteenth centuries. There is some debate as to whether or not the construction of sections of the revetments is a reflection of each plot owner being responsible for his own section, as Wallace suggested for Dublin, or whether it represents the division of work among gangs of labourers, appointed to various citizens, as Hurley suggested for Waterford.[118] A grant to Radulf le Hore of ground opposite St Saviour's, includes permission 'to take in as much of the land *rereward* on the bank towards the west as he may desire, but without damage to the citizens and town'.[119] *Rereward* probably means 'rearward'; the reference is confusing but it may imply that he had permission to reclaim land from the river. There are other references to land in this area which describe the Liffey located to the west, and may relate to the development of a small lane in front of the priory. In 1279, Claricia granted to Henry Fychet land that 'extended from the water of the Liffey on the west, to the highway on the east opposite the friars preacher, and from the land of Edward Colet to that of William Walerand, her father'.[120] Though it is impossible to make topographical sense of these co-ordinates, references to land grants beside St

---

113 See Alan Hayden, '9–12 Arran Quay, Dublin', in *Excavations 1990*, ed. I Bennett (Dublin, 1991), pp 27–8: L. Simpson 'Arran Quay, Dublin', *Excavations 1993*, ed. I. Bennett (Bray, 1994). 114 Hayden, 'Arran Quay'. 115 P. Wallace, 'Dublin's waterfront at Wood Quay: 900–1317' in G. Milne and B. Hobley (eds), *Waterfront archaeology in Britain and Northern Europe* (London, 1981), pp 109–18, at p. 112. 116 Hayden, 'Arran Quay'. 117 Simpson, 'Arran Quay'. 118 P. Wallace, 'A reappraisal of the archaeological significance of Wood Quay' in J. Bradley (ed.), *Viking Dublin exposed: the Wood Quay saga* (Dublin, 1984), pp 112–13, at p. 120; M. Hurley, 'Late Viking-Age settlement in Waterford city ', in W. Nolan et al. (eds), *Waterford: history and society, interdisciplinary essays on the history of an Irish county* (Dublin, 1992), pp 49–72, at p. 62. 119 *Ancient records*, i, *c.*1244–5, p. 85. 120 *Christ Church deeds*, 1279, no. 112.

Saviour's and/or on the riverbank are very common in the thirteenth century.[121] Radulf le Porter was granted by the city a plot of land, *c.*1238–9, on condition that he did not confer it on any religious order: 'ten feet of their ground, in breadth, opposite, the habitation of the friars preachers of the Holy Saviours, Dublin, towards the west, and in length from the street so far as the thread of the water of Avenlif'.[122] Approximately two years later, le Porter granted this plot of land with a 'stone house on the bank' to St Mary's and St Saviour's.[123] The land was then leased to Thomas of Lexington,[124] who may even have regranted it to St Mary's, who in turn granted it to Walter Hacket.[125]

Land located on either side of the bridge was divided into plots from a very early date. The 1213 agreement between the city and St Mary's included 'the land which is at the head of the bridge in the corner of the town of the Ostmen'.[126] The bridge was the main means of travel and communication between the suburb and the city on the south bank. In 1317, stones were taken from the bridge and St Saviour's priory in order to fortify the walls of the city on the south bank against the impending Bruce attack.[127] Of further interest are the grants of land on either side of the bridge: both Richard le Porter (*c.*1238–9) and John de Graunstete (in 1317) received land on the north and south banks of the river.[128] In 1347, Holy Trinity granted John de Graunstete land on the north bank, in front of the house of St Saviour's, for the construction of a chapel in honour of the Virgin Mary.[129] Some references to the chapel imply that it was actually located on the bridge, but it is visible on the northern abutment on Speed's map (fig. 1). The chapel functioned as a bridge chapel and officials probably collected tolls from traders and travellers as they waited to cross the bridge, or take the ferry to the city.[130] There may have been small shops or stalls on the bridge. References also suggest that fishing nets were hung on the western side of the bridge in order to catch salmon before they reached the other side.[131]

Land use next to the bridge was intensive, as can be seen on Rocque's map. One of the more interesting formations is the plots that adjoin the bridge on the north side. This valuable location was used to its greatest possible extent, in that the plots closest to the bridge faced the main street while those further along the abutments faced the quays, thus creating an additional lane or street (fig. 3). Although the map dates to the eighteenth century, this formation probably reflects the medieval settlement pattern. The shape of present-day

121 *Ancient records*, i, *c.*1239–40, p. 83.   **122** Ibid., i, *c.*1238–9, p. 84.   **123** *Chart. St Mary's*, *c.*1241–2, p. 475.   **124** Ibid., *c.*1260–1, p. 472.   **125** Ibid., *c.*1276–7, pp 470–1. **126** Ibid., 1213, pp 345–53.   **127** *Ancient records*, i, Appendix 1, 1315: attack of Edward Bruce, p. 546.   **128**   *Ancient records*, i, pp 112–13.   **129** *Christ Church deeds*, 1347, no. 236; J. Mills (ed.), *Account roll of the priory of the Holy Trinity, Dublin, 1337–46*, intro. J. Lydon and A.J. Fletcher (Dublin, 1996), p. 156.   **130** O'Sullivan, 'Dominicans', pp 95–6. **131** Went, 'Fisheries of Liffey', pp 186–7.

Arran Quay, as it approaches Church Street bridge, was influenced by these plots. This can be seen most clearly at the corner formed by Heather's Shoe Shop, where the street frontage moves back several feet. This alteration in the street frontage probably came about in order to accommodate the need for access and the lane created by the abutment plots. This provides a clear example of how medieval land use patterns have shaped the streetscape of the modern city.

OXMANTOWN STREET: THE MAIN STREET

Initial analysis had suggested a concentration of thirteenth-century land grants in the Broad Street or eastern part of Oxmantown, with a shift of emphasis in the fourteenth century to Oxmantown Street. While this analysis holds to a certain extent, closer inspection reveals that the distribution of material is quite even across the suburb for the early period and, in fact, there is a contraction of references to the western part of the suburb in the late medieval period. This may be a reflection of the source material. St Mary's records are concerned mainly with the thirteenth century and had they continued into the fourteenth century perhaps a very different image of settlement would be presented. In the late fourteenth century, the documents are primarily concerned with Oxmantown Street, with a particular focus on the lands around St Michan's church. There are references to men who represent the entire range of medieval crafts and occupations, holding land in this, the main street of the suburb. Shops were also located on the lands to the north of St Michan's (fig. 4).

The reputed foundation of St Michan's church (*c*.1095) is the earliest indication of settlement in the Oxmantown area.[132] St Michan's was to remain the only parish church on the north bank until the foundation of St Paul's and St Mary's in 1697. The 1095 foundation-date for St Michan's is derived from Hanmer's chronicle. Meredith Hanmer was prebend to St Michan's from 1595 to 1604, and Lawlor suggested that he might have had access to lost manuscript material.[133] St Michan's is listed among a number of churches associated with Dublin in a poem with an Armagh provenance, dated by Ó Corráin to *c*.1121–29.[134] The next reference to the church dates to *c*.1179.[135] St Michan's is the first church mentioned in the list and this precedence has

---

132 M. Hanmer, 'The chronicle of Ireland', in J. Ware (ed.), *Ancient Irish histories: the works of Spencer, Campion, Hanmer and Marlborough* (Dublin, 1663), p. 97. For discussion of the origins of St Michan's church, and settlement on the north bank prior to the coming of the Anglo-Normans, see Purcell, 'Oxmantown', chapters 1 and 2. 133 H.J. Lawlor, 'Note on the church of St Michan, Dublin', in *RSAI Jn.*, lvi (1926), pp 10–21, at p. 14; J. Bradley, 'The topographical development of Scandinavian Dublin', in F.H.A. Aalen et al. (eds), *Dublin city and county: from prehistory to present* (Dublin, 1992), pp 43–56, at p. 51. 134 D. Ó Corráin, 'Ireland, Wales, Man and the Hebrides', in P. Sawyer (ed.), *The Oxford illustrated history of the Vikings* (Oxford, 1997), pp 83–109, at p. 107. 135 *Alen's register*, p. 7.

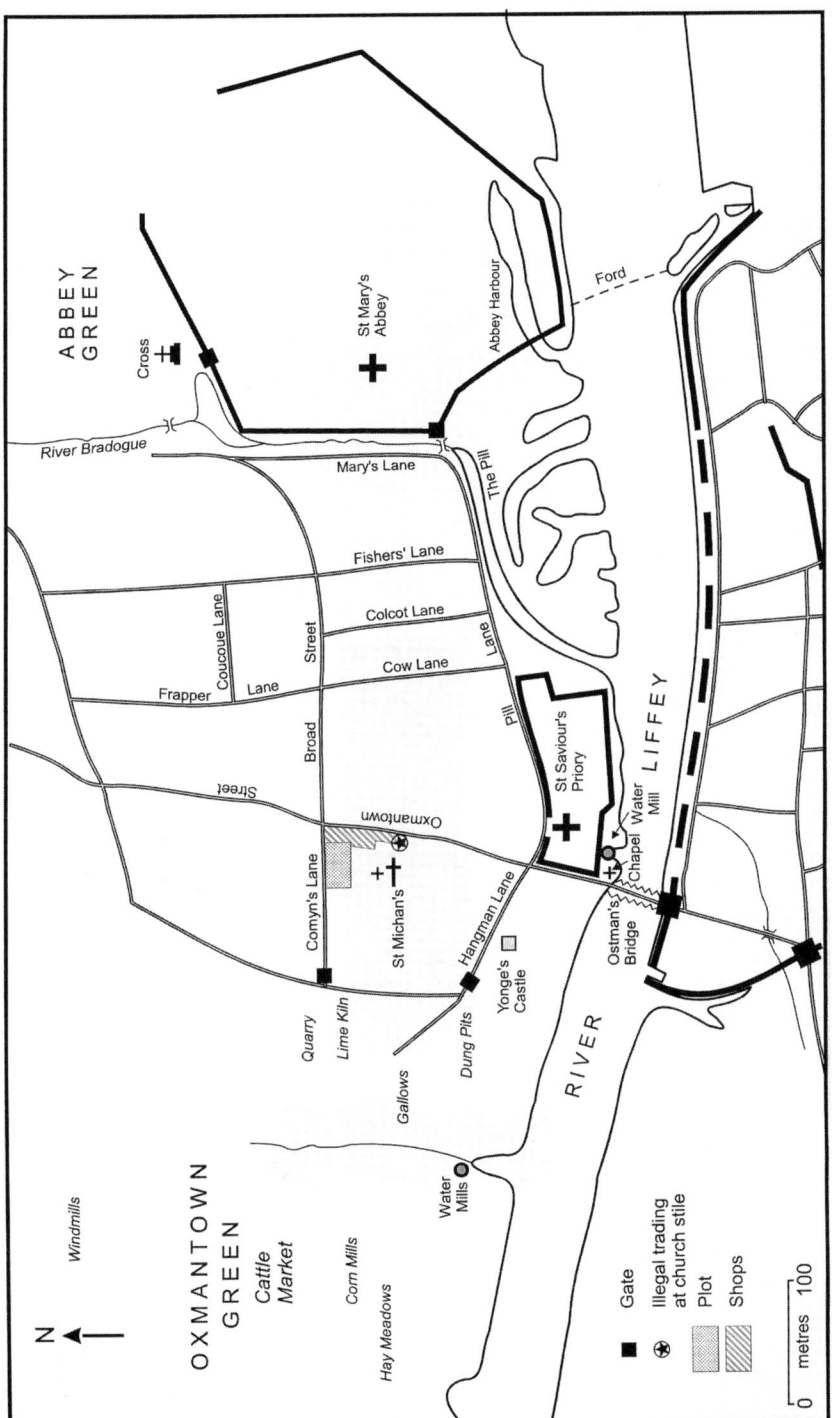

4 Sketch map of Oxmantown, c.1500. (Map based on Clarke and Simms, additions by Stephen Hannon, Geography Dept. UCD)

led to the suggestion that it was one of the older churches.[136] There is very little structural information available for the eleventh-/twelfth-century fabric of St Michan's. The present church was built in 1685–6 by the then rector, Dr John Pooley.[137] The arrangement of the church tower is deceptive: it is based on a fifteenth-century model and so looks medieval in date. Craig has drawn attention to a series of church towers from Dublin – such as St Michan's, St Michael's and St Audoen's – all of which share similar construction in the seventeenth century.[138] The vaults of St Michan's do not date to the twelfth century, as is often suggested, but are late medieval at the earliest. Craig maintains that the layout of the vaults tallies with the Renaissance plan of the church. He goes on to suggest that the new St Michan's was probably larger than its medieval predecessor and that it was certainly broader.[139]

St Peter's church in Waterford may be a contemporary of St Michan's. Both churches date to the late eleventh/early twelfth century and both had suburban locations. Bishop Samuel of Dublin and Máel Ísu, bishop of Waterford, were trained and ordained by Archbishop Anselm of Canterbury. Letters reveal that all three men remained in contact during the late eleventh and early twelfth century.[140] In this way, common architectural fashions or trends may have been transmitted. The alignment of the steps of St Michan's suggests that they preserve the outline of an earlier structure with perhaps a smaller nave. Excavation and analysis of St Peter's site in Waterford revealed twelve phases of development dating from the early twelfth to the seventeenth century.[141] St Peter's was located on the site of an earlier graveyard dated to the eleventh century and post-holes suggest the presence of a timber church. In the early to mid-twelfth century, a church with a rectangular nave and chancel was constructed, 6.2 m in length from east to west.[142] During the thirteenth century, both the chancel and the nave were expanded and a round apse was added.[143] In the later medieval period, the church was expanded eastwards so that it became a long rectangular building 26.05 m from east to west.[144]

The extent of St Michan's churchyard and cemetery may originally have been greater than it is today. On Rocque's map, the cemetery continues north-wards behind the large plot at the back of the plots that front on to Oxmantown Street (fig. 3). At an earlier date, the cemetery may have extended as far as

---

136 Lawlor, 'Note on St Michan's', p. 12; Bradley, 'Topographical development of Dublin', p. 51.   137 M. Craig, *Dublin, 1660–1860* (London, 1992), p. 41.   138 Ibid.   139 Ibid. 140 M. Rule (ed.), *Eadmeri Historia Novorum in Anglia* (London, 1984), pp 73–4 and pp 76–7. See also A. Gwynn, 'St Anselm and the Irish church', in G. O'Brien (ed.), *The Irish church in the eleventh and twelfth centuries* (Dublin, 1992), pp 99–115; Gwynn, 'Bishop Samuel', pp 81–8.   141 M.F. Hurley, and S.W.J. McCutcheon, 'St Peter's church and graveyard'; B. Murtagh, 'The architecture of St Peter's church', in M. Hurley et al. (eds), *Late Viking age and medieval Waterford* (Waterford, 1997), pp 190–227 and pp 228–43 respectively.   142 Murtagh, 'Architecture of St Peter's', p. 228.   143 Ibid., p. 231. 144 Ibid., p. 231.

Comyn's Lane. Excavations of a site in May Lane revealed burials, all of which were found in levels dating from the late medieval period.[145] No evidence regarding the boundary of the precinct of the site was uncovered and Conway suggests that it might lie under or close to modern-day May Lane (Comyn's Lane).[146] In 1996, a pre-development site assessment of 145–150 Church Street, north of May Lane, uncovered 'a layer of disarticulated human remains cut into the natural gravel to the immediate south of the excavated site'.[147] Subsequent excavation carried out by Meenan revealed a ditch located below layers containing thirteenth- and fourteenth-century pottery and animal bones.[148] This may in fact represent the boundary of St Michan's.[149] This ditch also contained six intact human burials and nine disarticulated burials.[150] The ground level of the present cemetery at the back of St Michan's is significantly higher than that of Bow Street, suggesting that there is probably a considerable build-up of burials on the site. In the medieval period, the church was accessible from both Oxmantown Street and Bow Lane. In 1347, Holy Trinity granted John de Graunstete licence to construct a chapel in honour of the Holy Trinity in St Michan's churchyard on the north side of the church.[151] All of this suggests that the churchyard may have been greater, and the church itself smaller, in the medieval period, for there would have been no room on the north side of the present church.

In 1458, permission was granted to John Chever, clerk and keeper of the rolls of the king and his chancery in Ireland, 'to found a chantry of one or two chaplains in honour of St Cithe (Sythe) the Virgin, at the altar of St Cithe, in the church of St Michan in the vill of Oxmantown'.[152] The south aisle of the chancel was dedicated to St Sythe, an East Anglian princess whose cult originated in Chich near Colchester, and is associated with Evesham, Worcester, Hereford and Aylesbury in the late eleventh and early twelfth century.[153] The dedication to the saint would further support a pre-Norman foundation date for St Michan's church. The guild dedicated to the Blessed Virgin and St Cithe was instituted in 1476.[154] It is difficult to determine the comparative wealth of St Michan's as a parish church. In 1306, it was valued at £4 8s. while St Michael's was worth £6 12s., and St John's 100s. 10d.[155] In 1339, St Michan's was able to render 2s., in line with other churches from within the

---

145 C. Conway, 'May Lane/Bow Street Dublin', *Excavations 1996*, ed. I. Bennett (Bray, 1997), p. 29.   **146** Ibid.   **147** D. Murtagh, '145–150 Church Street', in *Excavations 1996*, pp 21–2.   **148** R. Meenan, 'Old distillery site, Church Street, Dublin', in *Excavations 1997*, ed. I Bennett (Bray, 1998), p. 37.   **149** Ibid.   **150** Ibid.   **151** *Christ Church deeds*, no. 236.   **152** H.F. Berry (ed.), *Statute rolls of the parliament of Ireland: reign of King Henry VI* (Dublin, 1910), xii, p. 513.   **153** Bradley, 'Topographical development', p. 51, suggests that her cult spread through London.   **154** Colm Lennon discusses the foundation charter of this guild, in 'The foundation charter of St Sythe's guild, Dublin, 1476', *Archivium Hibernicum*, xlviii (1994), pp 3–12.   **155** *Account roll of Holy Trinity*, appendix, p. 192.

walls; for example, St John's 2*s*.[156] The extents at the time of the dissolution
record that St Michan's church held a number of properties in the suburb and
within the walls of the city.[157] The total value of these lands, including two
watermills, was £33 7*s*. 9*d*.[158] The original value may have been much greater,
given that many of the tenements in the extents are described as 'now waste'.

Oxmantown Street, the king's highway, is the location commonly given for
the entire spectrum of craft-workers across the medieval period and the list
includes blacksmiths, glassworkers, masons, tailors, dyers, skinners, hoopers,
carpenters, weavers, and bakers. St Michan's, as the only parish church on the
north bank of the Liffey in the medieval period, must have been a focus of
activity for these craftsmen. Holy Trinity continued to hold many of the properties surrounding St Michan's and a list of their tenants in 1542 includes
'John Goldsmith (tenant of the house above the church stile), John Pers and
John Baly (tenants of houses next to the stile)'.[159] On Speed's map, the
church's land on the north side extends behind the neighbouring houses,
while to the south there appears to be open access. On Rocque's map, the plot
on the north side abuts directly onto the churchyard, creating an entrance
with two other plots located directly in front of the church (fig. 3). Even
today, the gable end of the house on the north side of the church extends into
the churchyard.

The area north of St Michan's appears to have been a prime site in
Oxmantown, situated on the main routeway into the city (fig. 4). The history
of this area can be traced from the fourteenth to the early seventeenth century.
In 1306, John Serjant paid the prior of Holy Trinity 8*s*. for one messuage,
next to the cemetery of St Michan's.[160] John Serjant was mayor of Dublin in
1308. A century later, in 1407,

> John Ingoll and John Mole, chaplains [of Holy Trinity] release to Henry
> Marburgh, John Hothum, and William Poddyn, chaplains, six shops in
> Oxmantown, parish of St Michan, situate between the highway on the
> front and east, the land of Thos. Serjant held by John Fychet 'Deyer',
> on the west, St Michan's churchyard on the south, and the land of the
> said Thomas on the north.[161]

It would seem that the land held by John Fychet, dyer, formerly that of Thomas
Serjant, was located across the rear of a number of properties that fronted
onto Oxmantown Street. It is impossible to determine the size of this property,
but indications are that it was quite substantial. On Speed's map, the houses

---

156 *Christ Church deeds*, 1339, no. 232.   157 *Extents Ir. mon. possessions*, pp 6–8.   158 Ibid.,
p. 8.   159 *Christ Church deeds*, 1542, no. 1191.   160 *Account roll of Holy Trinity*, p. 192.
161 *Christ Church deeds*, 1407, no. 828. It would appear that the western plot was in the
hands of John Dyer by 1401; ibid., no. 810.

to the north of the church front onto Oxmantown Street only; no plot divisions are shown and no houses or buildings were located behind the main frontage (fig. 1). Keene has suggested that Speed may have exaggerated the extent of buildings along the street frontages in Winchester, and the same may hold true for his depiction of Dublin.[162] Rocque's map, however, depicts a complex plot pattern, suggesting that some of the plots to the north of St Michan's had the advantage of frontage on both Oxmantown Street and Comyn's Lane. There is also a large plot, located at the back, which may represent the land held by the Serjant/Fychet and Barnwall families. If Rocque's map is an accurate representation of the medieval plot pattern, then access to this land may have been via Comyn's Lane and/or a small passage from Oxmantown (fig. 3).

In Murtagh's excavation of 145–50 Church Street, two lime pits dating from the mid- to late thirteenth century were uncovered. He quotes the reference to the Fychet family, suggesting that it supports the association of the area with tanning.[163] Different craftsmen generally practised tanning and dyeing but, because their crafts are interdependent, they are usually found in close proximity to one another. Tanning continued in this part of the street into the sixteenth century: Holy Trinity granted a plot of land on the north side of St Michan's churchyard to Richard White, tanner.[164] Excavation of 145–50 Church Street also revealed a total of nineteen rubbish pits, the majority of which date to the thirteenth/fourteenth century, and some to the sixteenth century.[165] The finds displayed a distinct lack of personal goods and were composed mainly of domestic refuse, pottery, slates, ridge and floor tiles.[166] The proposed date of this material is important for it demonstrates that although most documentary references date from the late fourteenth century onwards, the lime-pits and rubbish pits provide evidence of thirteenth-century activity.

In the fifteenth century, many land grants are specified in relation to St Michan's and to the land held by John Fychet. In the sixteenth century, very similar notices are given, except that the land passed into the hands of the Barnwalls, who acquired the property *c.*1498.[167] A good description is found in 1539 when Holy Trinity granted to William Power, clerk, and Katherine, his wife, 'a tenement now held by them in the parish of St Michan, confessor, situate between the king's way, on the east, Barnwall's lands, on the west, St Michan's churchyard, on the south, and lessor's lands on the north'.[168] The Barnwalls were a major family in sixteenth-century Dublin.[169] It was common practice for families such as the Barnwalls, Dowdalls, and so forth, to hold estates outside the city of Dublin. On a smaller scale, *c.*1326, John Serjant was

162 Keene, *Medieval Winchester*, p. 34. **163** Murtagh, '145–50 Church Street', p. 21. **164** *Christ Church deeds*, 1539, no. 1175. **165** Murtagh, '145–50 Church Street', p. 21. **166** Ibid. **167** *Christ Church deeds*, 1498, no. 1109. **168** Ibid., 1539, no. 1174. **169** C. Lennon, *The lords of Dublin in the age of the Reformation* (Dublin, 1989); see especially chapter 1.

a tenant and farmer of Grange Gorman but he also had a messuage near St Michan's churchyard.[170] That families such as the Barnwalls occupied land in Oxmantown, and particularly in Oxmantown Street, suggests that this area was a valued location. The tenurial history of the large tenement to the north of St Michan's may be reconstructed as follows: the Serjant family in the fourteenth century, the Fychet family in the fifteenth century and the Barnwall family in the sixteenth century. The Barnwalls were still in possession of the tenement in 1576[171] (see fig. 4).

In the late fourteenth and early fifteenth century, references to shops emerge north of St Michan's and in front of the Fychet/Barnwalls lands. In 1407 there were six shops.[172] Oxmantown may have had shops from an earlier date, for there are references to a *cellarium* in the early thirteenth century,[173] though the matter is complicated since *cellarium* may mean a cellar, storeroom or shop. Throughout the fifteenth century, there were shops on Oxmantown Street. Holy Trinity granted two shops along with a garden to Margaret Dowoke, widow.[174] The abutment clause mentions the Serjant family, and demonstrates that its members continued to hold land in the area. At the time of the dissolution, St Michan's held two shops in Oxmantown.[175] The shops, located to the north of the medieval parish church, were an ideal outlet for the goods produced by the craftsmen who lived in Oxmantown Street. Craftsmen occupied both sides of the Street. In 1539, Holy Trinity leased to 'Gryffin O Powell, of Dublin, yeoman, and Margete Banen, his wife a messuage in Oxmantown, lately inhabited by William Smith, on the south side of St Michan's church, and on the west side of the king's pavement'.[176] One plot had the advantage of frontage on both Oxmantown Street and Broad Street:

> John Baret grants to William Foyl, of Dublin, merchant, a rent of 18*d*., issuing from a messuage in Ousmannestown, suburbs of Dublin, situate between the tenement of John Russell, mason, and Alice, his wife, on one side, and the corner of the highway to S. Mary's abbey on the west, and extending from the highway to Fynglas to the tenement of Stephen Tayllour; to be held at the services due thereout to the chief lords.[177]

This is the same William Foly, merchant, mentioned earlier who requested that his body be buried in St Saviour's priory. John Serjant, who held land across the street, witnessed this grant in his capacity as mayor of Dublin. The grant refers also to a mason living in the area. A test excavation directly opposite St Michan's, at 27–31 Church Street, was carried out in 1996; a layer

---

170 *Christ Church deeds*, c.1326, no. 570.   **171** Ibid., 1576, no. 1344.   **172** Ibid., 1408, no. 842, and no. 843.   **173** *Chart. St Mary's*, i, pp 495–6; *Reg. Omnium Sanctorum*, p. 496. **174** *Christ Church deeds*, 1481, no. 1032.   **175** *Extents Ir. mon. possessions*, p. 7.   **176** *Christ Church deeds*, 1539, no. 1174.   **177** Ibid., 1344, no. 628.

of dark clay was found containing animal bone, slate, mortar, oyster shells, flecks of charcoal and medieval and post-medieval pottery sherds.[178] Slate and particularly mortar were the raw materials of the medieval mason.

In 1533 it was ordained that 'no manner person ne persones, free ne unfre, dwelling within the franchaises of Dublin, whatsoever degree they be ... not to bought no manner of merchaundsne vytallis as cum throw Oxmantown pase Seynt Michans church styll, and sillyng to be done within the walls'.[179] The reference appears to imply that illegal trading took place at the church stile of St Michan's. It would seem that the residents, craft-workers and traders who lived along Oxmantown Street were quick to take advantage of their location on one of the main approach routes to the medieval town.

OXMANTOWN GREEN AND THE WEST

Though Oxmantown Green served a number of purposes throughout the medieval period, its primary function was as common pastureland. St Stephen's Green and Hoggen Green were also common pasturelands. In 1541, it was ordained that 'the market place of all cattle shall be in Oxmanton Green, and in no other place'.[180] Suburbs provided space for pens and stables and were therefore ideally suited to cattle and horse markets. In addition, part of Oxmantown Green, just beyond Hangman Lane, appears to have been a designated area for the disposal of dung. Initially, it seemed that this area was maintained for the inhabitants of Oxmantown. However, an ordinance issued in 1560 demanded that the residents of Cook Street, Merchants' Quay, and Bridge Street, along with those from Oxmantown Street, were to clear the dung from Hangman Lane.[181] This seems to imply that the residents of the south bank were also using these pits.

The grazing of cattle on the common pastures of the city was a privilege that was reserved for freemen of the city. Just like the fishing rights of the Liffey, Oxmantown Green was a heavily guarded resource. Ordinances were introduced in the sixteenth century to prevent the Irish and the unfree from grazing their cattle. Constables were appointed to patrol and protect each of the greens.[182] The constables appointed to protect Oxmantown Green in 1577 were John Ussher, John Quine, and Thomas Shelton. The latter actually lived on the Green. The Shelton family also held the gate and land on either side of Hangman Gate. A large number of tenants with cattle- or farming-related occupations were granted land in and around Oxmantown Green, particularly husbandmen, labourers and yeomen,[183] as well as tanners, leatherworkers and

178 D. Delany, '27–31 Church Street, Dublin', *Excavations 1996*, p. 21.   179 *Ancient records*, i, p. 396. The entry also mentions like dealings in Thomas Street.   180 Ibid., p. 411.   181 Ibid., ii, 1560, p. 9.   182 Ibid., ii, 1577, p. 116 and p. 120.   183 *Christ Church*

saddlers. The site along Bow Lane seems to have been ideally suited to the tanning process, as it was located near the Green, which provided space for working and drying leather on racks, and the stream would have supplied regular running water. The hazardous nature of the crafts practised in Oxmantown and the suburbs in general is underlined by the ordinance issued in 1577 forbidding the construction of 'fyrr and faggot reekes', within 8 fathoms of any dwelling house.[184]

Most of the earliest references to Oxmantown Green mention the quarry. In 1236, the citizens of Dublin granted to Randulf le Hore and William Russell 'a meadow extending, in length, from the old quarry of the Ostmen to Kilmehanoc, and in breadth, from the king's highway as far as the stream of the water of the Liffey'.[185] Kilmehanoc is used again as a reference point in 1248, when Holy Trinity granted to the archbishop 'a certain land in the tenement of Kilmehanoc'. A footnote describes Kilmehanoc as 'beside Oxmantungreen where the gallows is now'.[186] A grant of *c.*1290 implies that St Mary's held land in the vicinity of the quarry.[187] There was a quarryman living in the suburb at the time.[188] In 1342, John de Graunstete was granted the lime-pit near Oxmantown Green,[189] which he probably utilised in the construction of the chapel of the Blessed Virgin beside the bridge, and Holy Trinity chapel in the grounds of St Michan's. The pit was granted to John along with a curtilage formerly belonging to Henry Fychet, and another located near St Michan's churchyard. One can assume that the lime-pit was in close proximity to these lands. In fact, a later reference in the fifteenth century describes the pits in Hangman Lane, 'before the churchyard over the west part betwixt the old lime kyll'.[190] In the early seventeenth century, quarrying was still taking place on the Green as is evident from a grant to John Foster, alderman: 'permission to dig stones in Oxmantown Green sufficient to burn two hundred hogsheads of lime'.[191] This demonstrates continuity of usage throughout the medieval period, for quarries and lime-pits were valuable resources.

All of the early references to Oxmantown Green are concerned with specific features such as the quarry, lime kiln, Pole Mills and the windmill belonging to Holy Trinity (fig. 4).[192] In 1424, William White granted to Robert Chamer 'a messuage and garden opposite the 'Pole' water, near Oxmangrene, in the parish of St Michan's'.[193] A century later, in 1542, Oliver Stephens acquired the 'Poule Mill with the concourse of water thereto in the suburbs'. Stephens was bound to keep the premises in repair, providing milstans, coggs and rongs

deeds, 1476, no. 1007; ibid., 1514, no. 1124.   **184** *Ancient records*, ii, p. 134.   **185** *Ancient records*, i, 1236, p. 81.   **186** *Alen's register*, p. 71.   **187** *Chart. St Mary's*, i, *c.*1290–1, p. 500.   **188** *Reg. St John the Baptist*, 1283–4, no. 44, pp 24–5.   **189** *Christ Church deeds*, 1342, no. 233.   **190** *Ancient records*, i, 1486, p. 369.   **191** Ibid., ii, p. 481.   **192** *Christ Church deeds*, 1330, no. 578.   **193** Ibid., 1424, no. 888.

for the upkeep of the mill.[194] In the late fifteenth and particularly in the sixteenth century, references to the Green increase and become more general. Most references are found in the Christ Church deeds, and this either reflects an imbalance in the source material or marks a genuine increase in occupation. Oxmantown Green is cited to the south of some late fifteenth- and sixteenth-century land grants, which seems to suggest that the northern section of the Green was occupied. One of the earliest grants of a place called *le Ratownerewe*, with the Green on the south, specifies the dimensions of the plot, described at the time as vacant, length 64 ft and breadth 34ft.[195] This may indicate the deliberate carving up of land on the north side of the Green, but there are references which suggest that this part of the Green was already inhabited by this period.

In 1486 Holy Trinity made the following grant:

> To John Payne, of Tartayne, turner, a messuage and garden near Ostmantown Grene, near Dublin, the former situate between the messuage of Thomas fitz Robert, husbandman, on the west, that of John Walshe, woodcutter, on the east, the said green on the south, and the said garden, on the north; and the latter extends from the said messuage, on the south, to lessor's orchard, on the north; to hold for 40 years; rent 4 *s.* and a hen at Christmas. Lease to rebuild with mud walls and straw roof.[196]

John Payne, a turner, was granted land beside a woodcutter, and both their plots are located beside the orchard belonging to Holy Trinity. Although there are no direct references to woodland on the Green, its presence may be inferred from grants such as these. In 1560, Thomas Grace, a barber, was granted a house on Oxmantown Green, one of the conditions of the lease being that he was 'not to cut timber or trees without the lessors' [Holy Trinity] licence'.[197] This raises the possibility of woodland management on Oxmantown Green. Further indication of woodland located on the northwestern section of the Green may be inferred from the following grant:

> Lease to Hugh Brady, bishop of Meath, a nook, a plot of wood containing 3 acres, parcel of the main wood called Salcock's wood, Co Dublin, situate between the gripe of a double ditch, dividing it from the main wood, on the north and the east, and the scrubby park, part of John Kelly's farm, on the south, the highway from Dublin to Little Cabra on the south-west, and the long park, in Mr Agard's possession, on the north-west.[198]

194 Ibid., 1542, no. 1190. **195** *Ancient records*, i, 1400, p. 124. **196** *Christ Church deeds*, 1486, no. 1072. **197** Ibid., 1560, no. 1270. **198** Ibid., 1578, no. 1352.

At some stage, Salcock's Wood may have extended southwards to Oxmantown Green. Activities on the Green serve to reinforce the rural nature of medieval suburbs. The extents of St Mary's abbey mention the location of orchards, gardens and parks within the monks' precinct, thus highlighting the horti-cultural aspect of the suburb. Holy Trinity had an orchard, known as the Great Orchard, north of Oxmantown Green. In 1542, Holy Trinity leased the orchard, described as being 'situated beyond the houses of Oxmantown Green to Oliver Stephens'. The conditions of this lease state 'lessee is to cut and plant such trees as he thinks fit'.[199] Oliver Stephens had also acquired the Pole Mills on the Green from Holy Trinity.

It is possible to reconstruct the plot sequence of a number of lands located on the north side of the Green. One such sequence is as follows: Patrick Tasker's house, located next to Thomas Grace, barber, and next to Annyse Doyne's garden.[200] In 1545, John Kelly, the sexton of Holy Trinity, was granted Annyse Doyne's garden, described as the two messuages beside Thomas Grace, on the east, and his neighbour to the west was Mr Shelton.[201] In 1545, John Kelly rented the messuages for 16s., and when the grant was renewed in 1571 he paid 20s. Later still, in 1589, when his plots were granted to Peter Calfe, one of the Vicars Choral, he paid a rent of 26s. 8d.[202] This may suggest an increase in rental values, or perhaps that the plots had been developed, with the result that the value of their contents warranted a higher rent. In 1561, Thomas Walsh, a mercer, was granted the house and messuage inhabited by John Read, yeoman, situated beside the dwelling house of Tade Follam, on the east, John Benet's holding on the west, with the Green and the orchard to the south and north respectively.[203] In 1567, William Gibney, labourer, was granted the cart house on the east side of the plot held by John Read, with the plot belonging to Edmond Follam on the west. This grant also recounts that part of the cart house was kept for horses.[204] The Green provided ample room for the keeping of carts and horses. The grant also refers to the place where the hay is rich, which implies that certain parts of Oxmantown Green may have been maintained and harvested for hay. An earlier reference in the four-teenth century mentions the hay meadow near the fisheries of St Michan's.[205] There are references to named farms located in and around the Green. In 1543, Holy Trinity leased to Edmond Innose, a labourer, a house situated on Oxmantown Green, with the Green to the south, Mey's farm on the north, the great place on the east, and Guydo's place on the west.[206] The said Guydo of Swords also held a house in nearby Grange Gorman.[207] The Holy Trinity estate of Grange Gorman was located to the north of Holy Trinity orchard.[208]

---

199 Ibid., 1542, no. 1188. 200 Ibid., 1541, no. 1181. 201 Ibid., 1545–6, no. 1200; ibid.,1571, no. 1322. 202 Ibid., 1589, no. 1385. 203 Ibid., 1561, no. 1275. 204 Ibid., 1567, no. 1307. 205 Ibid., 1324, no. 218. 206 Ibid., 1543, no. 1192. 207 Ibid., 1563, no. 1288. 208 Ibid., 1561, no. 1271.

Holy Trinity was one of the main landholders on the Green, particularly in the northern part. St Mary's held land around the quarry, the area on the Green parallel to the northern end of Oxmantown Street, while the city held the lands in and around the gallows, running parallel to the southern end of the main street.

Although people may have always lived in and around the Oxmantown Green area, there was a definite increase in occupation in the late fifteenth and sixteenth century. The development of the green areas of the city began to alarm the municipality, and it ordered that no part of Oxmantown Green, Hoggen Green and St Stephen's Green was to be leased, as the greens were needed 'for people to take open air upon, and because the city was growing very populous'.[209] As noted above, John Foster was granted the quarry on Oxmantown Green on condition that he did not prejudice the walk, highlighting the recreational functions served by the Green. The Green provided ample space for civic and leisure activities: for example, the mustering of the guard, and on May Day the parading of the citizens of Dublin before the mayor. Oxmantown Green fulfilled many diverse functions both within the local community, and also within the broader community of medieval Dublin.

As the material from Oxmantown demonstrates, land grants contain a great deal of information, with regard to the people involved, their ethnic identity, and their occupation. They may also contain street names, information as to how they acquired those names, and how they changed. When collated land grants reveal concentrations in various streets and areas. In the case of Oxmantown three concentrations emerge: fishing associated with the eastern area of the suburb and St Mary's abbey; craftworking along Oxmantown Street, the main street of the suburb; and cattle-related activities around Oxmantown Green. Outlets for these goods and produce were provided by the trading that took place at the early market place at the eastern end of Broad Street next to St Mary's abbey, by the illegal trading at the stile of St Michan's church, by the shops located along Oxmantown Street, and by the cattle-market on Oxmantown Green. These concentrations follow a loose chronological pattern, the earliest settlement being around Broad Street and the abbey. In the thirteenth century, with the establishment of the Dominican priory of St Saviour's, there was a concentration of activity along the riverbank. There are references to grants in Oxmantown Street in the thirteenth and fourteenth centuries, but in the fifteenth and sixteenth centuries activity within the suburb contracted to this area. Oxmantown Green was a vital part of the suburb throughout the medieval period; in the fifteenth and sixteenth centuries there was an increase in occupation in and around the Green by a number of husbandmen, farmers and labourers, as well as by craftsmen who took full advantage of the resources of the Green.

209 *Ancient records*, ii, 1635, p. 253.

As Oxmantown was a suburb, it was of secondary or marginal importance to the town core area, and this is reflected in the documentary material which is predominately concerned with the walled area. Nevertheless, this material can be usefully employed to reveal much about the life of the medieval suburbs. It follows that the application of this form of analysis to the town core area of Dublin would be a most productive study.

ACKNOWLEDGEMENTS

I wish to thank Howard Clarke for his supervision of my thesis, and Stephen Hannon for additions to the maps based on the originals by Howard Clarke and Anngret Simms. I would also like to thank Kevin Murray and Donnchadh Ó Corráin who read draft versions of this article.

A much disputed land: Carrickmines and the Dublin marches

EMMETT O'BYRNE

In the middle ages, conquest and colonisation created frontiers between native and newcomer, stretching from Prussia to Palestine, across the Iberian peninsula and onto Ireland. Ireland's most important and also most neglected frontier was that formed by the Dublin marches – the lands that lay between the city of Dublin and the neighbouring Irish princes of Leinster. Here the frontier was an ethnic patchwork in which different racial groups lived side by side. So, naturally its politics were fluid and flexible. As in some other European lands, the newcomers showed over time that they could merge into native societies, adopting their language, customs, dress and laws. On the other hand, many native families were also able to trim their sails to the realities posed by the arrival of powerful newcomers. The lack of political uniformity in the Dublin marches ensured that this hybrid region was home to considerable ethnic diversity. Having said that, these lands were to remain a violent and a much-disputed interface between the rulers of Dublin and the Leinster Irish. The purpose of this article is to place Carrickmines in this context.

Today the two townlands of Carrickmines Little and Carrickmines Great are located in the parish of Tully within the Dublin barony of Rathdown. Originally, though, Carrickmines belonged to the northern half of the Irish kingdom of Uí Briúin Chualann, a land that straddled the modern Dublin and Wicklow border. The principal secular landowners of Uí Briúin Chualann were its kings, who were drawn from the Mac Gilla Mo-Cholmóc dynasty. Further, the Ostmen of the city kingdom of Dublin also had substantial lands in Uí Briúin Chualann. It was their arrival at Dublin in the ninth century, and presence thereafter, that forced the borders of Uí Briúin Chualann to contract dramatically. For by the eleventh century, Ostman colonists had settled throughout northeast Wicklow. The expansion of the Ostmen into Uí Briúin Chualann can be paralleled with the gradual extension of their lordship over Ua Cathasaig's kingdom of Saithne in north Dublin.[1] In the twelfth century, the retreating Meic Gilla Mo-Cholmóc looked south to the neighbouring Irish

---

1 M.T. Flanagan, 'Historia Gruffud vab Kenan and the origins of Balrothery', in *Cambrian Medieval Celtic Studies*, no. 28 (1994), p. 76.

kingdoms of Uí Garrchon and Uí Enechglais for compensation, forcibly establishing an overlordship over them.[2]

The most prominent Ostmen of Uí Briúin Chualann and owners of Carrickmines were the Meic Torcaill (Þorkellsons), kings of Dublin for most of the twelfth century. The extent of the Mac Torcaill lands has been defined as incorporating the parish of Tully and stretching to the Dargle river at Bray. In addition to this considerable swath of territory, the Meic Torcaill also seem to have held lands in Glencullen and near Powerscourt.[3] After 1171 the above-mentioned lands extending from Tully parish to Bray were later referred to in English documents as 'the lands of the son of Turchill'.[4] Although the Meic Torcaill had successfully expanded into the region, their prize evolved into a marchland, an interface between Ostman Dublin and the rising power of the Uí Chennselaig overkingship of Leinster. The ethnic character of the marchland can be seen in the land holdings surrounding Carrickmines. This point is amply illustrated in the pre-1169 grants to the priory of Holy Trinity at Dublin by both Irish and Ostman nobles. Before his death in 1087 at the battle of Ráth Édair, the Uí Chennselaig prince Donnchad son of Domhnall Remar made a grant to Holy Trinity of Clonkeen. On the other hand, the Meic Torcaill proved themselves generous patrons of Holy Trinity. According to King John's charter to the priory in 1202, Sighrahre son of Thorkill had earlier granted land centred around Laughanstown, an area between Carrickmines and Loughlinstown.[5]

The other great clerical beneficiary of secular largesse in the Carrickmines area before 1169 was the archbishop of Dublin. At the request of Archbishop Laurence O'Toole, Pope Alexander III on April 20 1179 took the archdiocese of Dublin into papal protection. From the place-names that made up the 1179 list of the archdiocese's lands, we can discern its landholdings in the Carrickmines area. Before 1169 the archdiocese owned considerable property in the parish of Kilgobbin, including the land of Balemochain. The latter seems to have extended over the modern townlands of Jamestown (parish of Kilgobbin) and Jamestown (parish of Tully), as well as taking in present day Ballyogan. And it is possible, though not certain, that the townlands of Carrickmines Little and Carrickmines Great at this time belonged to the greater Balemochain.[6] Moreover, close study of the archdiocese's lands here

---

2 C. Etchingham, 'Evidence of Scandinavian settlement in Wicklow', in K. Hannigan & W. Nolan (eds), *Wicklow: history and society* (Dublin, 1994), pp 121–2.   3 Ibid., pp 129–30.   4 E. St John Brooks, 'The de Riddlesfords', *R.S.A.I.Jn.*, lxxxi (1951), pp 115–38; L. Price, 'The grant to Walter de Riddlesford of Brien and the land of the sons of Turchil', *R.S.A.I. Jn.*, lxxxiv (1954), pp 72–7; C. McNeill (ed.), *Calendar of Archbishop Alen's register* (Dublin, 1950), pp 28–30.   5 *Alen's register*, pp 28–30; M.J. McEnery and Raymond Refaussé (eds), *Christ Church deeds* (Dublin, 2001), no. 364; F. Elrington-Ball, *A history of the County Dublin*, iii (Dublin, 1995), p. 66.   6 Ibid., pp 3–4; for the identification of Jamestown with Ballymochain, see R. Goodbody, *On the borders of the pale: a history of the Kilgobbin,*

reveals another layer of ethnic diversity amid the marchlands of south Dublin. It was only after July 1170 that the Ostmen granted Kilgobbin church to the archdiocese, but it is significant that Kilgobbin was formerly known as Tech na mBretnach, 'the house of the Welshmen'.[7] That Kilgobbin was connected with the Welsh points to the presence of a Welsh community there before 1169. The existence of a Welsh community at Kilgobbin receives further support from place-name evidence in the locality. Just to the north of Carrickmines was Ballybrenan (*Baile na mBretnach*, the town of the Welsh, now Brenanstown), while medieval Carrigbrenan (now Monkstown) also points to distinctly Welsh influences.

As demonstrated by Edmund Curtis, Seán Duffy and Marie Therese Flanagan, there can be no doubt as to the strength of the connection between the Ostman city state of Dublin and the Welsh kingdoms before 1169. For example, the origins of the Fitzrery family of Cloghran in north Dublin lay in the ruling dynasty of the north Welsh kingdom of Gwynedd. Indeed, a close study of the Fitzrerys reveals evidence that can be adduced to point towards a Welsh presence within the Ostman kingdom. Links between Ostmen and the ruling family of Gwynedd would seem to date back to the exile of Cynan ap Iago at Dublin after 1039. Cynan apparently married the deceased King Olaf's daughter Ragnailt and fathered with her the later king of Gwynedd, Gruffudd ap Cynan (*d.*1137). Although disputed, it would appear Cynan received lands at Cloghran as part of Ragnailt's marriage portion. These lands were to remain in Welsh hands, and those administering them in the thirteenth century would seem to have been known sometimes as Machanan/Makanen, probably a corruption of mac Cynan or 'the son of Cynan'. Whether this patronymic indicates descent from Cynan ap Iago is debatable, but what is crystal clear is that the royal family of Gywnedd kept a close eye on these lands. In 1218 Llywelyn ab Iorwerth of Gywnedd petitioned Henry III to pardon the fine due from his cousin Cynwrig, so that he could have entry into the Irish lands of the latter's father, Rhirid ab Owain Gwynedd. Remarkably, this cadet line was to hold their lands until the seventeenth century.[8]

The strength of the pre-1169 Welsh connection in north Dublin with the Ostman kingdom is clear, but there is also evidence for Welsh communities living under the Ostmen in the southern Dublin marches. There does seem to

Stepaside and Sandyford Area (Bray, 1993), p. 10, see also pp 11, 32. Charles McNeill takes a different view. He translates Balemochain as Baile Uí Ochain and takes it to be modern-day Ballyogan: see *Alen's Reg*, pp 3, 4 and especially n. 10. See also Ball, *A history of the County Dublin*, iii, pp 65–7, and also the map at the beginning of the volume; *General alphabetical index to the townlands and towns, parishes and baronies of Ireland* (Dublin, 1861), pp 204, 543. 7 *Alen's register*, pp 3, 28. 8 E. Curtis, 'The Fitzrerys, Welsh lords of Cloghran, Co. Dublin', in *Louth Arch. Soc. Jn* (1921), pp 13–15; S. Duffy, 'Ireland and the Irish sea region, 1014–1318', unpublished PhD thesis (University of Dublin, 1993), pp 4, 109–11, 231; Flanagan, 'Historia Gruffud vab Kenan and the origins of Balrothery', pp 71–94.

be a case that the ancestors of the fourteenth-century Walshes and Howels of Carrickmines and Balybrenan ('the town of the Welsh') were long established there before the 1169–70 watershed. According to Valentine Hussey Walsh, the Walshes of Carrickmines were descended from a David Walsh who was created Baron Carrickmines in the 1170s.[9] This statement seems unfounded on a number of grounds. Firstly, there is no such title, and secondly it could not have been made, as Carrickmines was church land. As for the patronymic of Walsh, it offers few clues as it simply denotes somebody of Welsh origin. Moreover, the usage of Walsh, Walshman or le Walleys to describe persons of Welsh ancestry tended to transcend all classes. In 1222 the high-born Rhirid, lord of Cloghran, was simply referred as Righerid le Walleys, meaning Righerid the Welshman. What is clear though is that the Walshes and Howels of Carrickmines were certainly very near kinsmen, if not forming part of the same extended lineage that dominated the Welsh community living on these lands.

The 1326 rental of the manor of Clonkeen shows Maurice Howel leasing Carrickmines and Balybrenan from Holy Trinity, while his kinsman Peter Howel was allowed to occupy nearby Ballymorthan. This rental further displays a community of Irish cottiers and farmers working the lands of Clonkeen, including some of the Okenan lineage.[10] There seems a distinct possibility that these Okenans are not of Irish extraction but of Welsh. Their patronymic Okenan would seem to be a rendering of Ua Cynan or 'descendant of Cynan', which is similar to the Machanan/Makanen that was used by the men of Gwynedd at Cloghran. In addition, the Howel patronymic clearly indicates descent from an ancestor who bore the Welsh forename Hywel. Hywel like Cynan was a traditional forename of the royal house of Gwynedd and there were at least two known Hywels of that dynasty, who had Irish mothers.[11] The first Hywel was the son of Owain, king of Gwynedd (r.1137–70), who was killed during 1170 in a struggle to succeed his father. According to Meredith Hanmer, Hywel's brother Rhirid (d.1215), lord of Cloghran, was the father of the second Hywel, an obscure figure. There is only one later reference connecting the Hywels or Howels with the lands of the lords of Cloghran. On 10 March 1276, Philip Howel and a Geoffrey Harold – perhaps of the Kilgobbin family – sat on the jury at an inquisition to determine the lands at *villa Walensis* held from the archbishop of Dublin by Elias le Waleys (the Welshman).[12] The land in question would seem to be Balibren (Baile na

---

9 V. Hussey Walsh, 'The Austrian branches of the family of Walsh', in *The Genealogist*, xvii (London, 1901), p. 217. According to Hussey Walsh, David was a brother to Philip Walsh of Castle Hoel, Co. Kilkenny.   10 J. Mills (ed.), *Account roll of the priory of the Holy Trinity, Dublin, 1337–1346* (Dublin, 1891) p. 195; *Christ Church deeds*, no. 570. 11 Flanagan, 'Historia Gruffud vab Kenan and the origins of Balrothery', p. 86; Sir James Ware, *Ancient Irish histories: the works of Spenser, Campion, Hanmer and Marleburrough*, 2 vols (Dublin, 1809), ii, pp 16–19.   12 H.S. Sweetman, *Calendar of documents relating to Ireland, 1171–1307*, 5 vols (London 1874–85), ii, no. 1283, pp 231–2.

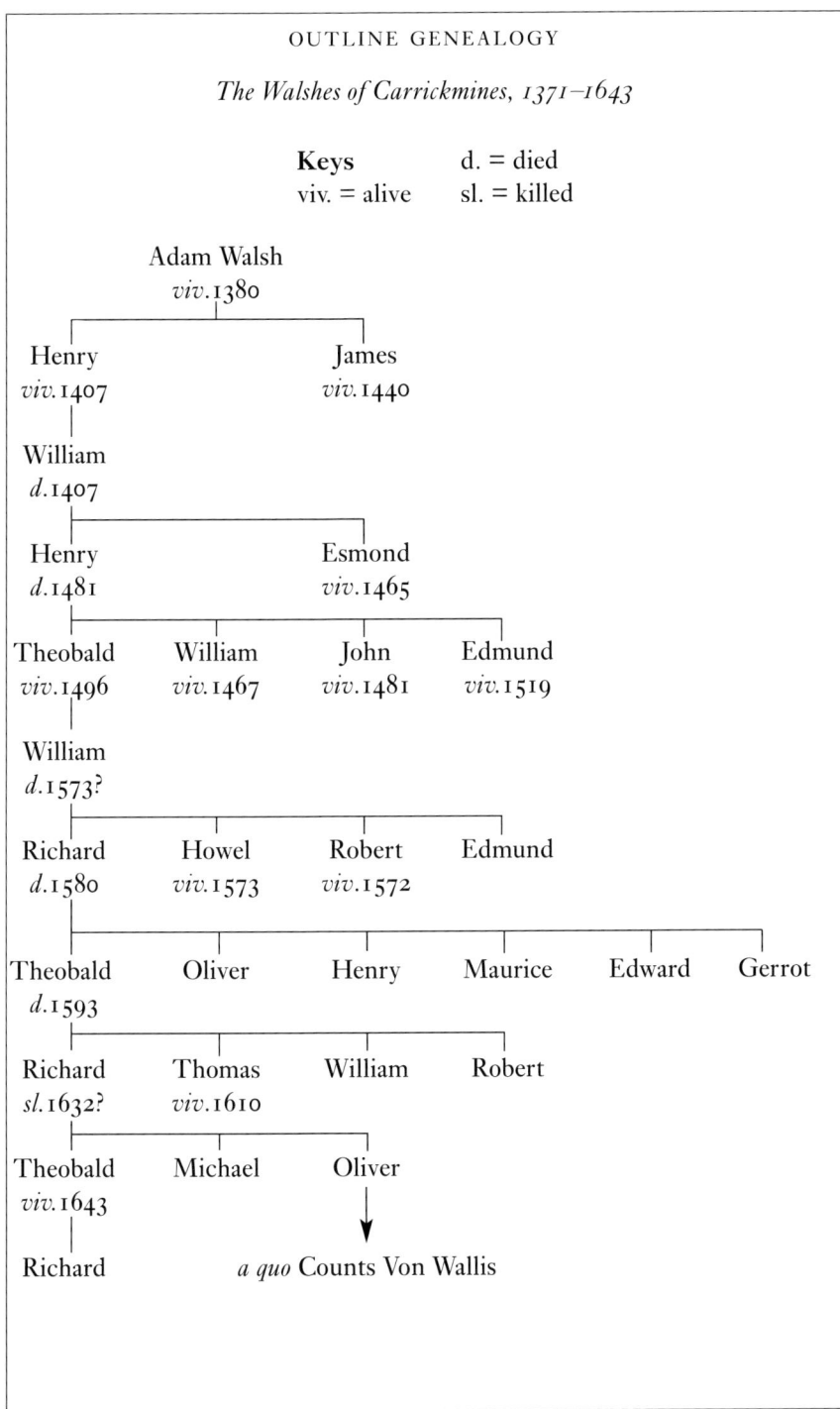

OUTLINE GENEALOGY

The Walshes of Carrickmines, 1371–1643

Keys   d. = died
viv. = alive   sl. = killed

Adam Walsh
*viv.*1380

Henry   James
*viv.*1407   *viv.*1440

William
*d.*1407

Henry   Esmond
*d.*1481   *viv.*1465

Theobald   William   John   Edmund
*viv.*1496 *viv.*1467 *viv.*1481   *viv.*1519

William
*d.*1573?

Richard   Howel   Robert   Edmund
*d.*1580   *viv.*1573 *viv.*1572

Theobald   Oliver   Henry   Maurice   Edward   Gerrot
*d.*1593

Richard   Thomas   William   Robert
*sl.*1632? *viv.*1610

Theobald   Michael   Oliver
*viv.*1643

Richard   *a quo* Counts Von Wallis

mBretnach, meaning town of the Welsh), now the modern townland of Walshestown located within the parish of Lusk in the barony of Balrothery East. This Balibren was undoubtedly the land of Righerid le Walleys (the Welshman) (*d*.1228), the lord of Cloghran who offered his homage to Henry III on 5 November 1222.[13] Therefore the Howels and Walshes seem to have sprung from the Welsh community living in the Carrickmines/Kilgobbin area during the pre-1169 era. The nomenclature of this community also indicates connections with the contemporary descendants of the royal house of Gwynedd located at Cloghran, suggesting that Ostmen may have settled some followers of these princes around the Carrickmines/Kilgobbin area.

However, the major turning point for the Irish, Welsh and Ostmen of the Dublin marches and of Uí Briúin Chualann was the arrival of Diarmait MacMurrough's English allies in 1169–70. The reactions of the Mac Gilla Mo-Cholmóc rulers of Uí Briúin Chualann and the Mac Torcaill kings of Dublin could not have been more different. This was largely due to their respective activities during the 1166 fall of MacMurrough. Then the Mac Gilla Mo-Cholmóc dynasty firstly proved fiercely opposed to the Leinster king. That changed after MacMurrough successfully encouraged O'Brennan to assassinate the rebellious king of Uí Briúin Chualann, allowing Domhnall Mac Gilla Mo-Cholmóc, MacMurrough's son-in-law, to take its kingship. On the other hand, the Meic Torcaill were long-time enemies of MacMurrough. After the murder of the king of Uí Briúin Chualann, they joined the high-king Ruaidrí O'Connor to force the Leinster king into exile. In September 1170 MacMurrough had his revenge, seizing Dublin from its king, Ascall Mac Torcaill. The end of Mac Torcaill kings of Dublin finally came in July 1171, culminating in their defeat by the English and Domhnall Mac Gilla Mo-Cholmóc and the later decapitation of Ascall in his own assembly hall.

In the past nationalist historians have tended to paint the effect of the English arrival upon the Irish in apocalyptic terms. What has been neglected is the continued survival of the old Ostman and Irish elites near Dublin and in East Leinster. Indeed, survival was ensured by their respective decisions to become anglicised to a degree. Domhnall Mac Gilla Mo-Cholmóc of Uí Briúin Chualann was successfully to span the ethnic divide. During the lifetime of Domhnall's son, Diarmait, their dynasty transformed itself into the Fitzdermots. Evidence of this can be shown in their names. Instead of being christened Domhnall or Diarmait, dynastic scions now bore names such as John, William, Robert and Ralph, the forenames of the conquerors. Their metamorphosis was so complete that without earlier evidence of their Irish lineage, the Fitzdermots were indistinguishable from the settler aristocracy. The only recorded trouble was either in the late twelfth or early thirteenth

13 *Cal. docs Ire.*, i, no. 1059, p. 162; Flanagan, 'Historia Gruffud vab Kenan and the origins of Balrothery', pp 90–1.

centuries when a Donohoe Mac Gilla Mo-Cholmóc killed Roger fitz Gilbert, an Englishman. By 1276–7, it was clear that the descendants of the Meic Gilla Mo-Cholmóc had travelled a long way. Then Ralph Fitzdermot was paid for defending the Vale of Dublin from the MacMurroughs, while Edward I in 1282 rewarded the Fitzdermots by declaring Ralph a knight. After this date the family subsequently declined in importance, selling off their remaining eight carucates in Uí Briúin Chualann sometime after 1305. But they remained thoroughly respectable: Sir Ralph's son John fitzRalph entered the service of the archbishop of Dublin and served in 1326 as the bailiff of the manor of Shankill.[14] They also seemed to hold onto some lands around Rathdown into the fifteenth century, for an unpublished pipe roll of Henry VI records a John son of Dermod behind in his rent in 1408. Even more remarkably it seems some of the Fitzdermots held land in north Dublin at Lusk until the middle of the sixteenth century, while William Dermot was appointed on May 4 1563 to the office of chancellor of Holy Trinity.[15]

Having said that, others were neither so lucky nor so prudent. Naturally, the Mac Torcaill kings were the major casualty of the conquest of Dublin. After the execution of Ascall Mac Torcaill in July 1171, the Mac Torcaill lands were declared forfeit. In north Dublin, they lost their extensive holdings at Portrane, Malahide, Portmarnock and Kilbarrack. By 1174, though, Hamund Mac Torcaill and his brothers had sufficiently rehabilitated themselves to have their Kinsaley lands confirmed to them.[16] In the marches of south Dublin, it was an entirely different story. There the Meic Torcaill were seemingly dispossessed of their lands wholesale, as Walter de Riddelesford I was granted their lands from Tully to Bray. As further punishment Strongbow also confiscated the properties of Sigerith and Torphin Mac Torcaill, granting them to the abbey of St Mary at Dublin. Perhaps after the rehabilitation of Hamund in 1174, the local Ostmen of Uí Briúin Chualann chose to acknowledge this process by granting Kilgobbin to Holy Trinity.[17] The partial restoration of the Mac Torcaill lands in north Dublin is consistent with the English favour displayed to other Ostmen. After the collapse of the Mac Torcaill hegemony, the Ostman families of Harold and Archbold became significantly more important. The large and extended Harold lineage was incorporated within the feudal settlement from early on, particularly on the lands of the archbishop, Holy Trinity and on those of the royal manors.[18] English favour

14 *Christ Church deeds*, no. 557. **15** J.T. Gilbert, *A history of the city of Dublin*, 3 vols (Dublin, 1854–9), i, p. 235; M. Griffith (ed.), *Calendar of Inquisitions* (Dublin, 1991), Hen VIII 6/7 (c), p. 4; *Christ Church deeds*, no. 1291; E. O'Byrne, 'War, politics and the Irish of Leinster, 1156–1606', unpublished PhD thesis (University of Dublin, 2001), p. 56. **16** *Christ Church deeds*, no. 1 (2). **17** *Alen's register,* p. 28. The text says that Ostmen made a gift of Theachabreatan by reason of their forfeiture. **18** K.W. Nicholls, 'Críoch Branach: the O'Byrnes and their country', in C. O'Brien (ed.), *Feagh McHugh O'Byrne: the Wicklow firebrand* (Dublin, 1998), p. 17; *Alen's Register,* p. 31; *Calendar of justiciary rolls,*

towards this community was evident by the incorporation of the Ostmen at a higher social level than most Irish, as evidenced by 36 identifiable Ostman rents for lands within the Vale of Dublin.[19] The emerging partnership between the English with the Irish, Welsh and Ostmen of the marches greatly facilitated the bedding down of the feudal settlement south of Dublin. However, it must be stressed that the Irish of east Leinster adopted English customs and practices to varying degrees. But in Dublin and east Leinster the colony prospered overall, living cheek-by-jowl with these communities. On the whole, this mutual toleration promoted mutual indulgence, resulting in a long-lived peace.

As for Carrickmines, a major change in its ownership came *c*.1185. The then archbishop of Dublin, John Comyn, came to an arrangement with Holy Trinity about the lands surrounding Carrickmines. In exchange for quit-claiming their rights to lands on Lambay island, Holy Trinity obtained further lands at Tilach (Clonkeen), along with other lands at Ballyogan and the land of Dromin, an area of land that lay between Carrickmines and present day Cornelscourt.[20] The grant to Holy Trinity by Archbishop Comyn of the archdiocese's lands at Dromin and Ballyogan was confirmed by Archbishop Luke about 1230. Much later on 17 September 1504, Archbishop William Fitzsimons was again to confirm Ballyogan and its vill to Holy Trinity along with Ballybrenan and St Brigid's chapel at Carrickmines.[21] But the earliest origins of Carrickmines Castle are to be found in the context of imminent danger from the Wicklow Irish. The long peace in east Leinster between the Irish and the settlers gradually crumbled after the extinction of the Marshal lords of Leinster in 1245. This led to the extension of English common law into Leinster, increasing racial tension between the two communities and shortening the paths to war.

The spark that ignited the Wicklow Irish was famine, resulting in war from 1269. Primarily, the object of Carrickmines Castle was to protect the Welsh farming communities cultivating the fertile land of south Dublin. Its defenders were naturally drawn from the Howels, Walshes and later the Lawlesses. Their nexus of common interests and ambition stretched westward across south Dublin to the Harolds, Archbolds and the remnants of the Meic Torcaill. Inevitably, the O'Byrnes and the O'Tooles cast envious eyes upon the rich cereal-growing lands that Carrickmines Castle sought to protect, threatening the existence of these communities. The need to stem the Irish tide was

1295–1303, p. 306; *Cal. justiciary rolls, 1305–7*, pp 476; *Cal. justiciary rolls, 1308–14*, p. 285; NAI, RC 7/13 (iv), pp 22–24; *Cal. docs Ire.*, ii, p. 313; J.T. Gilbert (ed.), *Chartularies of St Mary's abbey, Dublin*, 2 vols (London, 1884–5), ii, p. 349.   **19** L. Simpson, 'Anglo-Norman settlement in Uí Briúin Chualann, in K. Hannigan & W. Nolan (eds), *Wicklow: history and society* (Dublin, 1994), p. 203.   **20** *Alen's register*, pp 13, 16; *Christ Church deeds*, no. 44.   **21** *Alen's register*, pp 255–6.

paramount. Accordingly, Carrickmines was to assume offensive capabilities, serving from the late thirteenth century as a staging post for English expeditions to attack the Wicklow Irish. Its importance was not lost upon the Irish who saw it as a linchpin of the Pale's defences – one that had to be destroyed.

The emergence of Murchadh O'Byrne (*c*.1265–1338) heralded a much harder Irish line being adopted towards the settlers. From the surviving evidence, he with Fáelán and David O'Toole set about expelling the Welsh settlers from Wicklow, particularly the Fitzrhys family of Imaal and the Lawlesses of east Wicklow. For Maurice Howel, owner of Carrickmines, the fate of the Lawlesses was to be avoided. Accordingly, he sought to prop up the collapsing Lawless lordship against Murchadh, serving with Richard le Waleys and Henry O'Toole in late April 1309 on Lord Lieutenant Piers Gaveston's campaign against the O'Byrnes.[22] The government at Dublin clearly valued the service of the Howels. In 1314 the government pardoned the offences of Maurice and several kinsmen, including an Archebaud (Archbold) Howel, along with Richard le Waleys, Richard Roth le Waleys and Robert Lawless because of their service in Offaly and the Leinster mountains.[23] Subsequent events proved why Howel and his men were pardoned. In response to the defeats of the O'Mores in late 1315 and early 1316, Murchadh O'Byrne exacted a terrible revenge upon the settlers of east Wicklow. Before Lent 1316 he lined up with the O'Tooles and disgruntled elements of the Harolds and Archbolds to devastate the remnants of the Fitzgerald barony of Wicklow, culminating in the sack of the Wicklow town. The devastation wreaked by the O'Byrnes on the Fitzgerald Wicklow lands was so thorough that no rents could be collected from them that year. From the surviving evidence, Murchadh was steadily eradicating the English presence in east Wicklow, forcing their evacuation of lands and farms. This process starkly mirrored the tactics he employed against the settlers of Shillelagh in 1295–6. Hugh Lawless, leader of the settlers of east Wicklow, pleaded before Lord Edmund Butler in February 1316 for relief from the O'Byrne onslaught, graphically describing the terrible plight of the Wicklow settlers, caught in 'a confined and narrow part of the country, namely between Newcastle McKynegan and Wicklow, where they have the sea between Wales and Ireland for a wall on one side, and the mountains of Leinster and divers other wooded and desert places on the other where the said Irish felons live'. Lawless did not mince his words: 'by the malice and wantonness of the Irish of the mountains of Leinster, felons of the king, they have been expelled and removed from their fortresses, manors and houses up to the present, and many of the said faithful subjects of the king have been slain by the said Irish felons'.

22 R. Frame, 'The Dublin government and Gaelic Ireland, 1270–1361', unpublished PhD thesis (University of Dublin, 1971), p. 79. **23** *Cal. justiciary rolls, 1308–14*, pp 314–16.

The remorseless advance of Murchadh O'Byrne brought Maurice Howel back into Wicklow, serving from November 1316 to January 1317 as part of the garrison of Newcastle McKynegan in east Wicklow.[24] Howel again served as guardian of the Leinster marches during 1324–25, earning £26 13s. 4d.[25] In spite of Howel's service, the settlers in Wicklow steadily crumbled, allowing the O'Byrne horsemen waste the lands of Carrickmines and the rich farms of south Dublin.[26] Even though war was lapping against the walls of Carrickmines, successive priors of Holy Trinity continued to entrust Maurice Howel with the defence of their lands. In August 1329 he, with Thomas Harold and Thomas Archbold, served against the O'Byrnes,[27] while he delivered some O'Tooles into custody during 1334.[28] But after the middle of the 1330s, Howel and the priors became resigned to adopting a far more flexible approach towards the Irish. Between 1339 and 1344 the priory had intimate dealings with Irish dynasts such as Gerald son of Dúnlaing O'Byrne and 'Fynnok' O'Toole, and was engaged in trade for timber with the Irish.[29] The reality, though, was ceaseless Irish aggression. In 1344, John Chamburleyn, bailiff of Clonkeen, recorded payments in his account of 4d. to two men, who spent two nights on the top of the mountains, watching for Irish raiders.[30]

In response to the endemic violence, English policy was increasingly directed towards the establishment of friendly Irish in the lordships bordering Dublin. This policy may have been designed to prevent co-ordinated attacks of the Leinster Irish upon the English outposts. To cope with the growing strength of the Irish incursions into the Pale, Carrickmines Castle was refortified in early 1359. No doubt the importance of Carrickmines as a defensive site increased due to the policies of Justiciar Thomas Rokeby. In 1350 Rokeby had developed a new English policy directed towards the establishment of friendly lordships bordering Dublin. As part of this policy Rokeby, on April 23, presided over the election of Walter Harold as head of his sept. Interestingly, Walter Harold's electoral college consisted of electors drawn from the Archbold, Howel, Walsh and Lawless families, including Peter Howel, Richard fitz Michael Howel, Elias fitz Robert Walsh and Hugh fitz Robert Lawless, later constable of Newcastle McKynegan in 1353. These families with their backs to the wall – and the sea – had everything to fight for. It is likely there was little room for them among the plans of the O'Byrnes. Clearly, the Welsh and the Ostmen had developed a united front, resulting in the emergence of an overall captaincy of the borderlands of south Dublin.[31]

24 P. Connolly (ed.), *Irish exchequer payments, 1270–1446* (Dublin, 1998), p. 239.   25 Ibid., p. 303.   26 Simpson, 'Uí Briúin Chualann', p. 210.   27 Frame, 'The Dublin government', p. 255.   28 Connolly, *Irish exchequer payments*, p. 371.   29 J. Mills (ed.) *Account roll of the priory of the Holy Trinity, Dublin, 1337–1346* (Dublin, 1897; repr. 1996), pp 20, 36, 57, 61, 91.   30 Ibid., p. 64.   31 E. Curtis, 'The clan system among English settlers in Ireland', *E.H.R.*, 25 (1910), pp 116–20; Frame, 'The Dublin government', p. 340.

Rokeby was to go further and turn his attention to the Irish. After success against the O'Byrnes in July 1350, Rokeby, as part of this policy, presided over the election, sometime in autumn 1350, of his protégé, John mac Taidhg O'Byrne after a campaign into O'Byrne territory earlier in July.[32] Moreover, he appointed Aodh O'Toole (at an uncertain date) custos or keeper of the Dublin and Kildare marches,[33] a decision reflecting the archbishop of Dublin's earlier employment of Máelmorda O'Toole as constable of Tallaght Castle in 1326. The relative peace that descended on the Dublin marches was dependant upon the continued goodwill of the O'Byrnes. John O'Byrne stayed in English service until the summer of 1353, but determined to assert himself. Like his predecessors, John O'Byrne concentrated upon the consolidation of east Wicklow, but increasingly subjected the manors and farms of south Dublin to a regular nightly regime of terror and burnings. John's assertion of independence frightened other Irish leaders such as Muircheartach MacMurrough, king of Leinster. In 1353–4 Muircheartach, Ruaidhrí O'More and Aodh O'Toole all supported the government, contributing large forces to a major expedition into John's country. These efforts proved successful as John came to peace on 22 March 1354, surrendering 92 cows.[34]

By the summer of 1354 Muircheartach and John had joined forces in a campaign against the English, providing ample opportunity for their respective dynastic rivals to prove their loyalty to the English.[35] The war betrayed signs of extensive co-ordination with other Leinster dynasties. Muircheartach was quickly captured by Patrick de la Freyne, but John defeated Rokeby, besieging him in Wicklow Castle during October 1354. John apparently requested Muircheartach's release during the negotiations, but Rokeby brought Muircheartach by sea to Wicklow and executed him as a warning to John, an act that shocked not only the Leinstermen but Irish kings country-wide.[36] In response, the Dublin government led by Rokeby developed between 1355 and 1357 a series of defensive wards to protect the Palesmen, including Newcastle McKynegan, Kilmartin, Killoughter, Saggart, Powerscourt, Bray, Glenmore, Killiney, Ballycorus, Jamestown and Carrickmines.[37] This made Carrickmines Castle one of the most important fortresses of the southern Pale. Therefore, if the O'Byrnes and the O'Tooles wished to expand into the Pale, the onus was on them to destroy or occupy these forts, leading them to develop siege tactics.

---

32 Ibid. For the campaign against O'Byrnes, see pp 339–40.   **33** Connolly, *Irish exchequer payments*, pp 444, 455.   **34** O'More brought 68 light horsemen and 108 footmen, while O'Toole contributed 15 hobelars and 4 kerne and gained a fee of £8. 13s. 4d. And Muircheartach was drawing a fee at Michaelmas 1353. See Frame, 'The Dublin government', pp 350–2.   **35** Nicholls, 'Críoch Branach', p. 15; Frame, 'The Dublin government', p. 357.   **36** *Annals of Connacht*, s.a. 1354; *Annals of the Four Masters*, s.a. 1354; *Annals of Clonmacnoise*, s.a. 1353; *Annals of Ulster*, s.a. 1354; Frame, 'The Dublin government', pp 355–8.   **37** Frame, 'The Dublin government', p. 359.

The function of Carrickmines Castle was to block one of the more favoured routes into the Pale, resulting in the O'Byrnes and O'Tooles laying siege to it in July 1359. The siege was lifted by Justiciar James Butler, 2nd earl of Ormond, after bitter fighting that lasted some days. Although Nicholas Power and 32 of his men were wounded, Ormond managed to take some prisoners before the Irish withdrew.[38] Once Ormond was gone the O'Byrnes were back. Relief for Carrickmines eventually came with Ormond's victory in early August over the O'Mores and MacMurroughs.[39] This and the general peace that was made on 12 August 1359 persuaded John O'Byrne to abandon the siege. He then voluntarily submitted at Carlow and paradoxically earned a knighthood for his efforts.[40] With the O'Byrnes temporarily at peace, the Dublin government again strengthened Carrickmines, installing Sir John de Bermingham and his cavalry there in 1360 to resist the O'Byrnes and the O'Tooles.[41] The rare lull in border warfare was prolonged by the O'Byrne civil war that erupted after the death of Sir John O'Byrne in the late 1360s. This, however, did not prevent the O'Byrnes from exploiting the Dublin government's preoccupation with the Munster wars in the summer of 1370. Then they seized several English castles along the Wicklow coast before probing Carrickmines again. Prompt government action retook the castles, forcing Braen O'Byrne to come to peace on 27 March 1371.

Between 1371 and 1374 Carrickmines Castle was consistently in the front-line because of its position astride the gateway to Dublin. Naturally, Carrickmines was a popular target for O'Byrne attacks. The O'Byrnes may also have been encouraged by the extinction of the male line of the Howel family by 1372. The later occurrence of the names Howel and Maurice among the Walshes of Carrickmines suggests that their leaders probably had married Howel heiresses. The first mention of the Walshes occupying lands formerly leased by the Howels from Holy Trinity comes in May 1372. Then Holy Trinity leased Ballybrenan to Thomas Walsh, a chaplain of the priory, for twenty years at a rent of 4 marks per annum. This, though, was conditional upon Thomas building and maintaining a stone house at Ballybrenan.[42] Further, it would seem that a Hugh Lawless obtained a lease upon Carrickmines and its castle. Underlining its strategic importance, Carrickmines Castle was then placed under the command of John de Colton, treasurer of Ireland and later archbishop of Armagh, withstanding two long sieges.[43] For the O'Byrnes,

38 Ibid., p. 374.   39 Ibid., p. 372. There was a campaign against the O'Mores of Slemargy in 1359, see E. Tresham (ed.), *Rotulorum patentium et clausorum cancellarie Hibernie calendarium* (Dublin, 1828), no. 57, p. 69.   40 For the dating of John O'Byrne's knighting, see Nicholls, 'Críoch Branach', p. 16. See also *Rot. pat . & claus. Hib*, no. 7, p. 66.   41 *Rot. pat. & claus. Hib*, no. 91, p. 79.   42 For the use of Howel as a name by the Walshes, see the lease in 1538 of Kyllenyn by the priory of Holy Trinity to William McHowel Walsh: *Christ Church deeds*, no. 1168. For the grant of Ballybrenan to William Walsh see ibid., no. 717. 43 *Rot. pat. & claus. Hib*, p. 87.

Carrickmines Castle again proved a nut too hard to crack, but this did not prevent them from trying again. Carrickmines Castle was to essentially remain a cavalry base to strike out against the Wicklow Irish, housing 40 mounted Fingal archers for 15 days in October 1388 to resist the O'Byrnes and the O'Tooles.[44]

Carrickmines experienced another change of ownership after the expedition of Richard II to Ireland in 1394–5. Clearly, the king's experience in the Dublin marches determined his decisions, firstly, to confiscate Lawless and Archbold lands and, secondly, to grant them to Janico Dartas. On December 12 1395 the king confirmed these lands along with Hugh Lawless's lands at Carrickmines to Dartas.[45] Richard's grant indicates that the crown had exercised its right to Carrickmines, depriving Holy Trinity of its ownership. In turn Dartas may have confirmed Carrickmines and other lands to John and David Walsh, who held these lands from the crown by knight service. In turn these men seem to have allowed Henry fitz Adam Walsh to occupy Carrickmines Castle and work its attached lands. Henry fitz Adam was definitely in possession of Carrickmines by 11 March 1400, for Henry IV then granted 100s. from the revenues of the royal manor of Thorncastle to 'Henry Adamesone of Cairykmayn' for his good service.[46] The Walshes of Carrickmines were soon to prove their worth as guardians of the Dublin march. In 1401 the pressure from the Irish, under Domhnall and Donnchadh O'Byrne, rose dramatically. In 1401 Donnchadh decided to settle a large force of O'Meagher mercenaries, kinsmen of his wife, along the Dodder river just north of Bray. The implications were clear for the Walshes of Carrickmines and the farmers of south Dublin. Led by Lord Mayor John Drake, the Dubliners and the Walshes slaughtered the mercenaries in August 1401 in battle at Bloody Bank near Bray (now known as Sunny Bank).

This O'Byrne defeat was greatly to consolidate the emerging status of Henry fitz Adam Walsh of Carrickmines as guardian of the Dublin Pale. After 1401 the accumulation of crown and clerical lands by the Walshes within the barony of Rathdown increased. In 1407 the crown granted land at Balally to Henry fitz Adam's son, William fitz Henry Walsh. This grant though was subject to the building by William fitz Henry of a castle there.[47] William fitz Henry himself resided at Symondeston in Kiltiernan parish, holding it from St Mary's abbey at Dublin. Upon the death of William fitz Henry sometime in 1407, a panel of jurors including John Archbold and John Lawless took part in an inquisition to determine the extent of Walsh holdings at Symondeston.[48] Henry fitz Adam Walsh of Carrickmines then seems to have

---

44 Ibid, p. 136.   **45** E. Curtis, 'Janico Dartas, Richard II's 'Gascon Squire': his career in Ireland, 1394–1426', in *R.S.A.I. Jn.*, lxiii (1933), pp 186–8.   **46** A.E. Stamp (ed.), *Calendar of close rolls, 1399–1402* (London, 1927), p. 69.   **47** Goodbody, *On the borders of the pale*, p. 23.   **48** *Chartul. St Mary's, Dublin*, i, no. 256, pp 280–1. Between 1438–63 Abbot John

become the guardian of his son's recorded offspring, Henry and Esmond. Naturally, the eldest of these boys, Henry, became the heir to the lands occupied by both his father and grandfather. In December 1407, the young Henry's rights to Carrickmines were confirmed. Then John and David Walsh on December 20 confirmed Carrickmines to Henry fitz Adam before granting the rest to Maurice Walsh and John fitz Maurice Walsh.[49]

Henry succeeded to these lands while still a minor in 1420, becoming an important landowner within the Dublin marches.[50] There can be no doubt that the Walshes were aware that many saw opportunity in his minority. Clearly, the decisions of Henry's early career were subject to the counsel of his older relatives. With their advice ringing in his ears, the young man had the good sense to burn the candle from both ends, cultivating good relations with his Irish neighbours and the powerful James Butler, 4th earl of Ormond. Walsh adherence to Ormond was to earn them the enmity of Thomas fitzMaurice Fitzgerald, later the 7th earl of Kildare. Through his wife, Ormond had become the protector of the Kildare earldom upon the death of the 5th earl of Kildare on 13 October 1432, acquiring two-thirds of it, while one-third went to the widowed countess.[51] This was seemingly achieved with the blessing of Kildare, who realised his earldom's perilous condition: his brother and successor, John, would die soon after him,[52] and the next in line, Thomas fitzMaurice, Kildare's grandnephew, was still a minor. Initially, however, Ormond and Thomas fitzMaurice were friendly, as the young Fitzgerald heir spent some time living in the earl's household. Over time relations cooled, culminating in Ormond's banishment of Thomas fitzMaurice from Kildare, probably before Ormond's departure for England in the winter of 1434–5.

For the Walshes of Carrickmines and Kilgobbin, the feud had disastrous consequences. And it got considerably worse after Thomas fitzMaurice took refuge with the O'Mores and then with the O'Byrnes. While the Kildare heir was living under the protection of the O'Byrnes, he cultivated a partnership with Braen son of Donnchadh of Newrath, the most active O'Byrne warlord of this time. Not insignificantly, this Braen was married to Elizabeth O'More;[53] while Thomas fitzMaurice's first wife was allegedly Dorothea O'More. Therefore Thomas fitzMaurice and Braen were possibly brothers-in-law. One

White of St Mary's gathered the principal figures of the Walshes such as James Came of Kilgobbin and Conchobhar Came of Kiltiernan along with Henry Walsh–captain of the Walschemen–to determine the boundaries of Kiltiernan: *Chartul. St Mary's*, i, no. 288, p. 353. **49** Hussey Walsh, 'The Austrian branches of the family of Walsh', p. 217. **50** Elrington-Ball, *History of the County Dublin*, i, p. 99. **51** Edmund Curtis (ed.), *Calendar of Ormond deeds*, 6 vols (Dublin, 1932–43), iii, no. 99, p. 82. **52** Ibid, p. 86. **53** 'Genealogia Joannis Byrne armigeri apud Burdigalam in Galliarum Regna', Microfilm of MS 162, reel no. 971, Pos 8301. Conn O'Connor Faly, lord of Offaly (1458–1471), was also married to a daughter of O'More, probably Cétach. See *MacFirbis's annals*, s.a. 1462; *Annals of Connacht*, s.a. 1462.

thing is certain, though: before September 1440 they were both terrorising the Pale, particularly the Walsh lands. For burning the Kilgobbin lands of James Adamesson (fitz Adam) Walsh, Henry's granduncle, the pair were outlawed on 6 September that year.[54] Unsurprisingly, Henry was soon in royal service, earning 10 marks on 12 July 1441 as a reward for fighting the Irish.[55] Henry was also probably part of the large English hosting defeated in 1442 by the O'Byrnes in Wicklow.[56] As time went on, Henry came to an understanding with the Irish, tailoring their interests with his own. According to a later complaint levied against him in 1468, Henry spoke Irish, wore Irish dress and used Irish law whenever it suited his purpose. Moreover, Henry is reputed to have extensively rebuilt the castle in the form that it was to stand for the next two centuries, raising the finance through extortion and illegal appropriation of the revenues of Dalkey port.[57] However, Henry's cosy world was transformed by the pardon in 1452 of his old enemy Thomas FitzMaurice.[58]

This pardon and Ormond's death in August 1452 transformed Thomas fitzMaurice from an outlaw living in the twilight worlds of both Irish and English society into a major player within the English lordship. In spite of his pardon, Thomas fitzMaurice was denied his inheritance. The reason for this was the continuing Butler dominance of the English government. Fitzgerald fortunes further improved when Duke Richard of York was restored as lieutenant of Ireland in 1454, forcing James Butler, earl of Wiltshire and Ormond, on 15 April to surrender all claims to the lieutenancy. Thomas fitzMaurice responded to York's rise by supporting his cause. His success is confirmed by the fact that Thomas fitzMaurice was both 7th earl of Kildare and York's deputy by October 1454.[59] Now York's deputy, Kildare's attitude to the Irish changed; he distanced himself from the O'Byrne friends of his rebellious youth and embraced a future of service to the English crown. Kildare's policy of good government, self-interest, and affinity-building was similar to the old Butler policies. He knew that the vulnerability of the Pale and the government were linked to that of his own earldom, resolving upon the implementation to a two-pronged strategy to strengthen the English lordship in Ireland. Firstly, Kildare decided to develop the defences of his own earldom so that it would act as the Pale's shield, and secondly he turned his attention to the reform of the Dublin marches.[60]

A sign of Kildare's hard-line attitude towards the O'Byrnes was his beginnings of the refortification of the Pale's borders. The next step came in

---

54 *Ormond deeds*, iii, no. 135, p. 119.   **55** *Rot. pat. & claus. Hib.*, no. 13, p. 263; Connolly, *Irish exchequer payments,*, p. 478.   **56** *Annals of the Four Masters*, s.a. 1442.   **57** H.F. Berry (ed.), *Statute rolls of the parliament of Ireland, 1–12 Edward IV* (Dublin, 1914), pp 461–3; Ball, *History of the County Dublin*, i, p. 99.   **58** H.F. Berry (ed.), *Statute rolls of the parliament of Ireland, Henry VI* (Dublin, 1910), p. 94. See note 2.   **59** *Stat. Ire., Hen VI*, p. 301; *Annals of the Four Masters*, s.a. 1454; *MacFirbis's annals*, s.a. 1454.   **60** *Stat. Ire., Hen*

Emmett O'Byrne

1454–5 when the Dublin assembly legislated for the introduction of a series of anti-Irish laws. Another important event was the suspension, that Easter 1455, of the timber trade between the Wicklow Irish and Dublin as well as the cessation in September of the supplying of Wicklow Castle. These actions were presumably due to O'Byrne hostilities. This must be taken as the end of the O'Byrne alliance with Kildare. Another aspect of Kildare's reformation of the Dublin marches was his taking in hand of its prominent families. Without doubt there was a personal aspect to this, as it afforded him the chance to settle some scores with the Walshes of Carrickmines. In his 1456 parliament Kildare outlawed Henry Walsh of Carrickmines and his son William. Among others to suffer the same fate were Thomas Carrach (Walsh?) of Shanganagh, Maurice Walsh, Patrick Archbold, Geoffrey Harold, Esmond Harold and a number of Lawlesses. They were all to surrender themselves to the constable of Dublin Castle or risk attainder. There, Kildare would hear all complaints against them. If they defied the writ of the parliament, they risked a campaign being proclaimed against them. Moreover, their future release would only be guaranteed by the deposit of several hostages.[61]

In the event, Kildare made the Walshes of Carrickmines pay a high price for their pardon of 1458, forcing Henry, his son William, and the Harolds to attack their Irish friends.[62] As part of this programme, the Dublin assembly in December 1457 also prohibited Irish horsemen from staying within the walls of the city.[63] Further signs of Kildare's policy to increase the security of the Pale was his energetic programme of encastellation in the Dublin and Kildare marches to fence in the Irish threat. As in West Leinster, the government took action to curb Irish inroads into the Pale, ordering the building of Bray Castle in 1459. Henry Walsh of Carrickmines, though, made strides towards his rehabilitation by aiding Archbishop Michael Tregury of Dublin in 1460 to erect fortifications at Rathdown and Newcastle Lyons.[64] But later that same year he was again in trouble. Then a number of charges were levied against him for oppressing the English inhabitants of south Dublin and of repeatedly refusing to obey the writ of the county courts. Moreover, he was also accused of stealing the cattle of the government collector of the barony of Rathdown and of detaining them illegally. So serious were the nature of complaints, Henry was ordered to appear before Richard, duke of York and lord lieutenant of Ireland.[65]

In the 1460s, the crisis on the Dublin marches peaked. Since his arrival in Ireland in 1450, Archbishop Michael Tregury of Dublin had been intent upon the revival of his diocesan rights within the lands of the Wicklow Irish and the marchers, complaining to the pope in 1451 of the desolation of his

VI, pp 298–9.   **61** Ibid, pp 441–43.   **62** Ibid., pp 557–9.   **63** J.T. Gilbert (ed.), *Calendar of ancient records of Dublin*, 22 vols (Dublin, 1889–1944), i, pp 284–9, 298.   **64** *Stat. Ire., Hen VI*, p. 757.   **65** Ibid., pp 767–8.

archbishopric. In 1460 he obtained a grant for recovery of archiepiscopal lands. The archbishop apparently began to revive his rights in Harold's Country and O'Byrne's Country.[66] His plans badly backfired, ending in kidnap, an alleged beating and a dismal imprisonment at the hands of Patrick O'Byrne and Geoffrey Harold, who were later excommunicated for their actions.[67] The events of Tregury's kidnap may be connected to the Dublin assembly's prohibition in 1461 of communication between citizens and the Harolds.[68] Testifying to the ability of the Wicklow Irish to penetrate the Pale was their attack in 1462 upon Christ Church cathedral.[69] The northward march of the O'Byrnes received a setback in 1462–3.[70] Despite having routed Henry Walsh of Carrickmines and having captured some of his sons, the O'Byrne lord was killed at the moment of victory.[71] The death of their leader did not prevent the O'Byrnes from conducting a regime of extortion and ransom upon the people of the Dublin marches. For Henry Walsh of Carrickmines, who was coerced by Kildare to fight the Irish, the situation at times in Dublin marches must have been a nightmare. Before August 1464, Bray was taken by the Irish and then retaken by Thomas Fitzgerald, 8th earl of Desmond.[72] The pressure from the Irish proved too much, forcing Henry to ignore government direction and again treat with the O'Byrnes. This backsliding drew an immediate response from the mayor and citizens of Dublin, who campaigned against him and wasted his lands. In 1465 Henry had had enough and successfully petitioned Desmond for his pardon and those of his kinsmen as well as for the restoration of his property.[73] By 1467 Henry and his sons William and John had returned wholesale to their old habits, orchestrating the oppression of the people of Rathdown through a campaign of day and night larcenies and kidnappings. For this, they, along with their relatives of Kilgobbin and Shankill, were ordered to place themselves by 4 March 1468 in the custody of the constable of Dublin Castle. Again political expediency and military necessity was to combine to let the Walshes off the hook.[74]

During the 1470s, the Wicklow Irish and their allies threatened to eradicate any government control over the Dublin marches. Armed with the support of

66 *Calendar of papal letters, 1447–55*, x, p. 99; see J.H. Bernard, 'Richard Talbot Archbishop & Chancellor, 1418–1449', *R.I.A. Proc.*, 35 (1919/20); *Stat. Ire., Hen VI*, pp 768–73; H.F. Berry (ed.), *Registers of wills and inventories of the diocese of Dublin in the time of Archbishops Tregury and Walton, 1457–1483* (Dublin, 1898), pp xx–xxi. 67 *Alen's register*, p. 242. 68 *Ancient records of Dublin*, i, p. 309. 69 *Christ Church deeds,*. no. 297. 70 *Annals of Connacht*, s.a. 1463; *MacFirbis's annals*, s.a. 1463. It seems the unknown O'Byrne overlord was succeeded by Tadhg Mór, son of Braen O'Byrne of Newrath. *McFirbis's Genealogies*, Microfilm no. 473 (UCD), p. 475. However, William Harold and Robert Harold's burnings throughout 1463 ensured that the Dublin marches remained disturbed see *Stat. Ire., 1–12 Edw IV*, pp 67–9 and pp 215–17. 71 *Annals of Connacht*, s.a. 1463. 72 *Ancient records of Dublin*, i, pp 141–3. 73 *Stat. Ire., 1–12 Edw IV*, pp 399–401. 74 Ibid., pp 443–7.

Edward IV, Kildare and the Dublin council continued the existing construction of a defensive system around the Pale that would be less of a drain
upon English coffers. By 1470 the government's weakness was such that
Edmund O'Toole compelled Saggart to pay him a blackrent. Furthermore,
collectors of parliamentary subsidies in Harold's Country, lying between
Saggart and Kilmashogue, were afraid to perform their duties for fear that the
Harolds would deliver them to the Irish. No doubt this situation contributed
to the decree of Kildare's parliament of November/December 1470, com-
manding Saggart's townsfolk to abandon their agreement with the O'Tooles.[75]
Saggart paid the ultimate price for its compliance, when the O'Byrnes and
O'Tooles sacked it in 1471–2, forcing many to abandon it. The sack of
Saggart spurred frantic English activity to enclose the town with defensive
ditches, while a fortified dyke was dug from Tallaght to Saggart.[76] Indicative
of the confidence of the Irish of east Leinster and their alienation from the
English archbishopric of Dublin and the government was their attempt to
resurrect the dormant bishopric of Glendalough, which was granted papal
approval in 1481.[77] But Kildare stuck to his task, one of his most innovative
actions being to create an embryonic standing force to punish their incursions:
his parliament of 1471/2 granted him 80 archers for his retinue, 40 of whom
Kildare undertook to maintain. Three years later Kildare's parliament went
on to authorise the establishment of a permanent fighting force; the 'Fraternity
of St George', comprising 160 archers and 63 spearmen, whose captains
included Kildare's son, the young Gerald Fitzgerald. When the Irish did
penetrate these Pale defences, they were devastating, directing their venom
upon the Walshes of Carrickmines and Kilgobbin. As Kildare's clients, Henry
Walsh and his kinsmen bore the brunt of their wrath: in 1476, the O'Byrnes
and O'Toole destroyed Kilgobbin Castle, leaving Maurice Walsh destitute.[78]

The fortunes of the Walshes of Carrickmines were to improve after the
death of Kildare on March 25 1478. Kildare's son Gerald, elected to take his
place, sought to build upon the sound foundations laid by his father. Thus,
the emergence in 1478 of Gerald Mór Fitzgerald as 8th earl of Kildare and as
lord deputy, signalled the gradual rolling back of the O'Byrne tide from the
borders of the Pale. The opening shots of Kildare's offensive came in 1480,
when a royal service was proclaimed in Kildare against the Irish. That
September the young Kildare rode into the Leinster mountains, devastating
the O'Byrne lordship as well as seizing Leighlinbridge from Murchadh

---

75 Ibid., pp 664–9.   76 Ibid, p. 809. This coincides with the Dublin assembly's suspension
in 1471 of the cereal trade with the Irish of Glendalough, see *Ancient records of Dublin*, i,
p. 347.   77 *Alen's register*, p. 245; *Cal. papal letters 1471–84*, ix, part 2, p. 744.   78 *Stat.
Ire., 12–22 Edw IV*, pp xlv, 130–5, 516–19, 715–7, see also pp 444–5. Maurice was
described as Kildare's servant in 1467–8; Edmund Curtis, *A history of medieval Ireland*, 2nd
edn (London, 1938), p. 334.

Ballach MacMurrough, king of Leinster.[79] The punishment inflicted upon the Irish eased the pressure on the Pale considerably, rewarding Henry Walsh of Carrickmines with relative peace in his last years. Henry died shortly after bequeathing Carrickmines to his son John fitz Henry on October 16 1481.[80] In the protracted conquest of the Wicklow Irish, Kildare received sterling help from Theobald fitz Henry Walsh of Carrickmines, the successor of his brother John. In late February 1495 Sir Edward Poynings, lord lieutenant of Ireland, arrested Kildare, sending him to England in March for allegedly encouraging the resistance of the O'Hanlons of Orior as well as prompting his brother's rebellion.[81]

Instead of joining Kildare's supporters, Theobald fitz Henry Walsh of Carrickmines, and the Harolds, organised forces to resist the rebels, while the baron of Dunboyne led a campaign into Wicklow late in 1495, capturing Art O'Toole, a Kildare client. By the summer of 1496, Kildare was back in favour because nothing had been proved against him. Moreover, Henry VII came round to the realisation that Kildare was the only English magnate capable of governing Ireland in his name, and was a considerably cheaper option than direct rule, so he made a new concord with Kildare, whereby he was restored to the deputyship and granted any crown lands he could reconquer from the Irish. A fresh mark of the king's favour was Kildare's new wife, Elizabeth St John, the king's cousin. These new conditions ended the war of Kildare's brother, Sir James Fitzgerald, who submitted in July 1496. Kildare landed in Ireland in mid-September 1496. Characteristically, he quickly exerted himself, taking pledges from both English and Irish lords at Drogheda and Dundalk. In Leinster, where there was resistance, he retook Carlow from Murchadh Ballach MacMurrough of Leinster after two attempts, before embarking on a circuit throughout Leinster. Bereft of protection and without an option, Murchadh Ballach and Cathaoir son of Dúnlaing O'Byrne and other Irish nobles, dispatched envoys to make their submissions at Dublin during October 1496.[82]

As for Theobald fitz Henry Walsh of Carrickmines, he quickly made sure to return to Kildare's side to help him reduce the O'Byrnes to vassalage by 1505. Throughout the Kildare ascendancy, leading figures among the Walshes

79 A.J. Otway-Ruthven, *A history of medieval Ireland*, (London, 1968) p. 400; *Ancient records of Dublin*, i, p. 357; *The annals of Ross*, p. 46.   **80** Hussey Walsh, 'The Austrian branches of the family of Walsh', p. 217.   **81** A. Conway, *Henry VII's relations with Scotland and Ireland, 1485–98* (New York, 1972), pp 195–7; D.B. Quinn, 'The hegemony of the earls of Kildare, 1494–1520', in A. Cosgrove (ed.), *A new history of Ireland*, ii (Oxford, 1993), p. 641; *Annals of the Four Masters*, s.a. 1494. Sir James Fitzgerald is mentioned burning Meath in 1494. This reference must pertain to 1495. For the attainder of the Fitzgeralds, see D.B. Quinn, 'The bills and statutes of the Irish parliaments of Henry VII and Henry VIII', *Analecta Hibernica*, 10 (1941), p. 94.   **82** Conway, *Henry VII's relations*, pp 232– 5.

such as Howel, William and Walter remained steadfastly loyal to their masters, evidenced by their acceptance of gifts of horses and hackneys from Gerald Óg Fitzgerald, 9th earl of Kildare.[83] Upon Theobald fitz Henry's death, Carrickmines seemingly passed to his brother Edmund fitz Henry. By 1519 Edmund fitz Henry of Carrickmines had fallen out with Holy Trinity, as on 21 February 1519 was ordered by William Hasard (the later prior of Holy Trinity), to renounce his claims to the nearby lands of Keatingsland and Priorsland.[84] During the closing years of the Kildare ascendancy, during the 1530s, the Walshes showed their desire for the earl's continued favour by terrorising his enemies. During 1531–2, they, along with the Archbolds and Harolds, joined some of the O'Byrnes and O'Tooles to devastate the lands of Archbishop John Alen of Dublin, Kildare's enemy. Strangely though, the Walshes played no recorded part in the doomed Kildare rebellion of 1534–5 against Henry VIII, indicating that they had somehow managed to stay neutral.

Edmund fitz Henry of Carrickmines died at an uncertain date before 20 June 1537. Carrickmines then passed to his nephew, William fitz Theobald Walsh, the husband of Margaret Fitzwilliam of Merrion. This William fitz Theobald set about increasing greatly his land holdings in the aftermath of the Kildare rebellion. From Edmund fitz Henry, William fitz Theobald inherited his strained relationship with Holy Trinity. On 12 December 1539 Dean Robert Paynswicke asserted the priory's right to the temporalities due from William fitz Theobald's lands at Ballyogan, Ballybrenan, Smothescourt, Priorsland, Keatingsland and from St Brigid's church of Carrickmines.[85] To compensate himself, William fitz Theobald in the early 1540s developed substantial land holdings in Wicklow. This was largely due to dramatic changes in the political landscape of Wicklow. There the O'Byrne lordship under Tadhg mac Gerald O'Byrne of Kiltimon had become a great deal more accessible due to the emergence of good relations with the Dublin government. On 4 July 1542, Tadhg mac Gerald agreed to the gradual introduction of English rule into his lordship as part of the government's policy of 'Surrender and Regrant', which meant that the O'Byrnes had a great deal of autonomy over their own affairs. But, as time proved, the reality was to be otherwise, and as has been noted, the change in English policies, combined with the political fragmentation of the O'Byrne lordship, paved the way for its being replaced by an English seneschalcy.[86] Even before that date William fitz Theobald's land agents were active in the O'Byrne lordship. On 17 August 1541 he obtained a lease of 21 years to Kilpeadar, while in 1544/5 he received letters patent to 12 messuages and 620 acres at Kilpoole in O'Byrnes' Country.[87]

---

83 G. McNiocaill (ed.), *Crown surveys of lands, 1540–1* (Dublin, 1992), pp 319, 321–2, 327–8, 332. 84 *Christ Church deeds*, no. 408. 85 Ibid., no. 431. 86 *Calendar of Carew MSS, 1515–74*, no. 170, pp 193–4; Nicholls, 'Críoch Branach', pp 8, 16. 87 *The Irish fiants of the Tudor sovereigns* (Dublin, 1994), Hen. VIII, no. 246; Griffith (ed.) *Cal.*

Moreover, on 12 April 1542 William fitz Theobald also obtained a grant of the Shanganagh lands of his cousin Walter Walsh (*d*.1551), then a minor and later his son-in-law.[88] These acquisitions certainly proved expensive. On 12 May 1543 William fitz Theobald acknowledged a debt of 100 pounds in the Irish chancery court,[89] but this financial stringency did not prevent William fitz Theobald from expanding his landed interests. In 1548 he acquired a lease for 21 years of the tithes of the prebend of Rathmichael at a rent of £22 per annum.[90] By 1555 the Walshes of Carrickmines enjoyed a better relationship with Holy Trinity, as William fitz Theobald had his lease upon Ballybrenan, and the lands of Priorsland and Keatingsland – described as being in the fields of Carrickmines – confirmed for 51 years on 28 October. For Priorsland and Keatingsland, William was to pay 20*s.* per year, while he was to render 16*s.* 8*d.* for those at Ballybrenan. He was also obliged by Holy Trinity to mow the meadows and gather the tithes of Ballybrenan and deposit them at place called the Holy Stod.[91] Further information about William fitz Theobald's manor of Carrickmines can be gleaned from an inquisition dated 14 April 1570. This inquisition not only set out the lands of the manor, but it also outlined William fitz Theobald's outlying lands near Bray. According to the inquisition, William fitz Theobald's lands at Carrickmines were held by knight service and amounted to some 310 acres. Also attached to the manor of Carrickmines were a watermill, and 40 acres spread between Anowdon and Ballerowe, hamlets located close to the castle. From Thomas Butler, 9th earl of Ormond, William fitz Theobald held another 73 acres for the nominal payment of a red rose on St John's Day, while in the royal manor of Rathdown he held a further 36 acres at Crompestown (Cranestown?) directly from the crown.[92]

　　Political expediency forced William fitz Theobald of Carrickmines, like his ancestors, to become increasingly involved with the O'Byrnes of Wicklow. After the failure of the Kildare rebellion in 1535, the O'Byrne raids on the Pale had grown more frequent. These raiders were not drawn from the old O'Byrne lordly families, belonging instead to the rising house of Ballinacor at Glenmalure. For Aodh O'Byrne and later his son Fiach O'Byrne, the lords of Glenmalure, the collapse of the Kildare hegemony proved to be their opportunity. And such was their strength that William fitz Theobald of Carrickmines felt that impressive defences of his castle could not afford him adequate protection. Instead he took the diplomatic option, arranging the marriage of his third son Robert to Aodh's daughter Honora.[93] By the late 1540s, William fitz Theobald's involvement with the Irish was clearly

inquisitions, Hen. VIII 187/17, pp 107–8.　　**88** Griffith (ed.), *Cal. inquisitions*, Edw VI 36/8, p. 130.　　**89** Hussey Walsh, 'The Austrian branches of the family of Walsh', p. 217. **90** *Irish fiants of the Tudor sovereigns*, Edw. VI, no. 214.　　**91** *Christ Church deeds*, no. 1242. **92** Griffith (ed.), *Cal. inquisitions*, Eliz 49/37, p. 196.　　**93** Hussey Walsh, 'The Austrian branches of the family of Walsh', p. 218.

growing. Against the background of considerable disturbance, he was pardoned on April 3 1549 for unspecified behaviour.[94]

Due to political instability, William fitz Theobald walked a tight rope between the government and the Irish, tacking before the prevailing political winds. In 1558 he was pardoned for his involvement in the murder of Peter Talbot by some kerns.[95] On the other hand while he assembled his troops for the muster of the Pale on 13 July 1560, he clearly realised that the Dublin marches were becoming more disordered due to the ambitions of the O'Byrnes of Glenmalure and the O'Tooles of Castlekevin.[96] The disorder in the marches was confirmed in February 1566. Then Sir Nicholas Bagenal complained to Robert Dudley, earl of Leicester, of the continual robbing and killing within the English Pale, pointing specifically towards the lands of the O'Tooles, O'Byrnes and the Walshes.[97] Perhaps on foot of Bagenal's complaints, the lands of the Walshes, Harolds and Archbolds were committed in April to the charge of Thomas Fitzwilliam of Merrion, William fitz Theobald's kinsman. Indeed, government reports emphasised the closeness of William fitz Theobald and his relatives to the Irish, portraying him as their client. On 4 February 1567 Richard fitz Robert Walsh of Carrickmines was included in the pardon of Féilim son of Toirdhealbhach O'Toole of Powerscourt.[98] Another government document dated 29 December 1572 displayed the depth and intricacy of the relations between the O'Byrnes and O'Tooles and the marchers of south Dublin. In it William fitz Theobald, his sons and their relatives of Ballybrenan, Kilgobbin, Ballaly and Shanganagh were said to be near kinsmen of the Irish and were sworn to them. The Walshes were not alone in their allegiance to the Irish; other marcher families sworn to Aodh O'Byrne and Fiach O'Toole of Castlekevin were the Goodmans of Laughanstown, the Talbots of Fassaghroe, as well as the Harolds and the Archbolds.[99] Moreover, one of the Walshes of Kilgobbin acted as trustee to the later marriage agreement of Fiach O'Byrne and his wife, Rose O'Toole. The deepening confidence of the Irish leaders was clear when this Fiach penetrated the Pale defences in 1574, and set the town of Kilmainham aflame before retreating back into the mountains.[100] The frustration of the New English at their inability to contain the attacks of the mountain Irish was palpable. One of these disgruntled New English was John Crawhall of Ballyloghlan (Loughlinstown). That June, a party led by Crawhall violently protested before Lord Deputy Sir William Fitzwilliam about the ease of Fiach's success, accusing the old marcher families such as the Walshes and their neighbours of connivance in these attacks.[101]

94 *Irish fiants of the Tudor sovereigns*, Eliz., no. 265.   **95** Ibid., Eliz.,no. 275.   **96** *Acts of the privy council in Ireland, 1556–71* (London, 1897), p. 86.   **97** *Calendar of the state papers, Ireland, 1509–73*, no. 3, p. 289.   **98** *Irish fiants of the Tudor sovereigns*, Eliz., no. 994. **99** Lane-Poole MSS 5358.   **100** PRO, SP 63/45/41; PRO, SP 63/43/14; PRO, SP 63/45/46; PRO, SP 63/46/64.   **101** PRO, SP 63/46/51.

The date of Theobald fitz William's death is disputed. According to an inquisition of April 1570, he died on 29 September 1569, but he may have lived on until 1573. What is clear though is that Theobald fitz William was succeeded as lord of Carrickmines by his son, Richard fitz Theobald Walsh, husband of Eleanor Fitzeustace of Clongoweswood. Like his father, Richard fitz Theobald steered a diplomatic policy of self preservation through the competing ambits of a largely Protestant New English government at Dublin and Fiach O'Byrne, the leader of the Leinster Catholics. Indeed, the collective pardon of Richard fitz Theobald, Thomas Fitzwilliam of Merrion and James Goodman of Laughanstown on 7 December 1574 may have been in connection with the O'Byrne raids on Dublin that year.[102] On 10 September 1577 Richard fitz Theobald was again pardoned for unspecified actions.[103] Thereafter nothing was mentioned of him until his death on 10 July 1580, when he was succeeded by his son, the 28-year-old Theobald fitz Richard Walsh. This Theobald fitz Richard was to die at the age of 41 on 17 November 1593, having enjoyed a reasonably peaceful tenure of his Carrickmines lands.[104] Theobald fitz Richard, by his wife Eleanor Fitzwilliam of Merrion, left a male heir, Richard fitz Theobald Walsh.[105] According to the inquisition of 28 November 1593, Theobald fitz Richard passed a much reduced inheritance to Richard fitz Theobald.[106] But because the heir was a minor, the crown took his lands into its hands, housing a troop of horse there before the end of that year. Moreover, the wardship and forthcoming marriage of Richard fitz Theobald were entrusted to Peter Barnewall, a prominent Palesman.[107]

As the need to deal with the threat of Fiach O'Byrne and the Leinster Catholics grew, most of the Walshes of Carrickmines gave their allegiance to the Dublin government. During the Nine Years War of 1594–1603, Carrickmines Castle housed 60 calvarymen of the earl of Southampton, Shakespeare's patron. This, however, did not prevent the O'Byrnes from burning the village outside the castle during the night of 12 June 1599. The removal of the O'Byrne threat to Carrickmines finally ended with the surrender in March 1601 of Féilim O'Byrne before the Dublin council. The subsequent pardons of the rest of the Leinstermen reveal that some of the Walshes of Carrickmines and their kinsmen had fought against the government. On 5 May 1601, Maurice and William Walsh of Carrickmines were pardoned with the followers of Domhnall Spáinneach Kavanagh, king of Leinster. Their cousin Nicholas Walsh of Kilgobbin was later included in Féilim O'Toole of Castlekevin's pardon on 14 December 1603.[108] The end of

102 *Irish fiants of the Tudor sovereigns*, Eliz., no. 2534.   103 Ibid., Eliz., no. 3098.
104 Griffith (ed.) *Cal. inquisitions*, Eliz. 223/150, pp 295–6.   105 Ibid., Eliz. 139/94, pp 254–5.   106 Ibid., 223/150, pp 295–6.   107 *Irish fiants of the Tudor sovereigns*, no. 5966.
108 *Cal. state papers Ire., 1600–1*, no. 82, p. 89, no. 15, p. 152, no. 105, p. 240; *Irish fiants of the Tudor sovereigns*, no. 6517; *Irish patent rolls of James I* (Dublin, 1966), no. lxxviii, p. 33.

Carrickmines Castle came in March 1642. Then the castle fell to the English, culminating in the slaughter of all its estimated 300 inhabitants. The castle apparently was then blown up and razed to the ground, although some of the Walshes survived to remerge as the Counts Von Wallis in the service of the Austrian Empire.

The discoveries at Carrickmines offer us a rare chance to reassess the history of medieval Ireland, particularly in the marches of Dublin and Leinster. They allow us a fleeting glimpse into the world of the frontiermen who guarded the Dublin Pale. Also they throw us a lifeline to the world of the Leinster Irish. Much of the misinterpretation of the Leinster Irish arose because of where they dwelt, living well beyond the Pale in mountainous and densely forested regions that have been characterised as the angry world of the Celtic fringe. Indeed, the ruggedness of their homelands has reinforced their popular image of being wild and untamed. Usually our only glimpse of this society in its natural habitat comes from accounts of government campaigns into these lands. But rarely do we get a cogent picture of the world of the Celtic fringe interacting with the Palesmen. More commonly, we are presented with images of conflict. In Carrickmines we have been gifted one remarkable chance to reassess the history of the Dublin marches – it should not be passed up lightly.

English patron, English building?
The importance of St Sepulchre's
archiepiscopal palace, Dublin

DANIELLE O'DONOVAN

INTRODUCTION

The following paper is divided into three parts: the first is a discussion of the documentary sources which detail the history of the medieval archiepiscopal palace of St Sepulchre, Dublin; the second section looks at what remains of the medieval structure, and seeks to explain how this can be understood; while the third section is an analysis of how St Sepulchre's fits into the traditions of archiepiscopal and episcopal building in Ireland and further afield.

The see of the archbishops of Dublin, the palace of St Sepulchre, is better known today as Kevin Street Garda Station. It became a barracks for the Dublin Mounted Police in the early nineteenth century, when the archbishop moved to a more fashionable address on St Stephen's Green. The palace was the home of the archbishops of Dublin for six hundred years, broken only by a short period in the sixteenth century when the Lord Justice occupied the house, much to the annoyance of the archbishop who was forced to live in Tallaght on a permanent basis. The archbishops of Dublin were not only ecclesiastical office-holders, they also held key positions in government. The palace played host to spiritual activities, such as ordination of priests and synods, as well as temporal activities, which included the administration of manors and the holding of courts. St Sepulchre's was the home of a very high-ranking official, and the architecture of the palace, of necessity therefore, reflected this.

DOCUMENTARY SOURCES FOR ST SEPULCHRE

A palace outside the walls (fig. 1) We are told in many secondary sources that John Cumin 'planted the palace down beside the collegiate church' but I have been unable to locate the original source of this reference. The building of the palace seems to be inextricably linked to the elevation of the small parish church of St Patrick into a collegiate church by the first English archbishop of Dublin, John Cumin. Monck Mason tells us that in 1191: 'The

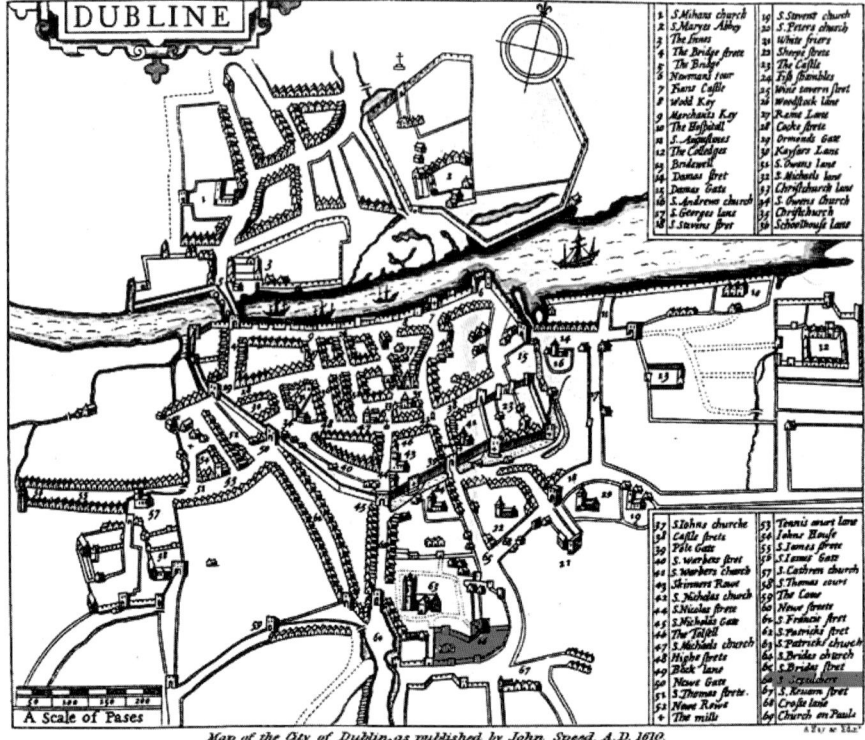

Map of the City of Dublin, as published by John Speed, A.D. 1610.

1 John Speed's Map of Dublin, St Sepulchre's highlighted in grey.

archbishops of Armagh and Dublin, together with the legate O'Heany, met at the cathedral of the Holy Trinity, from whence they made a solemn procession to the new built church in the south suburbs of the city of Dublin, which they dedicated to God, Our Blessed Lady Mary and St Patrick'.[1] Lawlor, in *The fasti of St Patrick's cathedral, Dublin*, suggests that from the beginning Cumin intended that St Patrick's should supercede Christ Church as the cathedral of Dublin.[2]

This may well have been on his mind, but there were a number of other reasons for Cumin's move. Some writers have made the mistake of thinking Cumin a Benedictine monk of Evesham; in fact he was a clerk, judge and court official for some twenty years before he was elected archbishop. He was made archdeacon of Bath in 1167 without being ordained priest, and spent much time abroad in the service of his king, Henry II. He was in the imperial

---

1 William Monck Mason, *The history and antiquities of the cathedral church of St Patrick from its foundation in 1190, to the year 1819* (Dublin, 1820), p. 2.   2 H.J. Lawlor, *The fasti of St Patrick's, Dublin* (Dundalk, 1930), pp 9–10.

court of Frederick Barbarossa during the papal crisis of the 1160s, in 1166 he was in Brittany with King Henry, and in November of that year he was sent to Rome to defend the king over his exile of Thomas Beckett. He was obviously a loyal servant of the king and an able statesman and administrator; it is certainly for this reason and not his religious credentials that Cumin was elected archbishop of Dublin at Evesham on 6 September 1181. Cumin, then, was a cosmopolitan figure who had experienced the luxury of some of the greatest courts in Europe. When he eventually came to Dublin in 1184 his palace was located behind St Michael's church at the southwest angle of Christ Church, probably near the site of the later Synod Hall. It is likely that his predecessor, St Lawrence O'Toole, had not furnished himself with a luxurious palace and, when Cumin moved his residence to a greenfield site next to the newly elevated St Patrick's church, he not only escaped the authority of the city provosts (by moving outside the walls) but provided himself with a palace suitable for a royal official of his rank. Grants made to the archbishop by John, lord of Ireland, gave Cumin further independence so that he could rule the manor of St Sepulchre as a Liberty. A papal protection of 1216 mentions 'the archbishop's houses and buildings at St Sepulchre's with the burgages and appurtenances',[3] suggesting that by the time Henry of London was made archbishop in 1213, St Sepulchre's was a substantial complex.

Accommodation within the complex of St Sepulchre's? There are a number of references in historical documents to different rooms in the palace, buildings situated around the palace, and to the gardens, orchard and pond. We learn from these records not only of the different rooms, but also of the functions they served, and these functions in turn reflect the lifestyle and responsibilities of the archbishop. The liberty status of St Sepulchre meant that the archbishop of Dublin was granted a branch of the crown's perogative. The archbishop exercised both temporal and spiritual authority over the citizens of the Liberty, which covered the manors of St Sepulchre, Tallaght, Rathcoole, Shankill, Ballymore Eustace, Castlekevin, Swords and Finglas (fig. 2). Both ecclesiastical and temporal courts were held at St Sepulchre's. A notice of 1529 of 'the order and time of the temporal courts of the archbishop of Dublin' states that: 'after the octave of Easter and Michaelmas the first session will always be held on Monday at the Palace of St Sepulchre for all tenants within the manor and liberty and for all the burgagers of the same by themselves or their attornies'.[4] The palace was well equipped to fulfill its function as a court, as we learn from a notice of 1377 to the effect that the king issued a pardon to 'the archbishop of Dublin for the escape from his gaol of St Sepulchre, Dublin, of one William, chaplain of Balinadon, convicted of

3 Charles McNeill (ed.), *Calendar of Archbishop Alen's Register, 1172–1534* (Dublin, 1950), pp 38–39.   4 McNeill, *Archbishop Alen's Register*, p. 291.

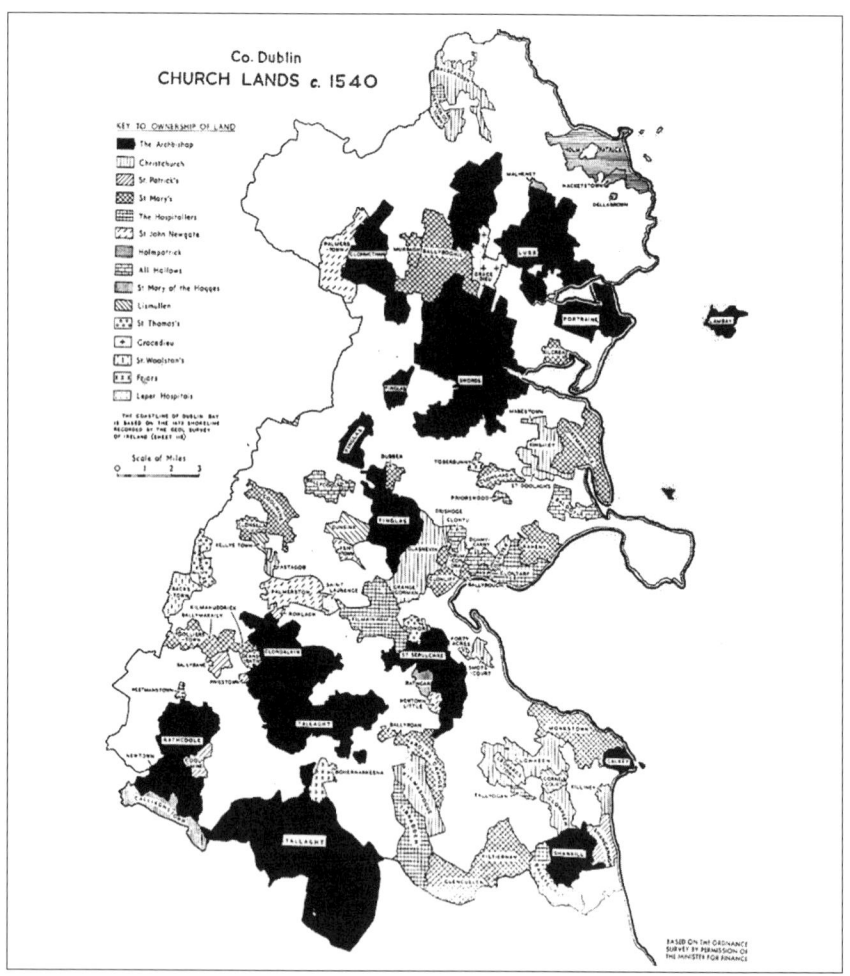

2 Map of church lands in the Dublin area (the archbishop lands in black) after Otway-Ruthven.

divers felonies, being immediately followed and captured and brought back to the said prison, whence he is now detained'.[5]

It seems that the prison was not the only place where people might be detained, for in 1302 a case is recorded in the pleas and plaints of Dublin of one Arnauld Chasserel, an unfortunate 'merchant stranger', who said 'that when he was seneschal of the archbishop of Dublin in this land, the purveyor and manager for the archbishop, appointed by him', the Dean and some of his associates 'finding Arnald near the lodging of the Dean near the church of St Patrick, on Sunday the feast of St John, took him by force and carried him to the prison of the archbishop in his manor of St Sepulchre, next to the lodging

5 *Calendar of Patent Rolls, Richard II, 1377–1381*, p. 55.

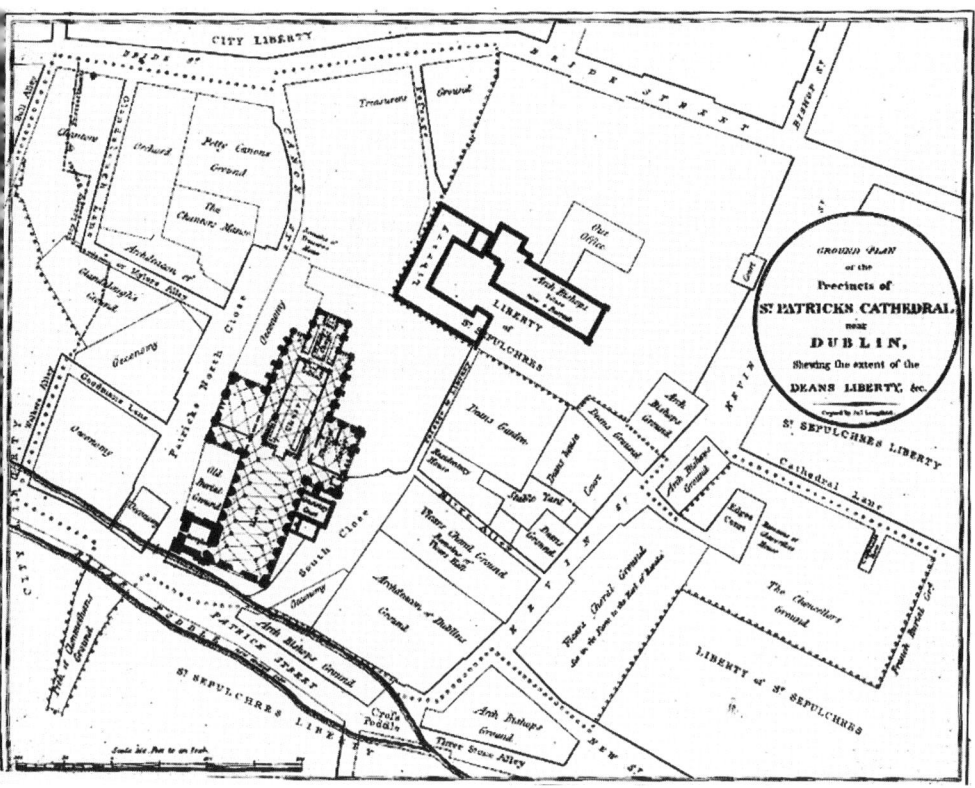

3 Ground plan of the precincts of St Patrick's cathedral by William Monck Mason, *The history and antiquities of the cathedral church of St Patrick* (Dublin, 1820).

of the Dean, and there imprisoned him and kept him for nine days ensuing'. When the case was heard the jurors said that the Dean was 'in no wise guilty, and as to the others, they had 'arrested him [Arnould] and put him in a certain room under charge of four serjeants of the archbishop, the doors of the room being locked and barred, for four days. And afterwards at the request of certain friends of Arnauld they allowed the serjeants to take him for the five succeeding days to a roomy place within the archbishop's house, forbidding him, however to pass those bounds'.[6]

The prison seems to have abutted one of the enclosing walls of the site, next to the Dean's manse, or so it seems from a petition of 1504 in which John Alen intends to build a house for the poor 'on a vacant site between the palace of St Sepulchre and St Kevin's Street, extending in length from the wall of the palace prison to the stone wall of the Dean's manse or manor on the west; in breadth, from the stone wall of the palace garden on the north to St

6 *Calendar of Justiciary Rolls 1295–1303*, pp 398–9.

Kevin's street on the south'.[7] In Monck Mason's plan of the site the court appears to be a separate building from the bishop's palace (fig. 3). This separation of the court may well have taken place in the post-medieval period, as the great hall would most probably have been used for the court and other administrative functions during the years we are interested in here. It is unclear whether the 'roomy place' in which Arnauld was detained was the great hall of the palace, but there is reference to a great hall at St Sepulchre's in the Irish patent roll for 1395.[8] In 1523 there is a reference to the 'inner room' of the palace, which may well refer to the archbishop's private chamber.

The best description we have of the palace is an inquisition of 1326, which describes it as: 'a stone hall badly roofed with shingles and unsafe, a chamber annexed, a kitchen and chapel badly roofed, of no value, because nothing could be got from them, they need great repair; there is a prison there now broken and thrown down'.[9] Could this damage have been done during the Bruce invasion? In 1316 there is as account of damage done to 'the gardens and orchards of St Sepulchre, injured by the king's army going towards Ulster to overcome the Scotch felons'.[10] In 1318 we find Edward II pardoning the citizens of Dublin for burning the city, and it is known that St Patrick's was damaged in these fires.[11] On reading a number of the descriptions of the archbishop's manors it becomes clear that the language used is very formulaic, so that the hall and chamber at Swords are described in the same way as those at St Sepulchre's, even though the buildings at these two sites are very different. The archbishop at the time of the 1326 inquisition was Alexander de Bicknor, and the inquisition was conducted because he was suspected of defrauding the crown; those surveying the lands may well have described them as being in bad condition so as not to give the king false hope as to the value of the land.[12]

A number of the buildings mentioned in the 1326 inquisition remain to be discussed. The palace kitchen is mentioned in a document dating from 1213–28 and seems to have been located near the edge of the site.[13] Better documented is the chapel, which is next mentioned in 1367 when a letter is dated there.[14] In the register of John Swayne, archbishop of Armagh (1418–39) is a document dated 1425 at Termonfeckin, County Louth; it is a testimonial 'of receipt by John Massum, priest of Armagh diocese, from Richard, archbishop of Dublin, of a subdeaconate on 28 March 1423, in St Sepulchre's Manor Chapel, Dublin'.[15] It seems, therefore, that the chapel was

7 McNeill, *Archbishop Alen's register*, pp 254–5.   8 Edward Tresham (ed.), *Rotulorum patentium et clausorum cancellariae Hiberniae calendarium* (London, 1828), vol.1, part p. 152. 9 McNeill, *Archbishop Alen's register*, p. 170.   10 'Pipe Rolls of Edward II', in *Report of the Deputy Keeper of the public records of Ireland*, no. 39 (1907), p. 65.   11 *Calendar of patent rolls, Edward II, 1271–1321*, p. 192.   12 Roger Stalley, *Swords Castle, County Dublin: an analysis of its history and architecture*, unpublished report (1986).   13 McNeill, *Archbishop Alen's register*, p. 53.   14 Ibid., p. 170.   15 D.A. Chart (ed.), *The Register of John Swayne, archbishop of Armagh and primate of Ireland, 1418–39* (Belfast, 1946), p. 41.

4 Beranger's engraving of the palace appeared in the *Hibernian Magazine*, October, 1771.

used not only for private prayer, but also administration and the ordination of priests. Monck Mason suggests that the palace chapel was converted into a parochial church in 1442 by Richard Talbot.[16] Certainly by the end of the seventeenth century there was no chapel, as Narcissus Marsh writes to a friend: 'though it may be called a palace for the stateliness of all the publick rooms of reception. Yet hath it no chapel or library belonging to it, nor indeed any convenient room to hold an ordinary study of books, so that mine lay dispersed in three separate rooms'.[17]

Building, rebuilding and restoration From the above accounts it is possible to conclude that the palace of St Sepulchre was a substantial complex of buildings, including a hall, a chamber, a prison, a kitchen, a chapel and an orchard and garden, all contained within a stone boundary wall. Before looking at a plan of the palace in search of medieval remains it is important to take account of the amount of rebuilding and restoration that has taken place over the last eight hundred years (fig. 4). Three medieval archbishops credited with works to the palace are John Cumin (1181–1213), Hugh Inge (1521–28)

16 Monck Mason, *Cathedral Church of St Patrick*, p. 9.   17 Muriel McCarthy, *All graduates and gentlemen: Marsh's Library, Dublin* (Dublin, 1980), p. 33.

and John Alen (1528–34). Cumin, as we have seen, is credited with establishing the palace on its present site, while Inge's work is made evident by the
presence of a doorway in the west wall of the palace with his coat of arms
above it. Finally, beside the 1326 commission copied into Archbishop Alen's
register, the scribe has noted that the palace was repaired by Alen in 1529.
In the seventeenth century, Archbishop Michael Boyle (1663–78) and
Archbishop Francis Marsh (1681–93) are both said to have enlarged, repaired
and beautified the palace, the latter at his own expense. In the early eighteenth
century Narcissus Marsh (1694–1702) built the library in the palace grounds,
and his successor, William King (1702–29), much altered the appearance of
the building and describes his work in many surviving letters.[18] One feature
mentioned by King but not in any medieval accounts is the tower, and to
complicate matters further King mentions an old tower which he implies has
been knocked down, and a tower that is still standing when he writes in 1713,
as he asks Marsh that he may be 'permitted to deposit some of his own books
in the lower room of the tower'.[19] This tower must have been in the northwest
angle of the palace, for the upper floor was an observatory and communicated
directly with Marsh's library. It was demolished in 1833 but the door that
opened into the tower can be seen on the first floor of the eastern wing of the
library.[20] This tower must be the block shown linking the library and the
palace in Monck Mason's plan of the site.

ST SEPULCHRE'S TODAY: A MEDIEVAL PALACE?

It is exceptionally difficult to tell anything about the date of construction of
the palace from looking at the fabric of the building. The only piece of cut
stone visible dates from the sixteenth century. How can we say that this
building is medieval? How can we say it was built by Cumin? The answer is
contained in the plan.

The plan At first glance the palace seems to be ranged around a roughly
rectangular courtyard with buildings of various shapes and sizes included in
the scheme (fig. 5). On studying the plan, however, it is possible to prove that
the palace was designed using a tightly planned geometrical method known as
ad quadratum (fig. 7). To discern this in the plan it is necessary to look at the
thick black lines indicating medieval masonry (and also to be willing to 'fill in'
the parts we must assume have been demolished). It becomes clear that at the
centre of the plan is a regular courtyard into which eighteenth-century

18 TCD MSS 1995–2008. 19 N.B and J.D. Newport-White, *An Account of Archbishop
Marshe's Library, Dublin* (Dublin, 1926), p. 7. 20 Newport-White, *Archbishop Marshe's
Library*, pp 37–8.

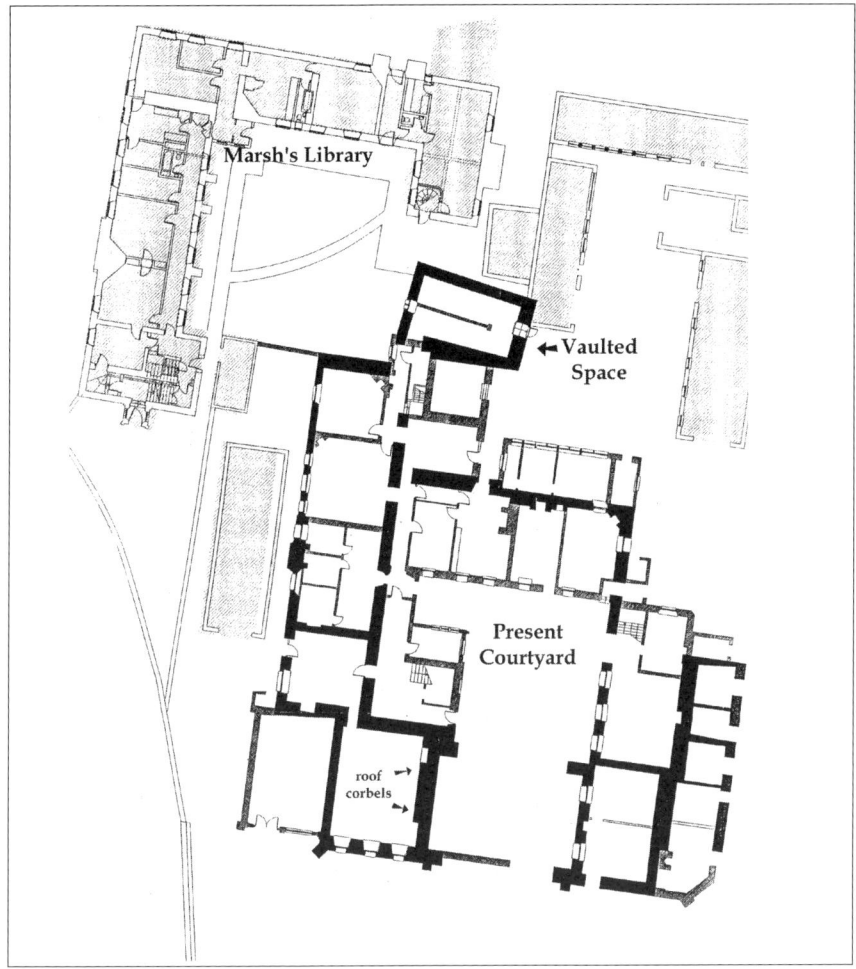

5 Plan of St Sepulchre's indicating the location of Marsh's Library, the vaults and the location of the courtyard as it exists today.

buildings have been slotted (fig. 6).[21] The depths of the ranges around this courtyard are determined in two ways; the narrower ranges in the east and west are laid out by the ratio of 1:1.414 (fig. 8) and the broader ranges are laid out by the ratio 1: 1.618 (fig. 9). The ratio 1:1.414 is the proportion of the side of a square as to its diagonal and may also be expressed as one is to the square root of two. The ratio 1:1.618 is achieved by dividing a square in half to create two rectangles; the proportion is the diagonal of the rectangle is to the side of the original square. The wall widths of St Sepulchre's pose some problems in

21 Drew, in his article 'Surroundings of the cathedral church of St Patrick de Insula, Dublin', *Irish Builder*, 33 (1891), p. 253, suggests that 'the lines of the old Manorial hall, with its ingle and cross screen of characteristic plan may still be traced' in the palace.

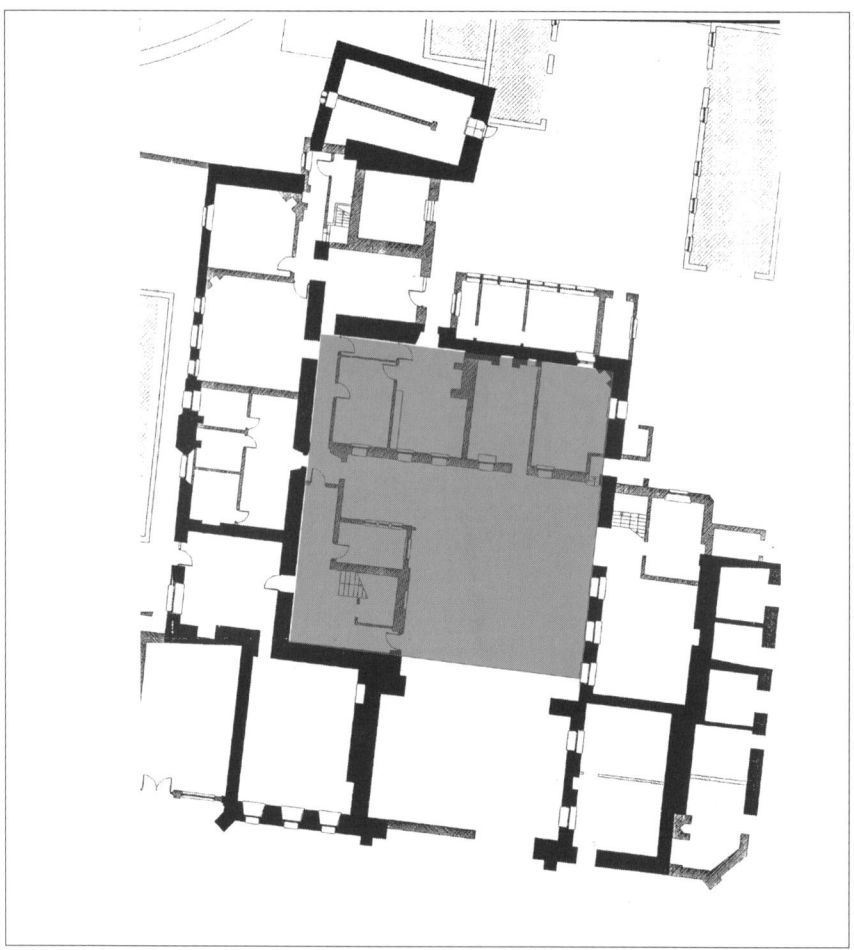

6 Plan with the original courtyard indicated in grey. This medieval courtyard is regular in shape and is indicated by the wall widths.

applying the scheme exactly. It is believed that when medieval builders laid out buildings in this way they used rope and pegs, put down a general plan on the ground and then built on this. The wall widths would not be strictly governed by the geometrical plan as the builders could have built inside or outside the lines. This would explain the irregularities at St Sepulchre's.

This proportional system seems to have governed the plan of St Sepulchre's and is by far the most logical way of explaining the widths of the rooms. The ad quadratum system was used throughout the middle ages and so is of no help in dating the building. However, there are certain assumptions that we may make about the palace upon understanding the proportional scheme. For the planning scheme to work, all of the buildings would have had

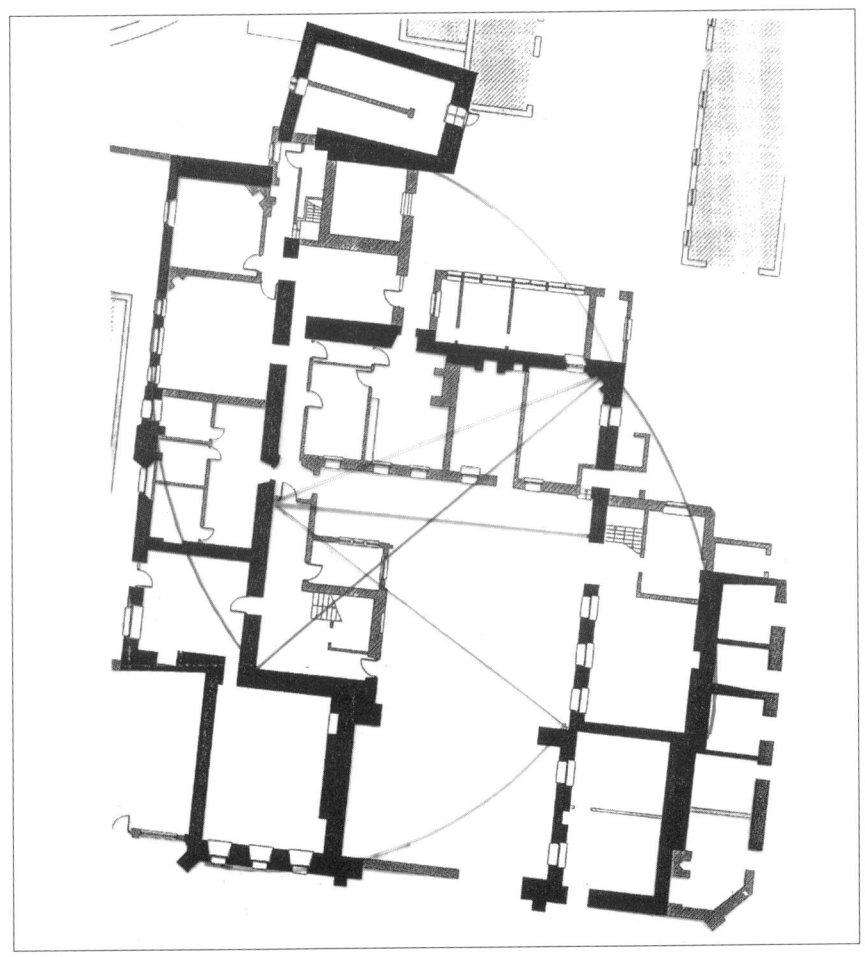

7 Plan with arcs indicating how the building was laid out.

to be laid out in one campaign. The angles and proportions are quite regular here which suggests the buildings are contemporary. Any patron willing to knock down part of the palace would certainly have been seeking to make it bigger, but all of the buildings appear to be governed by the original proportions (i.e., the medieval parts that survive). The medieval roof timber in the second-floor room at the southwest of the quadrangle needs further investigation. If there is enough timber remaining it may be possible to provide dates by dendrochronology (fig. 10). It is difficult to see how this room with its medieval roof relates to the cross-block that I suggest would have run east from it. If the plaster were removed we may see a blocked opening, or even blocked-up windows which would cast doubt on this cross-block to the east (unless this room was altered in a renovation subsequent to Cumin's time).

8 Plan with the north and south blocks highlighted.

We hear very little about the physical condition of the palace throughout the middle ages. Sir James Ware tells us that a number of archbishops improved the palace, but the first is Hugh Inge (1521–28) and the others are subsequent (fig. 11). Surely if there had been any great building campaign at St Sepulchre's, one of the greatest domestic buildings in the city, it would have been mentioned in some source. From this silence we can only suppose that the buildings erected by Cumin in 1190 were of such great comfort and elegance that they required only minor alteration, until the moment when the Tudor archbishop, most likely stirred by the great example set by his colleague, Cardinal Wolsey, set about a grand scheme of renovation.

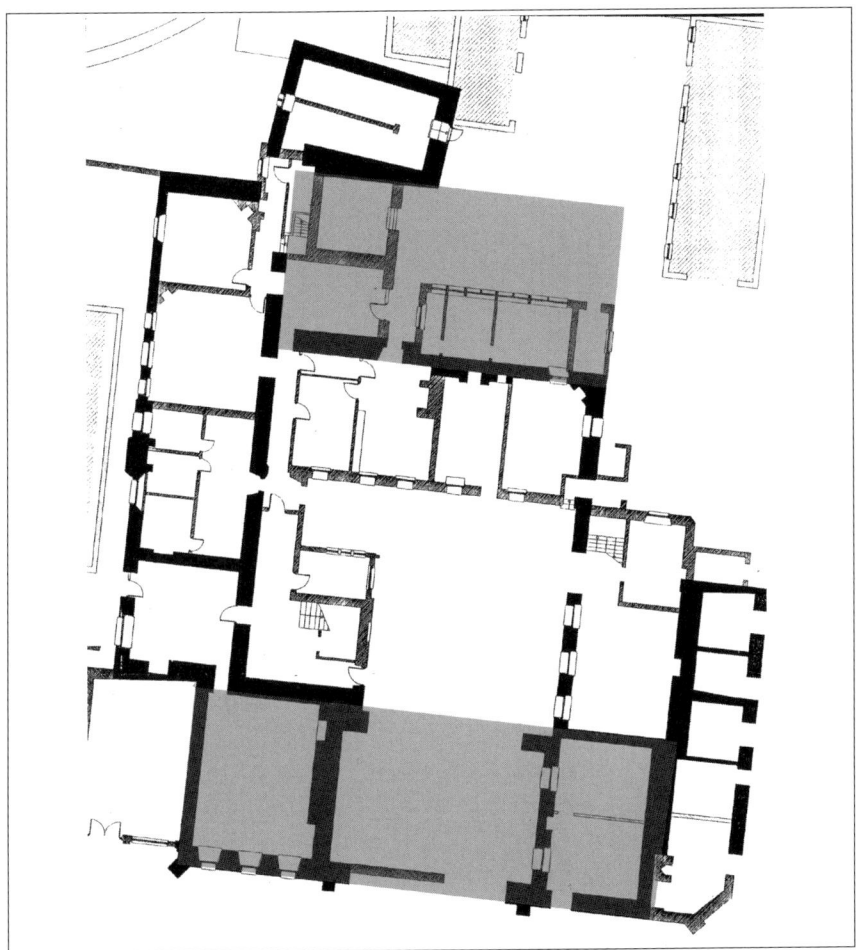

9 Plan with the east and west blocks highlighted.

ST SEPULCHRE'S IN CONTEXT: IRELAND, BRITAIN AND EUROPE

Does St Sepulchre's represent the standard plan for a bishop's palace of the late twelfth century, or indeed the early sixteenth? How does it relate to the other palaces put up by the archbishop of Dublin, or other bishops in Ireland? As many of the men who held the archbishopric were of English origin, should we look there for a model for the palace?

Swords Castle Swords Castle is known to have been started by John Cumin, the man credited with building St Sepulchre's. It differs from St Sepulchre's

10 The corbels and
roof timbers
concealing what many
believe is a medieval
roof.

11 Hugh Inge's
doorway in the west
wall of the palace.

12 A general view of the palace through the beautiful early eighteenth-century gates.

13 The 'crossblock' which has a medieval back wall and a late seventeenth or early eighteenth century front wall.

14 The back of this same crossblock with modern additions to the rear.

15 The east wing of palace with unusual outbuildings.

16 The gatehouse at Swords Castle with Dundry window dressings.

in being a fortified manor house, built for country living and the administration of the manor of Swords and a number of the archbishop's northern estates. The inquisition of 1326 also reported on Swords, where it was noted that the building was crenellated like a castle. There are far more agricultural buildings mentioned at Swords than at St Sepulchre's. The archbishop responsible for building Tallaght castle, Alexander de Bicknor, may well have been responsible for building a number of the buildings at Swords; Stalley suggests probably the chapel and the adjoining residence. The walls are of the fifteenth century, when we still find a number of archbishops spending time there (fig. 17), but Swords fell out of favour in the sixteenth century, and the castle was occupied by Dutch refugees.[22] The placing of the castle in line with the main street of the village of Swords probably dates from the earliest stages of development during Cumin's time. The gatehouse with Dundry probably dates from the time of Archbishop Fulk de Sandford or his brother John (1256–94) (fig. 16). When the site was excavated the most interesting ruins came from the chapel and adjoining 'residence' to the west where a beautiful tiled pavement was uncovered. The great hall is no longer standing but the windows can be seen in the outer wall to the west. Clearly the arrangement

22 Stalley, *Swords castle*.

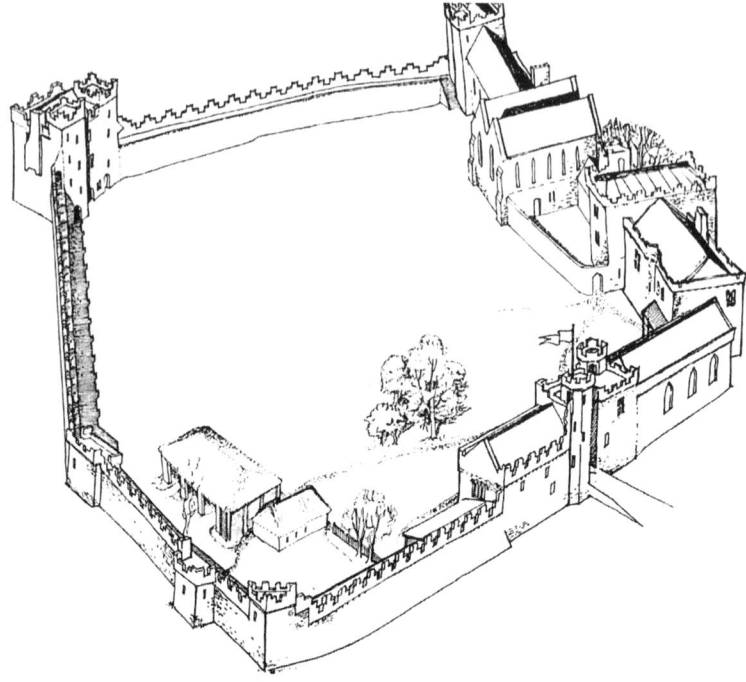

17 A reconstruction of the palace at Swords as it might have looked at its largest extent in the 15th century.

here does not reflect the tightly planned quadrangle seen at St Sepulchre's, as the buildings at Swords bear no formal relationship to each other.

The bishop's palace, Kilkenny It is thought that Bishop Geoffrey St Leger of Ossory (1260–1286) gave the original bishop's palace near the cathedral to the vicars choral when he founded them, so that they might use it as a common hall; and that he and his successors resided in their country manors until the new palace was constructed in the fourteenth century. The construction of the bishop's palace at Kilkenny is attributed to Bishop Richard Ledred (1317–60) who is said to have demolished three churches without the city walls in order to build the episcopal palace near the cathedral.[23] Two fourteenth-century elements survive within the palace, which externally looks to be eighteenth-century. One corner is occupied by a three-storey tower with an external staircase at the northeast corner (now lost), the ground floor is vaulted and this vault is carried on an hexagonal column. At the southeastern corner a two-storey hall is attached, the ground floor of which is vaulted, and

23 The Integrated Conservation Group, *The Bishop's Palace, Kilkenny. Conservation plan for the Heritage Council and the Representative Church Body*, Unpublished report, 2000, available from the Heritage Council, Kilkenny.

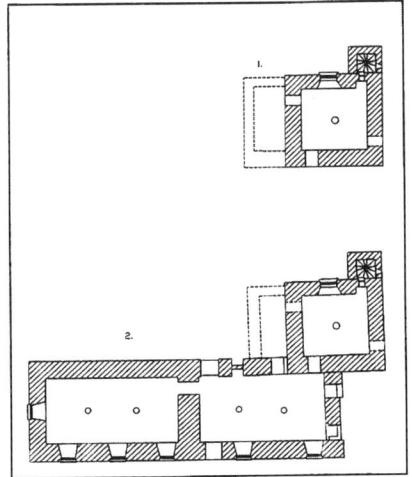
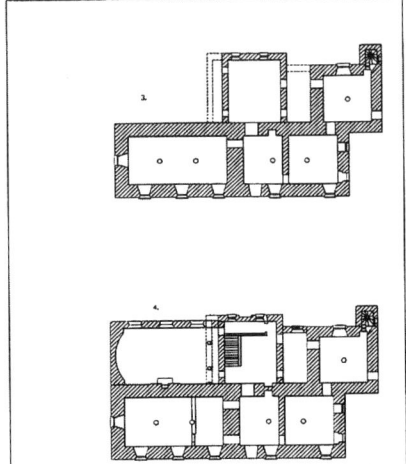

Plan 1

Plan 2

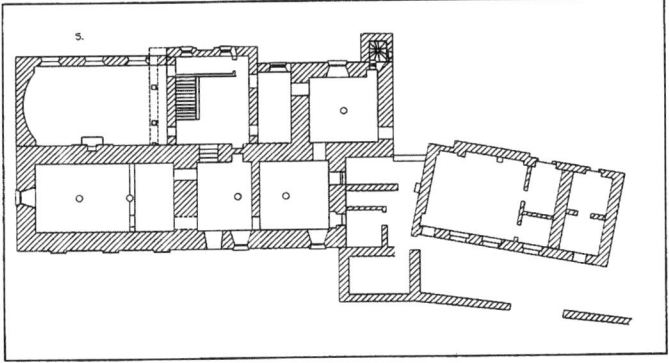

Plan 3

18 The bishop's palace, Kilkenny, a schematic ground floor plan charting the development of the palace; from the fourteenth-century tower and adjoining hall up to the mid-eighteenth century house.

again this vault is carried on pillars. A spine wall divides this vaulted ground floor in two (fig. 18). This hall arrangement, as we shall learn below, is the most common design for bishops' palaces in England during the twelfth, thirteenth, and fourteenth centuries, but the plan of the palace at Kilkenny bears no relation to that of St Sepulchre's, which does not fit into the mainstream of palace design during this period.

Continental bishops' palaces In the twelfth century a French bishop's palace was a two-storey block, vaulted at ground floor level and subdivided into a smaller and larger room at each level by a spine wall. The chapel may or may

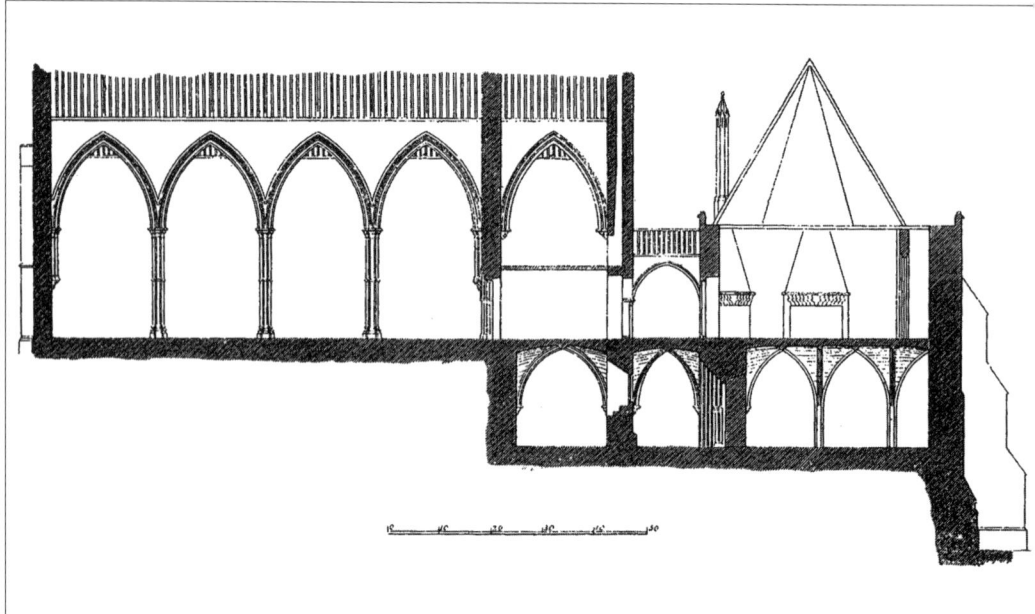

19 Longitudinal section through the west hall and kitchen at Lincoln.

not be absorbed into the main block.[24] This is the type of palace that John Cumin and Henry of London would have seen on their travels in France.

Bishops' palaces in England Michael Thompson, in his *Medieval bishops' houses in England and Wales*, suggests that in the eleventh and twelfth century the continental model for the bishop's house was the accepted building mode: vaulted ground floor with hall and chamber above. In the thirteenth century the ground floor aisled hall became popular. Often the bishop built a new hall next to the older, continental-style hall block, and used this older building as his private chamber.[25] This is believed to have happened at palaces like Lincoln and Wolvsey (figs 19 and 20). These two halls were often placed at non-regular angles, and do not form a regular court. Only in the fourteenth century do palaces ranged around formal courtyards become fashionable, and these are very different from St Sepulchre's. In fifteenth- and sixteenth-century courtyard houses the house itself is made up of two courts with a hall forming a cross-block between them and facing the entry gate. They are characterized by the use of brick, with stone trimmings, and often have ornamental brickwork. Hampton Court, Cardinal Wolsey's great house outside London, is a fine example of this trend.

24 Michael Thompson, *Medieval bishops' houses in England and Wales* (Aldershot, 1998), p. 31.

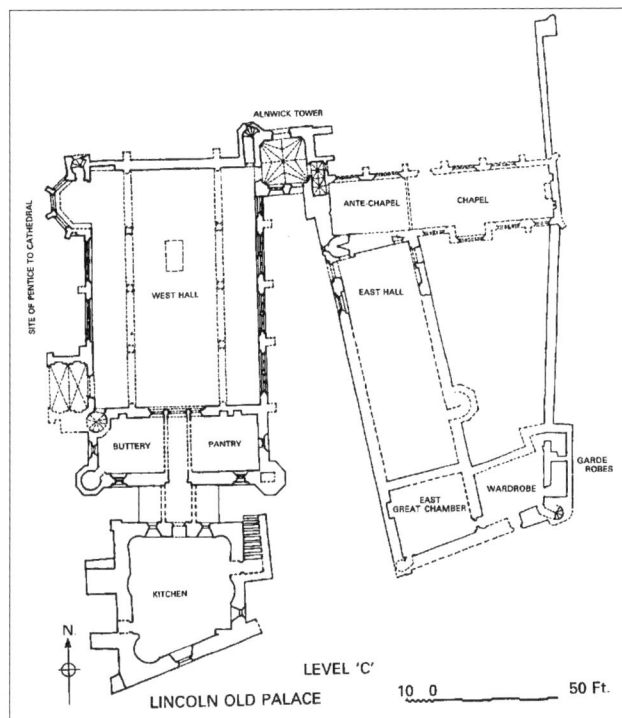

20 Lincoln: plan of the bishop's palace.

Where does St Sepulchre's fit into this pattern of building? Only two palaces seem to share common features with our palace and both of these were built by Bishop Roger of Salisbury (1102–39). The first is the see palace built at Old Sarum, which lies within the enclosure of the royal castle, which had been acquired by Bishop Roger (fig. 21). Michael Thompson describes it thus: 'Four ranges enclosed a small courtyard with a keep in the north-east projection from the enclosure as a kind of mural tower. Some or all of the ranges were two-storeyed and half the southern range at its east end was occupied by a two-storeyed chapel'.[26] The second courtyard house built by Roger is at Sherborne in Dorset (fig. 22). It is described by Thompson as: 'four ranges around a courtyard. The northern one was a two storeyed chapel and the southern parallel was a two storeyed hall … The keep with central division adjoins the hall at the south west corner'.[27] Thompson sees clear links to Benedictine monastic planning in these designs, with the church in the northern range and the hall in the southern range echoing the church and refectory in a Benedictine house; in a Benedictine monastery the abbot's house was in the west range, where at Sherborne we have the keep. These two palaces are considered very anomalous within the British tradition of episcopal domestic building, and so it is exciting to discover that something very similar

25 Ibid., pp 68–9.   **26** Ibid., p. 23.   **27** Ibid., pp 88–9.

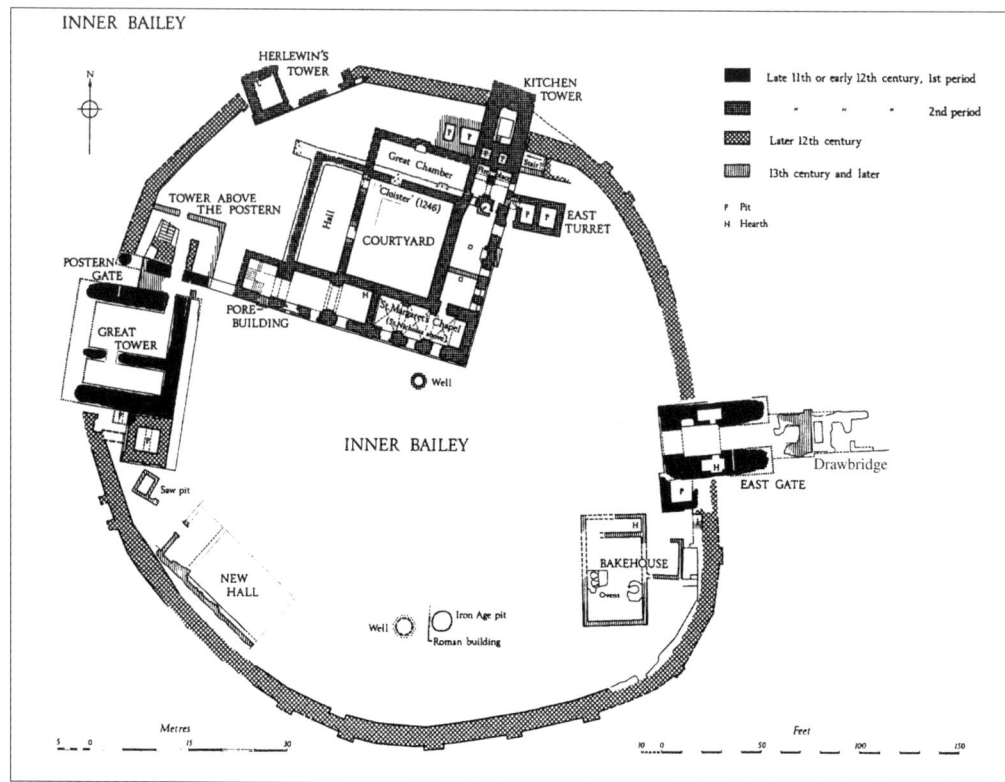

21 The plan of Old Sarum castle.

exists in Dublin. The link between these two English palaces and that in Dublin is that these two buildings also appear to be laid out *ad quadratum*.

In the light of the comparison between St Sepulchre's and Old Sarum and Sherborne, we may be able to understand better two features mentioned in primary sources as present in the Dublin palace. The first is the chapel, which in the two English examples is known to have been contained within the quadrangle and to have had a vaulted undercroft. The only medieval vaults remaining at St Sepulchre's are in the building to the north of the courtyard, which, with its east-west orientation, does seem to suggest itself as a chapel. We know from French and other English palaces that the chapel was often an independent structure, but in looking at the plan of St Sepulchre's it is clear that the cross-blocks which may have contained the chapel; those orientated east-west have been demolished but at one time these could easily have contained a chapel such as those at Old Sarum and Sherborne.

As to the tower, we see at Old Sarum that the tower was contained in the northeast angle of the palace, and that at Sherborne is in the southwest angle. At St Sepulchre's the tower is in the northwest angle. Could this be a 'mural

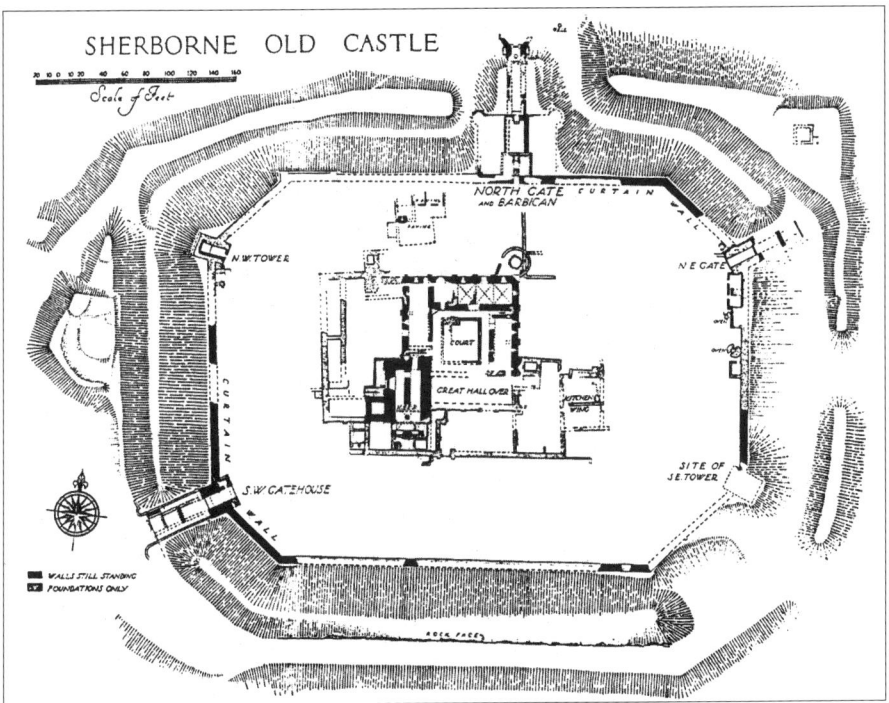

22 Plan of Sherborne Old Castle in Dorset.

tower' like those at Old Sarum and Sherborne? Could it be some kind of fore building, the standard entrance to a twelfth-century castle? These questions must remain unanswered, but this corner tower does strengthen the link with Bishop Roger's courtyard houses. Bishop Roger and Archbishop John Cumin lived at different ends of the twelfth century, so no direct link could have existed between them; however, during the years 1169–70 Cumin was an itinerant justice in Wiltshire, and so may have seen the castle at Old Sarum at first hand while it was still occupied by the bishop of Salisbury (before this site was abandoned for the new city of Salisbury where the present cathedral stands). Certainly we know that Henry of London was at the consecration of the new cathedral of Salisbury in the early thirteenth century: could he have undertaken changes to St Sepulchre's in order to bring it into line with the palace he had seen at Old Sarum?

CONCLUSION

From the above research it is possible to understand the palace of St Sepulchre in Dublin as a rich and important piece of medieval architecture.

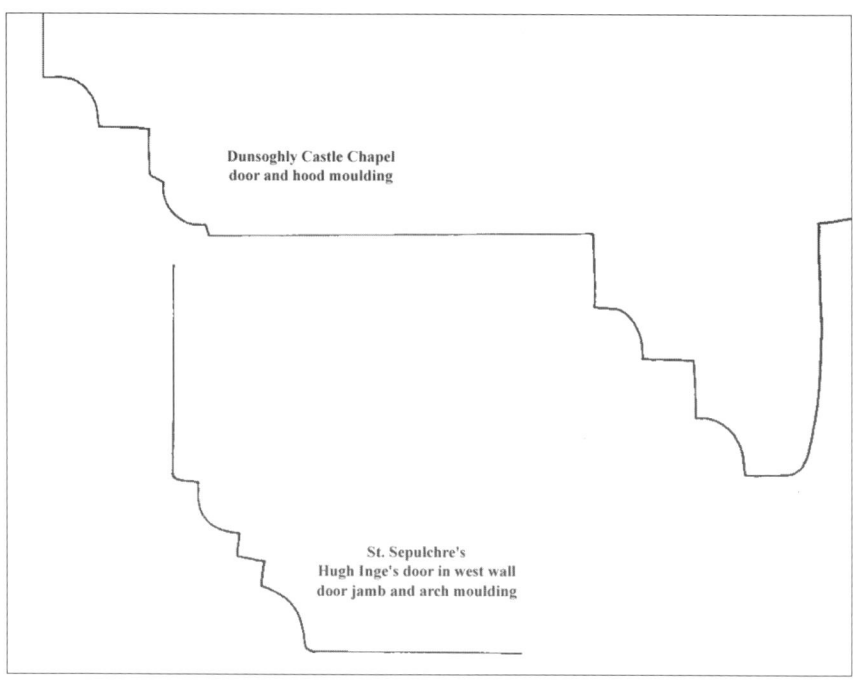

Dunsoghly Castle Chapel
door and hood moulding

St. Sepulchre's
Hugh Inge's door in west wall
door jamb and arch moulding

23 Moulding profiles from Dunsoghly Castle Chapel and Hugh Inge's door, St Sepulchre's

The palace is one of few surviving domestic buildings still situated in the heart of the city; the home of one of the highest ranking officials in the country, it played host to a number of different activities, not least the archiepiscopal court, priestly ordinations, administration, and entertainment. After over eight hundred years of habitation, and renovation, the palace retains a distinctive 'medieval footprint' evident in the plan of the building. The layout of the palace is unusual when compared with other bishops' houses in both Ireland and England, with just two other palaces closely resembling it, both also built in the twelfth century. Without further research into Irish bishops' palaces, it is impossible to say how St Sepulchre's might have influenced other medieval palaces in Ireland. Sadly no decorative elements survive from the first 450 years of the palace's existence, and without this evidence it is difficult to suggest, beyond the similarities in plan with Bishop Roger's two buildings, what the architectural pedigree might be. The only medieval element of the building to survive is the door in the west wall of the palace. Late Gothic in appearance, the door is a product of the Irish Gothic tradition. The moulding may be compared with that at Dunsoghly Castle (fig. 23) while the general layout of the door with three-centred arch looks like that at Slane College, County Meath.

How is one to answer the question: Irish building or English building? Irish mason or English mason? If we take the plan to be the only surviving element from the early years of the palace, we can see that this is monumental architecture, conceived in the Norman tradition. If decorative elements survived from this period, it is likely that they would reflect the Norman architecture seen in the earliest phases of Christ Church cathedral. Hugh Inge's door, on the other hand, is a typical piece of Irish late Gothic architecture. In general form it imitates the English 'Tudor' fashion of the time, but handling of the moulding with its simple profile, the floral decoration in shallow relief and the tapering of the chamfer plane at the bottom of the jamb mark it out as a piece of Irish decorative architecture.

ACKNOWLEDGEMENTS

Many thanks to the Irish Research Council for the Humanities and Social Sciences, Professor Roger Stalley, Dr Rachel Moss, Dr Arthur Gibney, John Cahill, and Aisling Ní Bhriain without whom I could not have done this research. Thanks to Dr Seán Duffy for his help and for allowing me to present this paper at the Medieval Dublin Symposium.

BIBLIOGRAPHY

Berry, Henry F 1898 *Register of wills and inventories of the diocese of Dublin 1457–1483*, Dublin.
Biddle, Martin 1986 *Wolvesey, the old bishop's palace, Hampshire*, HMSO. London.
Calendar of state papers, Ireland, 1507–1600, HMSO. London.
Close Rolls, Edward II–Elizabeth I, HMSO. London.
Craig, Maurice 1992 *Dublin 1660–1860*, 2nd edn, Dublin.
Drew, Thomas 1891 Surroundings of the cathedral Church of St Patrick de Insula, Dublin *Irish Builder*, 33, 253–5.
Evans, J. Wyn, and Turner, Rick 1999 *St David's bishop's palace*, CADW. Cardiff.
Gilbert, J.T. 1899–1944 *Calendar of ancient records of Dublin*, 19 vols, Dublin.
—— 1897 *Crede Mihi. The most ancient register book of the archbishops of Dublin*. Dublin.
Gwynn, Aubrey 1956 Archbishop John Comyn (Cumin) *Reportorium Novum*, vol. 1, no.2, 285–310.
Gwynn, Aubrey and Hadcock, R. Neville 1988 *Medieval Religious Houses, Ireland*, Dublin.
Handcock, W. 1991 *The history and antiquities of Tallaght*. repr. Dublin.
Harris, 1766 *History and antiquities of the city of Dublin*, Dublin.
Hembry, Phyllis 1978 Episcopal palaces, 1535 to 1660. In *Wealth and power in Tudor England, essays presented to S.T. Bindoff*, London, 146–166.
Holmes, Margaret 1988 The palace of St Sepulchre *DHR*, 122–126.
Jackson, Victor 1974–5 The palace of St Sepulchre *DHR*, xxviii, Dublin, 82–92.
The letters of Archbishop William King, unpublished, TCD MSS 1995–2008.

Lawlor, H.J 1908 A calendar of the Liber Niger and the Liber Albus of Christ Church, Dublin, *R.I.A. Proc.*, 27C, 1–93.

—— 1930 *The fasti of St Patrick's cathedral, Dublin*. Dundalk.

Mason, William Monck 1820 *The history and antiquities of the collegiate church of St Patrick near Dublin*, Dublin.

McCarthy, Muriel 1980 *All graduates and gentlemen, Marsh's Library, Dublin*, Dublin.

McEnery, M.J. and Refaussé, Raymond 2001 *Christ Church deeds*. Dublin.

McNeill, Charles 1950 *Calendar of Archbishop Alen's register, 1172–1534*, Dublin.

Patent rolls, Edward I–Elizabeth I. HMSO. London.

Pipe Rolls of Edward II 1907 In *Thirty-ninth report of the Deputy Keeper of the Public Records of Ireland*. Dublin.

Refaussé, Raymond and Clarke, Mary 2000 *A catalogue of the maps of the estates of the archbishops of Dublin, 1654–1850*, Dublin.

Robo, Etienne 1980 *Medieval Farnham*, Farnborough.

Sweetman, H.S. 1875–86 *Calendar of documents relating to Ireland, 1171–1307*. 5 vols. London.

Thompson, Michael 1998 *Medieval bishops' houses in England and Wales*, Aldershot.

Tresham, Edward 1828 *Rotulorum Patentium et Clausorum Cancellariae Hiberniae Calendarium*, vol. 1, London.

Ware, Sir James and Harris, Walter *The whole works of Sir James Ware concerning Ireland* revised and updated by Walter Harris, Dublin.

Watt, John 1998 *The church in medieval Ireland*, 2nd edn, Dublin.

White, Newport B. and White, Newport, J.D 1926 *Marshe's Library. An account of Archbishop Marshe's Library, Dublin*. Dublin.

White, Newport, B. 1936 *Irish monastic and episcopal deeds, 1200–1600*, Dublin.

—— 1943 *Extents of Irish monastic possessions*, Dublin.

—— 1957, The 'Dignitas Decani' of St Patrick's cathedral, Dublin, Dublin.

—— 1959, *Registrum dioceses Dublinensis: a sixteenth century precedent book*, Dublin.

Wood, Herbert 1930 *The court book of the liberty of St Sepulchre, Dublin*. Dublin.

Dublin's southern frontier under siege: Kindlestown Castle, Delgany, County Wicklow

LINZI SIMPSON

INTRODUCTION

This article describes the results of an excavation at Kindlestown Castle, Delgany, Co. Wicklow (RMP no. 8:17: N.G.R O279 211; figs 1–2; plates 1–5), carried out by the writer, on behalf of Dúchas: the Heritage Service (Licence no. 01E0844). The castle is located within a modern housing development called Dromont, off Kindlestown Road Upper, which leads from Greystones Upper to Delgany. The two-storeyed structure is rectangular in plan but only the north wall and part of the east wall stand to full height, as the south and west wall were comprehensively demolished sometime in the late seventeenth/ early eighteenth century (figs 3–5). These walls, however, were partially rebuilt in the nineteenth century to a height of 1.50m.

Kindlestown forms part of a recognisable group of castles in Ireland known as 'hall-houses' (Sweetman 1999, 89–104; McNeill 1997, 148–54). This type of building was at the lower end of the castle scale, essentially a domestic residence, which also has strong military capabilities. The defining characteristics can be summarised as a two-storeyed rectangular plan (often in proportions of 2 to 1), with a hall or living area at first floor level and an entrance at first floor level, accessed by some sort of external superstructure, the remains of which can sometimes be identified as beam-slots in the external face of the wall. The upper windows are invariably larger than the lower ones, attesting to the use of the first floor as the main living quarters. The castle at Kindlestown fits the general criteria of this type, as it is rectangular in plan and is also two storeys in height. The main room was the upper storey, which was supported by a strong barrel vault at ground floor level, spanning the length of the building. The doorway was in the east wall at ground floor level but there is some evidence to suggest that it is a later insertion. Other features of the castle include a projecting turret at the northwest angle, which houses a garderobe chamber (two separate latrines) at first floor and parapet level, the chutes of which exit through the main front northern wall. The east wall was originally a narrow service tower, which rose above the roof-line of the castle proper by at least one storey and which housed the mural stairwell, most of which is still in position. Part of the castle has only collapsed in recent years

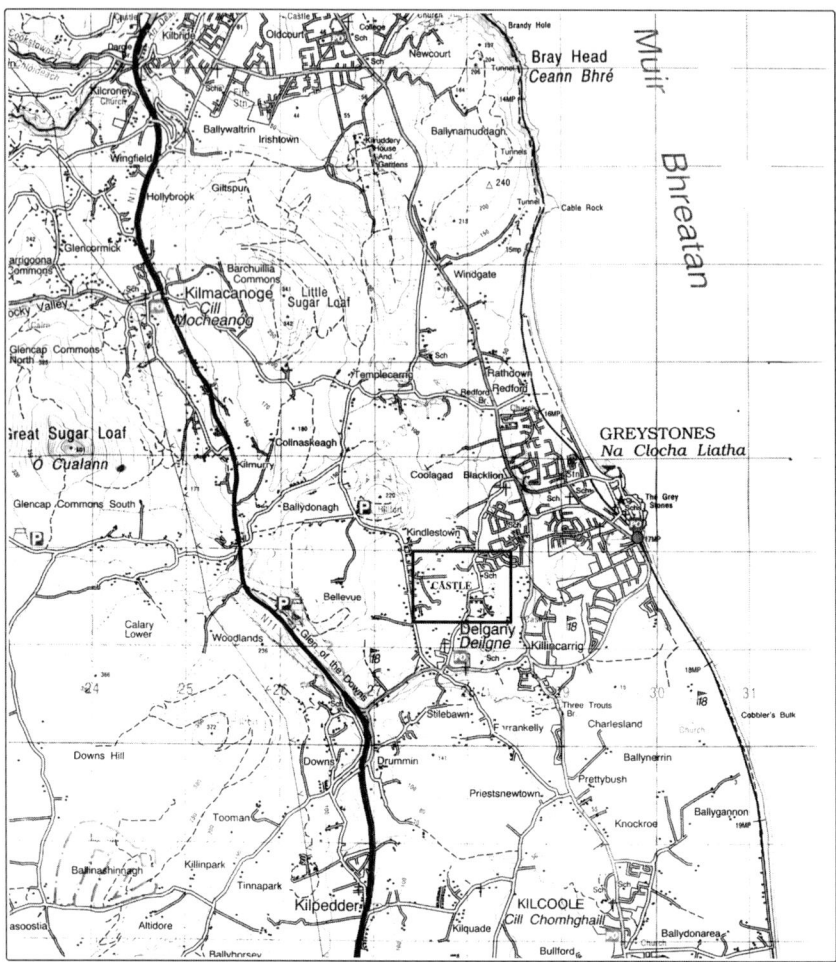

1 Site location

and this survives as three large hunks of masonry, at the eastern end of the site.

Although Kindlestown appears to fit into the general 'hall-house' typology, it is a late example of its kind. While most can be dated to the early or mid-thirteenth century, Albert de Kenley, from whom the castle took its name, probably started building the castle here in *c.*1300. Two construction phases are suggested in the build of the castle, that is, that the ground floor (including the barrel vault) was constructed first and the upper floor then added, perhaps by the Archbold family (see below) who probably occupied the castle from the mid-fourteenth century onwards. Kindlestown is also unusual as it originally stood within a large rectangular ditched enclosure, and an internal wet moat is still traceable on the northern and western side, lying 6.50m from the castle (figs 6 and 7; Grogan and Hillery 1993, 47). An archaeological assessment was carried out in the surrounding fields in 1991 as part of the new development but, although field ditches and dumps of building debris were noted, these were dated to the post-medieval period and no medieval deposits were located (Halpin 1992, 136). The area on the north of the castle was also under cultivation for potatoes in the relatively recent past, as traces of the 'lazy bed' system still survive as earthworks in this location. The castle is a National Monument, which is in a bad state of repair and Dúchas: the Heritage Service are due to carry out conservation works in the near future (fig. 8). The writer carried out an initial archaeological assessment in September 2001 and this was followed by the total excavation of the interior and a 1m-wide trench around the base of the castle. The excavation brief was to expose the surviving castle to foundation level (to aid repair) and

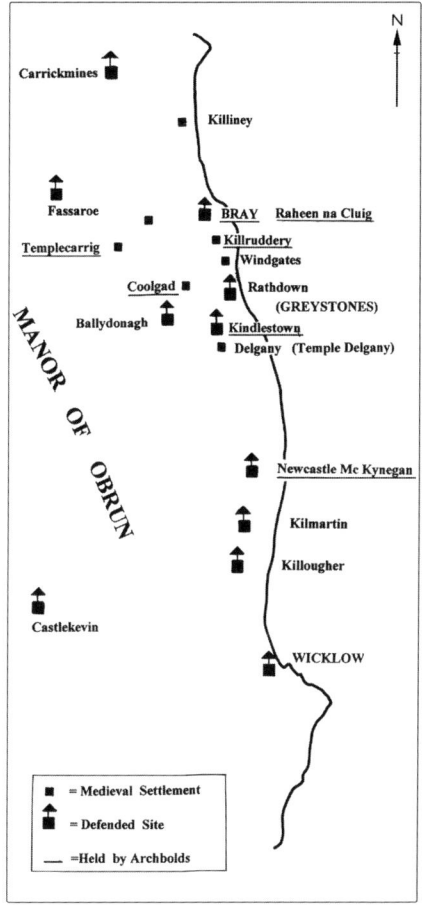

2 Historical map

to establish if any surviving floor levels were still *in situ*. This did not include a scaled surveyed of the standing building, which will be carried out at a later stage by Dúchas.

HISTORICAL BACKGROUND

Political history of the area

The Rathdown area Kindlestown Castle lies on the southern side of the mountainous ridge, known as Bray Head, which separates the town of Bray from Greystones and Delgany to the south (fig. 2). The castle is positioned on the lower slopes of Kindlestown Hill, but commands a good view of the surrounding countryside, as well as the coastline to the east. This region

Plate 1 Castle from the north

Plate 2 Castle from the south

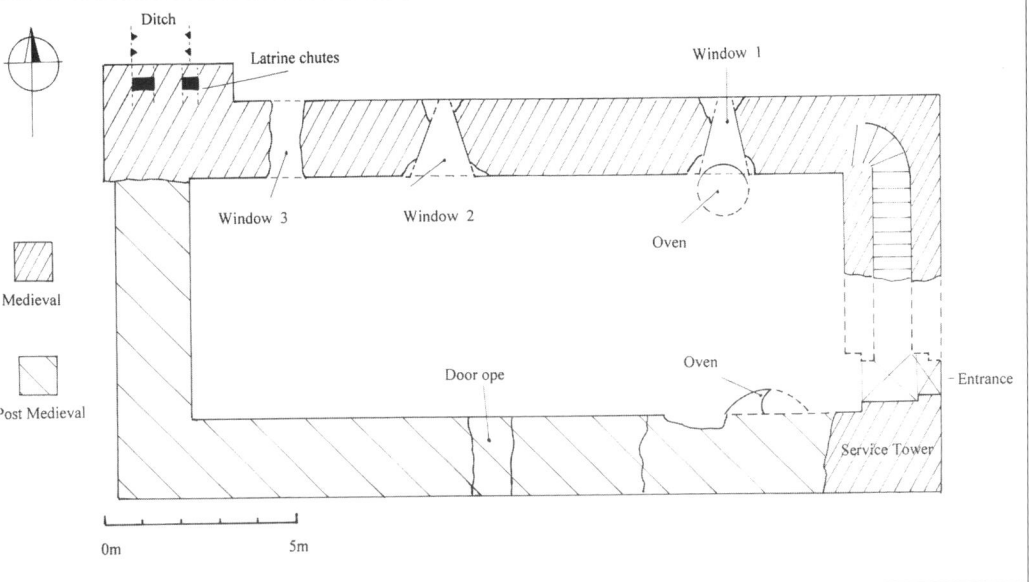

3 Floor plan, ground

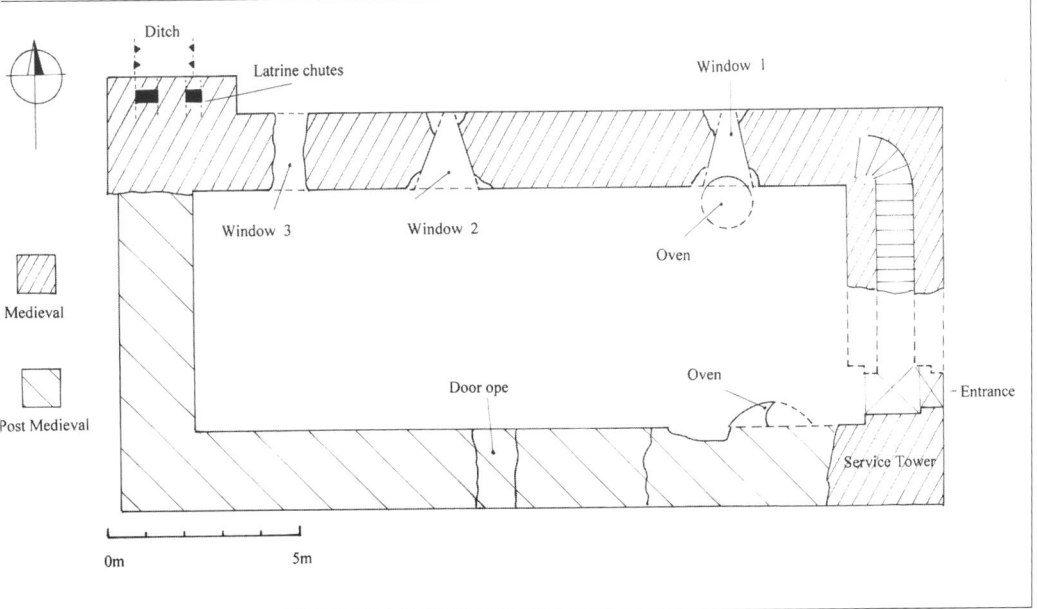

4 Floor plan, first

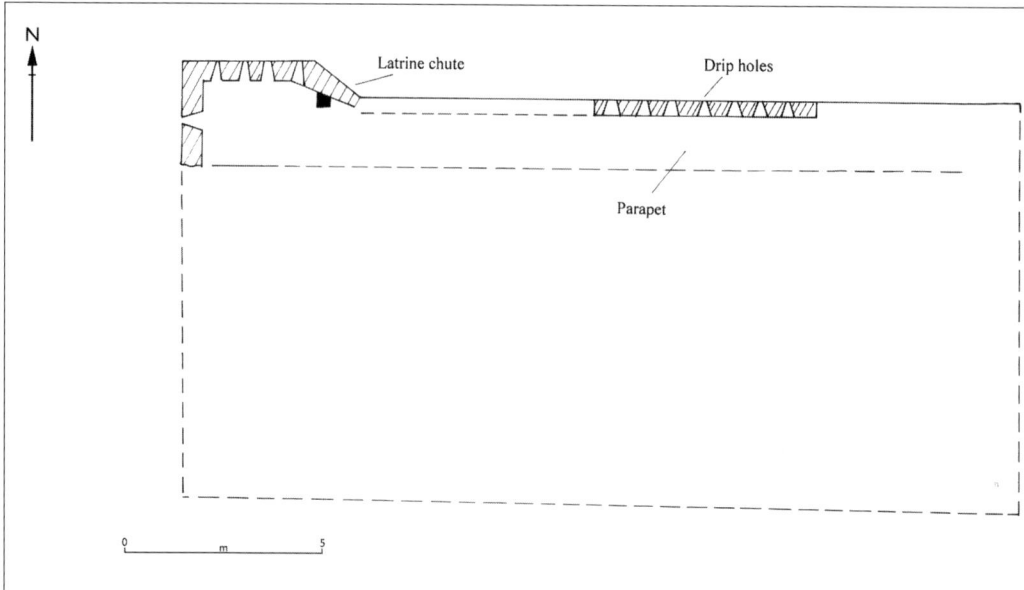

5 Floor plan, second

originally formed part of the vast territory of the Meic Gilla Mo-Cholmóc,
the Irish family whose caput on the southern side of Dublin was at Rathdown,
less than three kilometres to the northeast of Kindlestown (Simpson 1994a,
191–235). Domhnall Mac Gilla Mo-Cholmóc was chief of the dynasty at the
time of the Anglo-Norman invasion of Dublin in 1170 and he famously
supported Diarmait McMurrough (his father-in-law) and the new English
invaders, presumably in an attempt to maintain the family's prominent position
(Mills 1894, 161). As reward Domhnall's son Diarmait received his lands as a
fief under the new regime and thus continued in occupation of at least some
of the original family lands (Sweetman 1875–86, i, 356). The 'Normanisation'
of the family continued apace in the fourteenth century and, helped by a
marriage union with the Fitzgriffins, by the end of the fourteenth century, the
Meic Gilla Mo-Cholmóc were virtually indistinguishable from other prominent
Anglo-Norman families of the day. The acquiescence and co-operation of
Domnhall also had the knock-on effect of resulting in little displacement of the
existing population in the area, and thus the original tenants continued to
occupy the same lands after the invasion. This, in effect, guaranteed a relatively
peaceful assimilation of the old and the new in the immediate aftermath of the
events of 1170.

The medieval landscape The place-name 'Kindlestown' is very dominant
in the modern landscape, a reflection of the importance of the castle in the

Plate 3 Castle from the east

Plate 4 Castle from the west

Plate 5 The interior under excavation

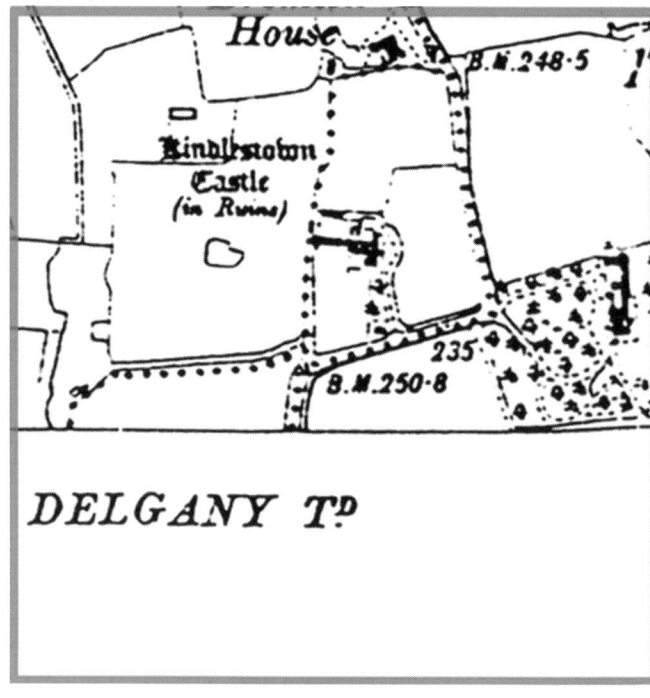

6 Detail of O.S., showing field boundaries (1909)

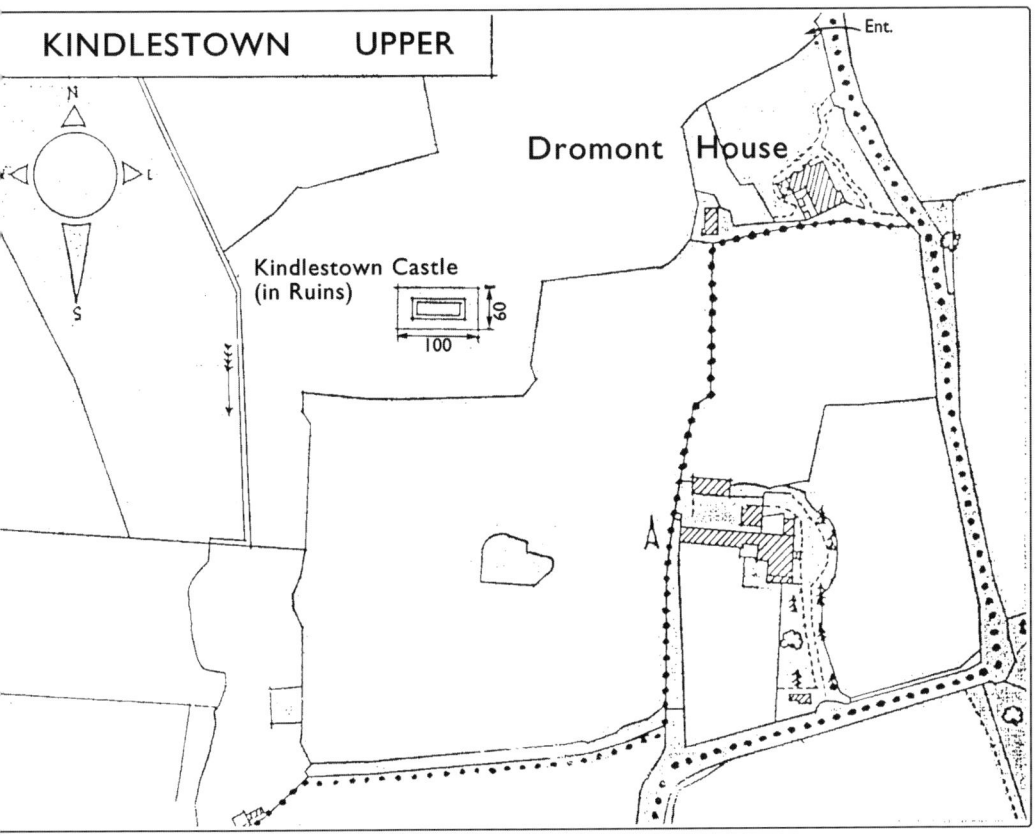

7 Map of castle, dated 1972

medieval times. Other place-names in the vicinity also reflect the rich and diverse settlement history of the area (fig. 2). Windgates, which originally referred to Kindlestown Road Upper (Price 1983, v, 325), is first recorded in *c.*1260 but the place-name is probably Viking in origin, incorporating the Norse word 'gata' meaning road (Gilbert 1889, 4; Price 1983, v, 235; Etchingham 1994, 117). Other medieval settlements in the area include Coolagad directly north of Kindlestown, and Templecarraig further north, as well as Ballydonagh (called Ballygunner in *c.*1225) to the northwest (Price 1983 v, 319). The place-name Coolagad is also Norse in origin (incorporating the element 'gata') while Ballydonagh probably incorporates the Viking personal name of 'Gunnar' (ibid.).

The areas of Dublin's southern hinterland which did not form part of the Mac Gilla Mo-cholmóg territory, were taken directly into the hands of the crown and these were divided into two large royal manors, Obrun and Othee,

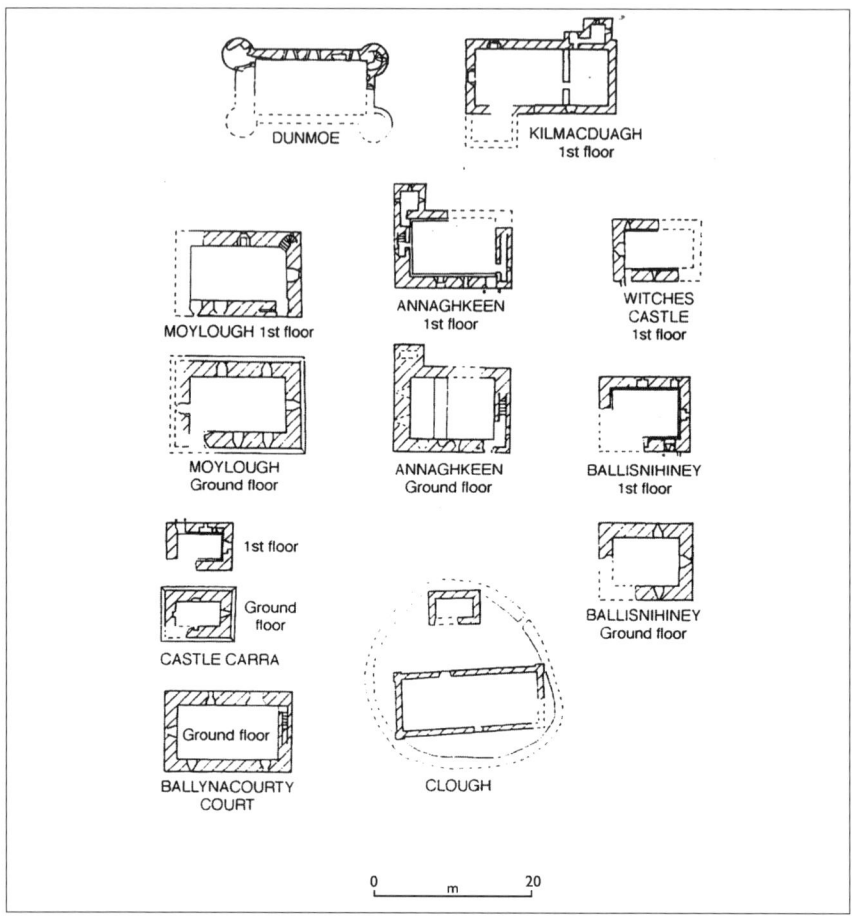

8 Assorted floor plans (after Mc Neill)

which functioned as huge administrative agricultural centres. Thus, throughout
the medieval period, this area was administered as part of County Dublin, as
Wicklow was only formed into a county in the early seventeenth century.
Although the royal manors tended to be occupied by the original pre-invasion
tenants, other lands were granted out by Strongbow to powerful Anglo-
Normans leaders of the day, as a reward for their loyalty. In the south
Dublin/north Wicklow area, Walter de Ridlesford, one of the most important
men of the invasion, received the manor of Bray and significant lands in the
surrounding countryside while Theobald Walter (Butler) was given the manor
of Arklow, to the south. Both these lords immediately established important
manors, which they filled with tenants from their lands in England. The
peaceful nature of the settlement of the southern hinterland was directly
reflected in the few military strongholds built as part of the initial invasion

campaign. The invaders were not conquering by military force, the result being that few mottes or stone castles were built in the early years. All this was to change, however, in the late thirteenth century, when the political climate changed dramatically for the worse (Simpson 1994a, 208–10).

War in the Leinster mountains Walter de Ridlesford, the man who had received the manor of Bray from Strongbow, had also received vast lands in Co. Kildare, the first consequence of which was the displacement of the original landholders there, the O'Byrnes and O'Tooles. They either shifted or were shifted *en masse* to the mountainous regions of Glendalough and Glenmalure, high in the Wicklow mountains. Here they settled on lands owned by the monastery of Glendalough, presumably under the protection of their kinsman Lorcán O' Toole, abbot of Glendalough and later archbishop of Dublin. Thus they occupied these lands peacefully in the initial years after the invasion. In 1216, however, the sees of Dublin and Glendalough were united as part of an attempt to bring both the abbey and the lands under the direct control of the Anglo-Norman archbishop of Dublin. By 1269 war had broken out and, exacerbated by severe weather and famine, this gradually gathered pace (Price 1983, xlix). Although the exact cause is not known, the first outbreak coincided with a vacancy in the see, which existed between 1271 and 1279 (Simpson 1994a, 208). By this date the archbishop's manor of Castlekevin (1.5 km from Annamoe) formed the central administrative manorial centre in the mountains and the O'Byrnes and O'Tooles were the main tenants there. It has been suggested that their rebellious activity was probably a reaction to crown officials attempting to seize control during the vacancy and perhaps trying to regularise their financial position. Thus, for the first time, the Irish of the mountains were in direct contact with the government officials (Frame 1971, 79). The result was a war in the south Dublin/north Wicklow area that was eventually to spread all along the Leinster mountains. This war continued throughout the medieval period and severely threatened the Anglo-Norman colony in Dublin.

The government reaction The government quickly mounted various military expeditions to crush these rebellions, usually with mixed results. In 1274 the government forces were soundly defeated but they did have notable successes under Robert d'Ufford and Geoffrey de Genville. There was relative peace after the brutal murder of the McMurrough brothers in 1282 but trouble broke out twelve years later in 1294 and this was to prove significantly more serious and enduring (ibid., 89). The crown's initial strategy was to attempt to root out the rebels and destroy their settlements, but this was operationally almost impossible to achieve from the outset, as they were simply not equipped for military campaigns in high-lying and inclement mountainous regions. The O'Byrnes, under Murchadh O'Byrne, retaliated by mounting 'smash and grab' raids, with increasing regularity and success, the result of which was the disintegration of the Anglo-Norman manorial system throughout the southern hinterland by the mid-fourteenth century (Simpson 1994a, 208–10).

By the late thirteenth century life was becoming increasingly difficult for the tenants of south county Dublin/north Wicklow but this also created an opportunity for 'frontier colonists' to expand their influence in the area (Simpson 1994a, 208–210). The result was the emergence of families such as the Harolds, the Mac Turkills and the Archbolds, who began to organise resistance and attempted to refortify the original Anglo-Norman settlement sites. These families were the descendants of the 'Ostmen of the vale of Dublin' who were an ethnically recognisable group of people, in the thirteenth century occupying the royal manors and renting their lands directly from the crown (Mills 1903–27, 35, p. 30; Simpson 1994a, 202). The vale of Dublin was also occupied by the remnants of possibly pre-Norman Welsh colonists, the Howels, Walshes and perhaps the Lawlesses, as well as the Irish tenants who had managed to hold on (O'Byrne 2002, 14). Stripped of the regimented security of the large royal and archiepiscopal agricultural manors, these people were cast adrift and left to get whatever they could from the land. Thus we find them in control of large chunks of the royal manors, paying large rents directly to the crown. Despite their continued occupation of the lands the hinterland was very difficult to defend since, as mentioned earlier, the peaceful nature of the invasion had resulted in few military earthworks or stone castles being built in the early years. Added to this was the fact that there was a distinct lack of powerful magnates, like Walter de Ridlesford, with the influence and money to defend their lands. A series of extents (accounts), dated 1326, indicate how difficult things were in the north Wicklow/south Dublin area by this date. Killegar, in Enniskerry, is described as waste, as were all the surrounding lands in the manor of Shankill, the main archiepiscopal manorial centre at this date (McNeill 1950, 170–98). The entire territory of Fercullen, which stretched from 'Berneceullen' to the west and Wyndgates (Greystones) to the east, an area that contained fifteen villages, was recorded as devastated and all the villages deserted, apart from the castle at Ballyteny (Powerscourt), which was held by the O'Tooles (Price 1953, 121). This was not to escape for long, however, as it was destroyed in 1316 only to be repaired by the crown shortly afterwards (Simpson 1994a, 219–22).

The destruction of Ballyteny castle probably occurred as part of the violent campaigns during the Scottish invasion under the Bruces in the early fourteenth century, which had a devastating effect on an area already in severe trouble. Murchadh O'Byrne was quick to take advantage and in 1316 he devastated east Wicklow with the O'Tooles and some of the Harolds and Archhbolds, burning all the major settlements including Newcastle McKynegan and Bray (Price 1953, 122). Although now technically enemies of the crown, the government desperately needed these men, the Archbolds, Howels, Lawlesses and Walshes, to defend these lands against the Scots, and so pardons quickly followed. This was well-illustrated in 1316 when David Archbold was put in charge of Newcastle McKynegan 'to suppress the malice of the Scottish and Irish felons and enemies of the king who were threatening to attack and besiege the castle'; a Rithnius (the Welsh forename Rhys?) Archebaud, presumably a relative, is recorded as holding the castle after David (Connolly 1998, i, 236, 239). The campaigns of the early 1300s certainly devastated the area as four years later, in 1320, Sir Hugh Lawless could not account for any of his lands in the north Wicklow area because 'of wars and invasion of the Scots and Irish rebels' (Curtis n.d., 10).

The fortalice system The construction of Kindlestown Castle, clearly a highly defensive dwelling, must be seen as a direct response to this dramatic change in the political situation. It represents a domestic dwelling in a frontier area, which was built by wealthy people, who could afford to build in stone. The crown actively encouraged this sort of building activity in the late thirteenth/early fourteenth century as it was recognised that the construction of such a castle could convert land previously uninhabitable into profitable land once again. An inquisition (a sworn inquiry usually undertaken on the death of the landholder to establish the heir and the crown's interest) dated to 1312 advised that it would be to the king's advantage to grant a certain individual forty acres of land in Saggart, as the occupier had built a castle there (pers. comm., Philomena Connolly†; NAI KB 1/1 M18). The eventual response of the government of Dublin was to establish a 'ward' or 'fortalice' system, which was first conceived in the early 1270s. These were designated strongholds, often pre-existing defensive structures, that could be garrisoned quickly in the event of a raid by the rebels. These were usually protected by between ten and twenty hobelars (light horsemen), as well as foot soldiers and archers (Frame 1971, 36). Thus initially, wards were established at Saggart and Baltinglass, on the west side of the Wicklow mountains, and at Newcastle McKynegan and the royal manor of Obrun, on the eastern side. Surprisingly, a ward was also established at Glenamalure itself, although this did not last long (ibid., 79; Simpson 1994a, 218–220).

The government policy of suppression of the Irish dynasties was generally successful from the 1270s onwards but, between 1355 and 1357, the justicar Thomas de Rokeby was forced to revive the fortalice system first used eighty years previously (Frame 1971, 122). De Rokeby set in chain a far more elaborate defence system, which saw a ring of fortalices or ward sites established around the base of the Wicklow/Leinster mountains in the 1350s. The new sites along the eastern coast included Newcastle McKynegan (a stone castle on a massive circular platform), Kilmartin (a polygonal ditched enclosure, which is still intact), Killoughter (a double moated site, which is partially intact),

Balyteny/Powerscourt castle (a stone castle, which is incorporated within Powerscourt House), Bray (a stone castle, the site of which is occupied by St Paul's church), Ballycorus (a stone castle, which survives as earthworks), Killiney (site unknown), Jamestown (site unknown) and Carrickmines (a stone castle with stone revettted earthwork attached, currently under excavation: Goodbody 1993, 16–7). The latter castle, held by the Walshes, was probably one of the most spectacular defences built against the O'Byrnes and the O'Tooles, its size bearing testimony to the problem the administration in Dublin faced. The position of the castle, on the main route from Wicklow to Dublin, meant it formed one of the first-line defences, combining as it did with the Pale ditch, a stretch of which still survives at Ballyogan. The recent archaeological excavations at Carrickmines have revealed a massive stone-revetted earthwork, which had a strong defensive gate-house and was surrounded by at least three substantial water-filled moats, the innermost two of which were rock-cut.

What is unusual is that Kindlestown was not warded at this time despite the fact that it was a strong castle, located within the frontier position, a perfect fortalice site. The answer may lie in the fact that, in the mid-fourteenth century, Thomas de Rokeby entered into an agreement with an O'Toole that he would maintain twenty hobelars and fifty armed foot soldiers to defend the English from 'Tallaght to Windgates [at Rathdown]', against the O'Byrnes (Frame 1971, 262). This O'Toole was presumably based in Balyteny at Powerscourt, a short distance from Kindlestown and this castle was evidently strong enough to protect the entire area at this time. The legal occupation of Balyteny by an O'Toole had its roots in a second strategy which was employed at the same time (1350–3), and saw de Rokeby attempting to buy off the rebels by placing them legitimately in control of the lands south of Bray. To this end, between 1353 and 1354, 'Odo Otothill' (Aodh O'Toole) was recorded as 'lately appointed keeper of part of the marches of Dublin and Kildare' (Connolly 1998, ii, 455). De Rokeby had less success with the O'Byrnes, although he presided over the election of John O'Byrne in 1350. However, the resultant peace only lasted three years after which time John returned with vigour to raiding and burning, proving the most significant threat to de Rokeby's plans (O'Byrne 2002, 14). The Archbolds proved particularly successful in holding their own and, eventually, their sphere of influence extended to nearly all of north Wicklow/south Dublin, from their main stronghold at Kindlestown Castle. The arrival of Richard II in 1394 threatened their earlier successes as he confiscated their lands, along with the Lawless and Walsh lands, all of which were granted to Janico Dartas (Curtis 1933, 187). The earlier tenants, however, including the Archbolds appear to have continued the occupation of their lands. The early fifteenth century saw a dramatic rise in the destructive activities of the O'Byrnes, under Domhnall and Donnchadh O'Byrne. Their expansionary attempts north of the Dodder culminated at the battle of the Bloody Bank in Little Bray, between the Dubliners and their allies the Walshes, and the O'Byrnes. The O'Byrnes were soundly defeated at this battle, ending their dominance in this area at this time (see O'Byrne above).

The rise of the house of Kildare in the mid-fifteenth century was to have a direct effect on the politics and land-holding patterns of the region. The young Thomas fitzMaurice FitzGerald (later to become the 7th earl), spent time under the protection of the O'Byrnes after falling out with James Butler, the 4th earl of Ormond and protector of the Kildare earldom. The bonds forged with the O'Byrnes of Newrath saw Thomas taking part in the raiding and terrorising of the southern hinterland, for which he was eventually outlawed (ibid.). However, the death of Ormond in 1452 accelerated him back into the political arena after which he began to distance himself from his former Irish allies. He set about reasserting control over the region and bringing the colonists, including the Archbolds, back in line. As justiciar, he enacted a statute which empowered him to seize unoccupied lands in the region and he began a massive refortification programme of the Pale (O'Byrne above). In 1456 he outlawed Henry Walsh of Carrickmines, Geoffrey Harold and Patrick Archbold and tried to push the Walshes against the O'Byrnes and the Harolds (O'Byrne 2002, 15). His politics were generally successful and after his death in 1478 he was succeeded as lord deputy by his son Gerald Mór, who continued the war against the O'Byrnes and O'Tooles. Gerald was successful in managing gradually to push back the O'Byrnes, as was demonstrated in 1482, when he seized the castle of Ballyteny (Powerscourt) from the O'Tooles and substantially rebuilt it. He also settled family members in the manor of Rathdown (ibid.), close to Kindlestown Castle, where they were presumably in close contact with the Archbolds (Price 1983, lxxxi; see O'Byrne above).

The Gabhal Raghnaill As stated earlier, efforts had also been made by de Rokeby to integrate the O'Byrne clan, although this had proved more difficult. The main branch was the *Gabhal Dúnlaing* of the *Críoch Branach* (an area of territory) but there were also between seven and ten sub-branches. The *Gabhal Dúnlaing* eventually occupied most of northeastern Wicklow strip, flanked on the west by the O'Tooles, who were lords of Fercullen and Fartry (in the Powerscourt valley and Roundwood area) by this date. The northern boundary was at the Glen of the Downs, although the entire area from the Downs to Shanganagh (Co. Dublin) became known in English records as 'O'Byrne's Country' (pers. comm., Emmett O'Byrne). On the southern side the dominance of the O'Byrnes stretched into Carlow, as far as Tullow. By 1405 the O'Byrne lords controlled the castle of Newcastle McKynegan, under the McMurroughs of Leinster but the sub-branch, the *Gabhal Raghnaill*, who were resisting the policy of government cooperation (O'Brien 1994, 306), began to grow increasingly powerful, led by the lords of Glenmalure. Thus it was recorded that, in 1466, the earl of Desmond (then lord deputy) led an army against the 'Branaghs' (O'Byrnes), passing from Wicklow to Bearnanagaoithy (Windgates in Rathdown) (Price 1983, iii, 225). It is evident from this that the earl took the Windgate/Templecarraig/Kindlestown route, which was the main route into Wicklow at that date, directly past Kindlestown Castle. That the O'Byrnes were an effective enemy was demonstrated when Edmund Óg O'Byrne (of the Downs branch), managed to enter Dublin Castle itself in 1533. From there, he rescued some of the prisoners, clearly posing a serious threat to the security of the colony (Price, ibid.). However, government forces did have their successes and in 1542 the O'Byrnes, under Tadhg Mac Gerard O'Byrne (lord of the *Gabhal Dúnlaing*), made a formal submission to the lord deputy, Sir Anthony St Leger. The following year the O'Byrnes were forced to surrender the castle and manor of Newcastle McKynegan (Price 1931, 135).

The integration policy The arrest of Gerald Mór FitzGerald by Sir Edward Poynings in 1495, for suspected treason, had a significant impact on the southern Pale as it left it totally unprotected from the continuing O'Byrne raids. Kildare managed to regain his former position in 1496 after which he returned to Ireland and redoubled his efforts to crush his old enemies, the O'Byrnes and Walshes a policy continued by his son Gerald Óg, the 9th earl. The failed rebellion, however, between 1534 and 1535 was to cause the Geraldine downfall and, as a knock-on effect, all of the lands in and around Kindlestown (but not including Kindlestown) were forfeited to the king, which included the three strongest castles of the district, Powerscourt, Rathdown and Fassaroe. The lands of Killegar/Enniskerry, Glencree, Kilmacanogue, and, closer to Kindlestown, at Coolegad, Coolakay, Templecarriag (the adjoining townland) and Coolnaskeagh were also all forfeited (Fitzgerald 1910, 132). Despite Kildare's aggressive method of dealing with the rebels, attempts were still made to promote co-operation between the government and 'Irish enemies' and to this end Turlough O'Toole (the elder) was granted the manor and castle of Powerscourt (Balyteny) in April 1542 while his brother Art Óg received the castle of Castlekevin, high in the Wicklow mountains. Turlough the elder travelled personally to court and received the grant directly from Henry VIII (pers. comm., Emmett O'Byrne). This cooperation, however, was confined to individual families: after 1535 the raids on the Pale increased in both number and intensity (see O'Byrne above). The source of these raids was now coming from the valley in Glenmalure (ibid.).

This policy of integration was also applied to the O'Byrnes of east Wicklow and in 1552 it was reported that 'the O'Byrnes and such other of Irish sort dwelling in the rest of Leinster and next to the Kavanaghs be of honest conformity' (Price 1983, iii, 227). The McMurrough-Kavanaghs, however, continued raiding in the area and are recorded as having taken Powerscourt Castle in 1556. Although the O'Byrnes of east Wicklow were being rapidly 'anglicised', the *Gabhal Raghnaill* under Hugh Mac Shane were resisting such moves and they began to capitalise on the war being waged against the policy of plantation by the O'Mores of Laois and O'Connor Falys of Offaly. However, it was Hugh Mac Shane's son, Fiach Mac Hugh O'Byrne, who was to have the most impact on the Wicklow area when he became captain of the *Gabhal Raghnaill* in 1579 (O'Brien 1994, 306). Fiach, married to Rose O'Toole of the O'Tooles of Castlekevin (his second wife), was to wage an intermittent but consistent war, which saw a pattern of submission followed by rebellion, depending on the political situation. His headquarters at Ballinacor (probably somewhere near Ballinacor House), at the mouth of the valley of Glenmalure, was his impenetrable fortress and the main target of the royal officials. From here he commanded an army, which controlled all the surrounding area and gave shelter to those in rebellion.

The end of Fiach's rule The government forces mounted a series of military campaigns to rout Fiach with varying degrees of success, as he proved difficult to defeat militarily and, more importantly, impossible to capture. Eventually, he was brought to heel by a series of negotiations, part of which involved the delivery of his son in May 1585, to Dublin castle in June, where he was executed the next month. Fiach was then forced to make a formal sub-mission before the Dublin council in November 1585. Despite this, he officially returned to war on 9 September 1596, an action precipitated by seizing the now government fort at Ballinacor, his former head-quarters (pers. comm., Emmett O'Byrne). Eventually, however, he was betrayed to Government forces in May 1597 and was swiftly killed. His surviving sons confirmed their submission in March 1601, finally ending the historic O'Byrne resistance (Price 1931, 161). Despite the co-operation of the O'Byrnes of east Wicklow, the submission of Fiach's sons in 1601 signalled the end of any remaining O'Byrne domination over parts of their old patrimony. Although the senior O'Byrnes and Fiach's sons managed to hold onto large estates, their title to the lands was signifi-cantly less secure. Most of this land had been declared forfeit for various acts of rebellion committed in 1580 or earlier and, as a result, there was great confusion in the early seventeenth century about land ownership.

A period of peace followed the submission of Fiach's sons in 1601, which was paralleled throughout the country, and this made the dramatic events of the 1640s all the more traumatic on the population of Ireland. The so-called wars of the 'three kingdoms' had a catastrophic effect in the south Dublin/ north Wicklow area, as elsewhere in Ireland, at this period. What started out as a civil war in England, between king and parliament, spread inevitably to Scotland, and across the water to Ireland. The Catholics in Ireland, both Old Irish and Old English, supported the king but the New English (in Ireland) were overwhelmingly supporters of parliament. This led inevitably to bloody civil unrest. The rebellion of 1641 was followed by serious civil disturbances, which saw the wholesale persecution of the Protestant population. The campaigns raged between both sides throughout the country culminating eventually in the arrival of the parliamentarians' leader himself, Oliver Cromwell. Although the duke of Ormonde was a Catholic royalist, the people of Dublin did not resist Cromwell when he landed at Ringsend in 1649. Cromwell's first campaign (between August 1649 and 1651), took him north-wards to Drogheda, where the town was taken in a bloody battle (Duffy 1997, 67). The sequence of events of the 1640s was to alter radically landholding patterns in the north Wicklow/south Dublin area, as lands were seized as part of the Cromwellian confiscations. As elsewhere in the country the land taken from the Catholic O'Byrnes was eventually granted out to Protestants.

History of Kindlestown Castle

The de Kenley and Mac Gilla Mo-Cholmóc connection Kindlestown Castle was built as a response to the political climate outlined above, the late thirteenth/early fourteenth century date for the castle corresponding to the beginnings of the disintegration of the Anglo-Norman colony in the area. One of the first references to the castle dates to 1377 but it was undoubtedly in existence well before this date (Price 1983, v, 322). It was known variously as 'Kenleystown', 'Kindlestown', and 'Kenliston', and, by the sixteenth century, 'Ballykenle' (ibid.). As it was the de Kenley name that became affixed to the castle it is most likely that this family was responsible for its con-struction and an Albert de Kenley can be identified in this area at the approximate time of its construction. Albert de Kenley was sheriff of Kildare in *c.*1300 and was directly related to the Mac Gilla Mo-Cholmóc family, as he was married to Joan, the widow of Ralph, son of John Mac Gilla Mo-Cholmóc. He got married without a licence from the king (as the king held the estate) and, as a result, was fined by the crown (Smal 1993, 34). The Mac Gilla Mo-Chomóc manor at Rathdown encompassed all the lands of the parish of Delgany and this must have included Kindlestown, which Albert evidently received at some date (Price 1951, 74). At the time of his marriage the heir, John, was a minor, and as a result, Albert also received custody of the Rathdown lands. Thus in the Irish pipe roll for 1296 Albert de Kenley accounts for £23 11s. 9d. for the rent of two parts of the manor of Rathdown, which belonged to Ralph, son of John (the younger John's father) (Mills 1903–27, nos 38–46, 38). Between 1299 and 1301 Albert de Kenley again accounted for two parts of the manor of Rathdown and Kylmanch (possibly Kilnamanagh in Glenealy), which belonged to Ralph, son of John before they were delivered to John, son of Ralph who was the last of the Mac Gilla Mo-Cholmóc family to hold Rathdown. Although these lands were delivered to the heir when he came of age in *c.*1301, de Kenley appears to have had additional lands in the Delgany area, which he probably received as a dowry from his wife. Some of these lands were at Ballygunner, as he is recorded as paying rent out of 'Balygonr' to the hospital of St John the Baptist in Dublin in 1304 (Price 1983, 5 322). Ballygunner can be identified as the modern-day Ballydonagh, on the north side of the Glen of the Downs, where Price identified the remains of a possible motte, although this has now been quarried away. However, there was no known stone castle or residence in this location.

That Kindlestown formed part of the Delgany/Ballygunner lands and was kept in de Kenley's hands is suggested by the fact that it did not appear to have formed part of the manor of Rathdown. Rathdown was conveyed by the heir, John, to Nigel le Brun in 1307, as le Brun accounted for '100 shillings for a licence to acquire the manor of Rathdown, of John son of Ralph, which is held of the king *in capite*' (Mills 1903–27, no. 39, 21). Le Brun also received eight carucates (*c.*240 medieval acres equates to one carucate) of additional land in the vicinity. By 1310, however, the manor of Rathdown was waste (ibid., no. 39, p. 60) and in 1330 'answers nothing for rents taken into the king's hands because Fromond le Brun, who held the manor of the king, alienated it in fee to Walter de Islep without licence' (ibid., no. 39, p. 96). The de Kenley lands at Ballygonner reverted to the king on de Kenley's death in the mid-fourteenth century; this is recorded in the pipe roll for 1340–1 in which Elias de Ashebourne accounts for the 'issues of the lands and rents, which belonged to the late steward of Albert de Kenley of Ballygonner, in the king's hands after divers debts in which Albert was bound to him on the day of his death, and the king committed the said Elias to hold the premises while in the king's hand and render 15 shillings yearly' (Mills 1903–27, no. 47, p. 44). This presumably included Kindlestown Castle.

The Archbolds at Kindlestown Kindlestown Castle was probably half built by the time of Albert's death and the name Kindlestown had already become affixed. It was evidently heavily defended and must have been under constant threat as, in 1301, it was recorded that the vills of Wicklow and Rathdown and other places were burned (Price 1983, lvi; Smal 1993, 35). Kindlestown was presumably a target and this is confirmed by the fact that the O'Byrnes managed to take the castle in 1377 (Price 1983, v, 322). Although it was recovered soon afterwards by the chancellor, Archbishop Wikeford, the incident is a clear illustration of how the castle, by this date, was clearly in the *terra guerre* or land of war (Price 1983, lxviii). Similarly, between 1370 and 1376 the O'Byrnes also attacked and took the castle of Newcastle McKynegan further south and, although they were eventually repulsed, in 1405 they returned and destroyed the castle (Price 1983, lxxii).

The Archbolds are first recorded in the district in 1314 when 'Reginald and Robert Archebaud and others of his family and name are rewarded for their warring with Irish felons in the Leinster mountains and are admitted to make fine for all trespasses and felonies to this day by pledge of Hugh Lawless' (Mills et al. 1905, iii, 318). From this time onwards they begin to expand rapidly and, by the end of the fifteenth and early sixteenth century, they managed to occupy nearly all the major centres including Kindlestown, Bray, Rathdown and Kilruddery, so that the area becomes known as 'Archbold's Country'. They connect into the Butler family who had an interest in Bray and play an active role in the defence of the surrounding country, on behalf of the crown. Thus, there were Archbolds running the royal castle of Newcastle McKynegan and Clonmore in Carlow in the early fourteenth century (Connolly 1998, i, 236, 239; ibid., ii, 359). Despite their sometimes official role, the Archbolds were kept in order by much the same device used against the O'Byrnes. They were forced regularly to submit hostages and their chiefs had to be officially ratified, as had the chiefs of the Lawlesses, Howels and Harolds (Frame 1971, 124–3).

The first reference to an Archbold at Kindlestown Castle is in 1399, when John Archbold is described as being 'of Kindlestown', suggesting he was residing there (Anon. 1889, 137, 40; Scott 1913, 225). In 1426, however, his son Patrick received the manor of Bray and, after this date, Kindlestown appears listed along with the assets of this manor. Patrick received the land at Bray from William Went and Richard Hackett, along with lands at Balymacrynan, Loghanbyrne, and Kylmasarny, all of which are in the parish of Bray (Anon. 1889, 137, 40). Most importantly, the grant was followed up in 1432 by a second grant from James Butler, the main landholder, for a rent of four marks, including the lands of Oldcourt at Bray (Scott 1913, 224). The Butler family had had an interest in the manor of Bray from at least 1311, when an extent (the financial account of the manor) of Obrun and Bray is recorded in the Red Book of Ormond (White 1932, 24). Curtis tells us that Theobald Walter (Butler) received the land in Bray from Philip de Rupella (Curtis n.d., 12) and a Richard de Rupella, presumably a relative, is recorded in the extent of 1311 (White 1932, 23). The ownership of Bray is difficult to trace after Christiana de Marisco (the de Ridlesford heiress) handed the manor back to the crown in the 1280s. The Archbolds, however, evidently held their lands directly from the Butlers as, in 1611, when attempting to secure some of their lands, the Archbolds claimed they had received the lands of Bray legitimately from the Butlers over two hundred years previously (Scott 1913, 226).

The Fitzwilliam connection A second family, the Fitzwilliams of Merrion and Dundrum, now comes into prominence in connection with the manor of Bray, and this adds to the general confusion. The Fitzwilliams appear to have received lands at Bray in 1423 from Philip Higdon (Scott 1913, 225; Anon. 1889, 131, 38) and this grant was evidently legitimate as in 1518 the Archbolds were forced to acknowledge the Fitzwilliams as their lords. In this document, 'Oliver Archbebold, son of Nicholas Archebold, Oliver Archebold, son of Simon Archebold, Edmund Archebolde and John, sons of Hebard Archebold … release and quitclaim their right of Myche Bree and Lytyll Bree' to Richard Fitzwilliam of Baggotrath. A related text states: 'Same grantors and Edward

Archebald, son of Tebet Archebolde … release and quit claim to Myche Bree and Litell Bray, Balirinle [Kindlestown], and Tampuldelne [presumably Temple Delgin, alias Delgany] (Anon. 1889, 207 62). Not only did the Archbolds agree to quitclaim the property, but they also agreed to pay rent, as in 1527 Walter Archbold is recorded as holding Bray from Fitzwilliam for a rent of a fresh salmon. The Archbolds were also bound to preserve the falcons, which nested every year in the manor of Bray, for the exclusive use of the Fitzwilliams (Scott 1913, 226). This connection with the Fitzwilliams is difficult to understand but it may have been associated with the original grant made by Strongbow, earl of Pembroke, to Walter de Ridlesford in 1173. It may suggest that Strongbow retained at that point some interest in the Bray area, which passed onto his heirs and was subsequently revived by them in the fifteenth century, perhaps in opposition to the Butler claim. What was most important was that the Fitzwilliam connection was clearly superior to the Butler, as the Archbolds reluctantly ended up paying rent to the Fitzwilliams. The Fitzwilliams were prominent in the politics of the area, as in 1566 a Thomas Fitzwilliam was recorded as the seneschal and chief ruler of the whole marches of Dublin, 'that is the barony of Rathdowne, the nations of the Washes, Asspolles and Harrolds' (Anon. 1889, 251 84). The land of the Walshes, Archbolds and Harolds were eventually committed to his care (see O'Byrne above).

The relationship between the Fitzwilliam and Archbold families was not harmonious and continual disputes are recorded in the sixteenth century, for example, the dispute between Thomas Fitzwilliam, Appolenar Talbot, and Margaret, his wife and William Archepole, son and heir to Patrick, concerning 'Moch Bree and Little Bree' (ibid., 245 81). However, the Archbolds always had problems with their titles, probably stemming originally from the confusion of the landholding arrangements of the late twelfth and thirteenth centuries. It is certainly of note that Walter de Ridlesford, the original recipient of the manor of Bray, never had proper title to the manor, the result of which was that the grant was much reduced when his son, also Walter, sought to get it ratified (Simpson 1994a, 196).

Kindlestown as part of the manor of Bray Little is known about Kindlestown in the fifteenth century after Patrick, son of John, received the manor of Bray in 1426. Nearly a hundred years later, in 1527, Walter Archbold is recorded as holding Bray, and he presumably also held Kindlestown Castle, although this is not specified. He died soon afterwards but had no heirs and, as a result, the lands passed into the hands of his brother, Patrick (son of Richard Archbold of Killruddery). Patrick died two years later, in 1529, but, however, did leave an heir, Gerald or Gerratt, who was only nine years old at the time (Curtis n.d., 13). As the heir was a minor, the property was taken into the hands of the crown until 1538 (Scott 1913, 277) but was managed directly by John Archbold, who was the son and heir of Hubert of Bray (then deceased). John is recorded as having granted half of the manor to William Ashepole of Kenlyeston in 1538, the same year Gerald came of age, although the circumstances are not clear. William subsequently granted it for nine years to Theobald Ashpole after which time it was supposed to revert to the heirs of Hubert (ibid., 7). This effectively meant there were two holders of the manor of Bray in 1538, the result of which was a division in the manor between Gerratt (the heir) and William (based on deeds held by the earl of Meath; ibid.). William, who lived in Kindlestown, held 'the castle of Much Bray, the watermill, with houses, garden tenements and cartilages, with appurtenances lying and being within the bawyn next to the castle and those half of all other lands, tenements, water and half the fishery' (ibid., 13). Gerratt held the other half of the lands and the fishery but it is not known where he lived, although it may have been Kindlestown also (ibid., 7, 13). The arbitrators of the partition were named as Raynold Talbot, James Goodman, James Blakeney and Stephen Fitzwilliam.

The documentary sources record that by 1560 William's half of the manor was held by Patrick Archbold, presumably the heir of Hubert (see above) to whom the manor reverted (after Theobald held it for nine years). The manor appears to have been divided again at this date, between Gerratt and Patrick (Curtis n.d., 7), although the reason for this is not clear. Patrick received the castle of Bray and fifty acres, but also sixty acres in Delgany and the castle of Kelleston (Kindlestown) with 180 acres (Griffith 1991, 172). Patrick died in 1560 and an inquisition was held the following year which established that the manor was held directly of the crown by knight service and that Gerratt and Patrick had split the manor as detailed above (ibid., 172). Patrick had evidently been in financial trouble as he had mortgaged his lands in 1560 by granting them to John Goodman Junior of Ballylaghan (Loughlinstown, Co. Dublin) and John Walsh of Kilcobban (Kilgobbin, Co. Dublin). Patrick's heir William was then eighteen but unmarried (Griffith 1991, 172). Patrick also provided the 'Breyes' (Little and Much Bray) for the use of his wife until she died and for the payment of his fines and for maintenance of his sons and daughters until the heir was twenty-three years old (ibid.).

William Mc Oliver Archbold of Kindlestown In 1568 the heir, William Mc Oliver Ashepol, was evidently living at Kindlestown as he is described as 'William Asspoll of Ballykenly' (Anon. 1889, 253 84; Griffith 1991, 243). The connection with the Fitzwilliam family remained strong as William, probably also in financial trouble, granted Michael Fitzwilliam of Donnamore Co. Meath and John Fynglas of Tibbersoule, Co. Dublin, one castle and all the messuages and lands, which he had in Miche Brey (Anon. 1889, 353, 84). His feoffes were James Goodman and John Walsh, who had both received lands in Bray from William's father Patrick (see above). As stated earlier William's holding at Kindlestown also had some connection to the earl of Kildare who was still receiving a rent from Kindlestown as late as 1568 (Mills 1994, 1240 [1029]). That William was an important man in the southern hinterland of Dublin is evident from the fact that 'William Ashepoll of Kenelestone' was recorded as sheriff of the county of Dublin in 1579 and, along with Marx Wycombe of Drynan, had been given a commission to execute martial law (Mills 1994, 3528 [2838]). Despite this, the year previous (12 May 1578) he had illegally entered and taken possession of the lands of Thomas Ashpole at Templedelgin (Temple Delgany), who was presumably a relative. Thomas had been attainted for treason and had been dispossessed of two hundred acres and a watermill (when William Skeffington was lord deputy and John Harold, sheriff of Co. Dublin; Griffith 1991, 243). William had entered the lands 'by what right the jury did not know' but which was presumably based on the fact that he had just come of age (he was now twenty three) and his family had held these lands for a considerable period of time. Eventually, in 1582, a pardon was granted to 'William Archbolde of Kynleston, Co. Dublin ... not to pardon any conspiracy or abetting of James Eustace, late Viscount of Baltinglas or William Nugent in their rebellions' (Mills 1994, 3864 [3329]). There was a family connection between the Eustaces and the Archbolds as William was married to a Talbot and the Talbots and Eustaces were strongly related through marriage (Fitzgerald 1910, 140). The family connection was probably closer than this as there was an allegation of bastardy made against Christopher Eustace in a suit between an Oliver Eustace and the said Christopher. The dispute concerned lands in Co. Kildare and at Kynleston (Kindlestown) Co. Dublin, which at this date were in the hands of William Archbold (Mills 1994, 6058 [6563]).

The lands that William's father Patrick granted to James Goodman and John Walsh of Kilgobban can also be traced, to a limited extent, in the documentary sources. Goodman died first, followed by Walsh, whose death is recorded in 1578. A Pierse Walsh was subsequently identified as John Walshe's heir and the association with the Archbolds continued as both William and Pierse enfeoffed Gilbert Talbot of Belgard, John Talbot of Rathdown and Edmond Birne of Rathdown of lands in the manor of Bray. William died in 1612 and an inquisition was held in 1621 (ibid.), when Patrick, his heir, was seised of half of Little Bray (which is still listed as in Co. Dublin at this date). This included two tenements, four tofts, and fifteen acres, all of which was held of the queen by one knight's service. Patrick was, at the time of William's death, of twenty-six years old and married (Griffith 1991, 400).

Patrick Archbold Patrick evidently lived in Kindlestown as in 1608 he is recorded as holding the castle (Griffith 1966, 153). In 1621, dogged by financial difficulties, he conveyed Kenleston (Kindlestown), Ballydonagh and Delgany (alias Temple Delgany) to Robert Kennedy, Sankye Silliard and Bernard Gratewell for a period of ninety-one years, although Bray is not mentioned (Curtis n.d., 16). Patrick subsequently died in March 1624, aged thirty-six and was succeeded by his son Edward who was probably quite young (ibid.). In this deed it is also recorded that Pierse Talbot and his heiress had received further security of Delgany as collateral, as they had purchased Ballydonagh and Kenlestown (ibid., 16). Thus the Tablots presumably held Kindlestown at this time, although the Archbolds continued to occupy it.

Disputes over title There had been repeated inquisitions into the title of deeds concerning Archbold property throughout the early seventeenth century, and these are documented in 1607, 1609, 1611, and 1629 (Documents in the possession of the earl of Meath, Kilruddery; Scott 1913, 148). The Archbolds always had problems proving title and the resultant inquisitions provide some information on the earlier landholding arrangements. In 1611 Patrick (son of William), in making a petition, claimed his ancestors held Bray from the Butler earls of Ormond for two hundred years (Scott 1913, 226). However, Patrick failed to establish this claim and was dispossessed of the hundred and twenty acres in Kenlestown (Kindlestown) and Coolegan (Coolagad) and sixty acres in Temple Delgany (Curtis, n.d., 15). The crown eventually granted his lands to Sir Henry Pierce (Scott 1913, 228–30) but, by 1620, Pierce had only managed to recover about sixty acres. The castle was evidently still an important residence at this date as in 1621 the castle of 'Kenliston and a watermill' was mentioned in a now destroyed inquisition of James I. Included in this was a total of four hundred acres, which were attached to the castle (Scott 1913, 228–30). This is the largest amount of land recorded attached to the castle and probably included Temple Delgany, Ballydonagh and Coolegad. Eventually Pierce granted his interest to Elizabeth Montgomery (Lady Brereton) who assigned it over to William Brabazon (later earl of Meath) in 1622. However, despite the fact that Brabazon had some sort of claim, the Archbolds had the stronger claim and, probably more importantly, possession of the castle. However, in 1625, Patrick's heir Edward Archbold of Delgany, then eighteen years of age, sold the manor of Bray to the earl of Meath, who was evidently amassing lands in the area (Curtis n.d., 17). His newly-acquired lands included Temple Delgany, Coolegad and Kindlestown Castle.

Despite the fact that Edward had sold the manor to the earl of Meath, the problem with title was still causing problems. A letter patent was eventually sent to Charles I in 1628 calling for an inquisition into the lands of Edward Archebold of Delgany, heir of Patrick (then twenty-one) to allow William, earl of Meath to purchase the manor of Great Bray (Bree and little Bree). The documents also record the fact that Sir Henry Pierce was falsely granted the manor for the term of 'one and twenty years for the yearly rent of seven pounds and twenty half penny Irish' (The letters patent were signed by Jacob Newman, who was responsible for much of the land reclamation around the

Temple Bar area of Dublin city at this point (Simpson 1994b, 8). Eventually, a second inquisition found in favour of the Archbolds but their lands, by this date, were heavily mortgaged to Robert Kennedy, Sankye Sillard, and Bernard Gratewell, as mentioned above (Curtis n.d., 16). The acquisition of the Archbold lands by the earl of Meath did not resolve the various land disputes, as a new dispute arose between the earl of Meath and the Fitzwilliams, the original claimants. As a result, the earl of Meath brought a case against Lord Fitzwilliam in 1637 (Curtis n.d., 2), an abstract of which survives as part of the Curtis transcripts. In this document, the title of the manor rests with William Ashpoll of Kenleston (this estate included 180 acres) and the Archbold lineage is recorded (see Appendix A). The opposing Fitzwilliam case is also listed and this records the descent from Sir Thomas Fitzwilliam to Oliver earl of Tyrconnell (Fitzwilliam) (see Appendix B; ibid. 8).

The Confederate rebellion and Cromwellian expeditions The land disputes were interrupted by the serious events of the early 1640s, which were to result in the destruction of many of the castles in the area. After Cromwell took Drogheda he marched southwards through Bray, Windgates, Delgany, Newcastle, as far south as Wexford, a route that would have taken him directly past Kindlestown Castle (Duffy 1997, 67). The present condition of Kindlestown Castle may suggest that Cromwell slighted it on his way past, although this seems unlikely given that it was in the hands of the earl of Meath who was loyal to Cromwell (as a result, his lands were declared 'unforfeited' in the aftermath of the war). There is little documentary evidence of destruction apart from a local tradition, which tells the story of the sacking of Kindlestown after the theft of Cromwell's favourite horse from Killincarraig castle, approximately one kilometre to the southeast. Henry Walsh of Carrickmines built this fortified house in the Jacobean style in the early seventeenth century and this still survives as a substantial ruin. The Confederates originally held it before it was seized and garrisoned by Cromwell and his forces, Cromwell reputedly spending the night there (Scott 1913, 171; Corlett 1999, 80). This small garrison was quickly besieged but they managed to hold out for three months before being relieved eventually by 1,500 reinforcements, who arrived from Liverpool and Chester (Scott 1913, 170). It is unlikely that a castle as strong as Kindlestown and located so close to Dublin would have escaped some destruction during these troubled times, in the period between the rebellion in 1641 and the siege of Limerick in 1691. The battle and siege of Carrickmines Castle in 1642, approximately eleven kilometres to the north, was the culmination of devastating campaigns in this area and one that must have resulted in the destruction of any defended dwellings in the vicinity. Specifically, in 1649 the duke of Ormonde sent instructions to Colonel Hugh O'Byrne to destroy Powerscourt Castle, as well as all other castles in the locality, to prevent them being occupied by Cromwell (Fitzgerald 1910, 138). This presumably included Kindlestown Castle although this is not recorded, unlike Fassaroe Castle, lying to the west of Bray, which was slighted at this time (Scott 1913, 170).

The deed of partition, 1666 That the castle stayed in the hands of the Brabazons is evident by the 'Deed of Partition, dated 1666', which was drawn up between the earl of Meath and Oliver Fitzwilliam, earl of Tyrconnell (viscount of Merrion and baron of Thorncastle/Stillorgan; Anon. 1889, 321 103) to resolve the original dispute. This was billed as the 'deed to end all disputes concerning lands of Great Bray, alias Bree' (Scott 1913, 230). In this deed the land of the manor of Bray was divided up but Kindlestown Castle remained in the hands of the earl of Meath.

Hearth money roll, 1668 The fate of the castle is difficult to trace from the mid-seventeenth century onwards, although it remained in the hands of the earl of Meath. The hearth money roll for County Wicklow, dated 1668, records that there were six houses in 'Kendalstown', none of which had a hearth perhaps suggesting that the castle may have been out of use by this time (Price 1931, i, 167). It is not clear, however, from the surviving castle whether it originally did have a hearth, as the most likely location was the southern wall, which does not survive. However, fireplaces were not necessarily present in stone castles: in the tower house at Clara, Co. Kilkenny there was only one fireplace at second floor level but the main chamber was serviced by a central fire or brazier, with smoke exiting out a louver or hole in the roof (Leask 1941, 93). Other castles similarly display no evidence of fireplaces, such as the hall-house at Rathlumney in Co. Wexford, which is very similar to Kindlestown, and the tower-house at Carrigaphooca, Co. Cork (O'Callaghan 1980–1, 3–5; Leask 1941, 91). The hearth roll gives other information about Kindlestown and the surrounding area. The two tenants mentioned at Kindlestown are David Tool and Bart Sillard, the former evidently an O'Toole while Bart Sillard was obviously a relative of Sankye Sillard, who had first received the castle in 1621 (Curtis, n.d., 16).

DEPICTIONS OF THE CASTLE

Cartographic sources The earliest map of the Delgany area is the half barony map of Rathdown, drawn as part of the Down Survey, under the direction of William Petty (1623–87) (Power 1994, 727). The map, dated 1652, delineates the parish boundaries and the townlands, as well as depicting large dwellings and some major topographical landmarks. Kindlestown is not depicted, perhaps suggesting that it was not occupied at this time, in marked

Plate 6 Du Noyer (A)

Plate 7 Du Noyer (C)

contrast to Killincarraig which is shown as a fine three-storey building, with a pitched roof, three turrets and a flag flying from the top: the house is described in the survey as 'the most remarkable building in this half of the barony' (ibid.). Kindlestown Castle is depicted on Jacob Neville's map of Wicklow, dated 1760, but this gives little information about the actual castle building, other than to register that it is there (Price 1983, v, 322). An estate map of Delgany, dated 1775, depicts the castle building but also shows houses on the northern and western sides, which had gone by 1838, as they are not shown on the Ordnance Survey (Halpin 1992, 48).

The antiquarian sketches by George Du Noyer Four antiquarian depictions of the castle by George Du Noyer survive, executed in the early 1840s (plates 6 and 7), and comprising three pencil sketches and one water-colour, which are currently in the care of the Royal Society of Antiquaries of Ireland. The depictions are particularly useful as they show the eastern end of the castle, before it fell sometime after 1913, when Canon Scott photographed the castle (Scott 1913). The drawings make it clear that the east wall was in fact a narrow service tower, which not only contained the stairs, but extended upwards beyond the main roof-line, the flashing of the pitched roof being clearly visible in the west face. The Du Noyer drawings also show the moat along the north side of the castle, as well as possible earthworks on the western side. The watercolour shows the castle from the southeastern side, with Kindlestown Hill and the Sugarloaf Mountain in the background (plates 6 and 7). This is the most finished of the depictions but the one in which Du Noyer uses the most artistic licence, when directly compared to the sketches taken at the same time. The castle is shown in an elevated, isolated spot in a classic castle pose, with no surrounding features such as the house known to have been located at the eastern side, or the field boundaries and trees. All these are faithfully recorded in the pencil sketches, which were probably taken to create this depiction (see below).

The angle taken obscures somewhat the true size of the ruin and the service tower, standing three storeys high, dominates. The presence of the mural stairs at the northern end of the tower is marked by four staggered slit windows, which extend from ground floor up and served to light the staircase to parapet level. The doorway at ground floor level survives as a large void although the straight jamb is visible on the southern side. Some of the quoins on the northeast corner had also been robbed out by this date. A second window in the east wall lit the mural chamber, which was located directly over the doorway at first floor level. This was probably some sort of guard-room but the window had been robbed out by this date. A third chamber must have existed that ran the length of the service tower at third floor level as there was a window in the west wall, which presumably lit the chamber. There appears to have been a projecting feature on the western side at parapet level, which may represent a machicoulis, a stone box, which projected over the top of the castle, through which missiles could be thrown (this survives as a hunk of masonry within the castle). However, this is a strange location for a machicoulis as there was clearly no door for it to protect. The only other feature visible is a stringcourse above which rose the parapet. The depiction shows the castle on an elevated site, flanked by a roadway on the eastern side (orientated north-south).

One of the pencil drawings shows a house to the east of the castle and this was two storeys in height with a steeply pitched roof (probably originally thatched), small windows and a chimney in both gables. This house is also shown in a second pencil drawing, which also depicts what appears to be a field boundary along the line of the present field boundary immediately south of the castle and a large pond some distance to the southeast of the castle, in the adjoining field. The fourth pencil drawing is taken from the northwest side, and thus the front of the castle is shown. Of most interest is the flashing on the service tower, the remains of the steeply pitched roof. This scar can be compared directly with the scar on Oldcourt in Bray, a castle probably similar to Kindlestown, which was also in the hands of the Archbolds in the fifteenth century. Du Noyer was also clearly aware of the moat on the northern side of the castle, as this is included.

Liam Price's field books Liam Price, the noted antiquarian of the Wicklow area, visited the site on at least two occasions and he recorded both these visits in his notebooks. In 1930 he found the site very overgrown with ivy and other vegetation but commented on the fact that the surviving north wall stood to full height up to the battlements, as it does today. He also noted the presence of a wet moat (he visited in October), which surrounded the castle and commented that much of the masonry of the castle appeared to have been removed by pick (Corlett and Weaver 2002, i, 90). Price visited the castle again three years later, also in October, in 1933 but this time in the company of Harold. G. Leask, the renowned castle expert (Leask 1941; Corlett and Weaver 2002, i, 90). During this visit Price recorded the remains of the plank-centring and also commented that Leask thought the castle may have been early thirteenth-century in date. Price also made an attempt to locate the line of the medieval road, which originally would have led to the castle but could find no indication of the route.

A DESCRIPTION OF THE CASTLE

Introduction Kindlestown Castle is a large imposing hall-house, which measures externally 21m east-west by 9.80m wide and stands *c.* 8m in height (figs 3–5). The north wall survives almost intact to parapet level while the

Plate 8 East wall foundation

southern end of the east wall also stands to first floor level, although in a
perilous condition. The southern and western walls were rebuilt in the nineteenth century and only stand, on average, 1.50m in height. These walls were
exposed during the excavation. The castle is two storeys in height and is built
of roughly cut/uncut grey limestone, bonded with a distinctive crude grey
mortar, which contained heavy grit/pebbles and shell inclusions. The walls
are over 2m in width and the quoins were originally of cut granite, the local
stone. The lower or ground floor level was roofed with a barrel-vault, orientated
east–west, which was original to the building and the northwest angle has a
projecting rectangular turret, which extends beyond the parapet level of the
northern wall. This houses two garderobe chutes at first floor level and a third
at parapet level. The eastern wall was originally a narrow service tower, three
storeys high, and this contained a stone staircase in the northeast angle, as well
as a small chamber at first floor level (plate 8). This service tower originally
extended an estimated 3.50m above the parapet of the main building and the
pitched roof of the castle abutted it directly (plates 6 and 7). The barrel vault
was lit by a series of three small rectangular slit windows in the north wall,
which widened into segmental-arched embrasures in the interior. All,
however, have been badly damaged. Four narrow rectangular slit windows also
lit the first floor level but the internal embrasures were much larger and at
least one preserves the remains of a window seat. The gap between the

windows in the central area at first floor level is very wide, perhaps suggesting that this level was originally divided into two chambers, east and west. The southern wall had a talus or basal batter while the foundations of the northern wall consisted of a series of stepped projecting offsets (plate 9). The excavation also revealed that the castle was roofed, originally in purple slate, complete examples of which were found throughout the deposits.

The enclosure The castle stood at the western end in a large rectangular ditched enclosure, which measured 52m east-west by 18m wide and which was still visible in 1991, marked by the surrounding field boundaries (fig. 7). Traces of an internal ditch and bank are now visible on the northern and part of the western side, although the southern side is very overgrown. The ditch is only 6.50m from the north wall of the castle, marked by a shallow but distinct depression, which is filled with nettles and measures at least 6m wide by at least 1m in depth. The ditch was bounded by an external bank traces of which survive on the northern side as a low mound. There also appears to be a causeway at the eastern end, although this may be more modern in date. The presence of the ditched enclosures may be deemed relatively unusual, as many hall-houses display no evidence of defensive enclosing earthworks or associated bawns, although Castleconor, Co. Mayo has similar earthworks (Sweetman 1999, 89). Previous archaeological investigation has revealed several fragments of worked stone, either original to the site or plundered from an existing medieval site somewhere in the vicinity. This was suggested by the discovery, by Christiaan Corlett, of a possible mortar (or bullaun) and a portion of a rotary quern stone amongst the rubble (Corlett 1999, 64). This was augmented during the excavation by the discovery of other worked fragments including a large rubbing stone. In addition to this, one of the granite steps of the staircase has a central perforation suggesting that it may be in a reused position.

Construction Phase 1 and 2 Two phases (Construction Phases 1 and 2) can be identified in the structure, suggesting that the upper storey was added to the castle. This can be summarised as a change in the type of stone used in the upper floor, a general thinning of the upper walls and a raising of the first floor level, a break in the render line in the front façade, and the use of putlog holes in the lower level, which are absent from the upper level (fig. 9). In addition, the exit of the chute of the latrine on the parapet corresponds to the building line, suggesting that this latrine was added in Phase 2. This combination of factors indicates that construction was halted after completion of the first floor, although it is not known for how long, and only at some later stage was the upper floor added. The break can be clearly identified on the internal side by a change in type of stone, which had a distinctive orange/red hue and was clearly from a different source. The walls were also thinner (0.40m) and, as a result, not as defensive (the thinness of the walls eventually

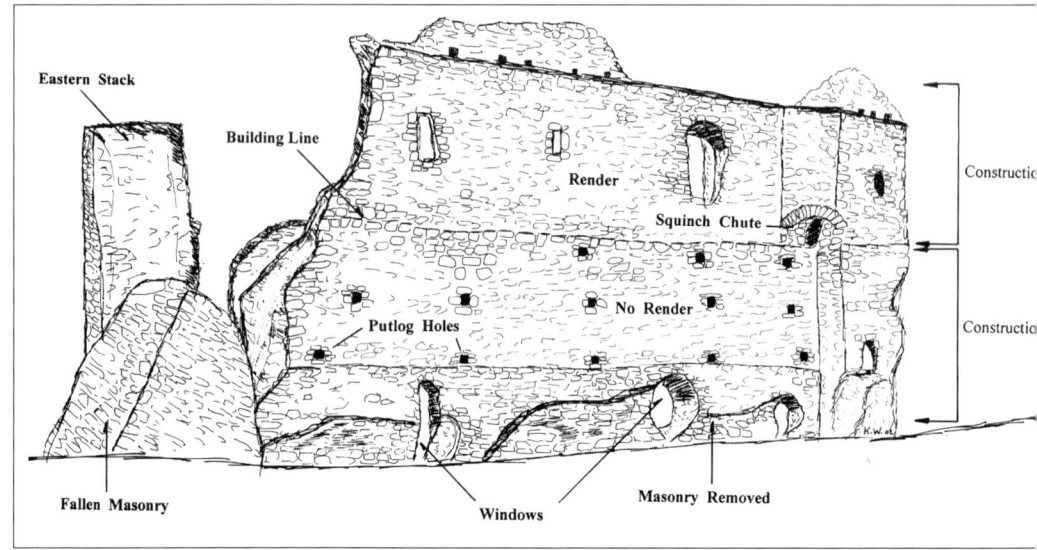

9 Construction level 1 and 2

led to the partial collapse of the eastern wall), and the offset which supported the first floor level was raised at least 1m beyond the top of the barrel vault. What is of note, however, is the fact that the mortar used in Phase 2 is very similar in type to that used in the first phase suggesting that the same source of lime was used.

The two phases can also be identified in the external façade in the form of a distinctive band of render which extends across the building. This suggests that the castle was completely rendered in Phase 2, but that the render adhered better to the upper levels because the mortar of the walls of this section was still fresh, unlike the lower Phase 1 portion (pers. comm., Ben Murtagh). Thus the render eventually fell off the lower section creating the visible 'band'. The regularly-spaced putlog holes in the lower Phase 1 section are conspicuous by their absence in the upper levels. Although it is probable that putlogs were used and subsequently neatly infilled, their absence from the upper level perhaps implies a change in the way the castle was constructed. The second phase of construction did follow the plan of the first and the northwest tower was completed with garderobes feeding into the already existing chutes of Phase 1. A third garderobe, however, was added at parapet level but this was clearly not in the original plan as the chute only extends through the Phase 2 portion of the wall, screened by a squinch arch. The entrance at ground floor level in the east wall appears to have been inserted in Phase 2 as the excavation revealed that the foundation of the eastern wall originally continued across the line of the doorway indicating that it was a solid wall (plate 8). This inserted doorway probably represents a deviation from the

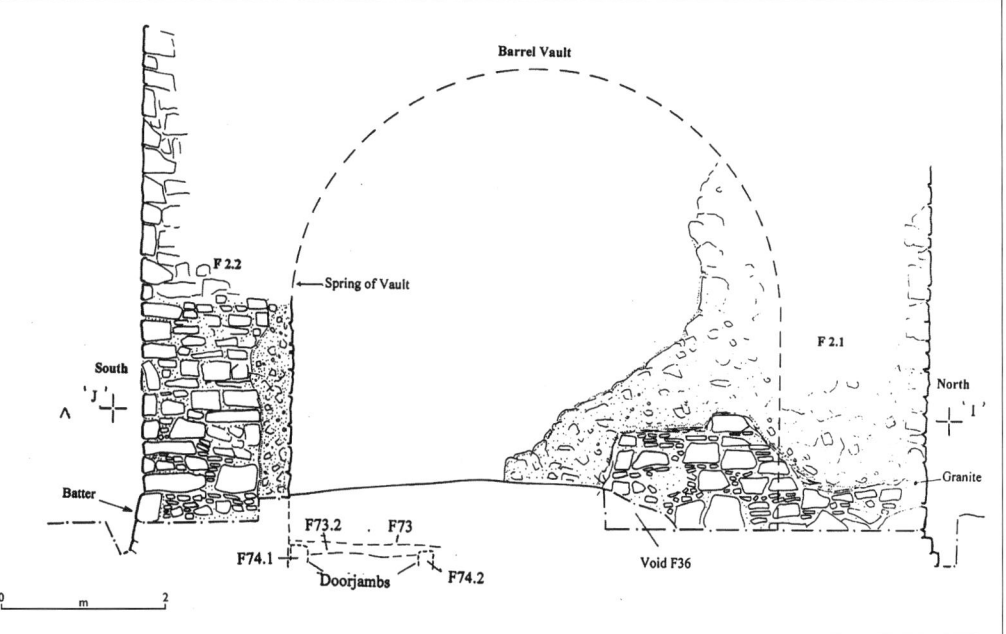

10 Elevation through the castle

plan to have a doorway at first floor level, as was typical of the hall-house type. However, this was presumably never built as the upper floor was added later.

The barrel vault The ground floor level represents Construction Phase 1 and this was composed of a full barrel-vaulted chamber, orientated east-west (plates 4 and 5; fig. 2), which was clearly original to the Phase 1 building as the northern haunch forms part of the core of the standing northern wall. The vault measured at least 5.15m in height and was constructed using plank-centring, a section of which survives in a patch measuring 2m square, which preserved the line of planks measuring 50mm by 80mm (fig. 10). There are also several open putlogs in the north wall, indicating that, at some stage, there was a scaffolding erected on the internal side. After the vault was con-structed the top of the vault and the spandrels on either side were probably infilled with clays to create a level platform for the floor of the great hall. This was suggested by the large quantities of clay found during the excavations, which was mixed with fragments of demolished barrel vault.

The north wall The north wall stands approximately 8m in height and is built of uncut limestone measuring, on average, 0.30m by 0.20m. The foun-dations are stepped on the external side, composed of two projecting offsets, varying between 80mm and 0.10m in width (plate 9). A white hard mortar is

Plate 9 North wall
foundation

used, which contains small stones and there are large visible lumps of lime, measuring 40mm in diameter. The scars of the barrel vault dominate the lower level of the internal face as this formed part of the main wall. The lower section of the external face of the wall was badly damaged when the facing stones were forcibly removed in a continuous strip, 1.40m in height, along the base of the wall. However, the remains of one granite quoin still survive on the northeast corner measuring 0.50m height by 0.40m in width by 0.20m in depth. There are also four regular rows of stopped putlog holes (0.20m square), the lowest level of which lies 1.70m above the present ground level. Corresponding but different putlogs are visible in the internal face. Three windows lit the barrel vault at ground floor level and these were small rectangular slit windows in the external face, which widened into larger embrasures in the interior, approximately 1.45m in width. The eastern window is the best preserved and this is roofed with two large slabs, orientated east-west and crowned by a pointed segmented arch, which is plank-centred.

Plate 10 The north wall (southside)

The western window is very damaged but appears to have been different in type, as it is positioned slightly lower than the other two windows and is smaller in size (plate 10).

Construction Phase 2 was marked by an increase in the survival of the white lime render, which is very visible as a band of colour extending across the façade at first floor level (fig. 9). This corresponds in the internal face to a change in the type of limestone used, which, as already stated, has a distinctive reddish hue (plate 3). A projecting offset marks the first floor level, which originally supported the floor and this is approximately 0.20m in width but was raised 1m above the top of the vault (plate 3). The front façade is broken by the three upper windows, which lit the first floor but, unfortunately, only the central ope survives intact as a small rectangular slit. All the windows widened into larger embrasures in the interior, which had pointed segmented arches but, unlike the ground floor level, had no plank-centring (plate 10). The eastern window (Window 4) is best preserved and this contains two small low window seats on either side. The western window (Window 6) is the best preserved but differs in type from the other windows, as does the corresponding window at ground floor level. The window is a long rectangular arrow loop, which is set within a square headed (rather than segmented arched) embrasure. This embrasure has a splayed jamb on the eastern side but is straight on the western. The floor level of the embrasure is at least 1m higher than the offset for the floor.

The upper level of the wall is crowned by a parapet wall, 1m in height, and the alure or walk-walk behind the parapet still survives, the sloping floor formed by the slated roof, which projects through the parapet wall and forms the external stringcourse. The slate in this section was far larger than the roofing slate proper, measuring, on average, 1m by 0.50m, evidently for increased stability. This type of alure, however, was somewhat unsatisfactory for two reasons; it was difficult to walk along (as it was sloping) and was inherently unstable (Leask 1941, 87–8). A series of rectangular drip holes was created in the parapet wall, which allowed the rainwater to drain down the front façade. Similarly, the squinch arch, which spanned the angle between the northwest turret and the wall proper, screened the chute from the garderobe at parapet level, which also drained down the front façade. The squinch arch is crowned with a pointed segmented arch, which is plank-centred in a similar fashion to the windows of the lower floor.

The northwest turret The northwest turret only projects out by 0.50m from the north wall and its primary function was to house the garderobe chamber at first floor level (plate 2), which contains two latrines. Two narrow slit windows lit the chamber but the window in the west wall was crudely con-verted into a gun loop sometime in the seventeenth century. The two latrine chutes measure, on average, 0.40m square and exit out through the main façade of the castle, the exits being located 2.20m from the present ground level. From here the waste was discharged into a leat or channel cut into the boulder clay, which presumably led directly into the surrounding moat (see below). There is at present no access into the garderobe chamber, which is rectangular in shape, roofed by a large segmental arch at the northern end with the remains of intact plank-centring on the southern end. Access to the chamber was *via* a round-headed doorway, at the western end, the base of which has been lowered in recent times.

The service tower The east wall originally formed a narrow service tower, which was approximately 2.55m in width and contained the mural staircase and a chamber at first floor level. This service tower projected above the line of the main parapet by approximately 3.50m (based on the Du Noyer drawings) and survived partially intact into the twentieth century. The staircase was at the northern end but most of this fell sometime after 1913 and survives on site as a hunk of masonry. The *in situ* section consists of a series of eight granite steps at least one of which is in a reused position as it has some sort of central perforation, 0.11m in diameter. The steps measure, on average, between 0.60m and 0.90m in length by between 0.40m and 0.55m in width although the full width could not be ascertained. The lower section of the staircase was orientated north-south before making a half turn to the west to allow access to the first floor level. The fallen corner preserves the roof of the

315

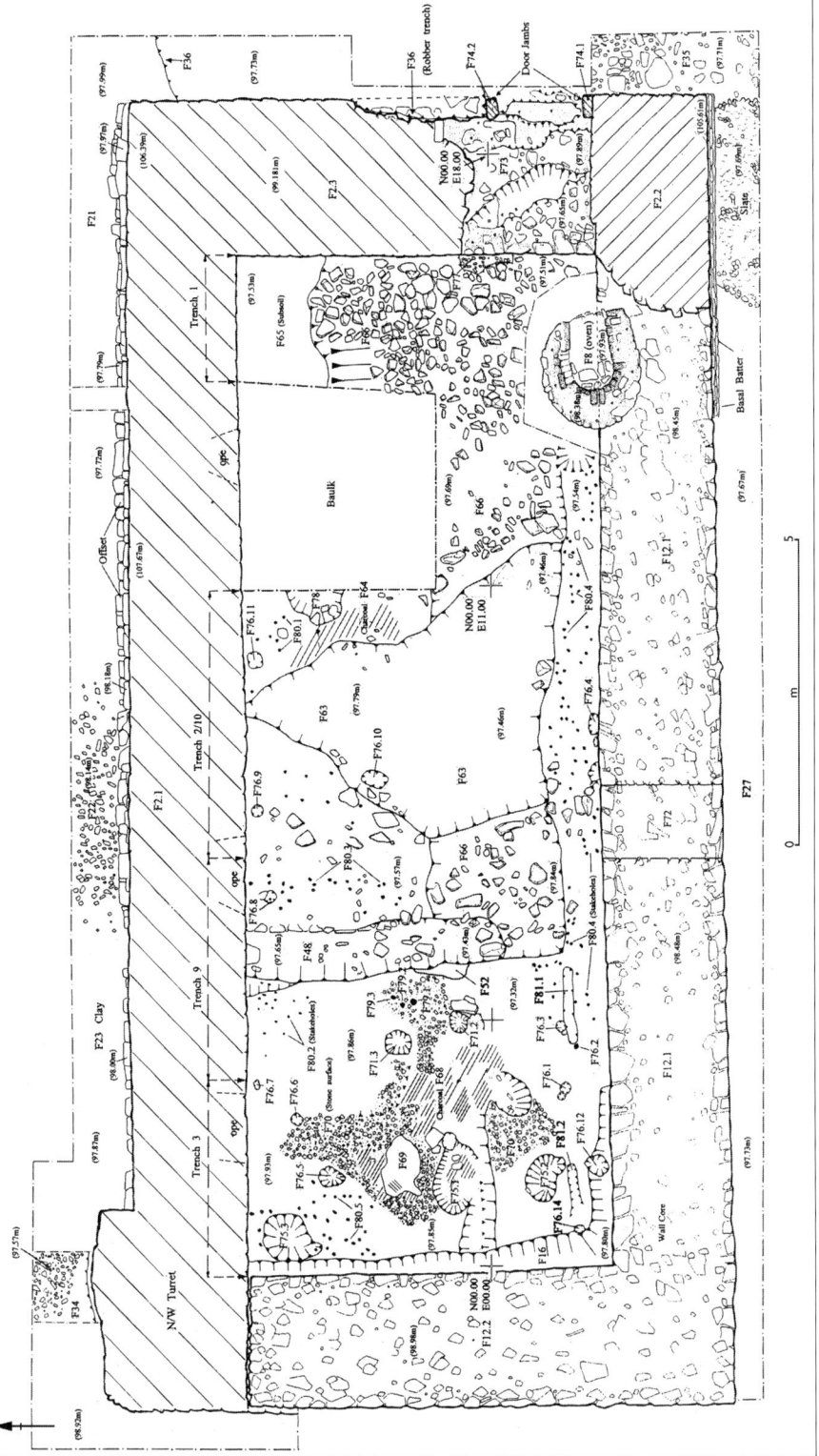

11 Excavation Level 1–5

mural staircase passageway, with segmented archways, when the staircase met the ground floor and first floor level. The staircase originally led into the vault *via* a passageway but this was broken through for the new doorway in Construction Phase 2 (plate 3), as the stone jambs of the new door were located during the excavation and these had disturbed the east face of the original wall (figs 10 and 11; plate 8). The southern side of the doorway was refaced and a small rebate still survives at the eastern end, which originally held the door. After the door was inserted it represented the main entrance into the castle, which also led to the first floor level *via* the stairs. There was a small chamber at first floor level, which was directly over the doorway as was suggested by the presence of a wall scar on the top of the stairs, which originally projected southwards.

The south wall The eastern end of the southern wall survives intact and this extends to full height, standing as an isolated stack. This preserves the remains of a large window at first floor level in the south wall, implicit in the remains of straight jamb. This jamb is at least 1.20m in height and is probably related to a window inserted at a later date, as the angle and type differed greatly from the embrasures of the windows in the north wall. Although the south wall was comprehensively rebuilt, the medieval foundations still survived at the eastern end, where the nineteenth-century wall was built directly on top. The original foundations were composed of large uncut lime-stone blocks, which measured on average 0.45m by 0.30m. This wall had an internal offset, which measured 0.10m in width by 0.20m in height and was completely sealed by a layer of redeposited boulder clay.

The rebuilt southern and western wall Both the southern and western walls were rebuilt in the nineteenth century, probably in an attempt to 'restore' the castle outline (fig. 12; plate 11). These walls, built to between 1m and 1.50m in height, are clearly different in type being of dry stone construction using no mortar. The lower levels of the southern wall are medieval in date but some of the new build has medieval mortar attached, as well as traces of wicker-centring suggesting that they came originally from the collapsed barrel vault. The western wall was mostly built anew, cut into a foundation trench but built over the original medieval foundations at the extreme northern end. This wall is slightly narrower in width than the original castle walls.

The collapsed masonry Several hunks of masonry from the collapsed eastern wall still survive on site and these probably fell sometime around 1913. The largest section originally formed the northeast corner of the castle, which contained the staircase and this has been described above. A second large section of masonry lies directly south and this contains the remains of what was originally a passageway, which led to the stairs. A third section of masonry

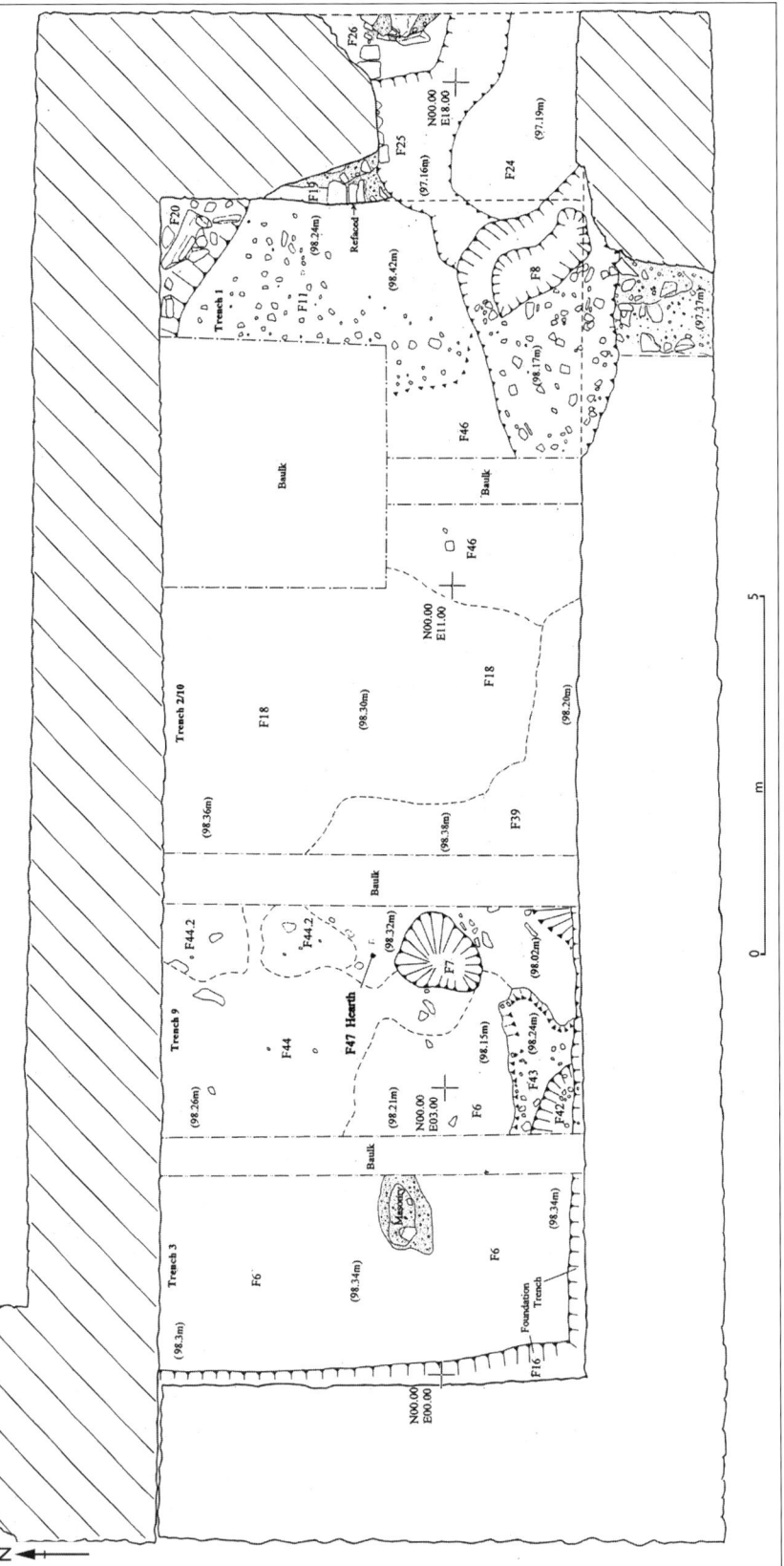

12 Excavation Level 6–11

Plate 11 The site from the east, before excavation

(F3.3) fell eastwards, into the interior of the castle and this appears to represent the remains of a small granite machicoulis or projecting 'murder hole'. These were usually positioned over the doorway but the Du Noyer drawings suggest that this one was positioned on the south side of the service tower.

DISCUSSION OF HALL-HOUSE TYPES

Introduction Kindlestown Castle can be identified as a 'hall-house', a type of castle first noted in England and represented by a stone hall, usually oblong in shape, which often had an adjoining chamber or solar. The main living space or hall was usually at first floor level and this was sometimes divided in two (O'Callaghan 1980–1, 22). This type first appears in Ireland in the early thirteenth century where they represented domestic residences with strong military capabilities. They appear as a specific type and can be recognised by various characteristics that they share. As with their English counterparts, they are usually rectangular in plan with proportions of two to one (although sometimes squat in plan; see Witches Castle, Co. Galway, fig. 94 in McNeill 1997, 148) and are normally two storeys high, with an entrance at first floor level (fig. 12). Access to the castle was *via* a wooden stairs, traces of which can sometimes be seen in the external façade of the castle in the form of beam slots. The first floor formed the main living area or hall and access to the lower level was often by an internal wooden stairs. As noted, hall-houses were dwellings, which had military features, both in their general 'castle' appearance and in their actual defensive elements, represented by solid stone walls, narrow defensive slit windows at ground floor level, as well as an entrance at first floor level. The upper levels invariably have thinner walls and larger windows, reflecting the domestic use of this part of the building. Thus the hall-house was primarily a domestic dwelling, housing a family rather than a military garrison. Although many of the surviving hall-houses are now in isolated positions with little evidence of stone or earthwork enclosing features, it is clear that they originally functioned as the medieval equivalent of the 'big house' forming the centrepiece of a domestic agricultural complex. These would have included ancillary buildings such as barns, stores, stables, etc.

H.T. Knox commented on this type of thirteenth-century castle in Ireland as early as 1909 and concluded that these structures were a distinctive early type whose distribution indicated a westerly concentration in Ireland. Leask also noted the 'oblong type', although he did not group them together as a specific type (Leask 1941, 101). McNeill discusses the hall-house in his recent book, under 'lesser stone castles', in which he examines their place within the castle-building sequence and lists eight examples out of a total of thirteen, which can probably be dated to before 1350 (McNeill 1997, 148–52). More recently, the Archaeological Survey of Dúchas: the Heritage Service, has identified more examples of this type during extensive fieldwork, and this has produced detailed information on distribution and type. Sweetman has since published the results of some of this additional information in his book on castles, where he devotes an entire chapter to the subject (Sweetman 1999, 89–104). While the westerly concentration identified by Knox is acknowledged, Sweetman provides additional examples in the east of the country, such as Delvin, Co. Meath and Kindlestown. Small clusters can also be identified in north Tipperary, Galway, Mayo and Limerick (ibid. 1999, 89; 1998, 13).

The military element was evidently very important in this new castle type and this is emphasised in their distribution pattern. The castles are concentrated along the west side of Ireland, in frontier country, which was still being conquered and settled in the mid-thirteenth century. It is certainly striking that there are few of these hall-houses in the central and eastern side of the country where the Anglo-Norman settlement was heaviest by this date. In addition, the examples that are found in the eastern side appear to be later in date, a symptom perhaps of the changing political climate, which saw rebellion in the Leinster mountains in the late thirteenth century. This appears to have caused a mini-revival of the hall-house type of which Kindlestown Castle was one.

Halls, moated sites, tower-houses, and seventeenth century halls The hall-house type can be compared directly to and probably originated from the halls that are often found as part of a castle complex, such as those at Trim, Co. Meath and Adare, Co. Limerick. This type of hall was also a 'compromise building', which balanced domestic considerations with real military needs. These buildings were usually rectangular in plan, often only two storeys high and they served a similar function, providing a place where people could gather and eat. However, these halls lay within the defensive enclosures, with less emphasis of the military capabilities of the building itself. The main difference between them and the hall-house was that the hall-house was the primary defensive element, which did not necessarily rely on outer defences. The other main difference was in the individual commissioning and building the castles; hall-houses appear to have been built by gentry as opposed to aristocrats, who are less likely to have left a trace in the documentary sources. This was certainly the case at Ballynacourty Court and Shrule in Galway, where the castles were built on land within the demesne lands of the de Burghs although the de Burghs are not recorded as residing there (McNeill 1997, 152). The use of the moat around Kindlestown is also significant as it reinforces Kindlestown as a hybrid type, straddling not only the hall-house typology but also a second type of site, the moated site, which emerges in Ireland in the late thirteenth/early fourteenth century. This type of site usually consists of a raised rectangular or square platform, surrounded by a water-filled moat and external (and sometimes internal) earthen bank. These residences were usually occupied by the colonial gentry and are found mostly in the southeast of Ireland (Barry 1997). In Wicklow, a variation of this type is noted, which combines the stone elements of a castle and water-filled moat, for example, Talbotstown, west Wicklow, which is stone-revetted with corner towers and Ballynagran at Glenealy, which has a strong gate-house on a platform 40m square (Simpson 1994a, 218). It is also of note that the strong castle at Rathdown was also on a platform, 50m square, which was also surrounded by a moat (ibid.).

The late date of Kindlestown is also interesting as it straddles the classic primary castle phase of the late twelfth/thirteenth century and the subsequent tower-house phase. Tower-houses were common in fifteenth- and sixteenth-century Ireland and can be best defined as fortified stone dwellings, often three to four storeys in height, which contain vaulted chambers, towers, mural passages and parapets. They are sometimes within a walled bawn or precinct, which may or may not have had protective towers or turrets on the angles. The use of the barrel vault at Kindlestown as a primary feature and a machicoulis attests to its lateness in the hall-house sequence but these are features that can be identified in the tower-house sequence. The mural staircase, with a half turn rather than a spiral arrangement, occupies a similar position while the service tower at the eastern end probably owes more in origin to the ecclesiastical belfry/residential towers of the fourteenth century than to any other form of architecture. The belfry tower in Carlingford, although it can be dated to the fifteenth century, is very similar in type to the upper façade (Phase 2) of Kindlestown, as it has a similar stringcourse and parapet wall. It is also interesting that the upper front façade of Kindlestown is very similar to Archbold's Castle in Dalkey, which can also be dated to the fifteenth century. Sweetman lays emphasis on the role that the hall-house played in the development of the tower-house type, suggesting that most of the 'tower-houses' which have been dated to the fourteenth century can be identified as hall-houses not tower-houses (Sweetman 1999, 103).

It is also interesting to note that a similar type of 'compromise building' emerges in the seventeenth century when additional 'halls' were added onto the side of tower-houses, increasing their domestic capacity and emulating, in some respects, the hall-house. The attached hall formed the primary residence at a time of relative peace in the first half of the seventeenth century but the military capacity was retained in the form of the tower-house. These additions were usually no more than two to three storeys in height and were of stone or earth and timber, the latter of which left little trace in the ground. Loeber identifies two such examples in Wexford, at Adamstone and Ballybrennan, both of which are described as barns suggesting that they were made of earth and timber (Loeber 1988–9, 68–9).

Parallels for Kindlestown Castle Kindlestown Castle fits into the classic hall-house type, the earliest phase of which probably dated to the late thirteenth/early fourteenth century while the upper storey is later in date (probably before 1377, when the castle as taken by the O'Byrnes). The castle is rectangular in shape in proportions of 2 to 1 but is a relatively large example, measuring externally 21m by 9.80m (average 11m by 6m; see McNeill 1997, 150 for table). The castle is vaulted at ground floor and was probably intended to have a first floor entrance, but, during the break in construction, a ground door was inserted into the eastern service tower. There is a projecting turret on the northwest angle and a service tower at the eastern end, which contained the half turn staircase. Kindlestown can be compared to many of the examples of hall-houses that have now been identified in Ireland. Galway has at least twelve hall-houses, many of which share similar characteristics with Kindlestown, for example, Annaghkeen Castle, which was built before 1350, but is similar in plan, measuring 11m long by 7.5m wide. It has a similar projecting turret (which has been added) but also has an intra-mural staircase (see McNeill 1991, 150; Sweetman 1999, 92). Kindlestown can also be compared directly to Moylough Castle in Galway, which is three storeys in height, the upper storey of which has been added. This castle also has an intra-mural staircase, which has half turn stairs, very similar to the stairs at Kindlestown. The windows are also very similar in size and shape (McNeill 1999, 91). Ballisnihiney, Co. Galway can also be compared directly to Kindlestown as it is one of the few castles that has a vault at ground floor level, which is original to the building (McNeill 1997, 149). This vault, however, was wicker- rather than plank-centred, unlike the vault at Kindlestown Castle.

There are approximately five hall-houses in Co. Tipperary, all of which were two storeys high with first floor entrances (Sweetman 1998, 15). Ballylusky is similar in appearance to Kindlestown as is Closhaskin, which had almost identical segmented-arched windows, which are also plank-centred (ibid. 1999, 94–5). There is also a significant concentration of hall-houses in Mayo, which suggests that some of the castles can be dated to the mid-thirteenth century, as the settlement of Connacht did not get underway until after 1230, notwithstanding earlier military campaigns. The Mayo examples are all typical hall-houses and have first floor entrance, which led directly into first floor halls, lit by defensive rectangular slit windows. The vault in Ballisnahyny, like Kindlestown, is original to the building perhaps suggestive of a slightly later date but this vault provides the roof of the first floor rather than the ground floor and so is different in type (Sweetman 1999, 95). In Co. Kerry, Ballycarbery hall-house dates to the late medieval period and this, like Kindlestown, also has a large narrow service tower at one end (ibid., 97). Although this is later in date than the service tower in Kindlestown, it does represent a similar type of device, which was used to house the staircases and probably contained small mural chambers. Dunmore, Co. Meath, which is probably of similar date to Kindlestown, also has a service tower, as well as rounded angle towers. This Castle is very similar in type to Delvin, Co. Westmeath (Sweetman 1999, 95). Rathlumney Castle in Co. Wexford bears the closest resemblance to Kindlestown Castle and the Prendergast family held this in the early thirteenth century. This building is rectangular in shape and is two storeys in height, with a garderobe chute in the northeast angle. The castle is unusual as it has an entrance and vault at ground floor level, the latter of which rises the full height of the building (ibid., 96). The windows are also round-headed segmented-headed, at least one of which was constructed using plank-centring as at Kindlestown. Rathlumney also had no evidence of a chimney and must have had a hearth in the centre of the hall (O'Callaghan 1980–1, 3–5). Kindlestown Castle may not have had a chimney either.

Closer to home, Oldcourt Castle in Bray, Co. Wicklow probably represents the remains of a medieval hall-house, which has been almost totally destroyed. All that survives is the narrow service tower, which was probably very similar in type to Kindlestown (see fig. 10 in Sweetman 1999, 103). It is also of note that the Archbolds held Oldcourt as part of the manor of Bray and may have built the castle there. The enclosing earthwork around Kindlestown Castle can probably be related to the political climate of the area in the fourteenth century as the use of a water-filled moat as a defensive earthwork became increasingly popular in the north Wicklow/south Dublin area at this time (Simpson 1994a, 218). As stated earlier, Rathdown Castle, to the northeast of

Kindlestown, stood within a large moated site, as did the castle at Ballinagran in Glenealy (ibid.). While many hall-houses are not associated with earthworks, some have been identified which did form part of a larger complex (Sweetman 1999, 89). These include Tomdeely in Limerick, which is very similar to Kindlestown and Park Castle in Galway. The latter stood within a moated site, suggesting that this castle could also be dated to the late thirteenth/early fourteenth century (ibid. 1999, 93).

THE EXCAVATION

Level 1=L13th/E14th century; **Level 2**=14th century; **Level 3**=15th/16th century; **Level 4**=E/M 17th century; **Level 5**=M17th century; **Level 6**=L17th/E18 century; **Level 7**=M18th century; **Level 8**=18/E/M19th century; **Level 9**=M/L19 century; **Level 10**=L19/E20 century.

Introduction The archaeological investigations at Kindlestown Castle consisted of the complete excavation of the interior of the castle and a 1m-wide trench around the exterior (figs 11 and 12). Initially, a total of three trenches, 3m in width (Trenches 1–3, from east to west) were excavated inside the castle and these formed the basis of the archaeological assessment carried out between 10 September and 5 October 2001. The continuous trench around the exterior of the castle also formed part of the assessment and this was divided into trench sections (Trenches 4, 5, 6, 7 and 8). On 8 October 2001 the assessment was extended to include the two areas in between the trenches and these were numbered Trenches 10 and 9, from east to west.

LEVEL 1 (LATE 13TH/EARLY 14TH CENTURY): PHASE 1

The western end of the castle: Trench 3/9 The excavation revealed that the medieval deposits within the castle were severely truncated and only a small section, 5m in width, survived at the western end (Trench 3; fig. 11). The castle itself was built directly on boulder clay, F65, which was hard yellow/orange clay, located less than 1m from the ground level. This boulder clay produced four sherds of medieval pottery, one of which could be linked with a sherd from a later context, F46 (Level 8), indicating that the deposits were very disturbed. A layer of redeposited boulder clay, F14, was laid on the surface at the western end of the castle and this abutted and sealed the foundations of the northern wall, F2.1. This clay surface was bright yellow in colour and contained a small area of stone mettling, F14.1, in the northeast corner, which measured approximately 2m square. The mettling, composed of small chips of limestone, evidently formed part of a floor although this was very truncated.

The stone surface A more defined rough mettled surface, F70, was located in the central area at the western end, also set into the boulder clay (Trenches 3 and 9). This was quite extensive in size, measuring roughly 4.40m east–west by approximately 4m in width. It was composed of small irregular-sized pebbles measuring, on average, 30mm in diameter, which were set very closely together. This surface appears to have represented one of the earliest floor levels within the castle.

The pit, F13 Additional activity was suggested by the remains of a shallow pit, F13, in the northwest corner of the castle, which measured 0.80m north–south by 0.60m wide and was 0.10m in depth. The sides were gently sloping and the base was flat, filled with pure brown sticky clay. The remains of a tree-bowl (F75.3) were identified within the pit and this had caused substantial damage. A series of twenty-nine post-holes (F80.5) were ringed around the pit and these were clearly related, although some extended on a north–south orientation. The post-holes measured between 80mm and 0.15m in diameter and all were filled with similar grey silt. They may have represented some sort of superstructure associated with the pit.

The hearth, F69 A substantial hearth F69 was located centrally placed at the western end of the castle, directly on top of the mettled surface F70. This was evidently the focus of activity at this end of the castle, surviving as an oval spread of charcoal and white ash, which measured 0.65m east–west by 0.35m wide and was not contained in any way. The primary deposit consisted of layers of pure charcoal, 20mm in depth, which were sealed by an off-white ash deposit, 10mm in depth. The cobbled surface, F70, and boulder clay beneath were fire-reddened, indicative of *in situ* burning and the hearth was evidently used more than once, as there were large spreads of associated ash and charcoal deposits, F68, which extended over a large area measuring 2.60m north–south by 2.20m wide. These deposits, between 10mm and 40mm in depth, included banded lenses of fire-reddened clay, burnt charcoal and ash. Analysis of the fill of the hearth suggested that it was a domestic food hearth, probably a roasting pit, which contained oats, wheat and barley. A large number of peas and beans were also located (see report on plant remains below). A second fire or hearth site was identified to the east (in Trench 9), suggested by the presence of a black burnt deposit, F52, which straddled Trenches 3 and 9 (plate 31). This deposit overlaid boulder clay directly and probably originally formed part of the charcoal and ash F68 spread. The F52 deposit measured 0.82m north–south by 0.62m in width and was, on average, 50mm in depth. It was composed of two bands of almost pure charcoal within a deposit of fine gravel and sand, which was light grey in colour. The upper band of charcoal measured 10mm in depth while the lower band measured 30mm in depth. A second floor of redeposited boulder clay F67 was identified in the central area of the castle (Trench 9) and this was

Plate 12 The hearth F64

stratigraphically equivalent to F14 clay at the western end (Trench 3). The floor F67 consisted of layers of redeposited yellow boulder clay, 0.20m in depth, which also included lenses of dark brown organic material. This floor also contained large charcoal flecks, some as large as 20mm in diameter, as well as one sherd of Dublin-type pottery. The most interesting find, however, was a coin of Edward I (F67.4), which was dated to between 1279 and 1302. A second coin of a similar date was also found but in a later disturbed context (F6). A third hearth site was suggested by a spread of fire-reddened clay, F64, in the central area (plate 12) and this measured at least 1.75m east-west by at least 1.40m in width, extending beyond the limit of excavation. The clay was fire-reddened to a depth of 30mm and was sealed by a thin layer of charcoal, 10mm in depth. It was truncated on the western side by the later F63 gully (see below).

The eastern end of the castle: the cobbled surface F77 As stated earlier few medieval deposits survived at the eastern end of the castle as this area was badly truncated by the later gully F66 and cut F63 (fig. 11; see below). A small patch of rough cobbling F77, that abutted the base of the east wall (F2.2), is probably all that remains of a primary stone surface. This surviving section measured 0.80m north-south by 0.22m wide and was composed of rough stones measuring, on average, 60mm in diameter and set closely together.

Discussion of Phase 1

Unfortunately, very little stratigraphy survived inside the barrel vault, which appears to have been continuously in use up until the seventeenth century at least. The mettled surface F70 is all that remains of an original floor surface at the western end of the castle but this was difficult to relate to the standing castle as the surface was not continuous and was confined to the central area of the barrel vault; thus it did not extend over as far as any of the walls of the castle. The clay deposit F67 produced one coin (F67.4) of Edward I, dated to between 1279 and 1302, and this fits into the general dating sequence of the castle. The position of the hearth and the associated deposits F68 on the stone floor may suggest that the surface was laid deliberately for the hearth, which evidently had more than one firing, as the deposits were banded. Analysis of the hearth material suggests that it was domestic in nature as it contained oats, wheat and barley, as well as peas and beans. The various other hearths spread around this end of the castle are also indicative of continual activity, although none of these hearths were permanent. The location of the hearth within the barrel vault is something of a puzzle as there is no known outlet for the smoke, although presumably the segmented windows may have functioned as crude chimneys. Also of note is the fact that there was no formal setting around the hearth, perhaps suggesting that it was temporary even though it did have more than one firing. Although excessive smoke was part of medieval life, it is possible that the hearth relates to a pre-vault phase, in use perhaps when the castle was being constructed. The builders may have cleared down to the boulder clay and then laid a rough surface from which to work. The presence of the redeposited boulder clay, F14, which was cut by the post-holes, probably represents part of this early activity. The cobbled surface, F77, at the eastern end of the castle probably represents a small section of the main floor of the castle but this was very rough in type. Only a small section survived and this was impossible to date, although the location of the surface indicates that it was medieval in date. In addition, the surface was truncated by the later activity, which could be dated to the seventeenth century

LEVEL I (LATE 13TH/EARLY 14TH CENTURY): PHASE 2

The internal division of the barrel vault The western end of the barrel-vault may have been divided in two or supported internally by two large post-holes, F71.1 and 2, which were positioned midway between the north and south wall (figs 11 and 13; plate 13). F71.1 lay at the western end, 2.10m from the west wall (to centre point of post-hole) and this measured 0.25m in diameter by 0.28m in depth, cut through the mettled surface, F70. The post-hole was filled with homogenous grey clay, which had occasional charcoal fleck and small stones. The remains of stone packing lay on the northern side

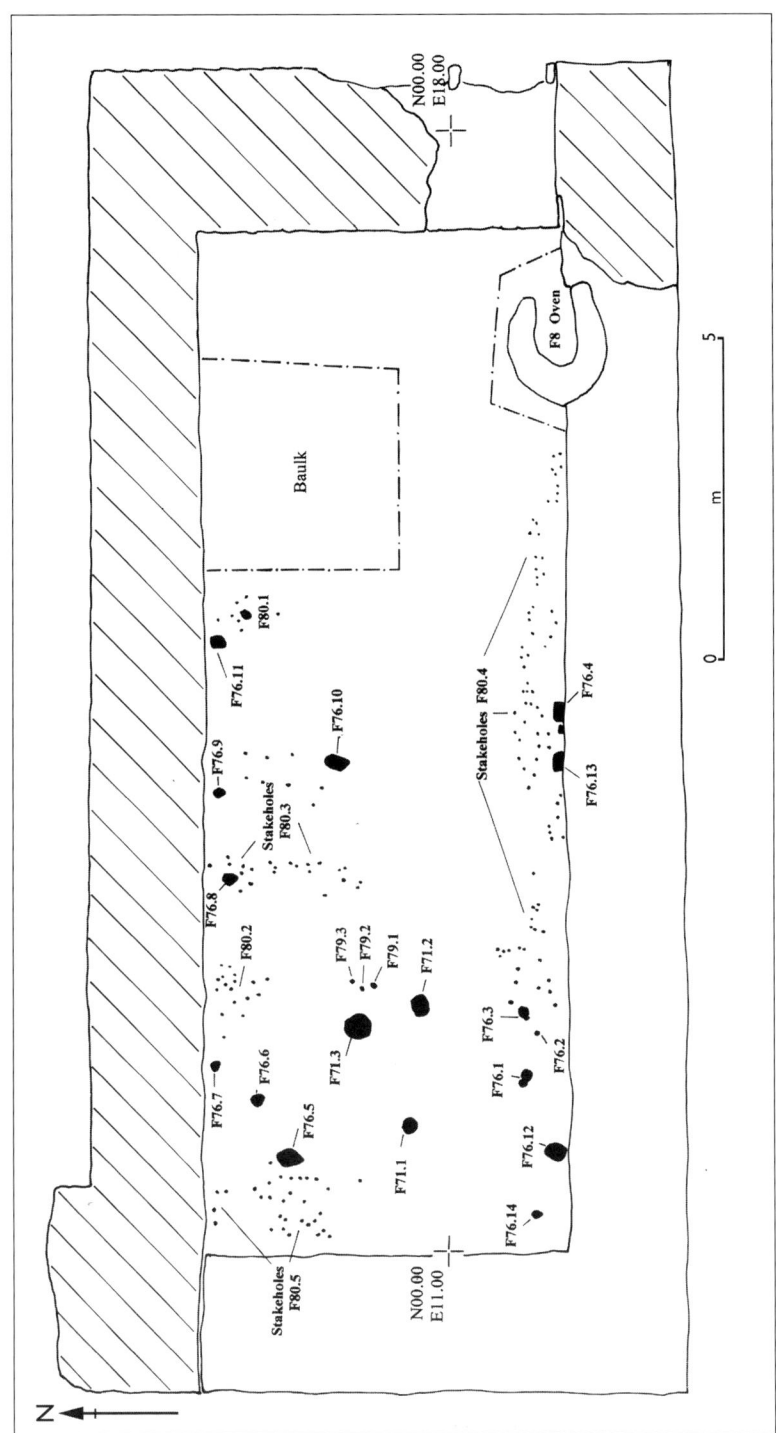

13 Plan of post-holes

F71.2

F71.1

Plate 13 The postholes
F71.1 and 2

comprised of several stones, the largest of which measured 0.37m east–west by 0.27m wide. The second large post, F71.2, lay 2m to the east and this measured 0.34m in diameter by 0.24m in depth, also filled with grey silt. This post-hole also had the remains of packing stones on the southeast side, one of which measured 0.43m long by 0.24m wide by 60mm in depth. It was located within a linear depression, F75.1, which measured approximately 1.37m east–west by 0.60m wide and was 0.25m in depth, filled with dark grey clay, which contained lenses of burnt material and charcoal, as well as fire-reddened clay. The depression was very irregular in shape and may have represented the remains of a later tree-bowl. A third large post-hole, F71.3, was slightly later in date as this post-dated the hearth F69. It lay north of post-hole F71.2 and measured 0.36m in diameter by 0.15m in depth, filled with a mix of clay and silt and numerous charcoal fragments. The function of this post is not clear although it was clearly structural in nature. It may have represented a replacement for either of the large posts F71.1 or F71.2.

Additional post-holes Three additional posts were identified in a cluster to the east, F79.1, 2 and 3, and these may have been related to the F71.3 post. F79.1 measured between 90mm and 0.10m in diameter and were filled with similar grey clay. A large number of additional post-holes were located cut into the boulder clay, all filled with similar grey clay. Although few patterns could be established, a line of large four posts (from west to east F76.7, F76.8, F76.9 and F76.11) could be identified along the inside of the northern wall, measuring between 0.19m and 0.30m in diameter and filled with grey clay. A fifth post, F76.6, to the south may have been associated with this group and this was 0.25m in diameter by 0.25m in depth. At least three large posts (F76.12, F76.13 and F76.4) were also identified along the southern wall, measuring between 0.15m and 0.40m in diameter and all filled with grey clay. These were similar in size to the scatter of large posts (F76.7, F76.1, F76.3 and F6.7), which were between 0.15m and 0.23m in diameter.

Other pits and depressions Several other depressions and pits were also noted at this level (fig. 11). F75.2 lay 1.05m to the south of the depression F75.1 and this measured 0.55m in diameter by 0.35m in depth, filled with grey clay with charcoal fleck. F75.3 represented the remains of a large tree-bowl in the northwest corner of the castle and this was very irregular in shape, cut through the pit F13 (see above). It measured 0.77m east-west by 0.60m wide and was 0.20m in depth, filled with a loose grey clay. F78 also represented a pit (Trench 2) cut into the boulder clay and this was located at the eastern end of the castle, near the hunk masonry that contained the machicoulis (F3.3). This measured 0.80m north-south by 0.60m wide by 0.25m in depth and was filled with grey sticky clay with charcoal fleck. A series of stones, which measured, on average, between 0.15m and 0.25m in diameter, were loosely piled up together. Two linear depressions may represent the remains of a slot trench, orientated east-west, at the western end of the castle. F81.1, the western slot, measured 0.80m long by 0.20m in width by 0.10m in depth, filled with grey clay. F81.2 lay to the east on the same alignment and possibly formed part of the same feature. This measured 1.20m long by 0.15m wide and was 0.12m in depth, also filled with grey clay. Both features were very shallow, suggesting that only the very lowest level survives *in situ*. However, they may represent the remains of a temporary wall slot or division.

Discussion of Phase 2

The large number of post-holes located within the western end of the castle is indicative of continual activity inside the barrel vault. Most of the post-holes can probably be dated to Phase 2 as many were cut through the mettled surface, F70, although others were cut through the boulder clay and their stratigraphic relationship is unclear. The size of some of the post-holes suggests that these were relatively flimsy posts, perhaps associated with storage racks, or lightweight internal divisions. However, some of the post-holes were very large (see below) suggesting some sort of large-scale activity. The positioning of the F71.1 and F71.2 was very striking, as they were almost centrally placed along the line of the barrel vault. The size of the posts indicates that they were structural in nature, the packing stones evidently supporting a large post. They may have represented an attempt to support the barrel vault although it is not clear why this would be necessary. The post-hole F76.10m was possibly associated originally with this arrangement but was truncated by the later gully F63. A series of large post-holes could also be identified along the north (F76.7, F76.9, F76.11) and south wall of the castle (F76.12, F76.2, F76.3 and F76. 4) and these may have represented part of this superstructure.

LEVEL 2 (14th CENTURY)

The east wall of the castle F2.2 The excavation revealed the foundations of the east wall of the castle and this established that the wall originally continued across the line of the later doorway (fig. 11; plate 8). However, the exposed base of the wall represented the very lower foundations and this stood only two courses in height, composed of small rough stones, measuring on average, 0.20m by 0.15m (fig. 11). In addition, this foundation, while containing mortar, was not as strongly mortared as the upstanding portion of the wall. The western facing of the wall was intact but the eastern face was disturbed by the insertion of the new doorway. The lower course extended beneath the south face of the entrance passageway (in the F2.2 wall), while the upper course abutted it directly. Thus the wall was originally bonded into the southern end of the east wall (F2.2).

The doorway F74 A set of stone doorjambs, F74.1 and F74.2, was identified in the east face of the service tower and this represented the new doorway at ground floor level (figs 10 and 11; plate 14). The doorjambs comprised two granite stones, which were set 1.45m apart, broken into the east wall of the castle. The northern jamb, F74. 1, measured 0.38m east-west by 0.20m wide by 0.18m in depth while the south jamb F74.2 measured 0.43m east-west by 0.20m wide by 0.18m in depth. The jambs were set deep into the foundations of the east wall and this was evidently to increase the height of the doorway, which was constricted by the existing barrel vault. The insertion of the jambs destroyed the eastern face of the main wall. A rough mortared mass of masonry, F73.2, was dumped down between both jambs at the same level, evidently for some sort of foundation and this measured 1.30m north-south by 0.60m wide by 0.25m in depth. The mass was of hard white mortar with irregular limestone of various sizes, some as large as 0.30m by 0.20m. This lump of masonry had no facing and possibly represented part of the demolished section of the east wall (service tower).

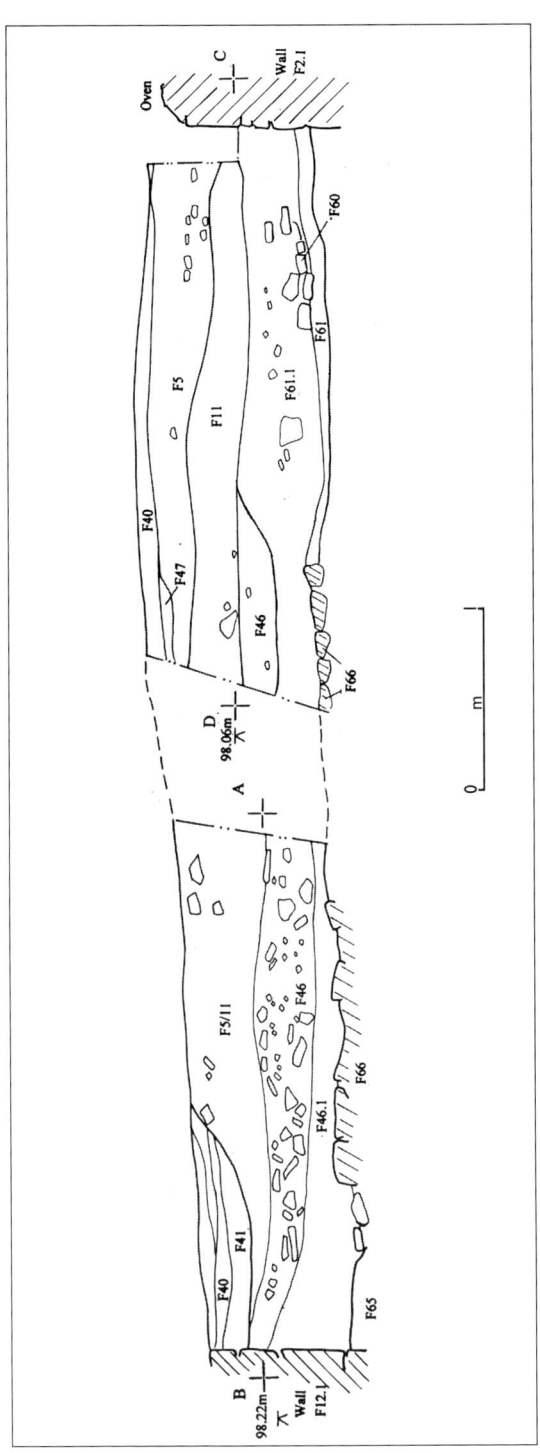

14 Section A–B and C–D

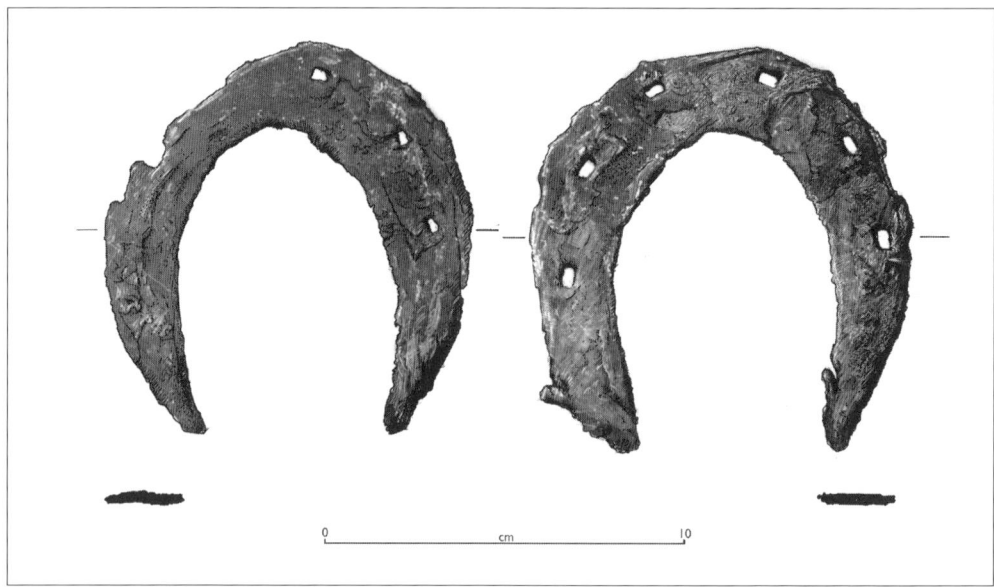

15 Medieval horseshoes, 2.1.1 and 2.1.2

Plate 14 The door-jambs F74.1 and 2

The surface F73 The remains of a new stone surface, F73, could be related to the doorway but this only survived as a small section measuring 1.73m north-south by 0.60m wide by 0.20m in depth (50mm above the jambs) (fig. 11). It was set into a clay deposit, 0.20m in depth, which sealed the demolished foundation of the east wall. This clay, F73.1, was yellow in colour and contained mortar flecks and fragments of limestone, which extended into the crevices of the south jamb of the passageway. The stones were generally irregular in shape at the southern end averaging 0.10m by 20mm and set on edge, abutting the south face of the entrance passageway. In the central area the stones are larger in size measuring between 0.30m by 0.22m and 0.10m by 0.10m. Most importantly, the surface abutted the broken-through section of the east wall (F2.2) suggesting that it was broken through prior to the insertion of the surface. The surface also abutted the southern face of the entrance passageway, which continued down for a further 0.26m in depth.

The slate deposit F29 A substantial deposit of slate chippings, F29, was found at the base of the southern wall, at the eastern end, in the trench that extended around the exterior of the castle (fig. 11). This deposit was composed of small numerous purple chips of slate, 20mm thick, in a dense deposit which was 80mm in depth. The deposit was scattered directly on the boulder clay and appears to have represented the residue of an original slate roof. The slate probably represents broken chips of slate, which were created during the construction of the roof. The deposit was similar in type to the F45 slate surface, which was reused in the post-medieval period (see below). The slate deposits F29 and F45 differed from the red heavy slate, which was found elsewhere in the castle, and as none of these had perforations or holes they were probably not roofing slate. To the north a deposit of large stones F35 was noted, lying on the boulder clay, at the northern end of Trench 7. They appeared to be natural boulders placed at the base of the castle but with no evidence of mortar. A clay deposit F37 sealed the stones (see below).

The garderobe deposits The excavation at the base of the northwest turret, on the northern (external) side revealed a pit feature F34, which probably represents a channel designed to catch the outfall from the garderobe chutes (fig. 11). This measured at least 1.20 east-west by 1m wide and was 0.40m in depth, cut directly into boulder clay, F33. The lower fill, F32.2, was medieval in date and this consisted of a light yellow/brown clay deposit, which contained inclusions of stone and organic material (see report on plant remains). Other inclusions included medieval pottery, charcoal, bone and metal, as well as one land snail shell. The remains of a second cut, F31.1, were also identified cutting through the upper levels of the garderobe chute, F34, and this represented a much later robber trench, excavated when the facing stones were robbed out from around the base of the castle. This cut was filled with loose rubble deposits, F31, which contained limestone fragments, mortar and stone.

Discussion of Level 2

The medieval deposits in the central area of the castle were almost completely destroyed in the post-medieval period by the gully, F66 (Level 4; E/M seventeenth century). However, the excavations at the eastern end of the castle did locate the original foundation of the eastern wall, which was removed when the doorway was inserted in Construction Phase 2 (fig. 10). The new doorway disturbed the eastern face of the wall and extended almost to foundation level, presumably to create a higher opening (2.20m in height), as the barrel vault restricted the height in this location. This new doorway was broken into an already existing mural passage, which was orientated north–south and housed the staircase, from first floor to barrel vault (as it was originally intended to have the doorway at first floor level). A new stone surface, F77, was also inserted positioned only 50mm above the level of the jambs. This, however, was badly truncated by later activity. The deposit of slate, F29, is also interesting as it was dumped directly over boulder clay, suggesting that it can be related directly to the construction of the castle, presumably when the roof was being put on. The deposit also suggests that the entire area was cleared of sod down onto the boulder clay during the construction phase. The gully located at the base of the northwest turret probably originally carried waste from the garderobe chutes into the surrounding moat, acting as a medieval sewerage system. The outfall presumably dripped down the wall and into the gully, thus eventually exiting into the moat. A thin lens of organic material was retrieved from this channel and this was analysed for plant remains (F32.2). The analysis found the remains of two seeds, one badly degraded cereal grain and a well-preserved oat grain (see report below). Both presumably originated in faecal material that passed through one of the garderobe chutes.

LEVEL 3 (15th/16th CENTURY)

The western end: Trenches 3 and 9 The cobbled surface, F70, and the spreads of burning, F68 and F52 (associated with the hearth F69), were sealed by a series of deposits, which can be dated to the fifteenth and sixteenth centuries. A spread of clay F50 was identified at the western end of the castle, which showed evidence of being burnt and which sealed the F52 burnt deposit beneath. This dump lay at the southern end of Trench 9 and was one of a series of clay deposits containing burnt clay material in this location (see F43 below). The spread measured 3m north–south and 1.60m wide and contained distinctive lumps of fire-reddened clay. These were probably derived from internal partitions within the castle, which would have been built of clay, held between upright posts and supported on either side by timber lathes (pers. comm., John Allen). The impression of some of the lathes is clearly visible in the clay fragments but there was evidently a fire within the castle, which burnt the partition and fired the clay, as the fragments are fire-reddened and scorched in some instances. These fragments are crude and contained vegetation and small pebbles (20mm) as a binder. The F50 spread was between 60mm and 0.20m in depth and consisted of mixed friable clay, which was brown in colour and contained large inclusions of charcoal, measuring, on average, 30mm in diameter.

Finds from this deposit included an iron key, as well as fragments of lead cames, presumably from leaded windows. This deposit also produced some animal bone and some stone but no ceramic material. The iron key is particularly important as it can be dated by comparison to the fifteenth century and provides a rough date for the deposit. It has a kidney-shaped bow and a well-preserved bit, which has three ward cuts (Anon. 1940, 141). The key is very similar in type to an iron key found during the excavations at Patrick Street, Dublin, which was dated to the fifteenth century (Walsh 1997, 138). The deposit F50 was sealed by F51 at the northern end and this consisted of a second deposit of clay, which was probably laid deliberately, within the sequence of clay deposition. This clay was light yellow in colour with few inclusions, apart from some large irregular-shaped stones and a lens of pure clay. There were occasional fragments of the burnt partitions, as well as lumps of charcoal and some slate. A sherd of Dublin-type pottery and an iron knife were found here, the latter having a well-preserved polished ivory handle. A small fragment of leather still survives between the blade and a handle, and this may represent the remains of a leather sheath. Similar knives have been found in Waterford and Temple Bar West, Dublin in contexts which date from the eleventh to the thirteenth century (Hurley et al. 1993, 454).

Discussion of Level 3
The findings from this level indicate that the vault had at least two clay floors and that clay and timber partition walls were in use somewhere in the castle, either in the vault or the main hall. These partition walls were evidently burnt and demolished, and the remains dumped in the vault to create a clay floor. This level also produced evidence of lead, probably derived from casement windows inserted into widened window-opes.

LEVEL 4 (EARLY TO MID-17th CENTURY)

The eastern end: Trenches 1, 10 and 2. The gully, F66 The eastern end of the castle was consistently in use throughout the post-medieval period, and a result the stratigraphy was dominated by a series of clay flooring deposits in this area. However, a major east-west gully, F66, was dug through the original castle deposits at this end sometime in the seventeenth century and backfilled with stones (fig. 11; plate 15). This gully was irregular in shape and measured

Plate 15 The infilled gully F66

14.20m east-west by between 2.20m (west) and 4.60m (east) in width and was at least 0.30m in depth, extending as far west as Trench 10. It was excavated through a deposit of large rounded boulders (between 0.30m and 0.40m in diameter), which appeared to represent a natural geological feature. The excavated trench or gully was then infilled with a deposit of loose limestone, which was within a layer of brown clay deposit, F66.1, between 0.10m and 0.20m in depth (at the southern end). The infilling of the gully with stone probably suggests it was for drainage purposes, which pre-dated the demolition of the barrel vault (as none of the limestone fragments within the fill could be identified as original barrel vault material). The finds included seventeenth-century pottery (Frechen, North Devon gravel free, a sherd of a Anglo-Dutch plate (*c.*1640)), one sherd of medieval pottery, flint, a knife blade, a nail and another iron object, and a badly fragmented sherd of glass. The bowl of a flat-heeled clay pipe, which can be dated to 1600–20 (pers comm., John Allen) was also found. Three sherds of glazed red earthenware were dated to the late seventeenth century from the very upper level. A substantial deposit of clay, F61 and F61.1, sealed the gully, and this deposit was between 0.10m and 0.30m in depth (plate 15). The clay was yellow in colour and was generally pure in type. It contained a few inclusions of gravel and was very similar to the other clay deposits at this end (F11 and F3). The upper deposit, F6.1.1, was very extensive in depth and was very similar in type to the F11 clay, which overlay it directly (see below).

Discussion of Phase 4

The function of the substantial gully F66 at the eastern end of the castle is difficult to establish. It was excavated along the line of what appears to have been a natural geological fault line and presumably had some sort of drainage function. It was filled with loose limestone boulders, which were probably designed to act as 'a soak-away' and trap water. None of the boulders had any mortar attached and there were no fragments of the barrel vault within the cut, suggesting that it was excavated when the vault was still in position and before it collapsed.

LEVEL 5 (MID- TO LATE 17th CENTURY)

The drain F48 The remains of a linear feature, F48, were identified in the central area of the castle and this was orientated north-south (fig. 11), measuring 4.90m long by 0.90m wide and between 0.45m and 0.60m in depth. This was probably some sort of soak-away or drain, which bisected the castle. It was cut through the F51 clays layers and was filled at the lower level, with black/grey organic deposit F54.2, which had lenses of charcoal, 10mm in width. The drain was sealed by an upper fill of sticky grey clay, F54.1, which contained stones of assorted sizes (some as large as 0.40m by 0.20m). The stones were haphazardly placed at the base of the trench with a concentration at the southern end (F54.3). This clay also contained lenses of burnt clay and mortar, as well as pebbles and animal bone. Also of note were large lenses of redeposited clay, presumably the underlying clays removed during the excavation of the trench. The linear feature was cut through the natural clays at the northern end (F67) and, at the lower levels, was edged on the eastern side with a series of small rectangular pieces of limestone, measuring, on average, 0.30m by 0.20m. There were also faint traces of stone edging on the western side but these had been partially disturbed. Four large irregular-shaped boulders, measuring 0.40m by 0.30m, were set along the top of the feature at the southern end, on the western side and this appeared to represent a later edging in stone, after the gully had begun to infill. The southern end of the feature was very difficult to define as it merged with the gully, F66, at the southern side.

The pit F55 and gully F63 The remains of a small pit, F55, in the northeast corner of Trench 9, were probably contemporary with the linear feature F48. This pit measured 0.30m east-west by 0.15m wide and was filled with a grey clay deposit, identical to the upper fill (F54.1) of the adjacent F48. The pit was filled and sealed by a spread of clay that measured 0.70m east-west by 0.48m wide by 0.32m in depth but produced no finds. The remains of a triangular-shaped cut, F63, were identified in Trench 2/9 and this was

Plate 16 The F63 gully

slightly later in date than the F48 linear feature, cut into the F64 burnt
deposit (fig. 11; plate 16). This cut measured 4.80m north-south by 4.20m
wide at the southern end, narrowing to 0.20m wide at the northern end. It
was at least 0.20m in depth, and was filled with hard yellow/grey clay, which
contained small irregular-shaped stones (between 50mm and 70mm in
diameter) and mortar fleck. At the southern end the deposit was dark grey in
colour but also had the same distinctive mortar fleck. The F48 linear feature
and the cut F63 were both sealed by a deposit of mixed clay, F62, which
contained stones and large fragments of charcoal and fire-reddened clay,
which was between 0.10m and 0.18m in depth. This deposit (similar to F18
see below) was probably used to level up the ground.

Discussion of Level 5
The linear feature, F48, probably also represented some sort of drainage
feature, orientated north-south but at least two phases could be identified, the

lower level and the later refacing in stone on the western side. The second phase caused damage to the original phase, which may have been medieval in date, as it was set deep into the boulder clay. The function of the second gully F63 is not known but it was also presumably for drainage purposes.

LEVEL 6 (LATE 17th/18th CENTURY)

The barrel vault was evidently demolished in the late seventeenth /eighteenth century as, from this level on, fragments of rubble from the vault can be found in all the succeeding deposits (fig. 12). The linear drain F48 and pit F55 were sealed comprehensively by friable clay deposits, F44, which measured, on average, 0.35m in depth and contained large (30mm) flecks of charcoal, burnt clay fragments, fragments of demolished barrel vault, as well as lenses of pure redeposited boulder clay, F44.2 (fig. 12). The finds included Leinster cooking ware (thirteenth/fourteenth century in date), clay pipe stems, as well as black glazed ware (seventeenth-nineteenth century), the medieval finds suggesting that some of the deposits were disturbed medieval soils. A large number of iron nails and rods came from this deposit, which also produced lead fragments (similar to those found in F50; Level 3). Also of note were three animal bones that had holes drilled through to make toggles (see bone finds below). The clay was probably introduced deliberately after the vault had collapsed to build up the ground level and provide a level surface. As the finds included large fragments of demolished barrel vault, some of which had evidence of wicker-work centring, F44.1, this deposit could be dated to some point after the barrel vault had been destroyed.

The fire-pit, F47 A small concentration of burnt and fire-reddened clay, F47, was identified along the eastern side of Trench 9 and this was suggestive of some sort of fire-pit or hearth. This was located 0.55m below present ground level and measured at least 0.60m north-south by at least 0.40 wide by 0.25m in depth. The clay was fire-reddened to a depth of 0.10m, sealed by layers of ash and charcoal and this hearth formed part of a general sequence of industrial activity, at this level; it may have represented the base of an oven.

The mound F43 A large mound of burnt material, F43, built up at the southern end of Trench 9 and this probably formed part of the general F47 deposit (fig. 12). The mound measured 1.70m east-west by 0.75m wide and was at least 0.20m in height. It was composed of layers of clay, which had large fragments of fire-reddened clay and a pronounced charcoal fleck. At the eastern end the remains of a patch of fire-reddened clay and charcoal suggest the presence of another hearth F43.1, which measured 0.30m north-south by 0.20m wide by 50mm in depth. The banded layers of charcoal suggest that there were several successive fires in this location. A small pit, F42, was cut

into the mound at the western end and this measured 1.10m east-west by
0.46m wide by between 0.15m and 0.20m in depth (fig. 12). It was filled with
dark brown silty clay with stone inclusions, 50mm in diameter but produced
no finds.

Discussion of Level 6
The barrel vault of the castle was comprehensively destroyed between Phases
5 and 6 and this resulted in the almost total destruction of the castle apart
from the northern wall and part of the eastern wall. The exact date of this
event is difficult to establish but it was probably in the mid- to late seventeenth
century. The south and west walls were destroyed, which resulted in the
destruction of the barrel vault but the masonry was then comprehensively
plundered. Much of the stone was within clay deposits and these may have
formed infill deposits on either side of the barrel vault. The castle was not
abandoned entirely after the destruction of the barrel vault, as evidence of
some sort of domestic activity is suggested by the hearth and mound F43.
This presumably took the form of oven activity, for which the ruined castle
was suitable, as it reduced the possibility of fire.

LEVEL 7 (18th CENTURY)

Structure A The eastern end of the castle was then divided into some sort of
chamber represented by the remains of two stone walls and a clay surface,
F61. This possible chamber measured 1.60m north-south and was delineated
by the stone walls, F59 and F60. F59 formed the southern extent, orientated
east-west and this measured 1.35m east-west by 0.40m in width but stood
only 0.20m in height. It was composed of irregular-shaped limestone set in a
very loose bond, which measured, on average, between 0.30m by 0.20m and
0.10m and 0.15m. The wall was mortared with hard cement like off-white
mortar, which contained small redbrick inclusions, and was set in a bedding of
this mortar. The second wall F60 was represented by a mass of mortared
stones also orientated east-west measuring 0.55m east-west by 0.40m wide and
lying just 0.45m from the north wall of the castle. This mass was formed by a
series of large pieces of irregular-shaped limestone measuring, on average,
0.20m by 0.25m, which were all mortared together. The mortar used was
friable, off-white in colour and similar in type to that used in the oven, F49
(see below). The facing stones of this wall had evidently been robbed out. A
new surface, F61, was laid within the chamber and this consisted of yellow
clay, which was between 40mm and 0.10m in depth. The southern wall, F59,
abutted the east wall of the castle, F2.3, at the eastern end but this section
appeared to have been refaced, F56.1, and bonded in bright orange clay, F19,
into which two large facing stones were set (fig. 12). The internal face of the

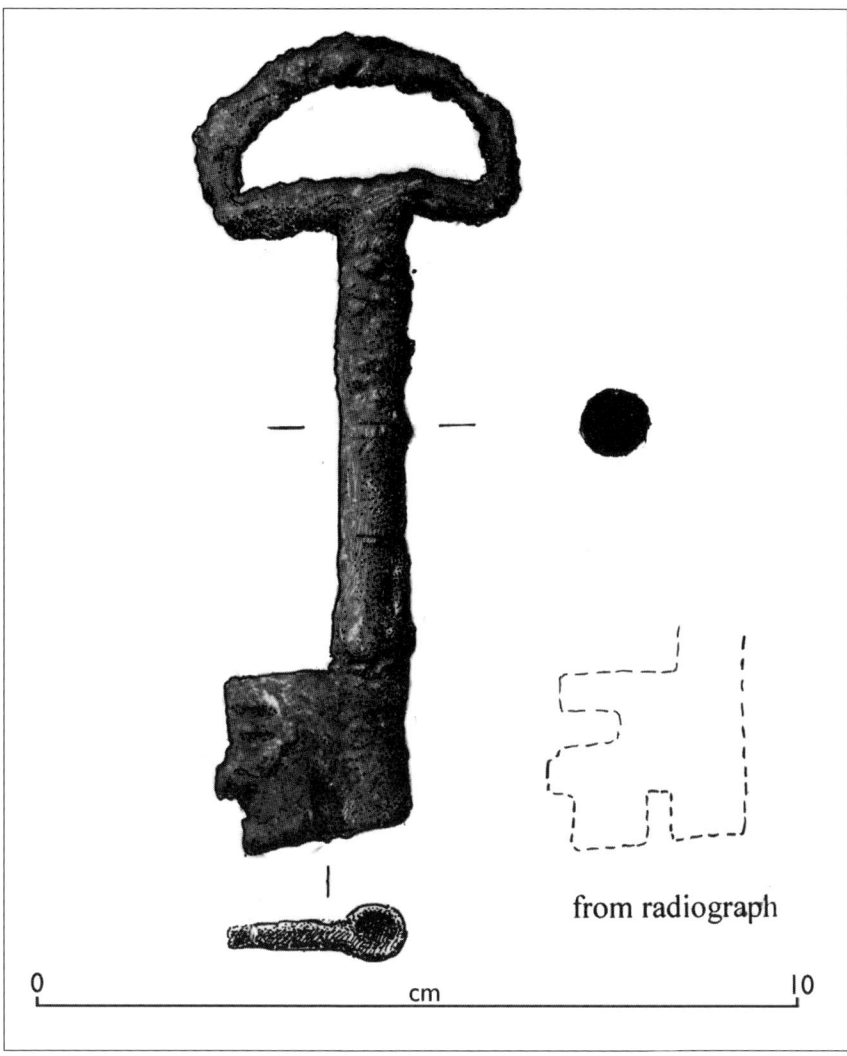

from radiograph

0   cm   10

16 Medieval key, 55:5

standing north wall in this location (the inner face of the barrel vault) was also rebonded with yellow clay at this time, probably when this chamber was constructed. The render of clay extended for 0.20m in depth into the wall.

The clay deposits A series of post-medieval clay deposits were identified at the western side of the castle. F15 overlay the natural clay and this consisted of a mixed deposit of clay, with lenses of beige clay and lumps of charcoal, as well as fragments of fire-reddened clay. This deposit was approximately 0.10m in depth and was very similar in type to F6, the main deposit of clay at this end of the castle. In Trench 9 this deposit was light brown in colour with large stones, which contained slates and some mortar. The F15 deposit was sealed on the east by F17, a second substantial deposit of mixed clay (Trench 3), which extended throughout the western end of the castle and measured between 0.15m and 0.22m in depth. This redeposited boulder clay was light yellow in colour and contained stones, as well as occasional flecks of charcoal. The stones were angular limestone, measuring, on average, 50mm in diameter. The F17 clay deposit formed part of a general dump of clays across the castle. F18 (Trench 9 and 2) was very similar in type and this was a yellow sticky clay deposit, which contained inclusions of charcoal fleck (20mm in diameter) and mortar fragments. Small stones were also found throughout, as well as a concentration of mortar fragments in the southeast corner of Trench 2/9. This deposit produced eighteenth-century pottery, as well as several medieval pottery sherds (a sherd of modern Chinaware was probably intrusive). A small concentration of burning, F39, was identified within F18 in Trench 2/9 and this measured 1.10m north-south by 0.68m wide. It was between 0.15m and 0.22m in depth and was composed of light brown friable clay with occasional charcoal fragments. However, it did contain large lumps of burnt clay presumably derived from the internal partitions found at the earlier levels.

Discussion of Level 7
The eastern end of the castle was sectioned off into some sort of small chamber, which was bounded by stone walls. These walls were comprehensively demolished but may originally have extended quite high as the inner face of the castle was repointed in clay to a height of 1.70m. The east wall was also repointed in clay, possibly because this wall had been damaged during the destruction of the barrel vault. Elsewhere, the earlier clay deposits were very disturbed in the eighteenth century, and thus they produced late seventeenth century as well as medieval pottery.

LEVEL 8 (MID-18th/19th CENTURY)

The central area A substantial deposit of mortar, F46, was identified in the central and east end of the castle, sealing the F66.1 clay deposits (fig. 14). This deposit represents parts of the demolished barrel vault, which was piled in a heap at the east end of the castle in a spread that measured 3m east-west by between 0.30m and 0.50m in depth. F46 was composed of loose limestone of irregular sizes most of which, however, averaged 0.20m by 0.10m. All the stones had mortar attached but were within a loose yellow clay deposit, F46.1, which had few inclusions and was similar in type to the general boulder clay deposits. It possibly represents clay packing used to infill the voids on either side of the barrel vault (pers. comm., Ben Murtagh). This deposit only produced two sherds of Leinster cooking ware and Dublin-type ware suggesting that the clay originally formed a medieval deposit. Fragments from the clay internal partitions were also found in this deposit.

The eastern end of the castle A substantial deposit of yellow clay F5/F11 sealed Structure A and the F46 stone deposits at the east end of the castle and this was very similar in type to the underlying F61 clay deposit. F11 was hard stoney clay, which varied in type across the eastern end but was between 0.40m and 0.60m in depth. The finds included Leinster cooking ware, as well as nineteenth-century. It contained few inclusions apart from small irregular-shaped stones, measuring, on average, between 60mm and 0.12m in diameter. The clay differed slightly over the demolished eastern wall where it was yellow, F24, and 0.25m in depth, with lenses of brown organic material and fine gravel. It also contained a large number of stones at the eastern end, as well as flecks of mortar. A band of bright yellow clay, F5, was also visually different and this was hard-redeposited boulder clay, between 0.10m and 0.15m in depth, which contained irregular-shaped stones and eighteenth- and nineteenth-century pottery. It corresponded roughly to the projected line of a wall F3.1, which lay to the west and was orientated east-west (see below). The remains of what appeared to represent a slate floor, F45, were uncovered set into the F5 deposit and this survived in a spread that measured roughly 1.60m square. The slate was very thin purple slate, which different in type to the heavier roof slate fragments also found throughout the deposits. One intact slate measured 0.26m by 0.18m and was rectangular in shape but the remainder of the chippings averaged 0.15m in diameter. A layer of black charcoal, F24, also lay within the F11 deposit and this was approximately 50mm in depth. This was pure charcoal in a spread that measured 1.20m north-south by 0.60m in width. It contained no finds and appeared to be dumped rather than the result of burning *in situ*.

The ovens F8 and F49 The F11 clay surface formed the floor of an industrial area at the eastern end of the castle, which included two brick ovens F8 and F49 (fig. 11). These ovens appear to have had a mixed use as a sample from the fills (F57) produced fifty-four seeds, which could be identified as a legume (peas/beans), sometimes used in the preparation of curries. The seeds, however, were in the process of being dried out perhaps for storage or planting rather than cooking. This was suggested by the fact they were complete and not fragmented in any way. The oven F8 was inserted in the south wall (F2.2) of the castle, at the eastern end and, as part of these works, the internal facing stones of the wall were removed in a stretch measuring 3.90m east-west by 0.90m in height (plate 17). The oven was oval in shape and measured internally 1.20m east-west by 0.70m wide (fig. 11). It was con-structed of a bright red late seventeenth/early eighteenth century handmade brick and survived to five courses in height, solidly and neatly built. The entrance flue was on the eastern side and this measured 0.60m in width by at

Plate 17 The oven F8

least 0.40m in height. Limestone flags formed the base of the oven but these
had been burnt black by successive burnings. In addition, the bowl of the
oven was packed with yellow sticky clay, which was caked onto the sides and
this evidently served as some form of lining. The remains of a ventilation
duct or possible flue were visible on the northern side, which allowed air (or
possibly bellows) into the oven. The brick was handmade and can probably be
dated to the late seventeenth/early eighteenth century. The largest example
measured 0.23m by 90mm by 60mm but the average brick measured 0.22m by
0.10m by 70mm. The brick were irregular in shape and the impressions of
grass could be seen in the underside where the brick were laid out in the sun
to dry. They were set in very fine sandy clay mortar, which was light beige in
colour and contained fine sand and small pebbles. The oven was filled with
layers of ash and pure charcoal, evidently associated with the last firing. The
charcoal and ash produced no finds apart from a series of curved red
earthenware pantiles most of which were scorched and burnt. These were
probably reused from an earlier building to roof the kiln. The fill, F58.1 and
2, consisted of layers of crumbly fire-reddened clay, which was mixed with
ash and charcoal, as well as numerous half bricks. The very basal deposit
F58.1 was a hard compact charcoal layer, which was fire-hardened and had
lenses of yellow ash. The upper deposit, F58.2, while similar in type, had less
charcoal and was more friable. Fragments of demolished barrel vault mortar

were also found within this deposit. The cut for the oven F8 oven was larger than the surviving oven and there may have been a second oven on the western side, although no trace survives. The construction cut was marked by a spread of gravel, F41, which was very coarse and contained different type of stones measuring, on average, 30mm in diameter. A second cut, F8.1, was identified on the eastern side of the oven and this measured 1.80m northeast/southwest by 0.70m in width by 0.30m in depth, filled with yellow clay. Two post-holes, F8.2 and F8.3, were identified at the north-eastern side of the oven, probably inserted in the final stages of use. These measured between 0.10m and 0.15m in diameter and were, on average, 0.20m in depth. Both were filled with black charcoal, similar to the fill of the oven.

The F49 oven A second oven, F49, was identified at this level, built into the northern wall of the castle, almost directly opposite F8. The F49 oven had been inserted in a cavity created through the base of a window embrasure (Window 1) but very little survived *in situ*. The exposed section was semi-circular in shape but it was presumably originally oval, like F8 (the southern end was not excavated). It measured internally 0.92m east-west by at least 0.80m wide and was composed of three courses of brick. The bricks used were hand-made brick, which were bright red in colour and similar in type to the bricks used in the F8 oven. Many of them were half and three-quarters in length, measuring 0.13m by 0.11m by 70mm, and all were badly decayed. They were mortared with a yellow crumbly mortar identical to that used in the F8 oven in the south wall. The fill (F57) of the oven was also similar in type to the deposits within the F8 oven. They consisted of layers of off-white ash and fire-reddened clay and a layer of black charcoal, 50mm in depth.

The wall cut F25 A large cut was evident over the eastern section of the castle wall (F2.3), almost vertically into the clay deposit F11 and the F24 deposit at the southern end (fig. 12). The cut was filled with mortar and limestone fragments, which were probably derived from the demolished east wall. The cut appeared to extend further eastwards beyond the limit of excavation and this was also filled with large lumps of limestone masonry, F26. This masonry spread measured at least 2.25m north-south by 1m in width and the mortar was white and cement-like, similar to that used elsewhere on the site.

The external north wall The excavation of the trench around the external side of the castle revealed the remains of a clay deposit F23, at the western end. This deposit was between 0.30m and 0.40m in depth and was composed of dark humic soil, which had built up against the robbed-out face of the wall. The finds included medieval pottery, as well as eighteenth- and nineteenth-century pottery; thus the deposit represents a disturbed medieval deposit, which included chips of limestone and fragments of mortar. Fragments of fire-reddened clay from wall partitions were also found within this deposit. At the eastern end the clay deposit was cut by a spread of limestone F22, which measured 3.50m east-west by at least 0.90m wide by 0.20m in height. It was comprised of small stones of various sizes but measured, on average, 0.10m by 0.15m, set within a mortar deposit. The deposits to the east of the linear feature F22 were composed of loose mortar and stone, F21, which was between 0.30m and 0.40m in depth. The mortar used was an off-white loose type and it contained fragments of glass, tin-glazed earthenware, blackware (eighteenth- and nineteenth-century in date), as well as medieval pottery. Fragments of fire-reddened clay from partitions were also found in this deposit.

Discussion of Level 8
The deep deposits of almost pure rubble (F46) were clearly derived from the collapsed barrel vault but this seems to have been dumped in one single event, perhaps to raise the floor level up and create a level surface. Most of the fragments of the barrel vault were presumably carried away for reuse, as F46 was mostly composed of loose mortar and chips of limestone rather than block. Both ovens (F8 and F49) were then constructed within the walls of the castle after the barrel vault was demolished. This was a common occurrence in the post-medieval period, when brick ovens were often built into external boundary walls or ruined castles, as they posed a serious fire risk. Both ovens were probably food ovens as F49 produced the charred remains of fifty-four legumes (beans or peas). Although these were probably used to flavour stews, in this instance their non-fragmented state suggested that they were being dried out in the oven either for storage or planting rather than consumption. The castle was still being plundered for stone at this date as a large cut/pit, F25, was identified over the eastern wall, which was filled with rubble. This rubble had no large stones, as these were presumably removed for re-use.

LEVEL 9 (19th CENTURY)

Clay deposits A second major phase of clay deposition was identified, which extended across the entire interior of the castle and could be dated to the nineteenth century (fig. 14). At the western end it was composed of a yellow clay deposit, F6, which was very mixed and contained lenses of clay and mortar, as well as hunks of masonry from the collapsed barrel vault (fig. 16). This deposit also had lenses of orange/yellow sandy clay and charcoal fragments, the latter of which were between 10mm and 30mm in diameter. The deposit also contained stone inclusions, which measured, on average, between 0.10m and 0.15m in diameter. A large number of fire-reddened clay fragments (partition walls) were also found throughout the deposits, as were numerous sherds of medieval pottery. These fragments of fire-reddened clay (partition walls), as noted earlier, are found throughout the deposits of the castle (F11, F5, F27, F46, F23, F21) and they are of assorted shapes and sizes but generally measure between 40mm and 0.10m in diameter. A large section of collapsed barrel vault, F6.1, was also identified within the F6 deposit, mortared together. This had impressions or traces of wicker-work centring. In the central area a substantial mixed clay deposit F10 was identified, which measured between 0.35m and 0.40m in depth. This was similar in type to F6 but contained noticeably less fire-reddened fragments of clay. Finds from this layer were mixed, indicating a date in the nineteenth century. At the eastern end of the castle the clay deposit differed slightly as it contained a substantial deposit of stone, F4, which may have formed a rough surface. This surface was composed of small chips of limestone, averaging 0.10m in diameter and set in a loose gravel deposit. This deposit also had lenses of rougher gravel, which was very similar to the gravel F41 associated with the ovens F8 and F49. A large iron key was found in this deposit.

Discussion of Level 9

Phase 9 represents a second phase of resurfacing inside the ruined castle and this consisted of deep deposits of clay across the interior of the castle (F6 and F10). These deposits, however, partially represent disturbed earlier layers as they contained medieval pottery. Also of note was the high frequency of burnt fabric fragments (from partition walls) at the eastern end of the castle, tapering off as the deposits (F10) extended eastwards. These deposits also contained large amounts of collapsed barrel vault.

LEVEL 10 (LATE 19th/EARLY 20th CENTURY)

The west and south wall of the castle, F12 The south and western wall of the castle were rebuilt sometime in the late nineteenth/early twentieth century to a height of approximately 1.20m (plate 18). As stated earlier the medieval foundation of the southern wall survived at the eastern end and this was reused as a foundation for the new wall but the west wall appears to have been replaced entirely, apart from the extreme northern end. The rebuilt walls measured between 1.90m (south) and 2.20m (west) in width and were of dry wall construction. Some of the masonry used was clearly derived from the collapsed vault, as there was evidence of wicker centring on some of the stones. The remains of a foundation cut F16 were evident for the western wall and the western end of the southern wall and this measured between 0.14m and 0.20m in width by 0.15m in depth (fig. 12). It was filled with brown clay, which contained one sherd of nineteenth-century glass as well as nineteenth-century pottery. The base of southern wall, F12.1, was founded on medieval footing at the eastern end and there was a modern ope F72 through the wall, almost centrally placed. This measured 1.12m in width but was crudely faced suggesting that it may have been put through at a later stage and then infilled. A deposit of brown/black soil, F27, built up against the external side of the southern wall F12.1 and this sealed the earlier slate deposit F29 (Level 2), which was medieval in date. This soil was between 0.30m and 0.60m in depth and contained inclusions of mortar and charcoal, as well as small stones and slate. The deposit contained Dublin-type pottery and porcelain, suggesting that it represented original medieval soil disturbed in the modern period. Fragments of the distinctive fire-reddened clay were also recovered from this deposit. The F27 deposit was sealed by F28, which was a mix of limestone and clay, and included lenses of humic clay. The stone was irregular in shape and measured, on average, 0.20m by 0.30m in diameter. The base of the western end of the southern wall, F12.1, and the west wall, F12.2, was not excavated out as the dry-stone wall facing was very unstable and there was a danger of collapse. The deposits consisted of the loose rubble F1 and lenses of dark humic soil, which contained numerous roots and modern finds.

Discussion of Level 10
The south and west wall were rebuilt in the nineteenth century, presumably in an attempt to restore the original outline of the castle. The walls were built along the line of the original walls but differed in type in their construction, as they were dry stone and not mortared. Thus there was no attempt to replicate the existing walls, the aim being to restore the outline of the castle rather than rebuild the ruin. The west wall was roughly butted onto the castle and was on a slightly different alignment while the southern wall was built along the line of the existing foundations, which were probably exposed to facilitate this.

LEVEL 11 (20th CENTURY)

The eastern end of the castle was sectioned off at this level and a rough clay-bonded wall F3.1 was built which incorporated the fallen hunk of masonry F3.3. The rough wall formed the southwest corner (1.40m east-west by 1.30m wide) of some type of temporary structure of which only the very foundations survived. The wall measured 0.90m in width but only one course was *in situ*, which was approximately 0.10m in height. It was faced on both sides but the central core was made up of large natural boulders. The northern facing was particularly neatly done and the stones measured 0.40m by 0.15m by 0.10m and were set on edge. The southwest corner was formed by a large granite stone, which measured 0.40m by 0.42m by 0.22m in depth, roughly squared. This can be identified as a quoin stone, presumably removed from the castle. The wall F3.2 foundation was not mortared but was set in a brown clay deposit F40, which was only 50mm in depth. The remains of a rough surface F9 were located within the angle of the wall and this was composed of long angular stones, averaging 0.20m by 0.10m, set roughly together. The F40 deposit contained modern glass and brick but the humic nature of the clay may suggest that animals were kept here.

The east wall The excavation along the external face of the east wall revealed the remains of yellow/brown compact clay, F38, which built up against the east wall of the castle at the northern end but contained modern finds. This was a pure deposit of redeposited clay, which contained inclusion of small stones, 20mm in diameter. A large robber cut, F36, truncated this clay deposit on the external side in what appears to have been an attempt to undermine the east wall, possibly with a view to collapsing it (fig. 11). The large foundation stones of the wall were removed and the core of the wall was carefully chiselled out, creating a large void. This cut measured at least 5m north-south by 1.50m wide and was over 0.40m in depth. The photographic sources suggest that the southern end of the east wall was still standing in 1913 but was evidently in a very dangerous condition.

The modern pits (late twentieth century) The remains of a modern pit, F20, were located in the northeast corner of the excavation and this was triangular in shape measuring 1.80m east-west by 1.80m by 1.36m (fig. 12). It was 0.35m in depth and was filled with loose masonry. A second pit, F7, lay in the central area, and this measured 1.70m east-west by 1.40m wide by between 0.74 and 0.90m in depth. This was very modern in date, constructed sometime after 1993. It probably represents some sort of children's hut.

SUMMARY AND CONCLUSION OF EXCAVATION

The excavations at Kindlestown revealed continuous occupation at the castle from the late thirteenth/early fourteenth century to the early to mid-seventeenth century, after which time the castle was ruined. Unfortunately, however, the deposits were very disturbed, apart from at the western end where a section survived intact. This area demonstrated that the original floor was a rough cobbled surface, set into boulder clay, which contained the remnants of a large hearth, thought to represent a domestic food fire (see below). The location of this hearth is something of a puzzle, as presumably, this would have generated considerable smoke if the vault had been completed by this date, although the small windows would have aided ventilation to some degree. The hearth, however, had no formal setting perhaps suggesting that it may have been in use during the construction of the castle. Several other temporary hearths were also located, which were probably related to the same activity. The hearth may have been associated with a variety of post-holes found within the castle, some of which may also have been related to temporary shelters on the site of the castle, perhaps during construction (as some of the post-holes pre-dated the hearth). Although some of the post-holes were in recognisable lines the large numbers make interpretation difficult. Two large posts in a central location were presumably associated with the barrel vault in some way and may represent the remains of a timber superstructure used to support it during its construction. Several rows of posts can be identified running east-west, along the walls at the eastern end but, unfortunately, the stratigraphy was removed further east by the post-medieval gully (F66) and it is not known if these posts continued along the length of the building. The posts were cut through the boulder clay and represent primary activity, perhaps when the castle builders were setting out the castle during the initial construction. The damage to the medieval deposits at the eastern end was, unfortunately, very considerable but a small patch of rough cobbling represents the original floor level.

The excavation also revealed that the eastern doorway, at ground floor level, was inserted in Construction Phase 2. This work disturbed the original east face of the wall and was broken through an existing mural passageway. The new doorway removed a section of the east wall and, with the associated stone surface, was positioned deep in the east wall foundations to allow for an increase in height. At the same time a channel was excavated at the base of the garderobe chutes in the northwest turret, and this was used to drain the waste from the latrines into the surrounding moat, traces of which are still in position on the northern and western side of the castle. This ditch is likely to be contemporary with the castle, and was probably water-filled, as suggested by the Du Noyer depictions. It may, however, have formed part of a much larger earthwork, perhaps suggesting that there was originally a bawn attached to the castle, which would have housed the ancillary farm buildings, including stables and outhouses. The excavation did produce evidence of occupation in the fifteenth and sixteenth century but, as the evidence is confined to the barrel vault (rather than the main living area), this evidence is very limited. The clay deposits from these levels suggest that there were internal partitions somewhere within the castle, constructed of clay on a timber framework. These partitions appear to have been burnt, presumably the result of a fire, and the remnants then dumped into the barrel vault as a rough floor surface. These deposits also produced evidence of leaded windows, which were also possibly destroyed in the fire. These would have been small casement windows, typical of the period.

The succeeding deposits were all post-medieval in date, detailing the continual occupation and use of the castle, even after it was slighted. It was still inhabited in the early seventeenth century when major works appear to have been carried out, perhaps in response to a problem of drainage. A large gully was excavated at the eastern end of the castle along the line of what appears to have been a natural geological feature, composed of rounded

Plate 18 The aerial view

boulders. The windows in the south wall may also have been enlarged at this date, as the remains of a large rectangular window are visible at the eastern end of the south wall, which is clearly very different in type to the segmented arched windows of the north wall. This conversion, from small defensive windows to larger domestic windows, was common in the early seventeenth century when a period of relative peace prevailed.

The castle was badly damaged in the (plate 18) mid-seventeenth century and was probably not habitable after this (as the west and south wall were comprehensively demolished). The remains of the hearth and a mound of fire-reddened clay may represent the site of a food oven or some sort of cooking activity, which was replaced by a rough chamber (Structure A) at the eastern end of the castle. This was evidently originally quite large as the internal face of the north wall was rebounded in clay at this time to a height of 1.70m and was possibly roofed. It was gone by the time that the two brick ovens were constructed in the ruins of the castle in the late seventeenth/early eighteenth century. The ovens, which were food ovens, were probably built by the occupants of the two-storey house depicted by Du Noyer, and were positioned in the castle to reduce the risk of fire, as was common practice. The fills produced the charred remains of peas/beans, which were being dried out for storage or planting. Despite this, these ovens were probably also used to bake bread. By the nineteenth century at least two substantial dumps of clay could be identified extending across the interior of the castle, indicating that the castle was still in use at this time. The southern and western walls were reconstructed at this time, as part of a general attempt to redefine the outline of the castle. The eastern end was then divided into some sort of rough enclosure, which incorporated fallen masonry and was probably used for animals as it contained a rich humic deposit. The final phase at the castle consisted of a series of pits, which were very modern in date.

THE FINDS

The pottery finds (by Clare Mc Cutcheon MA MIAI) A total of 122 sherds of pottery were recovered from the site at Kindlestown Castle. Following some re-assembly within and between contexts, this total was reduced to 112 sherds, of which 81 (72%) are medieval in date. The pottery was identified visually and the information is presented in Table 1. The number of sherds in each fabric type is listed along with the minimum number of vessels represented (MVR). No minimum number of vessels (MNV) could be given, as there was no absolutely quantifiable item such as a rim/handle junction present. The probable form of the vessel type is listed along with the date range of the distribution of the fabric type. Where diagnostic sherds have been found, the finds number is followed by R, B, H etc. for the rim, base and handle respectively. Where two or more sherds have been reassembled, the numbers are linked with a plus (+) sign. One sherd link between contexts was noted between F18 and F51. All of the wares from this assemblage are commonly found in excavations in Ireland. The apparent lack of fifteenth- and sixteenth-century pottery is also typical of excavations and as yet, no entirely satisfactory answer has been found to explain this lack of material.

Medieval ware

Leinster Cooking Ware: This is 'the single most widespread pottery type in Leinster' (Ó Floinn 1988, 340). It is characterised by large platelets of mica along with quartz and feldspar. Two rims, one with pinched decoration on the exterior and the second undecorated, but with a flat-topped profile, gives evidence of two cooking pots in Leinster Cooking Ware.

Dublin-type ware: The glazed ware in this assemblage is identified as Dublin-type ware as it is so similar to the wheel-thrown glazed ware found in Dublin in the thirteenth century (McCutcheon 2000, 122). Part of a strap handle was recovered with a single central incised line as decoration. One body sherd was decorated with a vertically applied brown strip while a second sherd showed a scar where an applied decoration had been present.

Table 1. Pottery identification, Kindlestown Castle

Fabric type	Sherds	MVR	Form	Date
Leinster Cooking Ware	12	2	Cooking pots	L12th–14th
Dublin-type ware	69	2	Jugs	13th
Total medieval	**81**			
Frechen	1	1	Jug	17th
North Devon gravel free	3	1	Bowl?	17th
Anglo-Dutch *c.*1640	2	1	plate	17th
Black glazed ware	10	2	Bowl	L17th–19th
Glazed red earthenware	3	1	Bowl	18th–19th
Bristol/Staffordshire slipware	4	1	Cup	18th
Porcelain	2	1	Cup	18th
Sprigged ware	1	1	Cup	19th–20th
Shell-edged ware	1	1	plate	19th
Transfer printed ware	3	1	Cup	19th
Chinaware	1	1	Cup	19th–20th
Total post-medieval	**31**			
Unidentified metalled waste?	1			
Stones with glaze	2			

Post-medieval wares

Only six sherds could be dated to the seventeenth century: a stoneware sherd from Frechen in Germany, three earthenware sherds from North Devon, so widely found in Ireland in the period, and finally, two sherds of the so-called Anglo-Dutch, a slip-trailed earthenware made primarily for the London market. The balance of the material ranges in date from the eighteenth to the twentieth century. In addition two pieces of stone were noted with apparent traces of a glass or glaze-like coating on them.

Clay building material (by Joanna Wren).

Introduction There are twenty sherds of clay building material in this assemblage, nineteen of which are from pantiles and one of which (01E0844; 1:14) is from a curved roof tile. All twenty sherds relate to the post-medieval phases of the site. The original Construction Phase 1 was roofed in purple slate, which was found throughout the deposits at this level.

Methodology The tiles were sorted according to fabric and form and were then weighed as the most accurate way of assessing quantity. The total numbers and weights of each form of tile were then recorded, according to feature. Within each grouping all percentages given below refer to weight. The material is divided for discussion on the basis of these fabric groupings and then ordered roughly chronologically. Dating is based on a combination of contextual information from this site and comparative material from other assemblages.

Curved roof tile One sherd (01E0844; 1:14) comes from a curved tile made in a smooth hard, pink/buff coloured earthenware, with inclusions of calciten (?) and unidentified grey and red stones. The writer has called this fabric K(indlestown) C(astle) T(ile) T(ype) One. Thin-section analysis would be necessary to establish an origin for this piece. Curved tiles originated in Asia Minor and have been in existence in Europe since the seventh century (Davey 1961, 149). They were used both on the body of the roof in combination with flanged tiles, and alone along the ridge. The flanged tiles were placed with their flanges facing upwards. The curved tiles then fitted over the sides of two flanged ones, holding them together. The majority of examples of this form of tiling found in Ireland date to the eleventh or twelfth centuries but examples are known in the post-medieval period. The sherd from Kindlestown was found amongst post-medieval material at the base of the northwest turret and was clearly from a disturbed context. (This may suggest that there was some sort of building, which had a clay tile roof in the vicinity, in the medieval period: this is unlikely to have been the original roof of the castle which appears to have been slated).

Sandy-red earthenware (pantiles) There are nineteen sherds of pantiles, which are a post-medieval refinement of the curved and flanged tiles. Both tiles are combined in one and they are attached to the roof with their long edges overlapping. All the sherds are made of sandy red earthenware fabrics and they probably include examples of both locally made and imported tiles (Wren 1997, 363). This type of pantile was first in use in Ireland in the early seventeenth century and continues in use throughout the eighteenth. Fifty-six percent of the sherds came from the fill of an oven (F8) in the south wall of the castle. This oven was made of hand-made brick dating to the late seventeenth or early eighteenth century. Another sherd came from the top of the drainage gully, which has been dated to the early seventeenth century. The presence of the pantiles suggests that there was a building at the castle in the seventeenth century which had a pantile roof. On the destruction of that roof the pantiles were possibly reused as the roof of the brick oven (pers. comm., Linzi Simpson).

Fragments of wall partition (by LS) A series of fire-reddened lumps of fabric were found throughout the deposits of the castle and these could be related to clay and timber partitions, which originally divided the castle into rooms. These partitions were of clay, supported by main upright posts, held in place by horizontal lathes (pers. comm., John Allen). The fragments were very fire-hardened and had obviously been heated to great temperatures, presumably during a fire. The fabric was dark orange/red in colour and had inclusions of large pebbles and stones. Vegetation-like impressions could be seen throughout the fragments, suggesting that grass or straw was mixed through. F6 (L9, L19th) produced the greatest number of fragments totalling seventy-three, while F23 (L9, 19th) produced thirty-four fragments also from a disturbed context.

The glass finds (by LS) The excavations at Kindlestown produced a small quantity of glass, most of which can be dated to the eighteenth and nineteenth centuries. Many of these fragments were from bottles, a large number of which came from a stone and mortar deposit F21 (Phase 8). A series of lead-cames was found in the deposits dating to the fifteenth and sixteenth centuries, which suggests that the castle did have leaded window at this date (see metal finds below). However, surprisingly, there were few sherds of early glass apart from two small sherds of thin green (iridescent), which may be medieval in date. These came from the seventeenth-century gully F66, but were possibly earlier in date.

The stone artefacts (by LS) A total of five stone artefacts were retrieved during the site clearance and these consisted of a possible mortar (or bullaun), a quarter of a mill stone, a rubbing stone, a spherical hammer stone and a possible window mullion, all of granite. The castle is built of limestone but the dressed stone appears to have been of granite although all of it has been robbed out, apart from one surviving granite quoin in the northeast corner. One large stone has at least two hollowed basins and this may represent a mortar, which was used in the preparation of ore smelting (Corlett 1998, 64). Alternatively, it may be a bullaun stone, since it has the typical artificially hollowed out hole or basin of these objects usually found associated with ecclesiastical sites (Edwards 1990, 116). The fragment from a millstone also suggests the presence of a mill close to the castle, which is mentioned in the historical sources. There is a small stream on the northern side of the castle, which may originally have powered a small mill, although no trace of this survives, either in the landscape or cartographic sources. The other stone artefacts include a spherical hammer stone, which is well worn and a very distinctive large rubbing stone, which has one large flat 'rubbed' surface. A third stone has what appears to be a bar-bolt slot (to hold a bar in a window) and this may suggest it was part of a granite window surround.

Slate (by LS) Over ninety fragments of slate were retrieved from the excavations, all with perforations at the top. The slate collection is composed of two different types, a heavy purple slate, which is roughly hewn and a lighter bluish slate, which splits better. The bluish slates are mostly rectangular in shape measuring, on average, 0.22m in length by 0.12m in width by 10mm in thickness and weighing, on average, 1kg. The slate was held in place by means of a circular perforation (5mm in diameter) at the top of the slate and most had hard white cement-like mortar attached (the overlapping line, where one slate overlapped another, is visible). The purple slates are far heavier and are more roughly hewn than the bluish examples and these represent the original roof of the castle. This slate was a heavy slate most of which has perforations, 6mm in diameter, to fix the slate onto the roof. The same type of slate (although in large slabs) is still *in situ* in the north wall where it projects through the north wall forming the stringcourse (through which drip holes extend). This slate is also used within the build of the wall. The tops of the slates are rounded rather than straight and there is a great variety of size, for example 1:75 measures 0.19m long by 0.15m in width by 0.15m in thickness while 1:67 measures 0.20m in length by 0.95m in width by 15mm in thickness.

Metal artefacts (by LS) The excavation produced a small collection of metal finds, which mostly consisted of various nails but also included keys, horseshoes, coins, a buckle, as well as various fragments of lead. The excavation produced five horseshoes, two of which (F2.1.1 and F2.1.2; fig. 15), are probably four-teenth-century in date (figs 3 and 4). Both F2:1:1 and F2:1:2 are very similar in type and both have three-on-three rectangular holes, with no separate countersunk or calkin (Type 4: Clark 1995, 97). The shoes were found within a wall cavity in the north wall and it is likely that they were found during metal-detecting activity and were placed there in the relatively recent past. One shoe (F2.1.1) is similar in type to a horseshoe found during excavations at Essex Street West, Dublin, which was dated to the fourteenth century (Simpson 1995, 80; for illustration ibid. 1999, 94–5). A total of two keys were found, one of which, F50: 5, can be identified as medieval in date (fig. 16). This has a D-shaped bow, a well-preserved bit with three ward cuts and a round-sectioned solid stem, which terminates in a rounded knob. This type can be broadly dated from the mid-thirteenth century to the fifteenth century (Anon. 1940, 140). The second key (F4.1) is a larger key, which is post-medieval in date and has a sub-rectangular bow and damaged bit.

Three coins were recovered, which is probably a relatively small number for the size and type of the site. However, the clay deposit F67, at one of the lower levels, produced an Edward I silver long-cross penny, F69.1 (1279–1302), which presumably relates to the primary phase of the castle. An iden-tical silver penny (although not in as good condition) was also found in a later deposit (F6.1), although this was clearly a disturbed location (identification by Cathy Daly). The third coin was found in the upper deposits (F1.17) and this could be dated to *c.*1860.

A total of three iron knives were also retrieved and this included what is possibly the best-preserved metal find from Kindlestown Castle. This is a whittle-tanged knife (F51.3) which has a particularly well-preserved polished ivory handle and triangular sectioned blade (Type D: Goddall 1990, 42). The knife contains a small fragment of leather with scored decoration at the junction between the blade and the handle and this may be all that remains of a leather sheath (fig. 17). The second knife, F18.16/66:16, is an iron scale-tanged knife which can be dated, by type, to the seventeenth century. The third knife is also a scale-tanged knife, which is almost complete and which has a triangular sectioned blade. This knife has a sub-rectangular shaped handle, which has three surviving rivets in place. Other metal finds from the castle included an incomplete trapezoidal copper alloy buckle (F21.1), a pin (F1.22) and a modern mount, (F1.22), the function of which is unknown, and a pin (F1.19).

At least four fragments of lead cames were retrieved from the excavation suggesting that windows of the castle were leaded at some time, probably in the late fifteenth/sixteenth century. All were similar in type and first appear in the deposit F50 (L3, 15/16th). The lead stripes were 'turned lead' and grooved (turned back on themselves) and at least two had the diagnostic H-section (Egan et al., 1986, 303). These probably held multiple small diamond-shaped windows known as 'quarries', which would have side-hinged casement openings (Roche 1996–7, 8; Hurley 1997, 126).

Bone objects (by Melanie Mc Quade) Two bone artefacts were found during the excavations, made from the metatarsals of sheep/goat. Both bones have small through perforations, which are centrally placed along their mid-shaft. The perforations are 2mm in diameter and are positioned 5mm apart. One of the objects (44:22), although not complete, appears to have been cut in a dorsal-distal volar direction (i.e., diagonally from front to back of distal shaft) creating a V-shaped cut that presumably had some function. The second artefact (44:21) is a complete bone, the distal epiphysis of which is unfused, indicating that it is from an individual under twenty months of age.

Analysis of faunal remains (by Melanie Mc Quade)
Introduction During excavations at Kindlestown Castle an assemblage of animal bone was recovered, which was retrieved by hand from features of medieval (late thirteenth/ fourteenth century) and post-medieval date. The presence of numerous small bones suggests that there was a high level of retrieval during the excavation. However, the paucity of fish bone may be due to the lack of sieved material. A total of 282 fragments were recovered, of which approximately 81% were identified to species and skeletal element.

Methodology The material was identified with reference to Cohen & Serjeantson (1986) and the comparative skeletal collection at the Natural

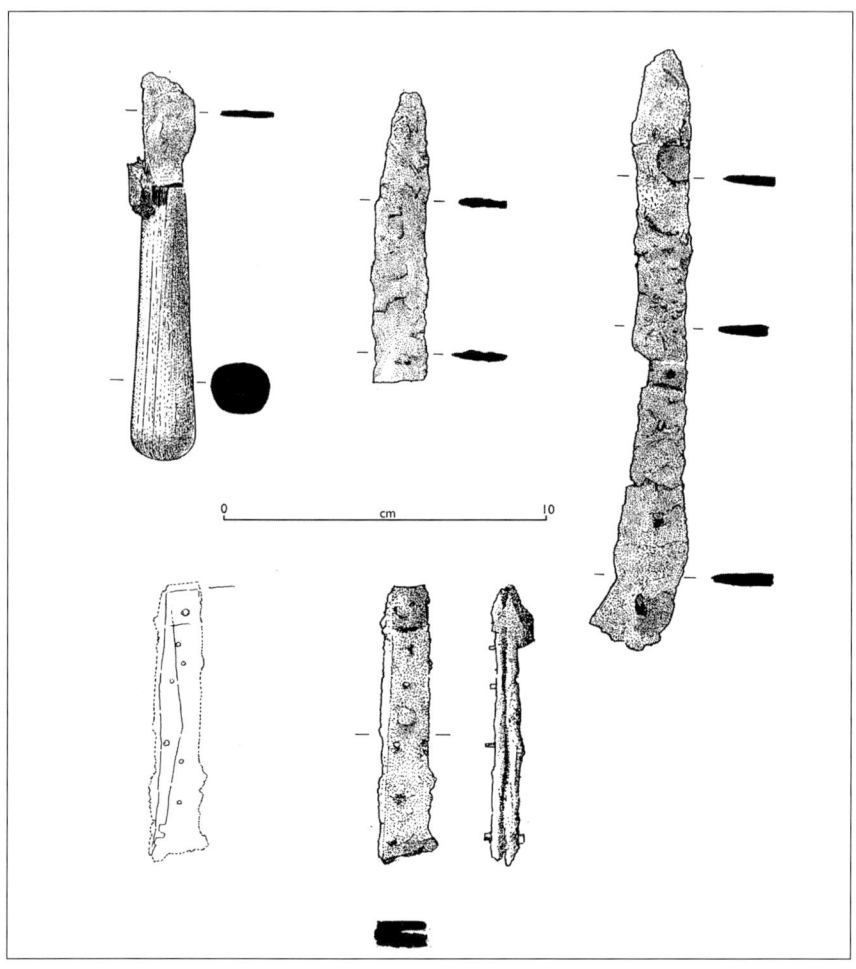

17 Medieval knife, with ivory handle, 51:3

History Museum. The fragmented condition of the samples hindered
attempts to differentiate between the remains of sheep and goat and, where
positive identifications could not be made (after Boessneck 1969; Prummel
and Frisch 1986), these species have been grouped together as sheep/goat.
Ribs and vertebrae were not identified to species and have been excluded from
fragment counts (tables 1 and 2). Long bone fragments that could not be
identified to species were classified by their size. The category 'large mammal'
covered cattle, horse and deer, the category 'medium mammal' covered
sheep/goat and pig. The minimum number of individuals (MNI) was calculated
on the most frequently occurring bone for each species, taking into account
left and right sides and the stages of epiphyseal fusion. Few complete bones

were present, but measurements were taken where possible using the methods outlined by von den Driesch and these are presented in the supplementary tables in the stratigraphic report (Simpson 2002; tables 3–8). Aging data was based on the stages of epiphyseal fusion and tooth eruption (after Silver 1969). Where relevant, the wear stages of mandibular teeth were also recorded (after Grant 1984).

Analysis: Medieval: A small collection of bone was recovered from F46 and this was probably medieval in date, as although the deposit is phased to Level 8, it represented the original barrel vault which had collapsed, the clay being used to pack around the vault. The species identified were sheep/goat (5), juvenile rabbit (2), rat (3), and jackdaw (1). Rabbit was introduced to Ireland after the Anglo-Norman invasion in 1169 and its presence has been noted at other contemporary sites (Bermingham 1995). Only two of the sheep bones, possibly from the same animal, provided any evidence of age. A proximally fused radius and a distally fused metapodial bone represent sheep over ten and 18–28 months respectively. There were no obvious signs of butchery on these bones. **Post-medieval**: The vast majority of the bones from Kindlestown Castle were retrieved from post-medieval features, which could be dated from *c.*1600 to the present day. The individual samples were very small and, consequently, yielded little information (table 1). The overall results of analysis are presented below.

Table 1. Total fragments identified to species in the various stages of the post-medieval period.

	Cattle	Horse	Sheep /Goat	Pig	Dog	Cat	Rat	Hedge-hog	Rabbit	Fowl	Pigeon	Kestrel	Starling	Fish
*c.*1600	7	3	16	4	I	–	–	–	3	3	I	–	–	–
7C	13	2	7	5	I	–	–	I	2	I	–	–	2	I
17/18	5	2	6	5	4	–	3	–	9	3	2	I	6	–
18–19C	7	I	I	8	–	I	2	–	4	–	–	–	2	–

Table 2. Total fragments and Minimum Numbers of Individuals (MNI) of the main domestic species identified in the post-medieval assemblage.

	Cattle	Horse	Sheep/Goat	Pig	LM	MM
Total	29	8	37	22	11	32
MNI	3	I	3	3		
Unid	79					

Condition of the material Despite being fragmented, the bone was generally well preserved. Only ten pieces had been weathered (F44, F66, F27, F23)
and five showed signs of gnawing and tooth marks from dog, cat and rodents
(F48, F27, F18). These had evidently been exposed for some time prior to
being sealed in their respective deposits. Several other fragments were
calcined (F21, F27), indicating that they had been burnt at a high temperature
prior to their deposition.

Species representation A wide variety of species were identified in the post-
medieval assemblage (table 1), but the majority of fragments were derived
from the main domesticates, of which most skeletal elements were present
(table 2). Brown rat was identified by the presence of a skull (F18) and it is
likely that the remaining bones from that feature are from the same individual. This species was only introduced to Ireland in the eighteenth century
and its presence provides a *terminus a quo* for these deposits (F5, F11, F18).

Aging data Aging data was limited by the small size of this sample in which
only a few individuals of each species are represented, and by the fragmentation of bones, many of which did not retain their epiphyses. Consequently,
it has not been possible to determine age profiles for the species represented.
However, a number of observations can be made from the available data.
Slaughter ages of 18–36 and 18–42 months are indicated for cattle represented by distally fused phalanges and unfused distal metacarpal and proximal
femur, with a fused femur indicating the presence of an individual over 42
months. Fused scapula, phalange and calcaneus represent sheep over 10, 16
and 30 months respectively, while a distally unfused radius is from an animal
under 36 months and a distally fused humerus is indicative of an individual
over 42 months. A pig under 12 months is represented by an unfused scapula
but a distally fused humerus and proximally fused radius are from pigs over
this age, while an unfused metatarsal represents an animal under 24 months.
The epiphyses of all of the horse bones (table 2) were fused, indicating that
none were from animals under 12 months of age, while radius and ulna on
which the epiphyses had fused are from a horse over 42 months. The dogs can
be aged between 13–16 months on the basis of a fused calcaneus and a
proximally unfused radius.

Butchery The wide range of skeletal elements found throughout this assemblage represents waste from initial butchery through to final meat consumption
stages. This indicates that during the seventeenth and eighteenth centuries
animals were either slaughtered in the vicinity, or that their carcasses were
imported whole and butchered in the locality. None of the horse bones show
evidence of butchery, but this was commonly encountered on bones of the
three main domesticates. The presence of midline chops on vertebrae
indicates that some of the carcasses were suspended prior to butchery, most of

which was done with heavy chopping knives, although a saw had evidently been used on a cattle femur (F23). Finer knife marks, created while removing flesh from the bone, were evident on scapulae and ribs and butchered fragments of long bone may be the result of marrow extraction. There was little evidence for butchery on the bones of the other species. Knife marks were only evident on one of the rabbit bones and these were created either by the removal of meat or pelts. Fine knife marks on a distal tibiotarsus of a domestic fowl (F44) probably result from removal of the lower leg prior to cooking. None of the goose or pigeon bones bore knife marks, but this does not exclude the possibility that these species may have been eaten.

Pathology Only two pathological conditions were identified on the bones in this assemblage. Irregular wear was noted on the fourth pre-molar and first molar of a mandible from a mature sheep/goat in which the third molar was present and at wear stage g (after Grant 1984). This anomaly is indicative of maloclusion, or abnormal bite. The second anomaly was an advanced infection, evident on the distal radius and ulna of a rat (F18), which may have been the cause of this creature's death.

Discussion A few bones were recovered from a feature of medieval date, but most of the faunal assemblage from Kindlestown is derived from post-medieval features, some of which post-date the occupation of the castle. The bone sample is too small to afford anything more than a tentative insight on the post-medieval diet or economy. However, a number of conclusions can be drawn from its analysis. The majority of bones were identified to cattle, sheep and pig, which gives an indication of their dietary value. Rabbit, fowl and pigeon may also have been exploited for their meat, but the other wild species probably represent animals and birds that once lived in or around the site. The recovery of only one fish bone, which could not be identified to species, is probably due to the retrieval methods employed on site, rather than an absence of fish in the diet. The withers heights of the species could not be calculated due to the paucity of complete bones in this assemblage. However, the measurements obtained are comparable to those from contemporary sites (McCormick and Murphy 1997). Bone fusion data is limited but indicates mixed slaughter ages for cattle and sheep and suggests that pigs were all under 24 months of age.

Analysis of plant remains (by Penny Johnston)
Samples: F69, Medieval hearth (L1, L13/E14th); F32.2, Base of garderobe chute (L2, 14th); F57, Post-medieval oven (F49) (L8, mid-18/E19th). **Introduction** A number of environmental samples were taken during the excavations at Kindlestown Castle, Wicklow. These comprised samples from the medieval hearth F69, from the gully F32 at the base of several garderobe chutes and the late seventeenth/early eighteenth century oven F49/F57. All

were examined for plant remains and the charred seeds extracted and examined. This report presents the results of that analysis.

Methodology The samples were collected as bulk soil, ranging in volume from one to three litres. These were processed using a simple flotation technique, and the floated material ('flots') were collected in meshes measuring 3000mm, while the heavy material that did not float ('retents') was collected in meshes of 1mm. Sorting and identification was carried out using a low-powered binocular microscope (magnification x4.8 to x56). The results of seed and chaff identification are presented in Table 1.

The features *F32.2 (sample from the gully, F34y, at the base of two garderobe chutes):* The remains of a steep-sided gully, F34, were located during the excavation around the exterior of the castle, at the northwest corner turret. This gully was at the base of two garderobe chutes and presumably carried the waste into the surrounding moat. Two seeds were found in this sample. One was a badly degraded cereal grain and the other was a well-preserved oat grain. Both may well have originated in faecal material that passed through one of the garderobe chutes. *F69 (sample from a medieval hearth, F69):* This sample was taken from a hearth composed of an ash and charcoal spread, with evidence of fire-reddening suggestive of *in situ* burning. The hearth was situated directly on boulder clay at the western end of the castle, within the barrel-vaulted ground floor. The sample produced edible plant remains and although these may have been deposited as tinder (Tierney and Hannon 1997), it is tempting to interpret the remains as either accidentally burnt food, or waste from food production that was thrown on the fire. This suggests that the area was used for food preparation. The position of the hearth within the barrel vault is something of a puzzle as there is unlikely to have been a flue or chimney in this location. The hearths may then have been in use during or prior to the construction of Kindlestown Castle as there was a break in the construction programme (L. Simpson, pers. comm.). *F57 (samples from a late seventeenth/early eighteenth-century oven):* Two samples were taken from a red-brick oven F49, which was inserted into the north wall of the castle. The brick oven was relatively large and measured internally 0.92m east-west by at least 0.80m wide. Three courses of brick survived, which were sealed by a fill of charcoal and ash. Two samples were taken, one from the upper fill and one from the base of the oven. Only the sample from the base contained the remains of charred seeds, suggesting that these were remains that were accidentally charred in the oven, and left on the base, before it fell into disuse. The upper fill was composed of sediment and other debris but this contained no plant remains.

The results The plant assemblage covers a diverse range of plant types, including cereals, legumes and seeds from wild plants, many of which were edible.

Cereals: Cereals were used for making breads, meals, porridges, gruels and soup bases (Sexton 1998a). Ten cereal grains were found in the hearth sample (F69), and two were recovered from the gully at the base of the garderobe chute (F32.2). The species found included wheat (probably bread/club wheat, *Triticum aestivum/compactum*), barley (*Hordeum vulgare*) and oat (*Avena* spp.). Even though only a small amount of these cereals were retrieved from the samples at Kindlestown, it is clear that oats were the dominant cereal (See table 1). Cultivated oats were introduced into Ireland in the early historic period (Kelly 1998), and they are frequently recovered in archaeobotanical assemblages dating to that period and later. The bread from oat flour is generally not of very good quality, as it does not rise very much but, despite this, travellers tales from the seventeenth century suggest that oat cakes were found in both rich and poor houses in Ireland (Sexton 1998b). As oats were a cheap and plentiful source of nourishment, they were widely used: cultivated oats dominated charred seed assemblages from medieval Waterford in both the Hiberno-Norse and Anglo-Norman periods (Tierney and Hannon 1997). Bread wheat and barley are also found in large numbers from many sites dating to the historic period and bread wheat becomes increasingly more frequent in the later medieval period.

Legumes: Many legume seeds were recovered from these samples but these were mostly concentrated in two different contexts, which fall into two distinct categories. The hearth sample (F69) was dominated by peas and beans, while the second category from the later oven (F57), may have been a flavouring or spice that was used in cooking. *Peas and Beans:* Sample F69: Peas (*Pisum* spp.) and beans (*Vicia* spp.) were introduced in Ireland in the early historic period (Kelly 1998) but their cultivation increased considerably in the Anglo-Norman period, particularly as they became an important part of the three-field rotation system of crop husbandry, which was practised extensively in medieval Ireland (Tierney and Hannon 1997). From the medieval period onwards, pulses were used as soup bases and thickeners (Sexton 1998b).

Indeterminate legumes: Sample F57: These seeds were recovered from the charred fill of a late seventeenth/early eighteenth century oven (F49), which had been inserted into the wall of the castle. The seeds were small, and despite being charred, they were well preserved. Small legumes are notoriously difficult to identify, as they have few defining characteristics and they are often categorised under the cover-all classification of 'Legume indet'. The seeds from this sample are all morphologically similar and the fifty-four seeds found probably represent a cache of one type of legume. As most of the seeds were intact, this suggests that they were not crushed or fragmented to put into food. They may have been left in the oven in preparation for storage or indeed for planting, before they were accidentally charred. A text by the seventeenth century English herbalist, Culpepper, recommends that seeds be dried before storage or planting, and 'you need not be so careful of keeping them so near the fire ... because they are fuller of spirit, and therefore not so subject to corrupt' (Culpepper 1995). Under high magnification, these seeds have a circular scar that resembles seeds from the *Trifolium* (or *Trigonella*) genus. It is therefore possible that these are the seeds of fenugreek; not the irregularly-shaped Mediterranean fenugreek, which is commonly used in curries today, but perhaps the native variety, Bird's foot clover (*Trifolium ornithopodioides*) which can be used in a similar manner to fenugreek in order to add flavour and smell to stews (Mabey 1972).

Wild Plants: The wild plants recovered from the samples from Kindlestown included fragments of hazelnut shell, black bindweed, knotgrass, wild radish and cornsalad, all of which were probably used as food. The members of the dock family (*Polygonaceae*), which included bindweed and knotgrass, are related to buck wheat, and many are edible, used predominantly in porridges and gruels. Hazel nuts have been collected as a foodstuff throughout history. A stash of nuts, carefully wrapped, was found during excavation of early eleventh-century Viking layers at Fishamble Street, Dublin where they formed an important part of the urban diet (Geraghty 1996). Hazel-nuts were a particularly good food to collect as they could be stored for a long time. The wild radish was a weed of crop fields but was also eaten as food in the medieval period (ibid.). As today, this would have been used as a tangy flavouring. Similarly, cornsalad, as the name suggests, was used in salads. Cornsalad also had several medicinal uses, which the herbalist Culpepper notes, although these generally pertain to the root and leaf, rather than to the seed (Culpepper 1995).

Conclusions The charred archaeobotanical remains from Kindlestown Castle were interesting and diverse, although not abundant. The seeds identified appeared to be predominantly from food plants, unsurprising as they were from samples taken from hearth and oven deposits, where food was probably prepared for consumption, as well as from a garderobe chute, where evidence of the aftermath of food consumption was found. The plant remains found included both cultivated and wild plants, and, despite the late date (thirteenth to eighteenth century) of these samples, it is clear that wild plants continued to be exploited, in particular, it seems, for the added flavour that they could give, to liven up sometimes jaded foods such as cereal-based gruels.

Feature no.		32	57	69
Sample no.		**3**	**2**	**5**
(Common Names)	(Scientific names)			
Cereal Grains	**Poaceae**			
Emmer/bread/club wheat	*Triticum dicoccum/* *aestivum/compactum*			1
Probable bread/club wheat	Triticum cf aestivum/compactum		1	
Hulled barley grains	*Hordeum vulgare*			1
Oat grains	*Avena spp.*	1		3
Probable oat grains	cf Avena spp.	1		
Oat embryo ends	*Avena spp. embryo ends*			1
Oat apical ends	*Avena spp. apical ends*			2
Oat/Rye grains	*Avena/Secale*			1
Indeterminate	Cereals Cereal indet.			1
	Leguminosae			
Legumes				
Pea species	*Pisum spp.*			7
Probable broad bean	cf Vicia faba			1
Indeterminate legumes	Legume indet.		54	7
Seeds from wild plants	**Wild Seeds**			
Hazel nut shell fragments	*Corylus avellana fragments*			7
Black Bindweed	*Polygonum convolvulus*			2
Knotgrass	*Polygonum cf aviculare*			1
Wild radish	*Raphanus raphanistrum*			2
Probable cornsalad	*Valerianella cf dentata*			1
Indeterminate wild seed	Seed indet.			1

APPENDIX

The transcripts found by Edmund Curtis and referred to earlier reveal details of the inquisitions into Archbold lands. The documents were in the possession of H.J. French (died April 1930) who made copies of the originals, which are held by the earl of Meath at Kilruddery. Liam Price appears to have obtained copies as they are currently in the Price Collection housed in the Royal Society of Antiquaries of Ireland (pers. comm., Chris Corlett). The documents consist of a copy of letters patent of Charles I, dated 1628, and various other documents relating to the title of Bray. Other deeds include a pedigree of the Archbold family, as follows:

Richard of Kilruddery
Patrick Ashpoll, died 20 (Henry VIII)
Gerard, (Gerratt) nine years old in 1529
Patrick, died 1560
William died 9 (James I)
Patrick, died 1624
Edward conveyed Bray to Sir W. Brabazon in 1625
William Asheploe of Kenlestown, died 1599
Patrick

Letters patent to Charles I, in 1628, called for an inquisition into the lands of Edward Archebold of Delgany, heir of Patrick (then twenty-one) to allow William, earl of Meath to purchase the manor of Great Bray (Bree and Little Bree). The description of the manor therein stated that it held a right of court, of Piepowder and fines and perquisities, as well as a market every Tuesday weekly and two fairs, one at Martinmas (11 November) and the other at May Day. The letter also included details of tanning (leather and hides) complexes, which were located somewhere in the manor of Bray.

The acquisition of the Archbold lands by the earl of Meath did not resolve the various land disputes, another arising between Meath and the Fitzwilliams, the original claimants. As a result, the earl brought a case against Lord Fitzwilliam in 1637 (Curtis, 'Title of Bray', 2), an abstract of which survives as part of the Curtis transcripts. In this document the title of the manor rests with William Ashpoll of Kenleston (this estate included 180 acres) and the Archbold lineage is recorded as above. The opposing Fitzwilliam case is also recorded (Curtis, 'Title of Bray', p.8) and this lists the descent from Sir Thomas Fitzwilliam to Oliver earl of Tyrconnell (Fitzwilliam):

Sir Thomas Fitzwilliam
Richard Fitzwilliam
Thomas M. Fitzwilliam
Oliver, now earl of Tyrconnell

ACKNOWLEDGEMENTS

The author would like to thank the excavation team for all their hard work: Bernice Molloy, Simon Dick, Colm Moriarty, Sarah Tobin, Kristina Olander, Tom Mohr, Bill Frazer and Nuala Hiney. All site drawings are by Kevin Weldon and finds drawings by Simon Dick. The author would also like to thank Ben Murtagh, Chris Corlett, Willy Cumming of Dúchas: the Heritage Service for help and advice during the excavation.

BIBLIOGRAPHY

Anon. 1889 *Calendar of ancient deeds and muniments preserved in the Pembroke Estate Office, Dublin.* Dublin. (Privately printed).
Anon. 1940 *London medieval catalogue.* London (repr. Ipswich, 1993).
Barry, T.B. 1977 *Medieval moated sites of southeast Ireland.* British Archaeological Report 35 Oxford.

Bermingham, N. 1995 Animal bones. In L. Simpson, *Excavations at Essex Street West, Dublin,* Temple Bar Archaeological Report 2 104–115. Dublin.

Boessneck, J. 1969 Osteological differences between sheep (*Ovis aries* Linne) and goat (*Capra hircus* Linne). In D. Brothwell and E. Higgs, *Science in archaeology,* 331–58. London.

Bourdillion, J. and Coy, J. 1980 The animal bones. In P. Holsworth (ed.) *Excavations at Melbourne Street, Southampton 1971–6,* BAR 33, 79–120, Oxford.

Clarke, J. 1995 Horse shoes. In *The medieval horse and it equipment, c.1150–1450.* 75–101. London.

Cohen, A. and Serjeantson, D. 1986 *A Manual for the identification of bird bones from archaeological sites.* London.

Connolly, P. 1998 *Irish exchequer payments, 1270–1446,* 2 vols. Dublin.

Corlett, C. 1999 *The antiquities of Old Rathdown.* Bray.

—— 1998 Recent finds from Co. Wicklow, *Wicklow: Archaeology and History* 1, 64–6.

Culpepper, W. 1995 *Culpepper's complete herbal.* Herefordshire.

Curtis, E. n.d Transcriptions in the possession of H.J. French (died April 1930) from originals held by the earl of Meath, at Kilruddery. These include documents relating to the title of Bray. Presently held by the Royal Society of Antiquaries of Ireland in the Liam Price Collection (pers. comm., C. Corlett).

—— 1933 Janico Dartas, Richard II's 'Gascon Squire': his career in Ireland, 1394–1426. *RSAI Jn.* 67, 186–8.

Davey, N. 1961 *History of building materials.* London.

Down survey, 1654–6, Parish and barony maps m. 2506, f.55. National Library of Ireland MSS.

Duffy, S. (ed.) 1997 *Atlas of Irish history.* Dublin.

Edwards, N. 1990 *The archaeology of early medieval Ireland.* London.

Egan, G. et al. 1986 Marked on milled window leads, *Post-medieval Archaeology* 20, 303–9.

Etchingham, C. 1994 Evidence of Scandinavian settlement in Wicklow. In Ken Hannigan and William Nolan (eds), *Wicklow: history and society* 113–138. Dublin.

Fitzgerald, W. 1910 The manor and castle of Powerscourt in the sixteenth century, formerly a possession of the earl of Kildare. *Jn. Kildare Arch. Soc.* 6, 127–139.

Frame, R., 1971 The Dublin government and Gaelic Ireland, 1272–1361, PhD thesis. Trinity College, Dublin.

—— 1981 *Colonial Ireland.* Dublin.

Geraghty, S. 1996 *Viking Dublin: botanical evidence from Fishamble Street, Dublin.* Medieval Dublin Excavations, 1962–81, C, 2. Dublin.

Gilbert, J.T., (ed.) 1884–5 *Chartularies of St Mary's abbey, Dublin,* 2 vols. London.

—— 1889 *Register of the abbey of St Thomas the Martyr.* London.

Goodall I.H 1990 Knives. In M. Biddle, *Object and economy in medieval Winchester,* 835–60. Oxford.

Goodbody, R. 1993 *On the borders of the Pale.* Bray.

Grant, A. 1984 The use of tooth wear as a guide to the age of domestic ungulates. In B. Wilson, C. Grigson, and S. Payne (eds) *Aging and sexing animal bones from archaeological sites.* BAR 109. London.

Griffith, M.C. 1991 *Calendar of inquisitions formerly in the Office of the Chief Remembrancer of the exchequer prepared from the MSS of the Irish Record Commission.* Dublin.

—— *Irish Patent Roll of James I: facsimile of the Irish record commissioners calendar prepared prior to 1830* with foreword by M.C Griffith 1996. Dublin.

Grogan, E. and Hillery, T. 1993 *A guide to the archaeology of County Wicklow.* Bray.

Halpin, A. 1992 in Bennett, I. (ed.) *Excavations 1991.* Bray.

Hurley, M.F et al. 1993 *Late Viking age and medieval Waterford, excavations 1986–1992.* 361–365. Waterford.

Hurley M.F. 1997 *Excavations at the North Gate, Cork 1994.* Cork.

Kelly, F. 1998 *Early Irish farming.* Dublin

Leask, H.G. 1941 *Irish Castles.* Dundalk.

Loeber, R. 1988–9 New light on Co. Wexford architecture and estates in the seventeenth century, in *Wexford Hist. Soc. Jn.* 14, 66–71.

Lydon J. 1994 Medieval Wicklow–land of war. In K. Hannigan and K. Whelan (eds) *Wicklow: history and society.* 151–190, Dublin.

Mabey, R. 1972 *Food for Free.* Glasgow.

McCormick, F. and Murphy, E. 1997 Mammal bones. In C. Walsh, *Archaeological excavations at Patrick, Nicholas and Winetavern Street, Dublin.* Dingle.

McCutcheon, C. 2000 Medieval pottery in Dublin: new names and some dates in S. Duffy (ed.) *Medieval Dublin I,* 117–125. Dublin.

McNeill, C. (ed.), 1950 *Calendar of Archbishop Alen's register, c.1172–1534.* Dublin.

McNeill, T. 1997 *Castles in Ireland.* London, New York.
—— 1990 The great towers of early Irish castles. In Marjorie Chibnall (ed.) *Anglo-Norman Studies XII, Proceedings of the Battle Conference 1989.* Woodbridge.
Mills, J. 1894 The Norman settlement in Leinster, *RSAI Jn.* xxiv, 161–175.
—— 1905 *Calendar of the justiciary rolls of Ireland.* 3 vols. Dublin.
—— 1903–27 Accounts on the great rolls of the pipe of the Irish Exchequer, *Reports of the Deputy Keeper of the Public Records of Ireland,* 35–54. Dublin.
—— 1994 (repr.), *The Irish faints of the Tudor sovereigns,* 4 vols, Dublin.
National Archive of Ireland, KB 1/1 M18 (pers. comm. Philomena Connolly†).
O'Callaghan J. 1980–1 Fortified houses of the sixteenth century in County Wexford in *Wexford Hist. Soc. Jn.* 8, 1–45.
O'Brien, C. 1994 The Byrnes of Ballymanus. In K. Hannigan and K. Whelan (eds) *Wicklow: history and society,* 303–39. Dublin.
O'Byrne, E. 2002 On the frontier: Carrickmines Castle and Gaelic Leinster. *Archaeology Ireland,* 16, no. 61, 13–5.
Ó Floinn, R. 1988 Handmade medieval pottery in S.E. Ireland – 'Leinster Cooking Ware' in G. Mac Niocaill and P.F. Wallace (eds), *Keimelia* 325–49, Galway.
Price, L. 1931 The Hearth money roll. *RSAI Jn.* lxi, 164–7, 172–8.
—— 1933 The Byrnes' Country in the sixteenth century: Part 1 *RSAI Jn.* 63, 224–43.
—— 1931 Notes on Fiach Mc Hugh O'Byrne' *Journal of the Kildare Archaeological Society* Vol. XI 2 134–75.
—— 1936 The Byrnes' Country in the sixteenth … century: Part 2 in *RSAI Jn.* 66, 41–66.
—— 1951 The grant to Walter de Ridlesford of Brien and the land of the sons of Turchil in *RSAI Jn.* 81, 72–77.
—— 1953 Powerscourt and the territory of Fercullen in *RSAI Jn.* 83 117–131.
—— 1983 (reprint) *The placenames of Co. Wicklow.* 5 Vols. Dublin.
—— 2002 *The Price notebooks,* ed. C. Corlett and M. Weaver. Vol. 1. Dublin.
Public Record Office of London, E101/244/6 (pers. comm. Philomena Connolly†).
Power, P. 1994 A survey: some Wicklow maps, 1500–1880. In K. Hannigan and K. Whelan (eds) *Wicklow: history and society,* 723–760. Dublin.
Prummel, W., and Frisch, H. 1986 A guide for the distinction of species, sex and body side in bones of sheep and goat. *Journal of Archaeological Science* 13, 567–77.
Roche, N. 1996–7 The glazing fraternity in Ireland in the seventeenth and eighteenth centuries. *Bulletin of the Irish Georgian Society,* xxxviii, 67–94.
Ronan M.V. 1930 The union of the dioceses of Glendalough and Dublin in *RSAI Jn.* 60 56–72.
Scott, G.D., 1913 *The stones of Bray.* Dublin.
Sexton, R. 1998a Porridges, gruels and breads: the cereal foodstuffs of early medieval Ireland. In M. Monk and J. Sheehan (eds) *Early medieval Munster archaeology, history and society.* Cork.
Sexton, R. 1998b *A little history of Irish food.* Dublin.
Simpson, L., 1994a Anglo-Norman settlement in Uí Briúin Cualann. In K. Hannigan and K. Whelan (eds) *Wicklow: history and society.* 191–235, Dublin.
Simpson, L. 1994b *Excavations at Isolde's Tower, Dublin.* Dublin.
Simpson, L. 1995 *Excavations at Essex Street West, Dublin.* Dublin.
Simpson, L. 2002 Excavations at Kindlestown Castle, Delgany, Stratigraphic report lodged with *Dúchas:* the Heritage Service and the National Museum of Ireland (Licence no. 01E0844).
Smal, C. (ed.) 1993 *Ancient Rathdown and Saint Crispin's cell.* Wicklow.
Sweetman, H.S 1875–86 *Calendar of documents relating to Ireland, 1171–1307,* 5 vols. London.
Sweetman, P.D. 1999 *The medieval castles of Ireland.* Cork.
—— 1998 Hall-houses in Ireland in *Archaeology Ireland.* 12, no. 45, 13–16.
Silver, I.A. 1969 The aging of domestic animals. In D. Brothwell and E. S Higgs (eds), *Science in archaeology.* London.
Schmid, E. 1976 *Atlas of animal bones.* Amsterdam.
Tierney J. and Hannon, M. 1997 The plant remains. In M. Hurley and O. Scully, *Late Viking age and medieval Waterford, excavations 1986–1992,* 854–893. Waterford.
Von den Driesch, A. 1976 *A guide to the measurement of animal bones from archaeological sites.* Peabody Museum Bulletin No. 1, Harvard, Mass.
Walsh, C. 1997 *Archaeological excavations at Patrick Street, Nicholas Street and Winetavern Street, Dublin.* Dingle.
White, N.B. 1932 *The Red Book of Ormond.* Dublin.
Wren J. 1997 The roof tiles. In M. Hurley and O. Scully, *Late Viking age and medieval Waterford, excavations, 1986–1992,* 361–365. Waterford.